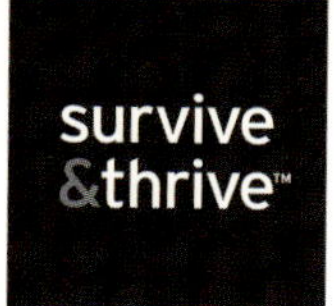

Create and Share Digital Photos

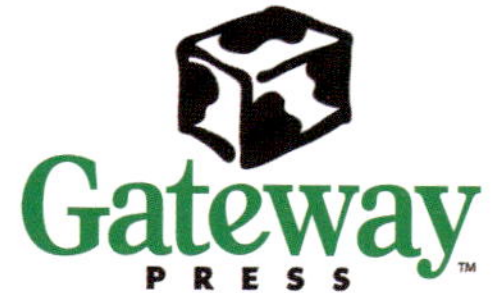

Notices

Create and Share Digital Photos
is published by
Gateway, Inc.
14303 Gateway Place
Poway, CA 92064

Version 1.0

ISBN: 1-57729-272-3

DATE: 5-13-02

Printed in the United States of America

Distributed in the United States by Gateway, Inc.

Welcome

From the introduction of Digital Photography in Chapter 1 through taking the next step in Digital Photography in Chapter 9, *Create and Share Digital Photos* provides you with what you need to know to acquire, organize, and enjoy photography with your PC. This product is designed to accommodate your learning style, and to make learning easy, interesting, and fun. You can stick to just the bare essentials or learn in greater depth by practicing key skills and applying your new knowledge. Our goal is to show you how technology can enhance your life, provide some fun, and open up new opportunities.

More Than a Book

Create and Share Digital Photos is more than a book; it is a blended learning system that also includes interactive CD-ROM and Internet presentations and activities. These tools all work together to provide a truly unique learning experience. The book presents technical information in visual, practical, and understandable ways. The CD-ROM extends the book by providing audio, video, and animated visuals of important concepts. Continue learning online by logging on to www.LearnwithGateway.com. The enrollment key provided with this book gives you access to additional content and interactive exercises, as well as reference links, Internet resources, and Frequently Asked Questions (FAQs) with answers. This Web site allows us to keep you updated on rapidly changing information and new software releases.

Classroom Learning

In addition, a hands-on training course is offered. Additional fees may apply. Our classes are ideal solutions for people who want to become knowledgeable and get up and running in just three hours. They provide the opportunity to learn from one of our experienced and friendly instructors and practice important skills with other students. Call 888-852-4821 for enrollment information. One of our representatives will assist you in selecting a time and location that is convenient for you. If applicable, please have your Gateway customer ID and order number ready when you call. Please refer to your Gateway paperwork for this information.

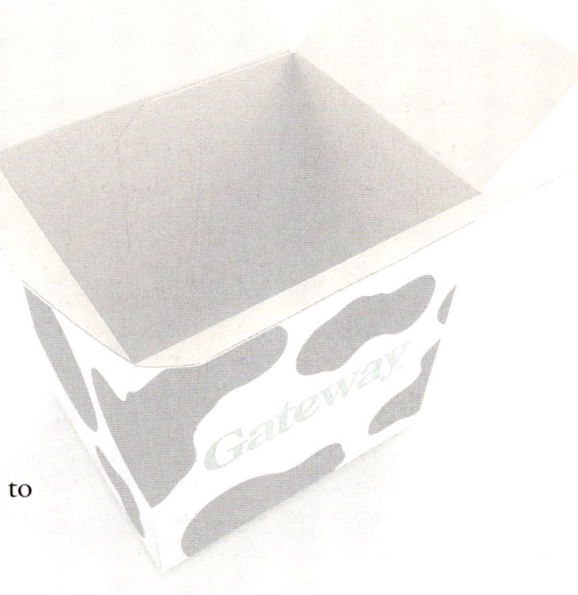

Learning map for Create and Share Digital Photos

This map shows how the elements of the Gateway Learning System work for you. The best of an easy to understand, highly visual book, the Internet and CD-ROM are all brought together to give you a unique and truly enjoyable learning experience. Notice how the interactive CD-ROM and Internet activities extend and complement the chapters in the book. Icons in the book will direct you to each element at the proper time.

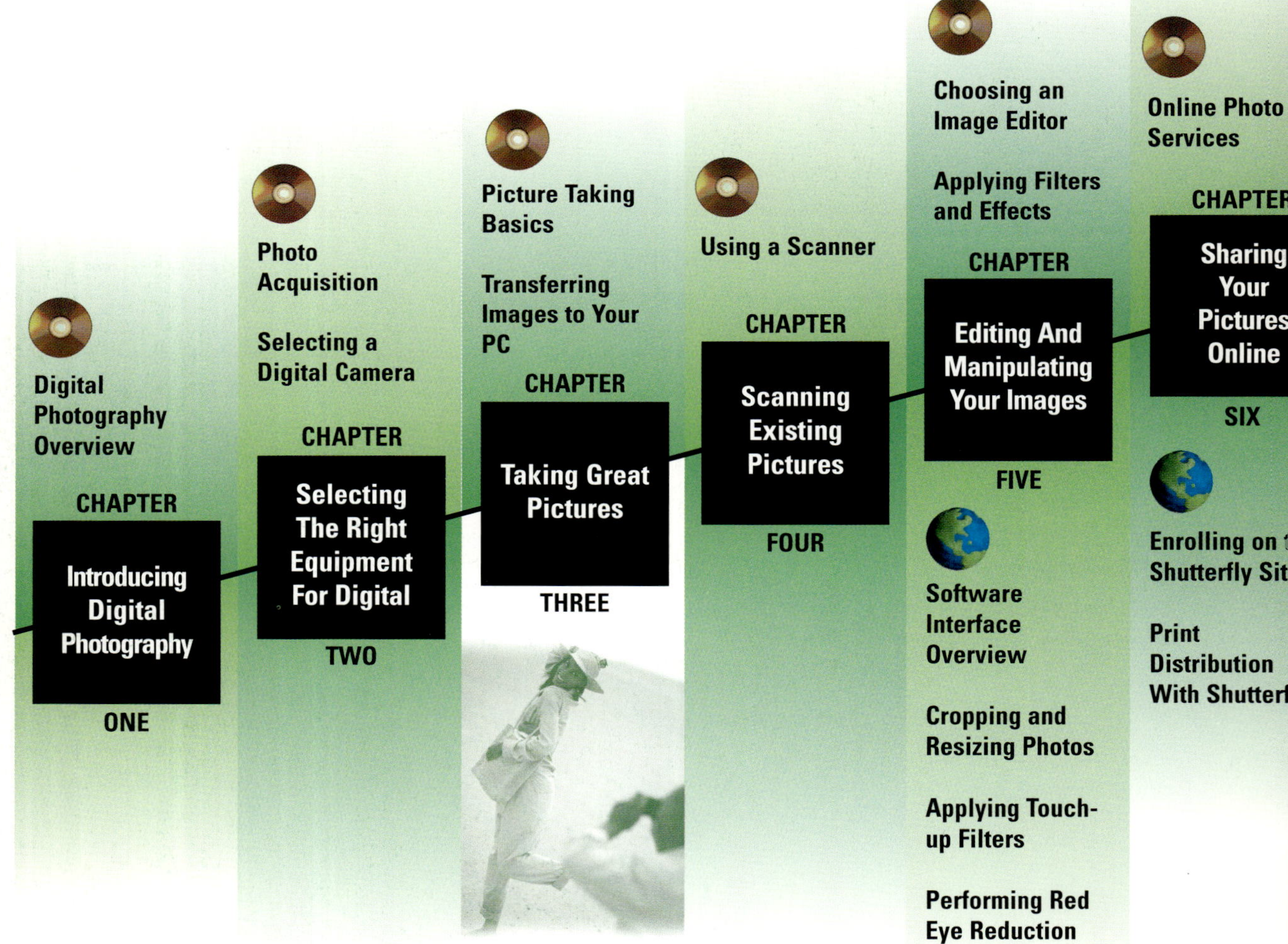

On Your CD Rom

On the World Wide Web

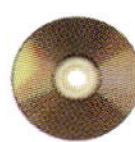

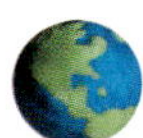

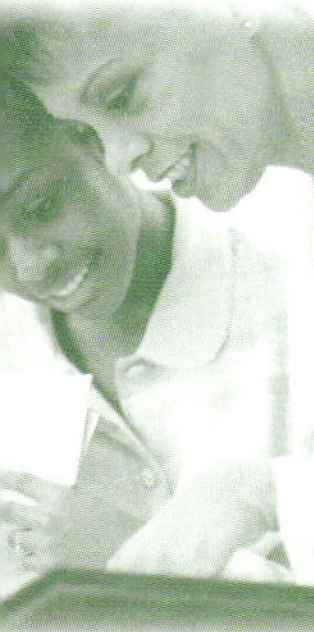

Organizing Images

Archiving Your Images

CHAPTER SEVEN

Printing Images

CHAPTER EIGHT

Organizing & Protecting Your Digital Images

CHAPTER NINE

Taking The Next Step In Digital Photography

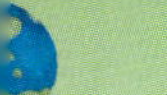

to Printing

ating pbooks With Gateway to Center

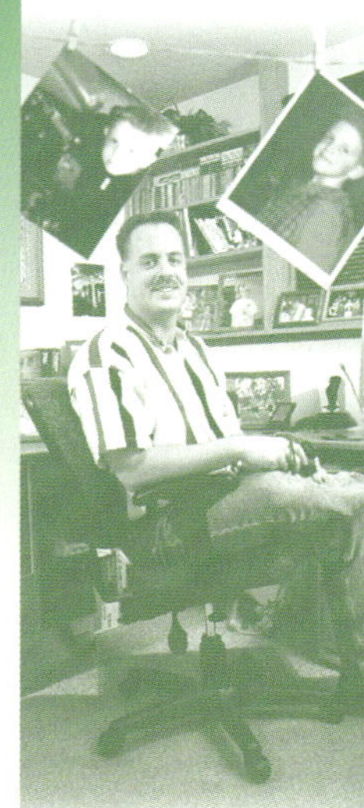

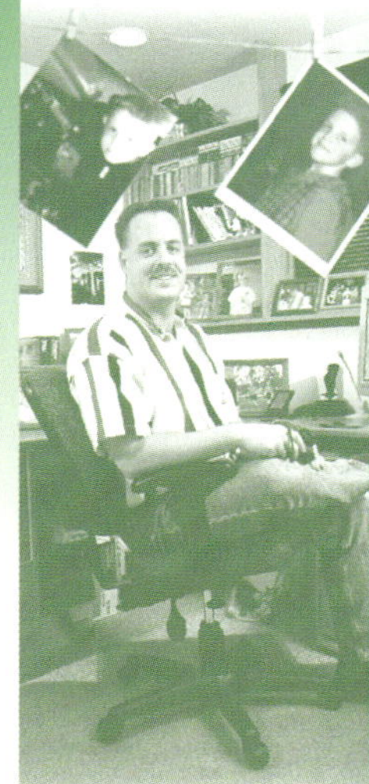

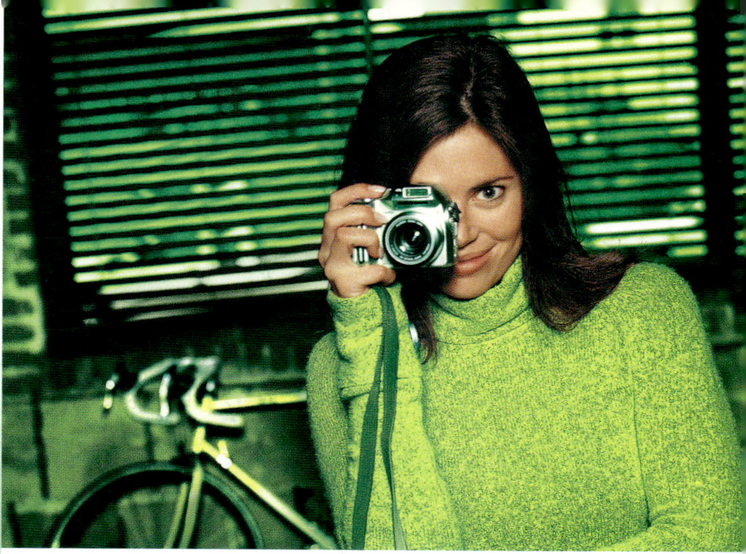

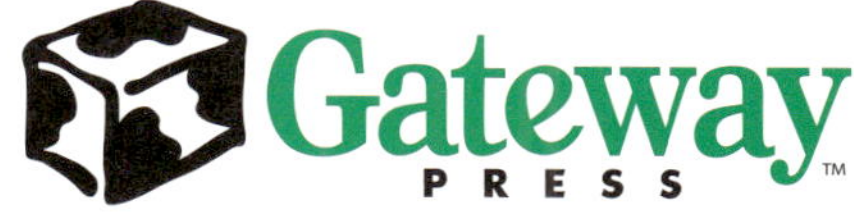

You can also take a Gateway class, and this is an ideal way to continue to expand your learning. Gateway instructors are dedicated to working with each individual and answering all your questions. You will be able to talk with other learners, practice important skills, and get off to a quick start. Additional fees may apply.

Call 888-852-4821 to enroll.

See you in class!

Contents

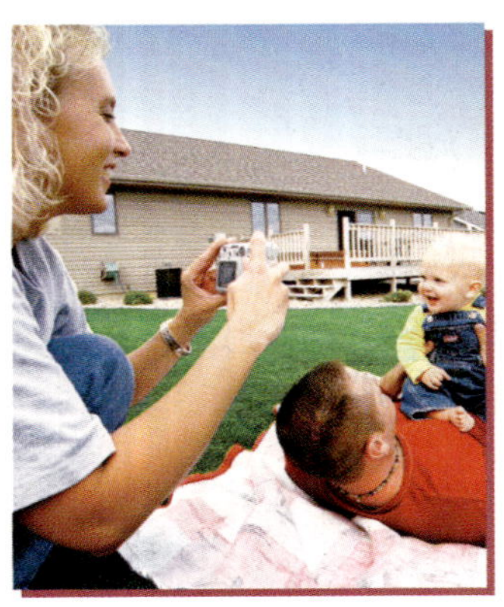

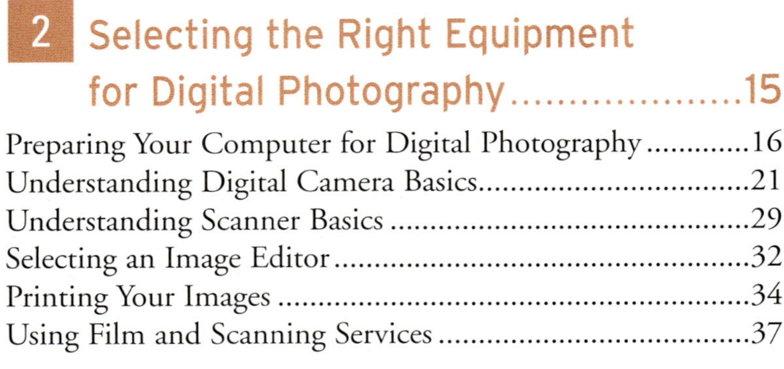

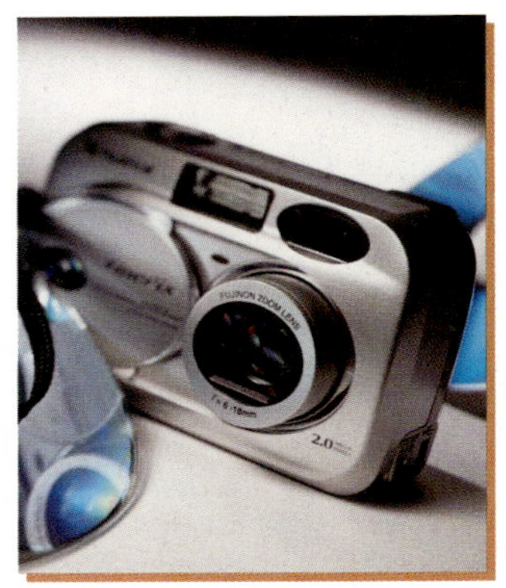

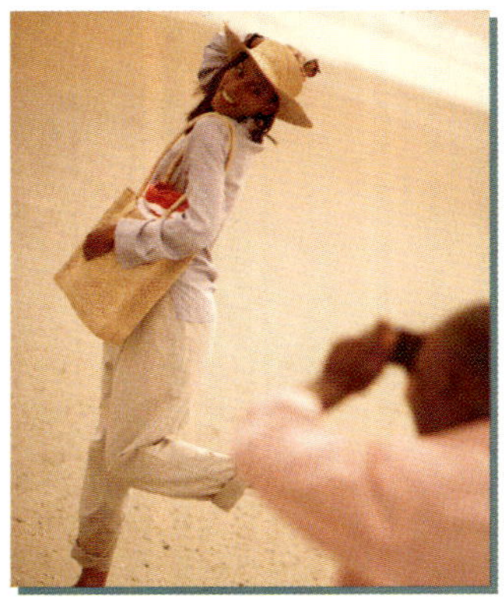

Contents

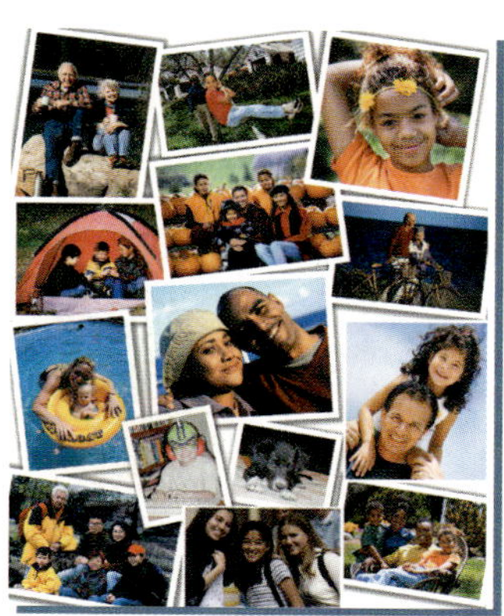

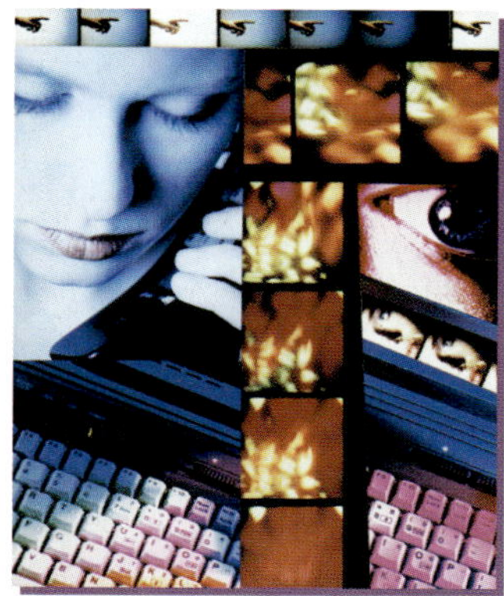

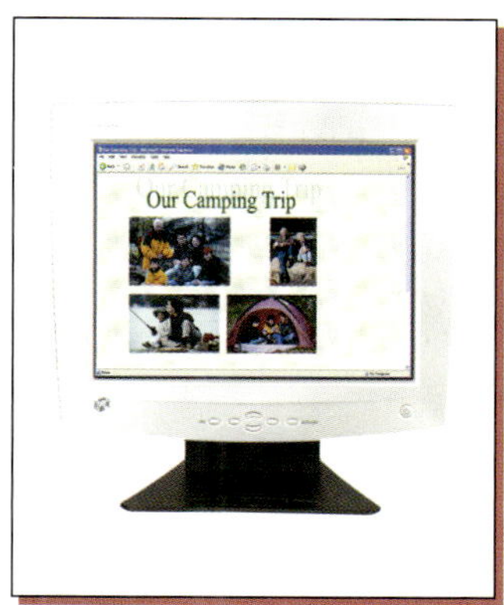

Contents

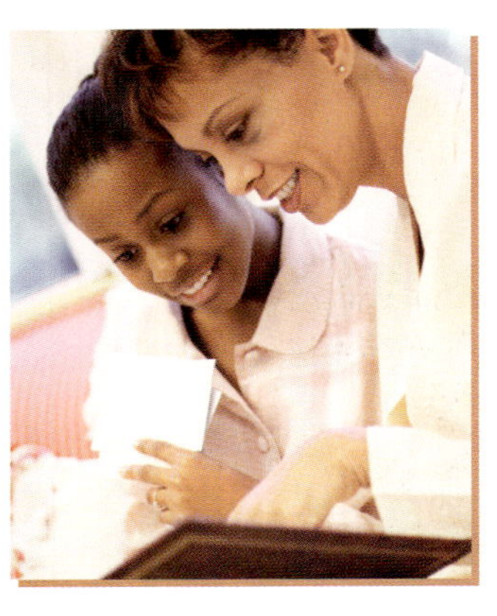

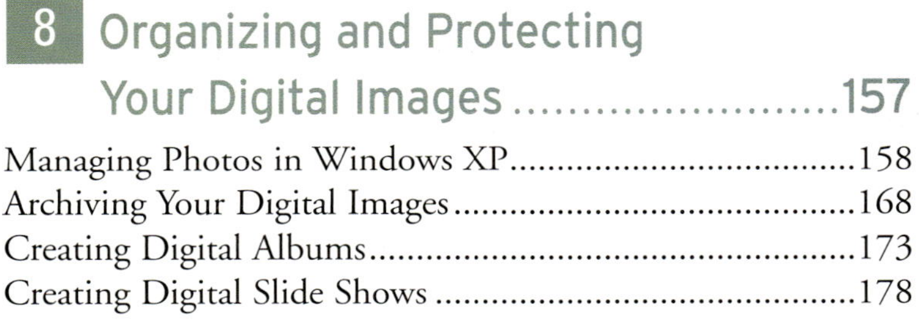

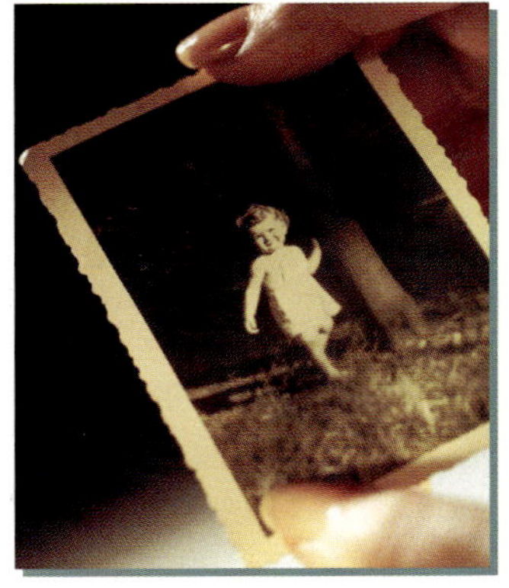

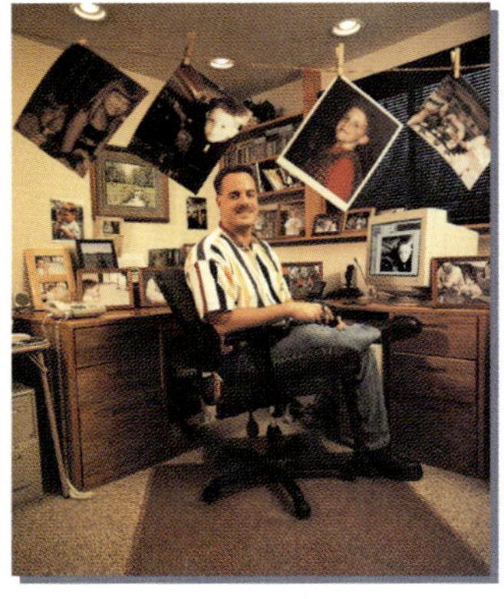

How to Use This Book

As you read the chapters in this book, you'll find lots of pictures, figures, and diagrams to help you visualize what you're reading. You'll also find numerous pictures, or icons, that serve as cues to flag important information or provide directions. Here is a guide to help you understand the pictures you'll encounter in this book:

A Note identifies a relatively important piece of information that will make things easier or faster for you to accomplish on your PC. Most notes are worth reading, if only for the time and effort they can save you.

A Warning gives notice that an action on your PC can have serious consequences and could lead to loss of work, delays, or other problems. Our goal is not to scare you, but to steer you clear of potential sources of trouble.

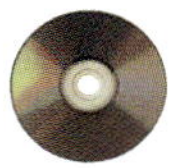

The CD-ROM flags additional materials including exercises and animations that you will find on the CD-ROM included with this book. Because some materials work better on your PC than in print, we've included many activities and exercises. These help you become more familiar with your system while practicing important skills.

In addition, many of the photographs that appear in this book are available on the CD-ROM. Simply click **Start Course**, then **Install Practice Files**, and the photos will be saved to your hard drive.

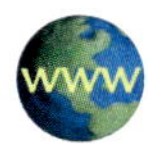

Because PC information and online resources are so dynamic, some material related to this book, including Web-based training, resides on the **www.LearnwithGateway.com** Web site. This allows us to keep that information fresh and up to date.

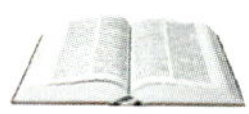

The *Survive & Thrive* series includes several books on topics from digital music to the Internet. Where other titles can be useful in improving and expanding your learning, we use the Book icon to draw those titles to your attention.

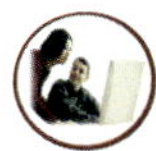

Gateway offers a hands-on training course on many of the topics covered in this book. Additional fees may apply. Call 888-852-4821 for enrollment information. If applicable, please have your customer ID and order number ready when you call.

You'll find sidebar information sprinkled throughout the chapters, as follows:

More About . . .

The More About . . . information is supplementary, and is provided so you can learn more about making technology work for you. Feel free to skip this material during your first pass through the book, but please return to it later.

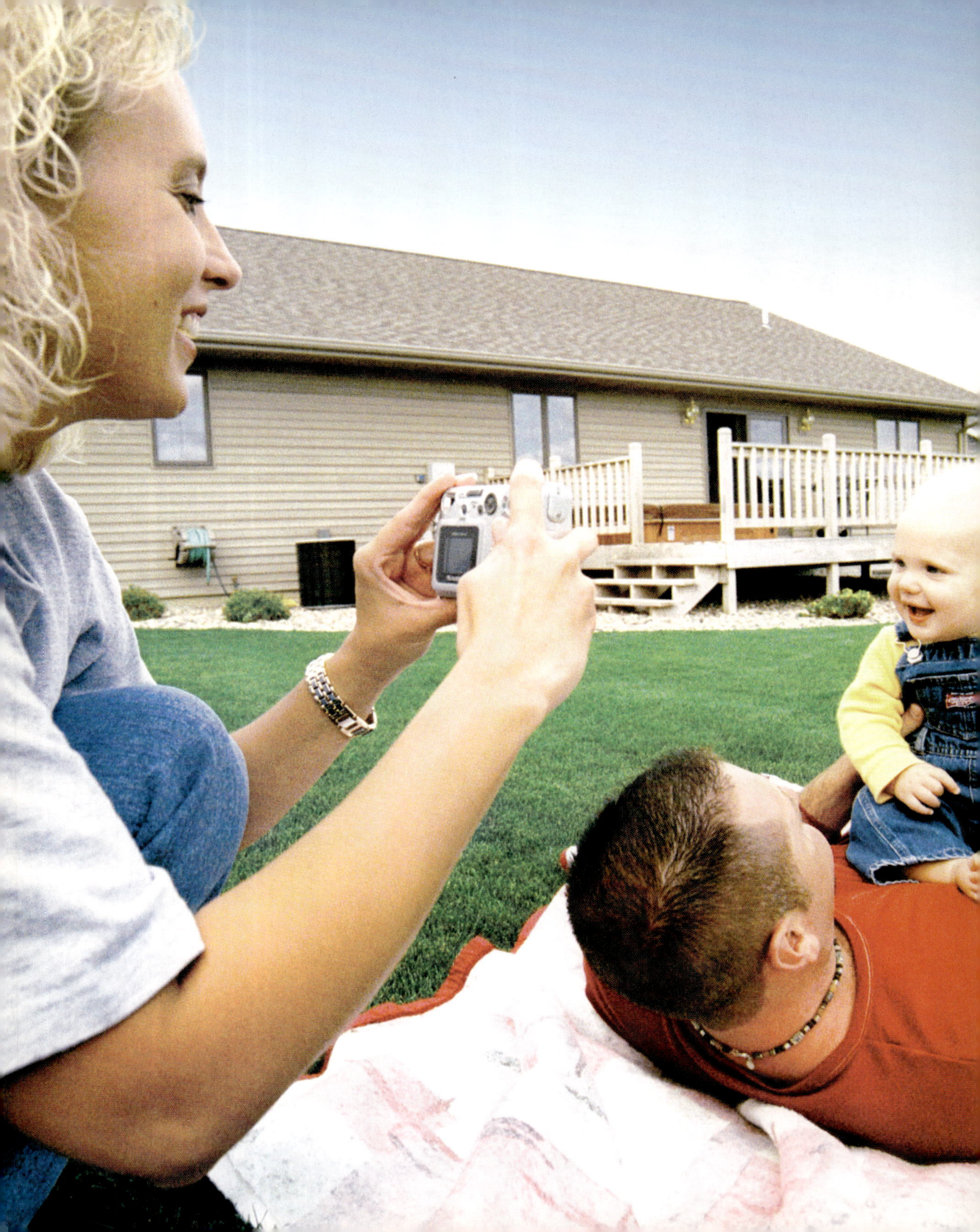

CHAPTER 1

Introducing Digital Photography

You have just entered the exciting world of digital photography. Improved personal computer technology, the Internet, scanning devices, and digital cameras enable us to stretch the boundaries of traditional photography. Professional darkrooms and messy chemicals are no longer requirements to create memories. Many software packages provide simple tools that turn static photographic images into exciting works of art. In fact, because of the advantages afforded by using a digital camera or other device, such as a scanner, to create digital images, you may decide to put away your film-based camera for good!

This chapter introduces you to the world of digital photography. In addition to learning what the phrase "digital photography" means, you'll discover all the fun things you can do with your digital images as well as the many sources of digital images, including pictures taken with a digital camera, images scanned in with a scanner, and others. You also learn about the many benefits of working with digital images. With digital photography, you can e-mail photos, create a snapshot book, order prints online, and more. Later chapters cover in detail how to perform all these fabulous things!

Learning About Digital Photography

The easiest way to describe digital photography is to compare this type of camera to a traditional camera. In fact, digital cameras are quite similar to their film-based counterparts, given that they include such familiar features as a lens, flash, and shutter. So what's the difference? The obvious one is that digital cameras don't use film to record the scene you are photographing. Instead, digital cameras use sensors, or *arrays,* called *CCDs* (Charge Coupled Devices) that convert light information from the photographed scene into a digital image.

Digital images are made up of individual picture elements called pixels. A *pixel* is a tiny dot of light that is the basic unit of measurement for images on a computer screen or in a digital image. These pixels combine to make the picture and are stored together as a digital file. Digital images can come from many sources (covered later), one of which is from a digital camera.

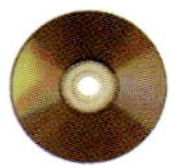

To learn more about the key features and benefits of digital photography, go to the CD-ROM segment *Digital Photography Overview.*

Digital photography involves using a new type of camera, a digital camera, to take pictures. This camera works like your computer; it takes the actual image (what you are photographing) and converts that image into a digital file. You can then use this digital file in many ways (see "What Can I Do With My Digital Photographs?" later in this chapter).

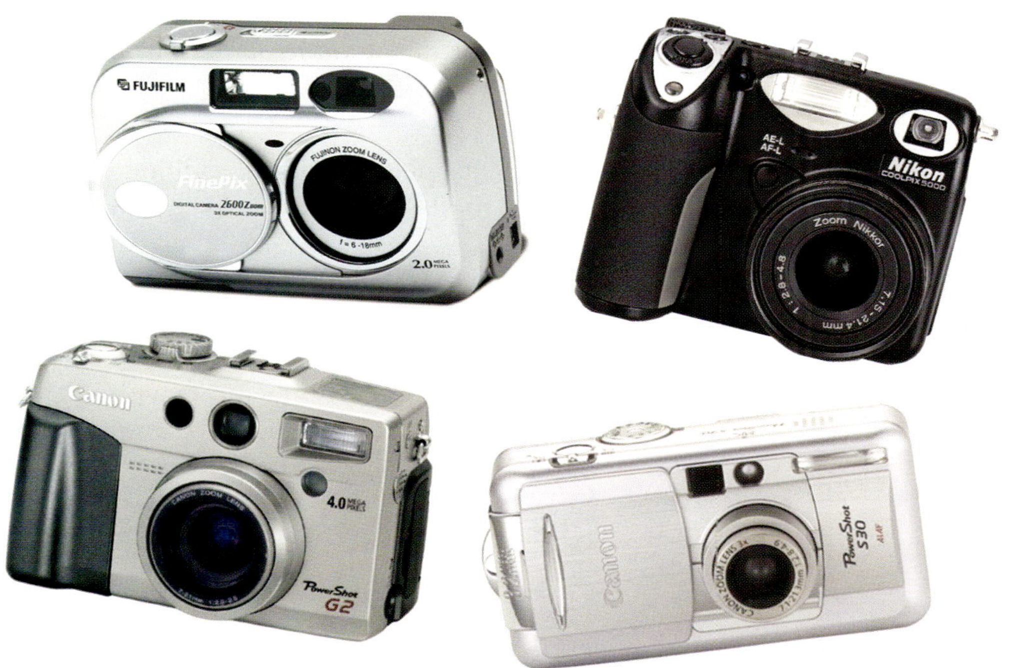

The quality of a picture is called its *resolution* and is a measure of the number of pixels per inch. The more pixels per inch in the image, the better the image quality. You'll learn more about image quality in Chapter 2.

The digital image is then stored as a file in your camera's memory or on a *memory card* (a removable disk that is similar to a computer floppy disk, but smaller) and can be transferred to your PC. The number of pictures you can take on your digital camera in one session will vary depending on the amount of available memory (be it inside your camera or in a memory card) and the resolution of the images. Because higher-resolution images contain more pixels, the files containing them are larger, and thus consume more space in your camera's memory or in your memory card.

Once you've filled the memory in your digital camera or memory card, sometimes referred to as a *memory stick*, you simply copy the images from your camera to your computer (called *downloading*). Then you can delete the images from the camera's memory or memory card, and voila, you're ready to take more pictures. You never need to pay for film again!

Discovering the Many Sources of Digital Images

Whether you're a seasoned photographer or a point-and-shoot person, creating digital images of your own is rather simple. You'll learn all about taking pictures using a digital camera in Chapter 3.

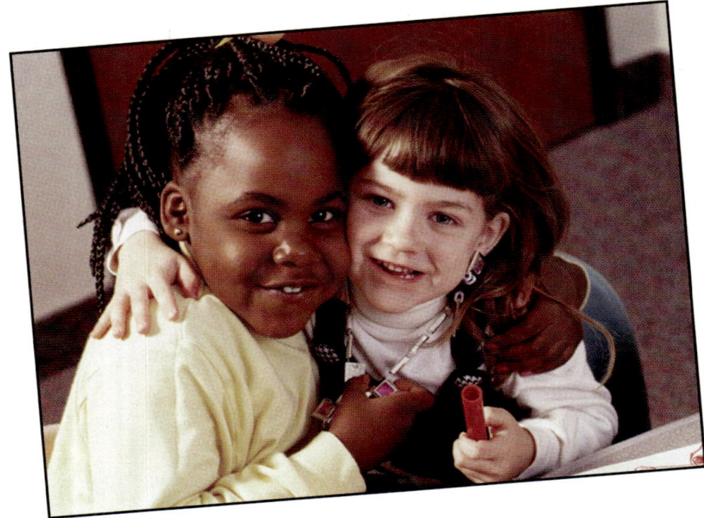

However, using a digital camera isn't the only way to create digital images. In fact, there are several different ways to obtain digital pictures, including scanners, online images, and more. The following list gives you a good idea of the many sources of digital images:

- **Using a scanner.** Suppose you're planning to attend a family reunion, and you want to create a scrapbook of old family photographs for the other attendees. Instead of paying to have the images reprinted at a photo shop, you can use a *scanner* to copy the images and save them as files on your computer. Then you can print the images using your own printer. Scanning existing pictures is the topic of Chapter 4.

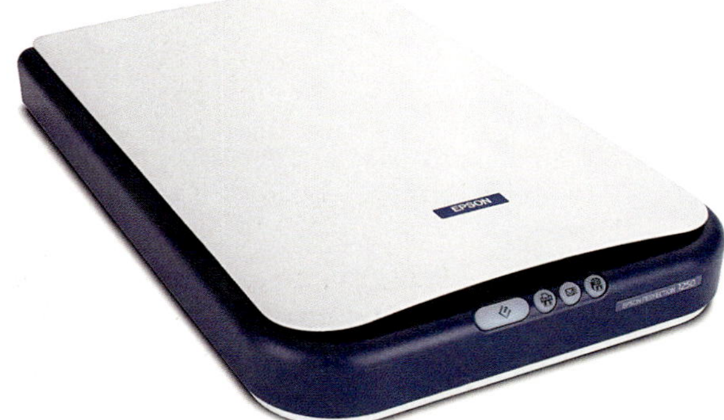

- **Using a CD-ROM.** Many photo-development services will place your images on CD-ROM when you develop film. You can then open these files from the CD and work with them on your computer.

Many new computers come with a CD-R drive; with this type of drive, you can record (or "burn") your own CDs. Because photo files can be quite large, storing them on CDs is a great way to keep your photos organized. You learn more about storing and organizing pictures, including using a CD-R drive, in Chapter 8.

- **Using the Web.** In addition to enabling you to receive your images on CD-ROM, many photo-development services will place your photos on a Web site, where you can view, download, share, and/or print them. Alternatively, some Web sites offer clip-art illustrations or photographs that you can download and use.

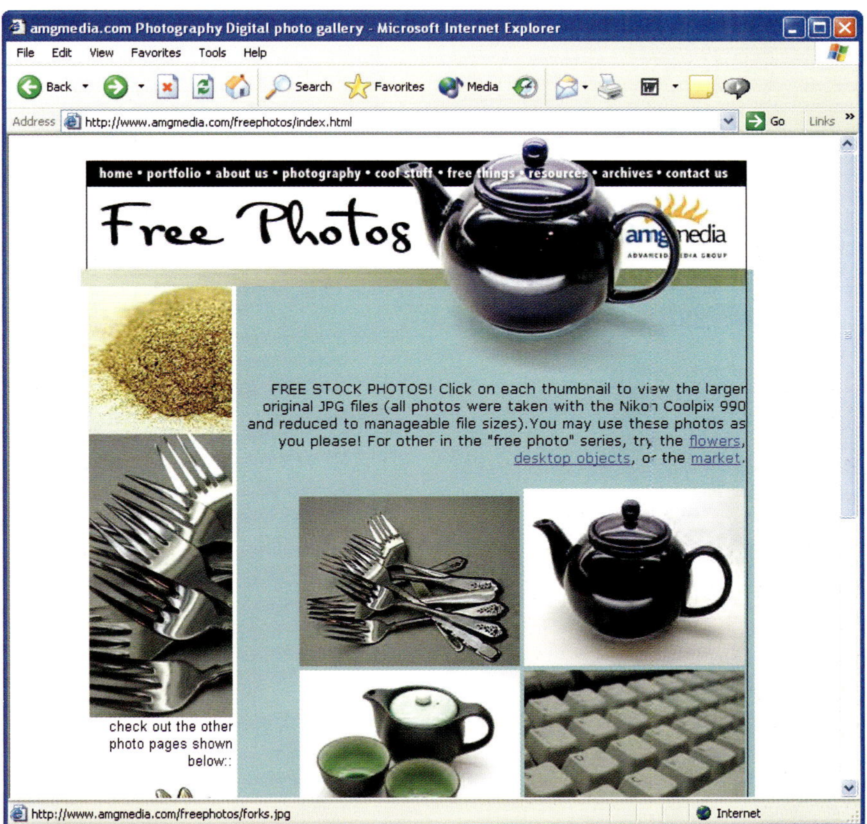

Some images are copyrighted. Just because you find a picture you like on the Web does not mean that you have permission to use that image as you see fit. Many clip-art and photo sites spell out what you can and cannot do with their images.

More About . . . Digital Photography without a Computer

Ideally, you have a computer on which to copy, edit, and print your pictures. But if you don't, you can still access some of the features and fun of a digital camera. Some cameras come with removable media, such as the Kingston CompactFlash and the SmartMedia cards. You can take pictures, store them on these media cards, and then take them to a local print shop.

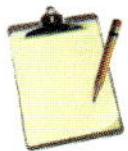

Throughout this book, when you see the phrase "digital image," it refers to pictures or illustrations from any one of these sources, not just pictures taken with a digital camera. Pictures taken with a digital camera are also referred to as digital pictures or photographs.

Why Go Digital?

Now that you have a good idea of what digital photography is, you can add up all the advantages. Doing so can help you evaluate whether it's worth purchasing a new camera (if you don't already have one). And if you do have a camera, you can gain a better understanding of how this new piece of equipment can make photography easier and more versatile.

Here are a few key advantages of using a digital camera versus a traditional one:

- **You can preview your picture immediately after taking it.** If you've ever picked up a pack of pictures at your photo shop, eagerly anticipating capturing that once in a lifetime moment on film and discovered only blurry prints of what might be your parents dancing at their 50th wedding anniversary, you'll appreciate this feature of digital cameras. You can preview your pictures immediately after you take them. If the picture isn't good, discard it and take it again.
- **You don't need to purchase film.** Because your pictures are stored in a digital format in the camera's memory or on the camera's media card, you can copy the pictures to your computer, clear them from memory, and take new shots.

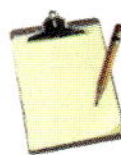

Take as many pictures as you want with your digital camera! Because you can discard the ones that don't turn out before they are printed, you don't have to worry about wasting film.

✦ **You can choose from several inexpensive printing options.** By being able to preview the image, you can print only the images you want using your own printer or using a special photo-quality printer. Alternatively, you can order prints online. If you are loyal to your local photo shop, you can take your images there, and have them create the prints. More options ensure you get *what* you want *when* you want it.

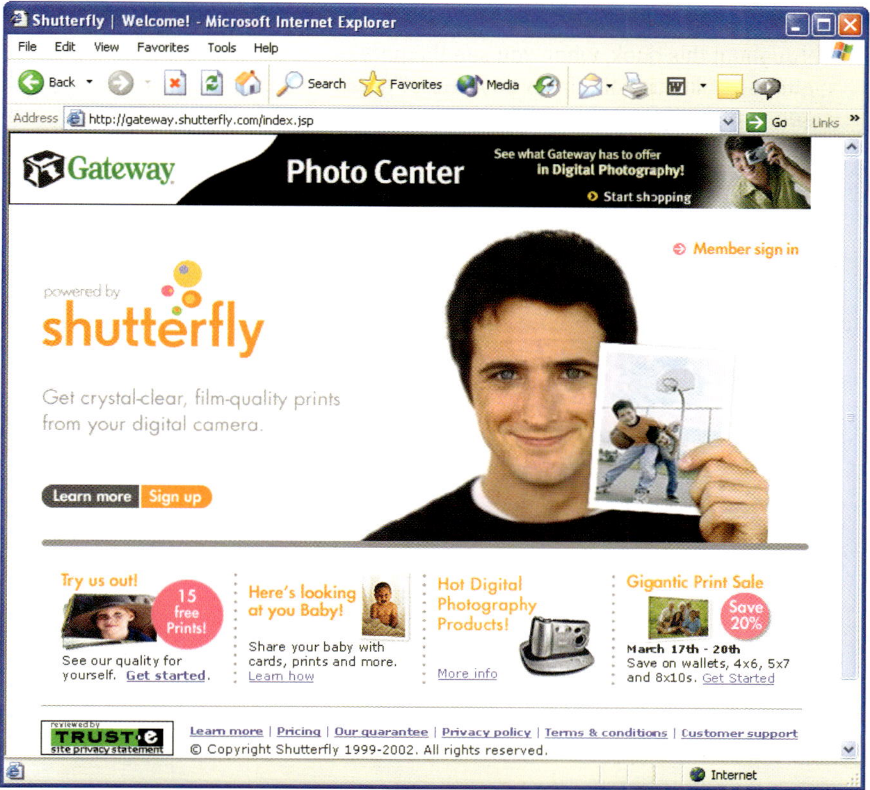

✦ **You can order the size and quantity of the prints you want.** If you commonly order double prints when you develop film from your traditional camera, you inevitably end up with 20 extra pictures that you don't really need. With a digital camera, you can select not just the quantity of each print, but also different sizes, including 5 x 7, wallets, and others.

✦ **Sharing your digital images is easy.** You can e-mail photos of your new baby to your sister in Antarctica. As another alternative, you can include photos on your Web page or within a document. Professional photographers especially benefit from this feature, because they can quickly broadcast their work to their customers. Sharing your images with others online is covered in more detail in Chapter 6.

Working with Your Digital Images

Because digital cameras are easy to use, with immediate results and endless editing capabilities, professional photographers were among the first to welcome digital photography. But even though they were among the first, professional photographers aren't the only ones who've found uses for their digital cameras. Let's explore some examples of using digital photography for your business or family photographs and documents.

In addition to highlighting some uses for digital images, this section also discusses some of the special techniques for enhancing or repairing pictures using special photo-editing software.

Photo Possibilities

Because digital photos are so easy to transfer to your computer, you can use them in countless ways. Here are just a few ideas to get your creative wheels turning for your own photographic works:

- **Business reports.** Pictures are a great way to improve the content and readability of many business reports, including newsletters, annual reports, and more. Do you want your clients to get to know you? Include your picture. Do you need to share complex plan or diagram with customers? Scan it, and then include it in the document. Regardless of your business, you can dress up reports by including photographs.

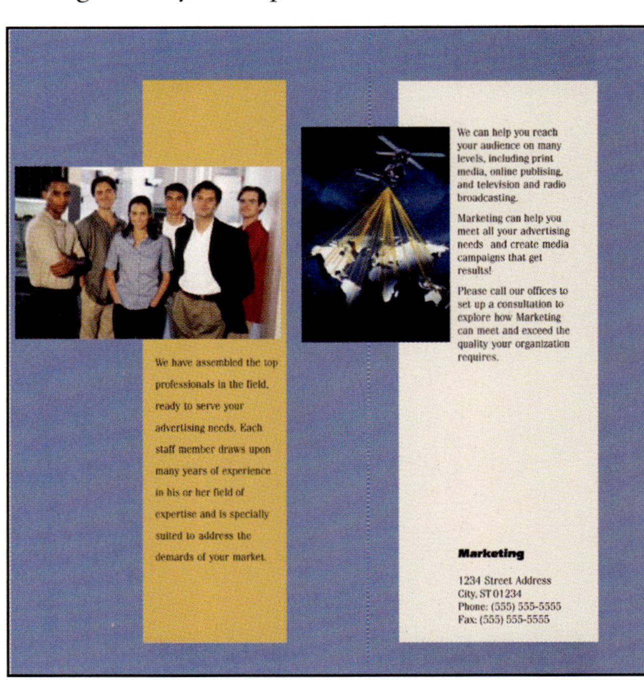

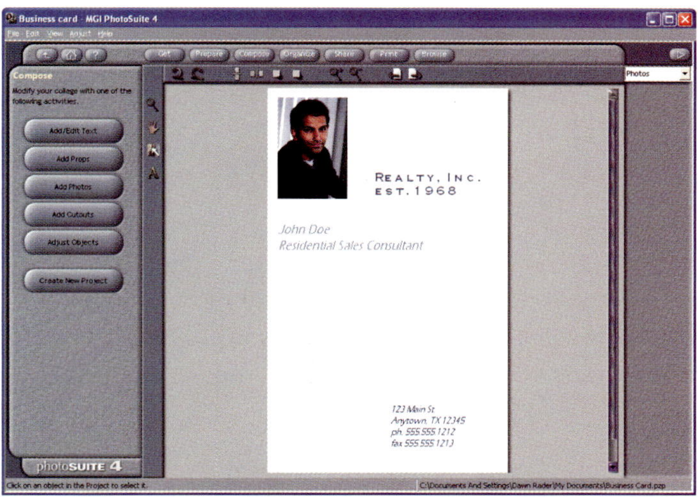

- **Business cards.** Personalize your business card by adding your picture or company logo. By including your picture, you make sure the recipient will remember your smiling face.
- **Product sales sheets and brochures.** If you are in sales, the old adage "a picture is worth a thousand words" couldn't be truer. You can show your potential clients with one or several pictures! For example, realtors use digital images to prepare virtual tours of the homes they're selling—providing a picture of hardwood floors and built-in bookcases makes for an easier sale than simply describing them.

Scientists and doctors use digital images, photographing microscopic subjects to study them in detail. Digital photography is even used in space. The Hubble Space Telescope, for instance, takes digital images that are then sent back to the space center and distributed to astronomers and the news media.

- **Web pages.** Liven up your personal or business Web page with photographs. For example, you can showcase your best-selling products on your business site, or include pictures of your pet on your personal page. If online auctions are your passion, you'll want to include one or several good pictures of the item you want to sell. Your imagination and the possibilities offered by the Web are limitless!

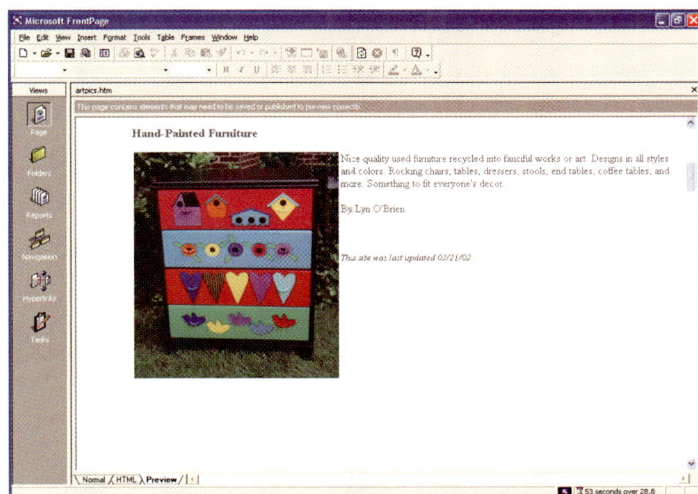

- **Family scrapbooks.** Scrapbooking is one the latest crazes. Just visit any craft store, and you'll see aisles and aisles of supplies. With a scanner or camera (or both), you can organize your photographic memories so that they tell a story. Using digital images, you can create a highlight book of your niece's high school years, or surprise your parents or grandparents with a family history, including scanned photographs of their storied past.

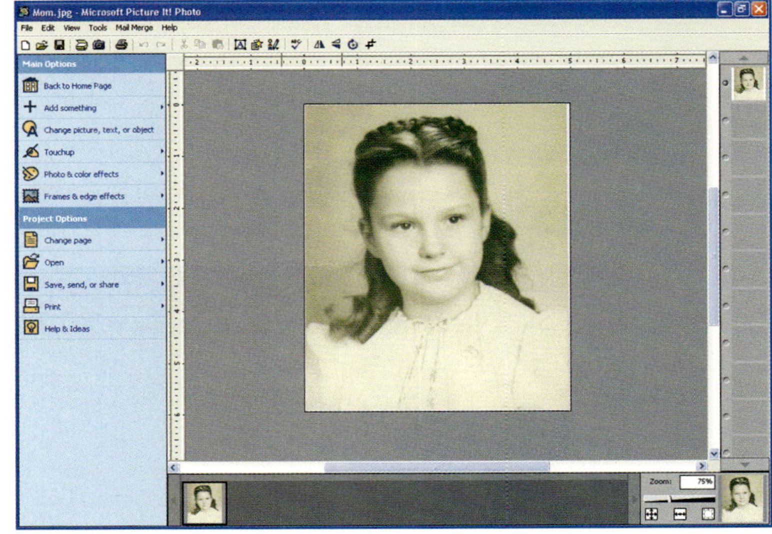

- **Cards, invitations, banners, and more.** With digital images, you can design your own holiday letter, including pictures of the family. Having a party? Create a fun invitation using digital photos. Or make a banner for an office party with photos of everyone in the company. You create many types of documents for entertainment and other purposes!

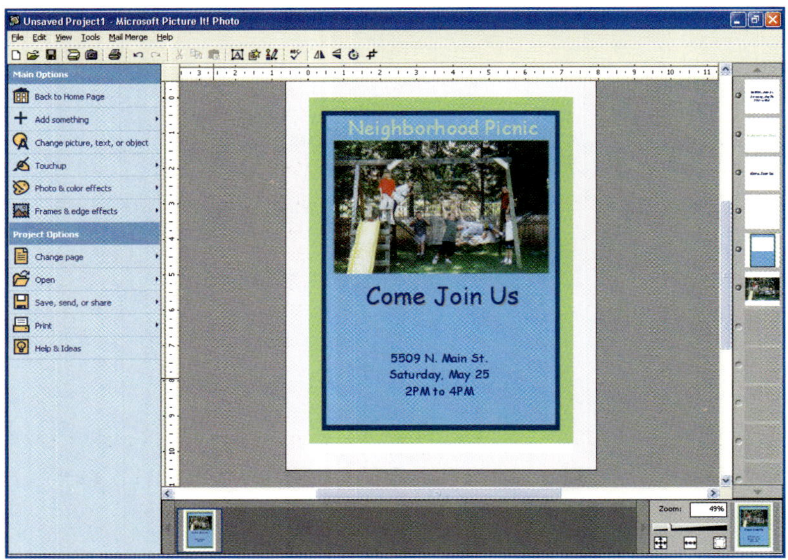

- **Craft projects.** In addition to printed projects such as invitations, you can also use your pictures for craft projects. For example, you can apply your images to memory quilts, t-shirts, mugs, and so on.
- **Slideshows and albums.** You can combine your pictures into a slideshow that you can play back, or use a picture album on your computer to organize your photos.

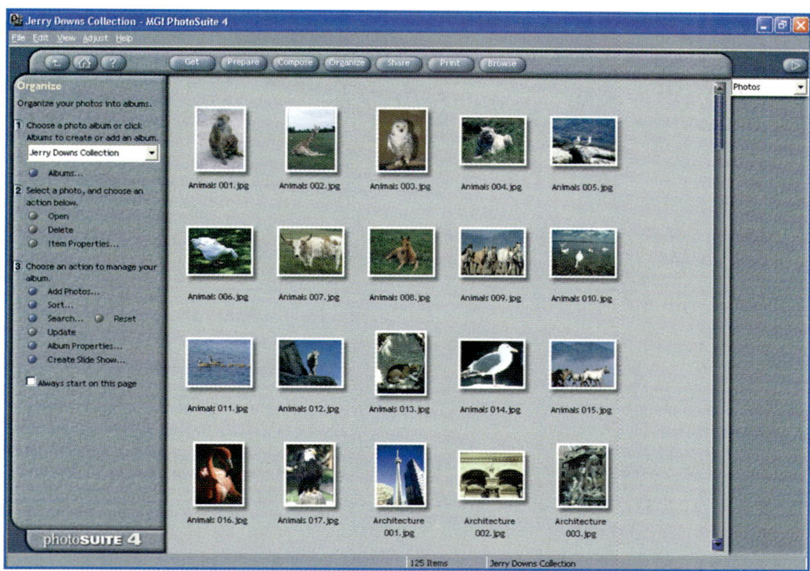

> **More About . . . Uses for Digital Photos**
>
> For insurance purposes, it's a good idea to keep a list of all your major possessions. That way, in case of a catastrophe, you have a visual record of the items that may have been lost or damaged. A digital camera is a perfect tool for this project; you can use it to photograph your belongings and insert the images into the document containing your list!

Editing Possibilities

In addition to the many uses for digital images, you also have a great deal of freedom in working with your digital pictures. The programs that enable you to edit digital images are called *image-editing programs.*

If you own a digital camera, it probably came with its own editing program, which you can use to manipulate your photos. Alternatively, you can purchase programs created by other companies if your needs are more advanced. Although the details of image-editing software are covered in Chapter 5, the following is a quick overview of the types of things you can do with image-editing programs:

- If your photos have flaws, such as red eye, you can correct them. You can also remove blemishes and wrinkles, giving yourself or a friend a virtual facelift!
- You can crop out portions of the picture to frame your subject better.

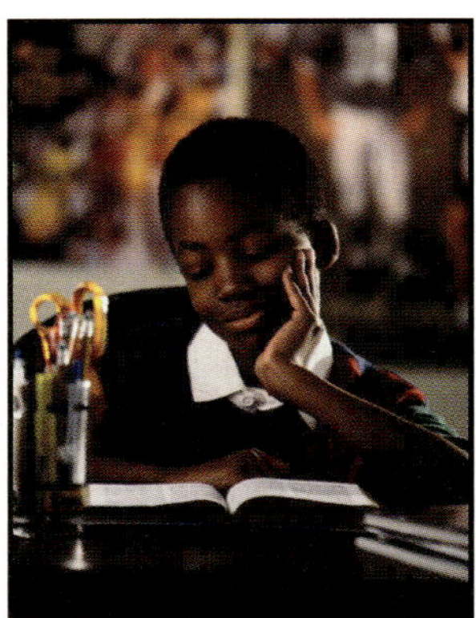
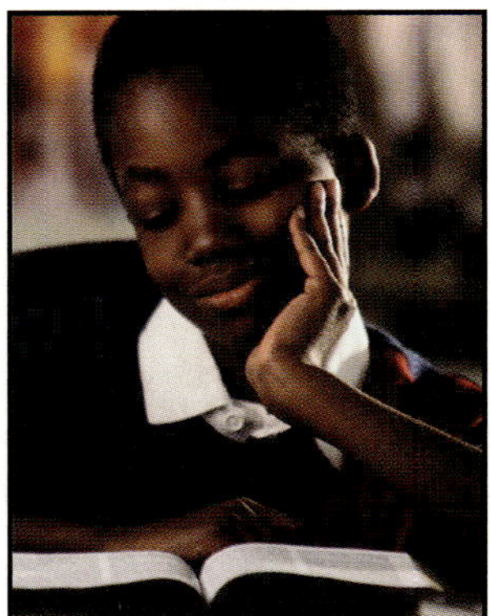

- You can change the orientation of the image by flipping or rotating it.
- You can apply special effects, such as converting a color image to black and white or warping the image.

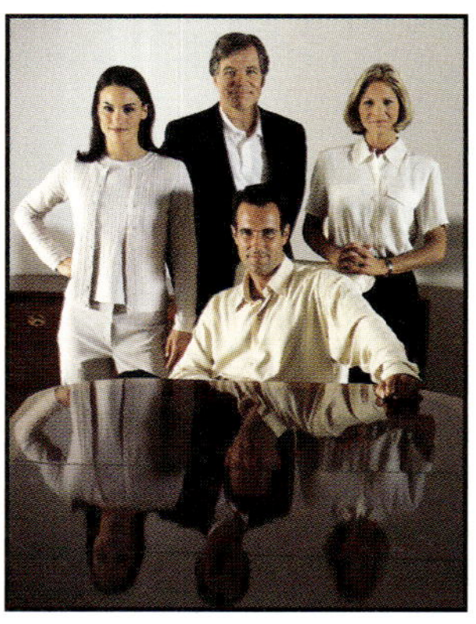
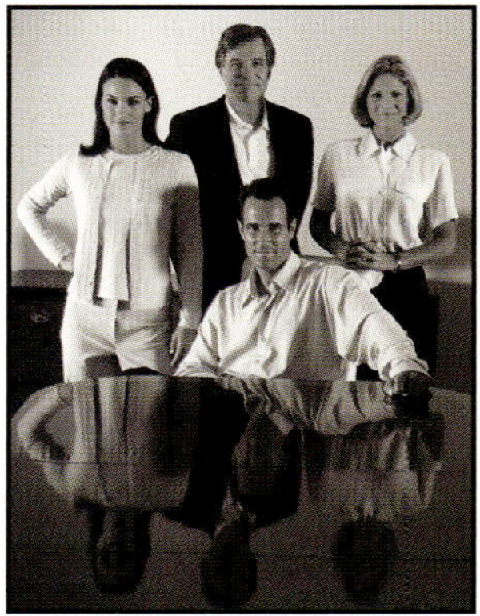

- You can repair old pictures that are torn or stained.
- You can manipulate pictures, adding or combining pictures to create a totally new picture. For instance, suppose that your friend cannot attend your wedding. You can take an existing photo of your friend and place them in a wedding picture just as if the friend was there!

To Keep on Learning . . .

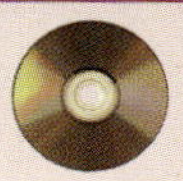

Go to the CD-ROM and select the segment:

- *Digital Photography Overview* to learn more about the key features and benefits of digital photography.

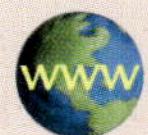

Go online to **www.LearnwithGateway.com** and log on to select:

- *Internet links and resources*
- *FAQs*

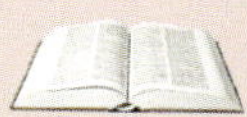

With the *Survive & Thrive* series, refer to *Use and Care for Your PC* for more information on:

- *Using a CD-R drive*

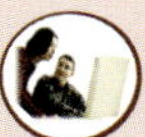

Gateway offers a hands-on training course that covers many of the topics in this chapter. Additional fees may apply. Call **888-852-4821** for enrollment information. If applicable, please have your customer ID and order number ready when you call.

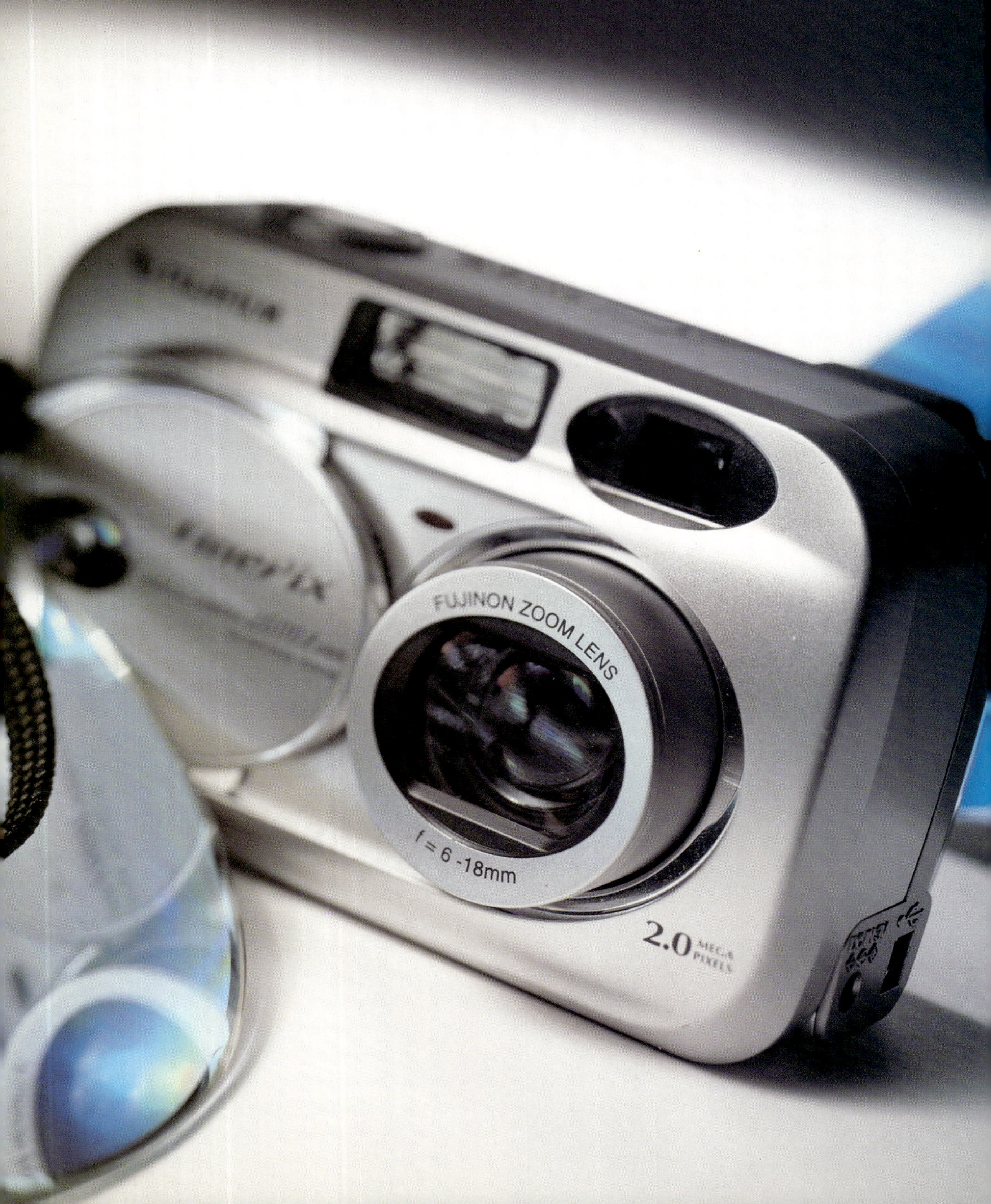
FUJINON ZOOM LENS
f = 6 -18mm
2.0 MEGA PIXELS

CHAPTER 2

Selecting the Right Equipment for Digital Photography

You may be intrigued enough about digital photography to start composing your shopping list, or you may already have made your purchase and are ready to go. Either way, this chapter provides an overview of all the hardware components you need, including what type of computer works best for digital photography. Later chapters go into more detail about each component. If you're thinking about purchasing, read this chapter to gain a good understanding of each type of component and the differences among them. If you already have your equipment, consider reading this chapter to learn more about your components. You may decide to purchase more equipment, or you may even realize you have features you didn't know about!

Preparing Your Computer for Digital Photography

As you know, a key component of digital photography—aside from the digital camera or scanner you use to obtain images—is your computer. In order to use your camera or scanner with your computer the computer must meet certain system requirements. For example, it must have a CPU (central processing unit) that is powerful enough to work with digital images. In addition, you need enough RAM (random access memory) and hard drive space. You'll also need to have a DVD (digital versatile disc) or CD (compact disc) drive, as well as the right type of connector on your computer to connect to your camera or scanner. Finally, the operating system on your computer must be able to support the use of cameras or scanners.

Both cameras and scanners have varying system requirements. To find out your camera or scanner's requirements, check its packaging or the detailed product information that came with it.

Most cameras (and other hardware add-ons) list the minimum system requirements. A computer that exceeds these minimum requirements will have better performance.

Finding Your System Information

If you're not sure about your computer's setup (that is, what types of hardware components it uses, how much RAM and hard-drive space it has, etc.) look at the paperwork from the computer manufacturer or seller. It should list all the computer components with detailed information for each one.

If you can't find your paperwork, follow these steps to get specific hardware information:

1. Click the **Start** button.

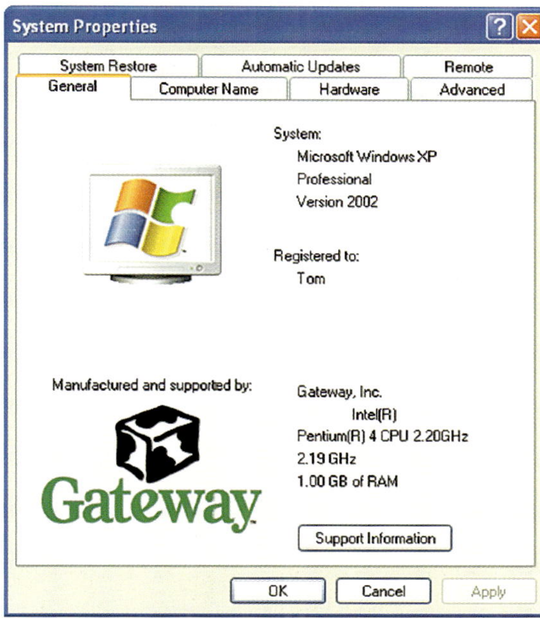

2. Right-click **My Computer** and then click **Properties** in the shortcut menu that appears. The System Properties dialog box opens with the General tab displayed. This tab lists the Windows version, processor type and speed, and amount of RAM.

3. Click the **Hardware** tab.

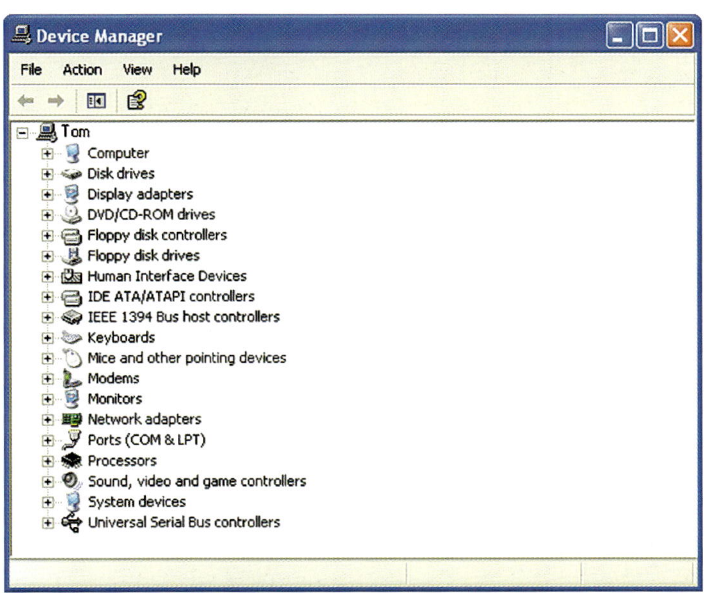

4. Click **Device Manager**. The Device Manager window opens, listing all the devices on your computer including hard drives, DVD drives, and CD drives.

5. To get detailed information about any of the devices on your computer, begin by clicking the plus sign next to that device's type.
6. Right-click the name of the device you want information about, and click **Properties** in the shortcut menu that appears.
7. The Properties dialog box opens, with several tabs of information about this device. Click the various tabs to gather the information you need.
8. Click **OK** to close the Properties dialog box.
9. Click the **Close** button to close Device Manager.
10. Click **OK** to close the System Properties dialog box.

The CPU

The *CPU* (central processing unit) is the core component of a computer. Sometimes referred to as the "brain" of the computer, the CPU interprets and carries out instructions, performs all computations, and controls the devices connected to the computer.

A variety of CPUs is available. One well-known manufacturer of CPUs is Intel®; another is AMD®. Each manufacturer produces various models of CPUs. For example, Intel produces Pentium® and Celeron® processors, and AMD sells Athlon™ and Duron™ processors.

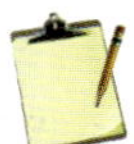

Laptops often use a different type of processor designed specifically for laptops.

CPU manufacturers often update their chips, making them faster and more powerful. CPUs have specific names to indicate newer models. For example, a current offering by Intel is the Pentium 4 processor.

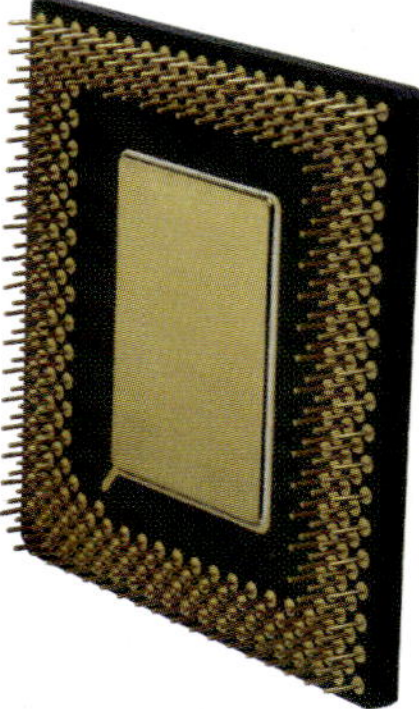

Figure 2-1 A CPU.

In addition to its type, a CPU's speed is important. The CPU's speed is the key factor in the overall speed of the computer. This speed is measured in megahertz (MHz) or gigahertz (GHz). *MHz* indicates how many million calculations a CPU can perform every second, whereas *GHz* indicates how many billion calculations a CPU can perform every second. As you might guess, the higher the number, the faster the computer.

The CPU is important when working with digital photography because of performance. The processor type and speed affect the overall performance of your computer. This, in turn, determines how quickly you can transfer your images from the camera or scanner to the computer, how quickly images can be opened and printed, and more. Because digital images can be quite large in size, performance is key.

Of course, faster is always better, but you don't need a top-of-the line computer to perform most computing tasks, including digital photography. For example, the FujiFilm FinePix 2600Zoom camera requires, at a minimum, a Pentium computer (any type) with a speed of 200 MHz or higher. Check your camera's owner's manual for more information.

RAM

RAM (random access memory) temporarily stores data, software, and the operating system while the computer is operating. RAM is a very important part of a computer; in most cases, the more RAM a computer has, the better and faster it performs, and the more tasks it can handle at the same time. RAM is measured in *megabytes* (M or MB) or *gigabytes* (G or GB).

As with CPU speed, the more RAM, the better. At the same time, you don't need the highest amount of RAM to enjoy digital photography. The FujiFilm® FinePix 2600Zoom in our example requires a minimum of 64 MB of RAM.

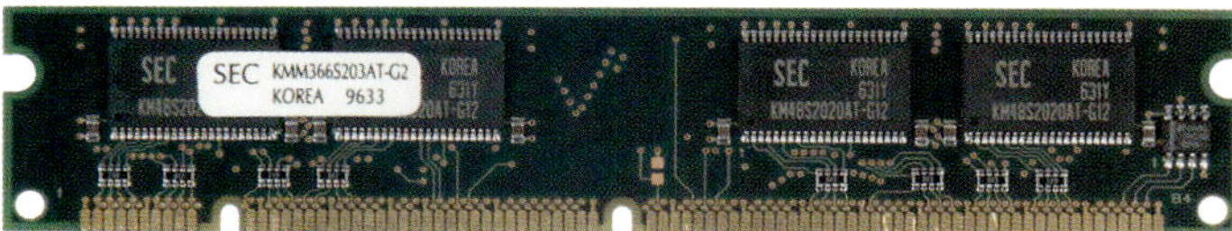

Figure 2-2 RAM.

Hard Drive Space

RAM is a temporary storage space on your computer where information is held as you are working on it. Your hard drive, on the other hand, is where you save information permanently—as a file with a particular name, on a specific drive, in a specific folder. Like RAM, the amount of storage space on your hard drive is measured in megabytes (M or MB) or, more commonly, gigabytes (G or GB).

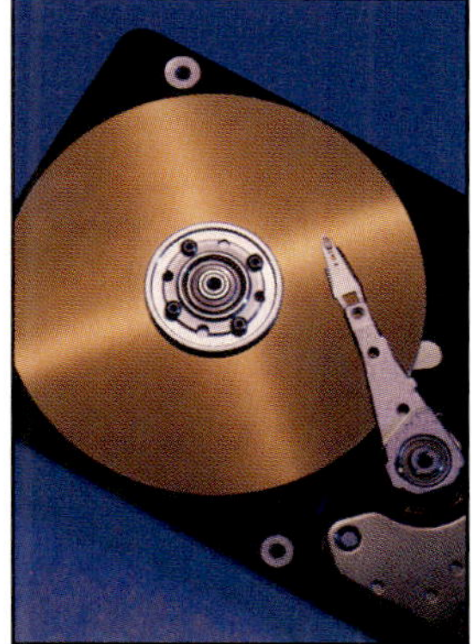

Figure 2-3 A hard drive.

It's easy to confuse RAM with the hard drive because the two are measured in the same way. Just keep in mind that hard-drive space stores information permanently, whereas information in RAM is stored only temporarily. In addition, you have quite a bit more hard-drive space than RAM.

With regard to digital photography, hard drive space is important for these reasons:

- Because picture files can be large in size, you need plenty of space on your hard drive to store them. You should probably have at least 140 MB or more of free hard drive space.

Besides your hard drive, you have other options for storing your files. For example, you can store them on CDs or DVDs. You can also compress your images so they consume less space. Chapter 8 goes into more detail about your storage options.

- You need space to store the program(s) you use to edit, print, and otherwise work with the pictures you create. (See the section "Selecting an Image Editor" later in this chapter for more information about these programs.)

CD/DVD Drives

Chances are, your camera or scanner will require your computer to have a CD drive or DVD drive, usually because the software for the camera or scanner is supplied on a CD or DVD. Also, when you install a camera or scanner, Windows uses a special type of file called a driver file. This file tells Windows the specific hardware details about your particular device. Drivers are also often supplied on CDs.

If the drives on your computer can be used to burn CDs or DVDs, you can also use them to store photos. You can learn more about organizing photos on CD or DVD disks in Chapter 8.

Connector

One of the most important things to check is how the camera or scanner is connected to your computer. Most connect with a standard USB (Universal Serial Bus) cable; you plug one end of the cable into the camera or scanner and the other end into the computer when you want to download or copy images from one to the other.

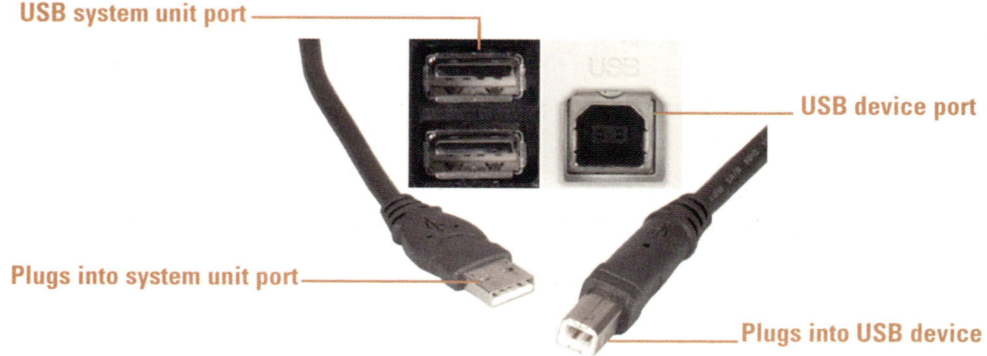

Most new computers come with several USB ports (generally four). If your computer is older, however, it may not. In that case, consider purchasing a camera that connects using a different type of cable or upgrading your computer to add a USB port (doing so is relatively inexpensive).

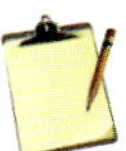

Ports are openings like sockets on the back or front of your computer. Older computers typically have one *parallel port*, which is most often used to connect a printer. These computers also have *serial ports*, used to connect other devices, such as mouse devices, modems, and so on. (Most computers have two serial ports.) Now parallel, serial, and USB ports are standard.

2

Windows Version

This book discusses digital photography in the context of the most recent version of Windows, called *Windows XP*. Windows XP includes several handy photo-handling features. For instance, you can plug in your camera and the Windows Plug and Play feature will automatically install the camera. When you take pictures, you can connect the camera and download pictures from the camera to the computer without any other software. Windows XP also includes a special My Pictures folder and picture-related tasks.

If you use an earlier version of Windows, however, you don't necessarily need to upgrade. Many versions of Windows provide support for digital photography, but it's a good idea to check your camera or scanner's documentation to ensure your version of Windows will work with it.

Understanding Digital Camera Basics

Just like a film-based camera, digital cameras come in all shapes and sizes, with many different features. Which camera is best for you depends on such considerations as what quality of pictures you need and how much money you want to spend. For example, if you're new to photography, digital or otherwise, a general-purpose model will probably suit your needs; most basic cameras take adequate pictures. If you're more experienced, however, you may want a model with more advanced features.

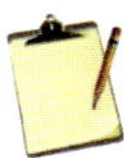

If you're thinking of buying a camera, you can use this section to help you select the model most suited to your needs. If you already have a camera, you can read this section to figure out what features it has; you may decide to upgrade as you become more experienced.

In any case, start with a good idea of what you want to accomplish with your camera. Then use the following list to understand the differences among cameras. This list gives you a good idea of what you need to take into consideration when choosing a camera:

- Picture quality
- File format
- Camera storage
- Storage media
- The display
- Camera size
- Camera features
- Power source
- Programs included with the camera

Where can you find all these details? If you've already bought a camera, this information probably appears somewhere in its packaging. If you're shopping around, read reviews online; they, along with camera advertisements, often provide detailed product information. The next several sections discuss in detail the main points in the preceding list.

Table 2-1 Digital photo camera specifications.

Camera	FujiFilm FinePix 2600	Nikon® CoolPix 2500	Canon® PowerShot S330	Canon PowerShot S30	Canon PowerShot G2
Digital zoom	2.5 x	4.0x	2.5x	3.2x	3.6x
Sensor resolution (effective pixels)	2 million	2 million	2 million	3.2 million	4 million
Optical sensor size	1/2.7"	1/2.7"	1/2.7"	1/1.8	1/1.8"
Optical sensor type	CCD	CCD	CCD	CCD	CCD
Light sensitivity	ISO 100	ISO 100	ISO 50-400	ISO 50-800	ISO 50-400
Still image format	JPEG	JPEG	JPEG	JPEG	JPEG
Lens aperture	F/3.5-8.7	F/5.6	F/2.8-F/4.7	F/2.8-F/8.0	F2.0-F/8.0
Camera flash type	Built-in flash	Built-in flash	Built-in flash	Built-in flash	Built-in flash
Storage Media	SmartMedia	CompactFlash	CompactFlash	CompactFlash	CompactFlash
Display type	TFT color LCD 1.8"	TFT color LCD 1.5"	TFT color 1.8"	TFT color LCD 1.5"	TFT color LCD 1.8"
Weight	7.1 oz	8.6 oz	9.2 oz	6.0 oz	14.8

Picture Quality

Cameras vary in the quality of the images they produce. Picture quality is measured in *pixels per inch (PPI)*. As mentioned in Chapter 1, a *pixel*, short for *picture elements*, is a tiny dot of light that is the basic unit of measurement for images on a computer screen or in a digital image. Digital images use millions of pixels to create an image; therefore, most cameras use *megapixel* to indicate one million pixels.

The more pixels per inch an image has, the better its picture quality (as shown in Table 2-1). For example, images generated by a 1.0-megapixel camera have fewer pixels than images generated by a 2.0- or 4.0-megapixel camera. Figure 2-4 shows photos captured with varying pixel settings.

Keep in mind that new cameras are introduced all the time. Expect to see cameras with even higher pixel ratings.

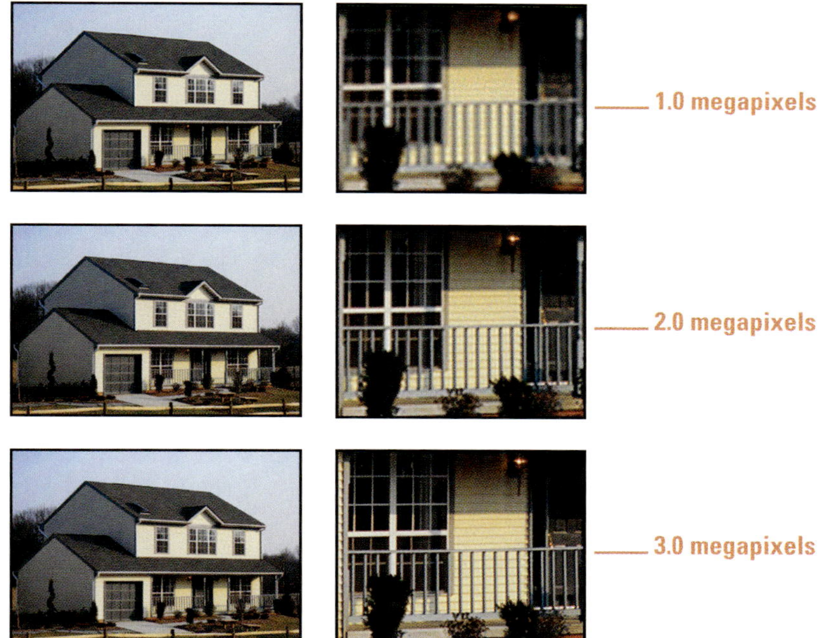

Figure 2-4 Image pixel comparison.

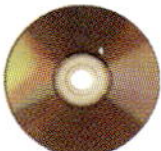

To learn more about digital cameras and how to make the right selection, go to the CD-ROM segment *Digital Camera: Selecting*.

File Formats

Some cameras enable you to save your pictures in different formats, which can come in handy depending on how you plan to use your images after you generate them. When you take a picture using a digital camera, the image is saved to a file, which you can then copy to your computer. Depending on the camera, you may have a choice of *file formats* that is, the format used to save the file, the most common of which is *JPEG* (Joint Photographics Experts Group). This format is among the most popular, not only for printed pictures, but also for pictures displayed on Web pages.

You may also be able to save images as *TIFF* (Tagged Image File Format) files, another popular type. These are often used for printed publications such as the pictures in this book.

If you are a novice, you don't have to worry about file formats. On the other hand, if you are a professional photographer or working on a project that requires pictures in a particular format, be sure to check out this feature.

Camera Storage

Digital cameras store images in their internal memory, on a removable card, or both. Storage is important because it determines how many pictures you can take and whether you need additional storage media.

Determining just how much camera storage you need can be tricky for a couple of reasons. One reason is that you typically have quality options when you take a picture; with the FujiFilm FinePix 2600Zoom, for example, you can take basic, normal, and fine images. The higher the quality of the image, the more pixels it has, and therefore the more space is needed to store it. Another reason is that your camera's overall quality—whether it's a 1-megapixel camera, 2-megapixel camera, and so on—affects the file size of the images it generates. Table 2-2 gives you an idea of how camera type and image quality can affect file size.

Check your camera manual for specific information about the approximate size of the image files your camera generates.

Table 2-2 How camera type and image quality affect file sizes.

CAMERA TYPE	IMAGE TYPE	IMAGE SIZE
3-megapixel	SuperFine	Approx. 2,002 KB
3-megapixel	Fine	Approx. 1,116 KB
3-megapixel	Normal	Approx. 556
2-megapixel	Fine	Approx. 770 KB
2-megapixel	Normal	Approx. 390 KB
2-megapixel	Basic	Approx. 200 KB
1-megapixel	Fine	Approx. 620 KB
1-megapixel	Normal	Approx. 320 KB
1-megapixel	Basic	Approx. 130 KB

Remember that you can take pictures with different quality settings. Higher-quality images take up more space in your camera's memory, which means you can take fewer pictures at one time. You can save space by deleting any pictures that you take and don't want. Also, you can clear the memory and start again by downloading the pictures from the camera to your computer.

Storage Media

Depending on what type of camera you have, you may be able to supplement its storage space by buying additional storage media in the form of removable media cards. The two most common types of media cards are CompactFlash and SmartMedia. You can also find cameras that use IBM® MicroDrives.

Not only does this type of media provide a great deal of storage space, but it also allows you to transfer the pictures on the media card to your computer or remove the media card and take it to a print service to have the images printed directly from it (see Chapter 7 for more on printing).

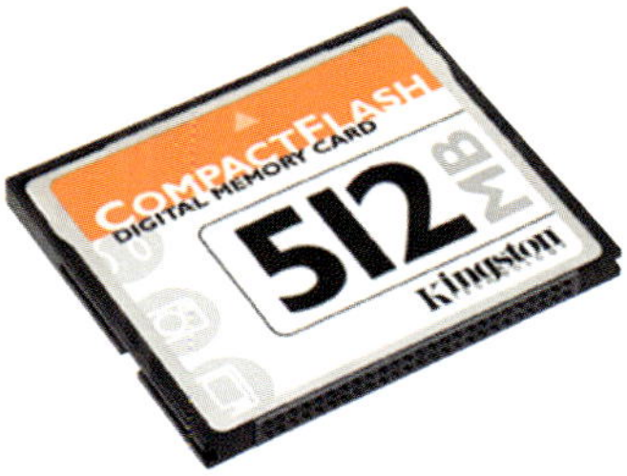

Figure 2-5 CompactFlash storage.

Removable media cards can store anywhere from 4 MB of image data to 512 MB. (Of course, cards that can store more data typically cost more as well.) Common sizes include 8 MB, 16 MB, and 32 MB.

It can be tricky determining how much storage space your removable media cards should contain. Both camera quality and image quality play a role in determining the size of the image files the camera generates, and the size of these image files dictates how much storage you need.

Chances are, your camera's manual has specific information about what type of removable media you can use, as well as approximate storage information. Using the example of the 2-megapixel FujiFilm FinePix 2600Zoom camera, Table 2-3 lists the number of images each size media card can store. (This table assumes the resolution of the images is 1600 x 1200.)

Table 2-3 Number of images various removable media cards can store.

Size of Card	Number of Fine-Quality Images	Number of Normal-Quality Images	Number of Basic-Quality Images
4 MB	4	9	19
8 MB	10	19	39
16 MB	20	39	75
32 MB	41	79	152
64 MB	82	159	306
128 MB	166	319	613

The Display

One of the neatest features of digital cameras is that they display your pictures right after you take them on an LCD (liquid crystal display) or similar display. This feature provides instant gratification—it allows you to see your photo immediately. These screens are usually 1.8 inches in size, but the size can vary. Some cameras also enable you to zoom in on your pictures using the LCD.

When selecting a camera, look at the display to make sure the view is sharp and big enough to get a sense of how the picture will look when taken. If you want to be able to zoom in, make sure the camera has this feature.

Camera Size

The size and dimensions of some digital cameras may surprise you; many aren't shaped quite like their film-based counterparts. The dimensions of a camera vary from model to model. Some are similar to a traditional camera, but others are more square in shape. If you're buying a camera, visit a store and handle it first to make sure you like how it feels in your hand. You may be most comfortable with one that is shaped similarly to your own film-based camera. The most comfortable are generally those that have metal bodies and a little extra weight.

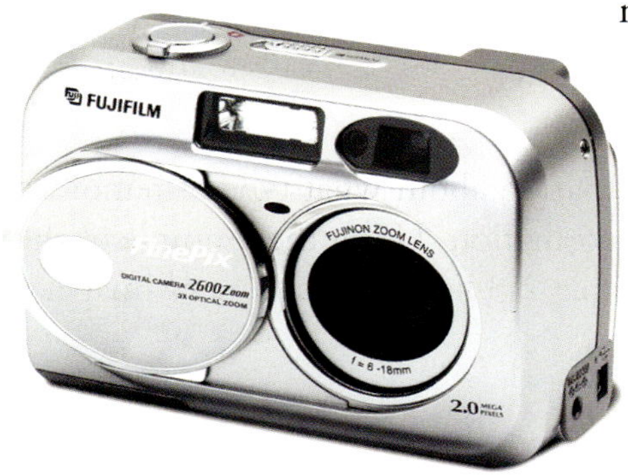

2

Figure 2-6 FujiFilm FinePix 2600 digital camera.

Camera Features

When comparing digital cameras, be sure to find out what type of lens and flash are used by each one, as well as what other features are offered. In certain respects, comparing digital cameras is similar to comparing their film-based variety. For example, when looking at a digital camera, ask what type of lens the digital camera has. Is it fixed, or can it be zoomed? If it's a zoom lens, what is the zoom range? Another important question to ask is what type of flash the camera has—automatic, manual, or both. Also, does the camera have automatic red-eye reduction?

More About . . . Lenses

When comparing digital cameras, you will see two types of zoom ranges cited: optical zoom and digital zoom. *Optical zoom* is the same type of zoom found on regular cameras. With an optical zoom, you actually change the range of space captured by the image sensor. *Digital zoom,* however, is actually a trick. This type of zoom photographs an entire scene, but saves only a particular part or expands a section by adding pixels. You can get the same effect by cropping the image in an imaging program.

Unlike film-based cameras, some digital cameras can also be used for audio/video recording or can function as simplified video recorders. Keep in mind, however, that a digital camera isn't going to replace your video camera. You can shoot short videos and capture pictures from the video to use as prints, but you won't get the full features of a video recorder in a camera. Also, digital videos are incredibly large in size. You will most likely be able to shoot only a short video clip.

Power Source

Most cameras use a rechargeable battery, and they may include a power adaptor (sometimes as an optional add-on). Many also come equipped to use AA or other readily available alkaline batteries. Digital cameras use up batteries quickly, and it may be more cost effective to invest in some rechargeable removable batteries or a special heavy-duty battery that attaches to the camera, such as Quantum's QB1 Compact. This type of battery is rechargeable, made just for digital cameras with a power adapter, and lasts for hours or even days, depending on use. When shopping for your camera, you may want to check to see if it has a port or adapter for such a power source.

Software Programs

Most cameras come with a driver, the file that tells Windows the particular details about this device. In addition, many cameras come with software that downloads the images from the camera to the computer and also enables you to edit and print the images. Popular software programs include MGI PhotoSuite 4 and Microsoft's Picture It!. You can find more information about software in the section "Selecting an Image Editor."

Accessories

In addition to the camera itself, you may want to consider buying some optional equipment. For example, as with a film-based camera, you may decide you need a carrying case, a tripod, extra batteries, and a power adapter for your digital camera. There are also special accessories for digital cameras, such as the following:

- Some Kodak cameras have a docking station that you can attach to your computer to make transferring images from the camera to the computer easier. The docking station isn't required, but it does simplify the transfer of images.

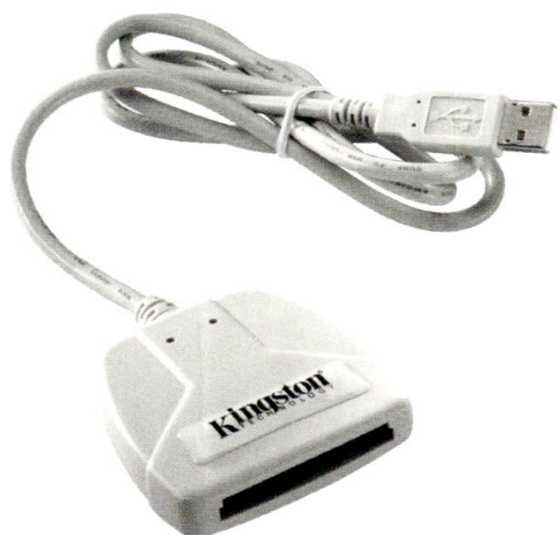

- Instead of docking stations, users can buy a memory-card reader that you can attach to your computer. You can then transfer images from your removable media card using this reader.

- Special photo printers enable you to print your digital images on paper that looks and feels like regular photographic paper. (See the section "Printing Your Images" later in this chapter for an overview of printing choices, as well as Chapter 7 for detailed information about printing.)

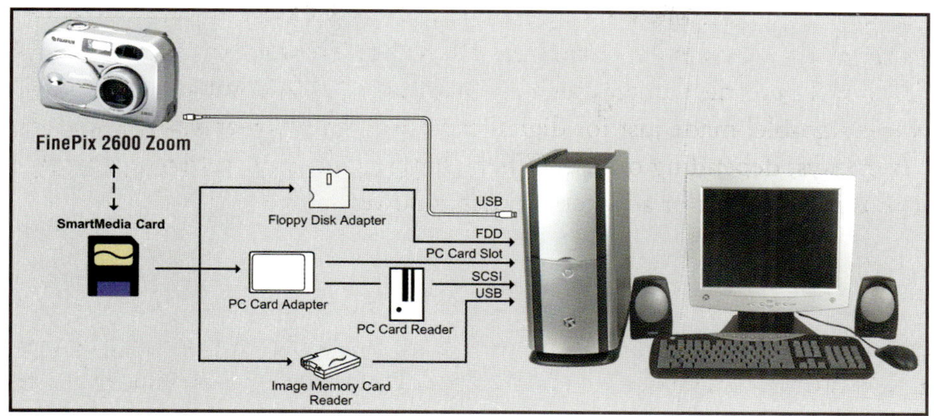

Here is an illustration of how the various pieces just discussed fit together to create a digital camera-to-computer connection.

Understanding Scanner Basics

As mentioned in Chapter 1, you can use a scanner to scan any type of document, including pictures, illustrations, maps, text, and so on. Once you've scanned an image, you can do any of the following:

- Insert the scanned image into a report, newsletter, brochure, order form, or any other type of document.

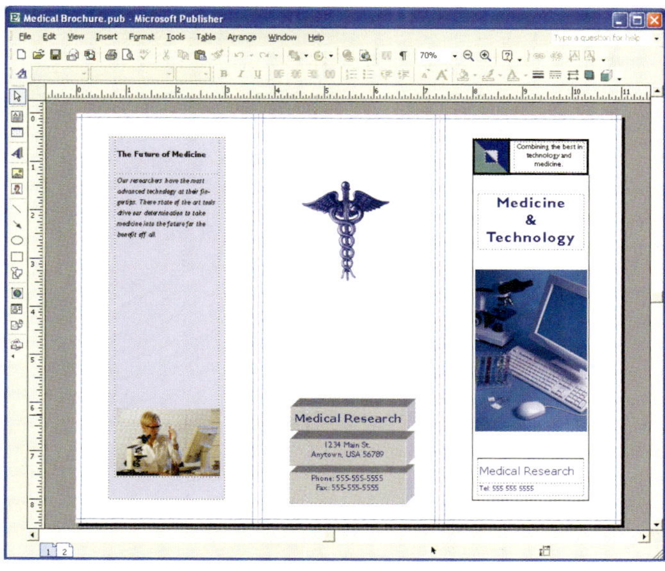

- Print the scanned image.
- Add the image to a Web page.
- Edit the scanned image, cropping parts out, adding text, and so on.

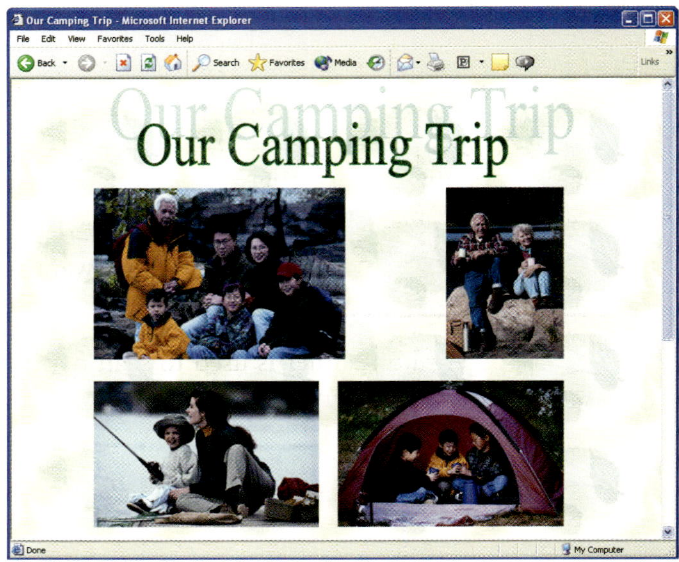

The following section provides a quick overview of different types of scanners. For complete information about using scanners as a source for digital imagery, see Chapter 4.

Types of Scanners

There are several types of scanners, including the following:

- **Flatbed.** The most common type of scanner is a *flatbed scanner*, which looks and works much like a copy machine. You place the image you want to scan on the transparent glass and close the lid. The scanner then scans the document using a moving light source, converts the image into digital format, and displays the image on screen.

When using a flatbed scanner to scan transparent images such as slides and negatives, the resulting image will sometimes appear to have concentric circles or rings on it that resemble a giant finger print. These are called Newton Rings and are a common problem when scanning transparent film media. If you are planning to buy a flatbed scanner that handles both pictures and transparent media, ask whether this is a problem for your scanner of choice. Most newer scanners have tried to solve this problem.

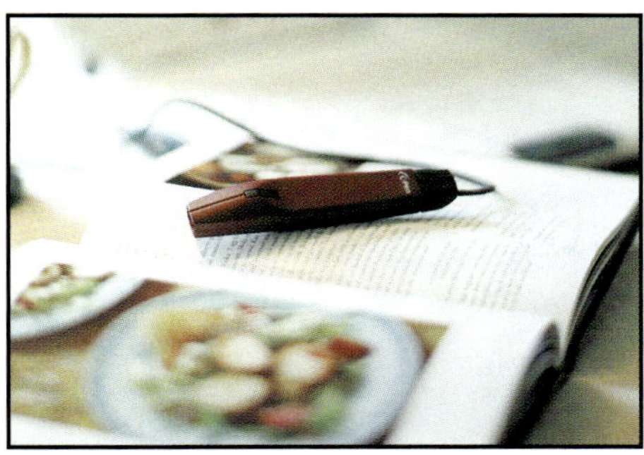

- **Handheld.** Another common type of scanner is a handheld scanner. This type of scanner sometimes looks similar to a pen, and it is most commonly used to scan text into the computer. You drag the handheld unit across the text you want to scan.

- **Film.** A film scanner is used to scan negatives and slides. You may consider buying a film scanner as you develop your digital-photography skills.
- **Sheet feed.** A *sheet feed* scanner is most commonly used for reflective material, such as transparencies.

In addition to choosing which type of scanner you want, you can also specify whether the scanner is to work in color or in black-and-white.

Image Quality

Like digital cameras, scanners vary in the quality of the image they produce. This resolution of a scanner indicates the quality, and the resolution is measured in pixels per inch, or *ppi*. As with cameras, the higher the resolution, the finer the detail in the scanned image. Generally, 300 ppi is adequate resolution for most users, but high-end scanners can produce scanned images with resolutions as high as 4000 ppi. You might need a higher quality scanner if you are doing professional artwork, detailed architectural prints, or other high-quality printed materials (for instance, a catalog).

More About . . . Image Quality

Another factor in image quality is *color bit depth*. A bit is the smallest unit of data that a computer can recognize. Color information is stored in bits; the more bits, the better the range of colors the scanner can read and represent. Color bit depth is covered in more detail in Chapter 4.

Scanner Features

When shopping for a scanner, you first select the type of scanner you want (typically flatbed for pictures). You then find one that can generate the level of quality you need for your scanned images. Once these two major decisions are made, you can start to compare the different features among scanners.

Chapter 4 covers in detail the different scanner features you can find.

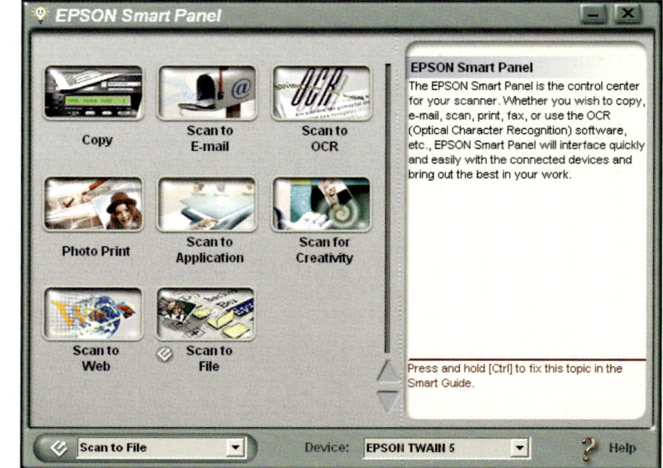

- **Scanning area.** This determines the size of the document you can scan. Most home and office flatbed scanners have legal-size scanning areas.
- **Scanning software.** Typically, scanners come bundled with software to handle the image once you've scanned it to your computer.
- **Connection type.** On newer computers, scanners are attached via a USB port. If you have an older computer, you can connect your scanner using one of the other ports such as the serial port. Or you may consider adding a USB port to your computer. This is a relatively inexpensive and easy upgrade.

Selecting an Image Editor

In order to *do* something with the images you take with your camera or scanner, you need some type of image-editing software. Image-editing software not only enables you to display the image, but also lets you print, save, and edit the image.

Here's some good news: Most cameras and scanners come bundled with their own software. For instance, if you buy an Epson scanner, it comes with a scanner program called ArcSoft PhotoImpression. You can use this program to view the scanned image, edit it, and save it. Likewise, Kodak cameras come with Kodak Picture Software, used not only to download images from the camera to the computer, but also to manipulate and save the pictures. Some companies, such as Gateway, bundle everything you need into one package. For example, if you purchase a Photo Solution, you may receive a camera, a software program, and extras, such as guides and photo paper.

If your camera or scanner didn't come with its own software, or if you find the software doesn't quite suit your needs, you can always purchase image-editing software on your own. Popular image programs include Microsoft's Picture It!®, MGI® PhotoSuite® 4, and Adobe® Photoshop®.

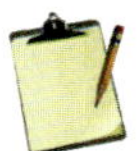

You'll learn more about using Picture It! and PhotoSuite 4 in Chapter 5.

All programs enable you to open, view, print, and save your images. Most enable you to perform the same set of basic editing tasks, including cropping, rotating, annotating, adjusting color, fixing red-eye, and so on. However, the programs differ somewhat in their look and feel, or interface. For example, compare Figure 2-7, showing Microsoft Picture It!, with Figure 2-8, showing MGI PhotoSuite 4.

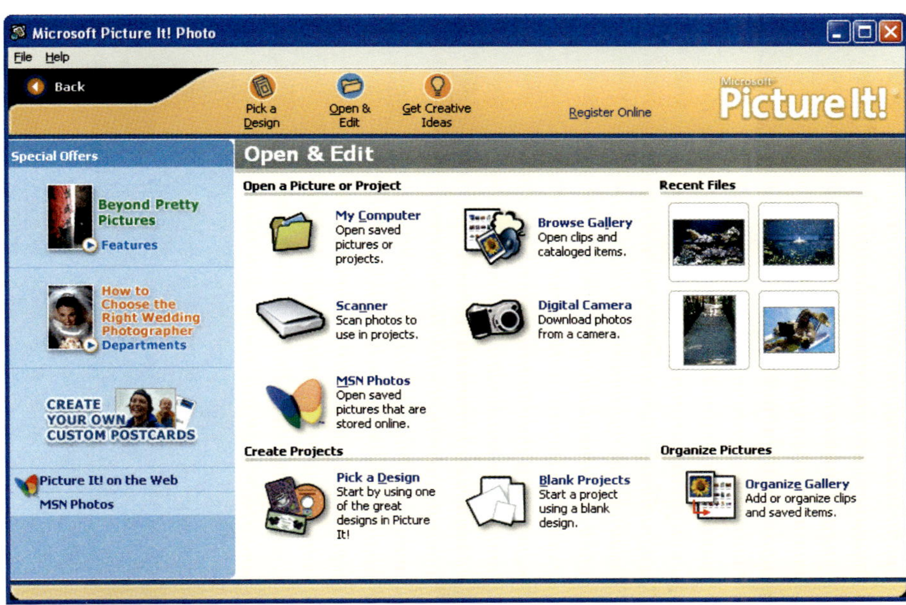

Figure 2-7 The Microsoft Picture It! window.

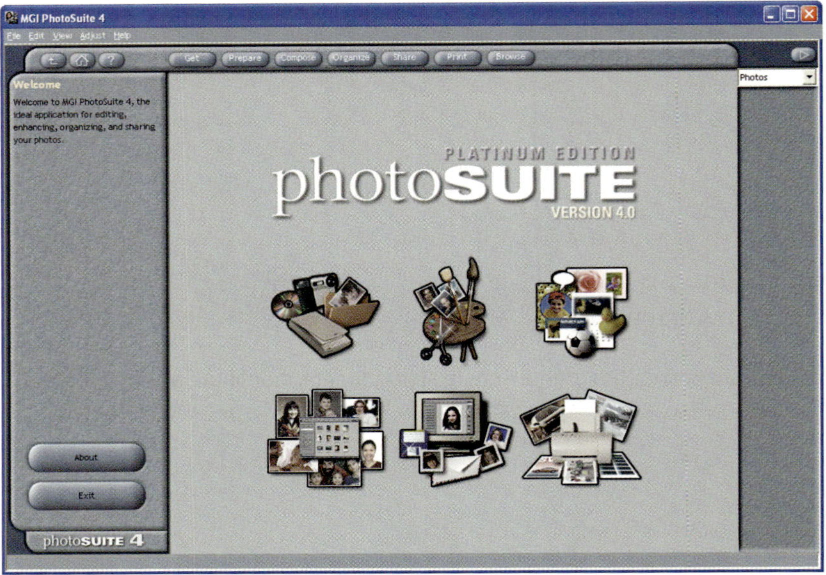

Figure 2-8 The MGI PhotoSuite 4 window.

The program you choose depends on your preference. If your camera or scanner or bundle came with its own software, it most likely will work well for you. As you become more experienced, you may want to consider some of the higher-end programs, such as Adobe Photoshop.

Printing Your Images

All your glorious pictures aren't much use if you can't show them off! Of course, one of the major advantages of digital photography is that you can include images in a document or Web page and send them via e-mail (covered in Chapter 8), but a brag book full of prints can't be beat. Fortunately, there are several printer options to choose from.

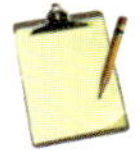

For specific details on printing your pictures, see Chapter 7.

Choosing a Printer

When choosing a printer, ask yourself the following questions:

- **What type of printer do I want?** These days, the two most common types of printers are *inkjet printers* and *laser printers*. Inkjet printers execute by spraying a fine, quick-drying ink onto paper. Laser printers, on the other hand, work more like copy machines. A laser beam burns special toner on the page to create the image. Inkjet printers are a popular choice because they are quiet and relatively inexpensive, especially if you want a color printer. In addition to inkjet and laser printers, special photo printers are available. These create print shop-quality picture prints on regular photo paper. You'll learn more about this special type of printer in Chapter 7.

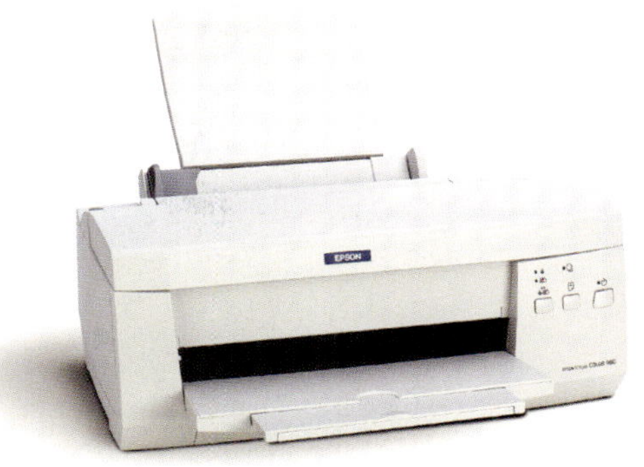

2

Several combination printer-copier-fax-scanner machines are now on the market. If you need an office machine that can perform multiple functions, check these out.

- **Do I need color?** If you plan to print photographs, you most likely will want a color printer. The most affordable are color inkjet printers, although color laser printers have become also become more reasonable as color printing has become more popular.
- **What level of quality do I need?** A printer's quality is determined by its resolution. For printers, resolution is measured in *dots per inch*, or dpi. Again, a higher number means a higher quality printed.

More About . . . Comparing Print Quality

When comparing print quality, you'll usually see resolution listed as 1200 x 1600 dpi. These two figures are the horizontal dots per inch and the vertical dots per inch. For example, you can expect to find printers with resolutions from 1200 x 600 dpi to 2400 x 1200 dpi on up. You may find it difficult, however, to translate such measurements into real results. If you are shopping for a printer, visit some retail stores and compare the printouts from various printers so you can see the difference.

- **How fast do I need my printer to be?** Printer speed is measured in the number of pages printed per minute (ppm). Laser printers are usually faster than inkjet printers. For both types of printers, you can expect to find speeds of 4-to-16 ppm.

Black-and-white printing is faster than color printing, so when comparing printers, you should check both the black-and-white speed and the color speed.

* **What type of connection do I need?** Printers commonly connect to computers via the parallel port, also called the *LPT* (line printer) port. Some, however, connect via a serial or a USB port. If you have just one printer, you likely have an available port. If you are adding a second printer, be sure you have an available port for it.

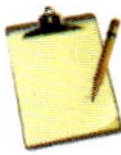

If you are printing on photo paper or labels, be sure you know which way to load the paper. Because you are printing on only one side of the page, the paper must be inserted properly. A good test is to mark an X on a plain piece of paper and then print something. You can then tell by the placement of the X which side of the paper the printer uses.

More About . . . Other Printer Features

Once you've narrowed down your options, there are a other printer features that you might want to consider before making your final choice:

* **How much paper does the printer hold?** If you print a lot of long documents, you don't want a printer that holds only a few sheets of paper. Look for printers that can hold between 150 and 200 pages.
* **Can the printer hold more than one kind of paper?** Some printers have multiple trays, enabling you to use one for plain paper and one for envelopes, letterhead, or other special paper. If your printer will be used in an office setting, even if it's a home office, this feature can be quite handy.
* **How is the paper fed into the printer?** Some printers use a tray that you slide into the front, whereas others use a tray above the printer that feeds the printer from the top down. Some people prefer one method to the other. Test out the printers on your short list to make sure it's easy to load the paper.
* **Can you print labels and envelopes?** Most printers enable you to print labels, which is handy for mass mailings. You should also be able to easily print an envelope, be it from an extra paper tray or through manual feed.
* **What controls does the printer have?** Expect to have an on/off switch as well as a reset button. The printer also should have some clear way to indicate problems like paper jams. Look for error buttons that clearly indicate the problem.
* **What are the costs of the supplies?** In addition to paper, you need to replace the ink cartridges for inkjet printers and the toner cartridge for laser printers. Check out the prices of the replacement cartridges that work for each printer model when shopping around.

Using Film and Scanning Services

If you want the results of digital photography but don't want to purchase a camera or scanner, you still have other options. For example, many film-development companies, such as Kodak, enable you to store digital versions of your film-based photo prints on CD-ROM or on the Web. Once your prints are digitized, you can print, e-mail, or modify them using your computer, just as you would if you had used a scanner or digital camera to obtain them.

If you need to scan an image only occasionally, you may not want to purchase a scanner. Fortunately, many copy and print stores offer scanners for customers' use. In most cases, you can use the same copy or print shop to print pictures, documents, photo calendars, brochures, or any other specialty item that might require a special type of printer. Many film-processing companies now have in-store scanners that you can use to scan your photographs and print copies of any size. Check your local drugstore for one of these kiosks; they are easy to use and convenient for creating Christmas cards, family photos, wallet-size pictures, or enlargements.

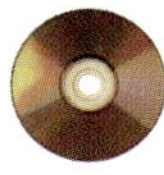

To understand the different sources of photographs that can be converted to a digital format, go to the CD-ROM segment *Photo Acquisition*.

To Keep on Learning . . .

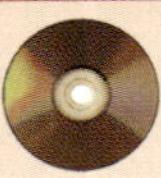

Go to the CD-ROM and select the segment:

- *Digital Camera: Selecting* to learn more about digital cameras and how to make the right selection.
- *Photo Acquisition* to understand the different sources of photographs that can be converted to a digital format.

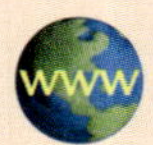

Go online to **www.LearnwithGateway.com** and log on to select:

- *Internet Links and Resources*
- *FAQs*

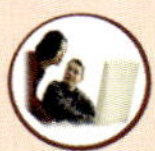

Gateway offers a hands-on training course that covers many of the topics in this chapter. Additional fees may apply. Call **888-852-4821** for enrollment information. If applicable, please have your customer ID and order number ready when you call.

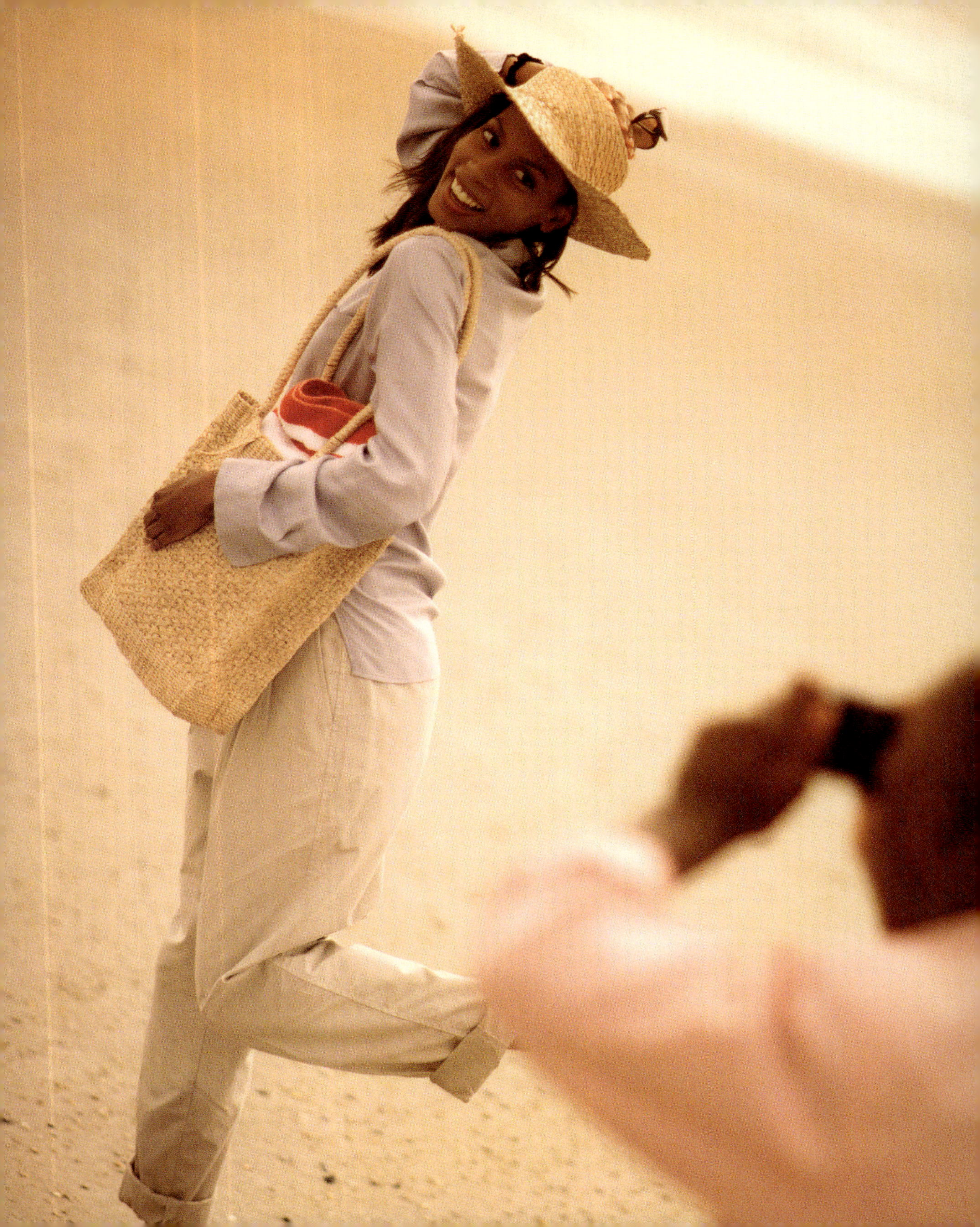

CHAPTER 3

Taking Great Pictures

By now, you've discovered the advantages of digital photography. You've also explored the equipment that enables you to enjoy working with your digital images. Now it's time to get down to the business of actually learning how to use your digital camera to take digital pictures.

In this chapter, you'll explore the various controls and buttons on your digital camera and discover what each one does. You'll also gain an understanding of basic photography principles. Then, you'll learn how to take various kinds of photographs using your digital camera, and you'll wrap up the chapter by studying how you can transfer the digital images on your camera to your computer.

Exploring Your Camera's Features

Unless you're an expert, you may view most of the dials, buttons, and other gizmos on your digital camera as mysterious at best. Getting a handle on how these features and settings work will pave the way to using your digital camera to its fullest potential.

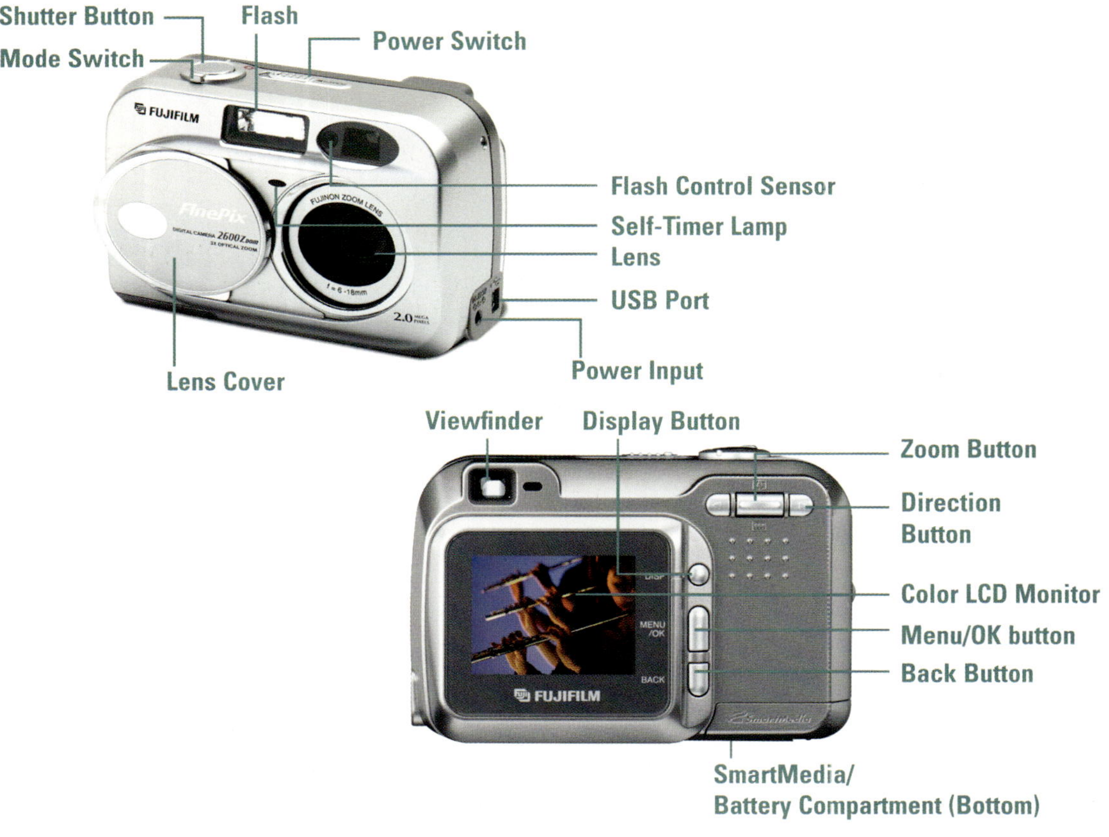

The features that are typically found in digital cameras include the following:

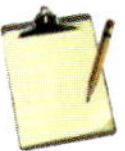

Every camera offers different features. Even when two cameras boast the same features, you probably access them in different ways. The best way to determine your camera's features and the best use of those features is to read the camera's user manual.

- **Lens and lens cover.** The lens and lens cover are easy camera features to locate on the camera's front side. To take pictures, you remove the lens cover or slide it to the side to expose the lens.
- **Power button.** To turn on your camera, you need to press the power button, which is typically located either on the side or top of the camera.
- **Connection port.** To transfer pictures from your camera to your computer, connect the cable to your camera's port. The port is usually found on the side of the camera. Refer to Chapter 2 for an illustration of ports and cables for digital cameras and computers.
- **Viewfinder.** The viewfinder is a tiny window on the camera's body that you look through to frame your shots. It is generally found on the backside of your camera.
- **Shutter button.** You press this button, which is almost always located on the top of the camera, to take a picture.
- **Flash.** You use a flash to illuminate the subject of your photograph if the lighting is too dark.
- **Mode switch.** Most cameras have several *modes*—one for taking pictures, another for reviewing or playing back photos, etc. You use the mode switch, typically found on top of the camera, to change modes.

Many digital cameras also feature a movie mode, which allows the camera to shoot short videos in addition to still photos.

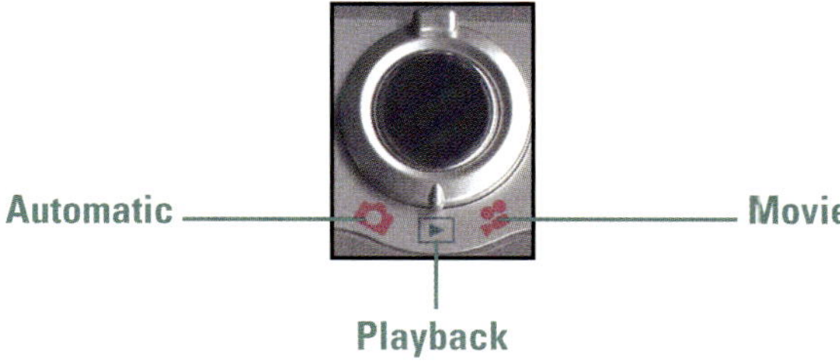

- **LCD monitor.** The LCD monitor shows you a preview of a picture you've just taken. You also have the option of switching to *playback* or *review* mode, enabling you to view the pictures currently stored on your camera.

- **Menu button.** Many cameras feature a menu button (or something similar) that enables you to access the commands on your camera, such as the Delete command.
- **Scroll buttons.** Scroll buttons, which usually look like arrows, enable you to navigate among commands or to move from picture to picture.
- **Media slot.** If your camera can use a media card such as a SmartMedia or CompactFlash card, it has a slot where you insert the card.
- **Battery compartment.** One source of a camera's power is supplied by batteries, which are stored here.

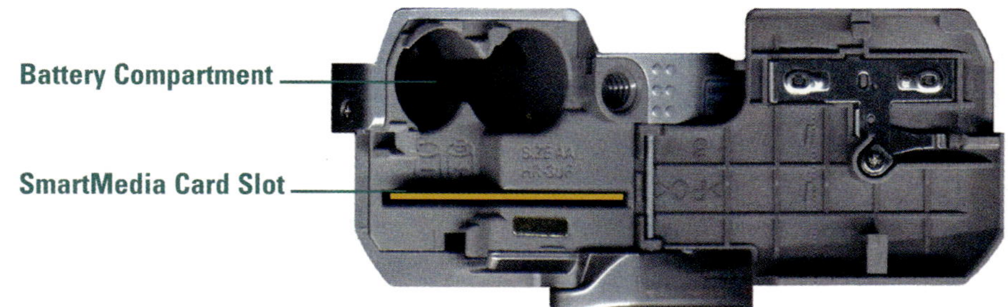

Before you can use your camera, you may need to take a few steps:

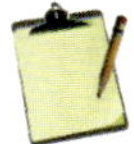

For specific instructions on completing each of these steps, refer to your camera's user manual.

1. If necessary, insert batteries into the camera's battery compartment (in some cases, you'll need to charge them first).
2. If your camera uses a media card, insert it in the appropriate slot.
3. You may need to set certain camera options, such as the date and time.

Understanding Basic Photography Principles

As with any new undertaking, one of the very first things you must learn about photography—digital or otherwise—is the vocabulary used by photographers. Learning just a few key photographic terms and concepts will help you decipher your camera's user manual as well as any articles or how-to information you encounter later.

This section introduces you to some of the key terms and concepts relating to digital and film-based photography. You don't need to master all these concepts in order to begin taking pictures with your digital camera. However, as you become more skilled, you'll appreciate this foundation.

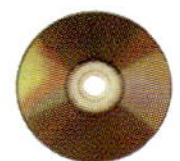

To learn how to take a great picture, go to the CD-ROM segment *Picture Taking Basics.*

Composition

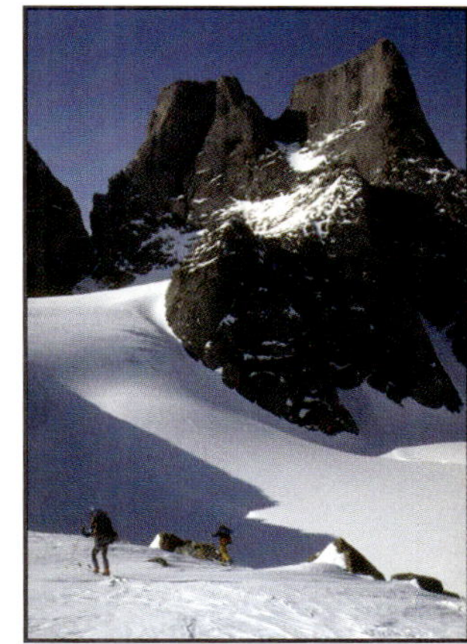

Composition refers to the way you frame the subject of your photograph, or *compose* your image. When composing images, the basic rule is to frame your picture for optimal presentation of its subject. To this end, most beginning photographers frame the subject in the center of the picture. As your photography skills advance, however, you may decide to experiment with other compositions. For example, you may decide to shoot your subject off-center to create a different balance in the picture. Alternatively, you may decide to include more of the background to better show the contrast between your subject and its surroundings. In the photograph shown here, the photographer has incorporated the landscape to convey the magnitude of the scenery in comparison to the people in the photo.

More About . . . Composition

Many professional photographers recommend that as you frame your image, you divide the scene into a grid (either into thirds or into a grid of nine squares). To achieve balance, you place your subject in either the left or the right third. You may want to experiment by framing the subject in different portions of the grid to see which placement gives you the best composition.

To aid you in this, some digital cameras actually overlay a grid pattern on the LCD screen or in your viewfinder, as is the case with the FujiFilm FinePix 2600Zoom camera's Framing Guideline feature. (To access this feature on the FinePix 2600Zoom, press the DISP button until the Framing Guideline option appears.) Check your camera's manual to see if it has a similar feature and, if so, how to use it.

Depth of Field/Focus

When you photograph a subject of any kind, you typically want that person or object to be in focus. Your digital camera uses a lens for focusing, a process that often occurs automatically. With your camera's manual controls, however, you can manipulate your image's *depth of field*—the area of the photograph that's in focus—by using zoom controls to change the lens's focal length and by adjusting aperture settings.

Zoom Controls

Focal length refers to the distance between the camera's lens and the film or digital sensors the camera uses to record an image. A shorter focal length yields a wider angle of view, meaning that the subject of the photograph will be relatively small in comparison with the background. A longer focal length, on the other hand, yields a narrower angle of view, which means that the subject of the photograph will appear larger in the frame.

If your camera has zoom controls, you can use them to adjust the lens's focal length. In fact, most digital cameras offer multiple zoom settings, usually indicated as 2X (a magnification factor of two) or 3X (a magnification factor of three). The higher the magnification, the closer the subject of the photograph appears.

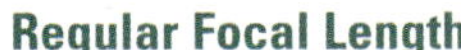

Regular Focal Length

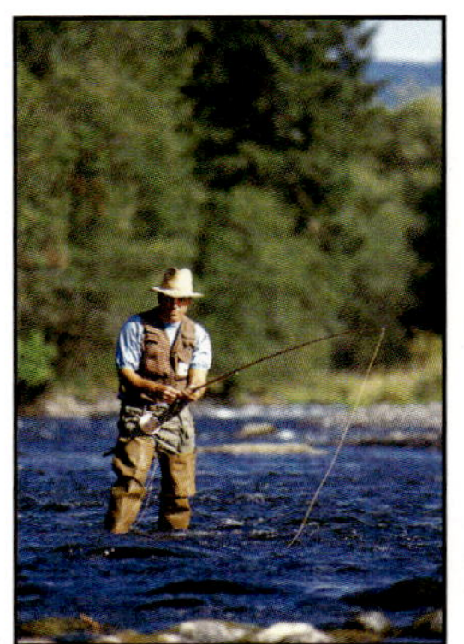

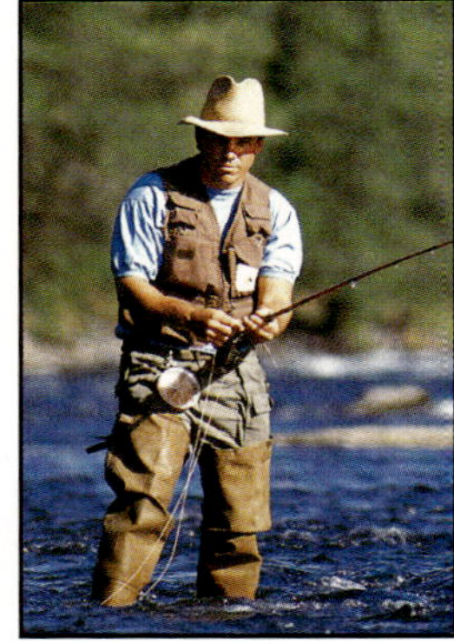

Zoomed Focal Length

Because digital cameras use smaller lenses than film-based cameras, the focal length and zoom are not the same as those used by 35mm cameras. For instance, the diagonal measurement of a digital frame is around 43mm, whereas the normal lens on a 35mm camera is around 50mm. To avoid confusion, most digital cameras give a 35mm equivalent instead of the camera's actual focal length.

Aperture Settings

In automatic mode, your digital camera sets the focus (and, by extension, the depth of field) automatically. In manual mode, however, you can tinker with the depth of field by changing the camera's aperture settings.

A camera's *aperture* is the opening through which light enters before striking the film or digital sensors. You can make the diameter of this opening larger or smaller by changing the aperture settings, also called *f-stops*. A lower f-stop indicates a larger aperture diameter, and vice versa. The photo shown next on the left has a small aperture and great field depth, whereas the photo on the right has a large aperture and shallow field depth. Although the two photos look focused differently, the camera was focused on the girl in each.

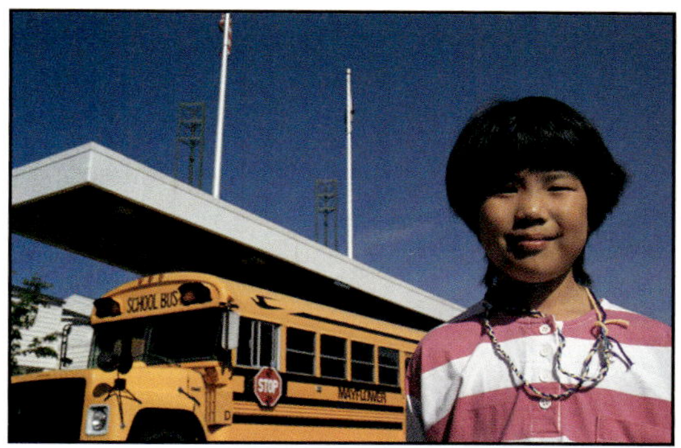

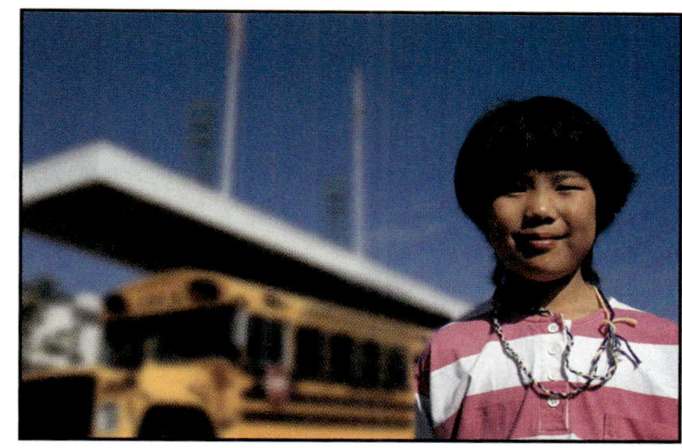

Aperture settings and how they relate to depth of field is an advanced photography subject. For now, just remember that your camera can use various aperture settings to achieve different effects in your pictures.

Exposure

In photography, be it digital or film-based, you must expose your camera's digital sensors or film to light in order to take a photograph. The term *exposure* refers to the amount of light allowed to travel through the camera's lens and aperture and strike its digital sensors or film when the shutter is opened.

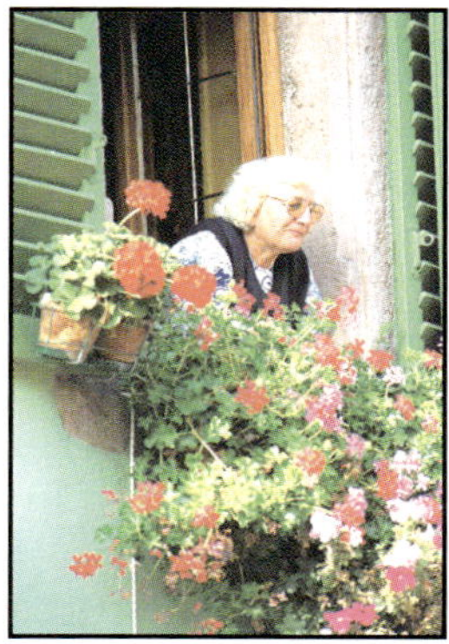

Overexposed

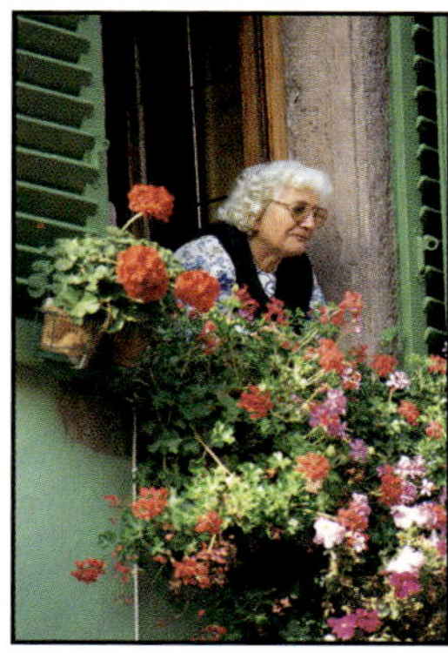

Proper Exposure

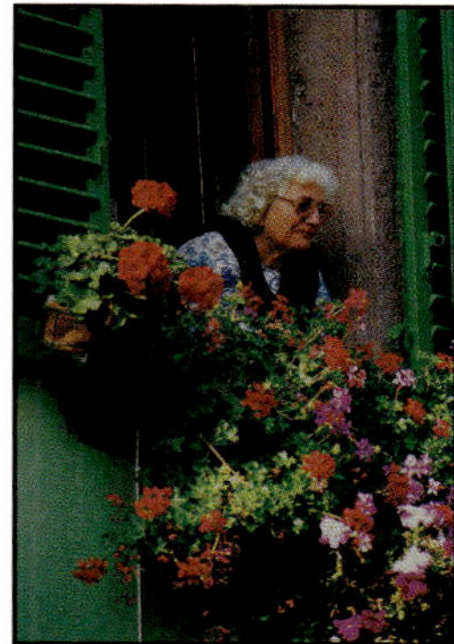

Underexposed

There are two ways to alter the amount of light that strikes the camera's digital sensors or film. One is to adjust the camera's aperture settings, increasing or reducing the amount of light that can pass through by making the aperture larger or smaller. The other is to increase or decrease the camera's *shutter speed*—that is, the amount of time the shutter remains open. The longer the shutter is open, the more light can pass through.

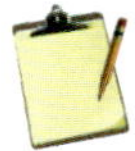

If you want to change your camera's aperture and shutter-speed settings manually, you may need an additional piece of equipment called a *light meter* to help you avoid *overexposing* your photograph (using too much light) or *underexposing* it (using too little light). Fortunately, most digital cameras have a built-in meter to handle that job for you.

Rather than make you adjust the aperture and shutter-speed settings manually, most digital cameras have an automatic-exposure mode that determines the best focus, aperture, and shutter speed for each picture. Some digital cameras, however, enable you to adjust the automatic exposure settings. If you're using the FujiFilm FinePix 2600Zoom, for example, you can adjust an Exposure Compensation setting to change the brightness of the image. This comes in handy when subject and background brightness vary greatly. In addition, some cameras have special exposure settings for various types of pictures, such as action shots, panoramic shots, portraits, and others. See the section, "Taking Specialized Photos," later in this chapter for more information.

Lighting and Flash

As you photograph your subject or scene, be sure to consider lighting. If you're outdoors, the sunlight overhead may be intense and cast shadows on your subject that may or may not be visually pleasing. If you're indoors, the lighting may be insufficient for correct exposure.

One way to adjust the lighting for your image is to move the subject to a position where the lighting is more pleasing or robust. Alternatively, you can use artificial lighting—be it lighting designed with photography in mind or lighting designed simply to illuminate a room—to enhance available light. Finally, you can use a built-in camera flash to supplement natural or available light.

Using a built-in flash often results in improved color, exposure, and picture sharpness, but it can also "wash out" your subject, making them blend in with the background. Many digital cameras feature automatic flashes, which are activated whenever the camera detects low-light conditions. In most cases, however, you can also use the camera's menu to adjust the flash settings.

Common flash settings include the following:

- **Auto.** Choose this setting if you want your camera to activate the flash when the lighting of the shot requires it. This is usually the default flash setting.

- **Red-eye.** When you photograph people in certain conditions (low light, for example), the use of a flash sometimes makes their eyes look red. When you select the Red-eye feature, the camera uses a pre-flash, which strobes immediately before you take the picture. This strobe occurs in addition to a regular flash, which strobes the instant the photograph is taken. As a result, red-eye is eliminated. The reason for the preflash is to cause the pupils of the subject's eye to shrink before the main flash goes off, thus reducing the chance that the light will reflect off the retinas in the back of the eye, which is the cause of red-eye in photos. See Chapter 5 for details on how to remove red-eye using image-editing software.

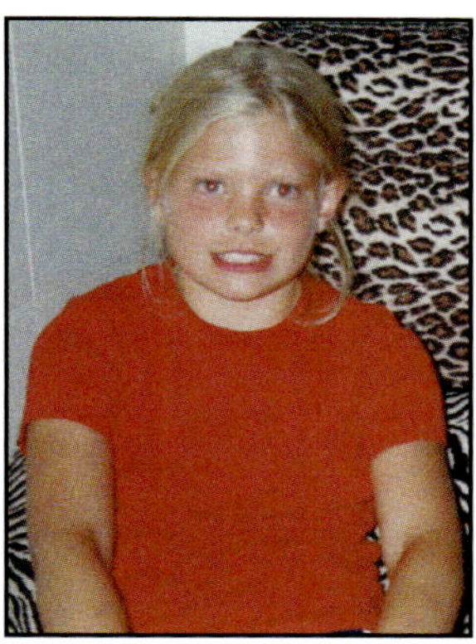

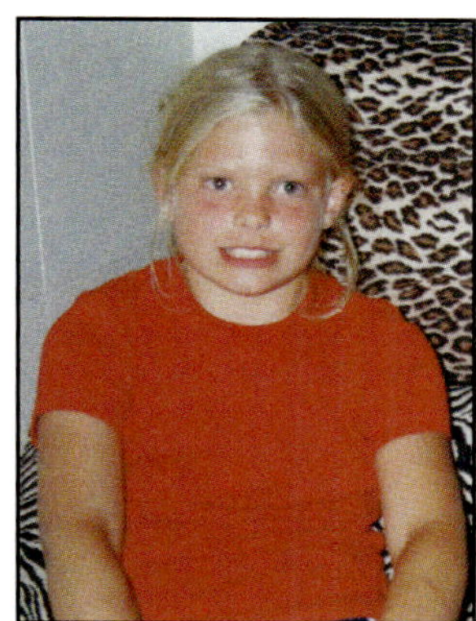

- **Forced or Fill.** Select this option when you want to use the flash regardless of lighting conditions. This is a good choice when you're shooting photographs in fluorescent lighting. Doing so will basically relight the scene using the color corrected light from the flash rather than allowing the lighting from the fluorescent bulb to cast its lovely green glow over your subject. It's also helpful for removing shadows when you shoot in bright light or sunlight.

- **Suppressed or Off.** Choose this option to disable or suppress the flash regardless of lighting conditions. You might choose this setting if you know that using the flash won't help (for example, when the subject is out of the flash's range) or when you're shooting photos at night and don't want the entire scene illuminated.

Taking Photographs

Using your digital camera to take photographs is extremely simple—especially if the camera is set to automatic mode. Once you've grasped the basics, however, you'll no doubt want to move on to more advanced photographic techniques. In this section, you'll learn how to take basic pictures, and you'll get a few tips and tricks to move you to the next step of digital photography.

Using Automatic Mode

Although the preceding section briefly discussed how you can change camera settings to effect focus, exposure, and flash, most digital cameras can adjust these settings automatically. In automatic mode, you only need to point and shoot to take the picture. You'll find that using your camera's automatic mode works for most pictures and frees you to concentrate on the basics of composing and shooting photographs.

To take a photograph in automatic mode, do the following:

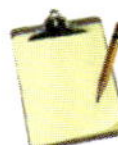

The steps outlined here are general ones and may differ somewhat from camera to camera. Read your digital camera's user manual for specific instructions on taking photographs.

1. Turn the camera on.
2. Set the camera to Automatic/Still image mode.

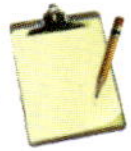

The FujiFilm FinePix 2600Zoom camera features a dial on top, with three icons. The icon that resembles a camera represents automatic mode; turn the dial to this mode.

3. Open the lens cover. If you can't get your camera to display or shoot an image, make sure the lens cover is entirely open. With some cameras, the lens cover must be pushed all the way open until it clicks.
4. Point your camera at the subject you want to shoot, using the viewfinder or LCD screen to center the subject.
5. Press the shutter button halfway down to engage the camera's auto-focus feature.
6. Press the shutter button the rest of the way down to take the picture.

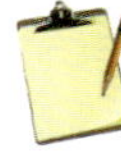

Most cameras' auto-focus features automatically focus on the object or person in the center of the viewfinder. You may decide, however, that you want to compose your image differently, perhaps with the subject to one side. Fortunately, many digital cameras offer a workaround.

7. Check the LCD screen to preview your image. You can either keep your image or discard it. (See the section "Managing Your Photographs" later in this chapter for more information about discarding images.)

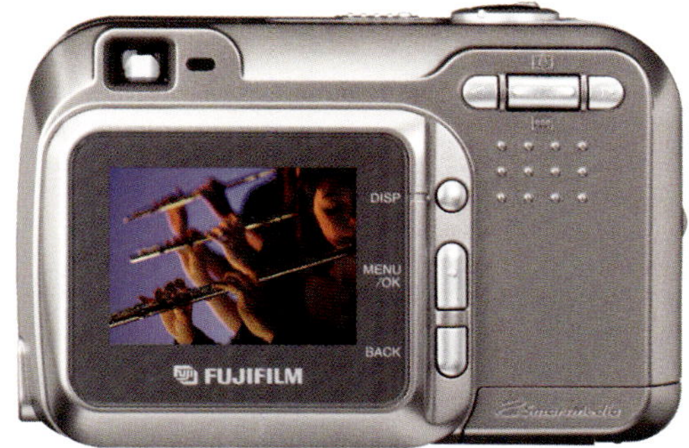

Using Zoom Controls

Once you've become comfortable using your camera in automatic mode, you're ready to start experimenting with other features such as flash settings, or zooming.

As mentioned previously, your camera uses zoom controls to change its focal length. A shorter focal length yields a wider angle of view, or *zooms out,* whereas a longer focal length yields a narrower angle of view, or *zooms in.*

To get the hang of your camera's zoom features, try the following:

The steps outlined here are general ones and may differ somewhat from camera to camera. Read your digital camera's user manual for specific instructions on using its zoom feature.

1. Point your camera at the subject, and preview the photo using the LCD screen.
2. Press the zoom button. You may see the current zoom settings on the LCD screen.
3. Press the zoom-adjustment buttons to change the zoom. Continue pressing the buttons until you're satisfied with the size of your photograph's subject in relation to the background.
4. Reframe your shot, placing your subject in the spot you want.
5. Press the shutter button halfway down to use the camera's auto-focus feature to refocus the shot at the new zoom level.
6. Press the shutter button the rest of the way down to take the picture.

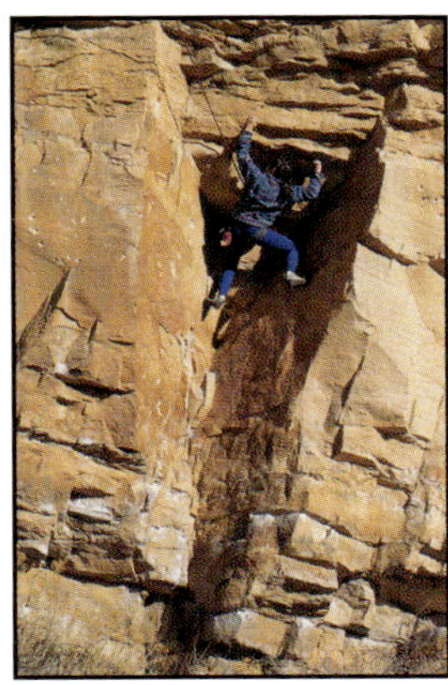

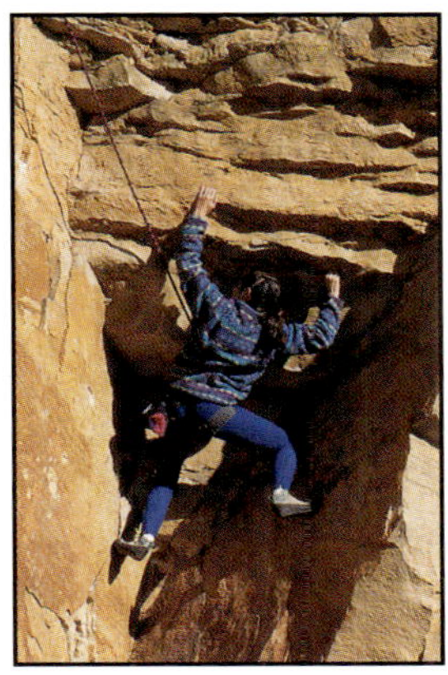

Taking Specialized Photos

As you become more adept at using your digital camera, you may want to extend your repertoire from simple snapshots to more specialized images, such as portraits, close-ups, nighttime scenes, or action photos. You can find entire books devoted to each of these subjects. This section briefly outlines a few things to consider when using a digital camera to capture specialized images. For more on image quality, see Chapter 2.

Of course, the best way to learn to shoot photographs of any kind, be they portraits or action shots, is to experiment. Fortunately, when you use your digital camera, buying film and paying for it to be developed is not a concern!

Shooting Portraits

Whether you're shooting your turtle or your Great Uncle Norm, you'll want to consider the following pointers when shooting portraits.

These tips apply whether you're shooting a posed portrait or a candid shot.

- **Use lighting to your advantage.** When you're outside, make sure that your subject isn't looking into the sun and that you are not pointing your camera into the sun. This can cause you to underexpose your subject because the camera will adjust itself to expose for the bright light of the sun. When you're inside, look for soft light, which you can often find by windows. In addition to placing your subject in flattering lighting, you may also want to use a flash.
- **Consider your background.** If you want the background to be part of the picture, use something simple. This ensures that the background doesn't detract from your subject.
- **Shoot from a good angle.** In most cases, the best angle is eye-level, but you can also get good shots by shooting from a higher point.

Lower camera levels can result in unflattering pictures.

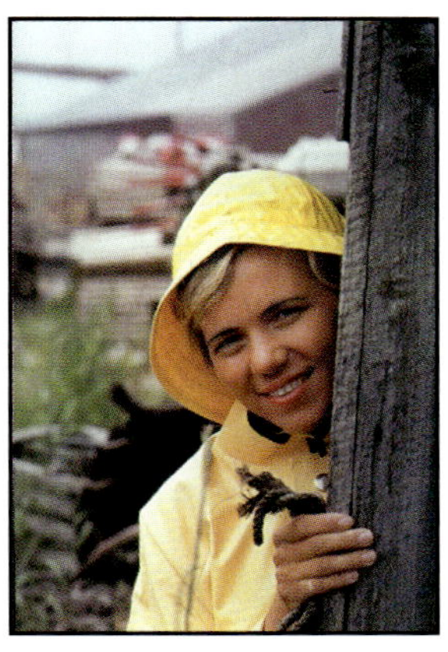

- **Capture your subject's personality.** As the saying goes, "the eyes are the windows to the soul." Focus on eyes to capture your subject's personality. You'll also find that capturing your subject in a relaxed pose improves your portraits.

Close-Up Photographing

Many small objects, such as flowers, insects, or coins, look best when photographed close up. You may also want to shoot portraits close up to truly capture the details of your subject's face. Regardless of subject, you'll find it easy to shoot close-ups using your digital camera's close-up mode. In this mode, the camera automatically adjusts the focus, flash, and zoom for best results.

The exact name of close-up mode varies from camera to camera. For example, the FujiFilm FinePix 2600Zoom calls this mode "Macro mode," whereas the Kodak DX3500 calls it "Close-up mode." Check your camera's user manual to see whether it offers any special modes for taking close-up pictures, as well as how to use them.

Here are a few things to consider when shooting close-ups:

- When photographing small objects close up, consider the background very carefully. It should be clean and uncluttered.
- If possible, lay the small object flat and photograph it from above. Try standing on a chair if necessary.

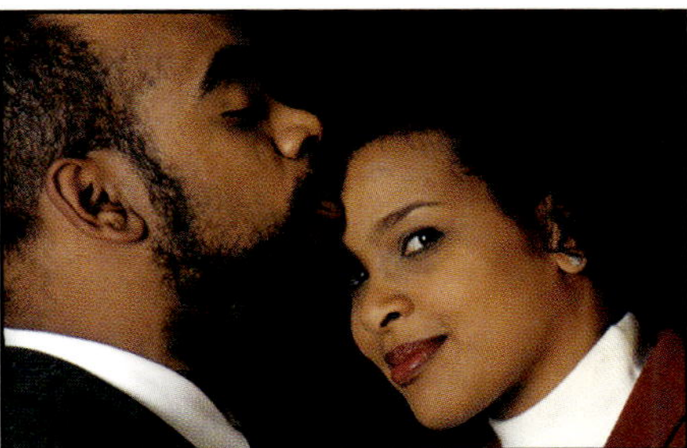

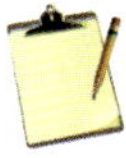

For telephoto images or extreme close-ups, you might consider purchasing an additional lens for your camera. Check with your camera's manufacturer to see what types are available.

Photographing at Night

Photographing at night presents a unique challenge. If you're photographing a nighttime scene that also features bright lights, your camera will most likely be fooled into thinking there's more light than there actually is and set the aperture, shutter speed, and flash accordingly. The result is an underexposed, potentially blurry image that leaves much of the scene in the dark.

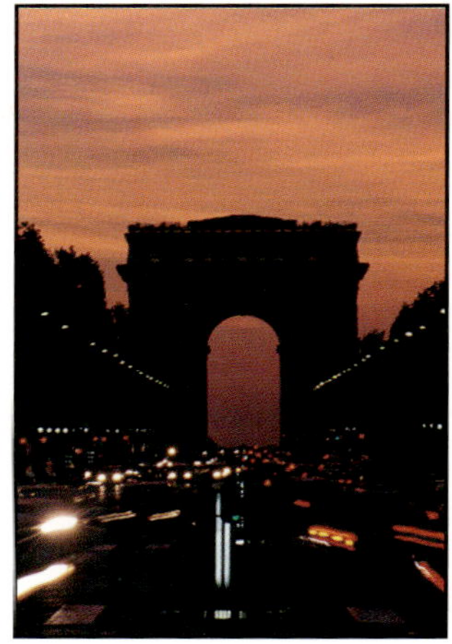

When photographing at night, try doing the following:

- Take a sample picture and preview the results. You can then make any necessary adjustments to the flash or exposure settings.
- If possible, mount the camera on a tripod to prevent movement. Even the tiniest camera movement can make the resulting photograph blurry, especially if the shutter speed has been reduced to accommodate low-light conditions.

Shooting Action Photos

Some of the most memorable pictures are those that capture one moment frozen in time—the winning shot in a basketball game, a downhill ski racer hurtling past a gate, a Formula One car hugging a hairpin turn. The key to taking action photos is to be ready for that magic moment. Here are a few tips:

- Get as close to the action as possible, both physically and by zooming in.
- Sit or stand at the ready, with your camera to your eye at all times. You never know when a dramatic moment will occur.
- Don't shoot just anything. Wait for something exciting to occur, like a runner sliding into second base or a dolphin breaching from the water.

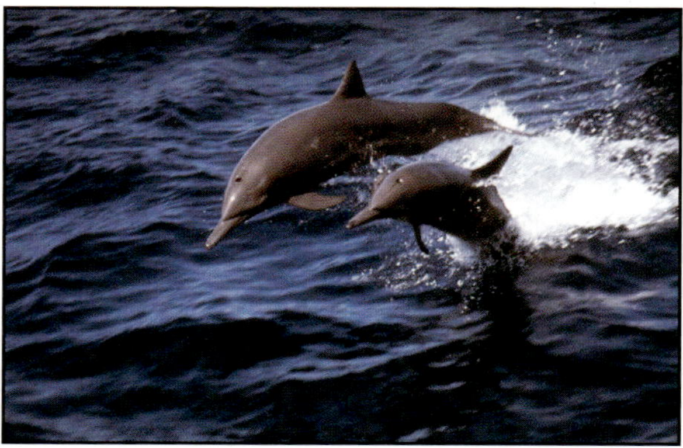

- Some cameras feature a multi-frame mode, which is useful for action photographs because it enables you to take a series of photographs by simply pressing the shutter button and holding it down. Check your camera's manual for information about using this mode.

- As you become more advanced, read up on the details of shutter speed (faster is better) and f-stops (lower numbers mean a larger aperture—and a better action photo).

Shooting Movies

In addition to enabling you to shoot photographs, many cameras also have a movie mode, which you can use to make short videos (from 20 seconds on up, depending on the amount of memory in your camera). To shoot a movie using your digital camera, follow these steps:

3

1. Switch your camera to Movie mode.

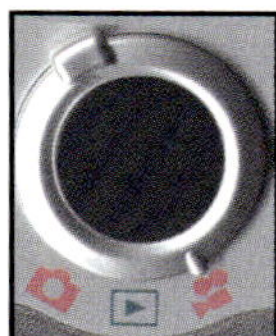

On the FujiFilm FinePix 2600Zoom camera, you change the mode dial to the button that looks like a movie camera.

2. Press the shutter button and release it to start shooting the movie. You should see REC on the LCD screen.
3. When you've finished shooting the movie, press the shutter button a second time.

Once you've shot your movie, you can preview it in Preview mode and transfer it to your computer, just as you would a still photograph. You'll learn more about previewing and transferring images and movies in the next section.

Windows XP includes a movie-editing program called Windows Movie Maker, which you can use to edit your movies.

Managing Your Photographs

Unlike film-based photographs, which must be developed and printed either by you or a photo lab before they can be seen, digital photos are available for viewing instantly. Adding to this convenience is the fact that if an image isn't up to par, it can be deleted from your camera's memory right away—no messy chemicals or hefty processing fees required. When your camera or removable media device finally runs out of memory, you can transfer the digital images you choose to save to your computer—which you can then use to store, manipulate, print, and e-mail your photos.

> **More About . . . Tracking Available Memory**
>
> Unlike a roll of film, which allows you to take only a set number of photographs (typically 12, 24, or 36), the number of photos you can store in your camera's memory or removable media device depends on how much memory you started with, as well as the image quality of the photographs you took. Fortunately, many cameras calculate how many more photos will fit in memory and display this information on the LCD screen. Additionally, most cameras display an error message when they've run out of memory.

In this section, you'll learn how to preview and discard images, as well as how to transfer images to your computer.

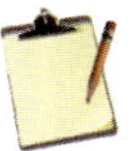

Take as many pictures as you want with your digital camera! Because you can discard the ones that don't turn out before they're ever printed, you don't have to worry about wasting film.

Previewing Photographs

With most digital cameras, you use one mode to take photos, and another—typically called Playback or Preview—to preview them on your camera's LCD screen. In this mode, you can scroll through all the pictures you've taken. To preview your images, do the following:

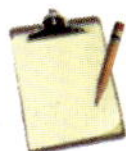

The steps outlined here are general ones and may differ somewhat from camera to camera. Read your digital camera's user manual for specific instructions on using it to preview your photos.

1. Switch your camera to Playback mode.

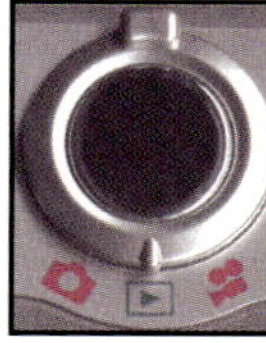

2. Press the Back and Forward buttons to scroll through your pictures.

Some cameras enable you to magnify a picture to view it in more detail. Check your camera's user manual for information about using this feature.

Deleting Photographs

No doubt, you'll take a photo that doesn't turn out as you expected—especially when you're getting used to using your new digital camera. Not to worry! You can delete any pictures you don't want, thereby freeing up space on your camera or removable media device for pictures that make the grade.

To delete images from your camera, do the following:

1. Change to Playback mode.

The name of this mode may vary by camera. Read your camera's user guide to determine which mode is used for deleting photos.

2. Scroll through your photos until the one you want to delete is displayed.
3. Press the Menu button.
4. Using the camera's arrow buttons, scroll to the Erase command (or a command with a similar name, such as Delete).

If you want to delete all the photos currently stored in your camera's memory, use the camera's menu to locate a command named Erase All Frames, Delete All, or something similar.

5. Press the Select button to select the command.
6. To confirm the deletion, use your camera's arrow keys to select OK or Yes.

Transferring Photos to Your Computer

Once you've taken a series of photos and deleted the ones you don't want, you can transfer the remaining photos to your computer. In addition to enabling you to store, manipulate, print, and e-mail your photos, transferring photos from your camera has the added benefit of allowing you to free up space so you can store additional photos in it.

Before you can transfer your photos to your computer, however, you must set it up to handle this operation. In this section, you'll learn how to configure your computer and camera for easy transfer, and how to use a variety of programs—including Windows XP, MGI PhotoSuite 4, and Microsoft Picture It!—to perform the transfer operation.

Setting Up Your Computer

Before you can transfer digital images from your camera to your computer, you must install the camera on your computer, just as you would a printer, scanner, or any other hardware device. The installation process copies the drivers your computer needs to communicate with your camera.

A *driver* is a software file that tells your computer's operating system all the important details about a device and how it works. The driver is what enables the digital camera to communicate with the operating system.

The first step in installing your camera on your computer is to use the connection cable that came with the camera to connect the camera (or removable media) to the appropriate port on your computer. (You may need to pull back a cover or slot to reveal the camera's connection port—that is, the hole the cable's connector is plugged into—as in the case of the Kodak 3500X, for example.) Most cameras or camera media connect to computers via a USB (universal serial bus) port. On newer computers, USB ports are generally found on the front of the computer (although some have USB ports on both the back and front or on the back only). If your port is on the back, it should be right under the cables for the mouse and the keyboard. For more information about cameras and ports, refer to Chapter 2.

After you've connected your camera to your computer, you'll use one of two methods to install it: Plug and Play setup or manual setup. Which process you use depends largely on what type of digital camera you have and which version of Windows you have on your computer.

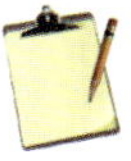

Try installing your camera via Plug and Play first. If that doesn't work, use one of the manual methods.

Plug and Play Setup

In many cases, Windows can recognize when a new component is added to your system and install it automatically. This is called *Plug and Play setup.* In this scenario, Windows queries the new device to find out details about it and then searches the driver files that were installed with the operating system for the one needed to communicate with that device. If Windows locates the driver file, it installs it on your system.

To use Plug and Play setup, you simply connect your camera or camera media to your computer. If Plug and Play setup is successful, a message appears in the notification area on the taskbar indicating that the hardware (in this case, your camera) was found and installed properly.

Manual Setup

Unfortunately, Windows doesn't always have the driver file you need to install a new component. In that case, you'll need to install the device manually. To do so, insert the CD-ROM or floppy disk that came with your camera in the appropriate drive on your computer. In most cases, a manual-setup routine starts automatically and walks you through the installation process. Simply follow the instructions that appear on your screen.

If the setup routine doesn't start automatically, you can still use the CD-ROM or floppy disk to install the driver with the help of the Windows Scanner and Camera Installation Wizard. Here's how:

These steps assume you have Windows XP installed on your computer. If you use an earlier version of Windows, start the Wizard by clicking **Start**, then **Settings**, and then **Control Panel**. In Control Panel, double-click the **Add New Hardware** icon to start the Wizard. Once the Wizard starts, the steps are similar to the ones outlined here, but the screens may look different. Simply follow the Wizard's prompts to install the driver from the disk.

1. Click **start**, and then click **Control Panel**. Control Panel opens.
2. Click **Printers and Other Hardware**. The Printers and Other Hardware window opens.

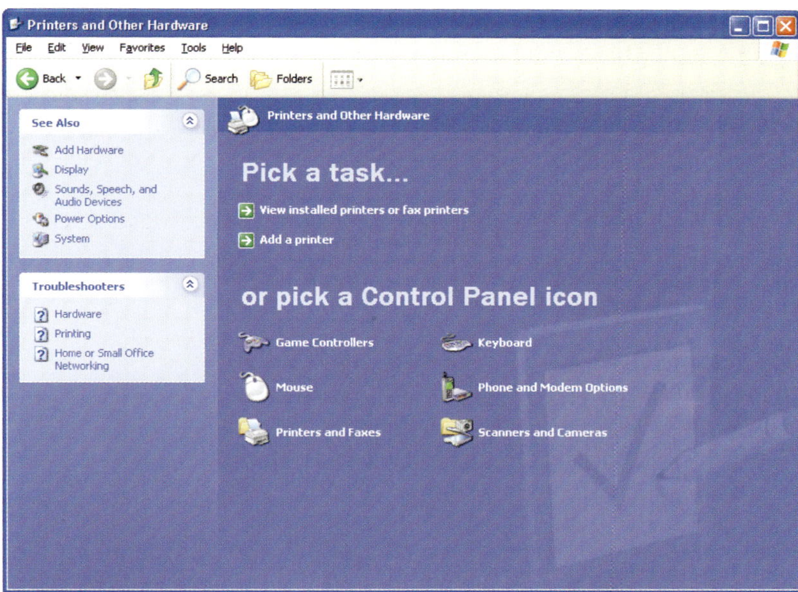

3. Under Pick a Control Panel Icon, click **Scanners and Cameras**. The Scanners and Cameras window opens, displaying any scanners or digital cameras currently installed on your computer.
4. In the task list, click **Add an imaging device**. The Welcome screen of the Scanner and Camera Installation Wizard appears.

5. Click **Next**. The second screen of the Wizard appears.

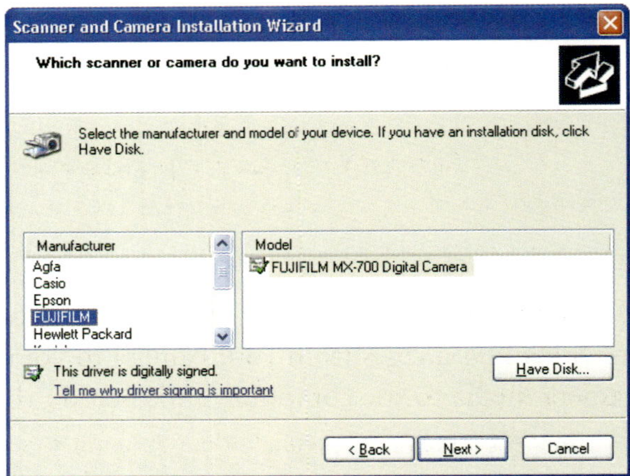

6. Insert the disk that came with the camera in the appropriate drive, and click **Have Disk**.

If you prefer, you can also see whether Windows has a driver that will work for your camera. To do this, select your camera's manufacturer from the list at the left of the screen and the camera's model from the list on the right. Click **Next**, and follow any instructions for installing a driver from among the drivers that come pre-installed with Windows.

7. The Install From Disk screen appears. Select the **Copy manufacturer's files from** drop-down list and click the drive containing the disk; then click **Browse**.

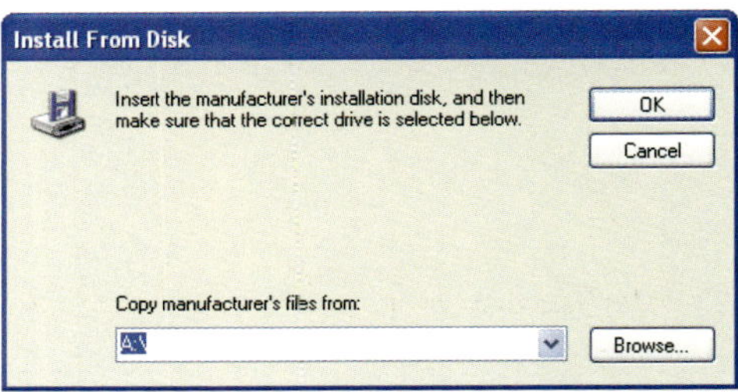

8. The Locate File dialog box appears. Select the driver file from the drive you specified in the preceding step and click **Open**.
9. Click **Finish**. Windows installs the appropriate driver for your camera.

If your camera didn't come with a CD or floppy disk, or if the CD or disk doesn't contain the driver file you need, check your camera manufacturer's Web site. Manufacturers commonly post updated driver files that you can download and install on your computer. To download the driver, follow the specific instructions on your manufacturer's site. Once the driver has been downloaded to your computer, note where it's stored and then select this location after clicking **Have Disk** in Step 6.

Once your computer has the correct driver installed, you're ready to transfer pictures from your camera to it. As mentioned previously, you can transfer photos using Windows XP or an image-editing program such as MGI PhotoSuite 4 or Microsoft Picture It!. You'll learn how in the sections that follow.

Some cameras require you to use their own transfer and editing programs, which are typically launched when you attach the camera or camera media to your computer. Even if your camera requires you to use its own software, you'll most likely be able to use the Windows XP Scanner and Camera Wizard to transfer pictures.

Transferring Photos Using Windows XP

Windows XP's Scanner and Camera Wizard leads you through the process of downloading images from your camera to your computer. Simply connect the camera or camera media to the computer, and then do the following:

1. Connect the camera media to the appropriate port on your computer and turn on the camera.

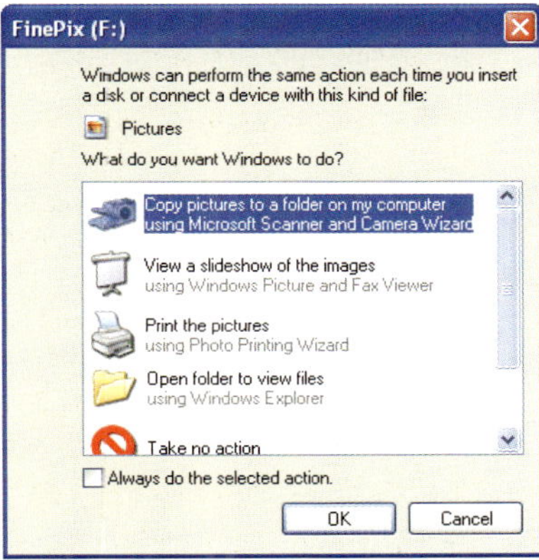

2. When prompted by the Removable Disk dialog box, select **Copy pictures to a folder on my computer using Microsoft Scanner and Camera Wizard** and then click **OK**.

3. Windows reads the camera or removable media and then displays the Wizard's Welcome screen. Click **Next**.

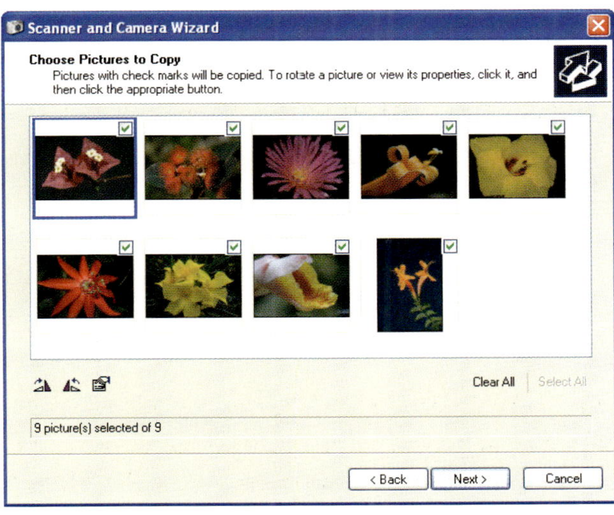

4. The Wizard displays thumbnail versions of each picture stored on the camera or the camera media. By default, all the images are selected. To prevent Windows from downloading an image, click it to cancel the selection; alternatively, click **Clear All** to clear all check boxes and then click the images you want. When the images you want to transfer are selected, click **Next**.

5. By default, Windows places all the selected images in a folder within the My Pictures folder, which is itself in the My Documents folder. To specify a name for the new folder, type it in the first text box or select a name from the drop-down list.

Every Windows XP user has a unique My Pictures folder that is the default location for storing images.

6. To specify an alternate location for the new folder, click **Browse** and navigate to the drive and folder where you want it to be stored.
7. To delete the pictures from your camera after they're copied to your computer, click **Delete pictures from my device after copying them**.

It's a good idea to delete the photos from your camera after they've been transferred; this frees up space for any new photos you take. The first few times you transfer pictures, though, you may want to leave them on the camera just to make sure the transfer goes without a hitch. Once you've verified that the images were transferred successfully, you can use the commands in your camera's menu to delete the images from its memory.

8. Click **Next**. The images are copied to the folder you've specified.

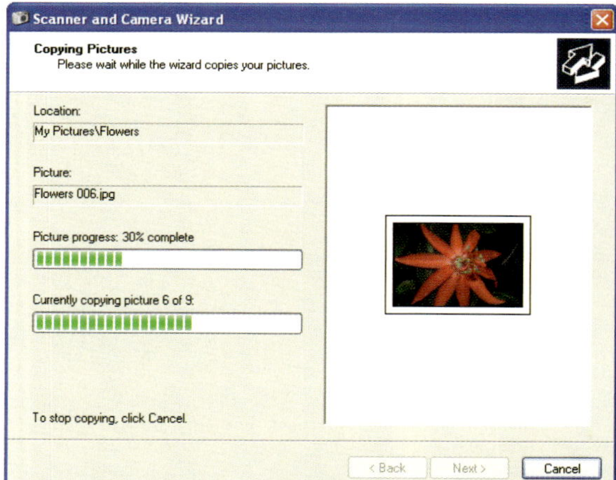

9. Next, you're prompted to select what you want to do next. You can publish the pictures to a Web site, order prints online, or do nothing.
10. Click **Nothing. I'm finished working with these pictures**, and then click **Next**.
11. Click **Finish** to close the Wizard. Once the images have been transferred to your computer, you can open the folder they're stored in and review, modify, or print them.

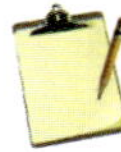

Most image-editing programs also allow you to transfer images directly from your camera to your computer

Now that you have downloaded your images to your computer, you are ready to enhance and print them. Chapter 5 covers opening and modifying pictures, and Chapter 7 outlines the procedure for printing your pictures.

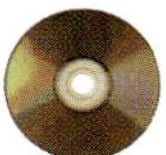

To understand how a picture is transferred from a camera to your computer, go to the CD-ROM segment *Images: Transferring to your PC*.

3

To Keep on Learning . . .

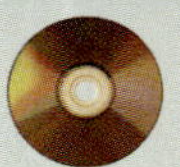

Go to the CD-ROM and select the segment:

- *Picture Taking Basics* to learn how to take a great picture.
- *Images: Transferring to your PC* to understand how a picture is transferred from a camera to your computer.

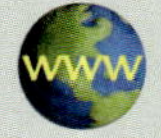

Go online to **www.LearnwithGateway.com** and log on to select:

- *Internet Links and Resources*
- *FAQs*

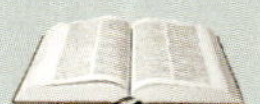

With the *Survive & Thrive* series, refer to *Use and Care for Your PC* for more information on:

- *User accounts*
- *My Pictures folder*

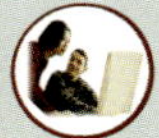

Gateway offers a hands-on training course that covers many of the topics in this chapter. Additional fees may apply. Call **888-852-4821** for enrollment information. If applicable, please have your customer ID and order number ready when you call.

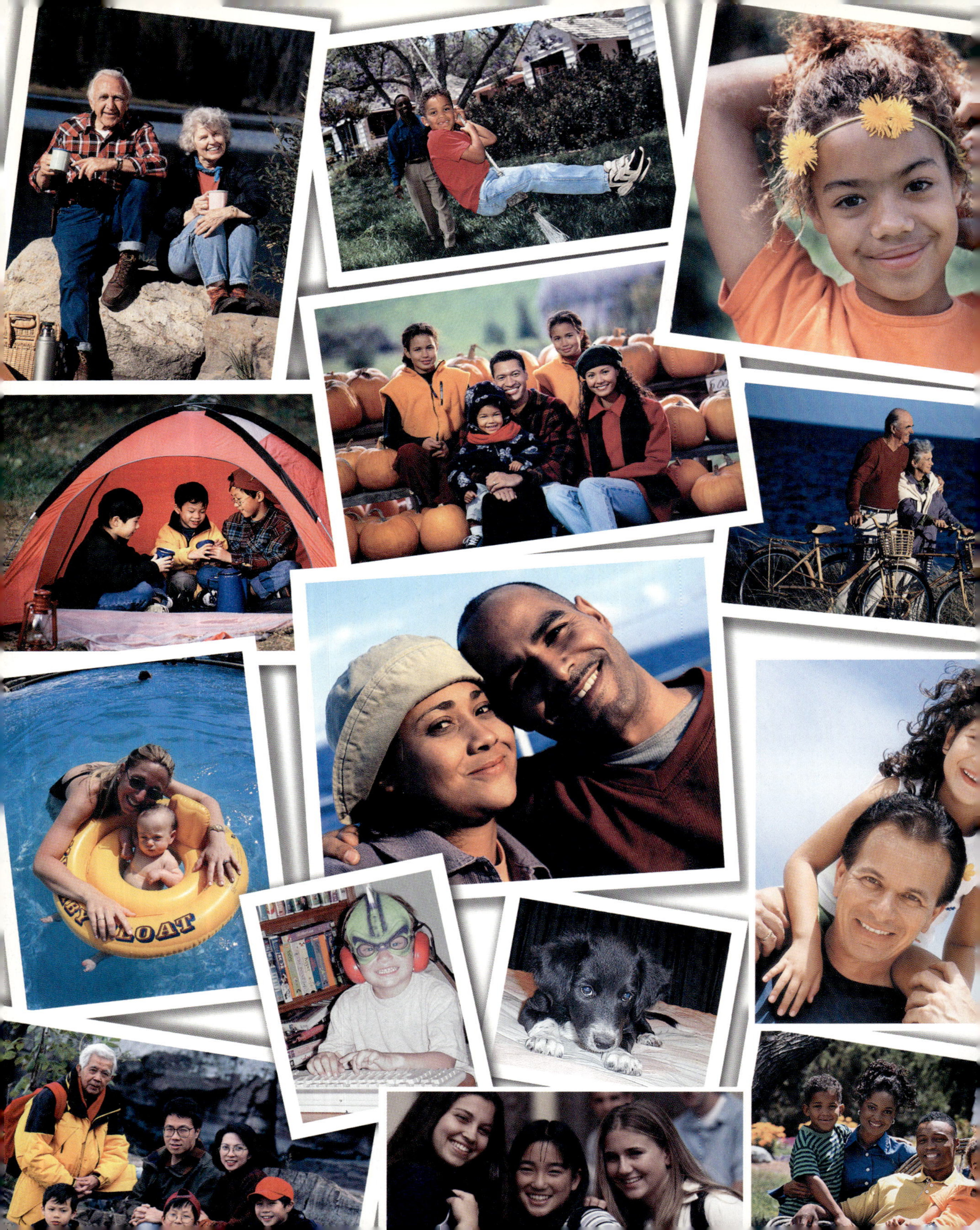

CHAPTER 4

Scanning Existing Pictures

Chances are you have some favorite photos taken with your film-based camera. Using a scanner, you can easily convert those photos to digital images and save them as files on your computer. Then, you can work with them just as you do the images you capture using your digital camera. For example, you can scan a photograph taken with a film-based camera at your family reunion and e-mail it to all your family members. Or, you can use your image-editing software to correct flaws in your photo prints, such as red eye, tears, or stains. The basics of using a scanner and the software that comes with it, as well as how to use a scanning service for the same results, are the topics of this chapter.

The specific steps for using your scanner depend on the make and model of the scanner and the software you use with it. Check your scanner's manual for detailed instructions.

Discovering What Your Scanner Can Do

You already know that a scanner can be used to convert photo prints or negatives into digital files that you can edit, insert into a document, e-mail to friends and family, add to Web pages, organize on your PC, print—the list goes on.

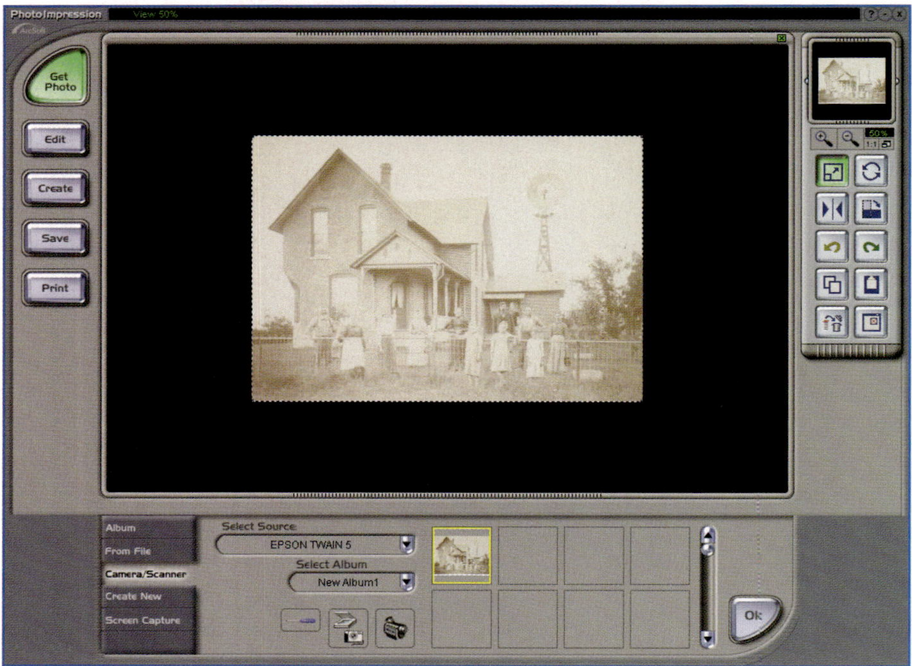

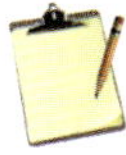

You can attach an adapter to some scanners that enables you to scan negatives and slides, as well as paper documents and regular photos. Some scanners, including the Epson Perfection 1250 Photo scanner, can scan both photographic prints and negatives; others can even scan slides.

But scanners aren't just for converting photographs into digital images. Suppose you're working on a user's manual for the nifty invention you've designed. You can use your scanner to convert hand-drawn line art into digital images that can be easily placed in the manual. Maybe your child drew a picture that you want to share with his grandparents; your scanner will convert that drawing to a digital file that you can then drop into an e-mail message.

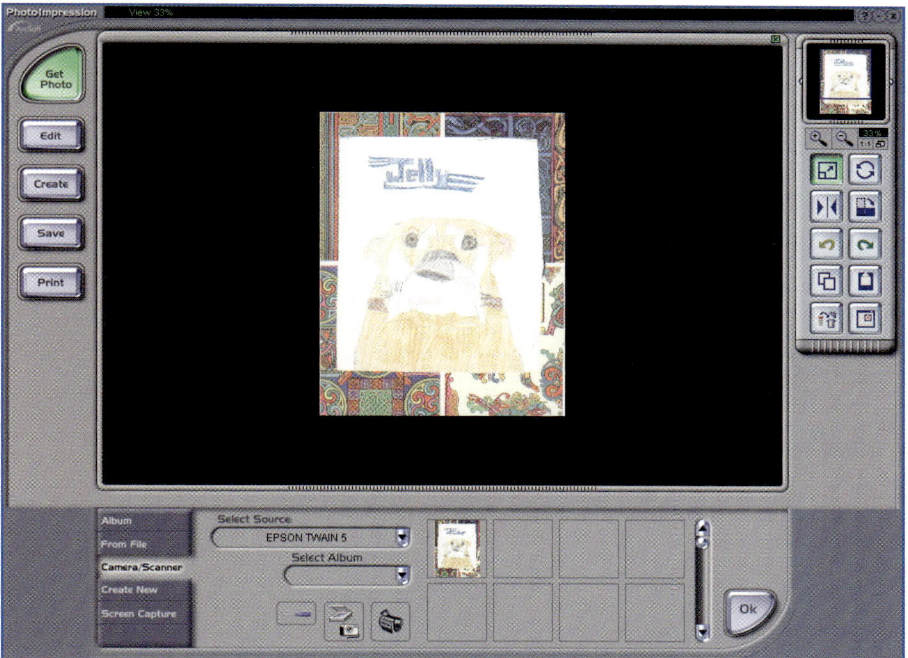

Scanners are also useful for digitizing important paper documents such as bank, financial and investment statements, receipts, tax information, and so on. That way, rather than—or in addition to—storing paper copies of your important documents, you can store them digitally on your computer.

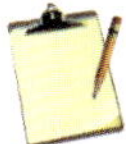

If you need to keep track of numerous contacts in the course of doing business, you might consider purchasing a business-card scanner to scan your contacts' business cards. You can then store the information from the card (the contact's name, company, phone number, and so on) in a contact-management program on your PC.

If you have fax software, you can even use your scanner to help fax documents from your PC. For example, suppose you need to fax a signed contract to someone. You can sign the contract, scan it, and then fax the digital file from your computer.

To fax a file from your computer, you need a fax modem and fax program. Windows XP includes a fax program, but you can also purchase separate faxing programs.

Alternatively, you can attach the scanned file as an e-mail attachment. Please refer to Chapter 2 about specifics on scanner hardware.

Connecting and Installing Your Scanner

Before you can use your scanner to convert your photo prints and other items to electronic files, you need to connect your scanner to your PC. Doing so is easy, requiring only two main steps:

- Physically connecting your scanner to your PC using a cable or other connection device
- Setting up your scanner to communicate with Windows

If your scanner comes with software, you also need to install the software. Do this after you set up your scanner so that the software can find and recognize the scanner. If you install the software first (without a scanner installed), the program may not recognize the device when you do add it.

Physically Connecting the Scanner to Your PC

To physically connect your scanner to your PC, you simply plug in all the various cords and cables. Follow these basic steps:

1. Connect the connection cable (chances are, one end of this cable is already attached to the scanner) to the appropriate port on your computer.

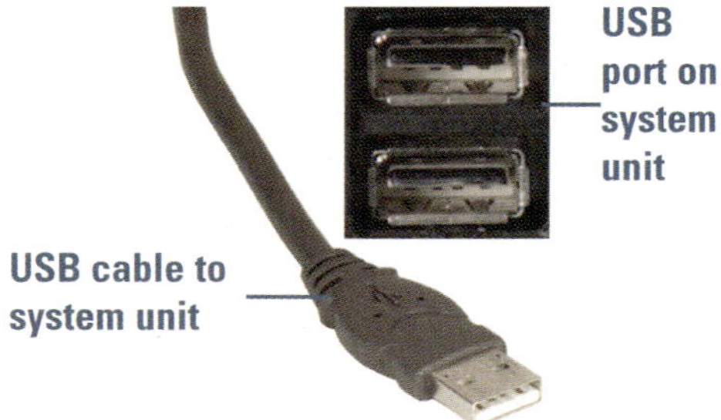

Many scanners connect with a standard USB cable. Most new personal computers have USB ports on the front of the computer (though they may be on the back, right under the cables for the mouse and the keyboard). If your computer is older, it may connect to the scanner via a different port and cable.

2. Plug the power adaptor into the scanner. One end looks like a regular outlet plug, whereas the other may contain a small circular plug similar to those found on power adaptors for stereos, cell-phone rechargers, and so on.
3. Plug the power adapter into a surge protector.

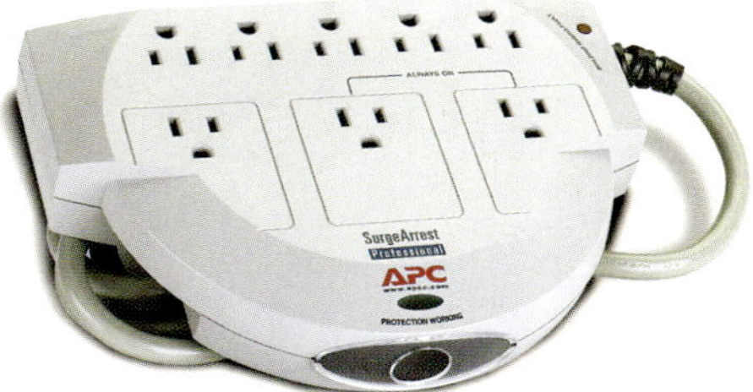

4

Setting Up Your Scanner to Communicate with Windows

After you successfully connect the scanner to your computer, it's time to install the scanner on your computer. The installation process occurs in one of two ways: through Plug and Play setup, or manually. Which process you use depends largely on what type of scanner you have and which version of Windows you use.

Plug and Play Setup

In many cases, Windows can recognize when a new component is added to your system and install it automatically. This is called *Plug and Play setup.* In this scenario, Windows queries the device to find out the details about it and, if possible, installs a driver for it. Windows comes with driver files for many different hardware types, including scanners.

A *driver* is a software file that tells Windows all the important details about a device and how it works. The driver is what enables the scanner to communicate with Windows. If a driver that matches is not found, Windows will offer to search for the appropriate file on a disk (use the one that came with the scanner). You can also find drivers at Web sites.

For most scanners, especially if your operating system is Windows XP, all you have to do is attach the scanner and plug it in, and Windows does the rest. To determine whether automatic setup is happening, check the notification area on the taskbar. You should see a message indicating whether the new hardware has been found. If Plug and Play setup was successful, then you are ready to scan; you can skip to the section, "Scanning an Image."

Manual Setup

Unfortunately, Windows doesn't always have the driver file you need to install a new component. Don't despair, however, you have some options. One of these is to install the device manually.

If your scanner came with a CD-ROM or a floppy disk—and chances are it did—you can usually install the scanner using that CD or disk. To do so, insert the CD or disk into the appropriate drive on your computer. The disk should start automatically and walk you through the installation process; simply follow the instructions that appear on your screen.

If the CD or disk doesn't start automatically, you can still use it to install the driver with the help of the Windows Scanner and Camera Installation Wizard. Here's how:

1. Click **start**, and then click **Control Panel**. Control Panel window opens.

These steps assume you have Windows XP installed on your PC.

2. Click the **Printers and Other Hardware** link. The Printers and Other Hardware window opens.

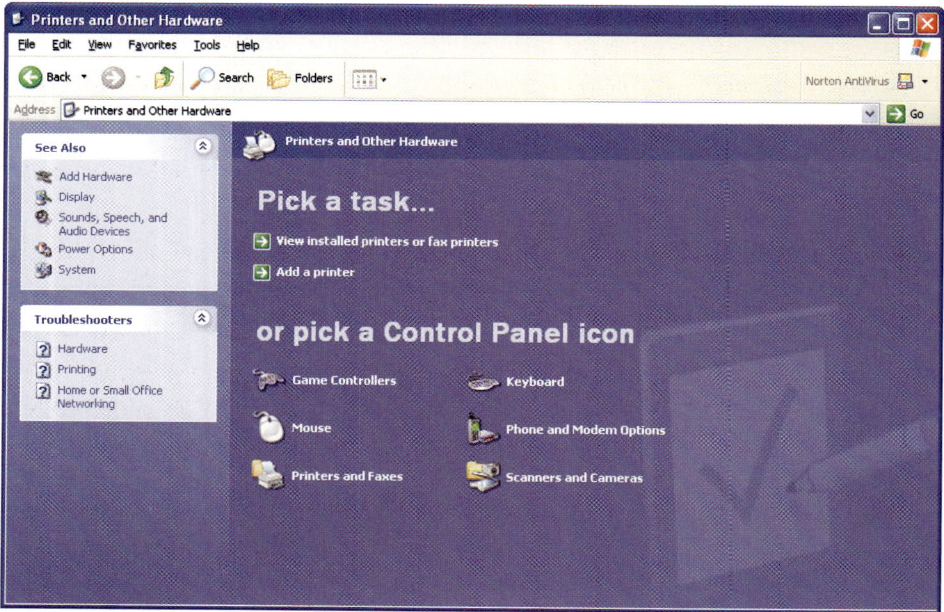

3. Under pick a Control Panel icon, click the **Scanners and Cameras** icon.
4. The Scanners and Cameras window opens. Here you see any cameras or scanners currently installed on your PC.

5. In the task list on the left side of the Scanners and Cameras window, click **Add an imaging device**. The Welcome screen of the Scanner and Camera Installation Wizard appears.
6. Click **Next**. The second screen of the Wizard appears.

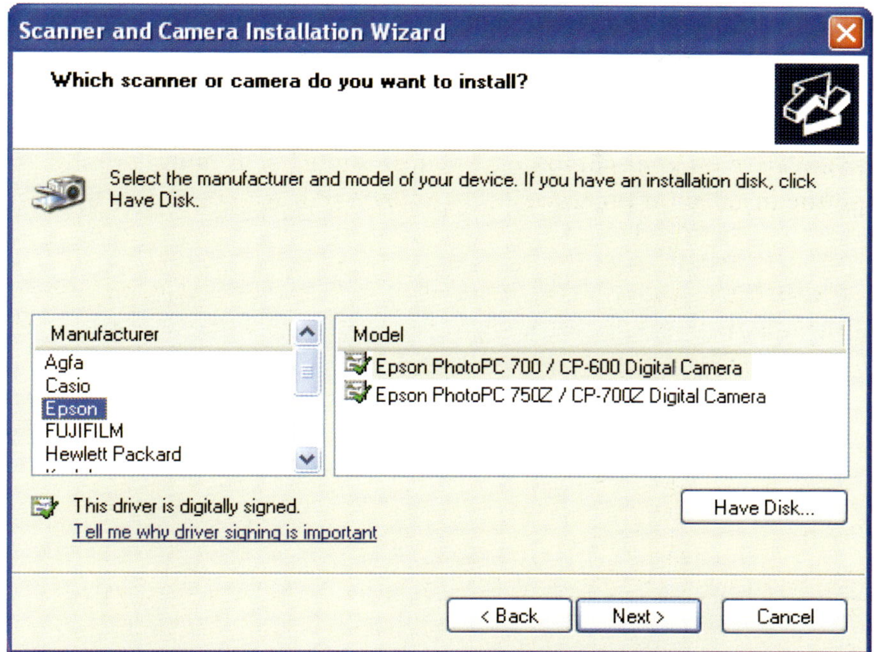

7. Insert the disk in the appropriate drive, and click the **Have Disk** button.
8. Click the drive containing the disk, and then click **OK**. Follow the steps that appear on the screen, clicking **Next** to move to each successive step.

If you don't have a CD or floppy disk, or if the CD or disk doesn't contain the driver file, check your scanner manufacturer's Web site. Manufacturers commonly have updated driver files that you can download and install on your computer. To download the driver, follow the specific instructions for that site. Once the driver is copied to your computer (downloaded), note where it is stored. Finally, then select this location after clicking Have Disk.

If the manufacturer's Web site doesn't have the driver you need, a generic driver may work with your scanner. Use the Scanner and Installation Wizard to install one:

As with the preceding steps, these assume you have Windows XP installed on your computer.

1. Follow steps 1 through 6 from the preceding list.
2. In the second screen of the Scanner and Camera Installation Wizard, scroll through the Manufacturer list until you locate the manufacturer of your scanner. When you find it, click it to select it.
3. Scroll through the Model list until you locate your scanner model. When you find it, click it to select it, and then click **Next**.
4. In case the scanner is not connected to your computer, the Wizard prompts you to connect it; do this now. Once the scanner is connected, click the port the device is attached to in the Available ports list, and then click **Next**.

To have Windows automatically check each port to see what devices are attached, click **Automatic port detection** and click **Next**.

5. Next, the Wizard asks you the name of the scanner. Enter a name to identify it (or use the one the Wizard suggests), and then click **Next**.
6. Click **Finish**. Windows installs the appropriate driver for your scanner.

Once your scanner is up and running, you're ready to scan documents, pictures, illustrations, etc.

Scanning an Image

Your scanner works a lot like a copy machine. You place the image you want to scan on the scanner's bed, and then scan the document. The scanner copies the image data, converts it to digital information, and displays it in the scanner's software program.

The specific steps for scanning—such as which command to select and the range of scanning options—vary across scanner models, but the basic steps are essentially the same. The steps that follow illustrate the general steps for a flatbed scanner. For specific information, check the manual for your particular scanner and scanner software.

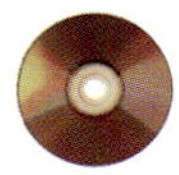

To gain an understanding of scanners and the steps to digitize a photo, go to the CD-ROM segment *Scanner: Using.*

1. Start the scanner program on your PC by double-clicking its desktop icon (if there is one) or by using the **start** menu. Click **start**, and then point to **All Programs**, then point to the scanner program folder and click the program icon. To use Epson's scanning tool, for instance, click **start**, **All Programs**, **Epson Smart Panel**, and then **Epson Smart Panel**.
2. The **Epson Smart Panel** program window opens. Click **Scan to File**.

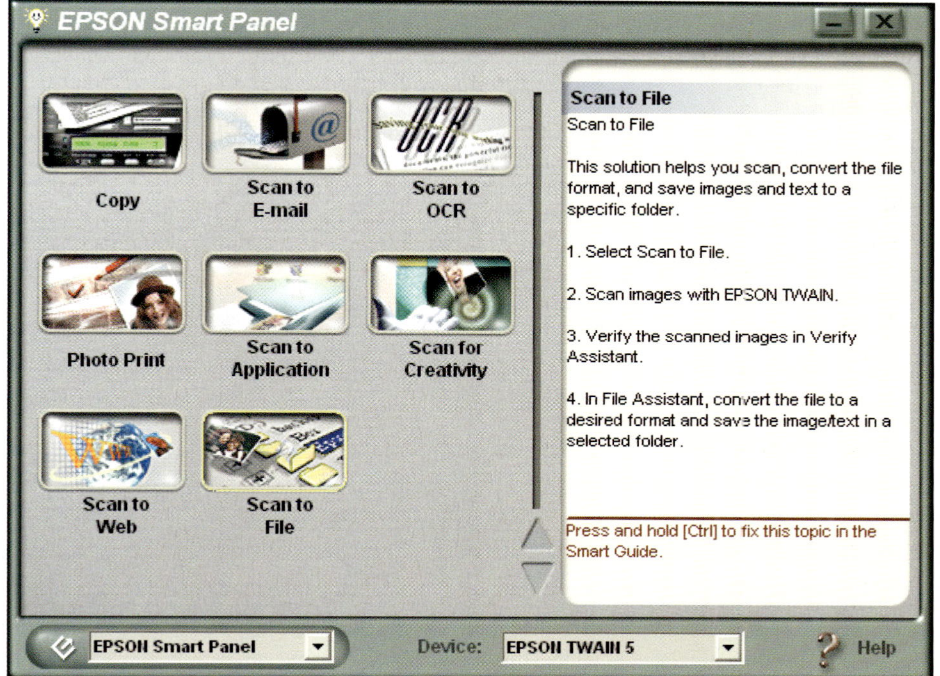

You may also be able to use your image-editing program to start a scan. See Chapter 5, "Editing and Manipulating Images," for help on these programs.

3. Place the image you want to scan face down on the scanner's view area. Place it in the top corner. (Check your scanner manual to find out where to place the image. Like copiers, the scanner usually indicates the start area with an arrow and includes paper dimensions.) Close the lid.

4. Set any available scanning options. For instance, you may be able to select what the scanned document will be used for (editing text or faxing, filing, or copying) and what type of image it is (black and white, color, etc.). You can also select mode (color, grayscale, or black and white), resolution, size, and other options. These options vary depending on the scanner. In Microsoft Office XP's scanning program, you can select the color (black and white, black and white from color page, color, or grayscale) as well as select options for the paper (whether it is double-sided, for instance).
5. Click the menu command or toolbar button needed to start the scan. Most programs include a menu command such as File, Acquire and a toolbar shortcut. Check with your program for the particular command to start the scan. In Epson's scanning program, you click **Scan**.
6. Some programs display a preview of the scan automatically. Others require you to click a **Preview** button to preview the scan, or to minimize the program window to preview the image. Others, like the Epson scan program, displays a preview automatically in the scanner program window.

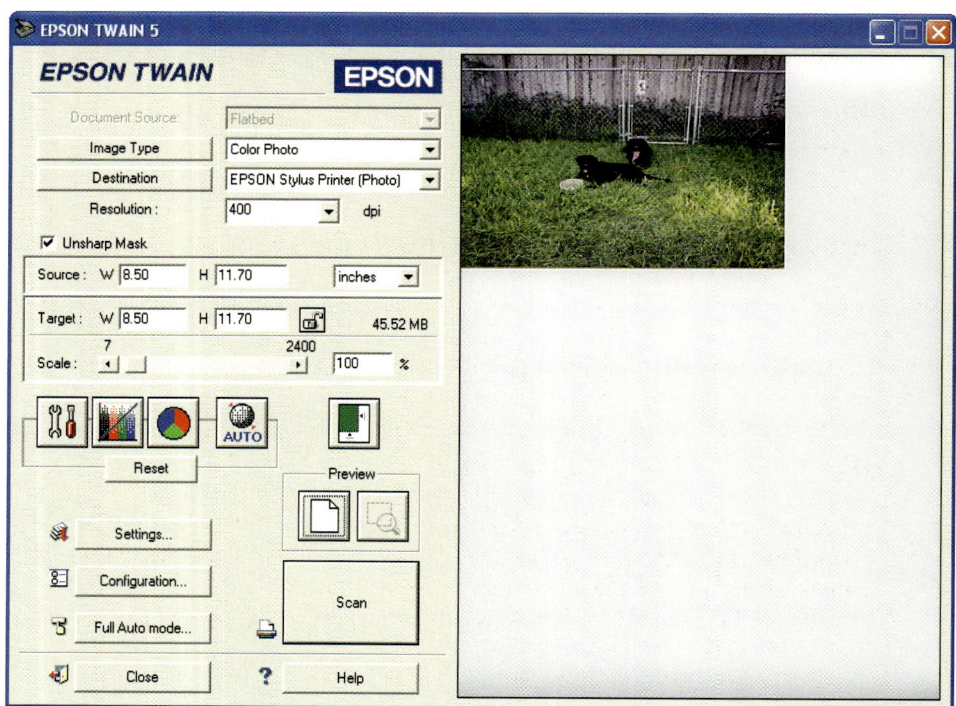

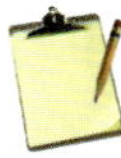

You may be able to scan documents from other programs. For example, in Microsoft Word for Windows, you can click the **Insert** menu, click **Picture**, and then **From Scanner or Camera** to access your scanner or camera from Word. You can then start the scan. The image is scanned directly to the document. You can then resize the image as needed and save the document.

Working with Scanned Images

Once an image has been scanned, you can manipulate the image using your scanner program. Although every scanner program is different, most enable you to edit the image in ways like the following:

You can also open and work with the scanned image in your image-editing program. See Chapter 5 for information on using this type of program.

- **Cropping the image.** Save just the portion of the image you want, and remove the rest.
- **Erasing part of the image.** Drag over any parts you want to erase.
- **Annotating the image.** Add notes to the image to call out points of interest. Alternatively, add text or freehand drawings to the image.
- **Flipping or rotating the image.** Rotate the image left or right; many programs enable you to select the exact degree of rotation.
- **Adjusting colors, brightness, and contrast.** Fine-tune these settings to improve the image, or distort the colors for effect.
- **Zooming around the image.** Zoom in or out for close editing work.
- **Printing the image.** Print a hardcopy of the printed image.
- **Saving the image.** Specify the image's file type, location, and quality. File types are covered in Chapter 2, as well as Chapter 5.

Because many scanner programs use a generic name for the scan (often the date), it's a good idea to resave the image using a more descriptive name. For example, "Mosaic Peace Stone" is more descriptive than "Monday, February 25." Doing so will help you identify this file later.

You can open an image in your scanner program and then use the program tools such as toolbar buttons to work with the image. In addition to using these toolbar buttons, you can also use menu commands to accomplish tasks. Check your scanner program manual for specific instructions on how to open and work with scanned images.

You can also open the image in an image-editing program such as Picture It! and use this program's tools to edit the image. Chapter 5, "Editing and Working with Images," covers how to open and then modify an image, including scanned images.

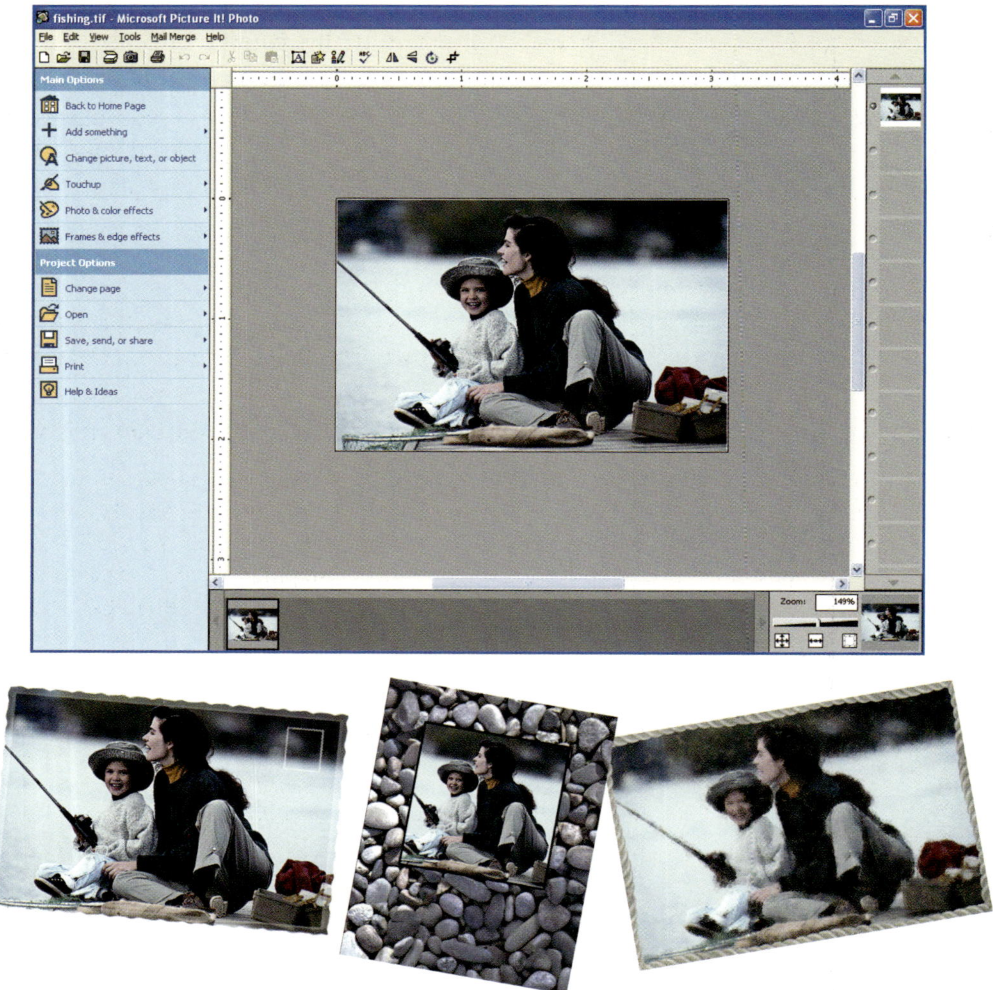

Figure 4-1 A scanned image open in Picture It!. Using menu commands and toolbar buttons, you can apply any number of effects to the image and accomplish several tasks with it.

The best way to learn about your scanning program is to experiment. Try out different features to see how they work. After all, you always have the option of undoing your changes (look for an **Undo** command on the **Edit** menu). And if you really mess up, you can simply scan the image again and start from scratch. For specific instructions, consult the manual for your scanner and scanner program or use the program's Help commands.

Using a Scanning Service

If you think you may want to scan images only occasionally, you may decide that buying a scanner seems wasteful. Alternatively, you may discover you need very high quality output—higher than most consumer scanners can provide. Either way, you may want to consider using a scanning service. Chances are your local print shop can provide this service for you. You can also find scanning services online from companies such as FujiFilm.

When using a scanning service, be it your local print shop or online, you provide the negative, image, or picture you want scanned. For a fee, the scanning service scans the item and provides you with a digital file—either on a floppy disk or on a CD. You can then open the images from the disk and work with them using your computer. For information about fees and services, check with your local print shop or on the Web.

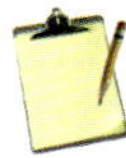

Be sure that your PC can read the type of media that the scanning service uses to store your images. For example, a popular storage format is Kodak's Photo CD; your CD drive must be able to read a CD (most new computers do). Check the documentation for your drive. Also, ask the scanning service. Sometimes you need to install a software program that enables you to read the images from the disk.

To Keep on Learning . . .

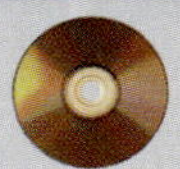

Go to the CD-ROM and select the segment:

- *Scanner: Using* to gain an understanding of scanners and the steps to digitize a photo.

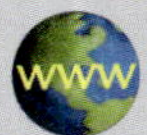

Go online to **www.LearnwithGateway.com** and log on to select:

- *Internet Links and Resources*
- *FAQs*

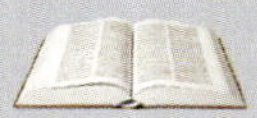

With the *Survive & Thrive* series, refer to *Use and Care for Your PC* for more information on:

- *Working with Windows XP programs*

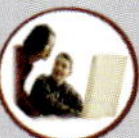

Gateway offers a hands-on training course that covers many of the topics in this chapter. Additional fees may apply. Call **888-852-4821** for enrollment information. If applicable, please have your customer ID and order number ready when you call.

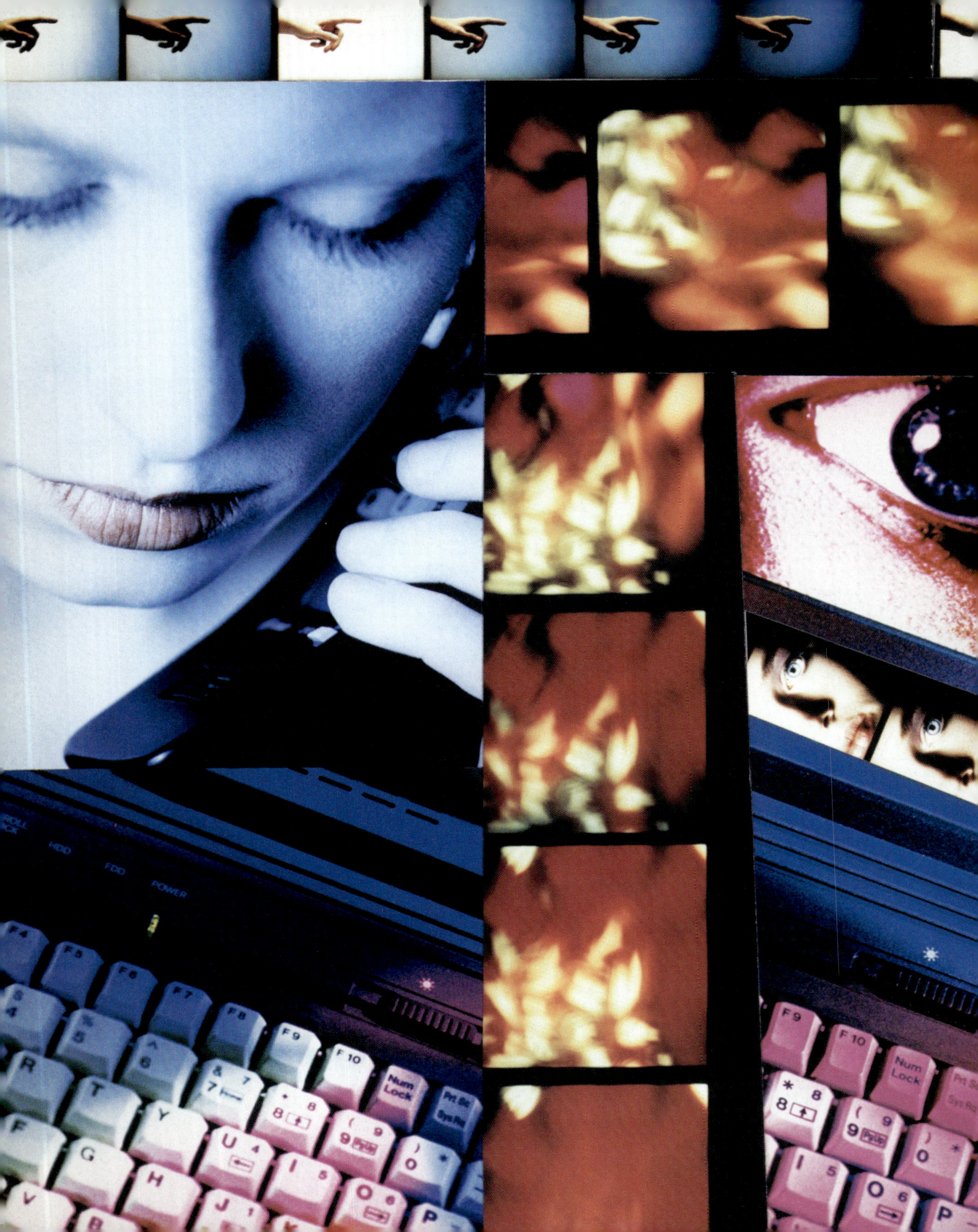
HDD
FDD
POWER
Num Lock
F9
F10

CHAPTER 5

Editing and Manipulating Your Images

Everyone has that one photograph that simply got away. Sometimes the photograph eludes you because you didn't have your camera with you. Other times you manage to snap the scene, only to discover that your thumb was covering the edge of the lens.

Image-editing software can't help you if you missed a shot because you forgot your camera. It can, however, rectify photographic mistakes like the thumb. Using image-editing software, you can crop out the offending digit, as well as correct images that are too dark or too bright, fix red eye, rotate images, and more. In addition, you can use image-editing software to apply a wide variety of special effects to your images. In this chapter you'll gain an overview of what you can accomplish using your photo-editing program, and you'll learn some specific skills that will help you perfect your images.

Understanding Image-Editing Basics

In Chapter 2, you were introduced to some image-editing programs. Many digital cameras or camera bundles include an image-editing program that will probably work perfectly for your needs. But, if your camera doesn't include an editing program, or if you think you'd prefer to use a different program, you can also buy one. Although each image-editing program on the market works a little differently, most offer the same basic set of features. For example, nearly every program, enable you to open, edit, organize, share, and print your pictures. However, image-editing programs often differ in precisely how each of these actions is accomplished.

In this section, you'll learn how to install and start an image-editing program, and you'll also preview some of the tools you can expect to find in one.

This chapter provides detailed steps for tasks using MGI PhotoSuite 4 and Microsoft Picture It!. If you use a different program, check its user's guide for specific instructions.

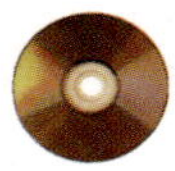

To learn more about image editors and their key features, go to the CD-ROM segment *Image Editor: Choosing.*

Installing the Program

Before you can use your image-editing program, you must first install it. The specific steps for this process differ from program to program, but in most cases starting the installation procedure involves the following:

1. Insert the program disk—typically a CD-ROM—into the appropriate drive on your computer.
2. Assuming the program disk is a CD-ROM, chances are it will start automatically and launch the setup or installation menu. From this menu, select the option to install the program.

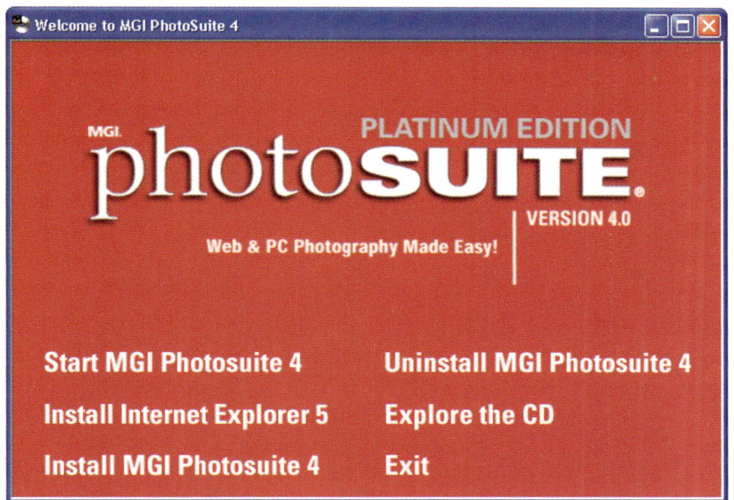

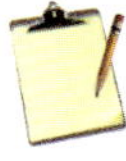

If your disk doesn't automatically play when you insert it, open My Computer and then double-click the icon for the drive you inserted the disk into (typically the CD-ROM or DVD drive). Look for a file called *install* or *setup,* and then double-click it to start the installation routine. Alternatively, you can click **start**, **Control Panel**, and then click **Add or Remove Programs**.

3. When your program's installation routine starts, follow the instructions to install the program, clicking **Next** to move from step to step.
4. When the installation process is complete, click **Finish**. An entry for the newly installed program has been added to the All Programs menu, and a shortcut to the program may have been added to your desktop.

Most software requires you to restart your computer after the program completes installation.

Most installation routines allow you to select a location for storing the program and its various files. You may also be able to specify what type of installation you want—for instance, typical or custom. With a typical installation, the most commonly used program tools are installed. With custom installation, on the other hand, you can select which of the various program components you want to install.

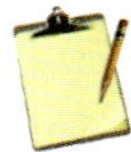

It's a good idea to choose typical installation when you're new to the program. You can always go back and use the installation disk to install other components after you've become more familiar with it

Starting the Program

Once your image-editing program is installed, you start it just as you would any other program. Here's how:

1. Click **start**, and point to **All Programs**.
2. If you see the program icon, click it. If the program icon is stored in a folder, point to the folder and then click the program icon. The program opens.

If a shortcut to the program was added to your desktop during the course of the installation routine, you can double-click it to start the program instead of using the start menu.

You may be prompted to register the program the first time you start it. Complete the information and register online if you choose.

Previewing the Program's Tools

When you start your image-editing program, it will probably display a Welcome screen with icons and/or *links* (underlined menu commands) for common tasks. These Welcome screens can help you familiarize yourself with your image-editing program. For example, Microsoft Picture It! displays a Welcome screen with options for picking a design, opening and editing pictures, and getting creative ideas.

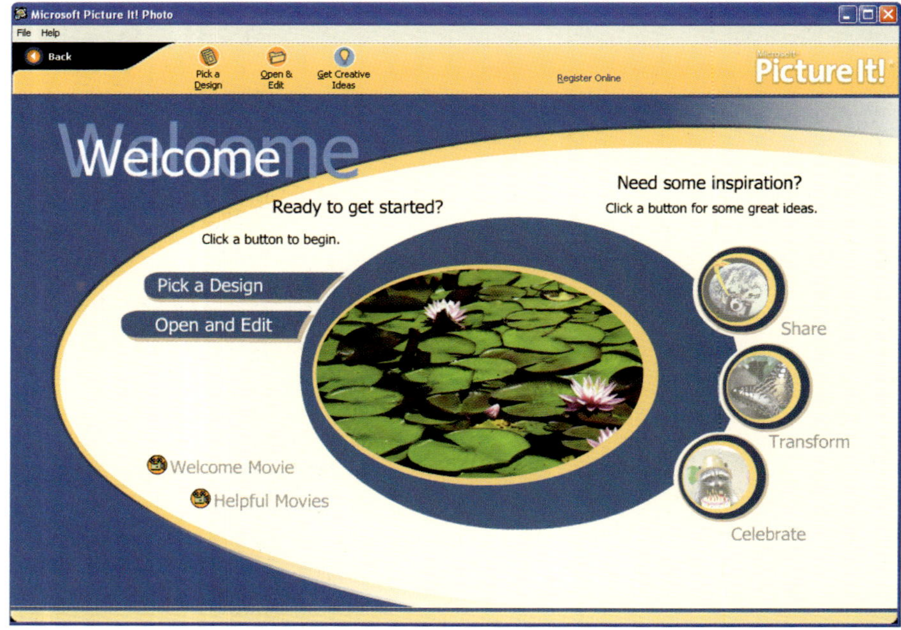

Some programs, including Picture It!, show a movie at startup before displaying the Welcome screen. This movie introduces you to the program's features, enabling you to familiarize yourself with the program. If you don't want to watch the movie, click **Skip Movie** (or a similarly named button) to skip it.

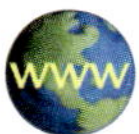

To learn about the key software features and navigation options for Microsoft Picture It!, go to the Web segment *Software Interface Overview* in the Picture It! course.

Likewise, MGI PhotoSuite 4 displays a Welcome screen upon startup, listing your main choices: Get (open pictures), Prepare (enhance a photo), Compose (create a project with your photo), Organize (sort photos and multimedia files into albums), Share (share photos online or through e-mail), Print (print pictures and projects), and Browse (search for pictures on the Internet).

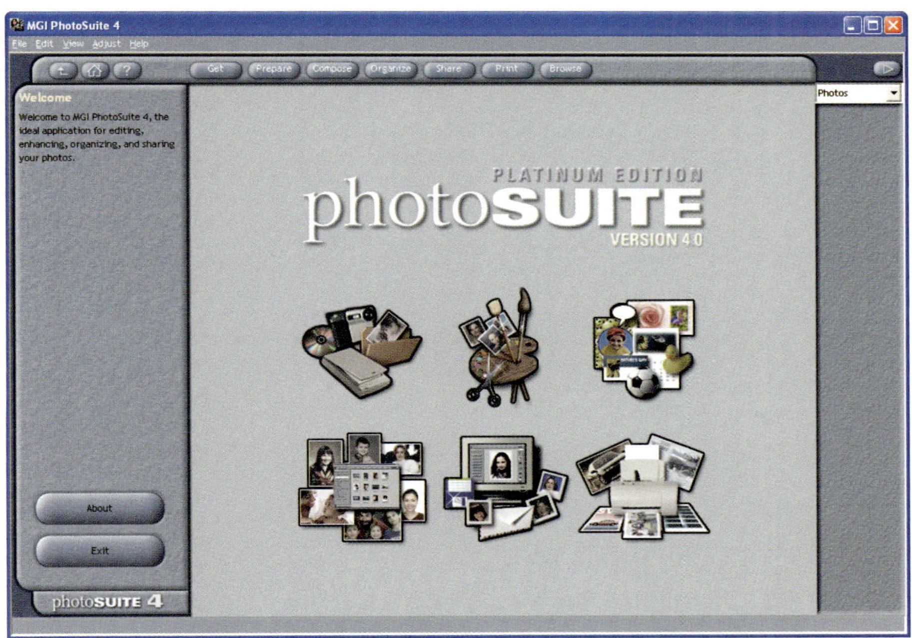

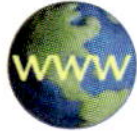

To learn about the key software features and navigation options for MGI PhotoSuite 4, go to the Web segment *Software Interface Overview* in the PhotoSuite 4 course.

5

Opening and Saving Your Images

Now that you're familiar with your image editor's program window and tools, it's time to get down to the business of using the program to work with your images. First, however, you must learn how to open images on your computer.

Before you can open an image on your computer, you must first download it from your digital camera, scan it using your scanner, or obtain it in some other way—perhaps by downloading it from the Internet or by copying it from a Photo CD. In many cases you can use your image-editing program to complete this task. Once the image is stored on your computer, you can use your image-editing program to open it.

In this section, you'll learn how to open images stored on your computer, and how to save the changes you make to them.

Opening an Image for Editing

Chapter 1 discusses the many different sources for digital images, including digital cameras, scanners, the Internet, and your computer. Most image-editing programs enable you to obtain pictures from these sources:

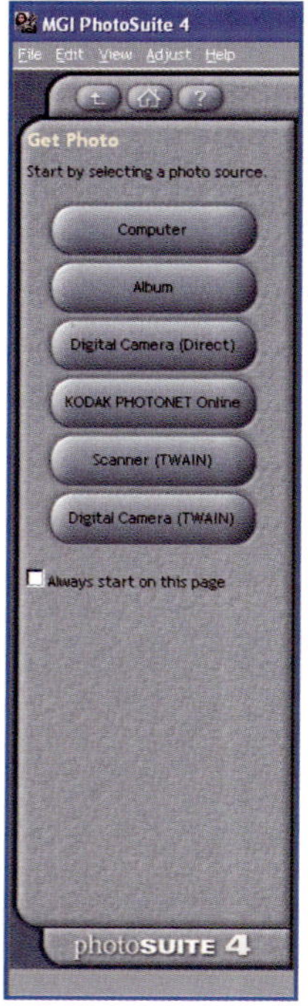

- **From your computer.** In most cases, you usually transfer your images from your digital camera or other device, such as a scanner, directly to your computer. You probably store images found on the Internet on your computer as well. Accordingly, you can use your image-editing program to open image files directly from your computer. When you choose this method, you select the drive and folder where your images are stored (this can include your CD-ROM drive), and then open the images.

- **From your digital camera.** Many image-editing programs enable you to download and open pictures directly from your camera. For help transferring pictures from your camera to your computer, review Chapter 3.

- **From your scanner.** In most cases, you can start a scan from your image-editing program, scanning the image directly into the image-editing program window. The option for doing this may be called "Scanner" or "TWAIN."

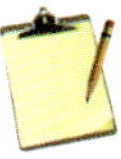

TWAIN is the official technical standard for scanning images. Almost all scanners come with a TWAIN driver (software that allows the device to communicate with the computer). This makes such scanners compatible with any other device that supports the TWAIN standard.

- **From the Internet.** You can use your image-editing program to access online photo and image sources and download image files to your computer.

Let's take a look at the most common method of opening pictures: from the computer. The following sections cover opening images using PhotoSuite 4 and Picture It!.

You may often want to open and work with several pictures at once or in order. Most programs enable you to open a set of pictures; you can then select which image you want to work with first. The image you've selected appears in the image-editing program's work area, while the remaining images are displayed in a "Library" or "tray." You'll learn how to open and manage multiple images in the following sections.

Opening an Image in MGI PhotoSuite 4

To use PhotoSuite 4 to open an image stored on your computer, follow these steps:

1. In the Welcome screen, click **Get**. PhotoSuite 4 displays the main sources for opening pictures (covered earlier in this section).
2. Click **Computer**. The Open dialog box opens.
3. Locate the folder that contains your image files.

By default, the Open dialog box in most image-editing programs lists only those files that are of a particular format. PhotoSuite 4 lists only PhotoSuite-format files. If the image file you want to open isn't listed but you know it's stored in the folder you've selected, click the **Files of type** drop-down list and choose the format of your image file.

4. Click the image file you want to open. The image is displayed in the Preview area of the Open dialog box. To select multiple files, hold down the **CTRL** key on your keyboard and click each file you want to open. If you select multiple images, no preview is displayed.

If you don't see the preview of an individual picture, be sure the **Preview** check box is checked.

5

5. Click **Open**. If you selected a single image file, it opens in the work area. If you selected multiple files, all open in the Library, with the currently selected image displayed in the work area.

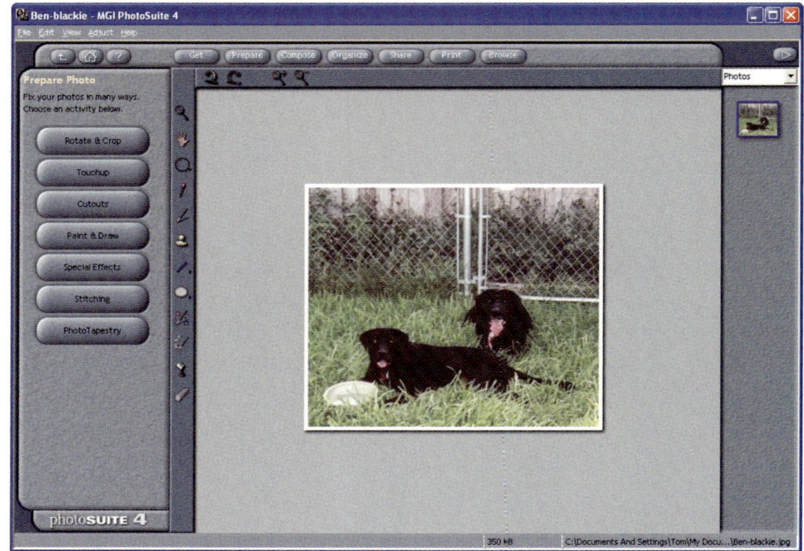

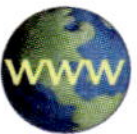

To practice opening a photograph on your hard drive with PhotoSuite 4, go to the Web segment *Photo: Opening* in the PhotoSuite 4 course.

Opening an Image in Microsoft Picture It!

In this section, you'll learn how to open pictures from My Computer. To open an image in Picture It!, follow these steps:

1. In the Welcome screen, click **Open & Edit**.

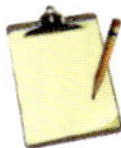

Picture It! lists recently opened files, which you can reopen by double-clicking. Picture It! enables you to open a picture from the Clipart Gallery as well.

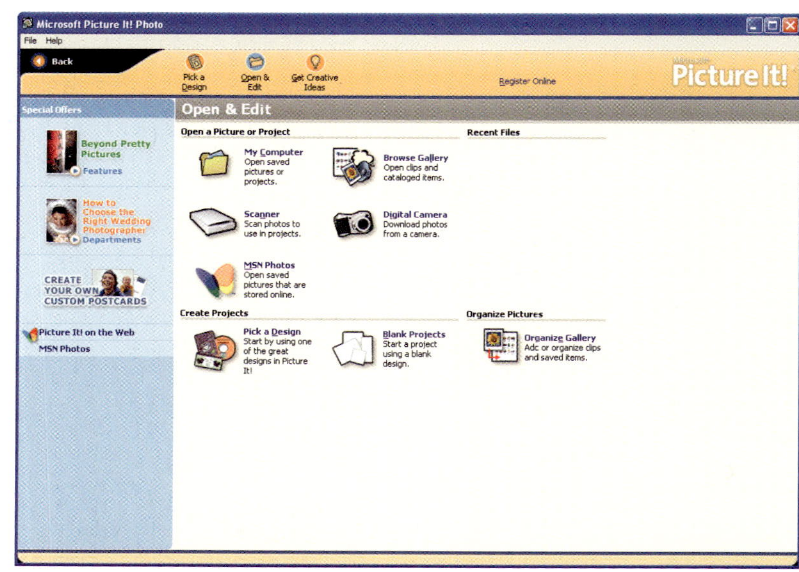

2. Click **My Computer**. The Open Pictures or Projects task pane opens.
3. Locate the folder that contains your image files.

4. Click the image file you want to open. To select multiple files, hold down the **CTRL** key on your keyboard, and click each file you want to open.

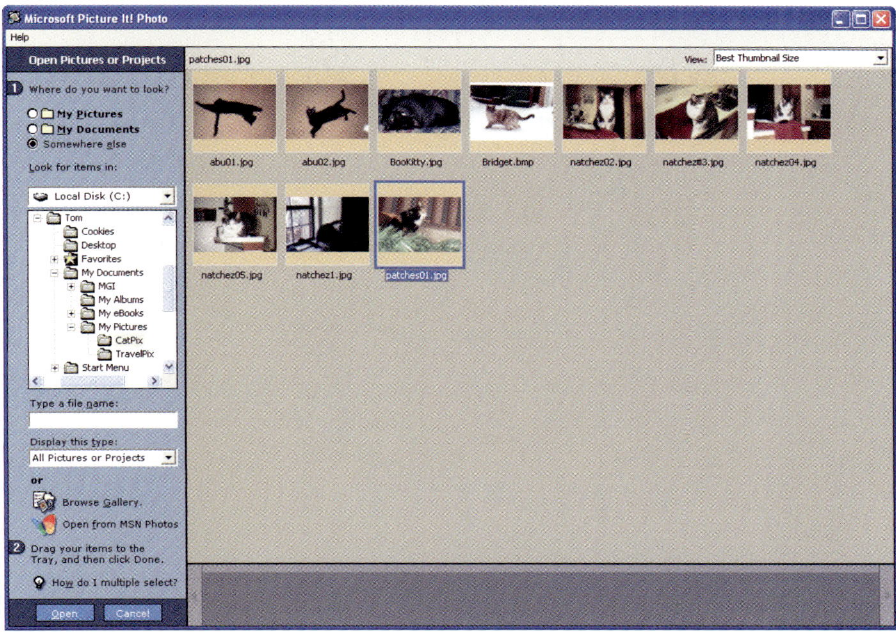

5. Click **Open**. Alternatively, drag the selected files from the main contents window to the tray. If you selected a single image file, it opens in the work area. If you selected multiple files, they all open in the tray, with the currently selected image displayed in the work area.

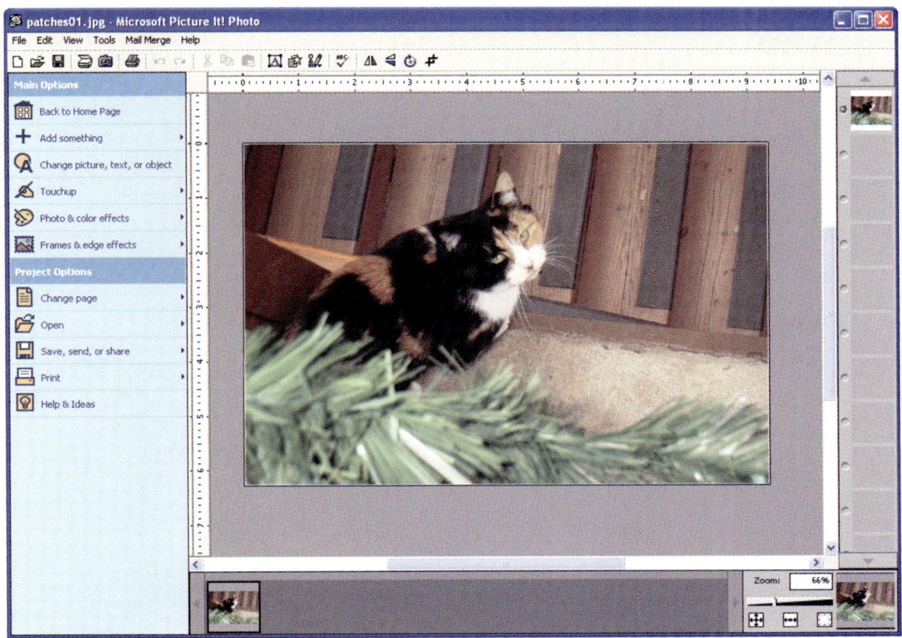

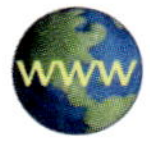

To practice opening a photograph stored on your hard disk drive with Picture It!, go to the Web segment *Photo: Opening* in the Microsoft Picture It! course.

Saving an Image

In most cases, before you begin to make changes to an open image, you should create a working copy of the image that's currently open. Any changes you make to the image occur within the working copy, while the original remains intact. You can then save the copy as a new file with a different name than the original. If your edits are a disappointment, this ensures that you can always return to the original and start over.

When you save an image file, observe the following guidelines:

- **Select the correct command from the File menu.** Click **Save As** the first time you save the file and give it a new name or store it in a new location, thereby preserving the original. Once you've saved the file using the Save As command, click **Save** periodically as you continue to edit the image.

Don't wait until you've made the final touches to your image to save it, and be sure to keep saving as you work. Otherwise, if some disaster should befall your computer (for instance, it loses power), all your work will be lost.

- **Rename downloaded images.** When you download pictures from a digital camera, their names are usually not very descriptive. For example, images can be named according to the date they were taken, or perhaps using a number scheme to identify the order in which they were taken. To help you remember which image is which, it's a good idea to save each image file using a descriptive file name.

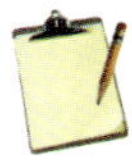

Even if you don't open pictures for editing and then save them, you should still rename your files if their names are not descriptive. This will help you keep your image files organized. You can rename files in a Windows folder by right-clicking the file, clicking **Rename**, and typing a new name. See Chapter 8 for more information about organizing image files.

- **Select a file format.** If your image-editing program saves image files using a proprietary file format by default, you might decide to change a file's format in order to share it with people who use a different image-editing program. The JPEG format is frequently used for images placed on the Web, because JPEG images are compressed and thereby require less space. The TIF and PCX formats are commonly used for printed illustrations. For more information about file formats, refer to Chapter 2. To change the file type, click the **Save as type** drop-down list, and then click the format you want.

Both PhotoSuite 4 and Picture It! include many options for saving, including saving a project or an album. You'll learn about some of these additional features in Chapter 9.

Saving an Image in PhotoSuite 4

To save an image open in the PhotoSuite 4 work area, follow these steps:

1. Click **File**, and then click **Save As**. The **Save Photo** dialog box opens.

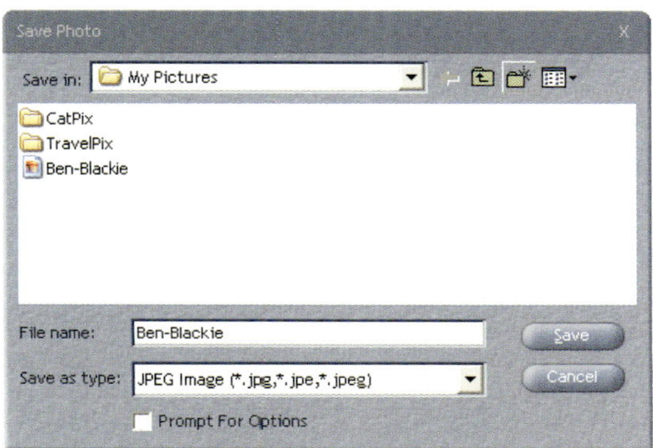

2. Navigate to the drive and folder where you want to store your image.
3. Locate and open the folder you want to save your image in.

If you want to create a new folder for your images, click the drive or folder the new folder should be placed in, click the **Create New Folder** icon, enter a name for the new folder, and press **ENTER**.

5

3. Type a name for the file in the **File name** text box. Make sure this name describes the contents of the image file.
4. Click **Save**.

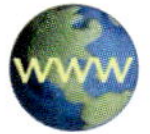

To gain practice saving photographs in different file formats using PhotoSuite 4, go to the Web segment *Images: Saving in Different Formats* in the PhotoSuite 4 course.

Saving an Image in Picture It!

To save an image open in the Picture It! work area, follow these steps:

1. Click **File**, and then click **Save as** to open the Save As task pane.

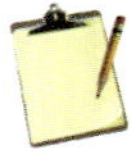

You can also use the commands under Project Options in the task pane to open the Save As task pane. Click **Save, send, or share**, and then choose **Save to my computer**. Finally, choose **Save as**.

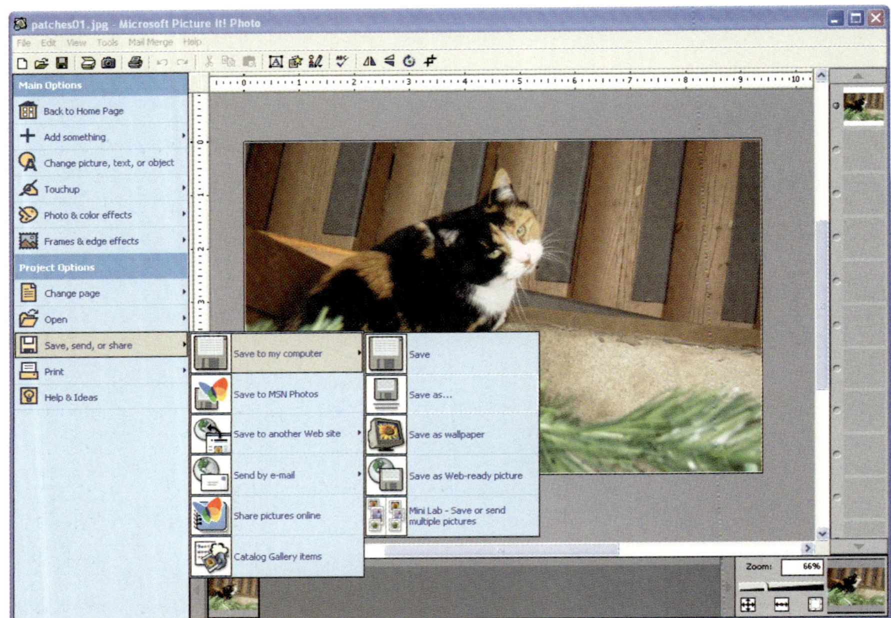

2. Locate and open the folder in which you want to save your image.
3. Type a file name in the **Type a name** text box. Make sure this name describes the contents of the image file.
4. Click **Save.**

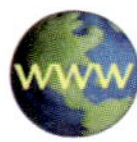

To gain practice saving photographs in different file formats using Picture It!, go to the Web segment *Images: Saving in Different Formats* in the Picture It! course.

Enhancing Pictures

Now that you understand the basics of your image-editing program—it's time to get into the meat of the program: using it to enhance your images.

One of the most common reasons to edit an image is to correct problems in it. For example, you may discover that the image is too light or too dark, that it lacks contrast, or that the eyes of your photograph's subject may appear to be red, a common problem with flash photography. You may want to eliminate unwanted elements of the picture and keep only part of it. In this section, you'll learn how to correct these common problems.

Most image-editing programs offer many more tools for fixing problem pictures than the ones covered here. For information about what other types of enhancements you may be able to use your image editor to apply, see Chapter 9. This chapter also includes a troubleshooting section for common camera and picture problems.

Adjusting the Color

Many features affect the color in your image, including brightness, contrast, and tint. If your picture is too dark, you can use your image-editing program to brighten it. Or perhaps the details in your image are not sharp—in that case, you can adjust the image's contrast. Finally, if you want to add a special effect, you can adjust an image's tint. In this section you'll learn how to adjust basic color settings using PhotoSuite 4 and Picture It!.

5

Every picture is different, so there are no set rules for determining what color settings will work best for you. To get the color in your image just right, you'll need to experiment a bit with the various settings. Don't be afraid; you can always undo your edits if you don't like the results. (You'll learn how to undo changes to an image file later in this chapter in the section "Undoing Editing Changes.")

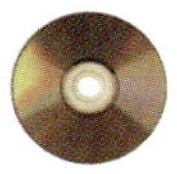

The photos used in the following exercises are available on the CD-ROM that accompanies this book.

Enhancing Color in PhotoSuite 4

PhotoSuite 4 can adjust the brightness and contrast in your image automatically, or you can use the program to adjust these settings manually. To instruct PhotoSuite 4 to handle color settings automatically, do the following:

1. Make sure the image you want to change is open in the PhotoSuite 4 work area.
2. Click **Touchup** in the Prepare Photo Activity Panel, and then click **Enhance**.

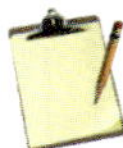

If the Prepare Photo Activity Panel isn't visible on your screen, click **Prepare** at the top of the PhotoSuite 4 window.

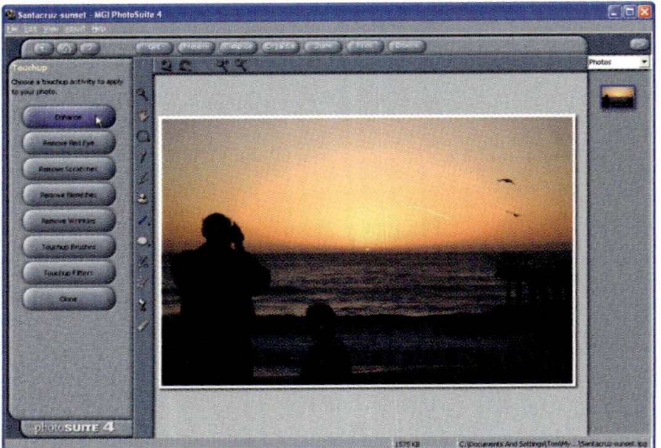

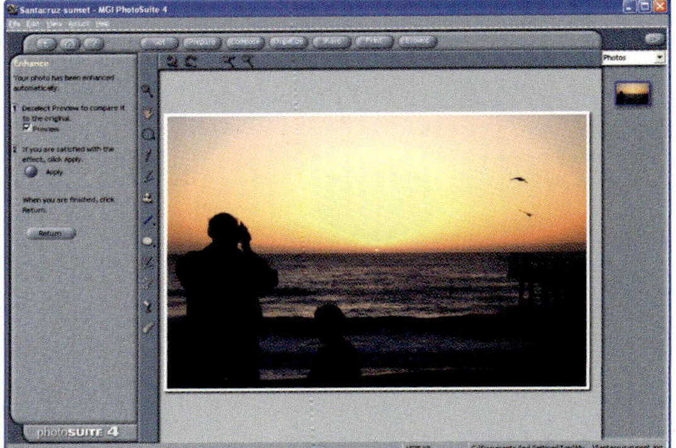

3. PhotoSuite 4 takes the necessary steps to enhance the image's color settings. If you like the results, click **Apply**, and then **Return**. To reject the changes, click **Return** only.

To adjust the color settings manually, you can use PhotoSuite 4 *touchup filters*. PhotoSuite 4 allows you to use several touchup filters, not just ones related to an image's color settings. For example, to sharpen or soften your image, you can use the Sharpen and Soften touchup filters, respectively.

Using the Fix Colors touchup filter, you can adjust the hue, saturation, and value of the colors to affect their shade and intensity. You can use the Color Adjustment touchup filter to adjust the amount of each of the three primary colors in the picture. To apply the Brightness and Contrast filter, follow these steps:

1. Make sure the image you want to change is open in the work area.
2. Click **Touchup** in the Prepare Photo Activity Panel, then click **Touchup Filters**. The Brightness and Contrast filter is selected by default.

To select another filter, such as the Fix Colors filter or the Color Adjustment filter, open the **Choose a touchup filter** drop-down list and click the filter you want to use.

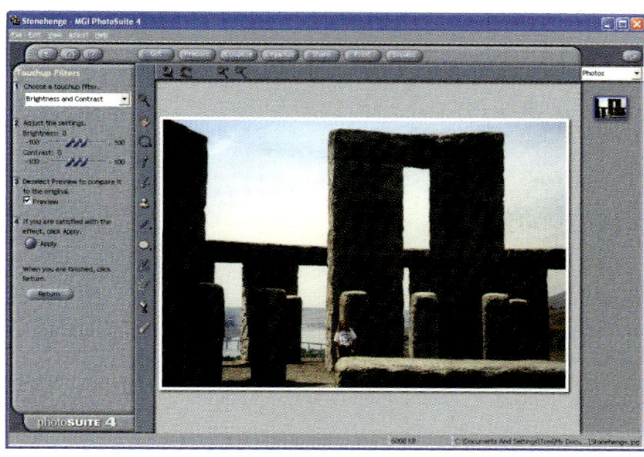

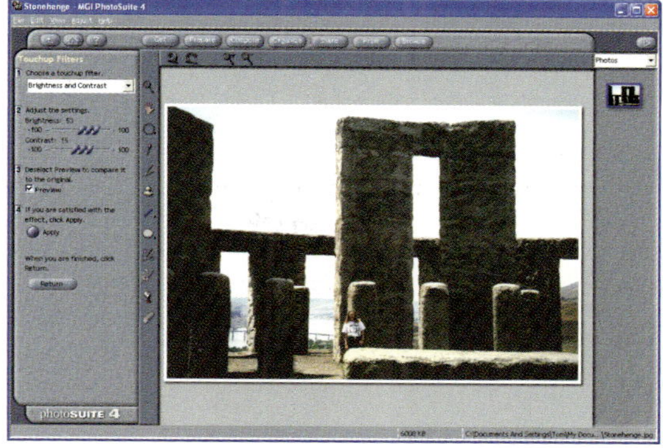

3. On the **Brightness** bar, click the plus or minus sign to increase or decrease the image's brightness. You can also use the slider bar to adjust the image as well.
4. Adjust the image's contrast by clicking the plus or minus sign on the **Contrast** bar.
5. If you like the results, click **Apply**, and then **Return**. To reject the results, click **Return** only.

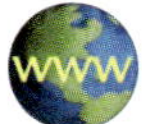

To gain an understanding of how to touch up a photograph with PhotoSuite 4, go to the Web segment *Touch-up Filters: Applying* in the PhotoSuite 4 course.

Adjusting Color in Picture It!

5

Like PhotoSuite 4, Picture It! affords you several options when it comes to adjusting the color in your image—and using them is just as easy. For example, to adjust image brightness and contrast automatically, follow these simple steps:

1. Make sure the image you want to change is open in the Picture It! work area.
2. Click **Touchup** under **Main Options** in the task pane.
3. Choose **Brightness & Contrast**. The Brightness & Contrast task pane opens, displaying settings for Details, Brightness, and Contrast.
4. Click **Automatic Fix**.

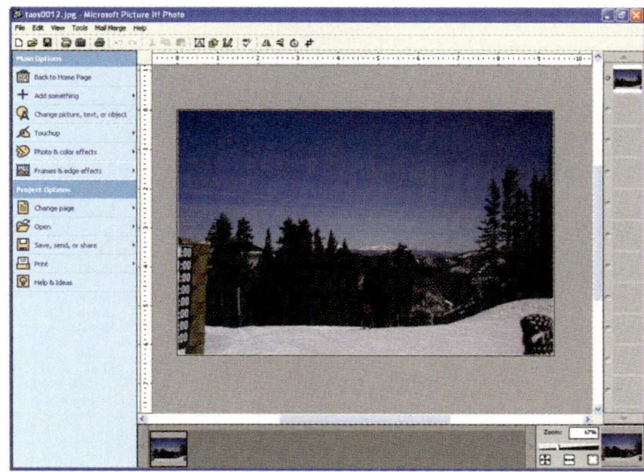

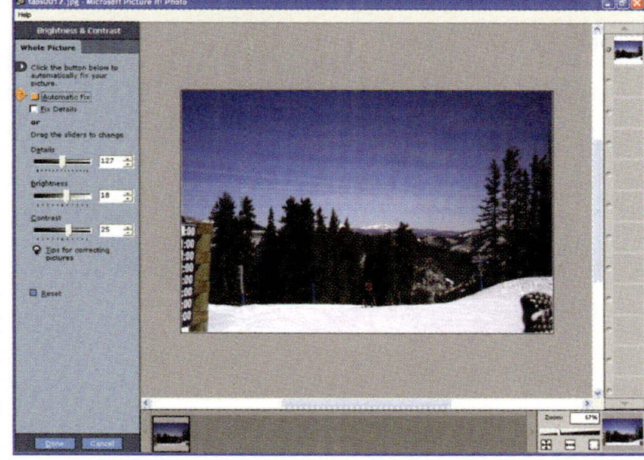

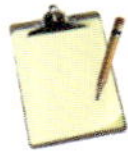

If you prefer to adjust color settings manually, drag the **Details**, **Brightness**, and **Contrast** slider bars until the image is the way you want it. Picture It! defines brightness as "the amount of light that appears to emanate from a color" and contrast as "the degree of difference between the lightest and darkest parts of an image." Details, on the other hand, redefines pictures with very dark and very light areas.

5. If you like the results, click **Done**. To reject the results, click **Cancel** only.

In addition to adjusting the brightness and contrast in your image, you can also adjust the tint either automatically or manually. Follow these steps:

1. Make sure the image you want to change is open in the work area.
2. Click **Touchup** under Main Options in the task pane.
3. Choose **Correct Tint**. The Correct Tint task pane opens, displaying settings for Color and Amount.
4. To instruct Picture It! to adjust the tint in your image automatically, click **Automatic Fix**.

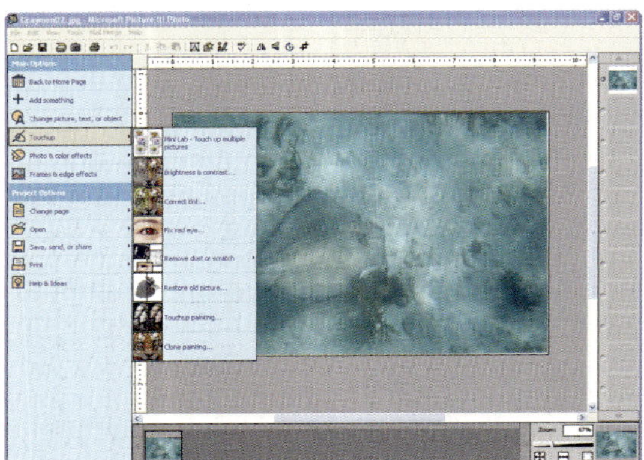

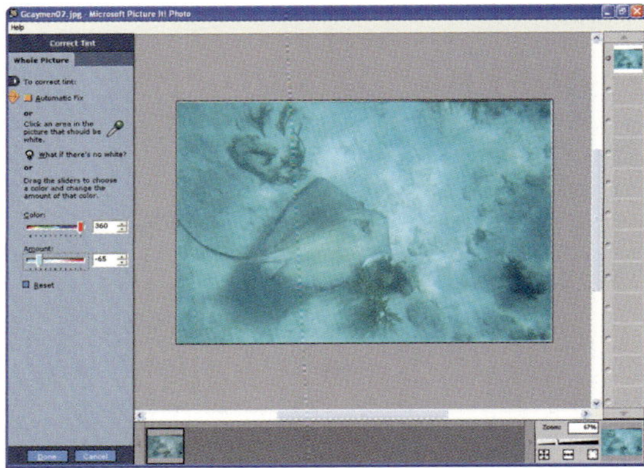

5. To adjust tint settings manually, drag the **Color** slider bar to select the color you want to change. Then, drag the **Amount** slider bar to add more or less of the color tint.
6. If you like the results, click **Done**. To reject the results, click **Cancel** only.

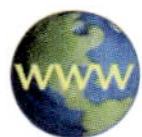

To gain an understanding of how to touch up a photograph with Picture It!, go to the Web segment *Touch-up Filters: Applying* in the Picture It! course.

Fixing Red Eye

Have you ever captured a perfect moment on camera, only to discover that your camera's flash turned your subject's eyes an unattractive shade of red? Fortunately, some cameras are designed to prevent red eye in flash pictures. If your camera does not have this option, however, or if you forgot to turn it on, then you can use your image-editing program to return your photographed subject's eyes to a normal color.

Fixing Red Eye in PhotoSuite 4

To fix red eye in PhotoSuite 4, follow these steps:

1. Make sure the image you want to fix is open in the PhotoSuite 4 work area.
2. Click **Touchup** in the Prepare Photo Activity Panel, and then click **Remove Red Eye**.
3. The Remove Red Eye Activity Panel opens. Click the Zoom buttons to zoom in on one or both of the subject's eyes.

You may need to scroll through the zoomed picture to view the subject's eyes.

4. Click the brush size bar to increase or decrease the size of the mouse pointer so that it's the same size as the eye you want to correct. To determine the mouse pointer's size, move it across the work area. The pointer appears as a circle with a crosshair.
5. Center the mouse pointer over the eye you want to correct, and click. You may need to click more than once to completely remove the red.
6. Repeat steps 4 and 5 for the other eye.
7. When you're finished, click **Return**.

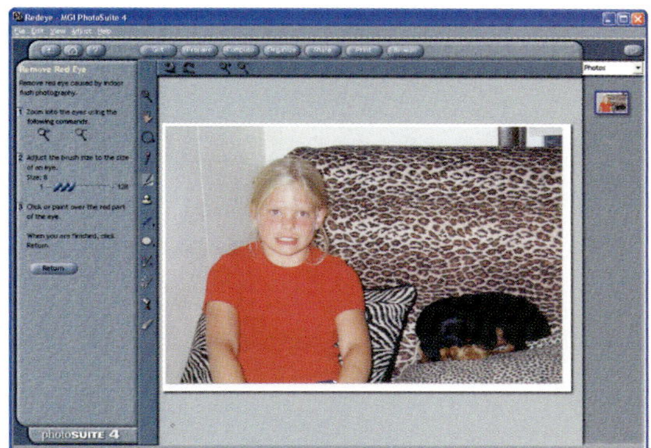

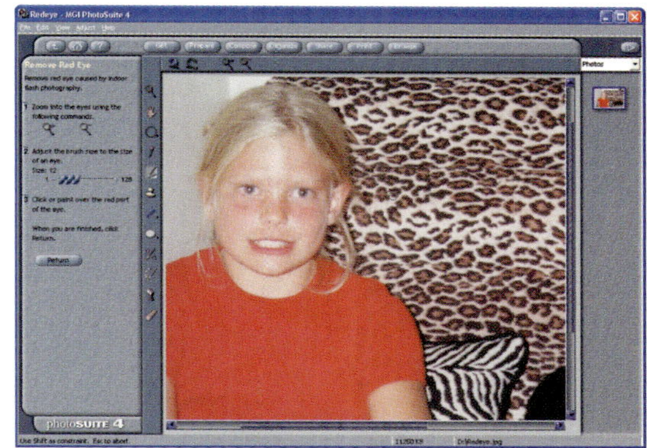

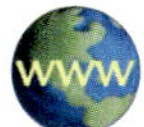

To be able to repair red eye conditions in a photograph using PhotoSuite 4, go to the Web segment *Red Eye Reduction: Performing* in the PhotoSuite 4 course.

Fixing Red Eye in Picture It!

Using Picture It!, to fix red eye, do the following:

1. Make sure the image you want to fix is open in the work area.
2. If the Fix Red Eye task pane isn't already open, click **Touchup** in the Main Options task pane, and then click **Fix red eye**.
3. Drag the zoom slider in the Fix Red Eye task pane to zoom in on the part of the image you want to fix.
4. Using the scroll bars in the picture work area, scroll so that you can see the red eye.

5. Place the round pointer over the first eye and click.
6. Repeat Step 5 for the second eye.
7. Click **Automatic Fix**.
8. Click **Done** to return to the main editing screen.

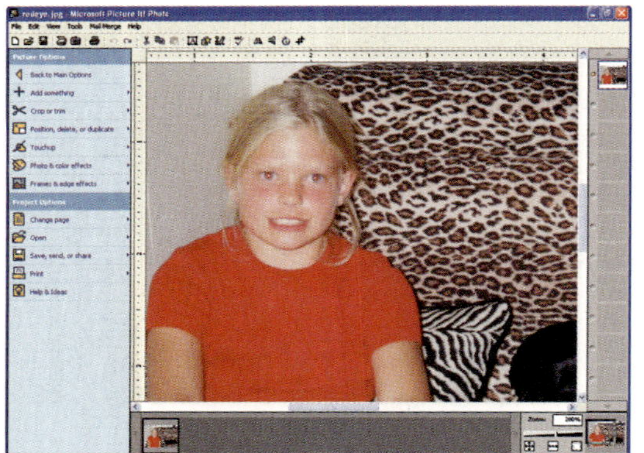

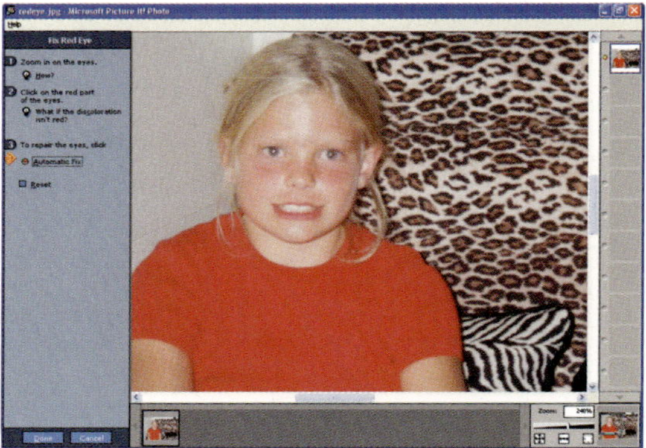

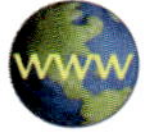

To be able to repair red eye conditions in a photograph using Picture It!, go to the Web segment *Red Eye Reduction: Performing* in the Picture It! course.

Cropping an Image

If you have an out of place object in the background of an image, or the subject isn't properly centered, you can cut out the unnecessary parts to better focus on your subject. Cutting out part of a picture is called *cropping*. As discussed in this section, you can use your image-editing program to crop your picture. You can even use special cutout features to create unusually shaped images such as stars or suns.

Cropping an Image in PhotoSuite 4

To crop an image in PhotoSuite 4, follow these steps:

1. Make sure the image you want to crop is open in the PhotoSuite 4 work area.
2. Click **Rotate & Crop** in the Activity Panel.
3. Click **Crop**.

4. Drag the resizing handles that appear on the border of the image so that the part of the image you want to keep is in the box.
5. Click **Crop**. The portion of the image outside the box is removed.

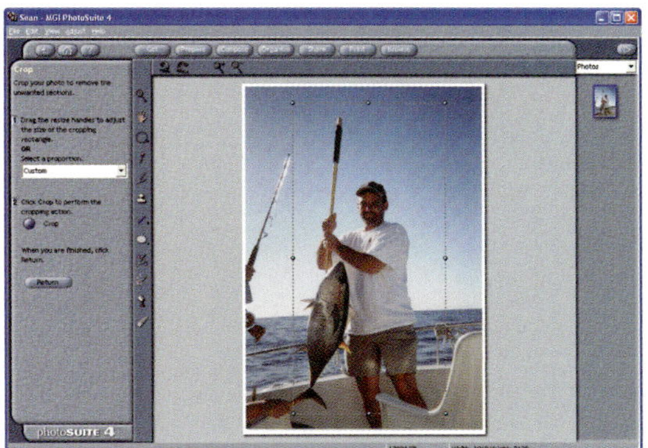

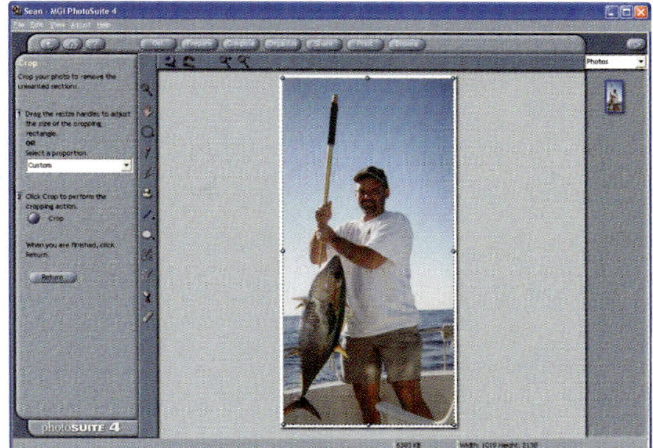

6. Click **Return**.

If you like, you can use a cutout to crop your image into a shape, such as a rectangle or ellipse. Alternatively, you can create your own shape using the PhotoSuite 4 freehand, magic wand, or edge finder tool. Here's how:

1. Make sure the image you want to crop is open in the PhotoSuite 4 wo-k area.
2. Click **Cutouts** in the Prepare Photo Activity Panel.
3. Select the cutout you want to use. Your options are rectangle, ellipse, freehand, magic wand, and edge finder.
4. Use the tool you chose to select the area of the image you want to keep.
5. Click **Make Cutout**.
6. Click **Cut to clipboard**. This allows you to paste the item to an existing or new image.

The software allows you to move, resize, rotate, as well as copy, cut or paste from the clipboard. It also allows you to sent the image to your Library or save the file.

7. When finished, click **Return**.

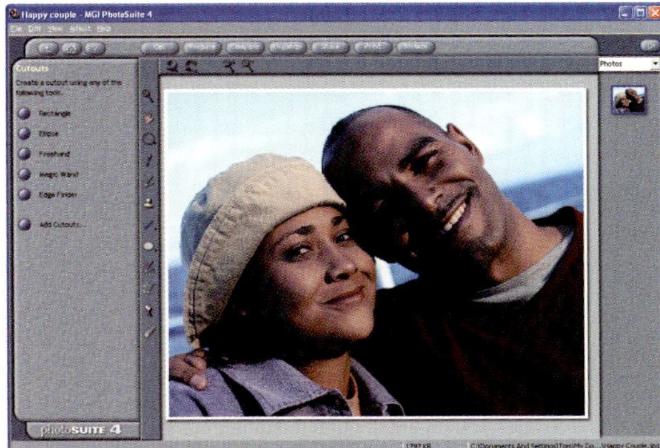

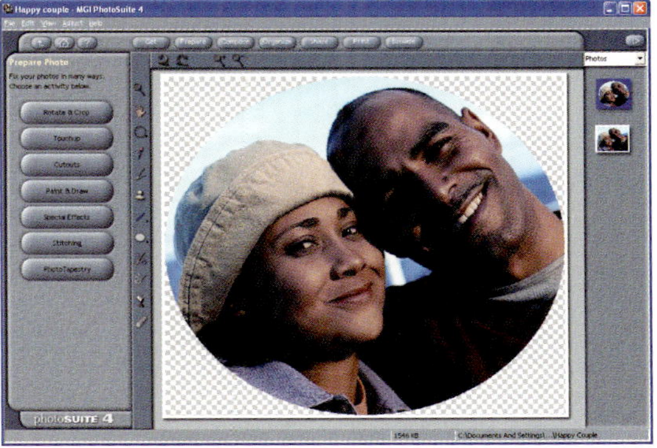

5

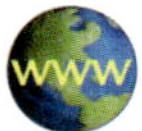

To practice cropping and resizing a photograph using PhotoSuite 4, go to the Web segment *Crop and Resize* in the MGI PhotoSuite 4 course.

Cropping an Image in Picture It!

To crop an image in Picture It!, follow these steps:

1. Make sure the image you want to crop is open in the Picture It! work area.
2. Click **Change page** under Project options in the task pane.
3. Choose **Crop page**. The Crop screen appears.
4. Drag the resizing handles so that the part of the image you want to keep is boxed. You can also drag the rotate handle to change the orientation of the cropped shape.

Like PhotoSuite 4, Picture It! enables you to crop your images using any of a series of predefined shapes, again called cutouts. Simply select the shape you want to use (your choices include ovals, hearts, stars, and other fun shapes). Then, drag the shape over the area of the image you want to keep.

5. When you're ready, click **Done** to crop the picture.

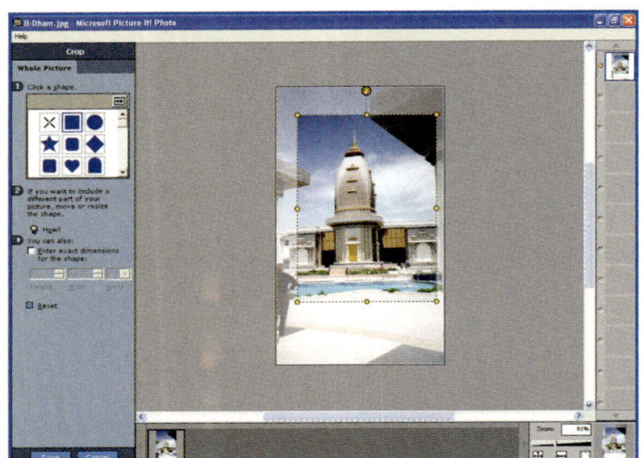

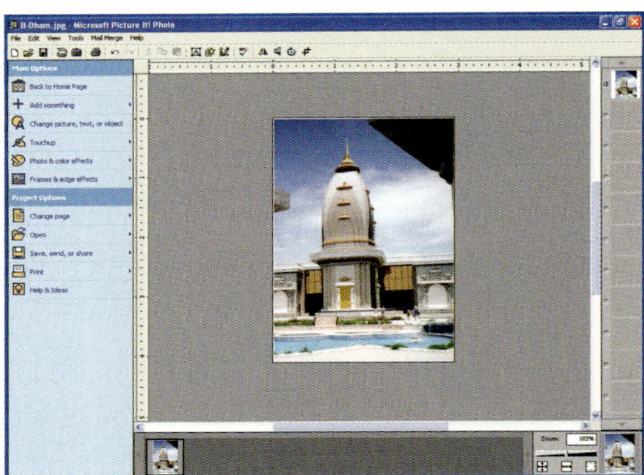

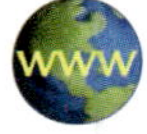

To practice cropping and resizing a photograph using Picture It!, go to the Web segment *Crop and Resize* in the Microsoft Picture It! course.

Rotating an Image

Sometimes digital images need to be rotated so they are displayed correctly on your monitor. For example, if you incorrectly place an image upside down on the bed of your scanner, simply use your image-editing program to rotate the image so that it's displayed properly. Additionally, if a photo is slightly crooked when scanned, you can rotate it in your image-editing program until it is set with the proper orientation.

Rotating an Image in PhotoSuite 4

To rotate an image in PhotoSuite 4, do the following:

1. Make sure the image you want to rotate is open in the PhotoSuite 4 work area.
2. Click **Rotate & Crop** in the Activity Panel.

If the Prepare Photo Activity Panel isn't visible on your screen, click **Prepare** at the top of the PhotoSuite 4 window.

3. Click **Rotate**.
4. Select a rotation angle, manually adjust the photo using the rotate handle, or use a preset rotation amount (90 degrees left, 90 degrees right, 180 degrees).
5. If you rotated the image manually, crop the image to the desired area as discussed in the previous section.
6. Click **Apply**, and then click **Return**.

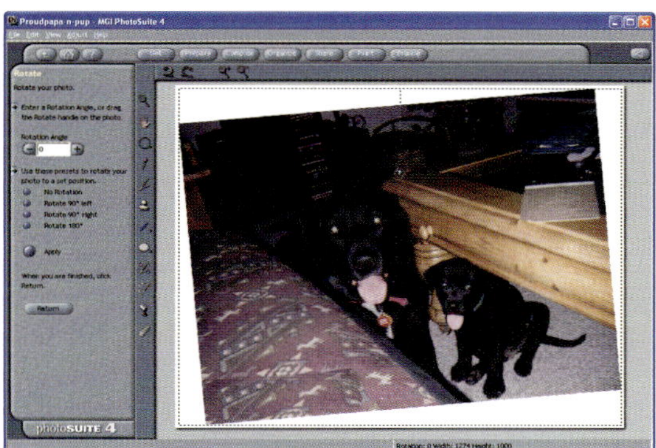

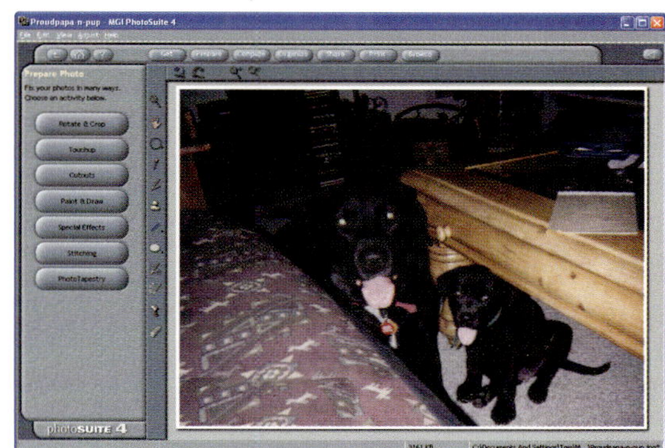

Rotating an Image in Picture It!

To rotate an image in Picture It!, do the following:

1. Make sure the image you want to rotate is open in the Picture It! work area.
2. Click **Change page** under Project options in the task pane.
3. Choose **Rotate page**.
4. Click the rotation you want: **left**, **half turn**, **right**, or **custom**.

5. Click **Done** to accept the change, **Reset** to undo the change and try another, or **Cancel** to return to the main editing screen.

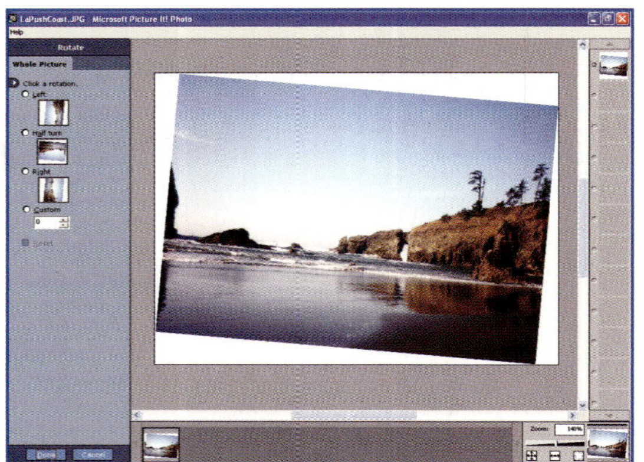

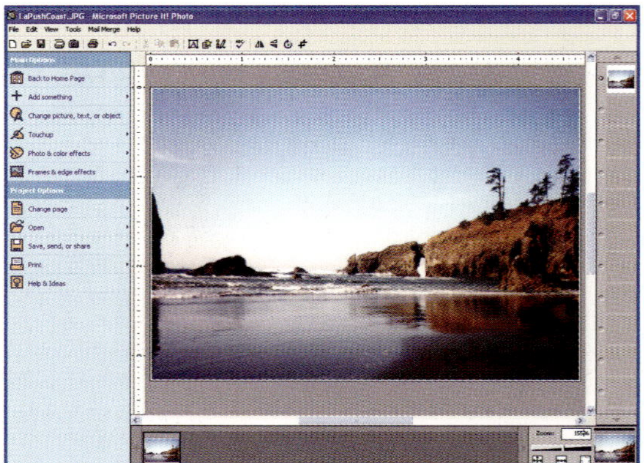

Adding Special Effects

In addition to enabling you to correct problems, your image-editing program can be used to add some fun and artistic effects to your picture. For example, you can convert a color photo to black-and-white, or add a sepia tone (a brownish tint) to your image to artificially age it. If you're really feeling funky, you can warp the picture, making it like a reflection in a funhouse mirror, turn the picture into a mosaic, add shadows, apply 3D effects, and much more. This section gives you a sampling of the many special effects available to you.

Using Color Effects

Just as you can use PhotoSuite 4 and Picture It! to adjust the colors in your image, you can use these programs to apply special color effects. For example, you can convert color images to black and white, or you can colorize parts of your image, perhaps by creating a sepia-tone effect or changing the color of your subject's eyes.

Applying Color Effects in PhotoSuite 4

To use PhotoSuite 4 to colorize an image, do the following:

1. Make sure the image you want to colorize is open in the PhotoSuite 4 work area.
2. Click **Touchup** in the Prepare Photo Activity Panel.
3. Click **Touchup Brushes** in the Touchup pane.
4. Select a touchup effect. For this example, we selected **Colorize**.
5. Click the brush size you want. If you plan to colorize a large portion of the image, select a larger brush; for detailed colorizing, select a smaller brush.
6. Click **Paint Color** and select the color you want to apply.

7. Colorize the image by dragging the brush over it.
8. Once you've completed the desired effect, click **Return**.

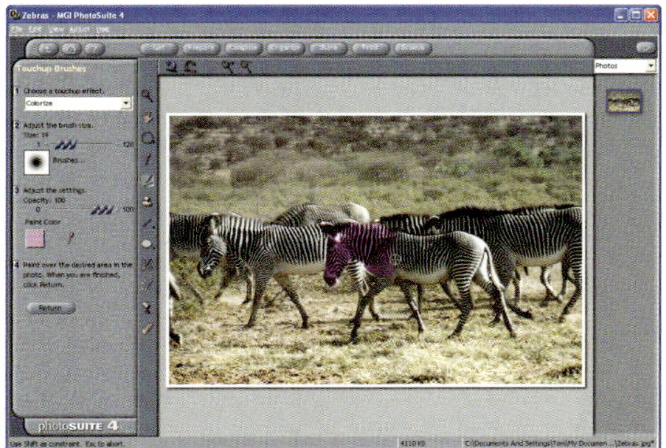

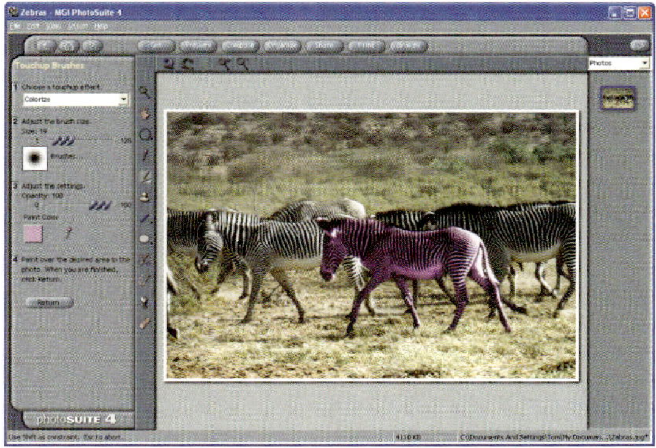

You can also use the tools alongside the work area to zoom in, select parts of the image, and apply special effects. If you aren't sure what a particular tool does, position the mouse pointer over it; its name will appear.

Applying Color Effects in Picture It!

To use Picture It! to convert a color image to black and white, do the following:

1. Make sure the image you want to convert is open in the Picture It! work area.
2. Click **Photo & color effects**.
3. Choose **Color or texture**.
4. Click **Black & white**. The Black and White screen appears, click the **Make black and white** button to apply the effect.
5. To revert to a color image, click the **Reset** button, to keep the image black and white, click **Done**.

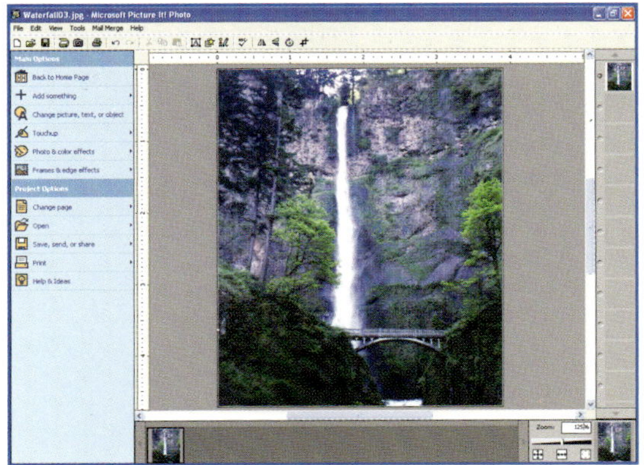

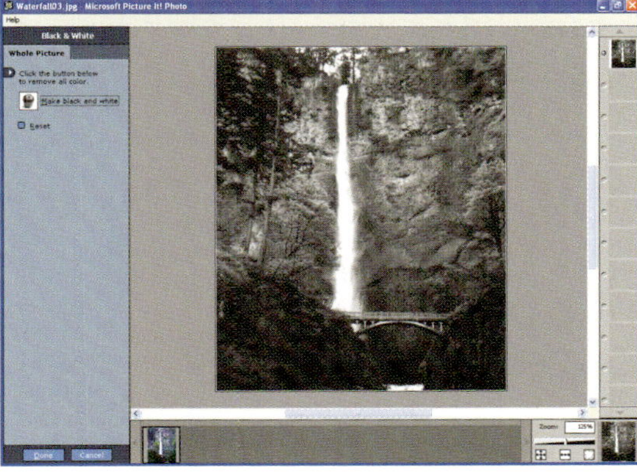

The Color or texture pane offers several options besides Black & white, including Antique, Change color, Colorize, Fill with color or text, Transparent fade even, Transparent fade gradual, and Negative.

Adding Other Special Effects

Color effects are just the beginning of an endless variety of special effects available to you when you use an image-editing program. This section gives you a brief overview of some of the other special effects you can achieve using PhotoSuite 4 and Picture It!.

The best way to learn how to use these features is to experiment! Try different features to see how the results look. If you don't like the effect, simply undo your changes (you'll learn how at the end of this chapter).

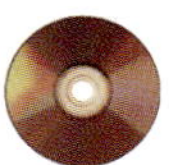

To explore the types of filters and visual effects that can be done on digital photographs, go to the CD-ROM segment *Filters and Effects*.

Adding Special Effects in PhotoSuite 4

Here are just a few of the effects you can apply using PhotoSuite 4 (for specific instructions on applying these effects, consult PhotoSuite 4 Help):

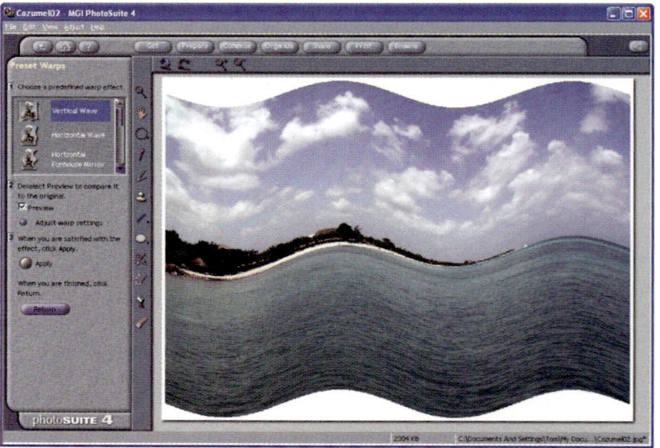

- **Special effects.** Apply any number of general effects to your image, including fog, glass, snow, and more. You can also warp your image (as shown here), using either preset or interactive warps. To apply these special effects, click **Special Effects** in the Prepare Photo Activity Panel, and then click the effect you want.
- **Draw effects.** Draw on your image using brushes and erasers as well as predefined shapes. Simply click **Paint & Draw** in the Activity Panel, and then select the tool you want to use.
- **Combine photos.** Using PhotoSuite 4's Stitching option, you can create panoramic sweeps. You will need several photos that were taken while panning the subject area. Alternatively, you can use create a photo tapestry which consists of hundreds of small thumbnail photos.

- **Touch-ups.** Remove scratches, blemishes, and wrinkles from your digital image using PhotoSuite 4's Touchup tools. Select Touchup from the Activity Panel and select the touchup option you want. The choices are: Enhance, Remove Red Eye, Remove Scratches, Remove Blemishes, Remove Wrinkles, Touchup Brushes, Touchup Filters, and Clone.

Adding Special Effects in Picture It!

Like PhotoSuite 4, Picture It! offers you several options for creating special effects, these options are accessed through the Touchup, Photo & color effects, and Frame & edge effects menus in the Main Options task pane. Here are just a few:

- **Illusions.** Adding such illusions to your images as bumps and craters, or boiling bubbles, is a snap. Simply click **Photo & color effects** under Main Options in the task pane, click **Photo & color effects**, then click Illusions, and then click the illusion you want.

- **Shadows.** To add a shadow to your image, click **Photo & color effects**, click **Shadow**, and then click the shadow you want. You can adjust the placement of the shadow by clicking the shadow line in your image and dragging it to a new position. To resize the shadow, drag the resizing handles.

- **3D Effects.** Applying a 3D effect to your image is simple. Click **Photo & color effects**, click **3-D effects**, and then click a style.

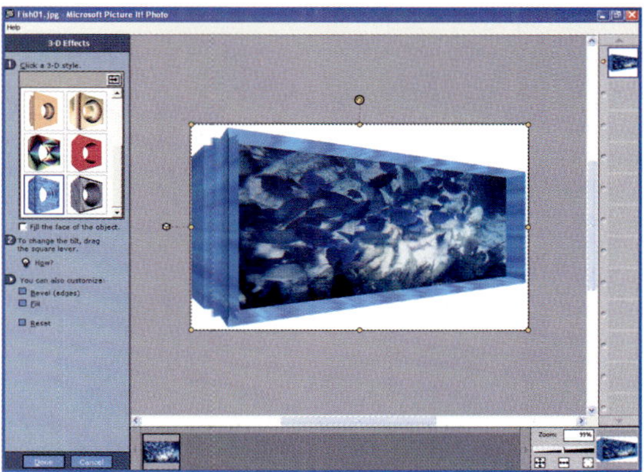

* **Frames and Edge Effects.** Add polish to an image by applying frame and edge effects. Frame effects add a digital picture frame around your image, whereas edge effects change the photo's edge; you can highlight or soften the edges or apply some other effect. To change the frames or edges of your picture, click **Frames & edge effects** and click any of the several options. A list of settings related to the option you've chosen appears; make your selections and click **Done**.

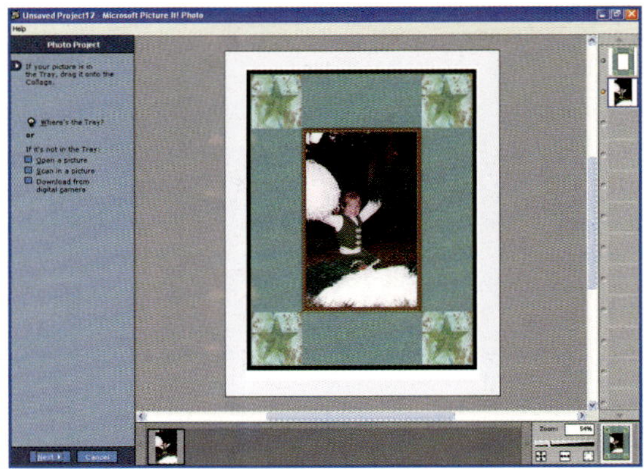

Undoing Editing Changes

Now you've done it. You've ruined a perfectly good image by adjusting its color and applying seven different special effects. What to do?

Fortunately, if you saved your edited image as a separate file as instructed earlier in this chapter, you can always scrap the edited version altogether and start over using the original (saving a new copy of it first, of course).

If you don't want to scrap all your work, however, you may be able to undo just a few of your changes. Many image-editing programs have an Undo command or button, which you can click to undo your most recent change. In some cases, you may be able to undo multiple changes, simply by clicking **Undo** multiple times.

Depending on what program you use, you may also be able to undo any changes you make before you even apply them. Many programs give you the option of accepting a change before making it official. You choose whether to accept the change, thereby implementing it for good, or to reject it and erase it from your image.

If you're ever confused about whether you've reverted to your saved image, you can always quit the program, selecting No when prompted whether to save the image.

To Keep on Learning . . .

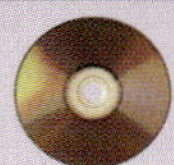

Go to the CD-ROM and select the segment:

- *Image Editor: Choosing* to learn more about image editors and their key features.
- *Filters and Effects* to explore the types of filters and visual effects that can be done on digital photographs.

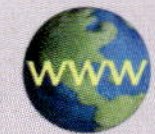

Go online to **www.LearnwithGateway.com** and log on to select:

- *MGI PhotoSuite 4*
- *Microsoft Picture It!*
- *Internet Links and Resources*
- *FAQs*

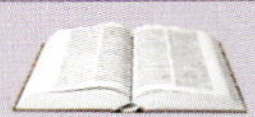

With the *Survive & Thrive* series, refer to *Use and Care for Your PC* for more information on:

- *Working with Windows XP applications*

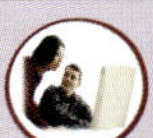

Gateway offers a hands-on training course that covers many of the topics in this chapter. Additional fees may apply. Call **888-852-4821** for enrollment information. If applicable, please have your customer ID and order number ready when you call.

5

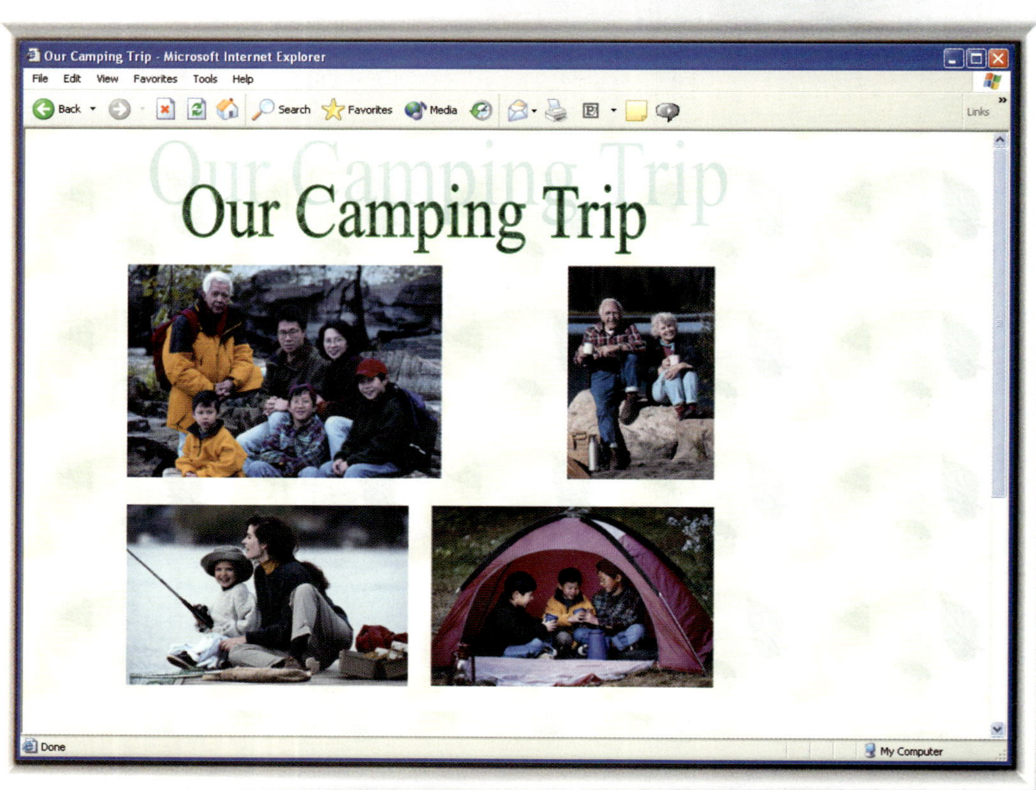
FPD1530
Our Camping Trip - Microsoft Internet Explorer
File Edit View Favorites Tools Help
Back
Search
Favorites
Media
Links
Our Camping Trip
Done
My Computer

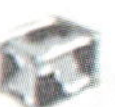

OSD
AUTO/SET

CHAPTER 6

Sharing Your Pictures Online

In the old days of film-based cameras, sharing pictures with friends and relatives around the globe involved paying for duplicate prints from your photo shop, not to mention shelling out for postage. This process wasn't terribly burdensome if you only wanted to send a single print to your sister in Nebraska. However, sharing photos of your newborn daughter with every person in your address book was another story altogether.

With digital photography, all that has changed. Thanks to the Internet, you can share your digital photos with as many people as you'd like by e-mailing them, using an online chat program, using an online photo service, or even creating your own Web site. You save time and money, and your friends can save your pictures of Junior to their computers.

Preparing Your Pictures

Before you use the Internet to share your digital photos with others, consider that the files containing digital images can be quite large, which means they can take a while to download via e-mail or to display properly on a Web site. This is especially true if the person you're sharing your digital photos with uses a dial-up modem to get online rather than a much faster cable modem or DSL (digital subscriber line) connection.

For this reason, it's a good idea to try to keep file size to a minimum when sharing digital photos online. One way to do this is to save your digital photos using a lower-quality setting. This reduces the image's resolution, thereby reducing file size. (You learned about resolution and quality settings in Chapter 2.) Besides, your recipients won't be able to notice the difference when they view the image onscreen. In fact, most images on the Web are at 72 pixels per inch (ppi), whereas print-quality images are around 300 ppi or greater.

If you've already photographed or scanned the image you want to share, try saving the image file at a lower resolution—for example, reducing a file with a resolution of 1024 x 768 to 640 x 480. The smaller image file will usually retain image quality that rivals the original when viewed onscreen, but it will take a lot less time to download to a computer. Be sure to check your image-editing application's documentation for the specifics on changing an image's resolution.

If you're not sure what resolution to use for sharing images online, try e-mailing a 640 x 480 image to yourself. Then, see how long it takes to download the message you sent. If you're satisfied with the amount of time it took to download the image, and the image's quality is acceptable, then you have your answer. Of course, you also need to take your recipients' connection speed into account. For instance, if you use a high-speed cable connection and your recipient uses a dial-up modem, the difference in download time will be drastic. Experiment with other settings until you find one that works for you.

In addition to reducing the image's resolution to enable your recipient to download it quickly, you should also consider the image file's format. If you send an image file that uses a format that your recipients' image-editing software can't read, then they won't be able to view your photograph.

Fortunately, as you learned in Chapter 4, most image-editing programs allow you to save images in a variety of file formats. Even so, it's a good idea to use one of the more common ones to share your images. The JPEG (Joint Photographic Experts Group) format is a good option, as most image-editing software can read it. As an added benefit, it reduces the image's file size while retaining its quality. In fact, most Web pages and e-mail messages that contain images use the JPEG format.

If you're sending several pictures via e-mail, consider compressing them into a folder rather than sending them separately. Chapter 8 covers compressing images in more detail.

E-mailing Your Pictures

The easiest and most common way to share pictures online is to e-mail them. Using e-mail to send your digital photos is free, easy, and instantaneous.

Before you can e-mail digital pictures, you must have an Internet connection and an e-mail account, as well as a program installed on your computer for sending and receiving e-mail. If your computer runs Windows XP, you already have an e-mail program: Outlook Express. Some image-editing software enables you to e-mail pictures from within the image-editing program itself. You must still have an e-mail program installed on your computer to do this; the image-editing program uses that program to create the e-mail message for you.

6

E-mailing with Outlook Express

To e-mail a digital photo using Outlook Express, and most other e-mail programs, you simply add the image file to an e-mail message as an *attachment*. Follow these steps:

These steps assume you use Outlook Express as your default e-mail program. If you use some other e-mail program, consult its help options or any documentation you may have to find out how to send files as attachments.

1. Start Outlook Express by clicking **start** and then **E-mail**. The Outlook Express window opens.
2. Click the **Create Mail** button on the toolbar. The New Message window opens.
3. Type the recipient's e-mail address in the **To** field.
4. Type any additional recipients' e-mail addresses in the **To** or **Cc** field. Be sure to type a comma before each additional address.

5. Type the subject of your message in the **Subject** field.
6. Click in the message area and type any text you want to include.
7. Click the **Attach** button on the toolbar. The **Insert Attachment** dialog box opens.

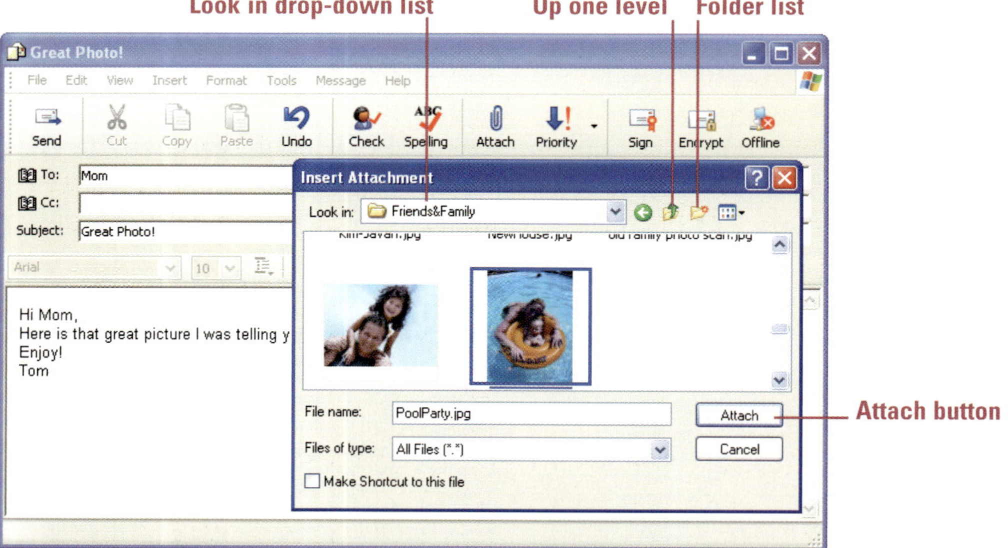

8. By using the **Look in** drop-down list and double-clicking folders in the folder list, navigate to the drive and folder that contains your image.
9. Click the folder you want and then click **Open** to display its files.
10. Click the image file you want to attach.
11. Click **Attach**. The name of the image file you've attached appears in your message's Attach text field.

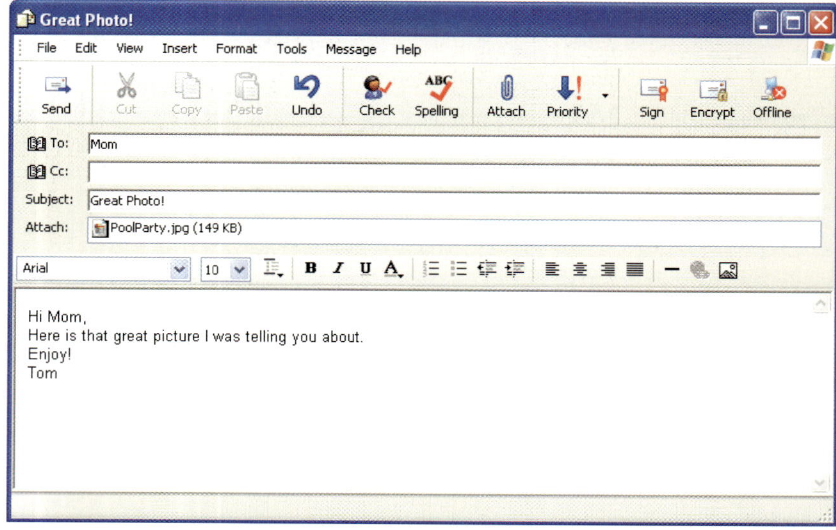

12. Click **Send**. If you're connected to the Internet, the message is sent, and a copy of it is placed in the Sent Items file.
13. If you're not connected to the Internet, the message is placed in your Outbox. When you're ready to send it, connect to the Internet and click **Send/Recv** on the main Outlook Express window's toolbar.

E-mailing from MGI PhotoSuite 4

Some image-editing programs, including PhotoSuite 4 and Picture It!, enable you to edit your image and then e-mail it directly from the program. (For more about using image-editing programs, see Chapter 5.) To e-mail a picture using PhotoSuite 4, follow these steps:

1. Open the picture you want to send in PhotoSuite 4, and make any changes you want.
2. Click **Share** on the Navigation bar. Options appear for sharing the picture.
3. Click **Send E-mail**. PhotoSuite 4 displays several send options. You can send the image as is, as a slide show, as a JPEG file, etc.

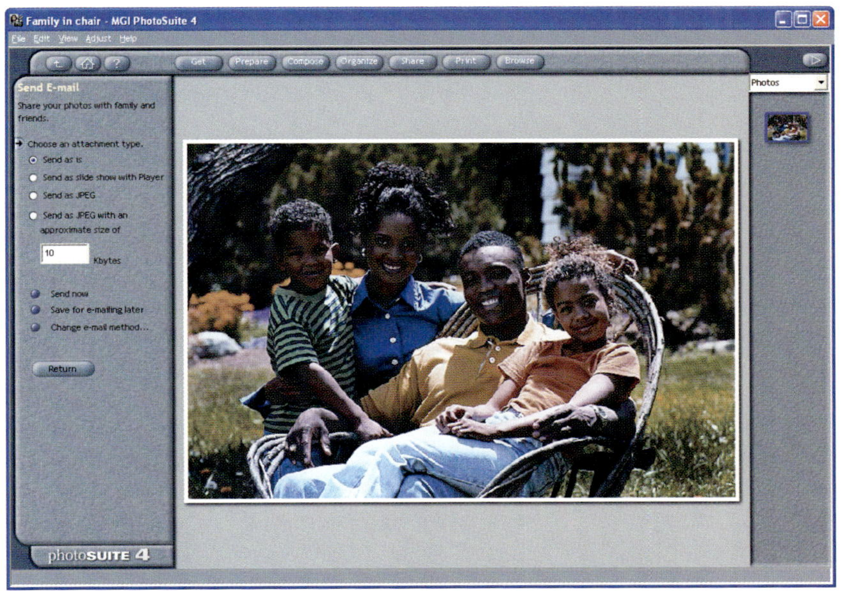

4. Click the send option you want to use.

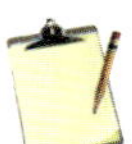

Consult PhotoSuite 4 Help for information on sending files in various formats. You can also learn how to save a file for e-mailing later.

5. Click **Send now**. A new-message window for your e-mail program opens with the image file attached.

6. Enter the recipients' e-mail addresses in the **To** field, separated by commas.

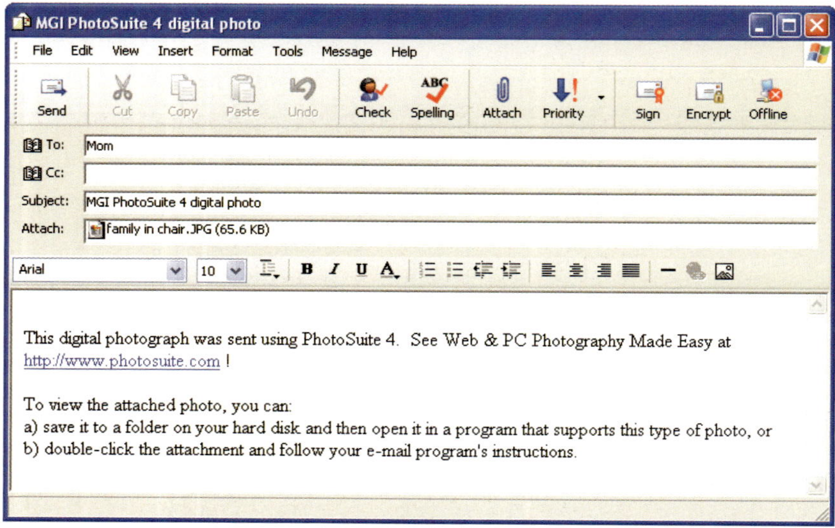

7. Click **Send**. If you're connected to the Internet, the message is sent immediately. Otherwise, the message will be sent the next time you connect and instruct your e-mail program to send and receive messages.

E-mailing from Microsoft Picture It!

You can use Picture It! to edit your image and then send it via e-mail directly from the program. (For more information about editing your images, see Chapter 5.) To e-mail a picture using Picture It!, do the following:

1. Open the picture you want to send in Picture It!, and make any changes you want.
2. Click **Save, send, or share** in the main window.
3. Choose **Send by e-mail**, and then click **Send as picture attachment**. The Send or Save for E-mail options appear in the task pane.

4. Use the **Click a picture size** drop-down menu to specify either how large the image file should be or how long it should take the recipient to download it. These settings are linked; by selecting a small file size, you decrease the download time. Likewise, if you choose a large file size, the download time increases. Click **Next**.

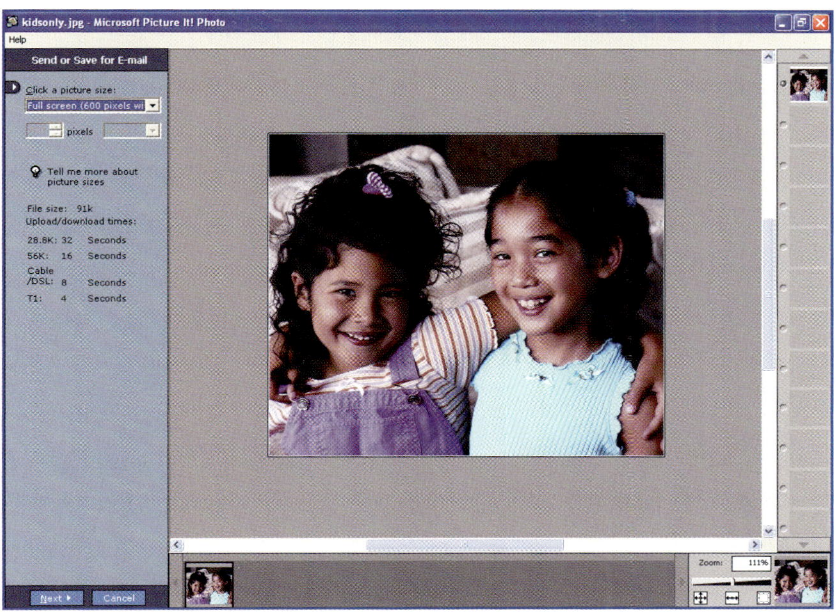

5. Click **Put the project in an e-mail message**. Picture It! creates a message in your default e-mail program (in our case, Outlook Express) with the image file attached. The message includes the subject, the attached file, and instructions for viewing the picture.

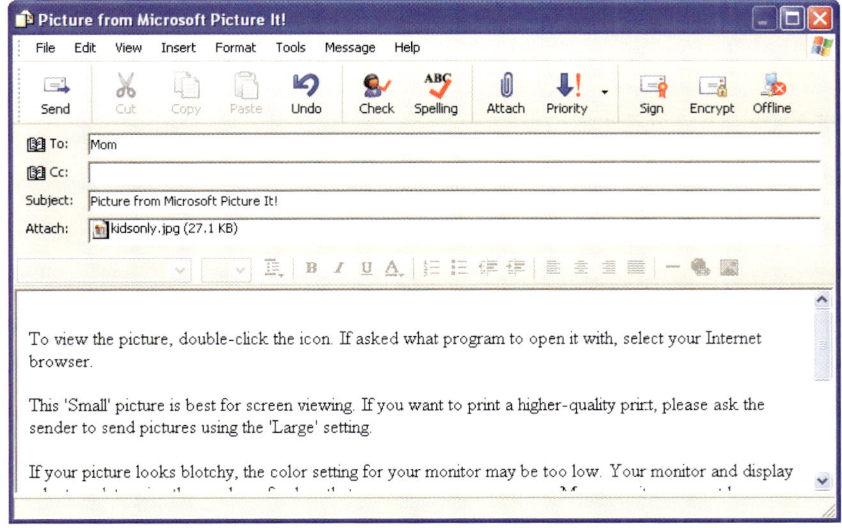

6

You can also choose to save the project to e-mail later if you are not online. Consult Picture It! Help for information on this option.

6. Type your recipients' addresses in **To** field.
7. Click **Send**. If you're connected to the Internet, the message is sent immediately. Otherwise, the message will be sent the next time you connect and instruct your e-mail program to send and receive messages.

Sharing Photos Instantly

Using e-mail is great, because it enables you to quickly and easily send messages to your friends and family. One drawback of using e-mail, however, is that you may not receive an immediate reply. In fact, depending on how often your recipients check their e-mail, it could be many hours or even days before they respond.

This is where instant messaging programs are useful. *Instant messaging* is a way of communicating with friends who are online at the same time you are. Using this type of program, you can have a real-time, private conversation, called a *chat,* with someone and send them files through this program. Currently, there are several instant messaging programs available.

If you want to chat and share files with friends online, they must use the same instant messaging system that you use.

Using Windows Messenger

Windows XP comes with a built-in instant messaging program. This program enables you to chat with other MSN® subscribers, as well as anyone with Windows Messenger installed on their desktop, any time you and they are both online.

Once you have your MSN account set up, you are ready to start sharing your photos using Windows Messenger. Here's how:

1. Click **start**, point to **All Programs**, and then click **Windows Messenger**. The Windows Messenger screen appears.
2. Click **Send a File or Photo**.
3. Select a contact from the Send a File dialog box, then click **OK**.

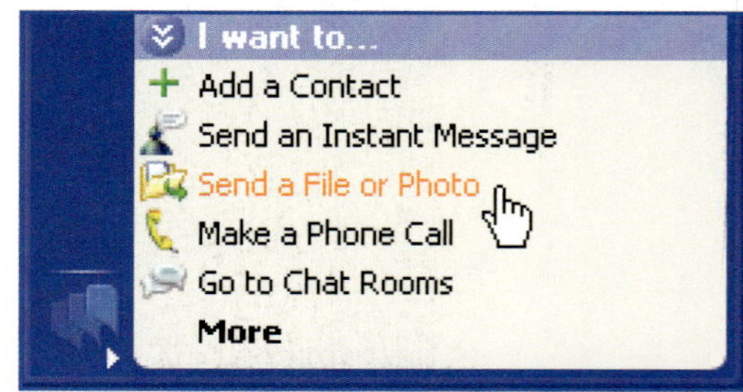

4. The Send a File to <Contact Name> screen appears. Locate the file on your PC that you want to send, and then click **Open**.

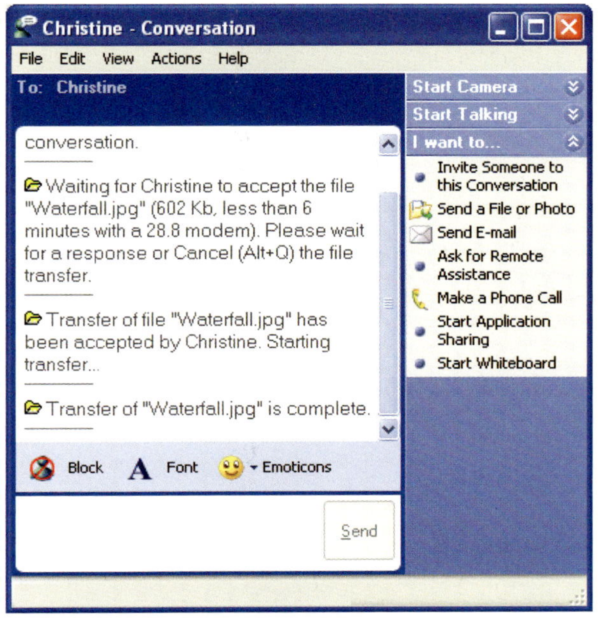

5. The Windows Messenger Conversation screen appears, notifying you that the program is waiting for the contact to accept the file. On the other end of the transmission, your online friend must click **Select** for the file to be sent. Once they do this, the file is sent and a delivery confirmation appears on the Conversation screen.

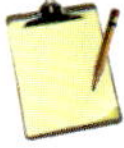

Instant messaging programs identify users by their screen names, similar to the way e-mail addresses are used. To find your friends, either ask them for their screen name or use the search feature in your program.

Using Online Photo Services

The Internet plays host to millions and millions of Web sites. Among these are sites designed for digital photographers like you. Using these sites, you can post pictures, get how-to information and ideas for creative photo projects, research reviews and specifications for specific cameras, scanners, accessories, and more. This section discusses the ways you can use online services to share your digital photos.

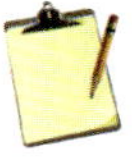

Many online photo services also enable you to order prints of your digital images. In fact, many image-editing programs, as well as Windows XP, provide handy links for accessing online printing services and ordering prints. Chapter 7 covers this topic in detail.

Each online photo service operates slightly differently, but you can get an idea of what these sites offer by visiting the Gateway Photo Center site. Here's how:

1. Start your Web browser, and type **http://gateway.shutterfly.com** in the Address bar.

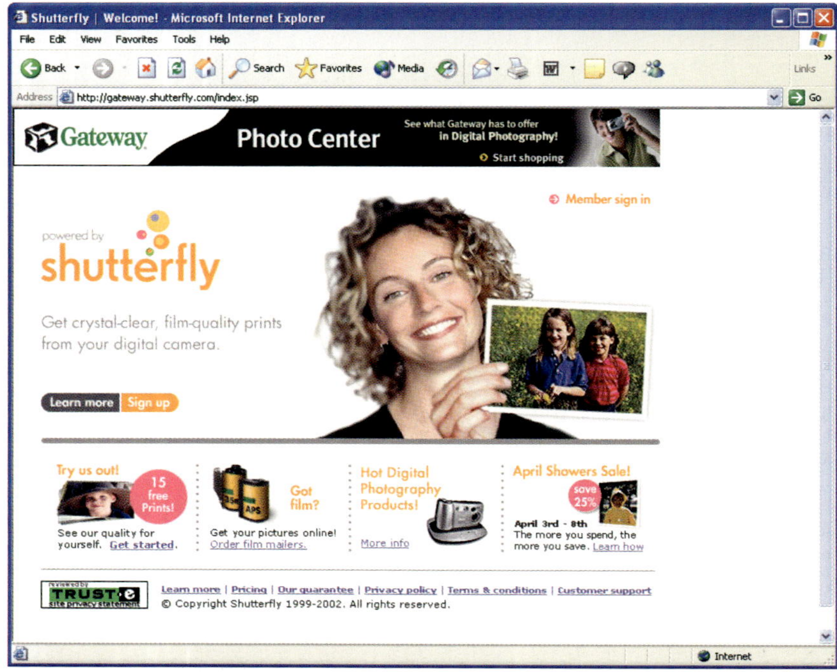

2. If this is your first time visiting the Gateway Photo Center, you need to set up an account. Click **Sign up**, and follow the instructions. If you already have an account, click **Member sign in**, and type your e-mail address and password.

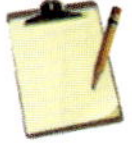

Most online photo services require you to set up an account to use their site, which is usually free. This typically involves providing your e-mail address, a password, and perhaps a few other details. You may also need to run an installation program to use some of the site's features. Check the instructions for setting up accounts at the site you plan to use.

3. Click **My Photo Center**. From here you can add pictures, view existing pictures, share pictures online, order prints, create cards, and much more.

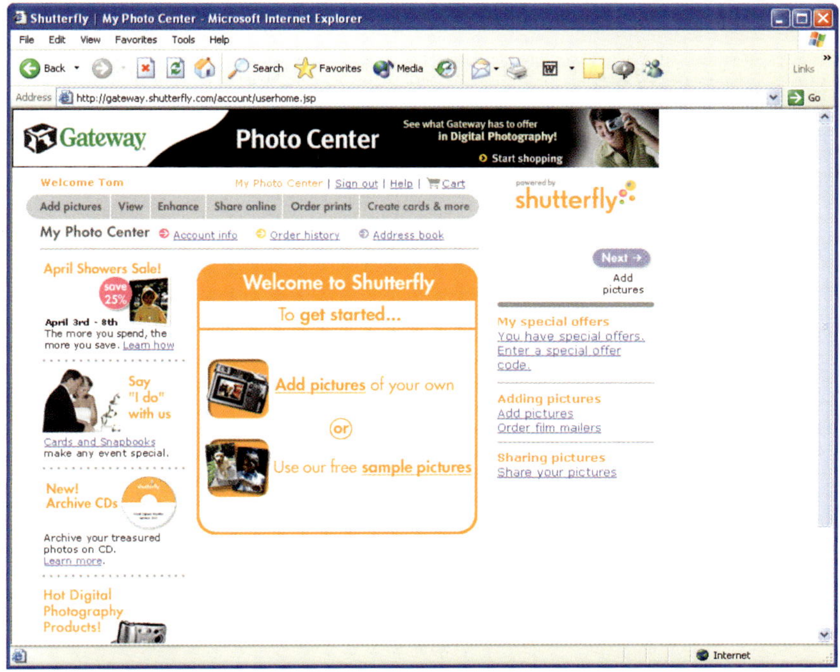

See the next section, "Sharing Pictures Online," for details on adding and sharing pictures.

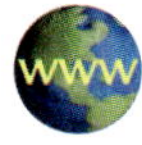

To learn more about the Gateway Photo Center, go to the Web segment *Shutterfly Site: Enrolling* in either the PhotoSuite 4 or Picture It! course.

6

Sharing Pictures Online

If you want to share only one or two photos with your friends or relatives, e-mailing the photos is usually the best way to go. If you want to share an entire album full of photos, however, e-mailing them can be time-consuming—especially for your recipients. After all, if downloading a single image file is time-consuming, downloading a dozen or more could take hours.

That's where online photo services come in. By posting your images on an online photo service's Web site, you can share as many photos as you'd like with whomever you'd like. Instead of sending your images to others, you invite your friends and relatives to view your page on the photo service's site. As an added benefit, many online photo services enable visitors to order prints of the photos they've been invited to view.

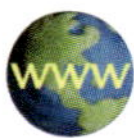

To gain practice printing from the Gateway Photo Center, go to the Web segment *Print Distribution* in either the PhotoSuite 4 or Picture It! course.

There are a few ways to post your photos on an online photo service's site. One is to go directly through the site itself; another is to use your image-editing program to post to the site. In the sections that follow, you'll learn how to post directly to the Gateway Photo Center, how to post to GatherRound.com from PhotoSuite 4, and how to post to MSN Photo using Picture It!.

If you purchased your MGI PhotoSuite 4 software with a Gateway photo package, you will have the Gateway Photo Center included in the software, instead of GatherRound.com.

Posting Pictures Directly to the Gateway Photo Center

To share your photos using the Gateway Photo Center, follow these steps:

1. Start your Web browser, and type **http://gateway.shutterfly.com** in the Address bar. (For help opening this page, see the section "Online Information Pointers" later in this chapter.)
2. Click **Member sign in**, and type your e-mail address and password.

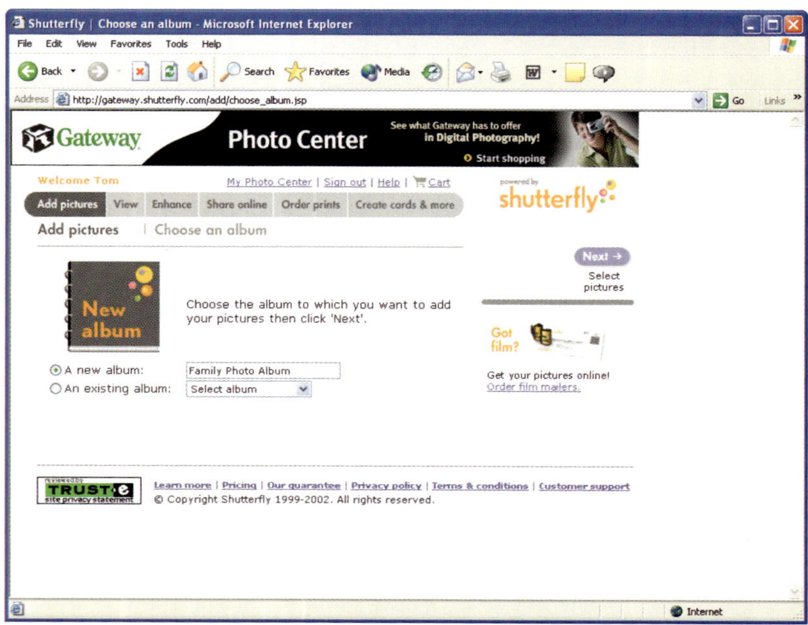

3. The My Photo Center window appears, click **Add pictures**.
4. Type an album name and click **Next**. The Gateway Photo Center will store your pictures in the album.

5. The Add pictures page is displayed, click **Choose Pictures**. The Add Pictures file dialog box appears.
6. Select the images you want to share (you can hold down the **CTRL** key to select multiple images in the same directory). Follow steps 5 and 6 for each file(s) you want to upload.

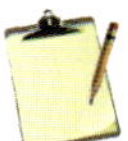

Depending on your Web browser, you may not be able tc choose multiple pictures at the same time.

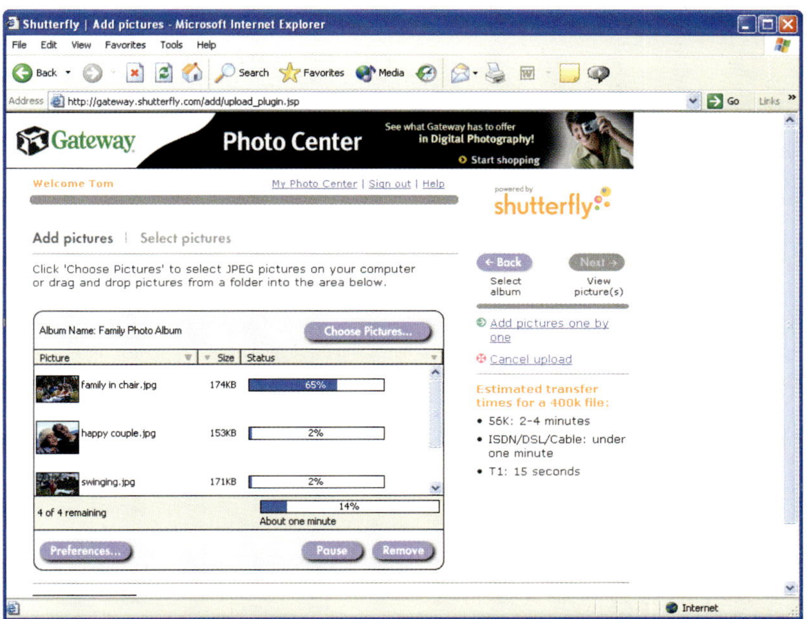

7. Click **Open**. The pictures are uploaded to the Gateway Photo Center. You see a progress window as the photos are uploaded. This may take awhile.

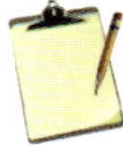

After the photos are uploaded, you can click **View pictures** to view your pictures online. You have lots of options once the pictures are uploaded. You can view them as a slideshow, enlarge them, add titles, delete them, order online prints, and more. Every service offers various features; check out what's available at your site of choice.

8. Click **Next**. The Pictures added successfully screen appears.

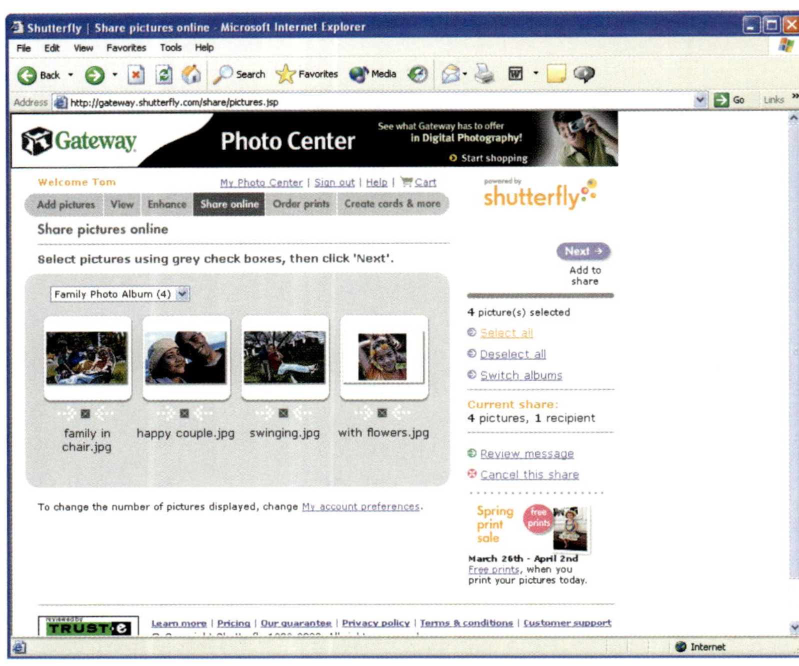

9. To share the album online, click **Share Online**.
10. Select the pictures you want to share by clicking in the box beneath each image and click **Next**.
11. Enter the e-mail addresses, a subject, and message for those you want to share pictures with. You can also specify whether a password is required.

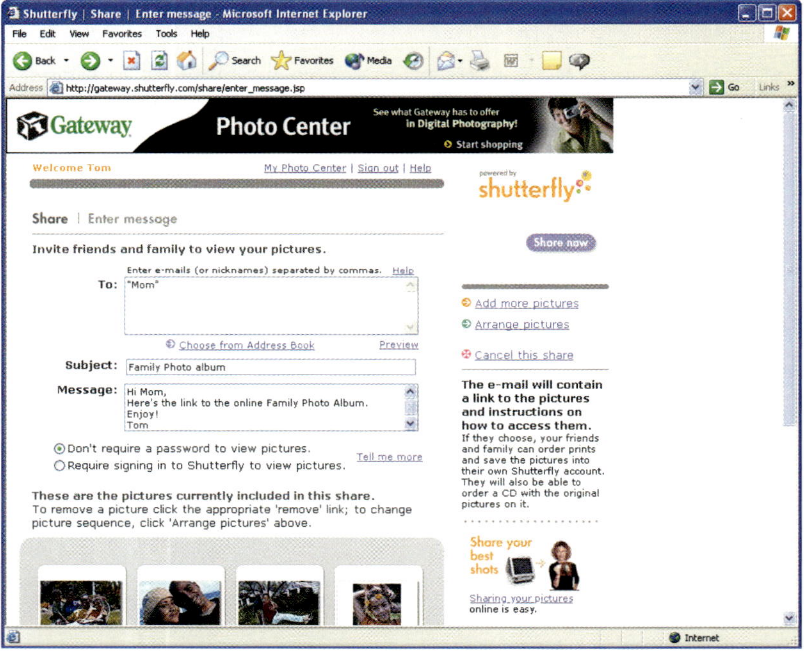

12. Click **Share now**. An e-mail message with a link to your online pictures is sent to all the recipients you entered. The recipients can click this link to view your pictures online.

The Gateway Photo Center isn't the only online photo site available. You can find others, each offering different services. Try out a few, and pick the one that offers the services that work best for you.

Posting Pictures at GatherRound.com from MGI PhotoSuite 4

As mentioned previously, you may be able to use your image-editing program to post your images to an online photo service's Web site. Using PhotoSuite 4, for example, you can post images to GatherRound.com. Here's how:

1. Open the picture (or pictures) you want to share in PhotoSuite 4, and make any changes you want.
2. Click **Share**.
3. The Save & Share Activity panel opens, displaying options for sharing the pictures. Click **Share Your Pictures At GatherRound.com**.

If this is your first time visiting GatherRound.com, you'll be prompted to set up an account. To do this, enter your e-mail address and password.

4. Follow the specific instructions in the Activity panel for sharing pictures online.

Posting Pictures on MSN Photos Using Picture It!

As mentioned previously, you may be able to use your image-editing program to post your images to an online photo service's Web site. For example, using Picture It!, you can post images to MSN Photos.

To post pictures on the MSN Photos site using Picture It!, follow these steps:

1. Open the pictures you want to share in Picture It!, and make any changes you want.
2. Click **Save, send, or share** in the main window, then click **Save to MSN Photos**.

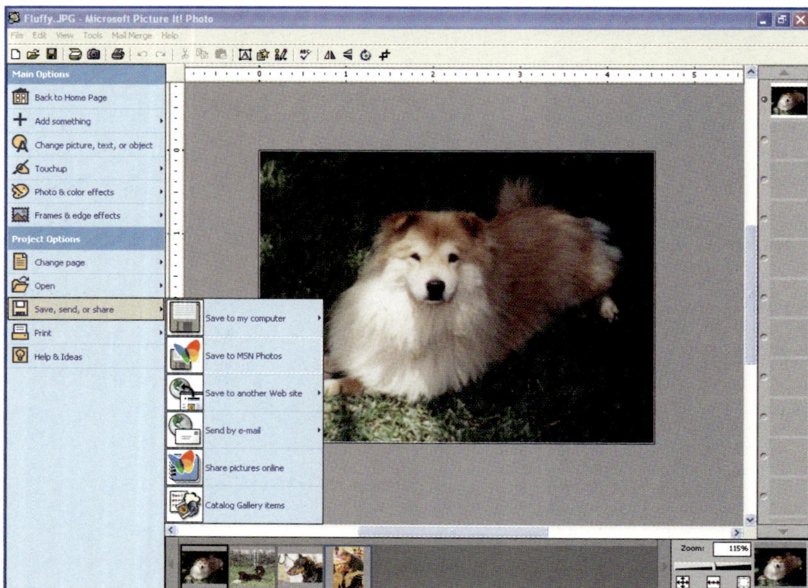

3. Specify whether you want to save only the current picture to MSN Photos or all the pictures in the Tray by clicking the proper radio button, and click **Next**.

To post pictures on MSN Photos, you must have a Microsoft .NET Passport account. If you don't have one, simply follow the steps in the .NET Passport Wizard to create one, clicking **Next** to move from step to step and then **Finish** to close the deal.

4. Click the **Click Here to Get Started** button.
5. Click **Continue**.
6. Click the folder you want to place your photos in, or, to create a new one, click **Create a new folder**. (If you create a new folder, type a name for it and click **Create**.) MSN uploads your photos (this may take some time).
7. Click **View your photos**.
8. To share photos in a folder, click to open the folder, select the photos to be shared, and then click **Share photos in this folder**.

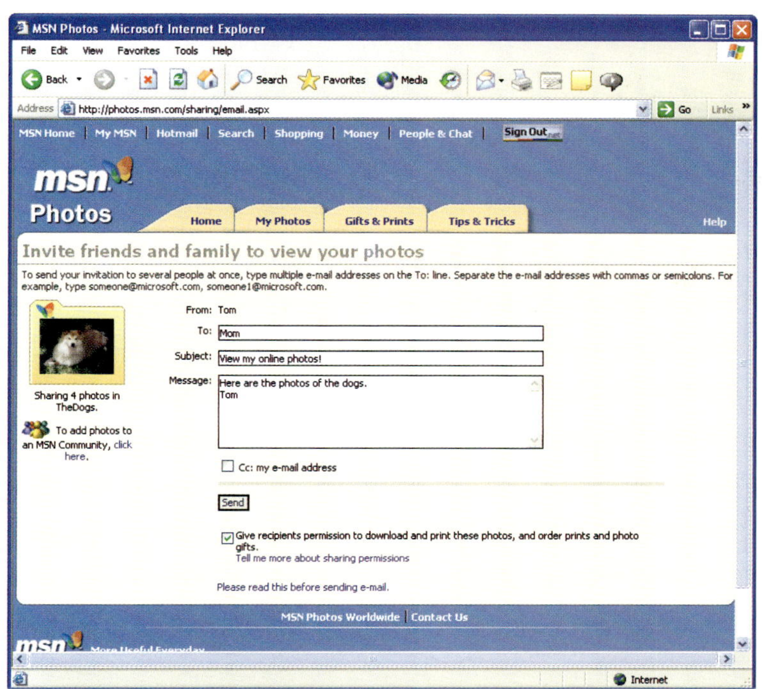

9. Enter the e-mail addresses, a subject or use default subject, and a message for those you want to share your pictures with.

10. Click **Send**. MSN Photos sends an e-mail message to all the recipients you've entered, with a link to your online pictures. The recipients can click this link to view your pictures online.

By default, your recipients can download and print any shared photos as well as order prints and photo gifts. If you don't want to grant your recipients permission to do this, clear the permissions check box.

Creating an Online Photo Gallery

If you've photographed a special occasion, such as a baby shower or a graduation ceremony, you might like to organize your images into an album to share online. Several image-editing programs, including PhotoSuite 4 and Picture It!, enable you to group a set of photos into a project or album and customize how they look, choosing from several designs. You'll learn how to create albums in Chapter 8.

After you've created a photo album, you can easily upload it to an online photo service site to share with your friends and relatives. To do so, simply follow your online photo service's steps for uploading albums.

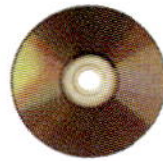

To learn more about online photo services and what they offer, go to the CD-ROM segment *Online Photo Services*.

Creating Your Own Web Site

Using an online photo service site is a great way to share your photos with others. Due to limitations, there's not much room for customization when it comes to the way your photos are displayed. If you want to display photos of your best friend's wedding, for example, you might want to add a special background to the page, noting the date of the ceremony and the names of the bride and groom. Most online photo service sites, however, don't allow for this type of customization.

Fortunately, with a little time and effort—not to mention some special software on your PC—you can create your own Web pages. Then, you can display your photos any way you like, using any color background, adding text, and even adding links to other sites if you so choose.

Of course, Web publishing is a book topic of its own—there are just too many options and programs to cover here. We can, however, give you an idea of what tools you'll need to publish to the Web and how best to use digital images on your Web pages.

- To create your own Web site, you need a program for creating Web pages. Popular programs include Microsoft FrontPage®, Macromedia Dreamweaver, and Adobe GoLive. These programs offer a wide range of tools for both beginners and experienced Web-page designers.

- To publish a Web page, you must have a Web service provider or Web host, which act as remote storage for your online files. Many of these services are free, but there may be limits on how large your site can be.

- Most Web pages contain a combination of text, links, and images. A *link* (also called a *hyperlink*) is a page element that a site visitor can click to quickly access another page on your site, or an entirely new site. Programs for creating Web pages include easy ways to insert links.

- Keep the images you include on your page small so they won't take forever to open on visitors' screens. Also, to ensure that all visitors to your Web site will be able to view your images, use an image file format that their browsers will be able to read, such as JPEG.

- The process for inserting images into Web pages depends on the program you use to create them. Typically, however, you click **Insert** and then **Picture**, or something similar. Once you've added the image to your page, you can resize it and move it as needed.

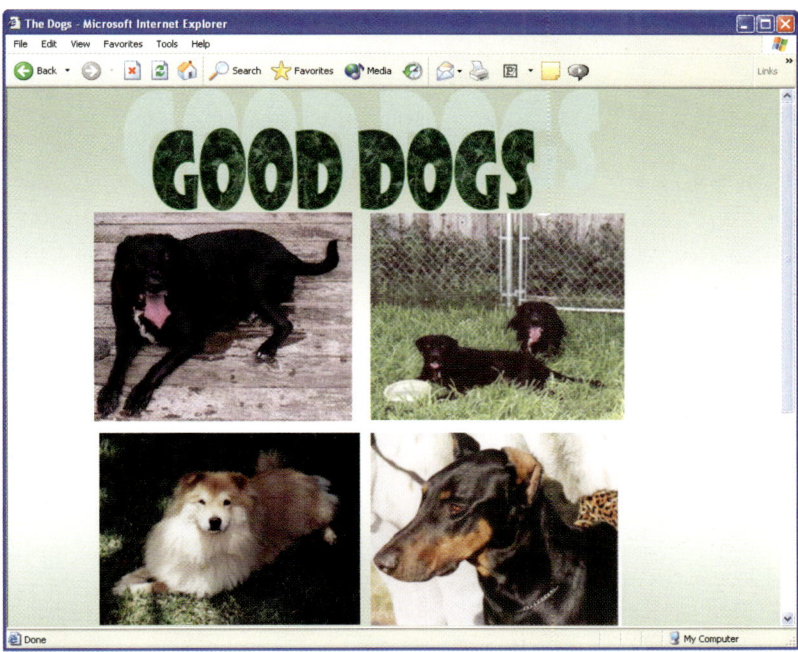

6

To Keep on Learning . . .

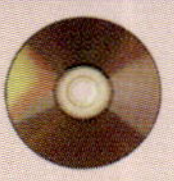

Go to the CD-ROM and select the segment:

- *Online Photo Services* to learn more about online photo services and what they offer.

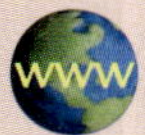

Go online to **www.LearnwithGateway.com** and log on to select:

- *Shutterfly Site: Enrolling*
- *Print Distribution*
- *Internet Links and Resources*
- *FAQs*

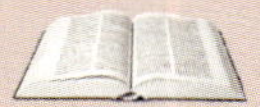

With the *Survive & Thrive* series, refer to *Communicate and Connect to the Internet* for more information on:

- Setting up an Internet connection
- Communicating with friends and family online
- Using e-mail programs
- Setting up your .NET account

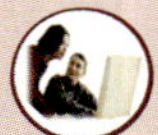

Gateway offers a hands-on training course that covers many of the topics in this chapter. Additional fees may apply. Call **888-852-4821** for enrollment information. If applicable, please have your customer ID and order number ready when you call.

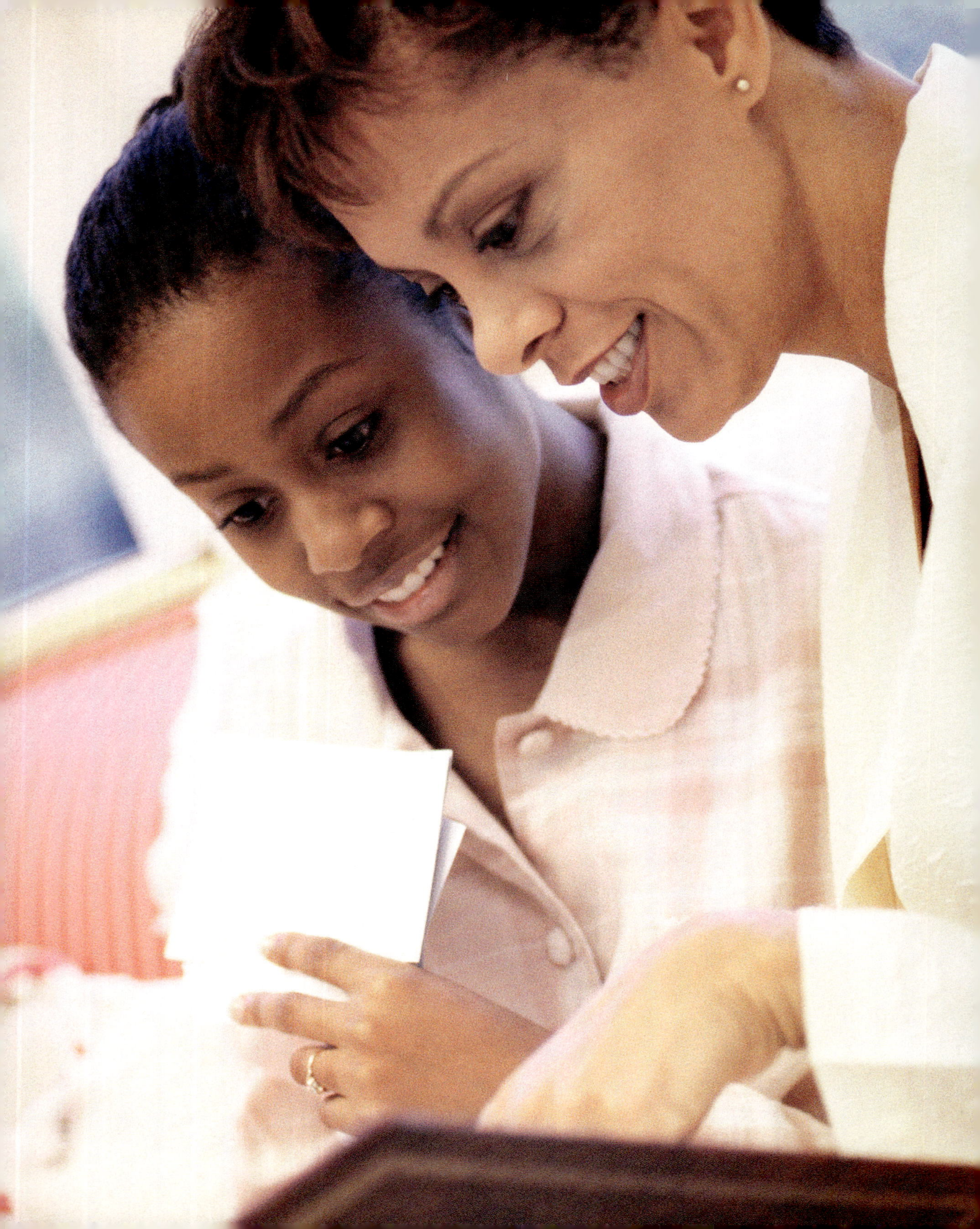

CHAPTER 7

Printing Images

You've used a digital camera or scanner to obtain digital images, a photo-editing program to touch them up, and learned how to share your digital images online. Now you're ready to share your pictures with your friends and family. This chapter covers the more traditional way of sharing photographs: making prints.

When it comes to printing digital images, you have many options depending on the equipment you have and the quality you want. You can print your pictures either with a regular printer or a special photo printer. Alternatively, you can take your digital picture files to a local photo store or send them to an online printing service and have regular prints made. Read on to learn the specifics of all these options.

Using Your Printer

One of the fastest and easiest ways to print a digital image is to use your printer, whether it's a regular document printer or a special photo printer. This section discusses both types of printers, outlines some considerations for getting the best-quality printout, and walks you through the process of printing your images.

Using a Standard Printer

If price and convenience are your primary considerations, you can print photographs using your regular document printer. Although you probably won't get professional-quality prints using this type of printer, you can still find many uses for the printouts you create with it, such as reports, family newsletters, informal invitations, and more.

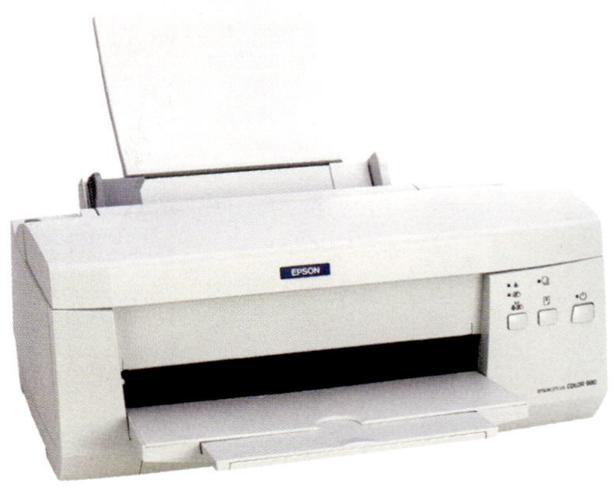

If you're using your regular printer to print your images, keep the following in mind:

- To print color pictures, you must have a color printer. If your printer is black and white, your color pictures will print in shades of gray.
- The quality of a printer's printout (the resolution) is measured in dots per inch (dpi). The more dots per inch, the finer the image. If you have a low-resolution printer (in the 300 dpi range), your printed pictures may look grainy—that is, the dots that make up the image may be visible.
- You can crop, rotate, fix red-eye, and adjust your images before printing.
- For better-quality photo prints, try printing on special photo paper and using the correct ink (see "Printing with the Right Ink on the Right Paper," later in this section for details).

Using a Special Photo Printer

If you want to create print-shop quality printouts of your images in the comfort of your own home or business, consider investing in a special photo printer. Photo printers offer several benefits, including the following:

- **Convenience.** Instead of taking your image files to a regular photo lab or ordering prints online, you can print high-quality photographs right from your desktop with the click of a button.
- **Quality.** With photo-quality paper, you can use a photo printer to create photo-shop quality prints.
- **No computer needed.** Most photo printers can print directly from a digital camera or memory card, which means you don't need your PC to make prints.
- **Portability.** The portability of photo printers comes in handy anytime you attend a family reunion or other event; you can take pictures with your digital camera and print your images on the spot to share with the rest of the family.
- **Small footprint.** *Footprint* refers to the space that a component takes up on a desk or other work area. Most photo printers leave a small footprint, meaning they are fairly small.

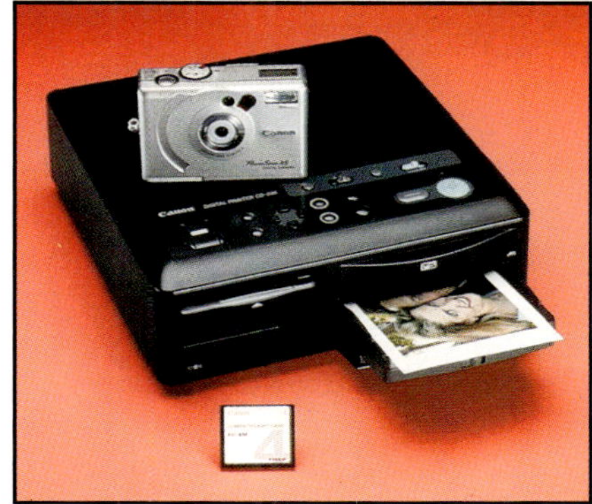

Photo printers are available at your local computer or electronics store and online. They come in a wide range of models, from the simple to the sophisticated. Of course, you can expect to pay more for higher-quality printers.

If you're thinking about buying a photo printer, you'll need to decide what type of printer best suits your needs. As you research and compare the many photo printers on the market, ask these questions:

- **Does the printer have to be attached to your computer to print?** Some printers must be attached to the computer in order to print, whereas others print directly from your digital camera or the digital camera memory card. If you want to use your printer while on the go, you'll be well served by a printer that can print directly from your camera or memory card.

- **How is the printer attached?** If the printer attaches to your computer, does it attach via a standard LPT (line printer) or parallel port, via a serial port, or via a USB (Universal Serial Bus) port?

- **What type of media can the printer read?** If your camera has removable media, make sure that the photo printer can read the type of media it uses. For example, if your camera uses SmartMedia cards, make sure the printer is compatible with them.

- **What size prints can you print?** Most low-end photo printers can print only 4 x 6 prints, the size offered by most photo labs. If you want larger images, check available print sizes for that printer.

- **How fast is the printer?** Some printers measure print speed as the time it takes to print a picture, whereas others measure it in pages per minute (ppm). You can find printers in the range of 12-to-15 ppm for black and white and 10-to-12 ppm in color.

- **What is the quality of the printout?** Quality, also called *resolution,* is measured in dots per inch (dpi); 2400 x 1200 dpi is common.

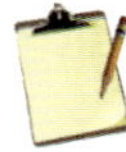

The best way to compare printout quality is to visit a computer-supply store and view the actual printouts from various printers. Otherwise, all the detailed specifications in the world won't help you choose.

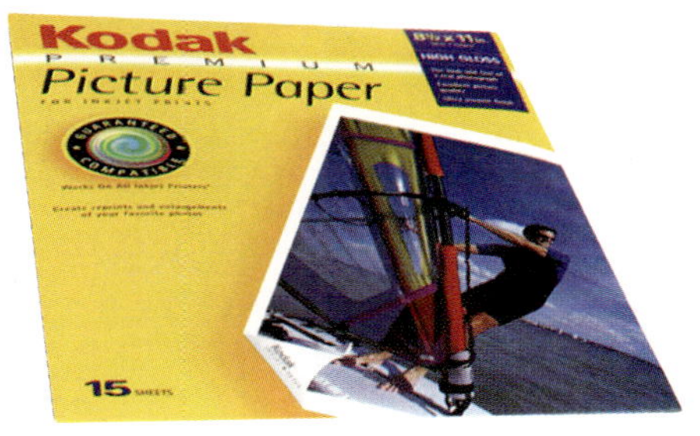

- **What supplies do you need, and how much do they cost?** The most costly component of photo printing is the ink your printer uses, not to mention the special photo paper you need for high-quality prints. Different printers use different types of ink and paper; check the prices of these items before choosing a printer.

- **What software is included with the printer?** Although, some printers come bundled with graphics software, most include the required drivers.

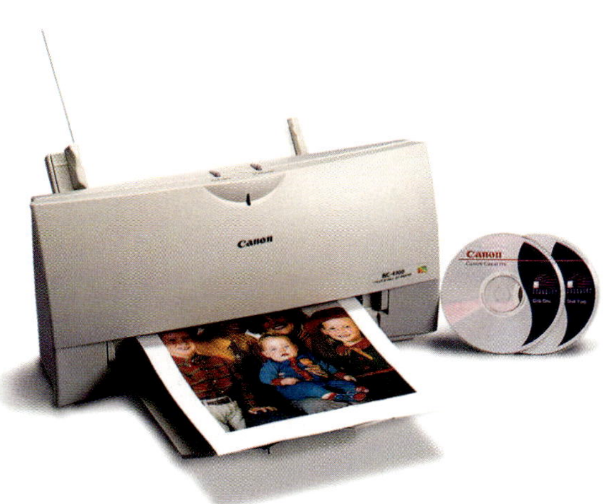

- **What are the system requirements for the printer?** Just as your PC must meet minimum system requirements in order to work with your digital camera or scanner, so too must it meet system requirements in order to work with a photo printer. Before buying a particular printer, be sure your system makes the grade.

- **What other equipment do you need?** If a printer cable is not included with the photo printer, you will need to purchase one separately.

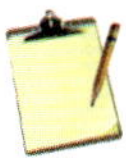

If you don't have a regular document printer, you might consider purchasing a printer that can handle both documents and photos.

Getting the Best Prints

Whether you use a document printer or a photo printer, you can make sure you get the best possible prints by correctly sizing the image, choosing the best paper and ink, and using the right printer settings.

Sizing the Image

Because most computer monitors display graphics at 72 dpi, most image-editing programs display image files at the same resolution—regardless of what resolution setting you used when you took the picture. If you chose a high-resolution setting, the digital image will simply appear larger on your PC's desktop (sometimes the size of a regular piece of paper); low-resolution images, on the other hand, will appear smaller. This is because high-resolution images contain more pixels than low-resolution images.

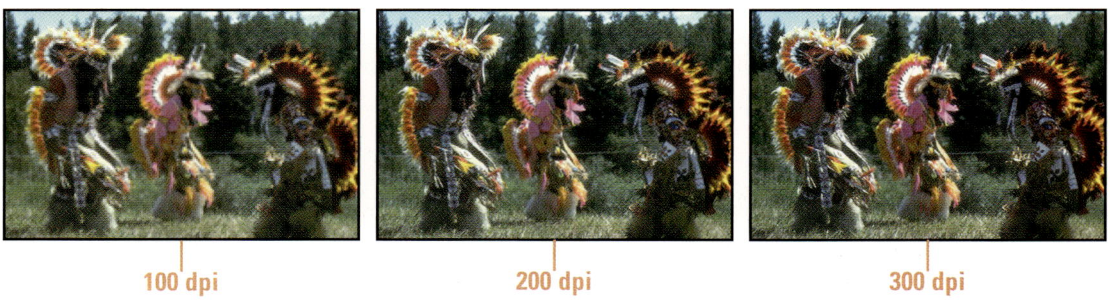

However, chances are that you will usually want your printed images to be smaller than they appear on your monitor at 72 dpi. For one thing, even high-resolution images appear grainy if they're too large. For another, it's hard to fit an 8 x 10 photo of your dog into your wallet. Fortunately, most photo programs let you specify how large you want your printed photo to be in inches; options typically include 3.5 x 5, 4 x 6, 5 x 7, etc. This doesn't change the number of pixels your photo contains but rather the amount of space those pixels occupy, in inches.

If your digital image is shaped oddly—that is, it won't quite fit into one of the available size options—your photo program may use a resizing algorithm to add or subtract pixels as needed.

Choosing the Best Paper and Ink

Regular paper is coarse and absorbs ink, often smearing the dots that make up a digital picture on an inkjet printer. Photo paper, on the other hand, is coated, and this coating prevents ink from soaking into the paper. The result is crisp dots and, thus, a clearer picture. For even better results, you can use special ink that dries quickly to prevent smearing.

To determine just what type of ink and paper you should use, check the documentation for your particular printer. Practically every printer manufacturer sells paper and ink designed to work with their various printers. It's usually best to stick with your printer manufacturer's line of products, but some third-party paper and ink products may provide adequate quality.

Using the Right Printer Settings

In order to obtain the best-possible photo prints using your regular printer or a photo printer, you'll probably need to adjust various print settings, such as paper type, print quality, and print mode. Available settings vary from printer to printer, but you can check your printer's settings by following these steps:

Changing a printer's settings affects all jobs you perform using that printer. Changing your regular printer's settings to handle dig tal photos may adversely affect the way in which regular documents are printed. To avoid this problem, you can usually change printer settings as you print, whether you do so using Windows XP or your photo-editing program. You'll learn how in the next section.

1. Click **start**, and then click **Control Panel**.
2. Click **Printers and Other Hardware**.
3. Click **View installed printers or fax printers**. A list of all installed printers appears.
4. Right-click the printer you're using. A shortcut menu appears; click **Printer Preferences**.

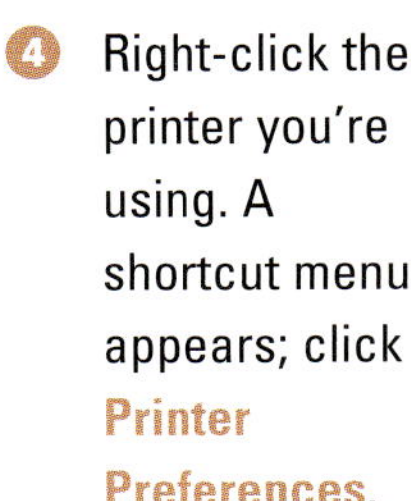

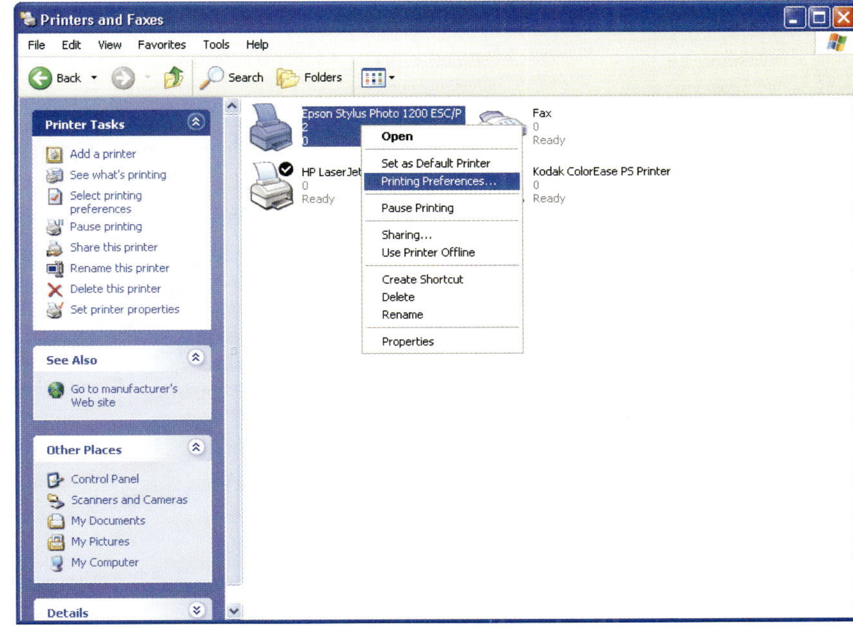

7

5. The Printing Preferences dialog box for the printer you selected opens. After clicking the **Paper/Quality** tab, you can select the paper source and the type of paper being used via the drop-down lists, and control the level of quality you want the print job to be (Best, Normal, Draft, or Custom) and whether the image should be printed in color or black and white via the radio buttons. Make changes as needed, and click **OK**.

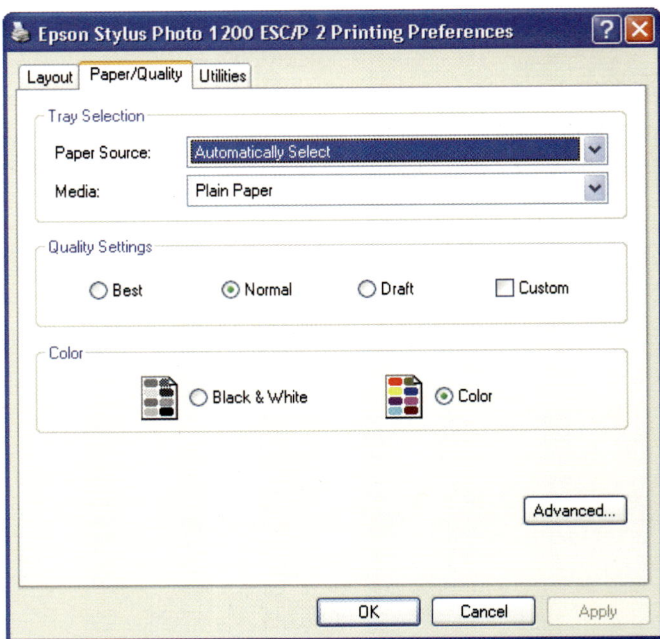

Your Printing Preferences dialog box may look different from the one shown here. For help with the settings available to you, consult your printer's manual or click the Help button (the one with a question mark on it) in the upper-right corner of the Printing Preferences dialog box.

Printing Pictures

You've decided what type of printer you want to use, you've properly sized your image, you've bought the correct paper and ink, and you've configured your printer to best handle printing digital images. At last it's time to print your images! You can do so using Windows XP's Photo Printing Wizard or using your photo-editing program's print feature. The following sections cover printing from Windows XP, MGI PhotoSuite 4, and Microsoft Picture It!.

Printing Pictures from Windows XP

To print pictures using Windows XP, do the following:

1. Select **start**, and then **My Computer**.
2. Open the folder or subfolder that contains the image files you want to print.

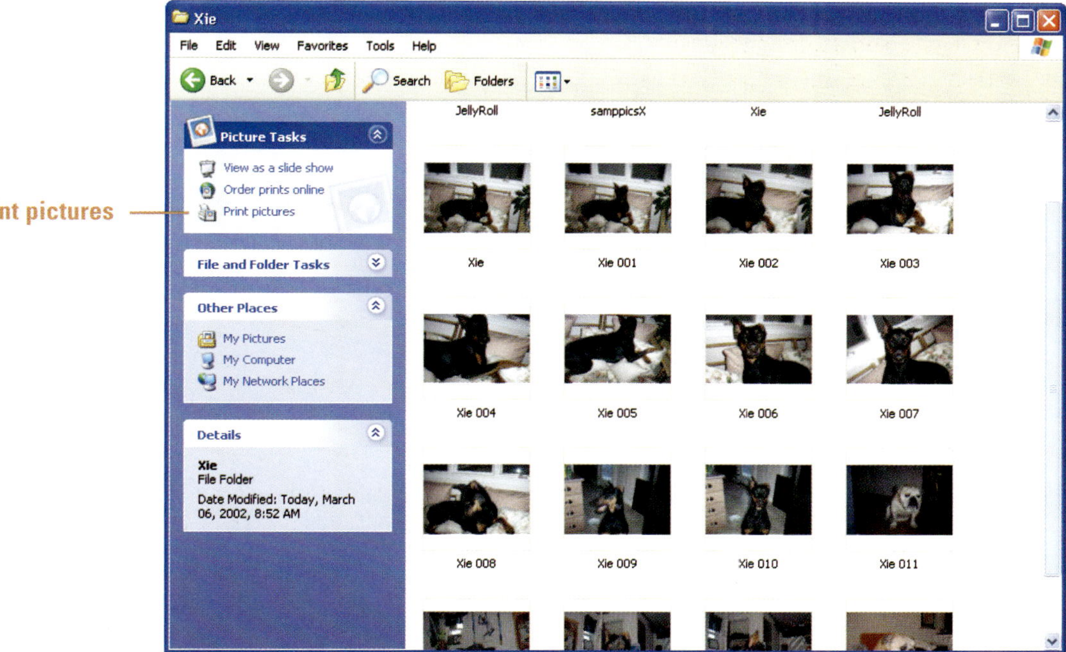

Windows XP provides a My Pictures folder within the My Documents folder, where you can store all your image files. Using this folder consistently ensures quick and easy file retrieval. For more information about organizing photos, see Chapter 8.

More About . . .Windows XP Features

With Windows XP, you can set up accounts for multiple users, and each user can customize many of the features of Windows, such as the desktop. Also each person with a Windows XP account has a My Documents folder with a My Pictures folder.

If you are working on a computer with more than one user account, you see the pictures in your account's My Pictures folder. To access pictures in another user's My Pictures folder, you'd need to log out and then log in as that user.

3. Click **Print pictures** in the Picture Tasks pane.
4. The Photo Printing Wizard starts, displaying its Welcome screen. Click **Next**.

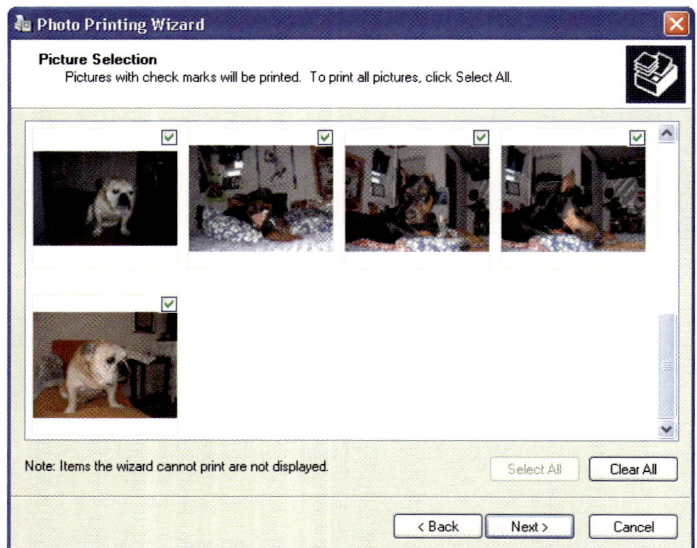

5. The Wizard displays a screen containing thumbnail images of all the digital pictures in the folder. To print all of them, click the **Select All** button. If you want to print only some of them, click the check boxes above the ones you want to print. When you've selected all the pictures you want to print, click **Next**.

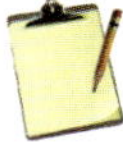

If you accidentally select an image that you don't want to print, simply click its check box to deselect it. To deselect all images at once, click the **Clear All** button.

6. Windows prompts you to select the printer you want to use. If the correct printer isn't displayed by default, click the down-arrow next to the default printer and select the correct one from the list. (If the printer you want to use doesn't appear in the list, it hasn't been installed yet on your PC. To install it, click the **Install Printer** button and follow the instructions Windows XP issues.)

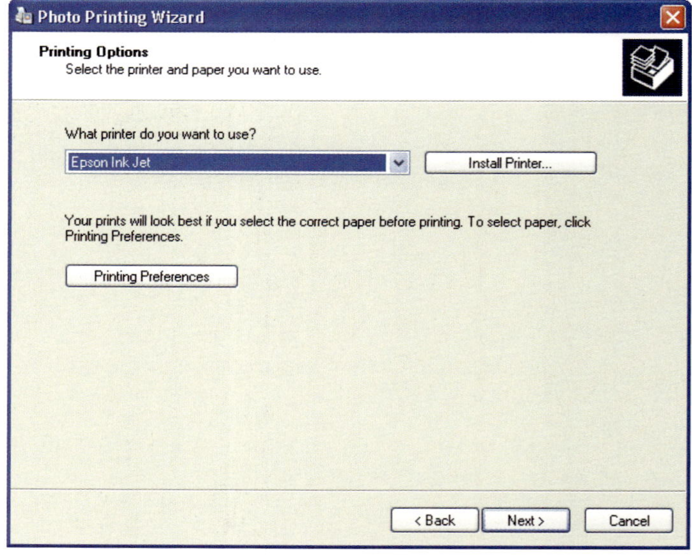

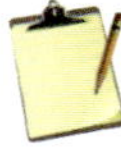

We mentioned in the preceding section that you can set printer preferences as you print; that way, you don't adversely affect the way regular documents are printed. To do this, click the **Printing Preferences** button. Then, in the Printing Preferences dialog box, adjust your printer's settings as needed, and click **OK**.

7. Click **Next**. The Wizard's Layout Selection screen opens, enabling you to select the size and layout of your pictures and preview your selection. Review the choices in the Available layouts section of the dialog box; once you've found a size and layout you like, click it. Your layout choice is highlighted once selected.

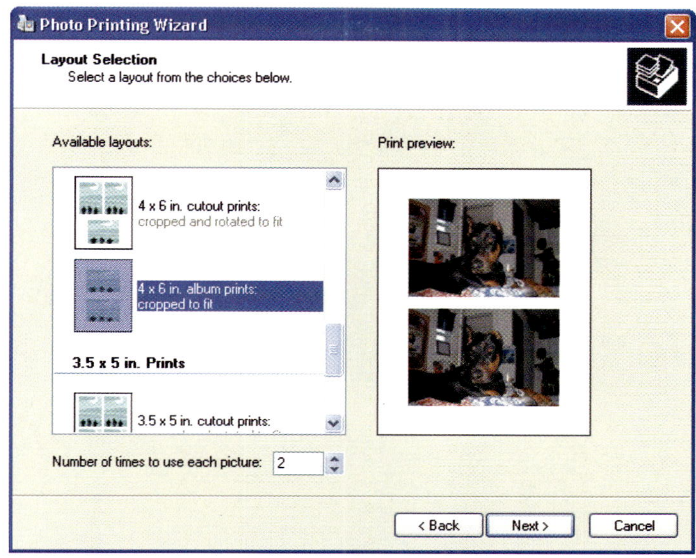

8. Specify how many times each picture should be printed. For example, to print two 4 x 6 album copies of each picture, click **4 x 6 in. album prints: cropped to fit** on the Available layouts section, then use the spin arrows or enter **2** in the Number of times to use each picture spin box. Click **Next**.

If you change your mind about a selection you've made in one of the Wizard screens, click the **Back** button to step backward through the Wizard until you locate the screen containing the setting you want to change. Change the setting as needed, and click **Next** to continue.

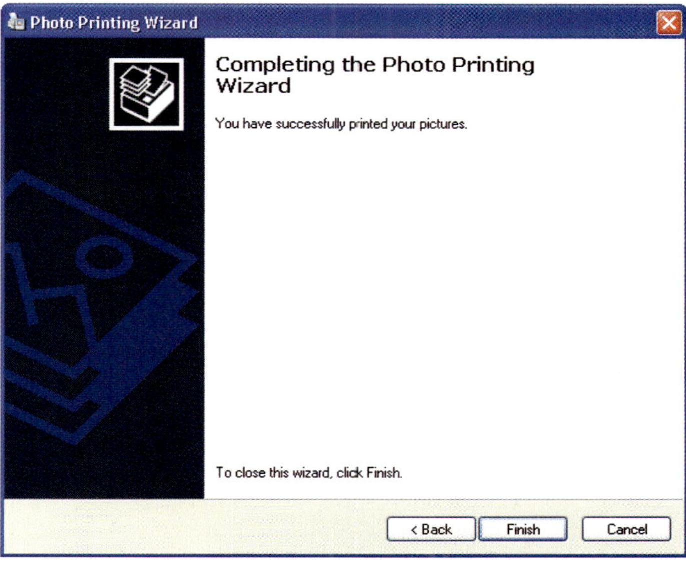

9. The pictures are printed, and the Wizard's final screen opens. Click **Finish** to close the Wizard.

7

Printing Pictures from MGI PhotoSuite 4

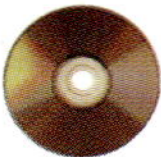

The photos used in the following exercises are available on the CD-ROM that accompanies this book.

To print pictures using PhotoSuite 4, do the following:

1. With the picture you want to print open in the PhotoSuite 4 work area, click the **Print** button.

If you need help opening image files in PhotoSuite 4, refer to Chapter 5.

2. Print options are displayed along the left side of the window; you can print single prints, print multiple prints, or order prints online. Click **Print**.

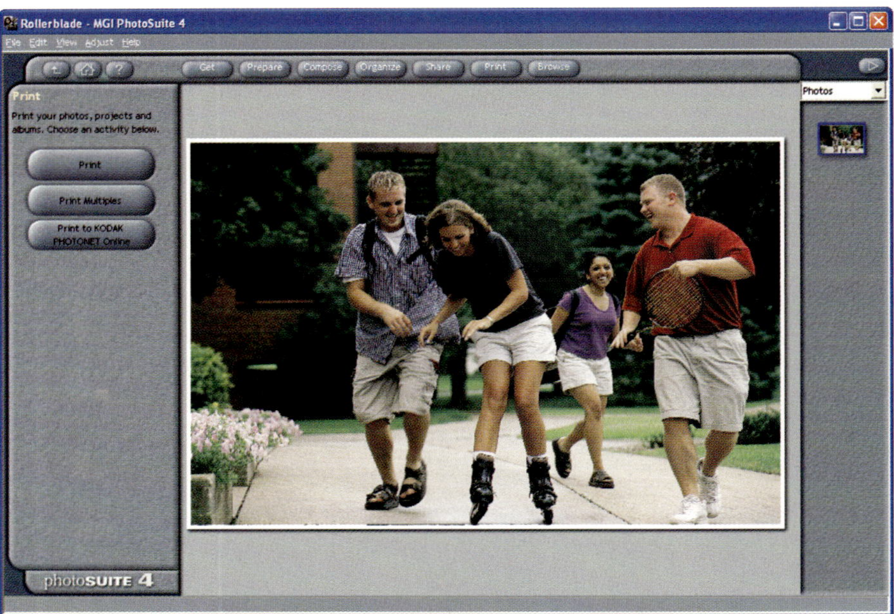

For information about ordering prints online, see the section "Ordering Online Prints," later in this chapter.

3. PhotoSuite 4 displays a series of Print Preview options. Here you can specify what printer you want to use, select the paper's orientation (portrait or landscape), establish the size of the printed image, specify how many prints of the image should be made, and more. Adjust these settings as needed.

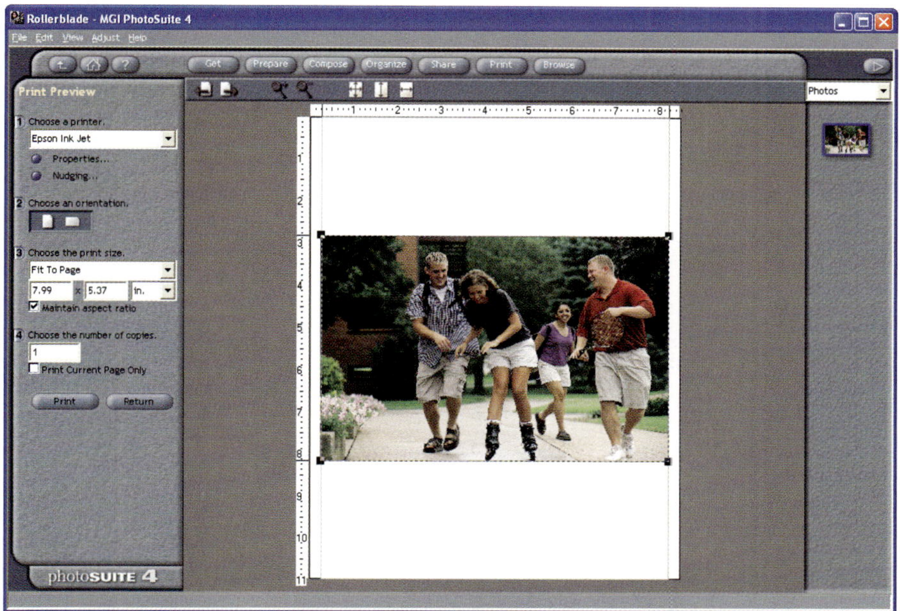

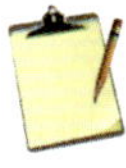

As mentioned previously, you can set printer preferences as you print; that way, you don't adversely affect the way regular documents are printed. To do this in PhotoSuite 4, click the **Properties** button in the Choose a Printer section of the Print Preview options. Then, in the Printing Preferences dialog box, adjust your printer's settings as needed, and click **OK**.

4. Click **Print**. The pictures are printed.

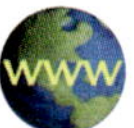

Go to the Web segment *Photo: Printing* in the MGI PhotoSuite 4 course to practice printing photographs using PhotoSuite 4.

Printing Pictures from Microsoft Picture It!

To print pictures using Picture It!, do the following:

1. After you've opened the picture you want to print, click **Print** in the Project Options area. A Print menu opens, containing options for printing on your printer, printing professionally online, and printing all your pictures.

If you need help opening image files in Picture It!, refer to Chapter 5.

2. Click **Print on my printer**. A submenu of printing options appears; for example, you can print on standard paper, labels or special paper, a multi-photo sheet, a banner or poster, an envelope, or an index sheet.

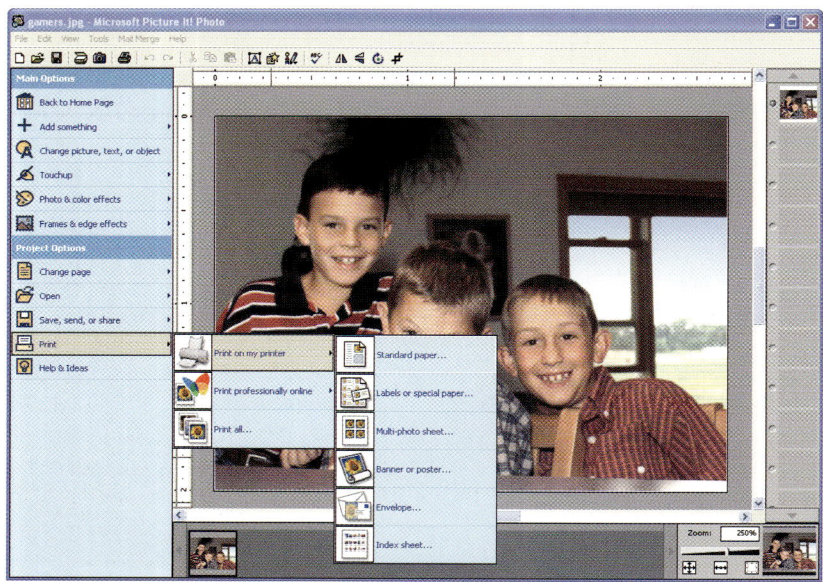

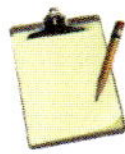

If you plan to print using paper other than standard paper, be sure to insert the correct paper type into your printer before printing the image.

3. Select your paper choice (in this case, Standard paper). Various print options appear in the Print task pane; these vary depending on your paper choice. For standard paper, you can select the printer to be used, the number of copies to be printed, the paper orientation (landscape or portrait), and the print size (fit to page, custom, 8 x 10, 5 x 7, 4 x 6, or 3.5 x 5).

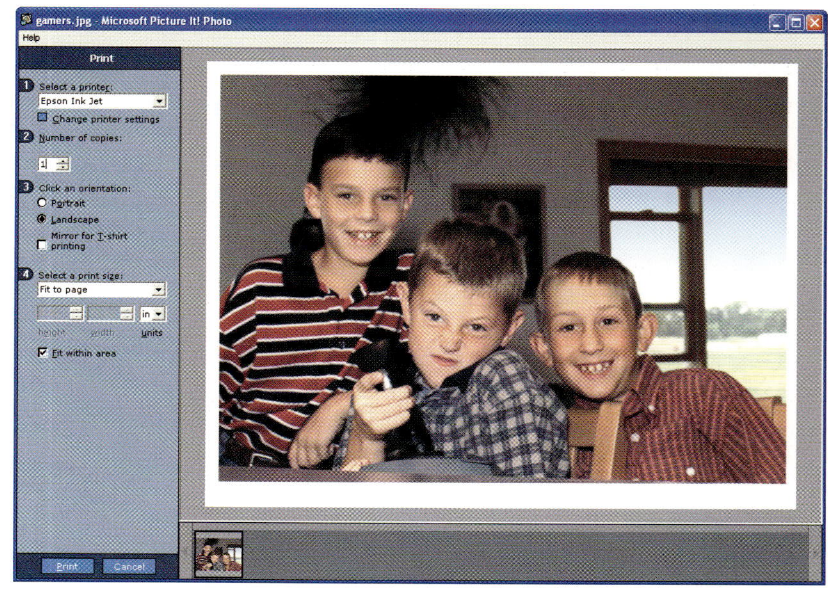

As with Windows XP and PhotoSuite 4, you can set printer preferences as you print; that way, you don't adversely effect the way regular documents are printed. To do this in Picture It!, click the **Change printer settings** option in the Print task pane. Then, in the Printing Preferences dialog box, adjust your printer's settings as needed, and click **OK**.

4. Make your selections, and click **Print**.

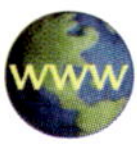

Go to the Web segment *Photo: Printing* in the Microsoft Picture It! course to practice printing photographs using Picture It!.

More About . . . Printing Multiple Pictures

With Picture It!, you can print several photos at once. To do so, first open all the photos you want to print. Then, in the Project Options area, click **Print**, click **Print All**, and then choose the type of paper you want to use (standard paper, labels or special paper, a multi-photo sheet, or what have you). In the Print All Pictures task pane, you can choose to print one picture per page or several pictures on each page; check the appropriate box. Then, in the Print task pane, select the printer to be used, the number of copies to be printed, the paper orientation (landscape or portrait), and the print size (fit to page, custom, 8 x 10, 5 x 7, 4 x 6, or 3.5 x 5). Finally, click **Print** to print the pictures.

Printing at Your Local Photo Lab

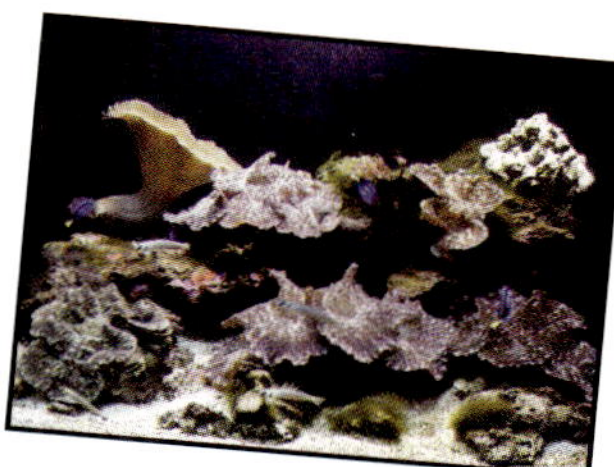

Suppose you've tried printing your images using your regular printer, but you decide you want enlargements or print-shop quality pictures. One option is to purchase a photo printer. But, as another option, you can have your digital images printed at your local photo lab—at a price comparable to that of film-based photo processing.

Many photo labs have self-service photo-processing kiosks, into which you can insert your camera's removable media card (for example, a SmartMedia or CompactFlash card) and then print pictures directly from the card. Alternatively, the photo lab may be able to print the images on your media card for you.

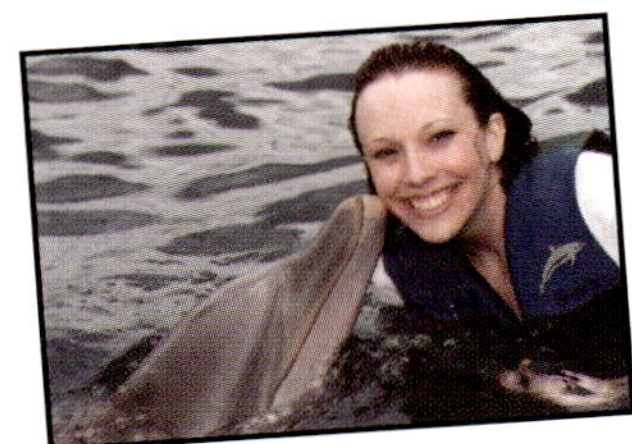

To find a reliable photo lab that processes digital prints, start with the lab you use to develop your film-based prints. Ask if they offer digital print processing and, if so, how it works. If your local lab doesn't provide this service, try other photo labs or drugstores.

In addition to enabling you to print photographs taken with your digital camera, many photo labs can convert photographs taken with a film-based camera into digital images. When you drop off your roll of film, you simply specify that you want your images to be digitized in addition to being printed; depending on your selection, these digital images are then stored on a CD-ROM or on the Web. You can copy these images to your computer, and then manipulate, edit, and e-mail them just as you would with digital images you obtained using your scanner or digital camera.

Using an Online Printing Service

If your local photo lab can't handle your digital media, don't despair. You can use one of the many online services to print your digital pictures. You simply upload the pictures from your computer to the online printing service's computer(s); the online service then prints the photos and mails them to you. Most of these services will also post them to a Web page for you to view. Of course, these services can't offer the one-hour turnaround time found at many photo labs, but you can expect to receive your photos within a few days.

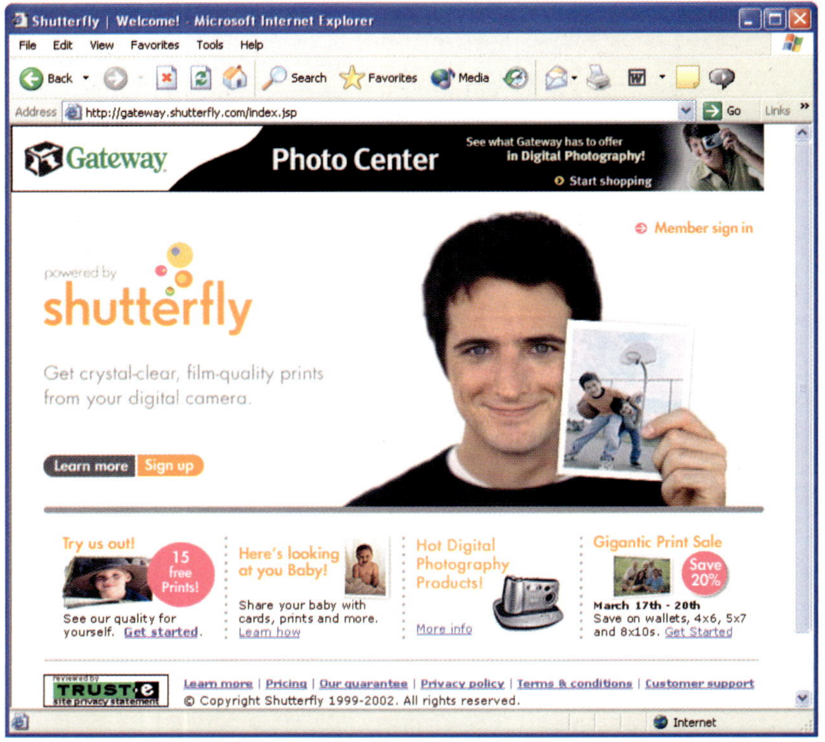

Turnaround time aside, online printing offers many benefits:

- **You can order copies of only the pictures you want.** Instead of having a whole "roll" developed, many online printing services will post digital copies of your prints to a Web site for you to preview. You can then decide which pictures you want printed.
- **You can order prints in various sizes.** These include traditional photo-print sizes (3.5 x 5 and 4 x 6), enlargements (5 x 7 and 8 x 10), and smaller sizes, such as wallet prints.
- **You can order multiple quantities of prints you like.** If you've ever ordered double prints when having regular film processed, you've probably ended up with extra copies of prints you don't like. When you process your digital prints using an online service, however, you can order one or more prints of any you like by viewing them online and choosing which ones you would like to order right from your own computer. You can also order many kinds of photo gifts like cards, mugs, and even framed prints from most of these services and have them delivered right to your home.

Online print services charge about as much as a typical photo lab, although you must also pay for shipping and handling. Some online print services, however, have introductory offers that enable you to receive several free prints so you can check their quality. Only after you've used all your free prints do you pay for processing.

One way to access an online printing service is to type its URL in your Web browser's Address field; you can then follow the site's directions to upload your image files. Be sure to first check out the site's printing charges, shipping charges, and turnaround time.

If you'd rather not hunt down an online print service on your own, however, you can use Windows XP or your photo-editing program to connect to one. The following sections cover using Windows XP, PhotoSuite 4, and Picture It! to order prints online.

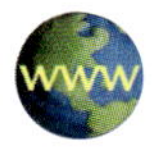

To practice creating a Snapbook of favorite photographs on the Shutterfly site, go to the Web segment *Snapbook: Creating* in either the MGI PhotoSuite or Microsoft Picture It! course.

Using Windows XP to Order Prints Online

To order prints online using Windows XP, you use the Online Print Ordering Wizard. Here's how:

You must be logged on to the Internet to complete this task.

1. From within **My Computer**, open the folder or subfolder that contains the image files you want to print.

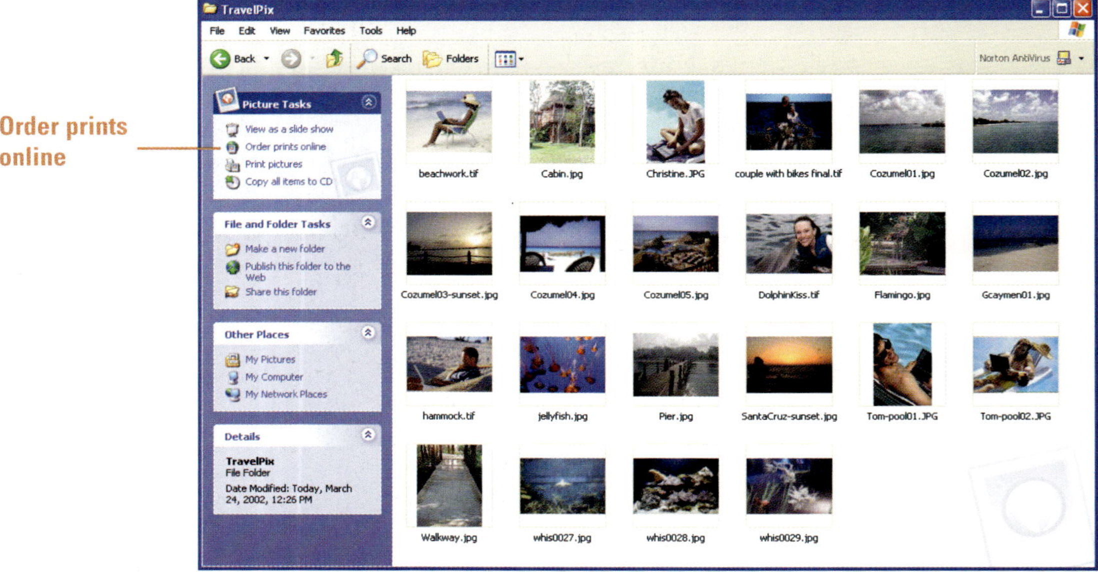

2. Click **Order prints online** in the Picture Tasks pane.
3. The Online Print Ordering Wizard starts, displaying its Welcome screen. Click **Next**.

4. The Wizard displays a screen containing thumbnail images of all the digital pictures in the folder. To upload all of them to the online print service, click the **Select All** button. If you want to upload only some of them, click the check boxes above the ones you want to upload. When you've selected all the pictures you want to upload, click **Next**.

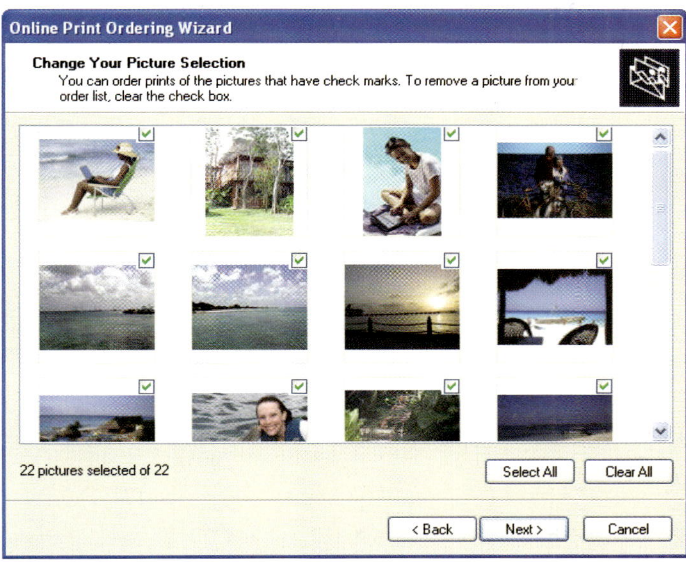

If you accidentally select an image that you don't want to upload, simply click its check box to deselect it. To deselect all images at once, click **Clear All**.

5. The Online Print Ordering Wizard displays a list of online print services. Choose the one you want to use, and then click **Next**.
6. Some online print services prompt you to set up a Microsoft .NET Passport account. To do so, simply follow the steps in the .NET Passport Wizard (which opens automatically) and click **Next** to move from screen to screen. You'll be prompted to provide your e-mail address, a password, and information about your location (country, state, and ZIP code).
7. Depending on which print service you select, you may be prompted to set up an account with that service. This process is similar to registering for a Microsoft .NET Passport account; you enter your e-mail address, password, and name.
8. Once you're logged on to the photo service's Web site, follow the on-screen instructions to order your prints.

More About . . . Ordering Prints Online

The precise instructions for uploading image files and setting print options vary depending on which service you use, but a few things are constant. For example, you can expect to select a size and quantity, as well as review pricing information, for each print. You'll also need to enter shipping and billing information. Once that's done, your picture files are uploaded from your computer to the printing service (depending on the speed of your connection, this can take a while). Once your order is complete, you can expect to receive your prints in the mail within a few days.

Using PhotoSuite 4 to Order Prints Online

To order prints online using PhotoSuite 4, do the following:

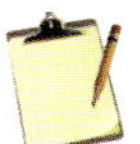

You must be logged on to the Internet to complete this task.

1. With the picture or pictures you want to upload open in the PhotoSuite 4 work area and tray, click the **Print** button.

   To open multiple pictures, hold down the **SHIFT** key and click on each picture file you want to open. The picture that is currently selected appears in the work area, with all other open pictures visible in the tray. For additional help opening image files in PhotoSuite 4, refer to Chapter 5.

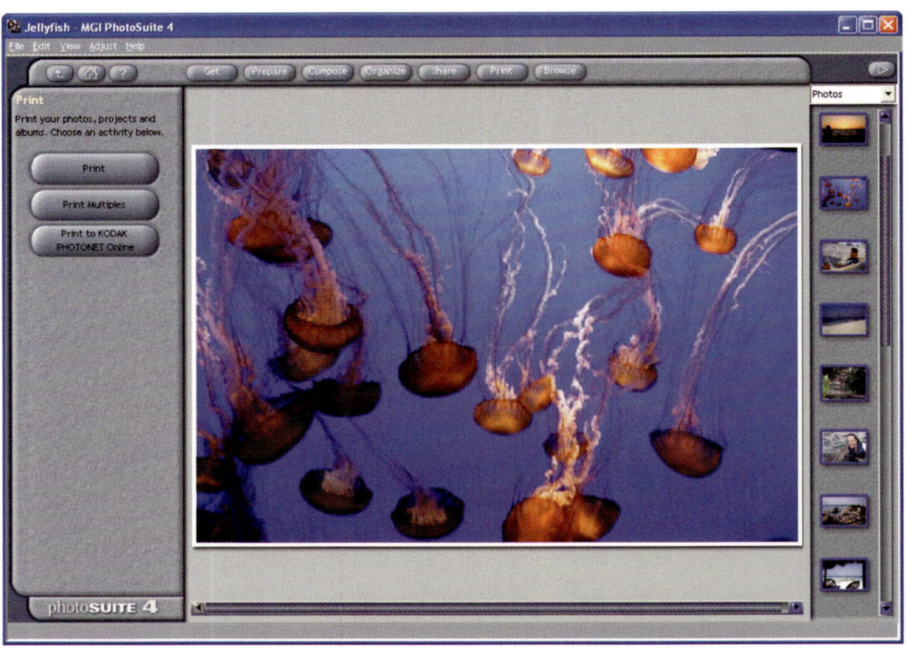

2. Click **Print to KODAK PHOTONET Online**. Once you're logged on to this Web site, follow the on-screen instructions.

If you purchased a digital photo solution pack that included MGI PhotoSuite 4 from Gateway, Inc., you will see a link named Gateway Photo Center. You can use this link to order pictures.

Using Picture It! To Order Prints Online

To order prints online using Picture It!, do the following:

You must be logged on to the Internet in order to complete this task.

1. After you've opened the pictures you want to upload, click **Print** in the Project Options area, click **Print professionally online**, and then click **Prints and enlargements**.

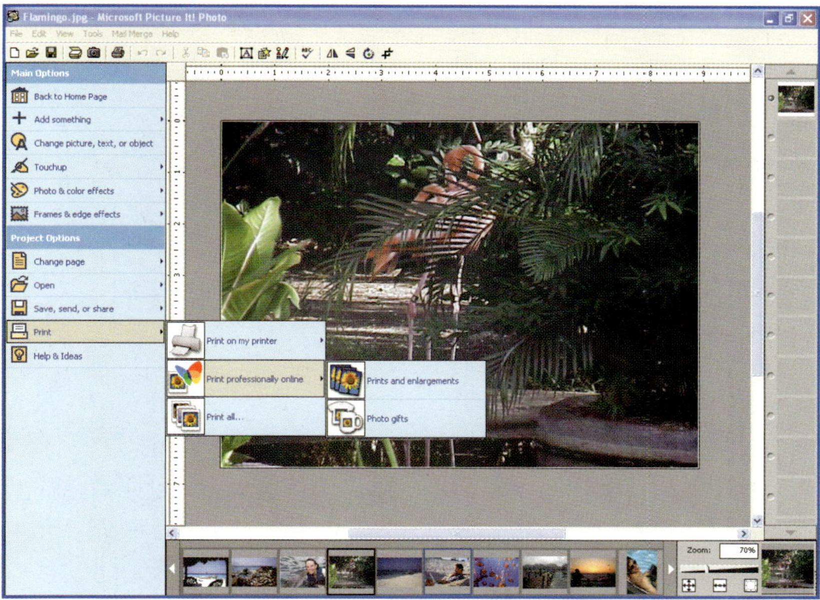

If you need help opening image files in Picture It!, see Chapter 5.

7

2. Specify whether you want to print the currently selected picture or all open pictures in the tray, and then click **Next**.

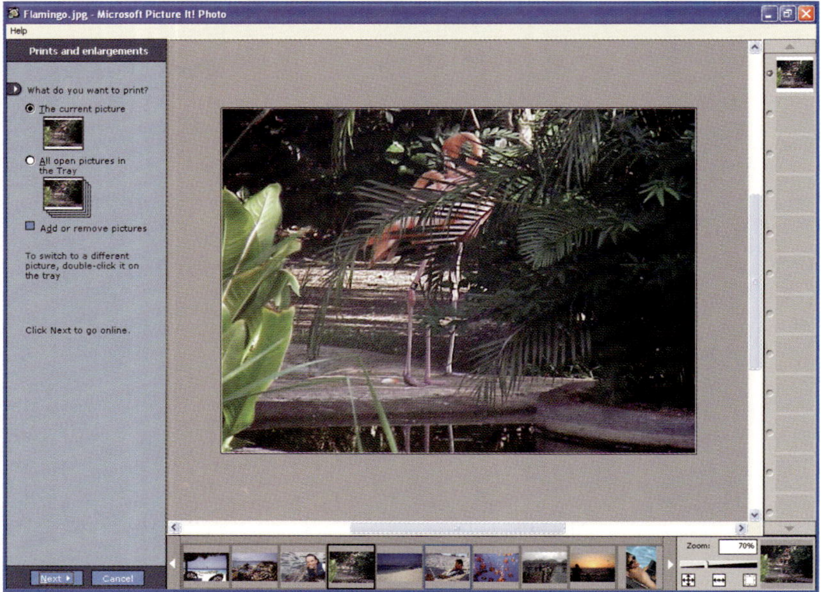

3. Follow the instructions in the Web page displayed on the right to select your print options and order your online prints. When you're finished, click **Done**.

> ### More About . . . Online Printing
>
> You can use your Internet browser to go directly to any online printing service and upload your pictures. You can also check the printing and shipping charges, review the turnaround time, and get detailed instructions on how to use the service. The steps vary from service to service, but should be fairly easy to follow, using the links at the site.

To Keep on Learning . . .

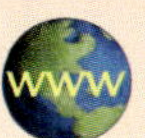

Go online to www.LearnwithGateway.com and log on to select:

- *Photo: Printing* in the PhotoSuite 4 course to practice printing using MGI PhotoSuite 4.
- *Photo: Printing* in the Picture It! course to practice printing using Microsoft Picture It!.
- *Snapbook: Creating* in either the MGI PhotoSuite or Microsoft Picture It! course to practice creating a Snapbook of favorite photographs on the Shutterfly site.
- *Internet Links and Resources*
- *FAQs*

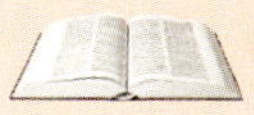

With the *Survive & Thrive* series, refer to *Use and Care for Your PC* for more information on:

- *User accounts*
- *Working with Windows XP*
- *Organizing your computer*

Gateway offers a hands-on training course that covers many of the topics in this chapter. Additional fees may apply. Call 888-852-4821 for enrollment information. If applicable, please have your customer ID and order number ready when you call.

7

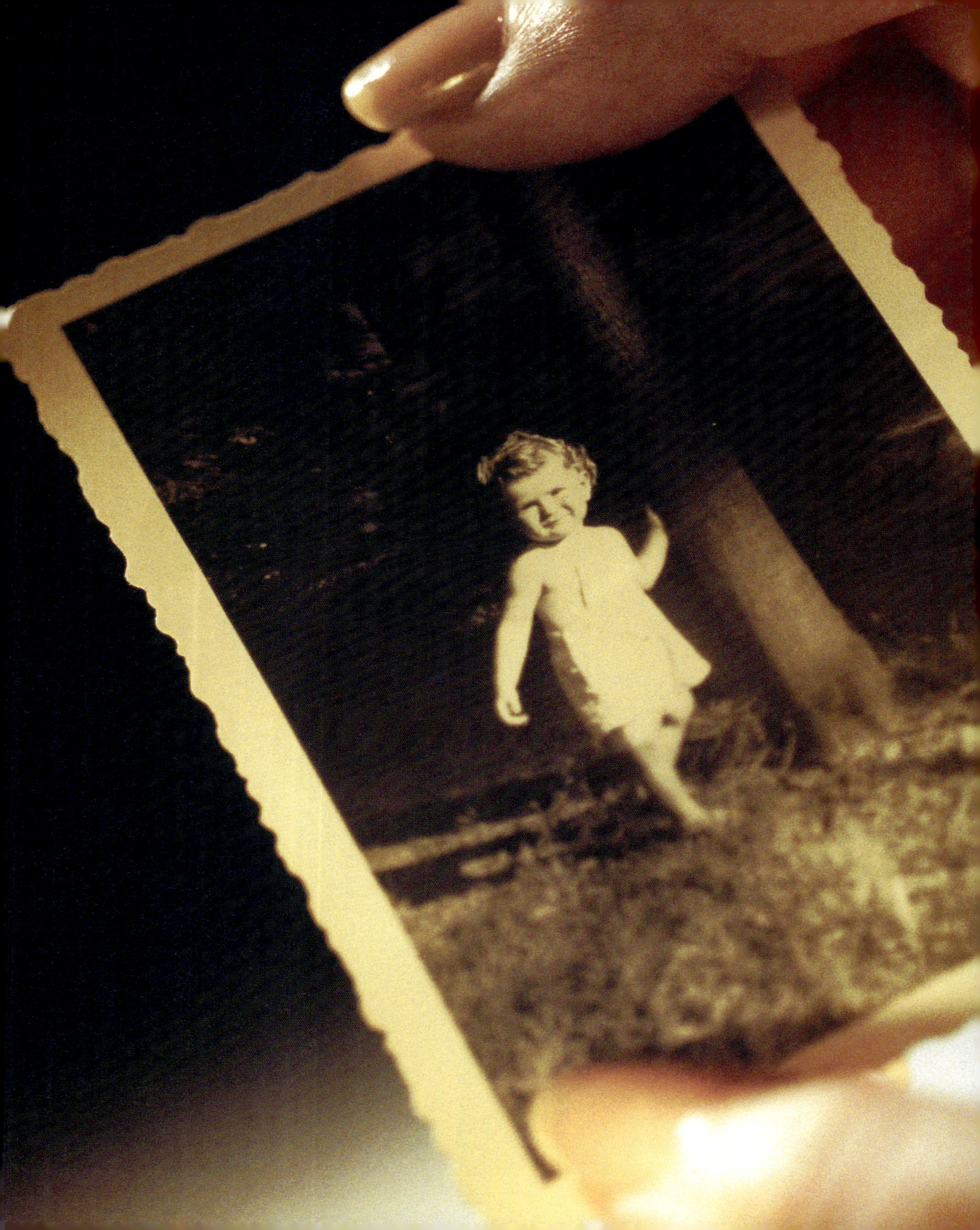

CHAPTER 8

Organizing and Protecting Your Digital Images

Many people use a photo album to organize and protect their print photographs. You may have one of your own. In fact, depending on how many photos you have, you may have several albums. Each album may represent a year in your life, or you may have albums containing photos from a single significant event, such as your wedding or your trip to Fiji.

Just as you organize your print photos into albums, you'll likely need some way to organize and protect the digital images stored on your computer. That way, you won't need to waste time looking all over your hard drive for a particular image. In fact, you can even group related photos into virtual albums that act much like their real-world counterparts. As an added bonus, you can create slide shows of those pictures to show to your friends. You may also decide to store your digital images on other media such as CDs or Zip disks, either to free up space on your hard drive or to have backup files in the event that something happens to the files on your machine. You'll learn how to do all this and more in this chapter.

Managing Photos in Windows XP

Chances are, you use a filing cabinet at work or at home to organize and protect important papers and other items. Most likely, this filing cabinet features two or more drawers, and each drawer contains folders. Each folder is labeled and has any number of related documents. For example, you may have a folder labeled "Tax Return," containing all your important receipts, bank statements, and a copy of the tax return you sent to the IRS.

Your computer's hard disk acts somewhat like a filing cabinet, enabling you to "file" your important documents—including digital images—in folders. Some of these folders, such as My Pictures, are created automatically by your computer's operating system (Windows); others you create yourself. You can even create subfolders and place them in the folders you create. With an organized folder structure, locating your digital images is easy.

In this section, you'll learn how to use Windows XP to keep your digital images organized. You'll learn how to manage your files by using folders to group related images, giving your images descriptive names, and deleting unwanted images.

Windows XP comes with a built-in thumbnail viewer so that you can see small versions of your images from the My Computer interface. To make use of this setting, click **start**, then **My Computer**. From within My Computer, select **View** from the menu bar, and click on **Thumbnails**.

Creating Folders

As mentioned previously, many versions of Windows, including Windows XP, include a special folder called My Pictures. One way to organize your photos is to store them all in this folder, much the same way some people store their photos in a shoebox. Doing this is certainly convenient, but just as digging through a shoebox to find a particular print can be time-consuming, so is sifting through image files in a folder to find the one you want.

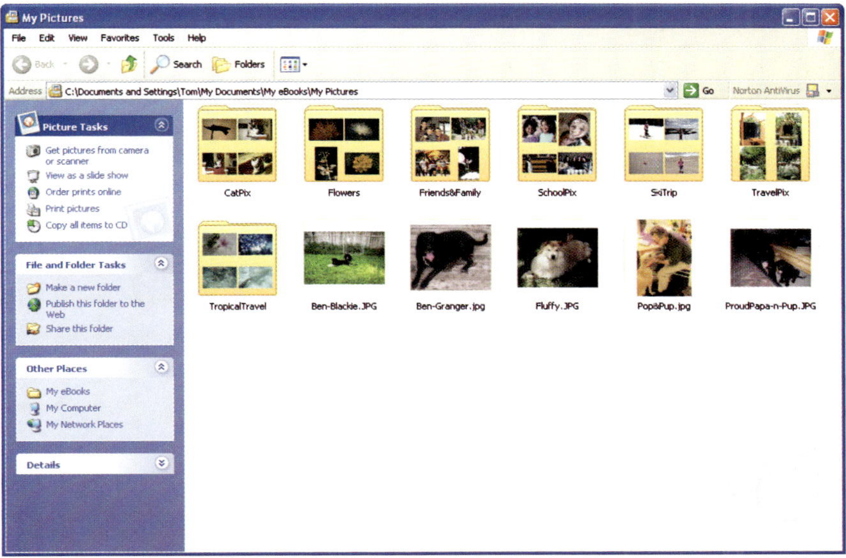

More About . . . The My Pictures Folder

Windows XP displays many picture-related commands in the Picture Tasks of the My Pictures folder's task pane. You can use these handy commands for working with your images. Selections include:

- Get pictures from camera or scanner
- View as a slide show
- Order prints online
- Print pictures
- Copy all items to CD

To remedy this problem, you can create subfolders within the My Pictures folder (or any other folder). For example, you might have one folder named "Trip to Paris," and in it you would store all the pictures from your recent visit to the City of Lights. You might have another folder named "Rover," containing all your digital photos of your dog. Or if you're putting together a scrapbook for a family reunion, you could store all the photos for that event in a "Reunion" folder. If your photos are well organized, you can easily find images you want to work with without having to conduct exhaustive searches through the recesses of your hard drive.

To create a folder within My Pictures (or within any other folder you choose) in Windows XP, do the following:

1. To open the My Pictures folder, click **start**, and then click **My Pictures**.
2. Click **Make a new folder** in the task pane. Alternatively, you can click **File**, **New**, and then **Folder**. A new folder is created within the My Pictures folder.

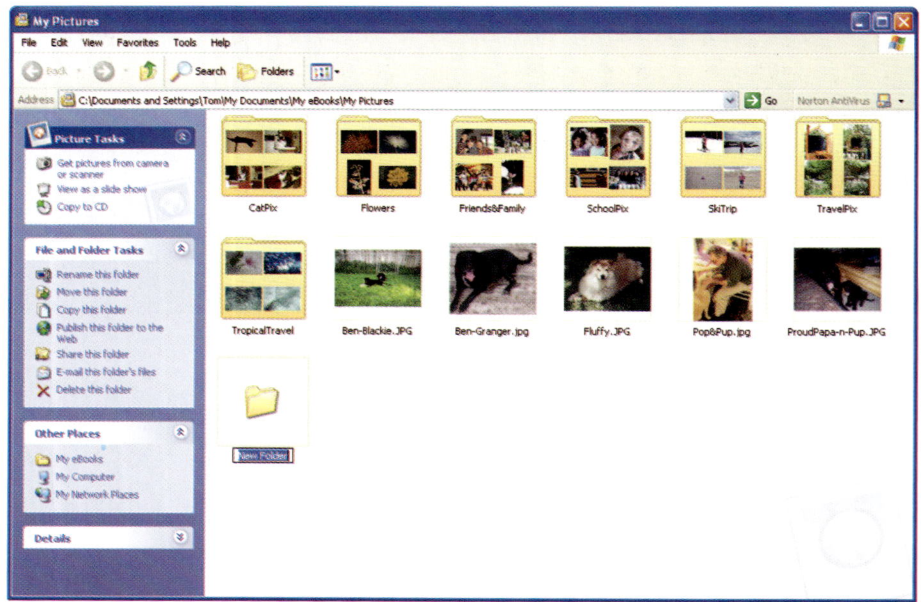

3. Type a descriptive name to replace the default name "New Folder," and press **ENTER**. (New Folder is already selected, so you can start typing immediately.) For this example, we'll call it "Fireworks."

Once you create a new folder, you can use it to store images or any other type of document or program you like. In fact, it's a good idea to create several folders in this manner, giving each one a descriptive name; then you can organize your images into the various folders to keep track of them.

Finding, Moving, and Copying Files

If you've already transferred photos from your digital camera to your hard drive, those images were most likely placed in a folder created by your digital camera software. The same goes for digital images you created using a scanner: The scanner software probably placed your scanned images in its own proprietary folder.

Consult Chapter 3 to review transferring images from your digital camera to your hard drive and Chapter 4 to review scanning photos.

Fortunately, you can easily move those files from their default locations to just about any other folder on your hard drive, including the one you created in the preceding section. Or, rather than move files, you might decide to copy them from one folder to another; that way, you have extra copies in case you need them.

Of course, before you can organize your image files, you must first find them. If you're not certain where your digital camera or scanner places image files by default, you can use Windows XP's Search Companion feature to quickly locate them. To use Search Companion, do the following:

1. Click **start**, and then click **Search**. The Search Results window opens.
2. Under What do you want to search for?, click **Pictures, music, or video**.

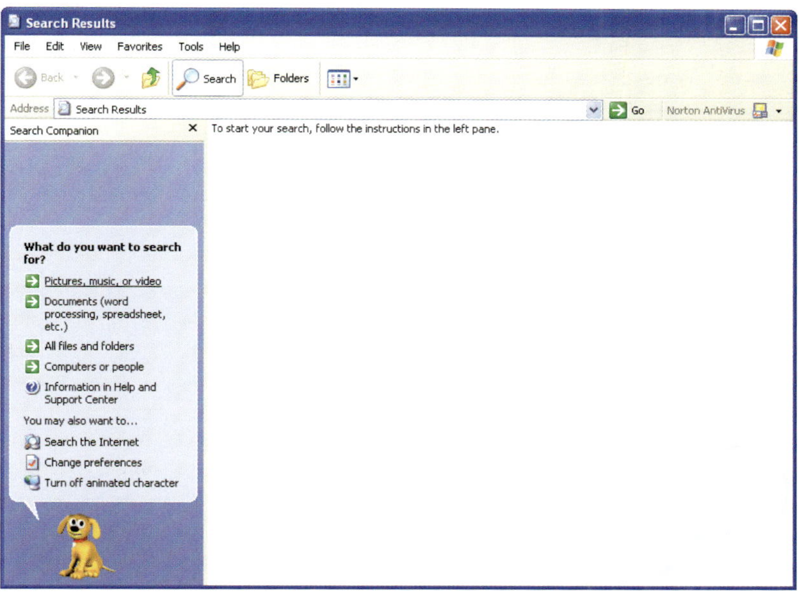

8

3. Under Search for all files of a certain type, or search by type and name, click the box next to **Pictures and Photos**, then click **Search**.

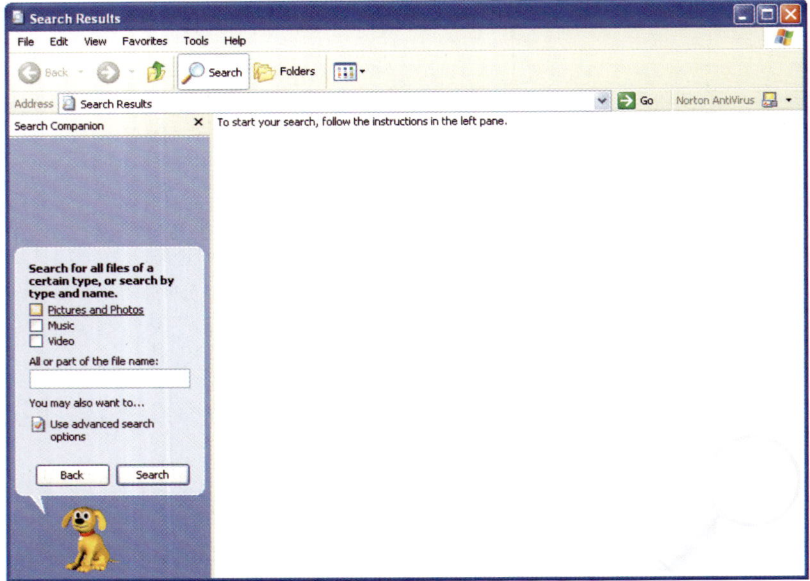

4. The search program searches for image files and then displays the results.
5. From here, you can access all picture and photo files on your computer.

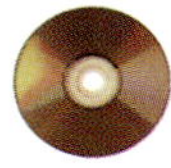

The photos used in the following exercises are available on the CD-ROM that accompanies this book.

Once you've found your image files, you can use Windows XP to move one or more of them to another folder on your hard disk. Here's how:

1. Locate and open the folder that contains the file or files you want to move.
2. Click any file you want to move. To select several files, hold down the **CTRL** key on your keyboard while clicking each file you want to move. If the files you want to move appear adjacent in the file list, you can select them all by clicking the first file you want to move, and while holding down the **SHIFT** key on your keyboard, clicking the last file you want to move.

If you want to move an entire folder and its contents to another folder, simply click the folder you want to move. To select multiple folders, use the method outlined above, clicking folders instead of files.

3. Click **Move this file** (or **Move this folder** if you selected a folder) in the task pane. (If you selected multiple files, click **Move selected items**.) The Move Items dialog box opens.

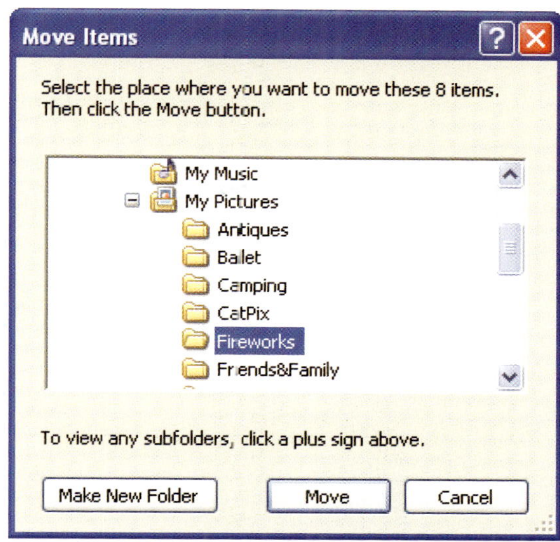

4. Click the folder you want to move the file or files into. To locate the folder, click the plus sign next to the drive where the folder resides. If the folder is a subfolder, click the plus sign next to its main folder to display it.

If you haven't yet created a folder for your image files, you can do so by clicking the drive or folder you want the new folder to reside in. Then, click **Make New Folder**, type a descriptive name for the folder, and press **ENTER**.

5. Click **Move**. The files are moved to the folder you selected in Step 4.

If you prefer, you can click **Edit** and then **Cut** to delete files or folders from their current location and copy them to the Windows XP Clipboard. Then, in the folder you want to place the images or folders in, c ick **Edit** and then **Paste**.

8

Copying files in Windows XP is similar to moving them. Here's how it's done:

1. Locate and open the folder that contains the file or files you want to copy.
2. Click the file, files, or folder you want to copy. (Refer to Step 2 of the preceding exercise for information about selecting multiple files and folders.)

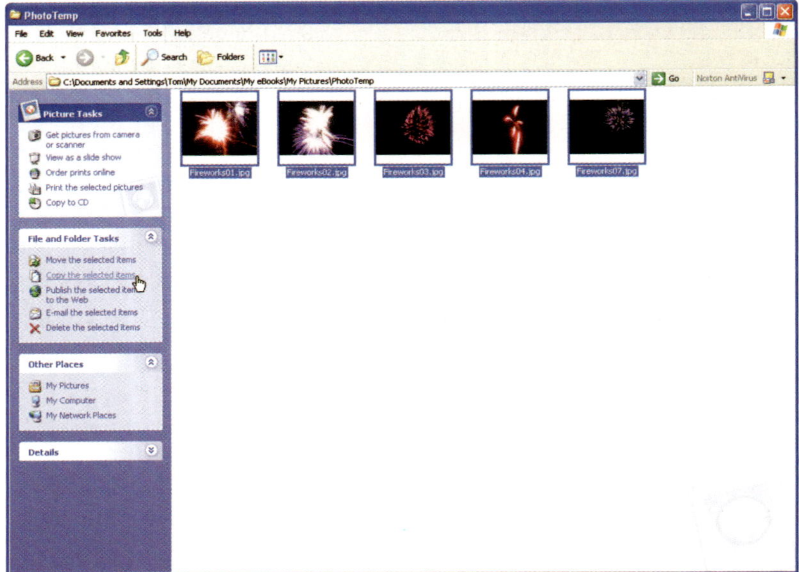

3. In the task pane, click **Copy this file** (to copy a single file) or **Copy selected items** (to copy multiple files). The Copy Items dialog box opens.

4. In the Copy Items dialog box, click the folder you want to move files into. (For help locating the folder, refer to Step 4 of the preceding exercise.)

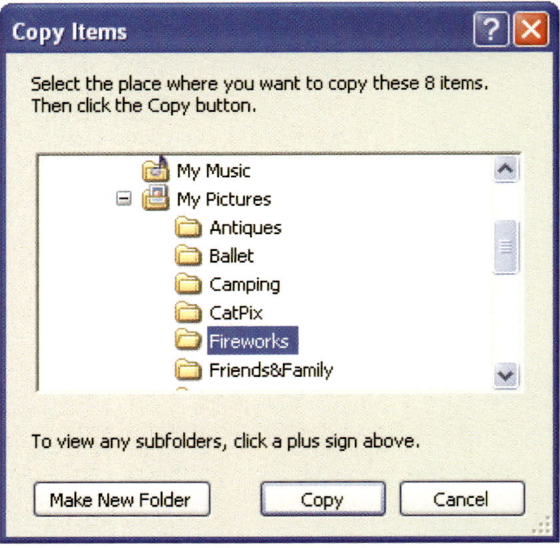

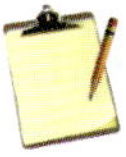

As with the Move Items dialog box, you can use the Copy Items dialog box to create new folders. Click the drive or folder you want the new folder to reside in, and then click **Make New Folder**, type a descriptive name for the folder, and press **ENTER**.

5. Click **Copy**. The files are copied to the folder you selected in Step 4.

As with moving files, you can use the Edit menu commands to copy files and folders from one folder to another. Simply click **Copy** instead of **Cut**, and proceed as in the preceding exercise.

Renaming Files

You've managed to move your digital images from their original location to the folders you've created. But how can you tell which one is which? Thanks to your digital camera's or scanner's rather bland default naming scheme, your image files' names just aren't very descriptive—at best containing the date the photo was taken and little else. If two images are transferred or scanned on the same date, the program simply appends a number to distinguish them, so that you have file names such as "Sunday May 18 (2)." Some devices provide filenames as nondescript as "Image001."

If you don't change the names of these files, locating one you need later on can be tiresome. That's why it's a good idea to develop a naming scheme for your image files. One possibility is to name your image files after the subjects of the photographs they contain, plus the date or event where the photo was taken. For example, rather than leave an image file with the default name "Sunday May 18 (2)," you might name it "Gramps Family Reunion" so you know the picture is of Gramps at your family reunion. If you took several pictures of Gramps, you could number each one within your naming scheme, as in "GrampsFamilyReunion1," "GrampsFamilyReunion2," and so on. Alternatively, you might decide to base your naming scheme on the folder containing the images you want to rename. Using the family reunion example, you might create a folder named "Family Reunion" and then name the photos in that folder "FamilyReunion1," "FamilyReunion2," and so on.

Renaming your image files does more than help you find the ones you like; it also helps prevent you from accidentally deleting files you want to keep.

To rename files using Windows XP, do the following:

1. Open the folder that contains files you want to rename.
2. Click an image you want to rename. (You can rename only one file at a time.)

❸ In the task pane, click **Rename this file**. (Alternatively, right-click the file and click **Rename** in the shortcut menu that appears.)

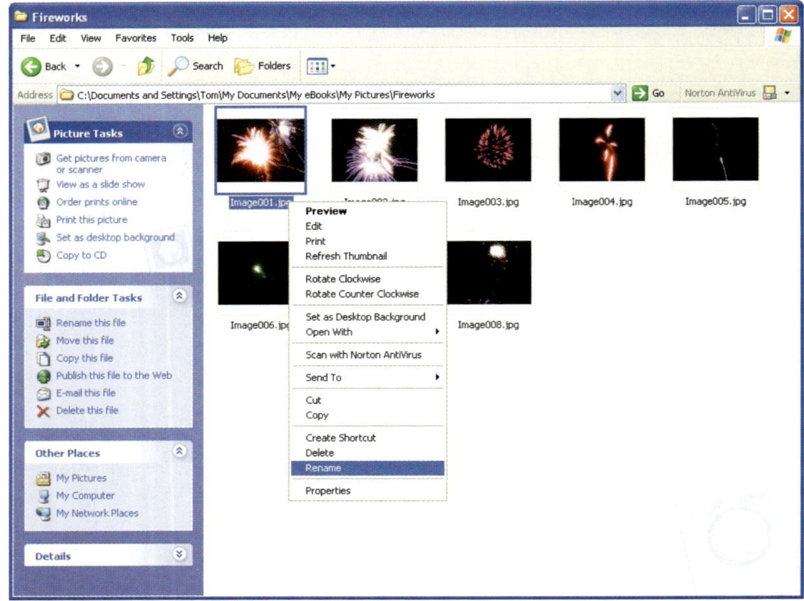

❹ The file name is selected; type a new name and press **ENTER** to rename the file.

Of course, finding a naming scheme that is specific enough for you to identify the file you want on the first try is a bit difficult. Fortunately, Windows XP enables you to view a small version of each image in a folder (called a *thumbnail*) alongside its file name. That way, if you have several photos of Gramps at the family reunion, you can scan these thumbnail images to locate the one you want. To configure Windows XP to display thumbnail images of each image file in a folder, you simply change to Thumbnail view; to do so, click **View**, and then **Thumbnail**.

Deleting Files

Digital image files are very large in size and can quickly fill up your hard drive. For this reason, it's a good idea to delete any image files you no longer need. Alternatively, you can copy your image files to a CD or some other media, as discussed in the next section, and delete them from your hard drive to make room for new files.

You can delete one file or several files at a time using Windows XP; you can also delete folders. Here's how:

When you delete a folder, you also delete all its contents.

1. Locate and open the folder that contains the file or files you want to delete.
2. Click the file, files, or folder you want to delete. To select several files, hold down the **CTRL** key on your keyboard while clicking each file you want to delete. If the files you want to delete appear adjacent in the file list, you can select them all by clicking the first file you want to delete and, while holding down the **SHIFT** key on your keyboard, clicking the last file you want to delete.

If you want to delete an entire folder and its contents, simply click the folder you want to delete. To select multiple folders, use the method just outlined, clicking folders instead of files.

3. In the task pane, click **Delete this file** (for a single file), **Delete selected items** (for multiple files), or **Delete this folder** (for a folder). Alternatively, right-click a selected file and click **Delete** in the shortcut menu that appears.

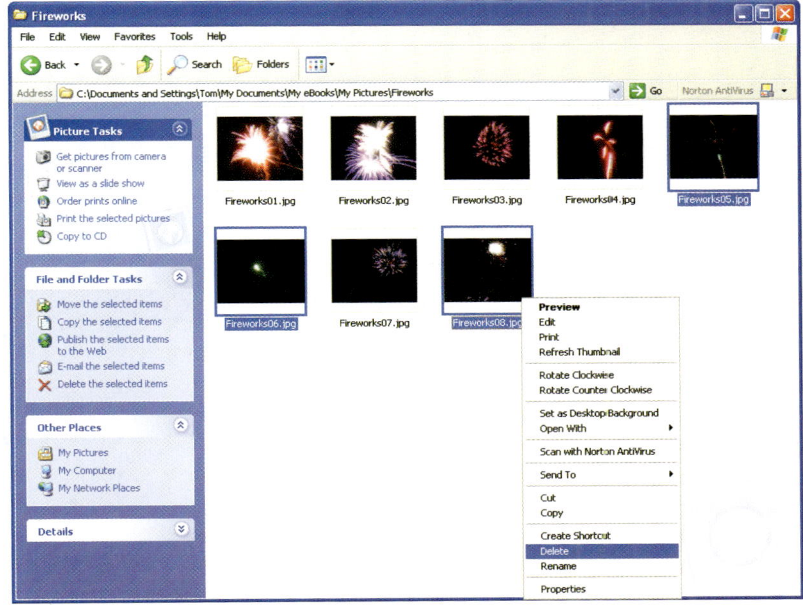

4. Windows XP asks you to confirm that you want to delete the selected files or folders. Click **Yes**.

When you delete files or folders in Windows XP, they're not removed from your hard drive right away, but are instead moved to the Recycle Bin. The *Recycle Bin* is a temporary storage location for recently deleted files, and you use it like the wastebasket beside your desk. If you throw away a paper document and decide later that you should keep it, you can always pull it out of the wastebasket—until you empty your trash.

Likewise, if you delete a file, you can recover it from the Recycle Bin until you tell Windows to empty it (or until Windows runs out of room in the Recycle Bin and permanently deletes files in it to free up space).

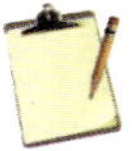

If you've deleted any files in error, you can retrieve them from the Recycle Bin. Simply double-click the **Recycle Bin** icon on your desktop to open the Recycle Bin window. Then click the files you want to restore, and click **Restore this item**.

Because your goal in deleting your digital image files is to free up space on your hard drive, you'll need to empty the Recycle Bin to seal the deal. To do so, simply double-click the Recycle Bin icon on your desktop to open the Recycle Bin window. Then click **Empty the Recycle Bin**. When prompted, click **Yes** to confirm that you want to permanently delete all items in the Recycle Bin.

Once you've emptied the Recycle Bin, you cannot retrieve any files you've deleted.

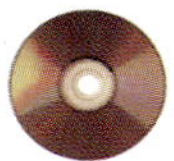

To gain an understanding of the benefits and guidelines for organizing your pictures, go to the CD-ROM segment *Images: Organizing*.

Archiving Your Digital Images

Just as you often keep negatives of your pictures as an archive in case something happens to your prints, you can *archive* your original digital image files. One major reason to do so is that image files are large and consume significant space. When you archive your digital image files you free up space on your hard drive, making room for other files. Another major goal of archiving files is protection: You can archive your favorite image files as *backups* in case the original files become damaged.

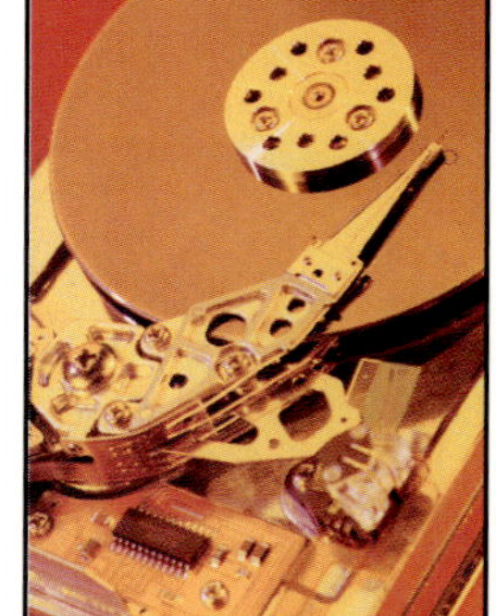

One way to archive your digital image files is to keep them on your hard drive, but in compressed format; that way, they consume considerably less space. Alternatively, if your computer has a drive that lets you record CDs, you can copy your image files to a CD and archive them that way. These options are discussed in the next two sections.

Archiving Images on Your Hard Drive

No matter how large your hard drive is, it will fill up if you add large numbers of image files to it. One solution is to add another drive to gain more disk space. Another is to store your images in a *compressed* (or *zipped*) *folder*. That way, the images remain on your hard drive, but in a different—and more compact—format.

Rather than using Windows XP, you can download programs from the Internet to compress (or *zip*) files. These include *shareware* programs, for which you pay a small fee, and *freeware* programs, which are free.

To use Windows XP to store images in a compressed folder, do the following:

1. Locate and open the folder that contains the compressed folder or any images you want to compress.
2. Click the image, images, or folder you want to compress. (To select multiple images or folders, hold down the **CTRL** key while clicking each item you want to compress.)
3. Right-click any of the selected files, click **Send To** in the shortcut menu that appears, and click **Compressed (zipped) folder**. Windows XP's built-in compression utility compresses and stores the images in a compressed folder within the current folder. A progress window indicates the progress of the compression operation.

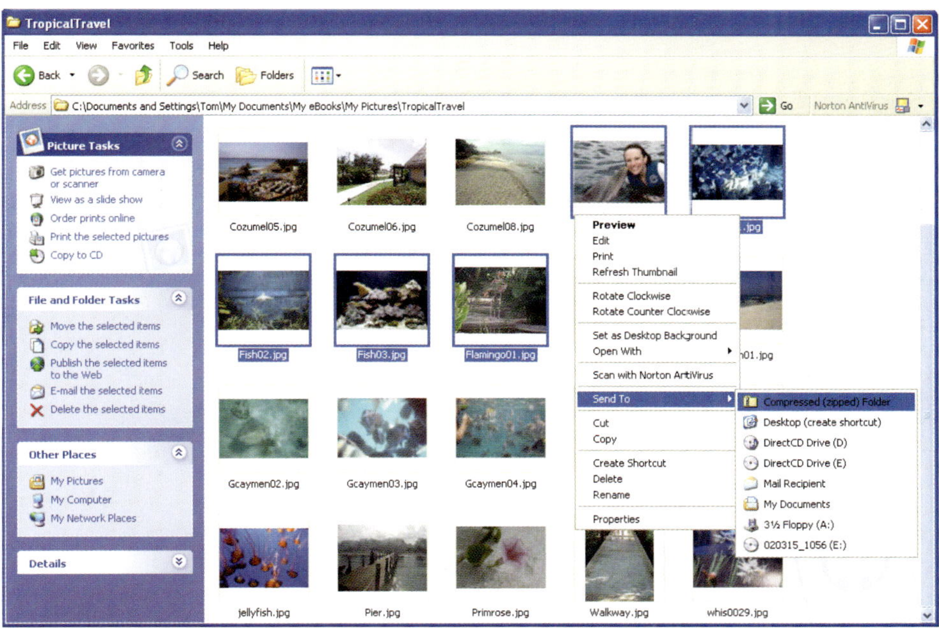

4. The compressed folder's default name usually consists of the name of one of the compressed images. To give the compressed folder a more descriptive name, right-click it and click **Rename** in the shortcut menu that appears. The folder's name is selected.
5. Type a new name for the folder and press **ENTER**.

When you send images to a compressed folder, they are copied, not moved. That means the original image files remain on the disk. To free up disk space, delete the original versions of the images you compressed. (To select multiple images, hold down the **CTRL** key while click each file you want to delete.)

As mentioned earlier in this chapter, files or folders that are deleted are not removed from your system but are moved to the Recycle Bin, where they continue to consume disk space. To permanently remove the files from your system, you must empty the Recycle Bin. For help performing this task, refer to the section "Deleting Files" earlier in this chapter.

Although you can't open images when they're compressed, you can uncompress or *extract* images when you want to work with them. To do so, follow these steps:

1. Locate and open the folder that contains the compressed folder with the images you want to extract.
2. Double-click the compressed folder. Its contents are displayed in a window, but the files aren't yet extracted.

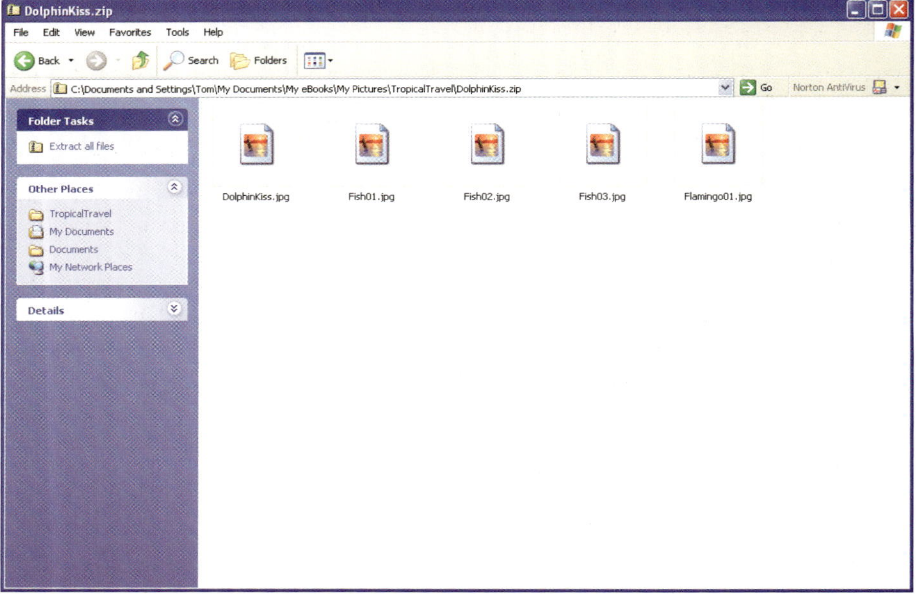

3. Select the file(s) you want to extract. (To select multiple files, hold down the **CTRL** key while clicking each file you want to extract.)
4. Right-click any one of the selected files and click **Copy** in the shortcut menu that appears.
5. Open the folder or drive you want to copy the files to.
6. Right-click in a blank area of the folder window and click **Paste** in the shortcut menu that appears. The files are extracted and copied to the open folder window.

Don't close the window with the compressed files before pasting them.

If you want to extract all the files in the folder, click **Extract all files** in the compressed folder window's task pane. This starts the Compressed (zipped) Folders Extraction Wizard. Read the Welcome screen and click **Next**. When prompted, select the folder you want to place the extracted images in, and then click **Finish**. The images are extracted and copied to the folder you selected.

Saving Images on a CD

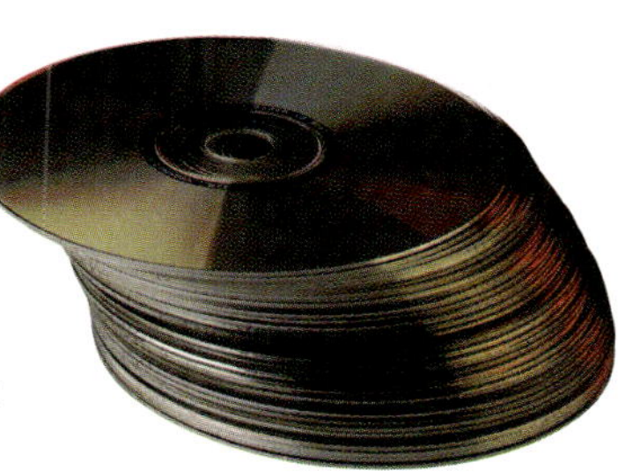

CD-ROM (short for *compact disc read only memory*) drives have been standard equipment on most computers for nearly a decade, making it easy to install programs, view data, and so on. However, CD-ROM drives have one major limitation. Although they can read data from discs, they can't write data to discs—which is to say that you can't use a CD-ROM drive to save data on a CD.

In recent years, technology has given rise to a new generation of *recordable* CD drives that not only read data from discs but also record data to discs. In other words, if you insert a blank CD into a recordable CD drive, you can copy information from your computer to the disc. With a recordable CD drive, users can back up data files, including image files, to CDs. By backing up your image files to a CD, you can free up even more hard-drive space than you can by compressing image files.

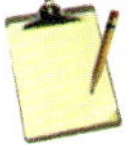

The advantage of using CDs instead of other storage media, such as floppy disks, to store your digital images is that CDs can store anywhere from 650 to 700 MB of data—the equivalent of nearly 500 floppy disks! That provides ample storage for your digital images.

There are two types of recordable CD drives:

- **CD-R drives.** A CD-R drive (R for *read*) can read data from CD-ROM discs and write to CD-R discs. A CD-R disc is a CD that can have data saved on it, or be *written to*, only one time. Once written to, a CD-R becomes a CD-ROM.
- **CD-RW drives.** A CD-RW drive (RW for *read-write*) has the same capabilities as a CD-R drive, but you can also use it to record data to the same CD multiple times. You can even erase a CD and reuse it. To take advantage of these additional capabilities, you must use a special type of CD called a *CD-RW*.

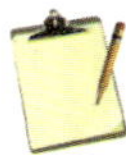

You can also record image files to DVDs (digital versatile discs), provided you have a recordable DVD drive installed on your computer. Because recording to DVDs is not yet a mainstream practice, this section focuses on recording to CDs.

You can use Windows XP to copy your images to a CD just as you use it for copying to any other type of drive. In addition to enabling you to archive images you no longer need, copying images to a CD is also a good way to create backups of your important image files—the ones you really don't want getting damaged or lost. If you like, you can archive copies of these files on CD, leaving the original versions intact on your computer. Here's how:

Some recordable CD drives come bundled with their own software for writing data to the CD, a process also known as *burning* the CD. Consult the user's guide that came with your computer to find out whether your drive requires you to use its accompanying software to burn files to CD rather than Windows XP. See the table at the end of the chapter for a reference to additional information on how to use a CD burner.

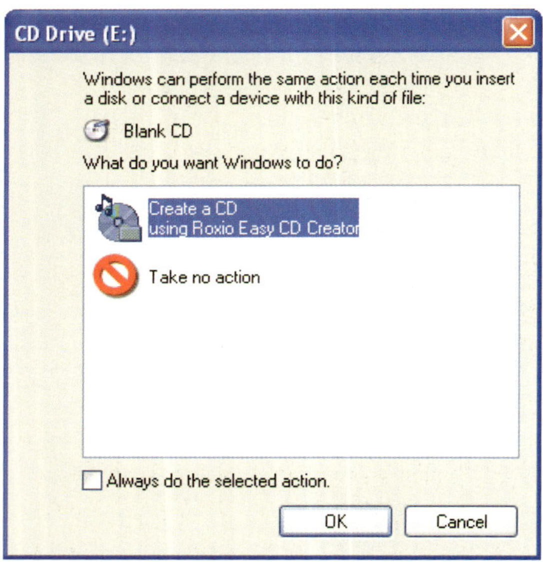

1. Insert a blank CD into the recordable CD drive. The CD Drive dialog box appears. Click **Cancel**.
2. Click **start** and then **My Computer**. The My Computer window opens.
3. Locate and open the drive and folder containing the image files you want to copy to CD.
4. Select the file or files you want to copy. (To select multiple images, hold down the **CTRL** key while clicking each file you want to copy.)

5. The step you take next depends on which folder your image files are stored in. If your pictures are stored the My Pictures folder, click **Copy to CD** in the task pane. If your pictures are stored in another folder, click **Copy this file** (for a single file), **Copy this folder** (for a folder), or **Copy the selected items** (for multiple files).

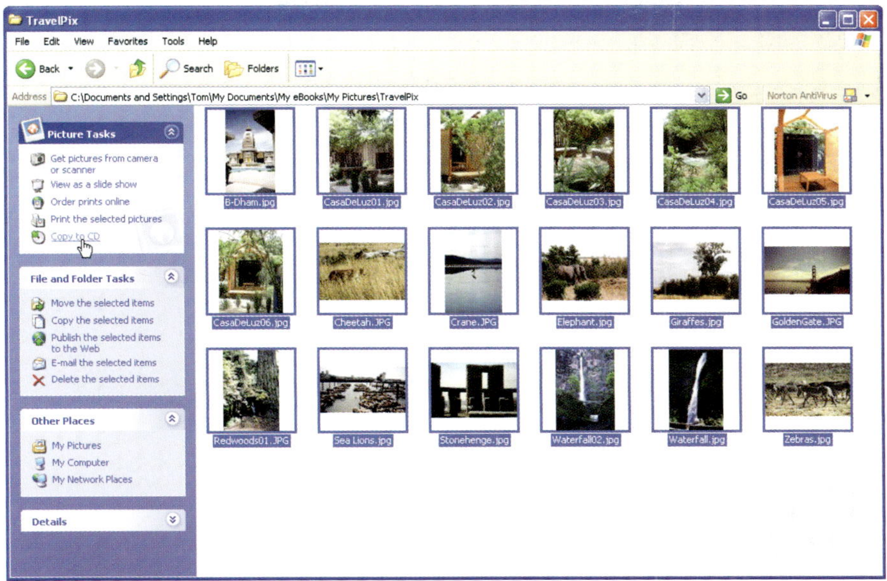

6. The Copy Items dialog box opens. Click the CD-R or CD-RW drive, and then click **Copy**.
7. The files are copied to the drive you selected in the previous step.

You can purchase blank CDs at computer stores, office supply stores, warehouse stores, and other places. Remember: CD-R drives can write only to CD-R discs, but CD-RW drives can write to both CD-R and CD-RW discs.

Because you copied the files to CD, rather than moving them, you must delete the originals from your hard drive and empty the Recycle Bin to free up space. (For help deleting image files and emptying the Recycle Bin, refer to the section "Deleting Files" earlier in this chapter.) Alternatively, you can leave the originals intact, and save the files on CD as backups in the event the original files become damaged or accidentally deleted.

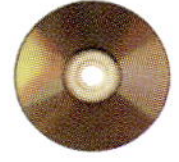

To learn about archiving and saving your pictures offline, go to the CD-ROM segment *Images: Archiving.*

Creating Digital Albums

Although using your computer's folder system or recordable CDs to store your digital images is practical. A more creative way to organize your images is by creating digital albums, much like the regular photo albums you use to store your photo prints. When you use digital photo albums, you select which pictures you want to include and arrange them in an order you choose. Both MGI PhotoSuite 4 and Microsoft Picture It! include features for creating photo albums. You'll now learn how to use these programs to accomplish this task.

Creating Digital Albums in MGI PhotoSuite 4

To create a digital photo album using PhotoSuite 4, do the following:

1. From within PhotoSuite 4, open the pictures you want to include in the album. The pictures are displayed in the Library.

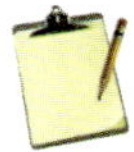

See Chapter 5 for help opening pictures in PhotoSuite 4.

2. Click **Organize**. In the Organize Activity panel, you can choose to open an existing album or create a new album.

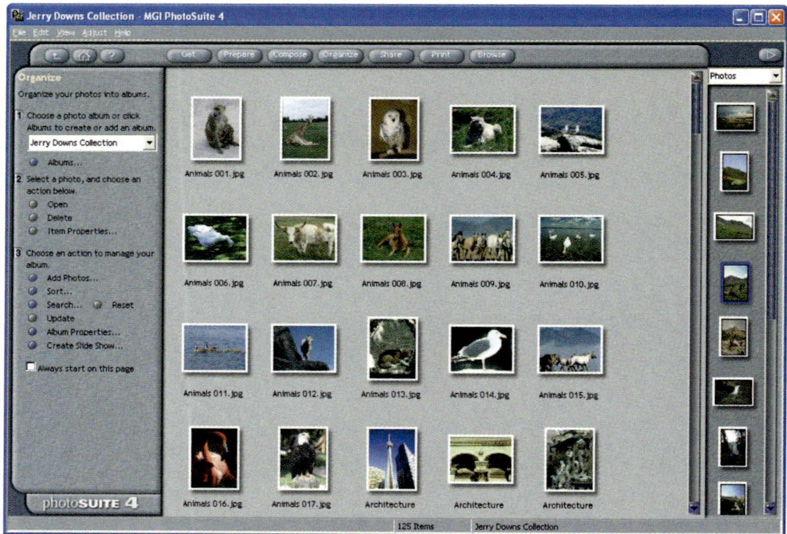

3. Click **Albums**. The Master Album dialog box opens.
4. Click **New**.

❺ Type a descriptive name for your album and click **OK**.

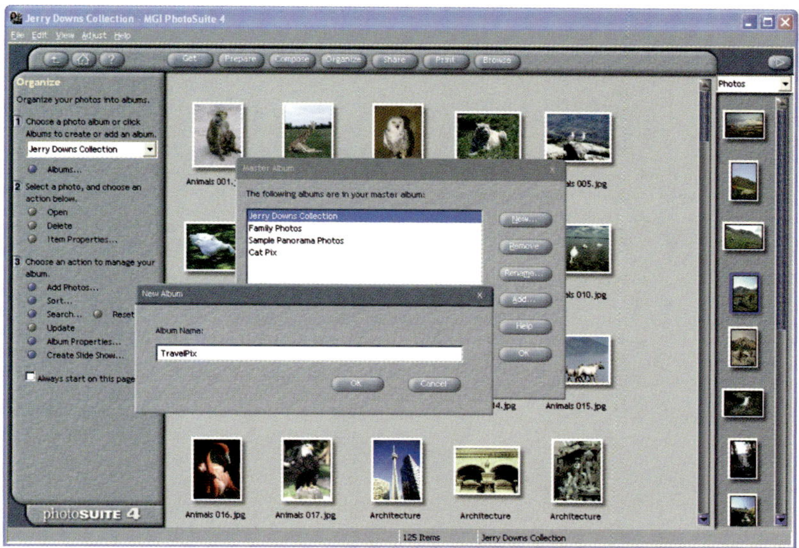

❻ Click your new album in the Master Album dialog box, and then click **OK** to open it.

❼ The album opens, and the next step is to add pictures.

❽ If you have images open, drag them from Library to the work area, arranging them in the order you want them to appear in the album. Alternately, click **Add Photos** in the Activity panel, then click **Computer**.

❾ The Add photo to Album dialog box appears. Navigate to the photos you want to add to the album, select them, and click **Add**.

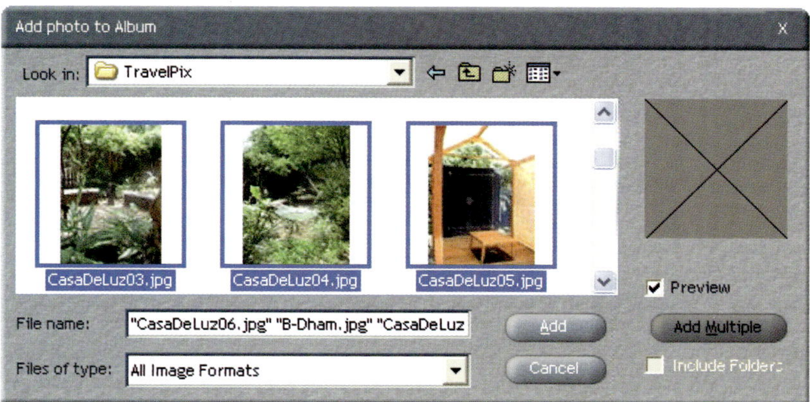

8

Once you've saved your album, you can select options in the Activity panel that enable you to delete pictures from the album, sort the pictures in the album, and set album properties (such as the size and whether a label is included). You can also print your album; refer to Chapter 7 for more information about printing.

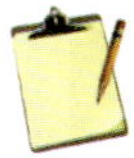

For information on other creative ideas, see Chapters 5 and 9.

Creating Digital Albums in Microsoft Picture It!

To create an album using Picture It!, do the following:

1. From within Picture It!, open the pictures you want to include in the album.

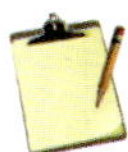

See Chapter 5 for help opening pictures in Picture It!.

2. The pictures are displayed in the Tray. Click **Pick a Design** in the Picture It! opening screen. A list of all the available design types appears.

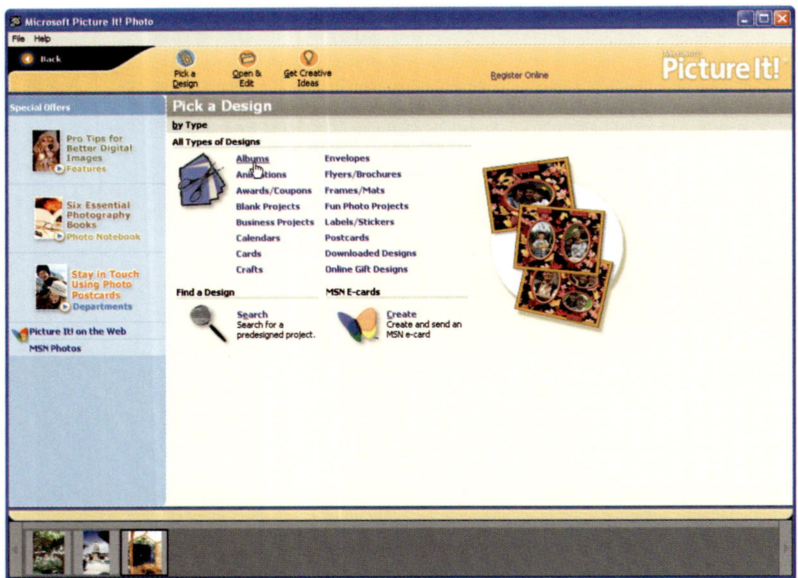

3. Click **Albums**.

4. Click **Album Pages** to view a list of design options for your album pages, including background images as well as placeholders for pictures. From the list that appears you can choose from several designs or themes, including Baby, Birthday, Family, General, Kids, Travel, Wedding, and Sports.
5. Click a design that relates to the photographs you want to include, and then click **Open**.

Although Picture It! displays several designs, some may not be installed on your computer. If you select a design that isn't installed, Picture It! prompts you to insert one of the program installation discs. Insert the disc and click **Retry**.

6. Drag a picture in the Tray to a placeholder on the album page; repeat for all placeholders on the page.

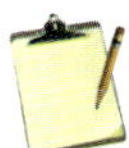

If you discover that you forgot to open a picture you want to include in your album, click **Open a picture** and add it.

7. If the album page includes any text placeholders, delete the text and replace it with your own. When each text box has been filled, click **Next**.
8. Drag a sizing handle to move or resize your images as needed. You can also flip images horizontally or vertically (refer to Chapter 5 for additional information on this action). When you're finished, click **Next**.

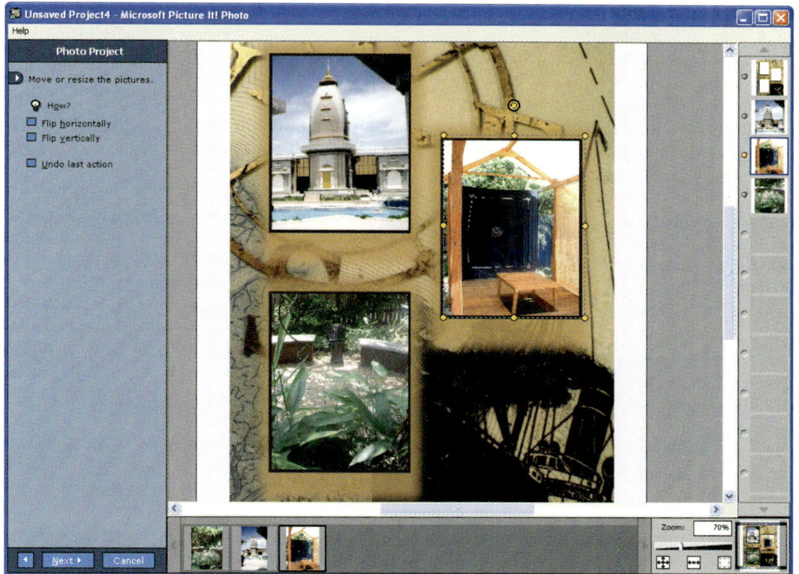

9. Click **Next**, then click **Done**.
10. Click **File** and then click **Save As . . .** navigate to the folder where you want the album stored and give it a descriptive name.

Once you've saved your album, you can add pages to it by repeating the steps just listed. When your album is complete, you can print it (refer to Chapter 7 for more information about printing).

More About . . . Microsoft Picture It! Designs

An album is only one of the projects you can complete using Picture It!. Others include cards, crafts, calendars, envelopes, papers, and collages. To experiment with these options, you can select them in the Pick a Design page. Alternatively, you can click **Blank Projects** in the Create Projects section of the opening Picture It! screen to choose from other options. For more information, consult Picture It! Help. You can also click **Get Creative Ideas** from the main screen.

Creating Digital Slide Shows

Even more exciting than creating digital photo albums is the ability to create slide shows of your digital photos; you can then use your computer to broadcast the slide show. In a slide show, each of the images is displayed full-screen on your computer, one after another. You can create a slide show of your images using Windows XP or your image-editing program.

A slide show is a great way to broadcast your photos over the Internet or share your photos via e-mail. Chapter 6 covers the specifics of displaying digital photographs online.

Creating a Slide Show in Windows XP

To create a slide show using Windows XP, follow these steps:

1. Place all the photos you want to include in one folder within the My Pictures folder.

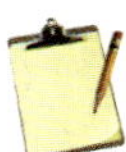

To access the slide show option in Windows XP, the photo files must be in the My Pictures folder or a subfolder therein.

2. Open the folder that contains these pictures.

3. In the task pane, click **View as a slide show**. Windows XP displays all the images in full-screen mode in a continuously running slide show.

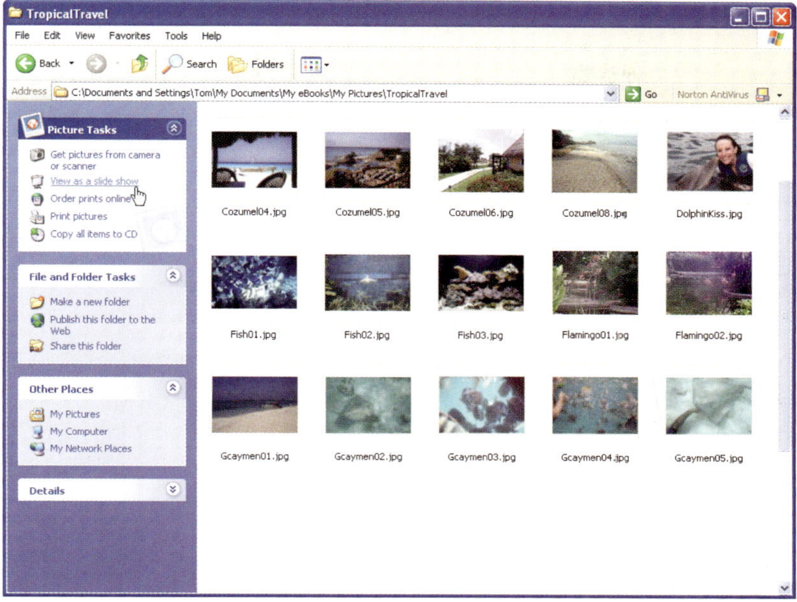

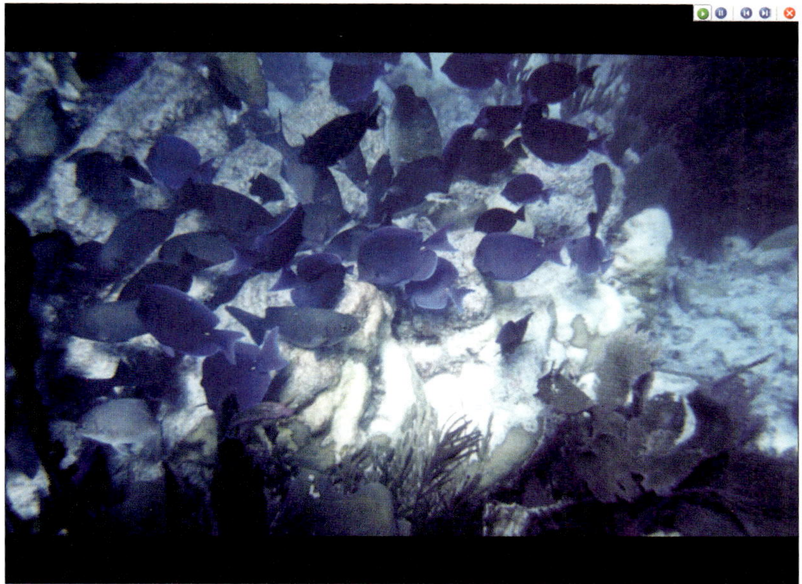

4. Move the mouse pointer to the upper right corner of the screen. A row of control buttons appears. Pause or close the slide show by clicking the appropriate button.

Creating a Slide Show in MGI PhotoSuite 4

To create a slide show in PhotoSuite 4, do the following:

1. From within PhotoSuite 4, open the pictures you want to include in the slide show. The pictures are displayed in the Library.

See Chapter 5 for help opening pictures in PhotoSuite 4.

2. Click **Organize**. The Organize Activity panel is displayed.

3. Click **Create Slide Show**.

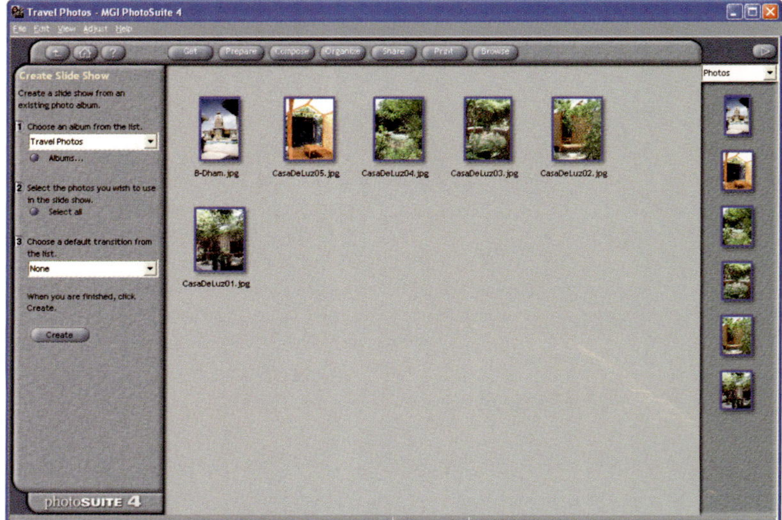

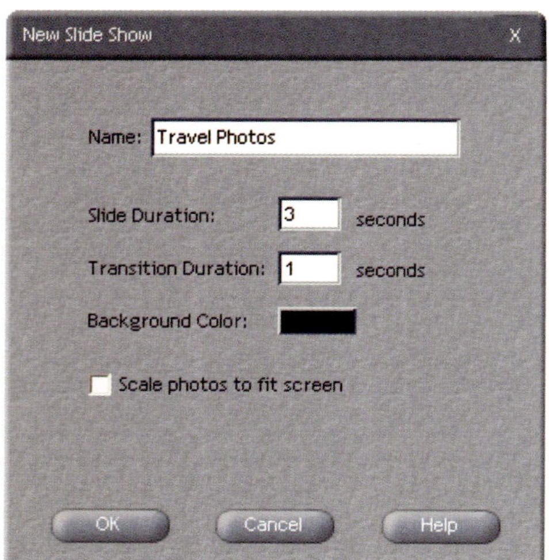

4. The Create Slide show Activity panel is displayed. You can choose to view items from an album, or select the images you opened in Step 1. After you've made your selection, click the **Create** button.
5. The New Slide show dialog box appears. From this screen, you can name the slide show; choose the duration of time each slide is displayed, the amount of time between transitions, background color, and whether to scale the photos to fit the screen. Select your desired settings and click **OK**.

6. The Edit Slide show screen is displayed. You can further customize the slide show with the options in the left pane or start the show with the buttons at the top of the screen, which work like standard CD or VCR buttons.

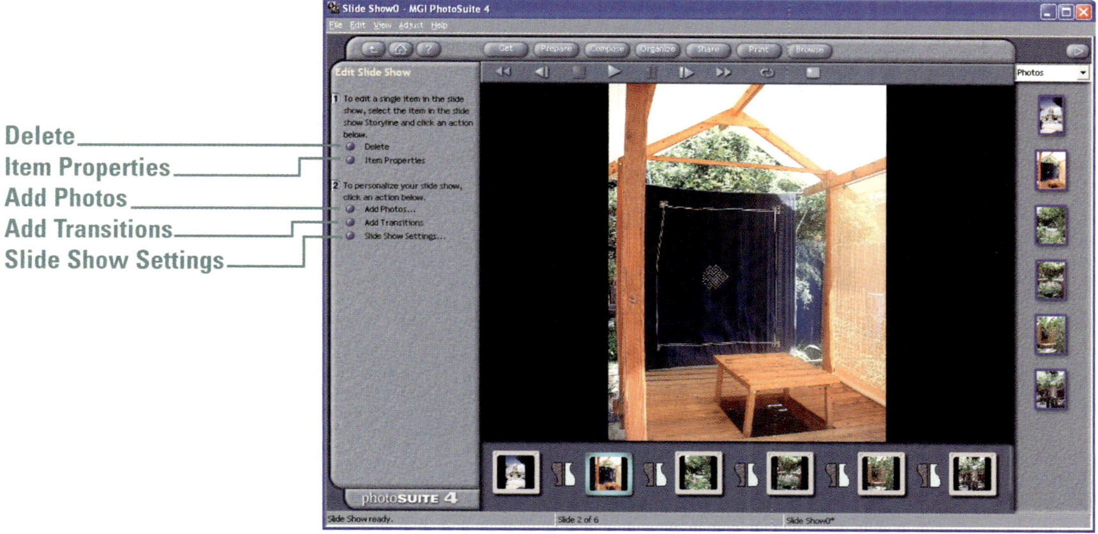

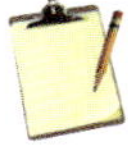

Use the approach just discussed when turning an album into a slide show; however, you can use a more direct approach using the Share Activity. Click **Share**, and then choose **Create From Scratch**. Set the options in the dialog box (slide duration, transition duration, background color, and slide show name). Then complete your slide show by adding your photos, and transitions.

Creating Slide Shows in Microsoft Picture It!

You can use Picture It! to create a flipbook (this is the same as a slide show). To do so, follow these steps:

1. From within Picture It!, open the pictures you want to include. The pictures are displayed in the Tray.

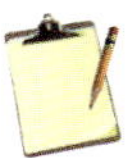

See Chapter 5 for help opening pictures in Picture It!.

2. Click **Pick a Design** in the Picture It! opening screen. A list of all the available designs appears.

3. Click **Animations**.

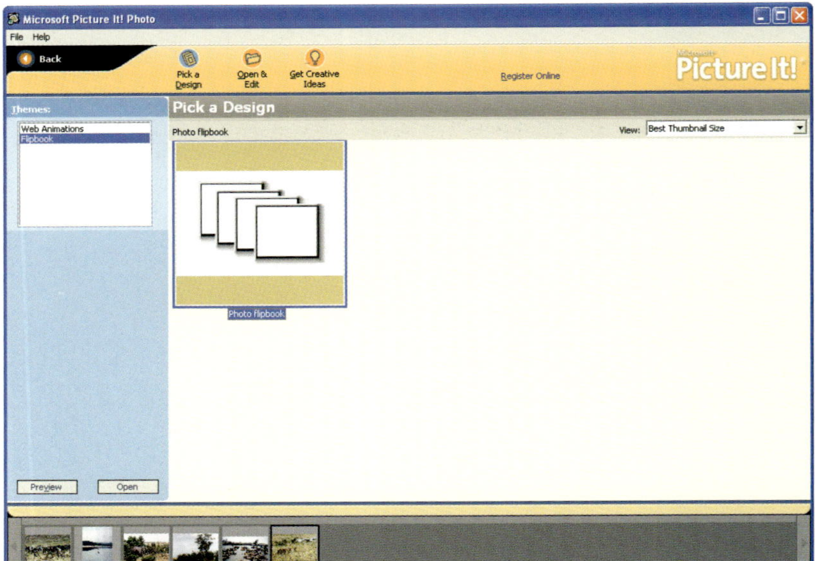

4. Click **Flipbook** in the Themes pane on the left, then select the Photo flipbook on the right, and click **Open**. The FlipBook Animation screen appears.

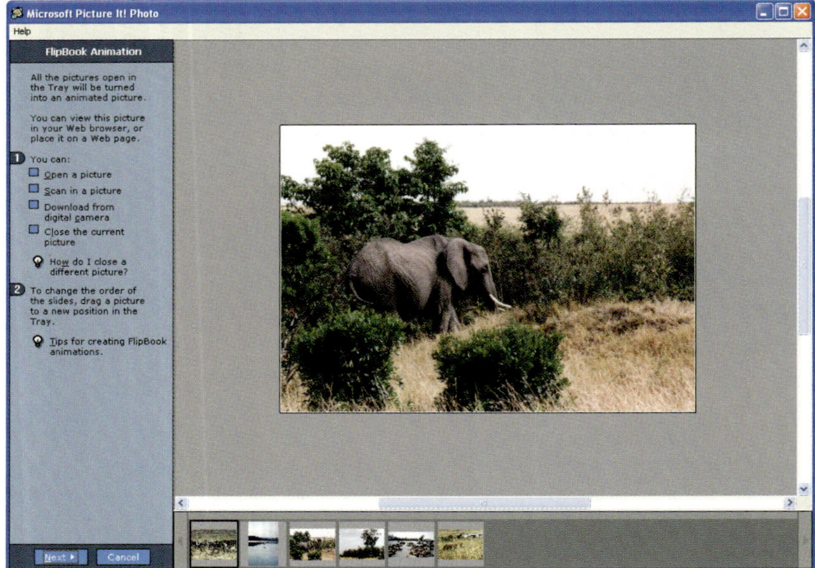

5. From this screen, you can select to add additional photos (from your computer, scanner, or digital camera), close the current picture, and change the order of the slides. Make any needed changes and click **Next**.
6. The next screen that appears allows you to choose whether you want a patterned or solid background. Select your desired background and click **Next**.

7. On the next screen that appears, choose your desired picture size, then click **Next**.
8. Next, choose the duration for the presentation and whether to play it once or loop continuously, then click **Next**.
9. On the next screen, the photos you selected are displayed as a flipbook. After you're done viewing the show, click **Save it**.
10. Navigate to where you want the flipbook to be stored, type a file name, then click **Save**.

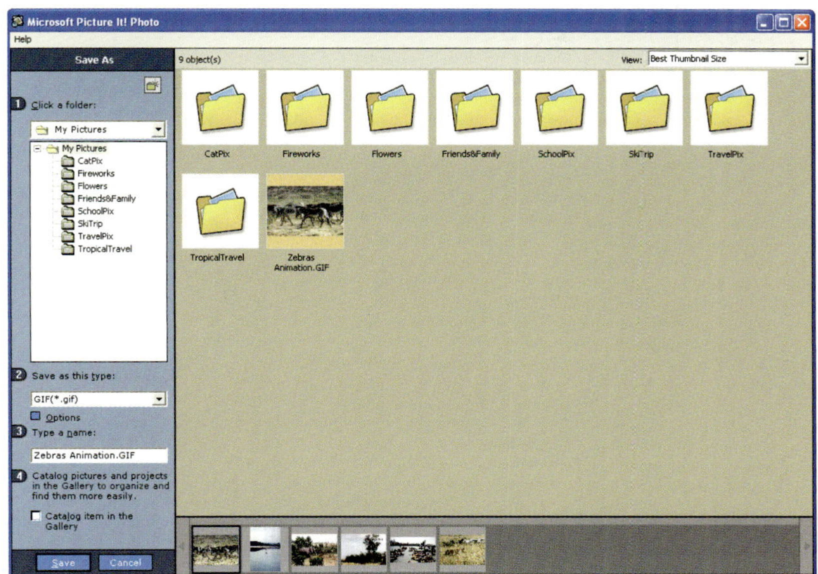

To Keep on Learning . . .

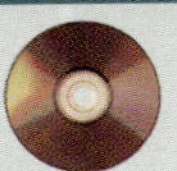

Go to the CD-ROM and select the segment:

- *Images: Organizing* to gain an understanding of the benefits and guidelines for organizing your pictures.
- *Images: Archiving* to learn about archiving and saving your pictures offline.

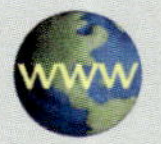

Go online to **www.LearnwithGateway.com** and log on to select:

- *Internet links and resources*
- *FAQs*

With the *Survive & Thrive* series, refer to *Use and Care for Your PC* for more information on:

- Folder structure and file management with Windows XP
- Using a CD burner

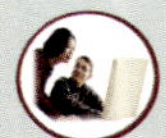

Gateway offers a hands-on training course that covers many of the topics in this chapter. Additional fees may apply. Call **888-852-4821** for enrollment information. If applicable, please have your customer ID and order number ready when you call.

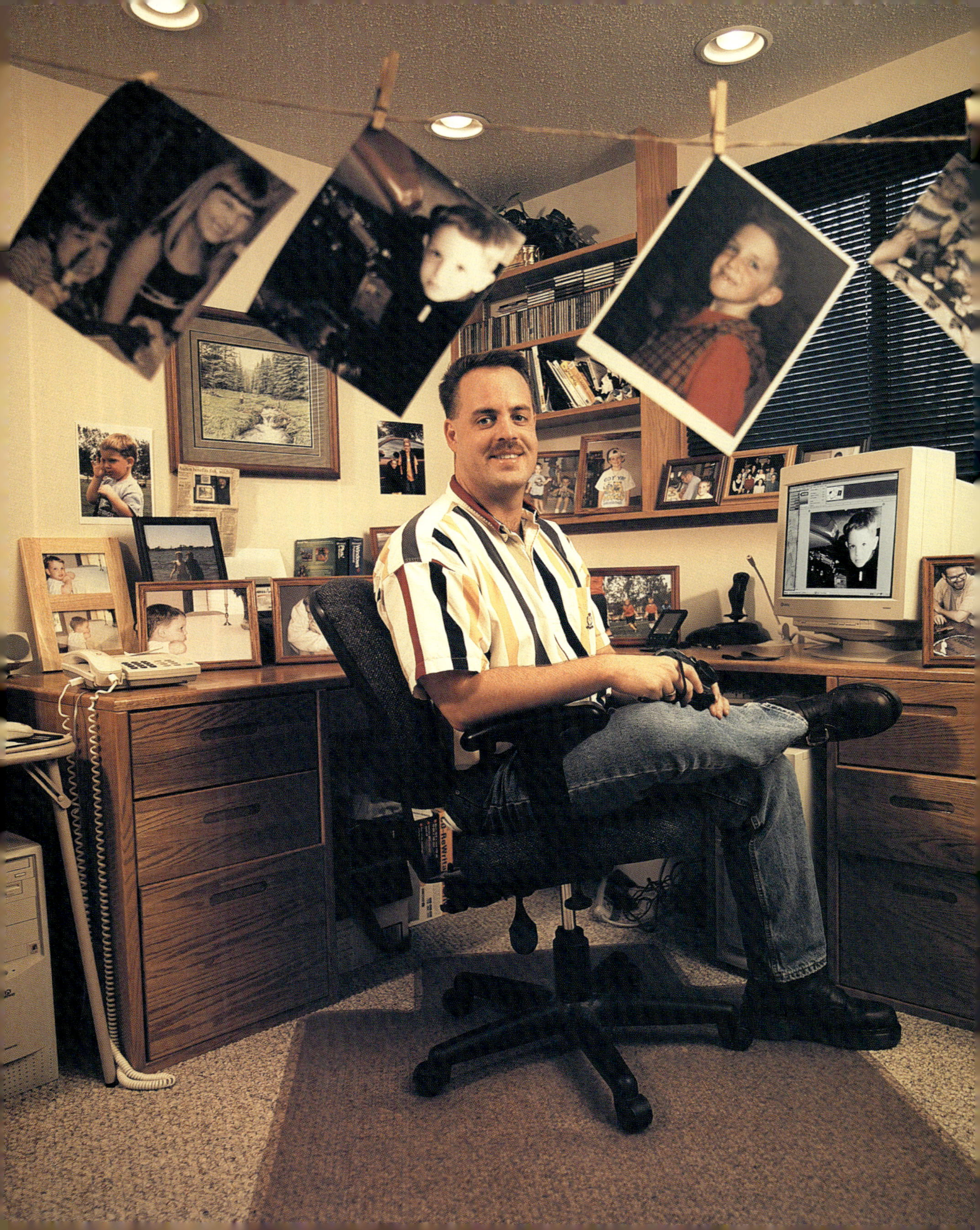

CHAPTER 9

Taking the Next Step in Digital Photography

Although this book provides a solid foundation for developing your skills in digital imaging, it only scratches the surface when it comes to the many options you have for producing exceptional digital images and the many creative things you can do with your photos. In this chapter, you'll explore features of digital cameras and image-editing software that can help you take digital photography to the next level. Then, you'll examine troubleshooting techniques you can use to rectify hardware problems (in particular, problems with your scanner or digital camera) as well as problems with your photos.

Exploring More Camera and Image-Editing Features

Now that you've mastered the basics of digital photography, you're ready to accept new challenges. In this section, you'll learn more about features of digital cameras and image-editing programs that can help you take that next step. You'll also learn about some Web resources you can use to expand your knowledge.

Exploring Your Camera Features

In Chapter 3, you gained some fundamental skills for taking digital photos. As you read Chapter 3, however, you probably sensed that most cameras—digital and otherwise—sport several additional features that you can use to refine your photographic technique.

Indeed, there are entire books devoted to the topic of camera technology and how it can be used to take good pictures—with tips and explanations about composition, special effects, lighting considerations, aperture settings, and more. See Chapter 3 for a complete discussion of these settings. Before immersing yourself in such a book, however, try the following:

- ✦ Read your camera manual. It may not be exciting reading, but it may be the best way to learn about additional features of your camera that will help you improve your photos.

✦ Read articles online or in magazines that describe some of the more complex photography concepts such as f-stops and shutter speeds.

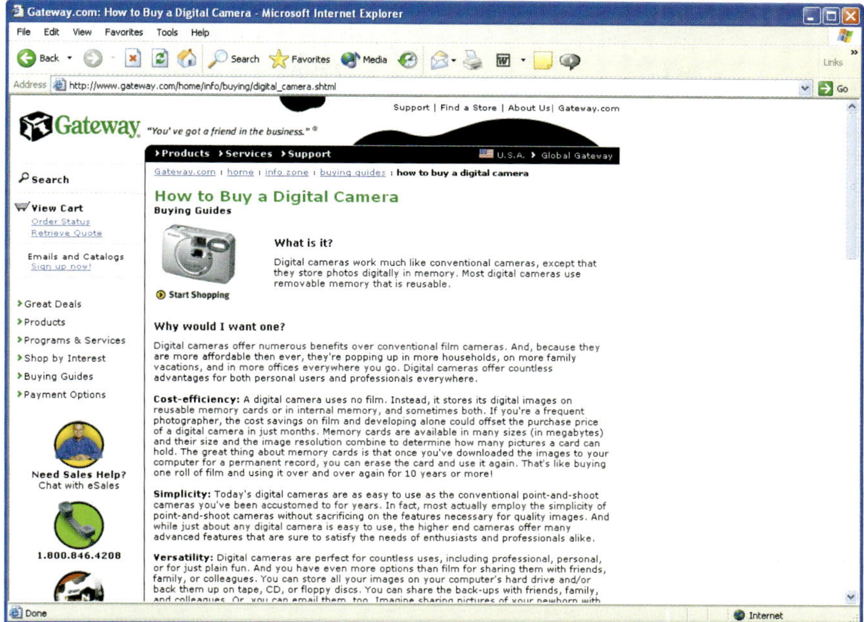

✦ Don't be afraid to experiment! You have nothing to lose. In fact, most of the best photographers will tell you there are no hard-and-fast rules when it comes to taking pictures. For the most part, you learn by trial and error.

✦ If you want to specialize in a particular type of photography (such as portraits, sports photography, or nature photography), investigate the camera features that work best for that type. If your interest lies in sports photography, for example, you'll probably want a camera with shutter-speed and lighting settings that differ from those you'd need if you planned to photograph bears in their native habitat.

Exploring Your Image-Editing Program

Of course, your digital camera isn't alone in offering advanced features designed to help you improve the look of your digital photos. Chances are, your image-editing program features all sorts of tools to help you get the most out of your images. You learned the basics of image editing in Chapter 5; what follows here is a sampling of ways you can use your image-editing program to improve your images.

For specific instructions on using your image-editing program to accomplish these tasks, read its user manual or Help. And don't be afraid to experiment!

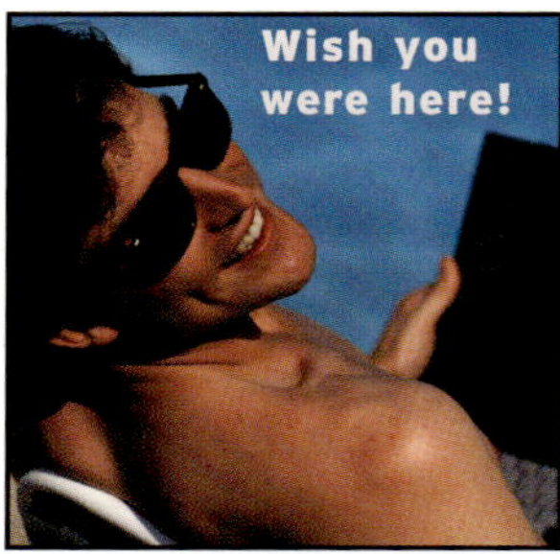

- **Annotate your images.** Add text, clip art, or other graphic objects to your image. You can also draw on the image using different brushes.

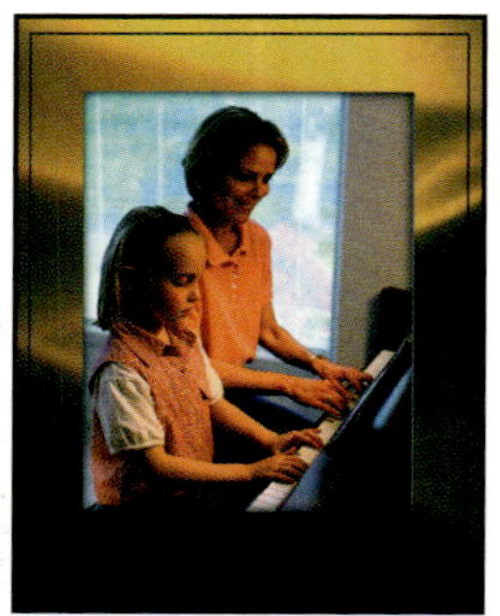

- **Add borders.** Add a border, frame, or mat to your picture, using the many patterns that range from checkered bars to fancy frames.

- **Apply filters.** Use *filters* to create special effects in your images. As an example, the Artistic Paintings filter in PhotoSuite 4 has been applied to the image shown here.

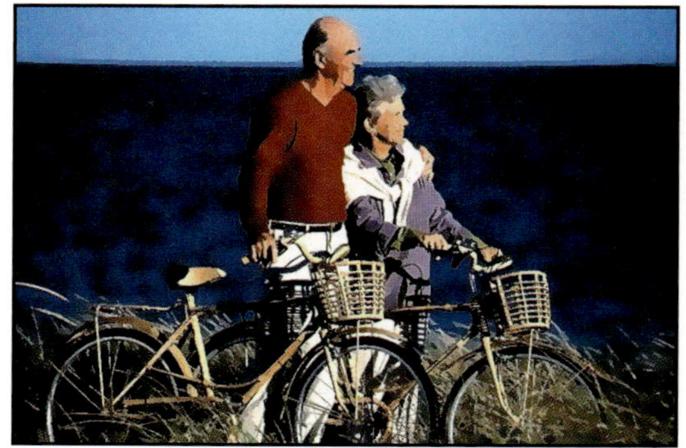

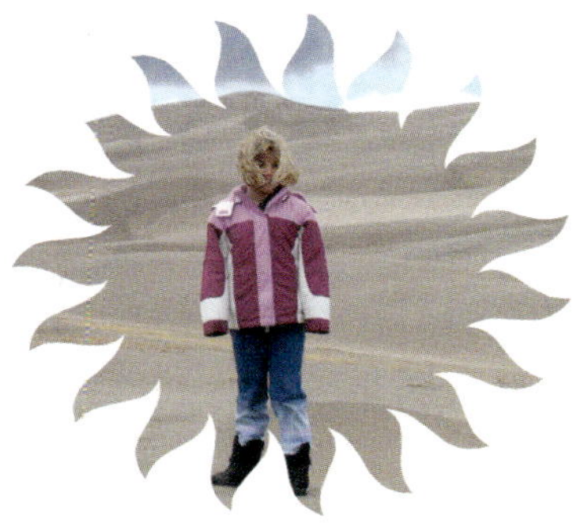

- **Crop the image.** Use fanciful cropping options to add interest to pictures for a scrapbook, for example.

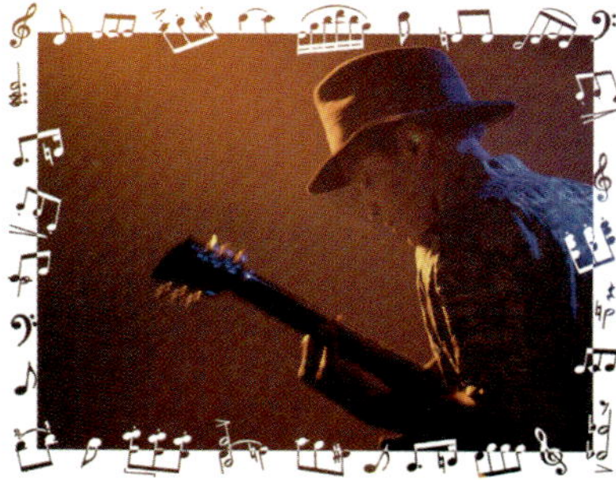

- **Apply edges.** Apply effects to the edges of the photograph itself. You can use unique designs, soft edges, or stamped edges, to name a few options.
- **Combine images.** Combine multiple images to create a new one.
- **Repair old pictures.** Repair old family photos marred by tears, stains, dust, scratches, or other blemishes. See Chapter 5 for a discussion on touching up images.

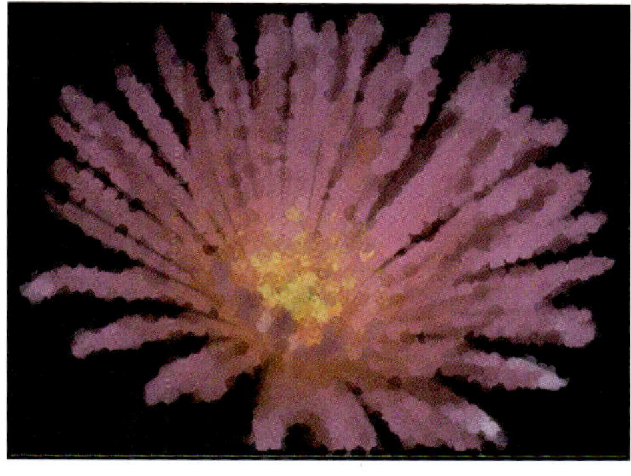

- **Apply special effects.** Create a photo mosaic or tapestry.

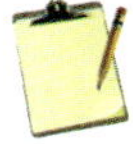

As your skills in digital imaging expand, you may want to consider using an image-editing program with advanced features, such as Adobe Photoshop.

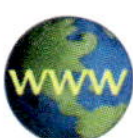

To learn more about creative ideas for digital photos, see the table at the end of this chapter.

Exploring Online Options

In Chapters 6 and 7, you learned how to share pictures online and how to use online printing sources, respectively. Not surprisingly, these aren't the only ways you can use the Web to enhance your digital photography experience. Consider the following additional ways you can explore the Internet:

- **Join an online photography discussion.** To share your interest with other photographers, consider joining one or several photography discussion groups (also called *newsgroups* or *forums*). You can also subscribe to photography-related *mailing lists,* which are newsletters that are e-mailed to you periodically.

- **Order or get how-to information about craft projects.** You can go online to learn how to make buttons, posters, mugs, refrigerator magnets, calendars, family trees, T-shirts, or just about any other items that feature your favorite digital photo.

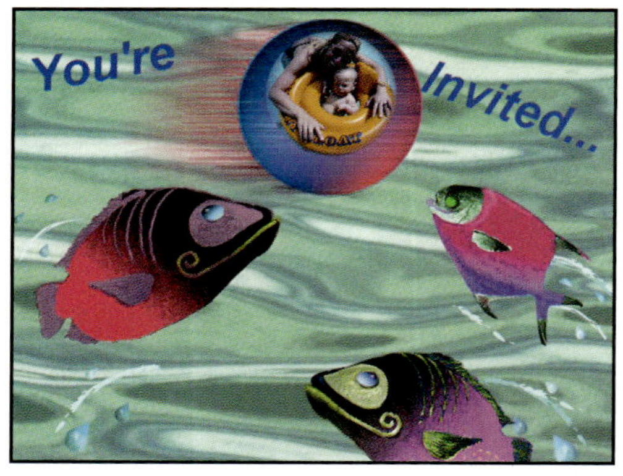

- **Create digital stationery.** Create and send picture postcards via e-mail, or learn how to print high-quality invitations or note cards that feature your photos.

- **Sell your photos.** Use an online auction site or create your own Web site to sell prints of your best photos.

- **Learn from other photographers.** There are numerous sites on the Web dedicated to all sorts of photography subjects. Visit other photographers' Web sites to see examples of excellent photography and perhaps read up on a few pointers. Additionally, most image editing programs come with sample photos that you can browse for inspiration.

- **Upgrade your digital-photography equipment.** As you gain experience in digital photography, you may decide you want additional equipment, such as a photo printer, special lenses, battery chargers, and so on. The Internet is a good place to look for advice as well as to comparison-shop.

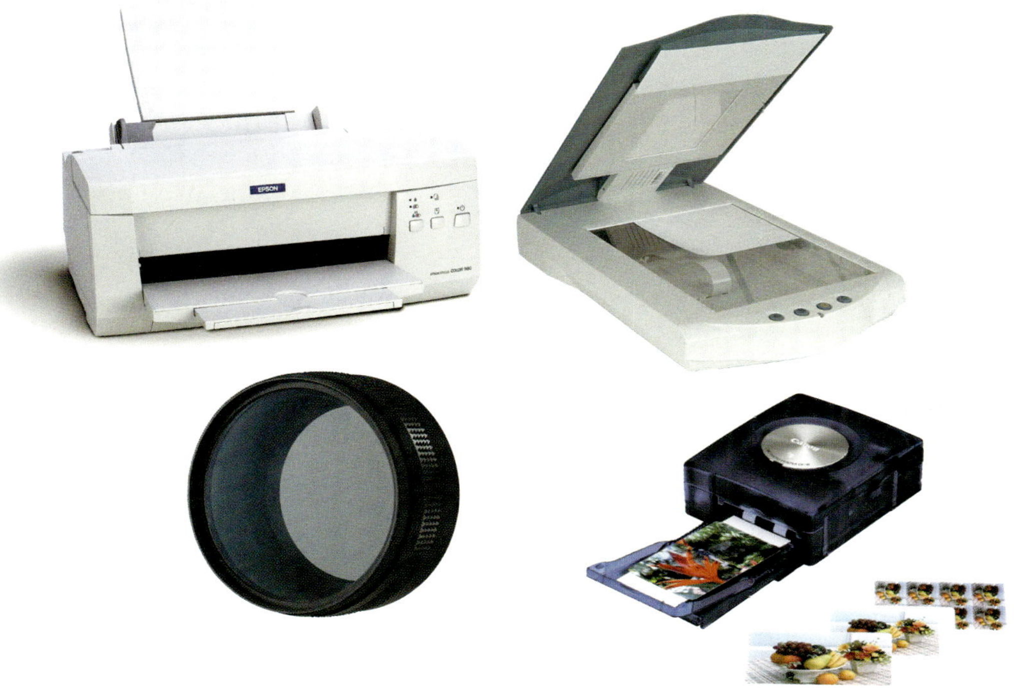

More About . . . Copyrighting Images

You should always add a copyright notice to any images you publish online. A photographer owns a natural copyright to his or her work whether the image is officially copyrighted through the government or not. However, recovering damages in a court of law may be more difficult if the work is not officially copyrighted.

For more addition on registering copyrights, contact the Register of Copyrights, The Library of Congress, Washington, DC 20559. You can also visit their Web site.

To officially register a copyright, you must fill out a form, pay a nonrefundable filing fee for each application, and submit a non-returnable copy of the image. You can also copyright a collection of images. Finally, some image-editing programs allow you to embed a message or copyright notice in the image itself for added protection.

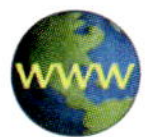

If you intend to sell your photos, or if you don't want them distributed without your permission, be sure to copyright them. See the table at the end of this chapter for more information on copyrights.

Troubleshooting Hardware Problems

You may occasionally encounter problems with your digital imaging equipment. Your camera may stop working properly or fail to communicate with your computer's operating system, your scanner may fail to scan an image you've placed on its bed, or your printer may fail to print your images. In this section, you'll learn how to rectify some of the equipment problems you may encounter.

Troubleshooting Camera Problems

When using your digital camera, you can prevent all sorts of equipment problems by adhering to these guidelines:

- Don't expose the camera to extreme heat or cold.
- Keep liquids (water, suntan lotion, soda, and so on) away from the camera.
- Keep the lens clean. You can clean it by gently blowing on it or by wiping it with a lint-free cloth. Don't use any type of cleaning solution!

If you've followed these rules but are still experiencing problems taking pictures with your camera, take the following steps:

1. Make sure the camera is turned on and that the lens is completely uncovered. (Be sure to remove or slide the lens cover to the side until it clicks into place.)

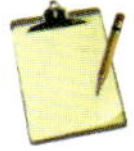

If the camera won't turn on, your batteries may be dead. Recharge or replace your batteries.

2. Make sure you're in the proper mode. If you're in Preview or Playback mode, you can't shoot pictures. Refer to Chapter 3 for more information about modes.

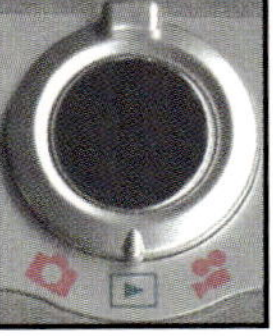

3. If the camera is on but you can't press the shutter button, it may be because the camera is busy doing something else. Wait until any lights on the camera stop blinking.
4. Determine whether you've run out of space to store images (the LCD usually displays an error message when this happens). If you have, delete images you don't want from the camera or media card, or download them to your computer to free up memory for additional pictures. Also, make sure your media card is inserted in the camera. If you forget to put it in, you won't be able to take pictures at all. Make it a habit to always check before setting out on any photography foray.

If your camera takes pictures as it should but you're having problems transferring your images to your computer, check the following:

1. Loose cables are a common source of problems. Make sure the camera's cable is plugged into the appropriate port on the computer and into the correct socket on the camera. If you're transferring images from a media card, be sure the media card is inserted properly. Try removing the card and reinserting it.

If you're using a media card, be sure it's compatible with your camera. If your camera only uses CompactFlash media, for example, you can't use the SmartMedia card.

2. Make sure the camera is turned on. Images can't be transferred if the camera is turned off.

If your camera still can't communicate with your computer to transfer images, you can use Windows XP to pinpoint the problem and locate possible solutions. Here's how:

1. Click **start**.
2. In the start menu, right-click **My Computer**, then click **Properties** in the shortcut menu. The System Properties dialog box opens.

Be sure to right-click **My Computer**. If you left-click it, Windows opens the My Computer folder instead of a shortcut menu.

3. In the System Properties dialog box, click the **Hardware** tab.
4. Click **Device Manager**. The Device Manager window opens.

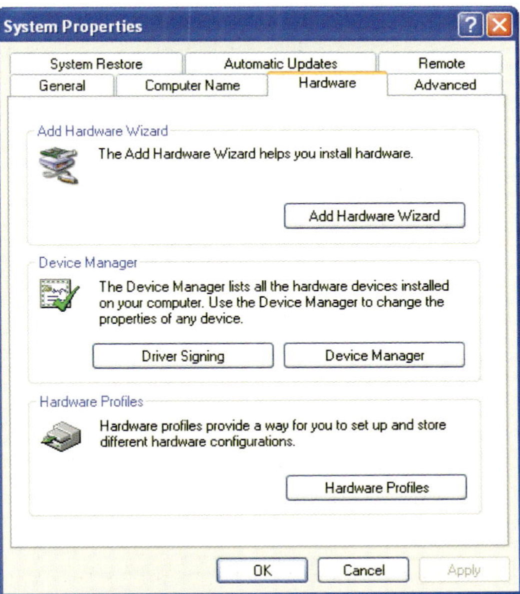

5. Click the plus sign next to **Imaging devices**. The Imaging devices list expands; you should see your camera listed.

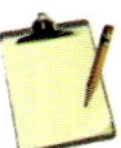

If your camera isn't listed in the Imaging devices list, click the plus sign next to **Universal Serial Bus controllers**. It may be listed there instead. If you don't find it there, the problem may be that the software that came with it hasn't been properly installed on your computer. Reinstall the software (refer to Chapter 3 for instructions) to see if that fixes the problem.

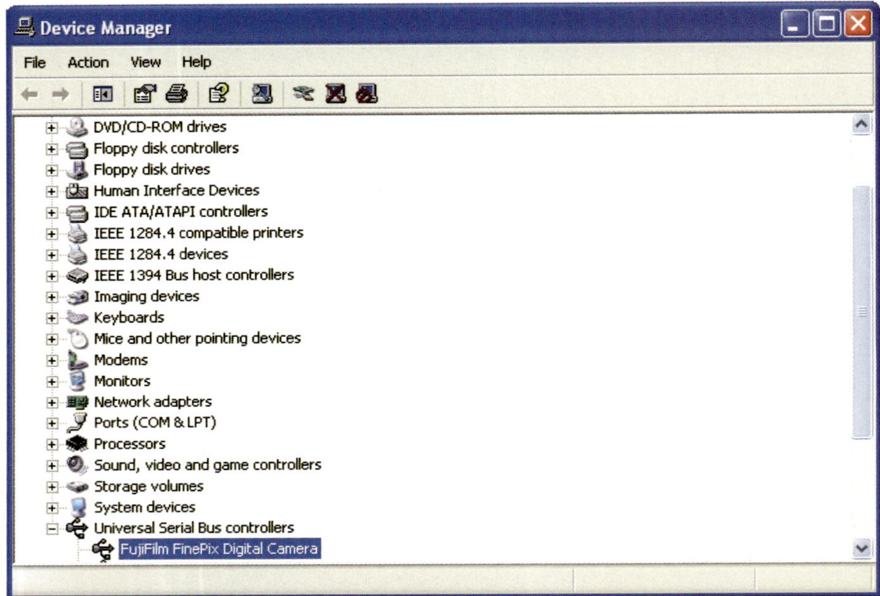

6. Right-click the camera name and choose **Properties** in the shortcut menu that appears.
7. The Properties dialog box opens, with its General tab displayed; this tab lists information about your camera. Click **Troubleshoot** to start the Troubleshooting Wizard.
8. The Windows Help and Support Center window opens. Click **I am having a problem with my camera/universal serial bus (USB) device**, and then click **Next**.

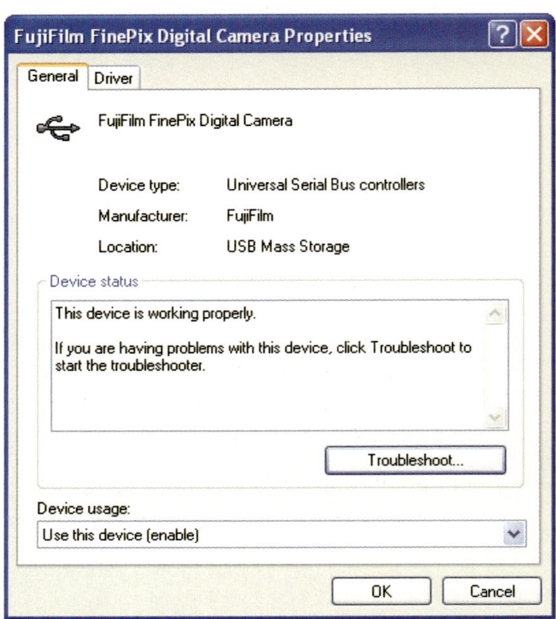

9. Read the information that appears, and select options to pinpoint the problem. After you select an option, click **Next**; the Wizard prompts you to choose among possible remedies. Continue choosing options and trying the remedies until the problem is resolved.
10. Click Close to close the Help and Support Center window.

Troubleshooting Scanner Problems

Just as you can use Windows XP to determine why your camera isn't communicating with your computer, you can use it to resolve problems with your scanner. In fact, the process of troubleshooting scanner problems is almost identical to the process of troubleshooting camera problems. Here's how it's done:

1. In the Device Manager window, click the plus sign next to **Imaging devices**.

If you need help opening the Device Manager window, refer to Steps 1–4 of the last exercise in the preceding section.

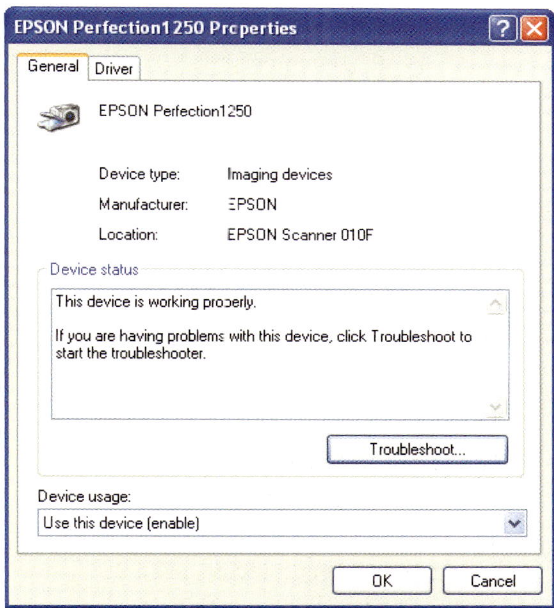

2. The **Imaging devices** list expands; you should see your scanner listed. Right-click the scanner name and click **Properties** in the shortcut menu that appears.

If your scanner isn't listed, the problem may be that the software that came with it hasn't been properly installed on your computer. Reinstall the software (refer to Chapter 4 for instructions) to see if that fixes the problem. Alternatively, uninstall and then reinstall the scanner's driver using the commands on the driver tab.

3. The Properties dialog box opens, with its General tab displayed; this tab lists information about your scanner. Click **Troubleshoot** to start the Troubleshooting Wizard.

4. The Windows Help and Support Center window opens. Click **I am having a problem with my scanner**, and then click **Next**.

Gateway computers have a customized version of the Windows XP Help and Support Center called the Gateway HelpSpot™.

5. Read the information that appears, and select options to pinpoint the problem. The Wizard first asks how your scanner is connected. Click **parallel port** or **USB**, as appropriate, and then click **Next**. The Wizard then asks you to double-check that the device is turned on and connected; do this and click **Next**. Follow each step, clicking **Next** to advance to the next screen, until the problem is resolved.
6. Click **Close** to close the Help and Support Center window.

Troubleshooting Printer Problems

If your printer isn't working, perform the following steps. After each step, try to print to see whether the problem has been corrected.

1. Verify that the printer is turned on (usually indicated by a light on the printer).
2. Press the printer's **Reset** button (or a similarly named button) to clear any errors.
3. Make sure there's paper in the paper tray. If the paper tray is removable, make sure it's inserted properly. Also, while inspecting the paper tray, make sure the paper isn't creased or torn, as this could cause paper jams.
4. Make sure that all covers, lids, doors, and other printer components are closed.
5. Make sure the printer's power supply is, in fact, supplying power. Plug something else into the outlet, such as a lamp, to see if it's working properly.
6. Check that there is ink or toner in the printer. If there isn't, replace the ink or toner cartridge (check your printer's user guide for instructions).
7. Disconnect and reconnect every cable connected to your printer. Be sure to disconnect and reconnect the cable connecting your printer to your computer at both ends. Types of printer cables include parallel, serial, USB, and power.

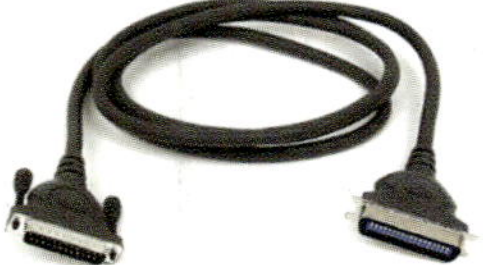

Parallel

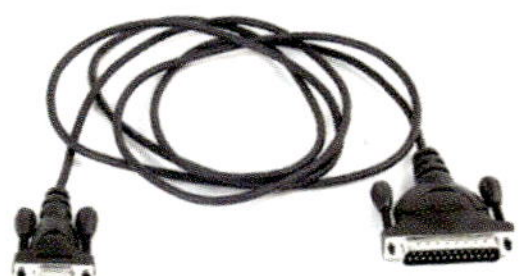

Serial

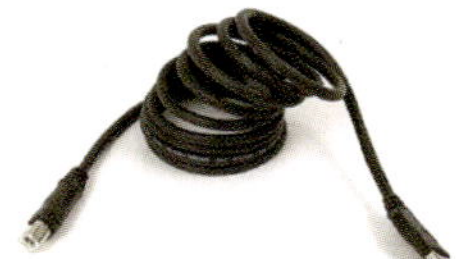

USB

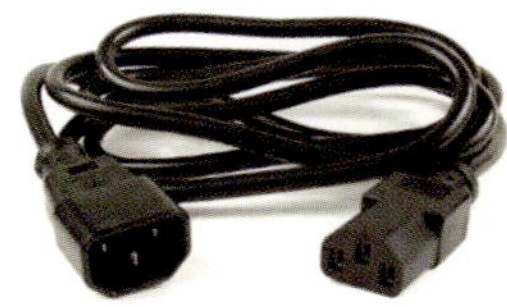

Power

8. Turn your printer off and back on three times. Wait about 15 seconds between switches. Cycling the power should clear the printer's memory; it may take three cycles to accomplish this.
9. Make sure your printer's software and drivers are installed on your computer. Try reinstalling them if they've become corrupted.

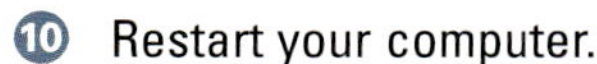

10. Restart your computer.

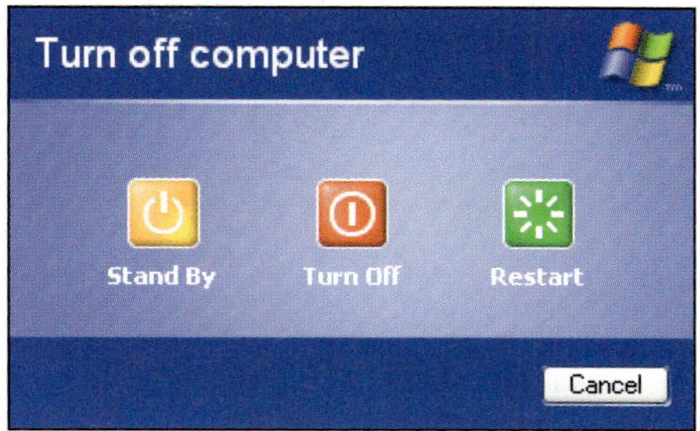

If your printer still doesn't work, you can use Windows XP's Troubleshooting Wizard to pinpoint the problem. Follow the steps outlined in the last exercise in the "Troubleshooting Camera Problems" section in this chapter, only at Step 5 select the printer as the imaging device you want to troubleshoot.

If your printer prints your digital images but the printouts are of poor quality, the printer probably isn't capable of printing high-quality images. To take an example, if your photo's resolution is 1,800 × 1,200 ppi, but your printer is only capable of printing at 300 dpi, that printer will render your image poorly on paper. Consider other printing options, such as online services or your local photo lab or print shop.

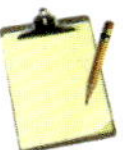

If you ordered prints of your images online and their quality is poor, you may need to shoot your photographs using a higher quality (resolution) setting on your digital camera. (Fortunately, most online photo services allow you to return fuzzy or bad pictures for a refund.)

Troubleshooting Picture Problems

One of the great things about digital photography is that you can use your camera's LCD screen to view your photos immediately after shooting them. This affords you the opportunity to immediately retake pictures whose image quality isn't up to snuff. Is there something blocking the picture (such as your finger)? If so, simply delete the image, move the offending digit away from the lens, and start again.

Unfortunately, the causes of some photo problems aren't always obvious. In following list, you'll discover what causes some common problems and how you can correct them:

- If the picture is too light, it may be because of your camera's flash. Try taking the same picture without the flash. Another possibility is that you were too close to your subject. If your camera has auto flash settings, use them for good exposure every time.
- If the picture is out of focus take it again, but this time be sure to press the shutter button halfway down to initiate the camera's auto-focus feature. Then press the button all the way down to take the picture.

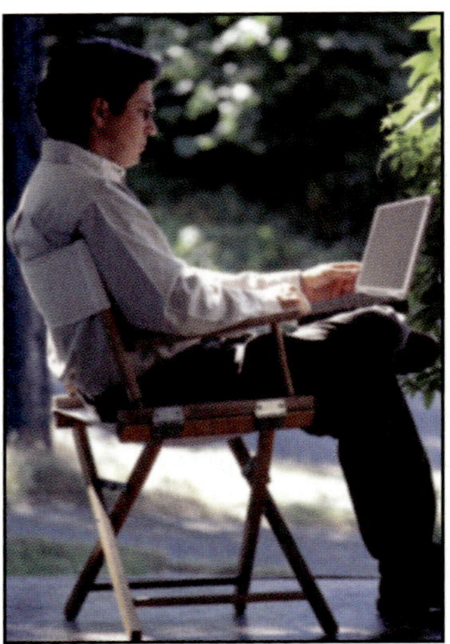

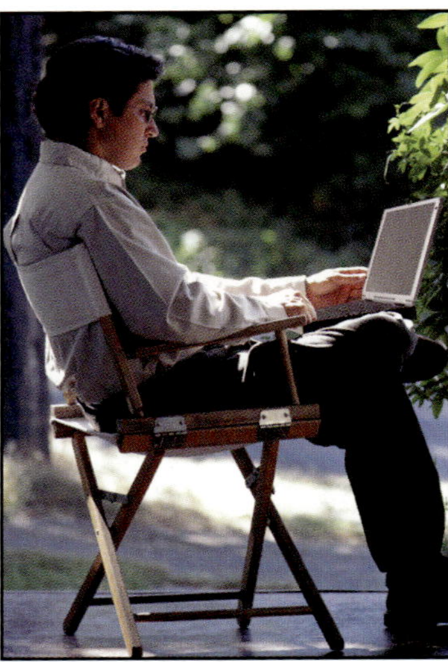

- If the picture isn't clear, make sure the lens is clean. You may also need to zoom in or out or stand closer or farther away to your subject. If you're photographing something in motion, make sure you hold the camera steady; you may even need to consider using a tripod.
- If the image isn't as sharp as you'd like, try shooting the picture at a higher resolution.

To Keep on Learning . . .

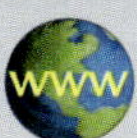

Go online to **www.LearnwithGateway.com** and log on to select:

- *Internet Links and Resources*
  - *Creative ideas for digital photos*
  - *Copyright information*
- *FAQs*

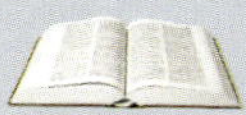

With the *Survive & Thrive* series, refer to *Use and Care for Your PC* for more information on:

- *Troubleshooting hardware devices*

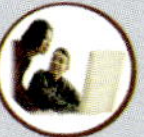

Gateway offers a hands-on training course that covers many of the topics in this chapter. Additional fees may apply. Call **888-852-4821** for enrollment information. If applicable, please have your customer ID and order number ready when you call.

Glossary

aperture The opening in a camera lens through which light passes to produce an image.

arrays Sensors in digital cameras that convert light information from the scene being photographed into a digital image. See *charge coupled device.*

automatic A setting available on some cameras that automatically sets the focus, f-stop, and depth of field. See *focus, f-stop,* and *depth of field.*

battery compartment The slot on a camera where the batteries are stored.

bit Color information is stored in bits; the more bits, the better the range of colors represented.

camera scroll buttons Buttons on a digital camera that enable the user to move among camera commands or pictures stored in the camera's memory.

CD-R drive A drive on a computer that can be used to copy information from a computer to a CD (compact disc) once.

CD-ROM drive A drive on a computer that reads CDs.

CD-RW drive A drive on a computer that can be used to copy information from a computer to a CD (compact disc) more than once.

charge coupled device (CCD) A light sensor in a digital camera.

CompactFlash One commonly used media card. See *media card.*

composition The organization of subject and background in a photograph. The way you compose your image.

connection port An interface on a computer to which you can connect devices with cables, plugs, and other connectors.

CPU Stands for central processing unit. The CPU is the core component of a computer. It interprets and carries out instructions and performs computations.

crop To remove a portion of an image.

depth of field The area of a picture that is in sharp focus.

digital album Like a conventional photo album, a way to present and arrange pictures in a digital format.

digital image Any image that has been created by a source, such as a digital camera, and converted electronically to be viewed on a computer. See *pixel* and *scanner.*

digital zoom A feature of some digital cameras that mimics optical zoom. With digital zoom, the camera photographs an entire scene but saves only a portion of it or expands a portion by adding pixels. The same effect can be obtained using an image-editing program. See *optical zoom.*

docking station A component that can be attached to a computer to transfer images from a digital camera to the computer.

download The process of copying images from a digital camera to a computer. Also refers to copying files from the Internet to a computer.

driver A file that tells the operating system the details of a particular hardware component, such as a printer, digital camera, or scanner. When the component is installed on a computer, a driver for it is copied to the computer.

dpi The standard measurement of resolution used with printed images; stands for dots per inch. Generally, a higher dpi indicates higher resolution. See *resolution.*

DVD A high-capacity optical storage media; a DVD looks like a CD.

exposure The process of exposing a camera's image sensor or film to light to create an image. Exposure is affected by settings such as focus, aperture, and shutter speed.

file format The organization of data in a computer file that enables a program to process it. Different programs can open and work with different file formats. Popular formats for digital image files include JPEG and TIFF. See *JPEG* and *TIFF*.

film scanner A device used to convert negatives and slides into digital files. See *scanner*.

flash A device used to produce a bright flash of light to illuminate the subject of a photograph.

flatbed scanner A device that converts text or images into digital files using a moving light source similar to that used by a copier. Flatbed scanners are the most common type of scanner. See *scanner*.

focal length The distance between a camera lens and the image the lens creates. A shorter focal length creates a wider angle of view, whereas a longer focal length creates a narrower angle of view focusing in on the subject of the photograph.

focus Adjustment of the distance setting on a lens to define the subject sharply. This can be done automatically or manually.

f-stop A manual setting whereby the diameter of the aperture is adjusted to change the depth of field. See *depth of field* and *aperture*.

handheld scanner A small device primarily used to scan text. See *scanner*.

hard drive A hardware component housed in a computer and used to store programs and files permanently.

image-editing program A program that enables the user to view, edit, and print digital images.

inkjet printer A device that works by spraying a fine, quick-drying ink onto paper. See *printer*.

JPEG Stands for Joint Photographic Experts Group. A file format often used for pictures posted on the World Wide Web.

laser printer A device that uses a laser beam to burn toner on paper. See *printer*.

LCD Stands for liquid crystal display. An LCD monitor on a digital camera displays pictures and messages.

lens A piece of glass on a camera used to collect and focus rays of light to form an image.

light meter An instrument that measures the exposure of light on a subject.

media card Removable media inserted into a digital camera to provide additional storage space. See *CompactFlash* and *SmartMedia*.

media slot A slot in a digital camera into which a media card can be inserted. See *media card*.

megapixel One million pixels. Megapixel is the unit used to measure digital camera quality; there are one-, two-, and four-megapixel (and higher) cameras. See *pixel*.

memory card A removable disk similar to a computer floppy disk that stores images taken with a digital camera. These pictures can be transferred from the memory card to a computer or photo printer. Sometimes referred to as a *memory stick*.

menu button A button on a digital camera that enables the user to access camera commands for setting the date, selecting the resolution, and so on.

mode A setting that affects how a digital camera works. Modes include picture mode, for taking pictures, and playback (review) mode, for reviewing pictures. Mode names vary from camera to camera.

open The process of making an image available to be edited.

optical zoom A lens on a film-based or digital camera that can be used to change the range of space captured by the camera's film or image sensor while keeping the image in focus. See *digital zoom*.

overexposing A condition in which too much light reaches the film, resulting in light, undefined images.

pixel From *pic*ture *el*ement. A tiny dot of light, which is the basic unit of measurement for images on a computer screen or in a digital image.

Plug and Play setup A set of specifications for automatic configuration of a computer to work with various devices, such as digital cameras.

port An opening on the back or front of a computer into which a cable can be plugged to connect a printer, digital camera, or other hardware component. Port types include parallel (or LPT) ports, serial ports, and USB (universal serial bus) ports.

ppi The standard measurement of resolution used with scanned images. Stands for pixels per inch. See *resolution.*

printer A device that prints text or graphical images from a computer. A printer can produce black or color output on paper and typically connects to a computer using a parallel or USB port. See *laser printer* and *inkjet printer.*

RAM Stands for random access memory. RAM temporarily stores data, software, and the operating system while a computer is operating. RAM is measured in megabytes (M or MB) or gigabytes (G or GB).

red-eye A common flaw in photographs in which eyes are displayed and printed as red. Most image-editing programs can correct this problem.

resolution The measure of a digital image's quality. For scanners, resolution is measured in pixels per inch, or *ppi.* For printers, resolution is measured in dots per inch, or *dpi.* Generally, a higher dpi indicates higher resolution. For digital cameras, resolution is measured by megapixel.

rotate The process of adjusting an image. This can be used to correct images that were scanned at an unsatisfactory angle.

save To copy an image to permanent storage. It's a good idea to save your original image, and then work from a copy.

scanner A hardware component that can convert documents and pictures into digital files. See *sheet feed scanner, flatbed scanner, film scanner,* and *handheld scanner.*

sheet feed scanner A device that can hold multiple sheets like a printer and is suitable for copying large text documents. See *scanner.*

shutter button A button on a camera that the user presses to take a picture. It is almost always on the top of the camera.

shutter speed The amount of time the shutter remains open to capture an image.

slide shows Presenting pictures where each of the images is displayed full-screen on your computer, one after another.

SmartMedia SmartMedia is a trademark of Toshiba. One commonly used media card. See *media card.*

TIFF Stands for Tagged Image File Format. A high-quality digital image format often used for pictures appearing in printed publications.

TWAIN The official technical standard for scanning images. Almost all scanners come with a TWAIN driver.

underexposing A condition in which too little light reaches the film, resulting in dark, undefined images.

USB Stands for universal serial bus. A type of port often used to connect scanners and cameras to a computer.

viewfinder A window on the body of a camera that the user looks through to frame and shoot a photograph.

wizard A feature that leads the user through a process step by step. For example, the Add Scanner or Camera Wizard enables the user to install a new scanner or digital camera.

Index

R

S

T

U

V

W

Z

Photo Credits

Mary Burmeister: 126, 127, 129, 147, 150, 151, 154, 160, 169, 179; **John C. Davidson:** 33, 91, 94, 96, 97, 98, 106, 147, 150, 151, 152, 153, 154, 159, 160, 164, 166, 167, 169, 179; **Daniel Gutierrez:** 105, 173, 182, 183; **Jennifer Herber:** 91; **Michael Kavcak:** 159, 160, 191; **Shelley O'Hara:** 9, 10, 49, 68, 69, 99, 100, 101, 129, 141, 142, 143; **Dawn Rader:** 76, 90, 91, 97, 102, 103, 104, 105, 107, 108, 129, 159, 160, 169, 173, 175, 176, 177, 179, 180, 181

GATEWAY, INC. END-USER LICENSE AGREEMENT

PORTANT - READ CAREFULLY: This End-User License Agreement (EULA) is a legal agreement between you (either an individual or an entity), e End-User, and Gateway, Inc. ("Gateway") governing your use of any non-Microsoft software you acquired from Gateway collectively, the OFTWARE PRODUCT".

e SOFTWARE PRODUCT includes computer software, the associated media, any printed materials, and any "online" or electronic cumentation. By turning on the system, opening the shrinkwrapped packaging, copying or otherwise using the SOFTWARE PRODUCT, you ree to be bound by the terms of this EULA. If you do not agree to the terms of this EULA, Gateway is unwilling to license the SOFTWARE RODUCT to you. In such event, you may not use or copy the SOFTWARE PRODUCT, and you should promptly contact Gateway for instructions returning it.

FTWARE PRODUCT LICENSE

e SOFTWARE PRODUCT is protected by copyright laws and international copyright treaties, as well as other intellectual property laws and treaties. The SOFTWARE PRODUCT is ensed, not sold.

GRANT OF LICENSE. This EULA grants you the following rights:

- **Software**. If not already pre-installed, you may install and use one copy of the SOFTWARE PRODUCT on one Gateway COMPUTER, ("COMPUTER").
- **Storage/Network Use**. You may also store or install a copy of the computer software portion of the SOFTWARE PRODUCT on the COMPUTER to allow your other computers to use the SOFTWARE PRODUCT over an internal network, and distribute the SOFTWARE PRODUCT to your other computers over an internal network. However, you must acquire and dedicate a license for the SOFTWARE PRODUCT for each computer on which the SOFTWARE PRODUCT is used or to which it is distributed. A license for the SOFTWARE PRODUCT may not be shared or used concurrently on different computers.
- **Back-up Copy.** If Gateway has not included a back-up copy of the SOFTWARE PRODUCT with the COMPUTER, you may make a single back-up copy of the SOFTWARE PRODUCT. You may use the back-up copy solely for archival purposes.

DESCRIPTION OF OTHER RIGHTS AND LIMITATIONS.

- **Limitations on Reverse Engineering, Decompilation and Disassembly**. You may not reverse engineer, decompile, or disassemble the SOFTWARE PRODUCT, except and only to the extent that such activity is expressly permitted by applicable law notwithstanding this limitation.
- **Separation of Components.** The SOFTWARE PRODUCT is licensed as a single product. Its component parts and any upgrades may not be separated for use on more than one computer.
- **Single COMPUTER.** The SOFTWARE PRODUCT is licensed with the COMPUTER as a single integrated product. The SOFTWARE PRODUCT may only be used with the COMPUTER.
- **Rental.** You may not rent or lease the SOFTWARE PRODUCT.
- **Software Transfer.** You may permanently transfer all of your rights under this EULA only as part of a sale or transfer of the COMPUTER, provided you retain no copies, you transfer all of the SOFTWARE PRODUCT (including all component parts, the media and printed materials, any upgrades, this EULA, and the Certificate(s) of Authenticity), if applicable, and the recipient agrees to the terms of this EULA. If the SOFTWARE PRODUCT is an upgrade, any transfer must include all prior versions of the SOFTWARE PRODUCT.
- **Termination**. Without prejudice to any other rights, Gateway may terminate this EULA if you fail to comply with the terms and conditions of this EULA. In such event, you must destroy all copies of the SOFTWARE PRODUCT and all of its component parts.
- **Language Version Selection.** Gateway may have elected to provide you with a selection of language versions for one or more of the Gateway software products licensed under this EULA. If the SOFTWARE PRODUCT is included in more than one language version, you are licensed to use only one of the language versions provided. As part of the setup process for the SOFTWARE PRODUCT you will be given a one-time option to select a language version. Upon selection, the language version selected by you will be set up on the COMPUTER, and the language version(s) not selected by you will be automatically and permanently deleted from the hard disk of the COMPUTER.

COPYRIGHT. All title and copyrights in and to the SOFTWARE PRODUCT (including but not limited to any images, photographs, animations, video, audio, music, text and "applets," incorporated into the SOFTWARE PRODUCT), the accompanying printed materials, and any copies of the SOFTWARE PRODUCT, are owned by Gateway or its licensors or suppliers. You may not copy the printed materials accompanying the SOFTWARE PRODUCT. All rights not specifically granted under this EULA are reserved by Gateway and its licensors or suppliers.

DUAL-MEDIA SOFTWARE. You may receive the SOFTWARE PRODUCT in more than one medium. Regardless of the type or size of medium you receive, you may use only one medium that is appropriate for the COMPUTER. You may not use or install the other medium on another COMPUTER. You may not loan, rent, lease, or otherwise transfer the other medium to another user, except as part of the permanent transfer (as provided above) of the SOFTWARE PRODUCT.

PRODUCT SUPPORT. Refer to the particular product's documentation for product support. Should you have any questions concerning this EULA, or if you desire to contact Gateway for any other reason, please refer to the address provided in the documentation for the COMPUTER.

U.S. GOVERNMENT RESTRICTED RIGHTS. The SOFTWARE PRODUCT and any accompanying documentation are and shall be deemed to be "commercial computer software" and "commercial computer software documentation," respectively, as defined in DFAR 252.227-7013 and as described in FAR 12.212. Any use, modification, reproduction, release, performance, display or disclosure of the SOFTWARE PRODUCT and any accompanying documentation by the United States Government shall be governed solely by the terms of this Agreement and shall be prohibited except to the extent expressly permitted by the terms of this Agreement.

LIMITED WARRANTY. Gateway warrants that the media on which the SOFTWARE PRODUCT is distributed is free from defects in materials and workmanship for a period of ninety (90) days from your receipt thereof. Your exclusive remedy in the event of any breach of the foregoing warranty shall be, at Gateway's sole option, either (a) a refund of the amount you paid for the SOFTWARE PRODUCT or (b) repair or replacement of such media, provided that you return the defective media to Gateway within ninety (90) days of your receipt thereof. The foregoing warranty shall be void if any defect in the media is a result of accident, abuse or misapplication. Any replacement media will be warranted as set forth above for the remainder of the original warranty period or thirty (30) days from your receipt of such replacement media, whichever is longer. EXCEPT AS EXPRESSLY SET FORTH HEREIN, GATEWAY, ITS SUPPLIERS OR LICENSORS HEREBY DISCLAIMS ALL WARRANTIES, EXPRESS, IMPLIED AND STATUTORY, IN CONNECTION WITH THE SOFTWARE PRODUCT AND ANY ACCOMPANYING DOCUMENTATION, INCLUDING WITHOUT LIMITATION THE IMPLIED WARRANTIES OF MERCHANTABILITY, NON-INFRINGEMENT OF THIRD-PARTY RIGHTS, AND FITNESS FOR A PARTICULAR PURPOSE.

LIMITATION OF LIABILITY. IN NO EVENT WILL GATEWAY, ITS SUPPLIERS OR LICENSORS, BE LIABLE FOR ANY INDIRECT, SPECIAL, INCIDENTAL, COVER OR CONSEQUENTIAL DAMAGES ARISING OUT OF THE USE OF OR INABILITY TO USE THE SOFTWARE PRODUCT USER DOCUMENTATION OR RELATED TECHNICAL SUPPORT, INCLUDING WITHOUT LIMITATION, DAMAGES OR COSTS RELATING TO THE LOSS OF PROFITS, BUSINESS, GOODWILL, DATA OR COMPUTER PROGRAMS, EVEN IF ADVISED OF THE POSSIBILITY OF SUCH DAMAGES. IN NO EVENT WILL GATEWAY, ITS SUPPLIERS' OR LICENSORS' LIABILITY EXCEED THE AMOUNT PAID BY YOU FOR THE SOFTWARE PRODUCT. BECAUSE SOME JURISDICTIONS DO NOT ALLOW THE EXCLUSION OR LIMITATION OF LIABILITY FOR CONSEQUENTIAL OR INCIDENTAL DAMAGES, THE ABOVE LIMITATION MAY NOT APPLY TO YOU.

Miscellaneous. This Agreement is governed by the laws of the United States and the State of South Dakota, without reference to conflicts of law principles. The application of the United Nations Convention on Contracts for the International Sale of Goods is expressly excluded. This Agreement sets forth all rights for the user of the SOFTWARE PRODUCT and is the entire agreement between the parties. This Agreement supersedes any other communications with respect to the SOFTWARE PRODUCT and any associated documentation. This Agreement may not be modified except by a written addendum issued by a duly authorized representative of Gateway. No provision hereof shall be deemed waived unless such waiver shall be in writing and signed by Gateway or a duly authorized representative of Gateway. If any provision of this Agreement is held invalid, the remainder of this Agreement shall continue in full force and effect. The parties confirm that it is their wish that this Agreement has been written in the English language only.

"Rev.3 9/24/98".

Mission

To help everybody unlock the power of their computer to achieve their fullest personal, professional and lifestyle potential.

Deep inside one of America's leading computer companies you'll find a group of very smart, very dedicated people who have nothing to do with manufacturing computers.

With fresh insights and breakthrough techniques, the Survive & Thrive team is transforming the way we acquire technology skills. And putting a human face on the digital revolution. Yours.

Topics

Look for these and other exciting topics from Gateway that will allow you to further explore the digital lifestyle and take advantage of the power of your PC.

- Windows® XP
- Digital Music
- Quicken®
- Microsoft® Word
- Digital Photography
- America Online®
- Microsoft Excel
- Digital Video
- Internet
- Microsoft PowerPoint®
- Microsoft Money
- Home Networking
- PC Security

THE LEGACY CONTINUES

USING THE HP 3000 WITH HP-UX AND WINDOWS NT

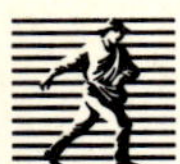

Hewlett-Packard Professional Books

Atchison	Object-Oriented Test & Measurement Software Development in C++
Blinn	Portable Shell Programming: An Extensive Collection of Bourne Shell Examples
Blommers	Practical Planning for Network Growth
Costa	Planning and Designing High Speed Networks Using 100VG-AnyLAN, Second Edition
Crane	A Simplified Approach to Image Processing: Classical and Modern Techniques
Fernandez	Configuring the Common Desktop Environment
Fristrup	USENET: Netnews for Everyone
Fristrup	The Essential Web Surfer Survival Guide
Grady	Practical Software Metrics for Project Management and Process Improvement
Grosvenor, Ichiro, O'Brien	Mainframe Downsizing to Upsize Your Business: IT-Preneuring
Gunn	A Guide to NetWare® for UNIX®
Helsel	Graphical Programming: A Tutorial for HP VEE
Helsel	Visual Programming with HP-VEE
Kane	PA-RISC 2.0 Architecture
Knouse	Practical DCE Programming
Lee	The ISDN Consultant: A Stress-Free Guide to High-Speed Communications
Lewis	The Art & Science of Smalltalk
Madell, Parsons, Abegg	Developing and Localizing International Software
Malan, Letsinger, Coleman	Object-Oriented Development at Work: Fusion In the Real World
McFarland	X Windows on the World: Developing Internationalized Software with X, Motif®, and CDE
McMinds/Whitty	Writing Your Own OSF/Motif Widgets
Phaal	LAN Traffic Management
Poniatowski	The HP-UX System Administrator's "How To" Book
Poniatowski	HP-UX 10.x System Administration "How To" Book
Poniatowski	Learning the HP-UX Operating System
Thomas	Cable Television Proof-of-Performance: A Practical Guide to Cable TV Compliance Measurements Using a Spectrum Analyzer.
Weygant	Clusters for High Availability: A Primer of HP-UX Solutions
Witte	Electronic Test Instruments
Yawn, Stachnik, Sellars	The Legacy Continues: Using the HP 3000 with HP-UX and Windows NT

THE LEGACY CONTINUES

USING THE HP 3000 WITH HP-UX AND WINDOWS NT

Mike Yawn
Senior Consultant
HP Commercial Systems Division

George Stachnik
Chief of Customer Communications
HP Commercial Systems Division

Perry Sellars
Account Support Engineer
HP Account Support Organization

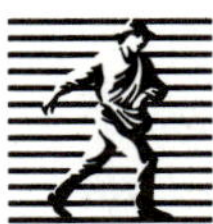

Prentice Hall P T R
Upper Saddle River, New Jersey 07458

Editorial/production supervision: Mary Sudul
Cover design director: Jerry Votta
Cover design: PM Workshop, Inc.
Manufacturing manager: Alexis R. Heydt
Acquisitions editor: Karen Gettman
Page layout/formatting: Bear Mountain Typography
Manager, Hewlett-Packard Press: Patricia Pekary

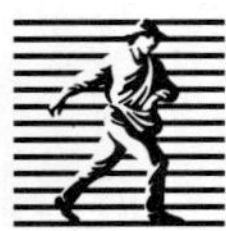

Published by Prentice Hall P T R
Prentice-Hall, Inc.
A Simon & Schuster Company
Upper Saddle River, NJ 07458

The publisher offers discounts on this book when ordered in bulk quantities.
For more information, contact:

Corporate Sales Department
Prentice Hall P T R
One Lake Street
Upper Saddle River, New Jersey 07458
Phone: 800-382-3419
FAX: 201-236-7141
E-mail: corpsales@prenhall.com

Printed in the United States of America

10 9 8 7 6 5 4 3 2 1

ISBN 0-13-259060-3

Prentice-Hall International (UK) Limited, *London*
Prentice-Hall of Australia Pty. Limited, *Sydney*
Prentice-Hall of Canada, Inc., *Toronto*
Prentice-Hall Hispanoamericana S.A., *Mexico*
Prentice-Hall of India Private Limited, *New Delhi*
Prentice-Hall of Japan, Inc., *Tokyo*
Simon & Schuster Asia Pte. Ltd., *Singapore*
Editora Prentice-Hall do Brasil, Ltda., *Rio de Janeiro*

For Debbie
-MY

For Monica, Ken, Andrea and Greg
-GS

For my Father and Mother
-PS

Foreword

The computer industry is always moving forward. Much has changed since the first HP 3000 was introduced in the 1970s.

HP 3000 customers are some of the most loyal in the world. Not because the 3000 was always first out of the starting gate with the latest and greatest technology, but because the technology was well thought out, integrated, and served a business need.

This integrated environment of the MPE Operating System, the TurboIMAGE database management system, and other subsystems and products such as VPLUS, COBOL II, and Transact, provided a great environment for the creation of high performance, business critical OLTP applications.

The new challenges of today require new approaches. The pace of business is much faster. The need to get answers faster has driven technology first from batch to on-line; and then from departmental, to enterprise-wide; and now to needing to be connected to suppliers and customers. Technologies such as Object Oriented languages and tools and the World Wide Web have emerged to help users respond to this new environment.

While some customers continue to find everything they need in the traditional MPE environment, others recognize the value of these new technologies, and want to know how to incorporate these technologies into an MPE environment.

In this book, Mike, George, and Perry will show you how to use some of these new technologies on the HP 3000, or to integrate your HP 3000 systems with other systems such as the HP 9000 or Windows NT servers.

While much has changed, some things have remained the same. Reliability, security, stability and data integrity are at least as important in this new paradigm as they were in traditional data processing environments. The HP 3000 still has a place in the data center of today and tomorrow.

Harry Sterling
General Manager
Commercial Systems Division

Preface

I began working for Hewlett-Packard in 1983. At that time, I knew almost nothing about the company's strategic commercial computing system, the HP 3000. In addition to taking the usual training courses, I was required to "tag along" with one of HP's sales people on a customer visit, so I could better understand how the machine was marketed to customers. The thing that I remember best about that day had nothing to do with the sales rep's presentation to the customer. Rather, it was the conversation that I had with him over lunch after we had left the customer's office. We were eating in a little place in downtown Chicago, and he had asked me if I had any questions. We were discussing some of the finer points of the HP 3000 strategy, when he made a statement that startled me.

"Well, the HP 3000's a great machine," he said, "But you know, of course that it's going away..." I must have looked a little dumbfounded. Remember, this was 1983.

"It is?" I asked.

"Oh sure," he replied, and proceeded to explain to me that the HP 3000 uses a 16-bit architecture. In those days the most powerful computer that Hewlett-Packard had was the 16-bit Series/70. "The rest of the world is moving to 32-bit architectures," he explained, citing several competitors who were already selling 32-bit products.

"Well, are we going to make the HP 3000 a 32-bit machine?" I asked. He smiled as if I were a five-year-old asking when Santa Claus was going to visit.

"No. You see, 16-bit architectures are completely different from 32-bit architectures. You can't magically turn one into the other." And then he told me how one of HP's biggest competitors had managed their transition from selling their older 16-bit products to the newer more powerful 32-bit machines. They had simply put the new, more powerful machines out on the market while jacking up the cost of support for the older architectures. This effectively forced their 16-bit customers into a corner. They could either undertake an expensive conversion, rewriting their existing application software to run on the new machines, or they could stay on the old architecture and pay the higher support costs. Either way, the competitor won. I noted that neither of these options seemed particularly attractive, and wondered how many of our competitor's customers had decided, as long as they were faced with a conversion anyway, to convert to a different vendor—like maybe HP. My friend from the sales force smiled.

"You're learning," he said. "When one of our competitors forces its customers through a conversion, that always creates opportunities for me," and he boasted that he had been able to steal some important accounts away from other computer companies because of this very issue. But in spite of this, he predicted that HP really had no choice. We have to build 32-bit products to be competitive—and since we can't make them compatible with the old 16-bit products, we would have to drop the HP 3000 line and move on to something new.

"You can't make a 32-bit purse out of 16-bit ear," he assured me. Sometime in the late 1980s, HP would come out with a new 32-bit computer, and then "force march" all the customers off of the HP 3000 onto a new 32-bit "box-to-be-named-later."

It was a prediction that I was to recall five years later, in 1988, when HP began shipments of computers based on its 32-bit "Spectrum" architecture. (Today it's known as "PA-RISC"). But unlike its competitors, HP designed its 32-bit PA-RISC machines to be upward compatible with the older 16-bit machines. This approach cost HP money—it took longer to bring the new machine to market. But, HP 3000 customers could, in most cases, run their 16-bit programs on new 32-bit computers without any conversion at all—not so much as a recompile. And as a result, even in spite of the delays, HP was able to bring its installed base to the new architecture with relatively few defections.

It's hard to overvalue HP's achievement with the HP 3000 and the PA-RISC migration. The computer industry had seen many new architectures come and go. But never before (or since) had a vendor brought a new architecture to the marketplace in such a way that customer investments in the old architecture were so completely protected.

"So much for the idea that the HP 3000's 'going away'," I thought to myself.

Soon after, my family and I moved to California, where I worked in the HP 3000 division. And one day, I got a phone call from an old friend from back east. He had left HP and was now working for one of the big database companies in the Bay area. We agreed to meet for lunch, and over our meal we talked about our respective employers. At one point he remarked, almost flippantly, "Of course, the HP 3000's a great machine, but you have to understand something."

"What's that?" I asked.

"It's going away," he responded.

I remember thinking, "Haven't I been to this movie before?" In between mouthfuls of pizza I asked, "What makes you say that?"

"Well," he responded, sighing in that special way that technical people sigh when they're about to explain an elementary truth to one of the uninitiated. "You have to understand that the HP 3000 uses that old clunky network-style database... What's it called again?"

"TurboIMAGE," I replied.

"Yes, TurboIMAGE. Now, TurboIMAGE was OK in it's day. But the world's changing. These days, everybody's moving to relational databases and client/server."

"Can't you do client/server with TurboIMAGE," I asked innocently?

Well, you *could* work out some way of doing it, I suppose. But all the client/server tools are based on SQL and the relational model. If you want to take advantage of all the tools and technologies that people are writing, you've got to move to an SQL database. And TurboIMAGE just isn't an SQL database.

"So what are you saying?"

"I'm saying that people are going to have to go through a conversion—they're going to have to convert their applications so that instead of running on top of TurboIMAGE, they'll run on top of one of the big portable databases, you know the ones I mean, and as long as they're converting anyway, a lot of them will simply move off of the HP 3000 onto another platform."

The logic was hard to argue with. The great client/server steamroller was just beginning to move across the face of the computer industry in 1988. But five years later, in 1993, HP had done the unthinkable. They had brought an SQL interface to TurboIMAGE (renaming it IMAGE/SQL in the process), and opened it up to the hundreds of PC-based client/server tools that had, by that time, flooded the marketplace. Once again, HP had acted in the interests of its customers—protecting their investments in the HP 3000 platform, databases, skills and software. HP had proven once again that just because technology was available on another platform, that didn't mean that HP's customers had to move there to take advantage of it.

As we move into the second half of the 1990s, I'm once again began hearing the same old refrain, "Well, you realize, of course, that the HP 3000's going away..."

"What is it this time?" I asked.

This time, the reason for all the hand-wringing in the HP 3000 community is UNIX. The industry seems to have been overrun in the last five years with consultants and other industry know-it-alls who, citing the benefits of open systems, will quote you chapter and verse a thousand reasons why every computer in your company will be running a version of UNIX before the year 2000. To be fair, the first time I heard this proclamation was back in 1990, when the smoke was supposed to have cleared by 1995. Now the date has been pushed back a little, but the message is the same: "the whole world's moving to UNIX (or more recently, the whole world's moving to NT). The HP 3000 is going away."

So what is it about the HP 3000 that seems to make it such a natural target for the doom-and-gloom-meisters of the industry? Surely there's no other platform that has been so doomed for so long, and yet, like that bunny rabbit in the TV commercials, still seems to be able to "keep going and going and going." What's so special about the HP 3000 anyway? And more importantly, how is the HP 3000 going to survive in a world that seems to be increasingly fixated on UNIX and open systems (or, if you prefer, NT and PC LANs)?

There was a time, not so very long ago, when the HP 3000 was Hewlett-Packard's single strategic computer system for commercial computing. Today, it shares that title with other HP products. Not so long ago, HP 3000 networking meant using NS (or predecessor DS), which was largely incompatible with other networks used by other systems. Today, the HP 3000 can easily share a network with PCs, with UNIX workstations and servers, or with many other kinds of computers. In the past, the HP 3000 had to be Hewlett-Packard's solution to virtually any commercial computing problem you might have. Today, given almost any problem, there's more than one way to solve it. The HP 3000 rarely represents the only answer. And the HP 3000 alone may not be the single best solution. *In fact, no single computing platform represents the single best solution to every problem.*

Real world problems call for real world solutions that take into account not just the technology that's for sale, but also the technology that you're using today. If the rise of UNIX and open systems has resulted in anything, it has made it easier and less expensive than it ever was in the past to operate a truly heterogeneous datacenter—one that uses lots of different kinds of computers together—leveraging the strengths (and weaknesses) of each platform to your best advantage. If there's a "single best solution" to every commercial computing problem—it's making different kinds of computers work together effectively. That, after all, is what "open systems" was originally supposed to mean.

Mike Yawn

Acknowledgments

Many people provided valuable assistance in developing the ideas that are described in this book.

Thanks to Bill Bennett, Gary Calomeni, and Vish Krishnan for discussions of the various aspects of creating portable software architectures. Thanks to Liz Sanville for information on language portability issues, and to Kevin Cooper for some BSD sockets tricks and tips.

Many people also reviewed part or all of the book in manuscript form and provided valuable feedback. Thanks to Bill Bennett, Kurt Guttenberg, Eero Laurila, Barry Lemrow, Steve Hoogheem and Debbie Yawn for this.

Thanks to everyone on the HP-Prentice Hall team that carried this book from the original idea to the finished product: Pat Pekary, Karen Gettman, Barbara Alfieri, Sophie Papanikolaou, Mary Sudul, and all the behind-the-scenes folks we never got to know.

Mike Yawn

I would like to thank the following folks for all of their support and help with this project.

First, my buddies in the Greenville, South Carolina office of Hewlett Packard who read and reread everything I wrote. I know you got tired of that.

Secondly to Roc Paez from the Fullerton, California office and Glen McNay of the Richmond, Virginia office of Hewlett Packard both of whom helped me so much in the security and disaster recovery areas.

I would also like to thank all of my friends on the Internet, Marybeth, Matt, Kelly and all the rest who always asked “how is the book coming”? This question kept my mind on what I had to do.

Last but definitely not least I would very much like to thank my family. My daughters, Carman, Caroline and Quinlyn along with my wife Julie. While it may seem like I am, believe me, I'm not permanently attached to the dining room table. I love you all so much!

Perry Sellars

My thanks to my wife, Monica, and my kids Ken, Andrea and Greg, for putting up with all the hours dad put into this project. Now we can get back to the fun stuff...

George Stachnik

Table of Contents

PART 1

A Short History of Information Systems

CHAPTER 1

The Computerization of Commerce

The tremendous changes that took place in society during the 1960's have been the subject of hundreds of books, speeches and articles. Some have focused on the upheavals in popular culture brought about by artists like the Beatles. Others have zeroed in on the sexual revolution, the hippie movement, or any of dozens of other aspects of society, all of which touch our lives to some extent. Now, thirty years later, many people have come to believe that the social, musical and sexual changes that began in the 60's have run their course. The Beatles have long since broken up. Sexually Transmitted Diseases and a resurgence of "family values" have put a damper on the sexual revolution. And the people that used to call themselves hippies now wear three piece suits and work for companies like IBM or HP. And yet there is one 60's—rooted revolution that is still being played out today.

In 1964, the International Business Machines Company, (IBM) announced the System 360. This was the first family of compatible computers, and the first to be based on integrated circuits. Many of the largest corporations in the world began to install these machines, and IBM soon found itself in a fast growing market, competing with companies such as Control Data Corporation (CDC), National Cash Register (NCR), and Honeywell, whose H-200 line was specifically targeted at IBM's older 1400 product line.

At first, there was great debate about how computing technology would affect our society and our lives. One point of view was that computers represented a dehumanizing force, and that human workers would be replaced by machines in many jobs, leaving in their wake an unemployed (and unemployable) workforce. Others claimed that computing technology represented little more than a high priced adding machine—a more efficient tool to use for bookkeeping. As computing became more cost effective, smaller businesses were able to mechanize their own operations. Then, as attention shifted from mainframes to personal computers in the eighties, computers became tools, not only for business, but for individuals as well. People found thousands of new applications and uses for the machines. Today, with the advent of the World Wide Web and other client/server technologies, personal computers are changing the way ordinary people buy goods, shop for services and pay their bills. And the firms that supply those goods and services, sensing that people will prefer to do business with companies that let them settle their accounts electronically, are scrambling to keep up.

The computerization of commerce, unlike many revolutions, has not taken place in a single "Big Bang." Instead, it has washed over the corporate world in successive waves: Each has altered the way that business could (and would) be conducted. Each has had a greater impact than the one before it. Virtually everybody who has worked with computers since the nineteen sixties has experienced the effects of these waves personally. If you worked for a large company that used mainframe computers and developed its own applications, you will recognize many of these waves at once, for you've probably experienced them directly. If you worked for a smaller company that didn't get involved with computers until less expensive machines (like the HP 3000) became available, or if you've depended on "packaged" application programs developed by third parties (as users of most HP commercial computers do), then you may have experienced the effects indirectly. Either way, if you've worked in the Information Systems (IS) industry during the past thirty years, then you've seen the following four great waves sweep across the industry.

The first wave, beginning the mid 1960's, began with the installation of large mainframe computers such as IBM's System 360 in many Fortune 500 companies, and the advent of the earliest batch processing systems. By the time Neil Armstrong took his walk on the moon, the "mainframing" of the Fortune 500 was well under way.

The second wave began in the 1970's, and was characterized by two key events. First mainframe based on-line transaction processing systems such as IBM's CICS arrived on the scene. By this time, most people who worked with business computers had come to believe that a large mainframe (typically from IBM) was the only kind of computer that was practical for managing the volumes of data generated by a multi-million dollar corporation.

Mainframes were sometimes "pitched" to the Fortune 500 as a means of taking advantage of their considerable size and financial resources to create a competitive advantage. Smaller companies simply didn't have enough money to be able to participate in the mechanization of commerce. This was true until the second key milestone of this wave, the advent of cheaper alternatives to mainframe hardware platforms. Digital Equipment Corporation (DEC) had been shipping minicomputers such as the PDP-5 since 1963. But the first 16-bit machine, the PDP-11/20 didn't become available until 1970. The HP 3000 was the first minicomputer to feature a data base management system (DBMS), and it might be argued that while other minicomputers found strong acceptance in technical markets, it was the IMAGE DBMS that made the HP 3000 so uniquely suitable for commercial applications.

A number of industry analysts predicted that networks of minicomputers would sweep mainframes from the computer marketplace by the end of the decade. Others predicted that batch processing would be a thing of the past in a relatively short time. Both predictions failed to come true. Instead, batch came to be used in conjunction with on-line processing. And in spite of the fact that business minicomputers were originally conceived as a less expensive alternative to mainframes, in the end they were more often installed side-by-side with mainframes.

The third wave began in the 1980's, with the advent of desktop personal computers (PCs) that were sufficiently powerful and easy enough to use to be practical in business environments. The roots of the PC revolution go back to 1972, when Intel introduced its model 8008 microprocessor. Microsoft was founded in 1975, and Apple Computer in 1977. But it wasn't until 1981, the year that IBM entered the Personal Computer (PC) marketplace, that the revolution really began to pick up steam.

In 1981, many seasoned IS executives had bet their careers on a concept that had become "conventional wisdom" in the IS industry, that a large mainframe was the only kind computer that made sense in a big company. A number of these people tried at first to ignore PCs, and a few even tried to ban their use. Both strategies failed. PCs invariably were accepted by end users and became commonplace on the desktop.

The fourth wave began with the introduction of standard operating environments such as UNIX into the commercial marketplace, and portable database management systems including Oracle, Sybase, Ingres, Informix and others. UNIX, originally developed by Bell labs, had been licensed to a number of other companies including Microsoft and Sun Microsystems.

Imagine a shellfish that has spent its life on the ocean floor. One day it finds itself hurled onto the beach by a wave. How should it adapt? Where does it begin? This is the kind of environment in which successful IS managers have been living (and even thriving) during the last half of the twentieth century. With the arrival of each new technological wave, IS managers and the corporations they work for have found themselves being hurled into entirely new environments (particularly competitive environments) and expected to survive and prosper. Each new technological revolution brings with it the same difficult questions:

> *"Can we use the new technology to get a competitive edge and make more money? And if so, how?"*
>
> *"How much will it cost us to invest in the new technology? What will happen if we choose not to invest in it? What's our exposure in the event that our competitors choose to invest in it, but we don't?"*
>
> *"Suppose we do choose to invest in the new technology. How do we get from the environment that we're using today (the old technology) to the new one? What do we do with our existing (legacy) systems?"*

A key part of every IS manager's job is to evaluate each new technology as it comes to the market. New technologies always get a lot of attention. UNIX, PC LANs, client/server, (including the World Wide Web), high speed internetworking, (including ***the*** Internet), various object technologies and data warehousing have all been championed during the last few years as the IS executive's savior.

It doesn't take a lot of common sense to see that, when a new technology becomes available on the marketplace, it is usually a good idea to bring it in house for evaluation against the above criteria. Too often, however, IS managers get caught up in the "hype" surrounding new technologies, and put them into production for other reasons...Whether the new technology is a hardware technology, (like RISC, or massively parallel processing), an operating system (like UNIX or NT), or a software technology (like client/server), you'll often hear arguments like these to justify putting it into production. And these arguments just don't hold water...

> *"My boss read an article in a business magazine that says that this new technology is going to become the dominant way of doing things over the next five to ten years. We have to put it into production, or we'll be behind."*
>
> *"Everybody else in our industry is using this technology. There must be a good reason. We better start using it too..."*
>
> *"The technology we're using now is old—it has been around since (fill-the-blank-with-the-date-of-your-choice). We need to get rid of it or we'll be the only ones left using it..."*

IS executives have to be concerned with new technology. If a new technology can be used to generate a competitive edge for your company, then it should definitely be investigated thoroughly, and if it turns out to be practical in your operation, implemented. But IS executives also need to be concerned with the existing older technologies that are used to run the company's day-to-day operations. Companies that have been in business for more than a few years are likely to be using older technologies: proprietary mainframes and minicomputers, host/terminal-based transaction processing systems and batch processing. These technologies may not be particularly glamorous. They may not do much for the IS manager's resume. But they work—every day. Part of the process of investigating a new technology is to determine how well (if at all) it can be integrated into the company's portfolio of existing technologies.

Too often, naive or inexperienced IS managers that have become excited abut the potential of a new technology will propose making it the basis of the company's entire information processing strategy. ("Our IS strategy is to use XXX everywhere, from the desktop to the datacenter...") This is rarely a good idea. Technologies are just tools to get the job done.

To see clearly how this kind of strategy goes wrong, imagine a master carpenter in ancient times. In his company, he has apprentices who've spent their lives learning to join wooden boards to one another by drilling holes through them and pounding wooden pegs into the holes. One day, his chief apprentice comes to see him. He's very excited because he has just come from the village, where he saw a demo of a new technology called "the hammer and nail". It was so amazing that he has brought one back to show the boss.

The master carpenter is amazed by what he sees—a tool that can be used to join boards without having to drill holes and cut pegs. Using the nails is a lot faster than joining the wood the old fashioned way, and the carpenter began thinking about the profits he would make based on the increased productivity of his apprentices. Of course, he would have to buy nails, but they are cheap and one bag looked like it held enough to last an apprentice for about a month.

Being a decisive manager, he calls a meeting of all his apprentices and announces, "From this point forward, our strategy for building things is to use only hammers and nails. No more pegs!" To ensure his policy is adopted, he collects all the braces, awls, chisels and other tools that his apprentices have been using to make pegs and drill holes for them, and issues each apprentice a brand new claw hammer and a big bag of nails.

A week later, he is paid a visit by an irate customer. This person had ordered a dining room table and 10 chairs, and the pieces had just been delivered. The customer first complemented the carpenter on what a fine job his apprentices had done joining the boards making up the table top, but then demanded to know why there were hundreds of "little iron circles" pressed neatly into the wood. The carpenter reassured the customer that those little circles represented the very latest in wood-butchering technology.

"They're called nails," he said, "And they are the very reason why the boards that make up your tabletop were joined so neatly, and, I might add, at such a reasonable price."

The customer complained, "Well, new technology or not, those circle-things will all have to come out. My children will eat at this table, and children spill things. Those iron circles will rust. I can't have rusty iron all over my good food! And that's not all. You've used these 'nail' things to attach the chair legs to the seats."

"What's wrong with them" the carpenter asked? "Aren't the chairs sound?"

"They're very sound," the customer replied. "But in one place there's a sharp iron point sticking out of the top of the seat. I ripped my pants and scratched myself on it. If I get sick you'll be hearing from my lawyer!!"

Unnerved, the carpenter promised the customer a full refund, and then went back to his shop to talk to the apprentices. He found the floor almost completely covered with bent nails. It seems that it had taken each of them a couple of days to learn how to use the hammers properly. It turned out that for every nail that had been hammered in properly, several had bent and had to be discarded. Some of his apprentices were now on their eighth bag of nails. "So much for saving any money," he thought to himself. In the end, the carpenter realized that although the new hammer-and-nails technology was an indispensable tool for some jobs, it wasn't necessarily good for table tops, chairs and certain other jobs. There, traditional hole-and-peg technology represented a superior way of doing things.

Information Systems works the same way. It's rarely a good idea to base your IS strategy on the latest and greatest technological tool. Instead, base your IS strategy on the needs of your business, and apply each technological tool where it makes the most sense.

CHAPTER 2

The First Wave: Who Survived It? Who Didn't?

Today, many IS executives are trying to figure out how to survive in a world that seems bent on turning itself completely upside down once every 18 months or so. Life in this kind of environment is exciting, volatile, complex, and maddeningly unpredictable. As IS planners look into the next century, the question on people's minds is less likely to be "how can we best do this job" and far more likely to be "how in the world are we even going to survive?"

In order to learn to be a survivor, it's instructive to look back at those who survived (or failed to survive) the technological waves that have rolled through the IS industry in years gone by. There is a great deal of "conventional wisdom" in the IS industry that new technologies are what makes IS departments successful. After all, the first companies to install on-line applications, use PCs, install LANs, or link UNIX workstations with servers have always been the ones we've read about on the front page of ComputerWorld. These IS managers are the ones that we see quoted in the press. But have these companies necessarily been the most successful? From a contemporary point of view, it's instructive to take a closer look at ways that our predecessors dealt with new technology. After all, as the old saying goes, those that fail to understand history are doomed to repeat it.

Batch Processing

The roots of the computer business can be traced all the way back into the 19th century. The invention of Charles Babbage's Difference Engine and Herman Hollerith's punch card tabulating machine arguably laid the groundwork for the first wave. In 1911, Hollerith's Tabulating Company merged with two other firms to form the Computing-Tabulating-Recording Company. In 1924, under the leadership of Thomas J. Watson, the company renamed itself International Business Machines, or IBM.

During the subsequent fifty years, the company would virtually invent the commercial computer marketplace. In 1948, they introduced an electronic calculator, and 1953 saw the first shipments of the IBM 701, a vacuum-tube based computer that had the then-unique capability of being able to store programs. But it was the development of the IBM 1401 that really got the first wave of computerization under way. First marketed in 1959, the company would sell over 10,000 of the machines to large corporations. The 1401 allowed companies to begin to exploit the batch processing capabilities of mainframe computers. Batch jobs were used to sort, process and bring some organization to the mountains of raw data that were accumulated by corporations as a by-product of doing business. There had always been a sense that this raw data could represent a valuable resource; it could be used to better understand the workings of the company and the marketplace in which it existed. Potentially, it could be used to run the company more efficiently (and therefore profitably), or to foresee trends in the markets that the competition might miss. The problem with these ideas was that prior to the advent of computerized batch processing, corporate information was processed using a variety of manual processes, handled by armies of clerks and accountants. It was numbingly slow, frequently inaccurate and prohibitively expensive, when it was done at all.

On the surface, the decision to mechanize these manual processes seemed like a classic managerial "no-brainer." On the strength of promises of huge savings, computerized batch processing was implemented at virtually every company that could afford it. It was well understood that the mainframe computers were very expensive pieces of equipment, but when the cost of the equipment was weighed against the money that would be saved by eliminating the manual processing, in virtually every case the decision to move ahead with the computers was made.

Hidden Costs

In spite of all the hardware developments that had been made in the first half of the twentieth century, the full-scale use of computers in business did not really become practical until the late 1960's. Until that time, there were a number of 'hidden costs' associated with using computers in business that made it difficult for companies to fully exploit computer technology.

In the engineering environment, where computers had found most of their early applications, the machines were typically purchased for relatively short-term projects. Applications rarely grew. Instead, they were replaced. But in the commercial world, it soon became apparent that exactly the opposite was true. Applications grew with the business, and there was often a need to move them to newer and more powerful computers. But in the early 1960's, computers were rarely compatible with one another. Moving up to a larger computer also meant rewriting the applications that ran on them.

This "hidden cost" of having to continuously rewrite application software in order to keep up with developments in the hardware acted to hamstring the development of commercial computing until the introduction of the System/360 in 1964. System/360 was the first family of computers that were compatible with one another, so that when a business outgrew one model of the S/360 line, it could replace it with a larger more powerful model without having to rewrite all the programs. IBM even marketed a System/360-based emulator for the 1401 to enable customers to move foreward from that product line. System/360 effectively kicked off the first wave of computerization, because it enabled businesses to write application programs secure in the knowledge that they wouldn't become obsolete when their business outgrew the capacity of their computer room.

In spite of this, there were still many hidden costs awaiting the unwary executive who waded into the waters of the first wave. Measured over the long haul, people-costs turned out to be one of the biggest expenses. Those who are old enough to remember the first wave of mechanization will recall the atmosphere of resentment that greeted the arrival of computing machines. Fear that computers were being brought in to replace human workers was commonplace. Manual processes that people knew, understood (and around which many had built their careers) were suddenly changed or done away with, for reasons that were difficult to comprehend at the time.

Chief executives pushed forward with the mainframing of their businesses, usually because those in the board room believed that it would ultimately benefit the bottom line. In some corporations, it did just that. The easy availability of cheap, well organized, verifiable reports enabled people to make better decisions and run the company more efficiently and effectively. This, at least, was the potential of mainframe based batch processing. But this potential was not always realized. Often, the old manual processes that were supposed to be replaced by speedier, more efficient batch jobs simply refused to die. Sometimes it was because people, perceiving that the acceptance of computers would cost them their jobs, fought the new batch processes in an effort to save their careers. But more often, the new systems proved to be their own undoing, as computerized batch systems were implemented quickly and without sufficient planning. The results were often efficient but ineffective. Manual processes had to be kept alive for years, operating in parallel with the new processes, and eating up any cost savings that the new processes were supposed to yield.

Lessons Learned

Those executives who survived the 1st wave did so because they grasped the first and most basic lesson of the computer age, which is that **Change is hard. Without proper planning and preparation, particularly on the human side, the implementation of any new technology will be more expensive, more complex and more time consuming than you thought it was going to be.** And the less you plan, the more expensive it will become.

These words of wisdom seem almost painfully obvious to today's owners of HP 3000 systems. But in the first wave, many hardware vendors sold their customers a story that claimed that the opposite was true; that computers represented nothing more than a more efficient way to keep the books. They claimed that implementing the new mechanized systems would be quick and easy. And the people who believed them frequently found themselves in search of new careers.

A second, and more important lesson learned in the first wave was that ***information (particularly in the form of application software), in and of itself, is valuable***. The fledgling IS departments, usually called Electronic Data Processing (EDP) in those days, did not understand this fact. Often, EDP departments operated as if the most valuable asset that they had was their computer equipment and technology. They invested heavily in managing (and learning to manage) the hardware more effectively. Even on the compatible S/360 computers, programmers were encouraged to use little "tricks" in their code to make more efficient use of the hardware. Programmers that could write in low level assembler languages were highly valued, and received top salaries because assembler language programs were, at least potentially, more efficient and made the best use of the hardware.

These programming practices had two undesirable side effects. First of all, they sometimes skirted the edges of IBM's promises of compatibility. Assembler language and low level supervisor calls (IBM called them "SVCs") were wonderful for writing applications that were fast. But the more one took advantage of these features, the more likely it was that the programs you wrote for one model of the S/360 line would fail to work properly on the next model.

More importantly, tricky programming practices made the code that much more difficult for other people to understand. At first, that was not perceived to be a problem. After all, the code had been written for the computer to execute, not for other programmers. But within a few years, the value of understanding how the code worked would be recognized. As business requirements changed, the code had to be changed as well, but by this time the programmers that had written the original code were often gone, having either been promoted or left the company. New programmers were hired, and these people had to learn the existing code before they could change it. Projects that ultimately boiled down to changing one or two lines of code wound up taking months because of the learning curve. By the end of the first wave, companies began to realize that the bulk of their programming dollars were being spent, not on new applications, but on maintenance of existing applications. And IS learned (sometimes the hard way) that application software which was easy to maintain had a lot of value.

Until the beginning of the first wave, the processing of corporate data was thought to be the province of low level employees—clerks and accountants. And ultimately, it was these people who really understood how the company worked. Without them, business would literally grind to a halt, and most managers understood that, at least dimly. But as the first wave rolled over the Fortune 500, the knowledge of how the company worked moved into IS. The routine work of running the business was now being done by application software, and nobody knew how the software worked except the people in IS. And so IS became very important.

Prior to the first wave, nobody had wanted the corporate data, because nobody had figured out any way to use it to make money, or to gain any kind of competitive advantage with it. But IS changed that. The first wave demonstrated clearly that information was valuable and that it could be used to save the company a lot of money. And so, in most companies, IS began to grow dramatically. In just a few years, IS would be recognized in most Fortune 500 companies as a strategic part of the enterprise, and shortly thereafter the title "Chief Information Officer," a title that was unheard of in the nineteen fifties, would enter the lexicon of the business world.

Relevance to Today's IS Manager

In some ways, things haven't changed much since then. Go to any computer industry trade show today, and you'll see demo after demo of computer products that can be used to develop applications software. Today the underlying technologies are more sophisticated that the ones used when Richard Nixon was in the White House. Graphical "point and click" user interfaces and object oriented programming languages certainly give today's programmers an edge over those of a generation ago. But implicit in every sales pitch is the idea that the product being sold reduces application development to a couple of mouse clicks. No planning, no design and no thought is supposed to be required. The result of using these tools in this way is the same as it was in the sixties. Batch systems that were implemented without adequate planning and preparation did not work. Client/Server systems that are implemented with the same lack of planning will ultimately suffer the same fate.

The underlying technology does not determine how difficult the change is going to be. When on-line processing was introduced in the second wave, when PCs were brought into the picture in the third wave, and when client/server and UNIX were factored into the equation in the fourth wave, the same principles still held. Whenever a new technology comes along, some vendors, in hopes of clinching a sale, will invariably promise that *this time*, change will be easy. Never was the phrase "Caveat Emptor" more applicable.

CHAPTER 3

Surviving the Second Wave

The second wave of computerization began to crest in the early seventies, when on-line transaction processing (OLTP) first became practical. Batch processing had delivered the potential to turn raw data into meaningful information. Now OLTP promised to deliver the information more quickly—in some cases instantly—to the people who needed it.

The 60's had been a rapid growth period for many corporations, and executives suddenly found themselves at the helms of very large and complex organizations. In the board room, there was a sense that management was out of touch with the day-to-day workings of the business—that things were out of control. Batch reports were typically too detailed to be of much help, and by the time you got hold of them, the information that they held was obsolete. To the chiefs of the corporate world, OLTP represented a way to regain control. "Imagine," they were told by the sales people, "being able, at the press of a button, to know exactly what is going on out there."

While IBM had been pushing the first wave forward in the 1960's, another company was quietly waiting its turn. Hewlett-Packard Company had been founded in 1938 by two engineers who sold electronic equipment out of their garage. By the 1960's, their company had also begun selling computers, including the HP21xx line. But part of the HP way was to stick to its strengths, and so the company remained focused on the engineering market until 1972, when

Hewlett-Packard brought the HP 3000 to the market. This machine was to be Hewlett-Packard's entry in the commercial OLTP computer marketplace.

Like IBM's S/360, the HP 3000 was a family of compatible computers with advanced features like a stack architecture and virtual memory. But unlike the S/360, the cost of an HP 3000 was comparatively low, at under $100,000 it was a fraction of the cost of a comparable mainframe. The HP 3000 used an operating system called the Multi-Programming Executive (MPE) which was designed for the HP 3000 specifically to maximize the throughput of on-line applications. Its COBOL compiler and IMAGE DBMS were unique in the minicomputer marketplace, and it used a technology called time sharing to allow transactions to be entered by multiple users simultaneously. This seems obvious today but in 1972 it was rocket science.

MPE was designed to manage the system resources (access to the CPU, memory and disks) and divide them up among the various users on the system. Its policy was (and is) to treat the most interactive users favorably. Users that entered shorter, faster transactions had a better chance of receiving the resources that they needed than did those users who entered transactions that took longer. MPE also supported a batch environment, so that the HP 3000 could be used for both batch and on-line processing simultaneously. But HP did not position the HP 3000 in the marketplace as a strong machine for batch processing. The early models of the HP 3000 were based on a 16-bit minicomputer architecture that simply did not have the raw performance required to support the kinds of batch workloads found on mainframes. (This stands in contrast to today's HP 3000s, which can outperform all but the most expensive mainframes.) But more importantly, the HP 3000 was optimized around the on-line environment. Batch processing was secondary.

At about the same time that HP delivered the HP 3000 to the market, IBM created a layer of system software for its mainframes to allow users to perform OLTP on the same machines that they were using for batch processing. The operating system used on mainframes at that time was an ancestor of the MVS operating system used on mainframes today. The new software for OLTP was called the Customer Information and Control System (CICS). Today, versions of CICS are available for a variety of computers, but in the early days, it was strictly a mainframe product. CICS was "layered" on top of the MVS system software that managed the execution of batch jobs. CICS and MVS work together to manage the mainframe's system resources. Table one contrasts this approach with that used by MPE on the HP 3000.

Table 3.1 Contrasting the MVS and MPE Approaches to Managing the OLTP Environment.

MVS / CICS Combination	MPE
Divides the computer system's resources among a number of "partitions." Each batch job is assigned to a dedicated partition.	Each batch job and on-line session owns a certain number of processes. Each process represents the execution of a particular program by a particular job or session, at a particular time.
On early versions of the operating system, the number of partitions was fixed. When MVS is introduced, the number and size of partitions becomes dynamic, changing in response to operator commands.	Each process is assigned a numeric priority when it is created. The initial value of this priority depends on whether or not the process is an on-line process. On-line processes receive higher priorities than batch processes.
Certain MVS subsystems, such as CICS, also receive a dedicated partition. On-line users share the resources associated with the CICS partition.	Each process's priority changes in response to the process's behavior. The more interactive a process is, the higher is its priority. System resources are routinely given to the highest priority process that is ready to use them.
MVS Operator commands are used to manage the number of partitions, and the way system resources are divided up among the partitions.	MPE operator commands are used to manage the batch and on-line environments.
The on-line environment is managed using CICS commands, which are different from MVS commands.	The on-line environment is managed using the same MPE commands used to manage the batch environment.
System resources are first distributed among the partitions, with one share going to the CICS partition. On-line users split up the resources allocated to CICS.	System resources are divided up dynamically among the batch users and on-line users. Normally, on-line users will always take priority over batch jobs, but exceptions can be created using operator commands.

The Pitfalls of OLTP

In the 1970's, on-line processing promised to deliver enormous competitive benefits to the companies that moved quickly to take advantage of the new technology. But just as "moving to client/server" has turned out to be a major stumbling block for many seasoned IS organizations in the nineties, “moving to on-line processing” was a journey that was fraught with pitfalls for the fledgling Electronic Data Processing departments of the seventies.

First of all, users had to decide between the two approaches shown in Table 3.1. The minicomputer approach used by HP represented the ‘hot new technology’ of the time. The “hype” that surrounded minicomputers at the time suggested that they would eventually replace mainframes—that the days of the expensive mainframe were numbered. But when the marketplace had an opportunity to vote with their dollars, the result was not quite so clear cut. HP did enjoy a good deal of success with the HP 3000. But at least in the early days HP scored primarily with small to midsize companies (notably manufacturers) that had not previously made a commitment to mainframe computing. By contrast, the trend among companies that were already running large batch applications was to implement their on-line applications under CICS, using the machines that they were already using for batch processing. In other words, the marketplace decided that there were situations where minicomputer technology made sense. There were other situations where mainframe technology seemed to represent a better fit.

As the second wave washed over the IS industry, some IS managers were able to manage the technological shift. Their careers flourished while others floundered or in a few cases even ended. The conventional wisdom in IS is that successful managers are the ones that make the most use of new technology. In fact, in the second wave, the successful IS managers were the ones that were able to overcome the pitfalls of the OLTP revolution. There were at least four major stumbling blocks.

First of all, some IS managers, believing that the new OLTP technology would sweep the old batch technology away behaved as if their batch systems had suddenly been rendered obsolete. The millions of dollars that had been invested in developing batch systems was treated as if it now had to be written off almost overnight. Projects to replace perfectly functional batch systems with on-line applications that essentially performed the same tasks were undertaken. From today's perspective, we can see that this point of view was nonsensical. Those IS executives that were able to see past the sales pitch could see that there were some business problems that were suited to on-line technology, and others that were more suited to a more traditional batch approach.

Secondly, in order to implement OLTP solutions, millions of dollars had to be found to invest in on-line technologies. The costs of terminals, minicomputers, more powerful mainframes and other hardware components of an OLTP solution were staggering, and these costs were often dwarfed by the costs of human resources. New people who knew how to use the on-line technology had to be hired, or the people that already worked for you had to be trained. Short-sighted IS managers who tried to trim the budget by cutting corners did so at their peril.

Third, with the advent of on-line technology, the demand for applications began to grow so quickly that the "Electronic Data Processing department," which by now had changed its name to "Management Information Systems" (MIS) or simply "Information Systems" (IS), found it difficult to keep up with it. People began asking for more applications, and it was taking IS longer to develop them. The term "application backlog" entered the jargon of the IS industry.

And fourth, (and perhaps least well understood at the time), there were the transitional costs. Companies needed to figure out how to make the transition to on-line systems without disrupting the day-to-day management of the business. This meant moving forward, not at the breakneck speed often proposed by the hardware vendor's sales rep (who was, after all, primarily interested in making quota), but rather at a slower, more prudent pace.

Today, from a contemporary perspective, some these problems seem almost laughable. But on the other hand, some of the issues that plagued the IS managers as late as 1976 are still with us today in 1996. For example, during an HP television broadcast conducted in February of 1996, over 90% of CEO's surveyed reported that the application backlog at their companies was six months or longer. The old saying that "the more things change, the more they stay the same" seems to be particularly applicable in IS.

The parallels between the "move to on-line" that took place twenty years ago and the "move to client/server" that's happening today are striking. In both cases, the driving force behind the technological shift is the desire to get information into the hands of the people who need it in a timely manner. In both cases, "hot new technology" prompted many IS managers to action. The successful IS manager's job is to perform an everlasting balancing act—adopting new technologies *where they make sense*, and continuing to use existing (legacy) technologies where *they* make sense.

In the technology-crazed nineteen nineties, the term "legacy system" has come to have a tawdry connotation. If all you know about technology is what you read in the business press, you might think that "legacy applications" don't do anything but cost money and create headaches. Successful IS managers know that the company typically runs on "legacy applications." Every legacy system was originally implemented to solve some kind of business problem. If it's still solving that problem effectively, then there's no reason to replace it. In other words, **changes in technology should not dictate what kinds of IS systems you decide to use. Technology should never drive your business. Your business should drive the choice of technology.** Successful IS managers don't replace a legacy system just because it's based on old technology. They will only replace it when it ceases to solve the business problem that it was built to solve.

This is not to suggest that new technologies shouldn't be used. Some IS managers who failed to survive the second wave did so because they behaved as if OLTP was a "fad," and that sooner or later everybody would go back to batch. The fact is that fundamental shifts in computer technology should always be investigated. OLTP certainly didn't turn out to be a fad. By the end of the seventies, virtually every company was using it, but not to the exclusion of batch processing.

The Importance of Integration

No single technology ever represents the single best answer to all of a company's business computing problems. This is a lesson that many of today's IS managers are painfully learning all over again. There is still no single best solution—not mainframes, not minicomputers, not personal computers, not UNIX, not the Internet and not NT. Each technology has its place. Each should be applied where it makes sense, and avoided where it doesn't. An important implication of this approach is the importance of systems integration. As new systems and technologies are brought on-line, they must be tightly integrated with legacy systems and technologies.

For example, there was once a major retailing company that had been in the forefront of the trend toward computerization in the late sixties. The company had been one of the first to implement batch-oriented systems to monitor customer accounts and track inventories. A nightly report, delivered to the company's buyers at eight o'clock each morning, told exactly how many items had been ordered and shipped the previous day, and how much inventory remained.

This company was blessed (or cursed, depending on how you look at it) with a very technologically savvy and forward thinking management team. And so, when OLTP became practical in the nineteen seventies, they decided to bring a new order processing application on-line. The on-line application would allow clerks working in the company's catalog order operation to take orders from customers over the phone, and be able to immediately tell the customers whether or not the items being ordered were in stock, and if not, how long the delay would be before they could be shipped. The benefit to the business, and the competitive advantage that would be gained over other, less technically advanced retail companies was clear.

At first, IS thought that the most difficult part of implementing the application would be the on-line technology upon which it would be based. This technology was brand new, and the company's staff of programmers, (who had by now accumulated years of experience with batch programming) had not been taught to use the new on-line tools. So, over the objections of the existing programming staff, a team of younger "hotshot" programmers was hired from the outside to work on the new project. Many of these new programmers had little practical experience. By and large, they had learned the new on-line technology in college. Some boasted some practical experience with small on-line pilot projects at other companies. But by and large, their experience with OLTP software was limited to "book-learning," and the building of small projects, often in a classroom environment.

It took just over 24 months to get the new application up and running, nearly twice as long as the original estimate, and in the end, the "newness" and complexity of the on-line technology didn't turn out to be much of a stumbling block. As the project developed, the biggest hurdle that had to be overcome turned out to be something that was at first thought to be a minor detail.

The on-line order processing application had to be integrated with an older batch system that managed each catalog order plant's inventory. For each order that was entered, the on-line application needed to check the inventories for the desired parts. The trouble was that inventory data was calculated by the older batch application, and the results stored off-line on reels of magnetic tape (state of the art in 1968).

The programmers that had been hired to work on the on-line system knew next to nothing about batch programming. ("They didn't teach it to us in college—they said it was obsolete.") They knew absolutely nothing about how this particular company's batch application programs worked. Even if they had understood the batch technology, they had neither the time nor the desire to learn the internal workings of the company's complex inventory system. Some acted as if the very idea of "dirtying their hands" with batch processing was beneath them.

After a number of fiascoes that put the project a year behind schedule, a team of older programmers who had worked on the batch application for years and understood it intimately were chartered to modify it to store certain key pieces of information on disk, where they could be accessed by the on-line application. By the time it was finally implemented competitors had all gotten wind of what the company was up to. By then, they had their own on-line catalog order systems under development, and in at least one case, up and running. The hoped-for competitive advantage of on-line catalog order processing failed to materialize.

I tell this story because it clearly illustrates the second fundamental lesson that successful IS executives learned during the second wave. **A key competence for IS is its ability to make old technologies and new technologies work together.**

There's more to the recipe for success than simply using new and old technology side by side. You can't build a wall between your legacy applications and your new applications if you expect them to work. The importance of application integration became even more apparent in the late 1970's with the introduction of the first database management systems.

Early Database Technology

The first OLTP applications had originally been developed around "flat" file systems (such as IBM's VSAM and HP's MPE and KSAM file systems). As OLTP systems became more complex, the limitations of file systems became apparent. Each on-line application "owned" its own set of files, and keeping many sets of files consistent with one another was time-consuming and complex. The first DBMSs represented a solution to this problem, because they enabled multiple applications to share a single physical copy of the data, while at the same time providing each application with its own unique "view" of the data. In this way, each application could be designed as if it still owned its own "files." If one application made a change to the database, that change would automatically be reflected in the views of the data that were used by the various other applications, because ultimately, they all shared just one physical copy of the data.

And again, the integration of new database technologies with older file-based technologies became a stumbling block. A key selling point for database technology in those days was that it would reduce the application backlog. Application development could be greatly simplified in a database environment because you didn't have to worry about keeping a lot of disparate files consistent with one another. Your DBMS took care of that. And in a world where all data resided in databases, it would have worked. The problem was most data in 1978 resided in flat files. Of course, you could move everything over from flat files to databases. But if you did, you'd have to rewrite all those flat file based applications—a proposition that was expensive, if not outright impossible.

In the end most companies wound up running a hybrid operation. New applications were built around databases whenever it was possible—but the new software often needed to make reference to some data items that resided in flat files which belonged to older legacy applications. The new technology was used when it made sense. The legacy technology survived as long as it continued to solve business problems, and as long as it could be integrated with the new technology.

Implications for Today's IS Managers

These are lessons that have profound implications for today's HP 3000 managers struggling toward successful implementations of software using client/server technologies. Today's trade shows invariably feature lots of demos of fancy application development tools that make it look like a programmer (or even an end user) can sit down at a desk and grind out all the applications you'll ever need in just a few minutes just by clicking the mouse a few times. You might wonder why there's an application backlog if new applications can really be built so easily. Today's problem is the same today as it was in 1982: building (or buying) new applications isn't the most important part of the job. The real key to success is making your new applications work together with your legacy applications. And today's solution to the legacy application problem has more in common with 1982's solution than you might think: there are really only two choices.

1. If the legacy applications are no longer effectively solving the business problems that they were originally designed to solve, then replace them and the system that they are running on. Or,
2. If the legacy applications are still doing the job for you, then keep them, and integrate them into the new client/sever environment.

CHAPTER 4

Treading Water In the Third Wave

In the 1980's, the computerization of commerce worked its way down from the Fortune 500 to the hundreds of thousands of small to midsize companies that form the backbone of the world economy. By this time even relatively small "ma-and-pa" businesses operating out of little more than store fronts could afford to apply computer technology to the problems of managing their affairs. In the minicomputer arena, HP brought new, less expensive models of the HP 3000 to the market, including a machine code-named "Mighty Mouse" that would support multiple users and fit under a desk. Other minicomputer vendors followed suit and big mainframe vendors had no choice but follow along. For years, IBM's mainframe strategy had been to bring bigger and more powerful machines to the market each year. Now they began to focus instead on smaller machines like the 4381 and the 9370, which offered compatibility with mainframes and price points closer to those offered by minicomputer vendors.

But all of this turned out to be little more than a warm-up for an event that would hit IS like a sledgehammer, forcing a total transformation of its values and its charter. A couple of engineers named Jobs and Wozniak were working for Hewlett-Packard when they came up with the idea of building a computer that was so small and inexpensive that it could be bought and used, not by a business, but by an individual. HP, (to its everlasting shame), didn't think that the idea had any merit, so the two engineers quit to form their own company, which they called Apple Computer. Jobs and Wozniak enjoyed a good deal of success with their brain-child, but it wasn't until the introduction of the IBM Personal Computer, or PC some years later that the impact of desktop computer was really felt in the IS department.

The third wave of the computerization of commerce was driven by the advent of these tiny machines. Up until now, the typical computer user had worked for a large corporation, and used the machines exclusively for business purposes. By the end of the third wave, it had become very difficult to form a clear picture of the "typical" computer user. What did "typical" mean when people used computers in every kind of business—from Fortune 500 companies to local car dealerships and real estate offices? How could you paint a clear picture of how computers were being used when people used them for every purpose imaginable, from business to education to games playing?

At first glance, there seems to be little reason for today's "typical" computer users to be interested in how IS departments had handled the issues arising from the computerization of commerce. And yet, just as many IS managers' short-sightedness caused them to paint themselves into one corner after another in the first and second waves, many of today's third wave computer users sometimes seem bent on using today's more powerful and less expensive computing technology to not only paint themselves into corners, but to saw the floorboards out from under themselves.

The Growth of "Soviet Style" IS Management

During the second wave, access to business computers was almost entirely governed by IS departments. IS typically had two charters—to safely store and manage the corporate data, and to provide application programs so that end users could access that data. We've seen how the second wave was characterized by the difficulties of integrating new OLTP technologies with older legacy technologies, with one result being the growth of the application backlog. IS's customers—the end users that worked in manufacturing, finance, personnel, purchasing or other areas—depended on IS to provide them with applications so that they could get their jobs done.

By the beginning of the 1980's, IS managers all over the industry were being told that their customers were not happy. The central issue seemed to be "who owns the information that we need in order to run our part of the company?" When end users wanted reports or the ability to work with information on-line, they had to pay IS to build or acquire the application software. And IS was taking longer and longer to deliver those applications. By the time end users were getting them, the business requirements that had led to their development in the first place had changed. They didn't need them any more.

During the first wave, IS had been able to keep up with the demand for applications because there were relatively few programs required and they didn't change very frequently. But in the second wave, the number and complexity of application software requirements exploded. Worse, most application programs had dependencies on other application programs. When you made any change to one, you often forced changes in others. The amount of maintenance programming that was necessary went up dramatically. When the demand for new applications rose by 10 percent, then the demand for programming hours could easily double or even triple. The application backlog grew until in many companies it was taking five years to design, code, test and implement new applications. Dissatisfaction from end users caused many IS managers to develop a kind of siege mentality about their jobs.

Faced with criticism from all over the company, IS had to find a way to get applications out more quickly. A great deal of effort had been spent on finding ways to make programmers more productive, starting with Structured Programming and Fourth Generation Languages in the 70's and continuing with Computer Aided Software Engineering (CASE) tools in the 80's. Each of these methodologies showed promise, but they worked best when they were used "in a vacuum"—that is, to develop totally new software projects from the ground up, without any dependencies on existing legacy software. But when they were applied in the real world, productivity gains often vanished in the learning curve and in the problems of integrating them with legacy applications and technology.

Each year, IS was faced with the same problem. It couldn't develop applications fast enough, and it couldn't figure out an effective way to speed up the development process. Most IS departments in the second wave responded in the only way that they could. Many IS departments began operating under what we'll call a "Soviet-style" of information management. They promised that next year things would get better if only the company would agree to fund the purchase of new computers, larger and more powerful than those that they had now, or those that the company had agreed to buy last year. These computers would, of course, be highly centralized and managed entirely by IS. End users couldn't use them or access their own information without IS's say-so (which was sold through the use of complex chargeback systems that nobody really understood, but which always seemed to charge more than you thought they ought to).

Of course, bigger and faster computers would not solve the problem. Applications weren't late because the computers were too slow. They were late because nobody had anticipated how complex the development and maintenance of applications would be, and how difficult it was to keep up with the demand for applications.

To angry end users, the introduction of personal computers must have seemed nothing less than a godsend. Like many revolutions, desktop computing got off to a shaky start. The first desktop machines were of little interest to business people; they required a lot of technical expertise to use and were often sold as kits. Their appeal was primarily to engineers, technicians and hobbyists. The addition of the first spreadsheet packages, notably Visicalc, made a big difference. Desktop computers began to make their way into the offices of a few adventurous accountants and stockbrokers. But with the advent of the IBM PC and the Lotus 1-2-3 spreadsheet package, the floodgates opened. Almost overnight, personal computers arrived on the desktops of executives throughout the business world. Granted, most CEOs had neither the time nor the inclination to learn to use them. Most wound up being used as little more than expensive paperweights or boat anchors, but IBM's name had brought a new level of respectability to desktop computing. Together with Lotus 1-2-3's innovative integrated approach to spreadsheets and graphics, the IBM PC represented a solution to a thousand and one little business problems, one that people could use without having to deal with Soviet-style IS at all.

Predictably, the advent of desktop computer technology was at first perceived, from IS's perspective at least, to be at best a threat and at worst nothing short of disastrous. Even the most myopic IS managers understood that bringing PCs into the enterprise could result in chaos. When the OLTP wave had swept through the corporate world in the 1970's, the IS department had to adapt—but at least it had control over the acquisition of hardware, software and technology. IS could decide *how* to adapt. But when the PC wave arrived in the 1980's, IS departments worried, with good reason, that they were losing control of the buying decisions. Computer hardware had long been the biggest line-item in the IS budget. PCs were nearly cheap enough to cover out of petty cash; an end user could buy one without consulting anybody in IS. Computer buying decisions and technology choices began to move from the IS department to accounting, to personnel, to manufacturing and to anywhere else in the corporation where people thought that they needed a computer.

In some companies, IS managers argued that, since PCs were computers, IS needed to have complete control over the purchase of all PC hardware and software. But these arguments carried little weight with end users, and invariably the availability of inexpensive PCs took the hardware buying decision away from IS. But much more importantly, it also took control of the applications away from IS. And when IS lost control of the applications, it also began to lose control of something much more important: the data.

There had been only one way for second wave computer users to access their data, through applications provided by IS. But applications were now available from a bewildering variety of sources. Programmers who worked on mainframes during the day were grinding out desktop packages at night and on weekends, and selling them through every imaginable channel. PC software companies were springing up overnight (with many disappearing just as quickly). A few end users were even using languages like BASIC to write their own applications. Slowly, IS began to understand that data that was owned by these applications was beyond

IS's charter to "manage and safely store" corporate data. It was data that, in the second wave, would have been turned over to IS to manage. Now, for better or worse, it was entirely under the control of the end users.

As IS began to lose control of the data, the *consistency* of the data began to become an issue all over again. In a second-wave world, when somebody from personnel had a question about the company's employee base, they knew where to get the answer. They might not have liked the idea that IS had the answer "locked up in the mainframe," but at least they knew where to look for it. But in a third-wave world the answer might not be on IS's mainframe. Part of it might be in a minicomputer run by manufacturing, or in a spreadsheet stored on a PC on some accountant's desk. Worse, there might be an answer in all three places and the answers that you got from each of the three sources might not agree.

From the beginning of the first wave, the whole point of using computers in business had been to get control of the information, so it could be used to run the company more efficiently and effectively and gain a competitive advantage. But now the response to IS's Soviet management style was making it difficult if not impossible to get answers to questions. Just as the breakup of the Soviet Union led to chaos in parts of Eastern Europe, the destruction of IS's information monopoly was creating Soviet style chaos in the third wave of the computerization of commerce.

Short sighted IS managers continued to behave as if their primary responsibilities were the selection, purchase and maintenance of the corporate computer systems. But the more visionary IS professionals began to see a different vision of IS and its responsibilities. In the second wave, IS managers had envisioned using DBMS technology to manage all the corporate information in a single centralized database, where it was easily managed by IS professionals, and where data consistency would cease to be an issue. In the world of the second wave, IS seemed to be making progress toward that ideal, but the chaos of the third-wave shattered it. Corporate data was being manhandled by end users in countless spreadsheets and PC-based files. There was no going back. IS now owned only the data and applications that were stored in the datacenter (now prophetically re-christened "the glass house") but each year the use of desktop applications (and data) grew, while the growth of centralized IS applications and data virtually stopped.

Clients and Servers—File Servers

Soon, end users began to realize that the act of putting PCs on their desktops had gotten them more than they had bargained for. In divorcing themselves from IS, they had gotten custody of a part of IS's charter. Now they bore the responsibility of managing those computers and the data that was stored on them. Invariably, novice computer users responded to this new responsibility with a shrug. "Hard disks must be backed up regularly," they were told. In fact backups were done sporadically, if at all. Inevitably the day came when a hard disk drive would crash, and important information would be lost. Novice users invariably expressed amazement and even indignation that there was no way to recover it. Suddenly, secretaries found themselves being pressed into service to put in long hours backing up hard disks using slow, cumbersome and unreliable floppy disks. Inevitably, the end users who had most loudly demanded the divorce from IS now came to realize that IS had been adding some value all along. They still wanted control of their data, but they weren't so sure that they wanted to be in the data management business.

As end users made greater use of their PCs, they also began to see that IS had added value in another way. It began when some end user would acquire a particularly useful collection of data and use it to create a spreadsheet on their PC. The spreadsheet would contain a number of mathematical formulas to make a complex series of calculations against the original data. End users would use this to analyze market trends and better understand the company's business. So far so good. But soon the spreadsheet would be shared among other PC users each of whom would make his own copy (typically on a floppy disk) and store it on his or her own PC. Of course, each user's requirements were a little different, so some of them made changes to the formulas. Before long, parts of the spreadsheet were being copied into word processing documents that were being passed up through the management chain, and the data was used to make important business decisions. As time went on, the original data upon which the spreadsheet was based became outdated. But the spreadsheet was designed to purposely hide the "raw data" from the user; all they saw was the results of the calculations. So this little detail didn't stop people from continuing to use it. Sooner or later, some enterprising users took it upon themselves to bring the original data up to date. But by now there were hundreds of copies of the spreadsheet on people's desktops. And each copy had its own collection of formulas.

End users had begun the third wave because they wanted better control of their data. But they didn't really want to have the responsibility of managing the data on their desktops. And before the end of the decade, a technology came along that seemed to represent a neat compromise between the tyranny of Soviet IS and the confusion of the PC world. Personal Computer based Local Area Networks (PC-LANS) such as Novell's Netware were designed, built and marketed with end users who were struggling through the chaos of the third wave in mind. The typical PC LAN environment works this way.

Every user has a PC on his or her desktop. In PC/LAN terminology, these PCs are referred to as "clients." Each of these client PCs uses a popular desktop operating system (typically Microsoft's MS-DOS and Windows), with its associated application programs (Spreadsheets, Word Processors and so forth). Each has a hard disk installed inside of it. (In MS-DOS terminology, this hard disk is often referred to as the "C-drive" or simply as "C:"). Users can store data and applications on their own hard disks, just as they always have.

PC LANs require that the office install at least one an additional PC called a "server." Like the client PCs, the server has a hard disk installed inside of it. But unlike the clients, the server is not used to run business applications. Instead, it uses a specialized operating system called a "Network Operating System" or NOS. (Novell's Netware is an example of a NOS). Networking cable is used to connect the server to each of the client PCs.

When an end user powers up the client PC on his or her desk, signals are sent across this cable to the NOS. The end result is that the end user's client PC now appears to have more than one hard disk installed on it. In addition to the internal (C:) drive, the client now appears to have one or more additional hard disks, (in a PC environment they are each assigned one-letter names ending with a colon, in accordance with MS-DOS conventions—for example, F:, G:, K:, and so on).

The important thing to understand about these additional disk devices is that they are shared among all the end users with client PCs. That is, prior to the use of the PC/LAN, if one end user created a spreadsheet and stored it on their PC, there was no way to share it without making a copy of it on another PC. But with a PC/LAN, the file containing the spreadsheet could be stored on a shared drive. The spreadsheet file would then be immediately available for use by other users at other client PCs. Any change that's made to the spreadsheet would be reflected at everybody's desktop.

Similarly, PC/LANs also allowed end users to share printers and other devices. Until now, each desktop computer user that wanted to be able to print spreadsheets and word processing documents needed to buy a printer and connect it to his or her own PC. PC/LANs meant that printers and other devices could be connected to the LAN and shared among all the clients.

Servers that are used in this way are typically referred to as "file servers." Today, file servers are used in virtually every business that uses computers. There are many other client/server technologies available today aside from file servers, and we'll discuss some of them in the next chapter of this book. For now, it's important to understand that the availability of file servers represented the first step in making desktop computers truly practical not just for individuals, but also in organizations—including fairly large organizations. First of all, the use of file servers had the potential of getting end users out of the data management business. As long as critical data was stored on people's desktops, each end user had to accept the responsibility for managing it. But by storing critical files on the server, the responsibility for managing it could be shared. Secondly, the use of file servers could potentially solve the data consistency problem. As long as end users could access files, spreadsheets and documents on a file server, there was less need to make copies of them, and therefore fewer opportunities for the data to become inconsistent.

File servers, based on popular PC/LANs like Novell's Netware solved some of the short term problems presented by the third wave. But they also acted to create a heightened awareness of the problems that hadn't been solved. PC/LANs had allowed PC users to share files and devices with one another. But this technology did not allow users to access the data that was owned by the IS department.

When end users first began creating spreadsheets, they had based them on relatively small samples of "raw data." This data was typically keyed into the spreadsheet programs by hand. As desktop computers became more powerful, it became possible to build larger and more complex spreadsheets. It became desirable to base the spreadsheets on larger samples of raw data, samples too large to key in by hand. If you were looking for raw data that described an entire industry, it was sometimes possible to buy it from a company that specialized in selling information. But (as was more likely) you were looking for raw data that described the operations of your own company, there was only one place to look—your own company's IS department. The third wave had begun as a messy divorce between IS and the end users. Now it began to look there might be a reconciliation. In the divorce, the end users had given IS custody of the corporate databases. But now they found that they needed them.

Reconciling IS and End Users

In the second wave, databases such as IBM's IMS and DB/2 or HP's TurboIMAGE had been very attractive to IS managers because they could be used to share a single consistent copy of the data among disparate applications. Now, it was reasoned, this same technology might be used to maintain consistency between the data that IS owned and the data that the end users owned.

In the waning days of the third wave, the task of integrating desktop data with the databases used on mainframes and minicomputers was difficult if not outright impossible. The technology simply wasn't there yet. The problem was that the desktop machines were based on architectures that had little in common with the larger machines used by IS. The idea of architectural standards, which was to drive the fourth wave, was as yet unheard of.

By the time the third wave ran its course in the end of the 1980's, most corporations were using (whether they knew it or not) a bewildering array of different DBMSs and file management systems, each of which were tied to particular applications running on particular hardware platforms. IS visionaries were looking for a technology that could be used to provide each end user and each application with its own view of the data, regardless of whether that data was physically stored in PC-based MS-DOS files and spreadsheets, mainframe-based VSAM files and IMS databases or minicomputer based KSAM files and TurboIMAGE databases. And that technology simply did not exist at that time.

If an end user wanted to create a spreadsheet based on a large sample of data from IS, they needed to extract the data from the files or databases on the mainframe(s) or minicomputer(s) and copy it to their own PCs. This operation could be complex and time consuming, and it did not solve the problem of keeping the data on the desktop consistent with IS's data, which changed constantly. Of course, you could put in special procedures to keep the two copies consistent—but inevitably, somebody asked, "Didn't we put in database management systems specifically to solve the data consistency problem?"

Lessons Learned

Those IS managers whose careers survived the third wave did so because they grasped its most fundamental lessons. Traditional IS managers were most comfortable keeping everything on their centralized computers, where they could most effectively manage it. But the application backlog had rendered that technology paradigm unworkable.

At the same time, even the most vociferous advocates of desktop computing and PC/LANs had to admit that there were some situations in which the IS approach seemed to make more sense. Early attempts to mount high-volume transaction processing applications on PC/LANs had met with mixed results, and most people agreed that these kinds of applications probably needed to stay on larger computers, at least for the moment.

This all boiled down to a realization that the things that IS had learned in the first and second waves were still true. **There was still no single computer technology that represented the best solution to every business problem, and the most important part of the job (and the one that was most frequently forgotten in all the excitement over new technologies) was making the new technologies work effectively with the old.**

Third-wave-styled desktop computer turned out to be the technology of choice for some applications—particularly word processing, spreadsheets and graphics.

These tasks typically required limited access to corporate data, and they heavily leveraged the technological benefits of desktop computers. But second-wave-styled OLTP was still the best way to process large volumes of business transactions. And there was even still a place for first-wave-styled-batch processing; nobody could see any advantage to running a five hour sort on somebody's desktop.

The successful IS manager had to know when to apply each technology. More importantly, the focus of IS's charter had begun to change radically. In the first and second waves, IS's attention was primarily directed at controlling the purchase and management of all computer processing and equipment. But in the third wave **the most important thing was to provide access to the corporate data to anybody who needed it, while simultaneously protecting its consistency and integrity.**

People in the end user departments were demanding that IS make it possible for them to use their PC's to access and even change the corporate data that IS had kept "locked up" in the mainframe. Smart IS managers began to realize that they had lost control of the hardware and of the applications. Now they needed to focus on controlling the technologies that desktop applications would use to access IS's data, regardless of whether it was stored in a mainframe or in a minicomputer.

The stage was set for the arrival of the fourth wave—UNIX and client/server.

CHAPTER 5

UNIX, Client/Server and the Fourth Wave

As data migrated out of the glass house and onto people's desks, the transition from a centralized computing paradigm managed by IS to a decentralized paradigm managed by end users was anything but smooth. Whenever proper backup schedules, disaster recovery plans and other system management practices fell by the wayside, valuable data was eventually lost. The causes included everything from operator errors, ("I thought that 'formatting' a disk meant re-aligning all the paragraphs in my word processing documents!") to power surges, network outages and hardware failure.

The availability of file servers (see Chapter 4) helped to get end users out of the data management business, but this technology required the use of PC/LANs. People became dependent upon networks, and interruptions in network service became increasingly expensive and unacceptable. The need for network management was recognized, but network managers were (and are) highly skilled individuals. The idea of hiring a network manager for each small PC/LAN did not seem feasible.

In spite of all these problems, people pressed ahead with the decentralization of information management. File servers proliferated and applications based on file server technology began to appear. Many small companies tried to run their businesses entirely on PC/LANs. The success of this approach varied with the size of the organization, the scalability and quality of the application, the network and the PC hardware.

A whole new school of thought about Information Technology had emerged. Many people (particularly those in younger organizations that had no dependencies on big centralized mainframes or minicomputers) came to think that the centralized approach to information management (derisively referred to as "big iron") was simply obsolete, and that the best way to manage the enterprise's data was to distribute it across many small servers, held together with local area networks. The client/server approach using PC servers seemed to work pretty well with relatively small applications and small numbers of users.

Scalability of Client/Server Applications

In the early 1990's PC servers had become popular with small businesses and small organizations inside of large businesses. When small organizations grew, they became big organizations with more complex requirements for managing information. But the PC LAN approach to building applications did not always scale up very well. Early attempts to implement large-scale, mission critical applications on file servers met with results that were mixed at best. There were several points at which failures could have disastrous consequences.

Disk mechanisms, with their complex design, many moving parts and fine tolerances seemed to be particularly troublesome. While microprocessor technology had advanced by leaps and bounds throughout the nineteen eighties, disk technology had advanced at a slower pace. Most of the advances in disk technology were in capacity and miniaturization, rather than in reliability and performance. For example, the earliest PC hard disks could hold only a few million characters. Twenty megabyte drives were considered large. By the mid nineties, you could buy disks that could hold billions of characters for less money, representing roughly a thousand fold increase in capacity. But because the new devices could hold much more data, the consequences of disk failures were that much more serious. When one failed you could potentially lose a lot more data. In order to keep pace, the new disks would have to be a thousand times more reliable than the old ones. And they simply weren't. Later technological advances, such as the development of RAID drives were helpful. But reliability wasn't the only thing standing between PC servers and large mission critical applications. There were also performance issues.

To understand why performance is such a critical issue in a client/server environment, imagine for a moment that you're taking a trip to the bank. Furthermore, imagine that your bank has a guarantee that its tellers have been specially trained to process any transaction in under a minute. At first glance, you might think that this means your bank visit will be over in a minute or less. But if a whole bunch of people show up at the bank just before you do, they'll form a line. You might spend a short time with the teller, but only after standing in line for 15 minutes.

Disk drive performance works in much the same way. The new high capacity disk devices could hold up to a thousand times more data than the older drives, but they were not a thousand times as fast as the old drives. In standalone configurations this didn't represent much of a problem. Suppose a user entered a transaction on a PC. A request to access the data (a "disk input/output operation," or "disk I/O") would be generated by the PC's operating system software, and sent to the PC's internal hard disk. The amount of time that it took for the disk mechanism to act upon and satisfy the I/O would be very short, typically measured in milliseconds. As long as each PC user was only using data stored on his or her own PC, the difference between 1 millisecond access times and 100 millisecond access times was unimportant. No end user would ever be likely to notice the difference.

But in a client/server environment, disk performance was more likely to become an issue, particularly with large complex applications. When a disk was installed on a PC server, it represented a resource that had to be shared among all the users on the network. It had to keep up with the demands, not of a single user, but of all the client PC users.

In order to be suitable for large scale mission critical applications, a client/server system has to be able to keep up with the demands of end users. Whenever the user of a client PC would click his mouse button to enter a transaction, the client PC would send one or more signals called "packets" across the network. When these packets arrive at the server, it would process the transaction. To do this, a number of hardware and software components of the client/server system come into play. For example, the transaction must be transmitted across the network. That takes a certain amount of time. When it arrives at the server, the server's processor (typically an Intel 486 or Pentium) will take a certain amount of time to process the transaction. Most transactions require some data from the server's disk drives. Accessing the disks takes time. Each of these steps is handled serially, one after the other. The transaction's response time is the sum of the times that it takes each of the components to do its job. If one or more components takes an inordinately long time, response time gets worse (longer).

For commercial applications, it's typical for the disk (or disks) to become a bottleneck. To understand why, consider the demands placed on the server by a large scale application. An individual user might generate a few transactions each minute. A large network might have hundreds or even thousands of users, all sending multiple packets to the server each minute. Each transaction could generate multiple I/O requests on the server. A server that's trying to run a large mission critical application might be called upon to process an average rate of 2,000 I/O's each minute, with "gusts" up to 3,000 or more depending on the application and the number of users.

The number of I/O requests that a server can satisfy per minute (or per second) can vary wildly. The specifications for disk drives are very technical and based on benchmarks that may bear little or no relationship to the workload imposed by a particular application. Generally speaking, PC disk drives based on early 1990's technology could handle a steady diet of about 1500 I/O's per minute, with gusts up to about 1800, not quite half the rate required by large client/server applications.

In the same way, other shared resources can become bottlenecks that constrict client/server performance. For example, the network itself represents a shared resource in a client/server environment. The rate at which data that can be transmitted across the network is limited. If the network becomes too busy, then users issuing transactions must wait, and response times will suffer.

The number of business transactions that a server can respond to each minute depends on a number of variables, including the complexity of the application and the speed of the whole client/server computer system (including the network, the processors and especially the disks). Even though one request can be processed in a matter of milliseconds, if the demand sometimes outstrips the server's ability to keep up, the server will operate with a backlog of requests.

It's not unlike what happens when a whole bunch of people show up at the bank. Just as people will line up to be serviced by the teller, a server will line up backlogged requests and process them one at a time. It could take many seconds or even minutes before the server is able to grind its way through a queue of backlogged requests. The result is long (perhaps unacceptably long) response times for transactions. All these reasons contributed to the poor scalability of early PC file servers.

On large mainframes and minicomputers, scalability problems can often be solved using parallel resources. To understand how this works, let's return to the bank for a moment. What does the bank manager do when the line gets too long? He puts more tellers on the floor. With several tellers operating in parallel, the line moves much faster, because as a group they can process more transactions each minute. In the same way, when computer performance suffers because of a disk bottleneck, one solution is to add more disk drives and spread the data across them. This solution works as long as the server's architecture is sophisticated enough to allow the disks to operate in parallel. That is, it must be able to process multiple I/O requests at the same time (one on each drive). This is how most minicomputers and mainframes work. For example, the HP 3000 architecture was designed specifically to allow multiple drives to be active at the same time. Unfortunately, early PC operating system software was not this smart. Even if there were multiple disk drives on the server, technical shortcomings in PC system software forced the server to access no more than one drive at a time. Imagine a bank with several tellers, but as soon as one of them begins working with a customer, the others go on a break. Such a bank would be no faster than a bank with one teller. Similarly, on early PC servers with multiple disk drives, the queue of I/O requests moved along at much the same rate that it would if there had been only one drive.

The demand for solutions to these problems was the driving force behind the development of the client/server technologies that characterized the fourth wave. People were looking for a server platform that could work with desktop client systems, and still scale up to the heights achievable by minicomputers like the HP 3000 or mainframes. Today, there are almost as many definitions of the term "client/server" as there are people working in the IS industry. You can "do" client/server on almost any platform you can think of , including the HP 3000. But in the early days of the fourth wave, "client/server" and "UNIX" went together like ham and eggs. In order to fully understand why this was so, it's necessary to first understand a few fundamental facts things about UNIX.

The Beginnings of UNIX

UNIX is an operating system that was originally developed by engineers at AT&T. It has, at its root, a single unique characteristic—portability. Portability means that it is relatively easy to implement a UNIX-based operating system on any hardware architecture. Most operating systems (including MPE/iX) don't work that way. They are written with a particular hardware architecture in mind. Since MPE/iX was designed specifically for HP's PA-RISC architecture, implementing an MPE/iX operating system on some other architecture (such as Intel Pentium chips) would involve completely re-designing MPE/iX.

UNIX, on the other hand, was originally designed to be independent of the hardware architecture. This is an extremely important characteristic for hardware vendors (such as HP). To see why, imagine for a moment that you are the president of HP. One day your best engineers burst into your office to inform you that they've just invented a new computer chip. It has everything that you could ask from a microprocessor—it's many times faster than anything that you (or your competitors) have been able to bring to the market thus far, plus it's reliable and it promises to be inexpensive to manufacture. Seeing the potential, you're overcome with excitement, and just as you're about to call the financial department to authorize hefty bonuses for each member of the engineering team, they explain to you that there's a fly in the ointment. This new chip is not compatible with any existing chip. And that means that there's no existing operating system that customers can use to take advantage of the new chip's power.

This is very bad news, because before you can bring your new chip to market, you must first write an operating system for it. Operating systems have always been written in low level assembler languages. It looks like you'll have to dedicate a large team of very expensive operating systems specialists to the project for a period of several years. Aside from the expense, there's now a huge risk involved. By the time the new operating system is ready, your new chip might no longer represent a quantum leap in technology and performance. By the time you can bring it to market, it may be just another ho-hum computer system. What you really need is a way to bring a new operating system to your new chip very quickly.

UNIX represents a solution to this problem, for two reasons. First of all, you don't have to write the UNIX operating system yourself. The source code for UNIX can be licensed.[1] Secondly, unlike other operating systems, UNIX wasn't written in a highly complex, low-level assembler language. Most of UNIX was written in a high-level language called "C." In order to create a UNIX operating system for your new chip, you need to write a C compiler for it. Writing a C compiler is not a simple task, but it's a lot simpler than writing an entire operating system from scratch. Once you have the compiler, creating a UNIX operating system for your new chip becomes a relatively straightforward affair—not simple—but well understood by UNIX engineers. Better still, by saving the cost of developing a new operating system, you can sell your new UNIX-based computer for less money, making you more competitive in the computer systems marketplace.

UNIX has been popular with engineers, (particularly those that work for hardware vendors) for many years. It has been around in one form or another almost as long as mainframes, but until the late 1980's, it was used primarily for technical applications. Commercial IS managers tended to shy away from UNIX-based systems until the 1990's. This is in spite of the fact that they were (and are) relatively inexpensive. The trouble with UNIX was that it was less reliable than traditional proprietary commercial operating systems like IBM's MVS or HP's MPE/iX. Also, early implementations of UNIX lacked many of the features that were deemed critical in commercial environments.

But in an era of downsizing, many IS managers became very focused on lowering costs, and interest in UNIX grew quickly. By the end of the 80's, UNIX vendors recognized that there were great opportunities for them in the commercial computing marketplace, and many commercial applications were written for UNIX computers. IS managers told HP (as well as the other UNIX vendors) that they liked the low cost of UNIX systems, and the wide range of applications that were quickly becoming available for the machines. They needed to be made more reliable, and equipped with the features that commercial IS managers had come to take for granted in the commercial environment.

1. Originally the rights to the UNIX source code were owned by AT&T. In the 1990's they were sold to Novell. At this writing they have been transferred to X/Open.

UNIX vendors (particularly Hewlett-Packard) moved quickly toward meeting these requirements and by the mid-nineties hundreds of thousands of HP 9000 UNIX systems were being installed in businesses all over the world. Other vendors had similar successes. Most of the commercial applications used on UNIX are based on relational database management systems from companies such as Oracle and Sybase. Many (perhaps most) UNIX applications are based on the traditional host/terminal paradigm typically found on more traditional mainframe and mini-computer systems. But UNIX really began to attract attention as a commercial platform when it was shown that client/server applications could potentially be scaled up more effectively when UNIX-based systems were used than they could with PC servers.

The word UNIX became synonymous with an information management strategy that was called "open systems." Open systems is based on the idea of standards. Standards are so ubiquitous in today's complex world that we tend to take them for granted. For example, when you plug a toaster into a wall socket in your kitchen, you know that it will work because all electrical outlets deliver a standard electrical voltage and accept plugs of the standard size and shape. As long as the manufacturers of toasters comply to the standards, you can buy your toaster from any company you like and be confident that it will work with the wall sockets in your house (at least as long as you don't move to another country, where the standards may be different).

Up until now, the commercial computer industry had gotten by with very few standards. Each computer vendor created its own proprietary computer architectures, having little in common with one another. When a company made a commitment to use a particular application, it locked itself into the particular architecture that the application used, because applications are tightly coupled with the architectures of the computers upon which they run. And this in turn locked the company into a single hardware vendor, because each computer architecture was supported by one and only one vendor.

UNIX promised to change that. When a customer committed to an application, they were still locked into a particular architecture, namely UNIX. But they were not locked into a particular vendor because many different hardware vendors sold UNIX systems. UNIX applications tended to be available on a variety of hardware platforms from different vendors. If a customer had a falling out with one UNIX vendor, they could turn to another.

Smart IS managers had realized that their success would now hinge in large measure on their ability to make different kinds of computers work together. In the third wave, the lack of standards had made it difficult to integrate Personal Computers into information systems based on other platforms and architectures such as

HP 3000s and mainframes. A fast growing group of IS managers and hardware vendors (especially HP) rallied around UNIX as the fastest way to solve the fundamental problems of the third wave. The plan was to run commercial UNIX applications on the desktop.

Client/Server in the UNIX World

When the invention of microprocessors made desktop computing possible, UNIX-based desktop computers followed very quickly. These desktop machines (called UNIX workstations) became very popular in engineering environments. HP moved into this market with its Series 700 models of the HP 9000 line. The 700s were based on the same PA-RISC hardware technologies found on HP 9000 UNIX servers and on the HP 3000. Graphical user interfaces like X/Windows and Motif made it easy to use UNIX workstations to run multiple applications at the same time.

In the PC/LAN environment, the term client/server had typically been used to describe the use of file servers. In the UNIX environment, the term came to denote any one of dozens of ways of using desktop UNIX workstations together with more powerful UNIX servers. For example, using a technology called the Network File System (NFS), UNIX machines could share files with one another in much the same way as PC-based file servers. This meant that applications running on UNIX-based desktop machines could be used to access data residing in files stored on UNIX servers. Servers could share files with other servers using the same technology.

Many commercial UNIX applications required end users to use terminals to log onto UNIX systems and access the applications. But if UNIX computers were connected via a network, users could use a technology called Telnet to logon from one UNIX computer to another. UNIX workstations could be used as terminals (using Telnet) while running applications at the same time (using GUIs such as X/Files could be copied between UNIX computers using the file transfer protocol (ftp). Most relational database management systems (Oracle, Sybase, etc.) included client/server components to allow databases to be accessed across a network.

In the early days of the fourth wave, UNIX systems enjoyed great technical advantages over PC based systems. Furthermore, UNIX servers did not suffer from the same scalability problems as PC servers. UNIX's I/O subsystem organized disks into groups called "file systems," which could be accessed in parallel. Also, UNIX's portability guaranteed that new servers based on the latest and fastest performing chip architectures would always be available, regardless of what hardware vendor took the lead in the ongoing race to build the fastest chips. PCs were limited to chips based Intel's architecture. This meant that the speed of UNIX servers was limited only by the ingenuity of hardware engineers. With the introduction of the Corporate Business Servers, HP began selling HP 9000 servers that were as powerful as traditional mainframes.

But UNIX's greatest appeal in the early days of the fourth wave was simply this: UNIX computers came "from the factory" with virtually all the networking technology built in and pre-installed. And, with a few exceptions, UNIX-based client/server technology worked across vendor boundaries, so customers could combine low cost desktop UNIX workstations from one vendor with powerful servers from another vendor. This stood in stark contrast to the PC world, where client/server technology was an "add-on" that had to be purchased separately, installed and configured, and the servers were based on the same architecture as the client machines. MS-DOS, the foundation of PC architecture had been found to have some serious technical limitations. For example, it could not take advantage of RAM sizes in excess of 640K without using special programming calls. UNIX had no such limitations.

The term "open systems" had originally been used to denote a strategy of using standards to make computers from different vendors work together. But now, it came to mean using UNIX machines throughout the enterprise—from the desktop to the datacenter. This strategy gained very broad acceptance in the early nineteen nineties. UNIX was, for all practical purposes, the only operating system that had shown it could run well both on the desktop and on a large powerful server. By 1990, many IS managers were installing UNIX systems, not because they were cheaper, but because they believed that UNIX systems represented the easiest way to get to a client server environment, and eliminate the chaos that had followed in the wake of the third wave. Client/server, they believed, could only work on UNIX and would not ever be practical on other architectures. From about 1990 to 1992 the computer industry press fairly glowed with articles that suggested, at least implicitly, that UNIX would become the only feasible operating environment before the middle of the decade. It really looked for a while like UNIX would "take over the world"—at least the world of IS.

The UNIX Juggernaut Stumbles

UNIX advocates had envisioned a world where all operating systems (or at least all the ones that mattered) were based on UNIX. There was no place for MS-DOS, MS/Word, MPE/iX or MVS in this vision. Some believed that UNIX workstations would inevitably replace PCs based on MS-DOS and MS/Word on the commercial desktop, and that all server processing would eventually move to UNIX-based machines.

By 1994, it was clear that things weren't going to work out quite that way. This is not to say that there was anything wrong with UNIX. Instead, IS managers saw that just as on-line had failed to sweep batch processing from the data center, just as minicomputers had failed to replace mainframes and PCs had failed to replace minicomputers, UNIX would fail to replace all the technologies that had come before it. Rather, UNIX would take its place beside all these other technologies.

The idea that UNIX would become the dominant operating system on planet earth was predicated on the notion that UNIX workstations would replace PCs on the commercial desktop. In spite of all the technical advantages of UNIX workstations, most commercial users stubbornly stuck with their PCs. Applications were the primary reason why. During the third wave, a number of very strong PC-based business applications (Lotus 1-2-3, Freelance, WordPerfect, MS/Word, AmiPro and PowerPoint among many others) gained wide acceptance among commercial users. It became clear that if UNIX was going to replace MS-DOS on the desktop, a means would have to be found to run these applications on UNIX workstations.

Some software companies attempted to port their applications from PCs to UNIX workstations. Others tried to emulate the entire Intel/Microsoft environment under the UNIX umbrella. Both approaches met with mixed results. Eventually it became clear that replacing PCs with UNIX workstations would mean abandoning applications in which users had invested a lot of time and sweat equity. And the vast majority of PC users simply didn't seem to be willing to do that.

Today, the vast majority of UNIX workstations are being sold into technical environments, and being used to run engineering applications. Microsoft, Intel, HP and other companies have moved forward to solve many of the technical issues that hobbled early PC servers. New operating system software, particularly Microsoft's NT, has addressed many of the scalability and reliability issues associated with MS-DOS. At the same time, sales of HP 9000 servers continue to accelerate year by year, with most servers going into commercial environments, running business applications.

Lessons Learned

At first glance, we appear to be right back where we were at the beginning of this chapter. At the close of the third wave, IS managers were trying to figure out ways to use the strong desktop applications running on PCs with the data that they had stored on other machines, including mainframes and HP 3000s. We said that UNIX had appeared to represent a solution to this problem, but the solution turned out to be unworkable. Or did it?

The key strength of the open systems strategy is not UNIX. It is standards. Standards are what allowed different UNIX systems to work with one another. And today, standards are what has finally made it possible for PCs, minicomputers, workstations and mainframes to work together. As late as 1992, if you wanted to take a standards-based approach to client/server, you had little choice but to move to UNIX, because UNIX was driving the process of defining the standards. But over time, most of the standards that made UNIX an open system in the first place have been implemented on other platforms as well.

For example, it was (and is) easy to network UNIX systems to one another because they all support the same networking standards. Virtually every UNIX LAN was based on IEEE 802.3, or Ethernet. Data is transmitted across UNIX LANs using a mechanism called Transport Control Program / Internet Protocol, or TCP/IP. Today, TCP/IP is the foundation for internetworking, the technology that underlies the Internet.

The Internet is a vast collection of networks that are connected to one another. At the birth of the Internet, the technology required to put a computer on the internet was only available on UNIX systems. Today the Internet is connected to PCs, NT Servers, HP 3000s, UNIX servers like the HP 9000, and countless other kinds of computer systems. The Internet is a useful tool because of technologies like html and the World Wide Web, BSD Sockets, NFS, ftp and TELNET. These technologies are all based on TCP/IP, and are all available on a wide variety of platforms including NT, HP 3000s, PCs, Mainframes and UNIX computers. The POSIX standard for basic operating system functionality (IEEE 1003.1) was originally written in an effort to unify the various versions of UNIX. Today it is supported, not only by most UNIX operating systems, but also by MPE/iX, by IBM's MVS, by Microsoft's NT, and by a number of other non-UNIX operating systems as well.

UNIX may have failed to replace all the other computer architectures used in the IS world. But today there are thousands of commercial applications available for low-cost UNIX servers like the HP 9000, far more than for any other platform. UNIX has succeeded in "taking over the world" in spirit, if not in actual fact. Ten years ago it would have been very difficult, if not impossible, to build a network encompassing PCs, HP 3000s, HP 9000s and Mainframes. Today such a feat is routine. Heterogeneous networking is a fact of life. We have UNIX to thank for this.

CHAPTER 6

The Age of Interoperability

The fundamental concept of client/server has changed subtly since the mid eighties. Originally, client/server meant connecting similar machines to one another via a network so they could exchange data with one another. Today's definition is almost the same—only the word "similar" is missing. Today, it's not unusual to see a PC client working with an NT server, an HP 9000 UNIX server, an HP 3000 server, a mainframe server, or all of the above. We live in an age that is not dominated by any individual operating system or computer architecture. It is the *Age of Interoperability.*

SuperServers

Today, HP 3000s, HP 9000s and many other computer systems can act in the role of traditional host computer systems and in the role of large scale servers at the same time. A computer *system* is one where the same physical machine is used to store the data and execute the application. For example, mainframes and HP 3000s have traditionally been used primarily as computer systems, with the applications running on the same machine on which the data is stored. On the other hand, a computer *server* is a computer that is simply used to store and provide access to data. The applications that act on that data are typically executed on other computers called clients. Clients are usually desktop machines. But they don't have to be. And an HP 9000 can act as a client by requesting data from an IMAGE/SQL database on an HP 3000.

Today's HP 3000s and HP 9000s are highly scaleable *systems*; they are often used to run large scale mission critical applications using traditional terminal based technologies, (such as VPLUS on the HP 3000, or curses on the HP 9000). But at the same time, they can also act as highly scaleable *servers,* providing access to data on behalf of applications running on clients. In this book, we'll use the term "Superserver" to denote a computer that can be used as a system and as a server simultaneously, while supporting mainframe-class workloads in either (or both) environments.

When PCs first arrived on the scene, IS managers recognized that their success depended in large measure on their ability to make these new machines work with their existing mainframes and minicomputers. In the fourth wave, some companies found that they could substitute relatively inexpensive UNIX servers for traditional platforms. But many other companies found that the cost and disruption of "moving to UNIX" outweighed the benefits. Now, finally, the advent of UNIX-style standardization to non-UNIX platforms has finally made it possible to have the benefits of client/server without the disruption.

For thirty years, people in the computer industry have been talking about which operating system was going to eventually become dominant. In the seventies, IBM convinced many in the Fortune 500 that MVS was the only operating system that could support the needs of a large corporation. In the eighties, Microsoft took the spotlight away from IBM with MS-DOS and MS/Word. In the nineties, UNIX began to look like a smart bet. And today there are some that believe Microsoft's NT will ultimately win the operating system wars.

And yet if you take the long view of IS's history, the lessons learned in the past tell us that it's extremely unlikely that any operating system will ever really "win". IS strategies that are based on the notion of moving all computer processing to one particular architecture or to a single operating system are usually not very practical, regardless of whether the target OS is UNIX, NT or even MPE/iX. The reasons are not hard to grasp.

First consider the case of a company that has legacy applications running on an older platform such as a mainframe or an HP 3000. If IS adopts an OS-centric strategy of moving all processing to UNIX, NT or whatever, then the legacy applications must either be replaced or ported to the target operating system. If the legacy applications are no longer cost-effectively solving the business problems that they were designed to solve in the first place, then replacing them makes sense. They should be replaced. But if the legacy applications are still doing the job, then the benefits of porting them or replacing them rarely justify the cost of doing so. No matter how you approach it, changing applications is disruptive to the business and costs a great deal of money. In the end, if you're lucky, the end result is new applications that do exactly what the old applications did. So what's the point?

What about companies that have no legacy applications? Here too, an OS-centric strategy makes no sense in the nineties. It might have been smart back in the seventies, when most of today's IS managers were "learning the ropes." Back then, the high price of hardware meant that most corporations could only afford to use one computer, and hardly anyone was brave enough to use more than one kind of computer. So an OS-centric strategy made a lot of sense. IS invested a lot of time, to ensure that they would choose the right computer with the right operating system. It was a critically important decision because they recognized that in the future it could seriously hamper their ability to grow and evolve. If they began by buying a mainframe to run manufacturing, then it was a sure bet that when they needed a Financials package or a human resource management system, they'd be limited to packages that ran on mainframes. Buying and learning to manage additional computers and networking them with the mainframe were both technically difficult and prohibitively expensive propositions. But look at how things have changed in the nineties. Today, computer hardware is much cheaper. Networking different kinds of systems with one another is de rigeur. There is no longer any reason to limit yourself to the applications that happen to run on one platform or another. Choosing the right platform is no longer the key to success. The important thing is not the operating system. The important thing is the network.

Client Server Evolution

When the client/server wave first appeared on the IS horizon, it looked like it would sweep all the older platforms and technologies aside, (a pattern that has repeated itself over and over again). Now client/server can be seen in its true light, as a process of evolution, not revolution. Customers that have been availing themselves of applications that run on mainframes and minicomputers (including UNIX servers) have no reason to worry about being locked out of the client/server world, because there is a well understood process for evolving into client server environments without walking away from your investments in more traditional technologies. Typically client/server evolution takes place in a series of five steps. It's not necessary to go through all five steps. Steps can be skipped or rearranged, depending on your business needs.

The first step is the ***installation of desktop computers*** in the office. As we've seen, IS rarely has the opportunity to plan or control this step. The low cost of PC hardware and software guarantees that this will happen with IS or without them.

The second step is to ***provide host application access***. This typically involves the use of terminal emulation software such as WRQ's Reflection Series, to allow the desktop computer users to take advantage of existing terminal based applications. Using Microsoft Windows, users can access these applications residing on legacy platforms like mainframes, HP 3000s or HP 9000s, and simultaneously be running PC-based applications like word processing and spreadsheets. If terminals have been used in the past to access these applications, the same terminal cabling can be leveraged for use with the terminal emulation software.

The third step involves ***installing a LAN*** that connects the desktop computers to one another and to the legacy computers. In the case of the HP 3000 and 9000, the necessary LAN software is bundled with the operating system at no additional charge. The LAN opens up the possibility of using the desktop computers as clients, together with full time servers such as NetWare PC servers, or together with any or all of the legacy systems acting as SuperServers. Here are some examples of ways that this can be useful. First of all, LAN access to the Superserver is much faster than access via serial interfaces. So host application access across a LAN is much faster and smoother. Technologies like ftp can be used to make host data available to PC applications more quickly. Software is available to make many Superserver platforms (including HP 3000s and HP 9000s) emulate Novell NetWare servers, so the mission critical data on these machines can be accessed from people's desktops as if it were on a Novell PC server. Internet technologies like the World Wide Web (www) become available in this environment. Web Browsers such as Mosaic or Netscape can be used to access www servers which could be outside the corporation on the public internet, or they can reside on HP 3000 or HP 9000 SuperServers inside the company. Printers like HP LaserJets can be attached directly to the LAN and accessed from any of the computers connected to the LAN. (Network printing is supported on MPE/iX as of release 5.5).

The fourth step involves ***integrating the data base environments*** on the various platforms. For example, Microsoft has made a strong commitment to a technology called Open Data Base Connectivity (ODBC) that allows its PC based products (MS/Word, MS/Excel, MS/Access, among others) to be used with various kinds of databases. ODBC is also supported by many other PC applications (Lotus 1-2-3 for Windows), and application development tools (such as Visual Basic, PowerBuilder and QBE). For example, ODBC can be used with MS/Word to create word processing documents that include information culled from IMAGE/SQL databases residing on HP 3000s, Oracle databases residing on HP 9000s, MS/Access databases residing on PC servers or all three. Similarly, Oracle has a technology called Oracle/Net that can be used to tightly integrate IMAGE/SQL databases on HP

3000s with Oracle databases on other platforms such as NT or the HP 9000. Similar technology exists for Sybase databases.

The fifth and final step is the implementation of ***distributed processing***. Using a technology such as OSF's Distributed Computing Environment (DCE), applications can be distributed across multiple computers and multiple computing architectures. This ultimately puts the desktop computer user in charge. From the desktop, the user can access data and programs across different kinds of computers without ever having to be so much as aware of whether he or she is using an HP 3000, an HP 9000, an NT or UNIX server or even a mainframe.

And in the final analysis, that is what client server was supposed to be all about.

IS's Responsibilities In the Age of Interoperability

IS began with a twin charter—to manage the data and to provide the applications necessary to run the business. Today, IS still provides some of the applications. The information flow that drives most large business organizations typically originates with a small number of large mission critical applications maintained and managed by IS professionals. These applications could be based on client/server technology, but they are frequently based on older host/terminal computing paradigms. Data flows from these applications on a daily basis in a great, slow moving river. Today, end users are demanding to have access to that river of data from their desktops. And today the technology exists to give them that access without compromising the data's integrity.

There are basically two approaches that can be taken to give end users access to the data. One is to use client/server technology to give them access to "live" databases on production SuperServers. These databases are typically being updated simultaneously by mission critical legacy applications. This approach may be workable, but it requires a lot of careful management. Giving end users access to your production SuperServers means allowing them to place workloads on these machines. And since much of the client/server work involves the processing of ad hoc queries, this workload is often unpredictable. In order to prevent wild variations in performance on the Superserver, clients must operate in highly controlled and restricted environments that may not meet the needs of the business. Careful management and control is a must. The second approach is called "data warehousing", and in simple terms, it involves periodically copying the raw data from production databases on the Superserver into client/server databases on full time servers. These databases are designed around the needs of by client/server users, and optimized to be used by them.

In both approaches, IS must continue to take responsibility for managing the data and the applications on the SuperServers. In a client/server world, IS bears new responsibilities:

1. **Physical and Logical Data Integrity**. IS has been using proper backup schedules and other basic system management practices since the sixties to ensure the integrity of the data. In a client/server world, these practices must be extended beyond the "glass house" and out to the client systems. Today, there are software solutions in place that can manage heterogeneous networks.

2. **Security**. Many client/server tools can be used to not only examine, but also to update the data on the Superserver. If your end users have a business need to do this, then remember that giving client/server users full access to production data on SuperServers does not mean an end to security. If anything, it means that more attention must be paid to security and data access controls than ever before.

3. **Data Availability**. High availability was once a euphemism for keeping the system up and running. Today things are more complicated. That are three aspects to data availability that must be managed—performance management, planned downtime and unplanned downtime. Performance is critical because your Superserver may be "up and running," but if client/server users have placed unexpected and uncontrolled workloads on it, then its performance will suffer. If performance is so poor that users of mission critical applications cannot get their jobs done, then for all practical purposes, that system is down. Planned downtime happens when the data is unavailable because of backups or other routine maintenance. Today, technology exists to minimize planned downtime through the use of on-line backups. Unplanned downtime happens when data is unavailable because of some kind of unexpected failure. You cannot prevent unplanned downtime, but you can have plans in place to ensure that your staff can recover from failures quickly. Today, there are many new technologies in place (SharePlex/iX for HP 3000s, MC/ServiceGuard for HP 9000s) that use redundant components and even redundant systems to minimize the time lost to unexpected failures.

4. **Maintenance of Traditional Host-Based Applications.** Some IS managers, focused on the need to move to a new technology, have acted to "freeze" expenditures on traditional host-based applications. This is a

mistake. In order to move forward into the client/server world, traditional host applications must be maintained in ways that are compatible with client/server access. That is, host-based software must be "well-behaved" in a client/server environment. This could mean tweaking the design of host based data bases to make them more usable for PC users. Database locking strategies are particularly important when you have no way of predicting when (or how) users will access your data.

5. **The need for host-based software.** Client/server does not eliminate the need for host based software. Rather, client/server tools provide new ways of creating and running applications that can access data stored locally, on servers, or on SuperServers. Some business problems (graphics, word processing, presentation management) are best solved using the graphical user interfaces and desktop processing power of PCs. Others (simple transaction processing) may be more cost effectively solved using simple transaction processing techniques that date back to the seventies. The trick is to approach each business problem separately, and apply each technology where it makes sense to do so.

System Management has always been a key part of the IS manager's job. In the age of interoperability, system management does not stop at the door of the glass house. The "system" that is now being managed extends out through the network to PCs and other desktop devices. And every aspect of IS's job must reflect this extension. Backup strategies, disaster recovery plans, and other system management practices all need to be reevaluated, and every step of the way IS must ask "What about the network? What about the PCs?"

CHAPTER 7

The HP 3000 And the 21st Century

We've seen how the computerization of commerce has washed over the IS world in a series of waves. Today's IS executive must learn to adapt in an environment that is focused on entirely different issues than his predecessor of twenty, or even ten years ago. In the past, IS had to worry about choosing the right operating system. Today, IS must be much more focused on how it will make different applications running on different computers work together.

In this chapter, (and in the remainder of this book) we will focus on how this applies specifically to the HP 3000. How does the HP 3000 fit into a heterogeneous network? What does the future of MPE look like? We'll also begin to focus on the tools and technologies used to design and develop applications. Which ones make the most sense in an open systems world?

In 1990, the term "open systems" was synonymous with "UNIX." Today, we know that open systems is the strategy that made client/server practical on UNIX systems. The open systems strategy now represents a standards based approach to making different kinds of computers work together to solve a common business problem. UNIX may (and often will be) a part of the solution. But the open systems strategy, as it applies to today's IS environment, is applicable on the HP 3000 as well as it is on UNIX systems such as the HP 9000 and on NT systems such as HP's NetServers.

Is MPE/iX an Open System?

Today, the term "open systems" has now come to mean much more than a dependence on UNIX. From 1990 onward, a number of characteristics were attributed to UNIX systems which, it was believed were unique to UNIX systems (and always would be). Some UNIX advocates talked about these characteristics as if they represented a kind of "manifest destiny," a guarantee that UNIX would become the dominant operating system in the commercial computing world. Today, some of these characteristics are just as applicable to HP 3000s as they are to UNIX systems. Others are not. Some of them are important to IS executives trying to put together and manage heterogeneous networks. Others have become irrelevant. We'll explore each of these characteristics in some detail:

- Freely distributed source code
- Software is available on more than one platform
- Application Portability
- Interoperability
- Commodity-priced hardware
- Adherence to standards
- Specifications are not under the control of any single vendor
- Common User Interface
- Common Management Interface
- Compatibility over time

Freely distributed source code. One reason for UNIX's early popularity was because AT&T made the source code for the UNIX operating system freely available, not only to hardware vendors, but also to universities. This led to the creation of various flavors of UNIX, since it enabled students (and others) to modify the source code and create their own unique UNIX operating systems, (a valuable exercise for computer science students hoping to find employment as engineers with one of the major hardware vendors). Many hardware vendors (HP included) modified the "standard" UNIX source code before selling it for use with their own chips. Today, although most UNIX systems can trace their roots back to the beginnings of UNIX, there are significant differences between HP's HP-UX,

IBM's AIX and Sun's Solaris, just to name a few of the more popular UNIX implementations. Efforts are underway to re-unify the UNIX world. A comprehensive standard for UNIX systems, originally called Spec1170, now called UNIX95, has been ratified by the major standards bodies. In February of 1996, HP-UX 10.10 became one of the first UNIX systems to fully support this standard. There are no plans to bring MPE/iX into full compliance with UNIX95, because HP does not plan to remake MPE/iX into a UNIX operating system. The strategy continues to be to enhance the HP 3000 in ways that make it easier to use it together with other computers, particularly UNIX machines like the HP 9000s and NT Servers such as HP's NetServers. Full UNIX95 compliance is not necessary to meet these objectives.

Software is available on more than one platform. To have the vendor independence that open systems promise, the software you depend on for day-to-day operations must be available on alternative platforms. The open systems interfaces (including POSIX, IMAGE/SQL, BSD Sockets and others) that were brought to MPE/iX with releases 4.5, 5.0 and 5.5 make it much easier for software vendors to leverage their development dollars on the HP 3000 platform. So for example, because Oracle VII is key to many HP 3000 users, HP worked with the Oracle company to ensure that it was available on MPE/iX within 90 days of its availability on HP-UX. As the applications software market shakes out, an increasing number of software vendors have determined it is not economical to support their application on every flavor of UNIX out there. There is a movement toward major UNIX platforms, particularly the HP 9000. There will always be a greater choice of applications on the HP 9000 than there is on the HP 3000. Once again, this does not mean that HP 3000 users should plan to abandon the platform. The key to success is not to try to move everything to one platform, but to use networks to make disparate platforms work together effectively.

Application Portability. Even if the commercial software that you purchase is available on multiple platforms, what about the software you develop yourself? Open systems interfaces on the HP 3000 offer protection for your investments in such software by ensuring that your well-written software can be ported in a straightforward manner to other open platforms, including the HP 9000, should the need arise. One way to accomplish this is by adherence to standards, but as we will show, you cannot always create a sufficiently robust application while staying completely within the areas covered by standards. Long before the term "open systems" was coined, good developers were adopting coding practices that would make moving the code between platforms easier. Open systems have not lessened or removed the need for this type of programming discipline. We will examine in detail the application design and coding practices that facilitate porting of code from the HP 3000 to other platforms, (and vice-versa).

Interoperability. Software availability across platforms and portability between platforms should be a concern if you think you may one day change your computing platform altogether. A far more common trend is to supplement your existing systems with additional systems that may or may not be of the same type. In this case, you should be concerned primarily with whether or not your existing HP 3000 systems will be able to work with newer systems. You must decide what level of interoperability is required for your particular environment. Some examples of technologies required are the ability to transfer files (FTP or DSCOPY), the ability to send messages (NetIPC, Berkeley Sockets), and Remote Procedure Calling capability (such as the Opens Software Foundation's Distributed Computing Environment, OSF DCE). Some interoperability issues are hardware related: Can the same terminals talk to all of our systems (which may require 3270 protocol, HP Block Mode terminal support, VT100 emulation, etc.). Can tapes created on one system be read on another? HP remains committed to continue to enhance the HP 3000 for a standards based approach to interoperability with other key computer systems, especially the HP 9000 and HP NetServers.

Commodity-priced hardware. In an open systems market, hardware vendors must be very price competitive. Many UNIX applications are available on multiple hardware platforms. Therefore hardware vendors are more likely to have to compete with one another, and this has the effect of keeping prices low. However, it's a mistake to attribute this downward trend in hardware prices solely to UNIX and open systems. Vendors of UNIX systems don't just compete with one another, they compete with vendors of proprietary systems like the HP 3000 as well. In fact, the trend toward low cost hardware was well under way before open systems ever appeared on the scene. RISC hardware and client/server software architectures have had more to do with the reduced cost of computing. When all costs are considered—hardware, software, support, training, staffing—it becomes clear that the best way to keep costs down is to move away from OS-centric IS strategies that tie you to any single architecture, regardless of whether that architecture is MPE/iX, HP-UX, or NT. The OS is not the important thing any longer.

Adherence to standards. This is now widely recognized as the single most important feature of open systems. But which standards? What level of adherence to those standards is required? Does adherence to standards represent any kind of guarantee that a system will be cost effective, or even that it will work?

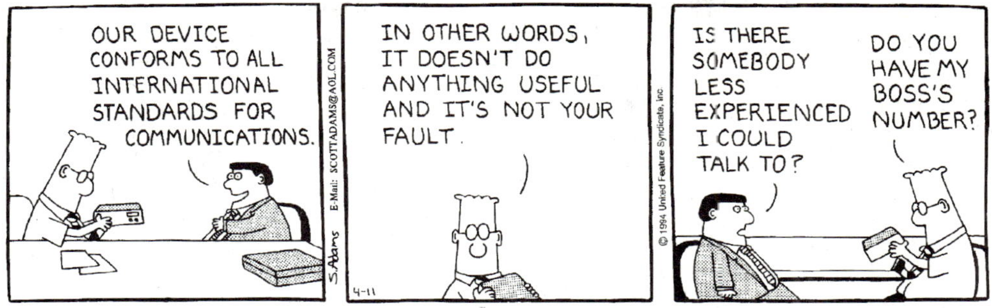

Figure 7.1 DILBERT reprinted by permission of United Feature Syndicate, Inc.

An important thing to realize about standards is that although they are necessary, they are not always sufficient. In the best of all possible worlds, software standards would be defined so rigorously that adherence to them would guarantee that the code you write will be portable to other standard platforms. But the truth is that many standards are not so well defined. Today, porting code from one UNIX platform to another is not typically as easy as UNIX advocates have made it out to be. There are many areas of functionality (GUIs, for example) for which there are multiple standards, not all of which are supported on every UNIX platform. There are other areas for which no standard exists, or for which the standards are not sufficiently complete to allow the creation of robust applications that avoid the use of non-standard constructs.

For two examples of this, consider POSIX and SQL. The POSIX (Portable Operating System Interface) group of standards have gone through several iterations, and even now are not sufficiently robust for most application developers to create applications of any complexity without straying outside of the standard features. SQL (Structured Query Language) is even worse; the SQL standard defines a base level of functionality that every database vendor has found it necessary to expand, frequently in incompatible directions. As a result, applications that was written for a particular SQL database (Oracle, for example) cannot easily be converted to run on a different SQL database. The effort involved can be just as much as it would take to convert and IBM IMS application to run on TurboIMAGE.

Commercial applications written on top of a POSIX compliant operating system (regardless of whether that operating system is based on UNIX, MPE/iX or NT) and an SQL compliant relational database (regardless of whether that database is Oracle, Sybase, IMAGE/SQL or some other) will, in almost all cases, need to take advantage of OS features and database features not defined by those standards. So, for example, developing on UNIX and Oracle may promote portability, but it is no guarantee. Likewise, developing on MPE/iX and IMAGE/SQL is not an insurmountable barrier to portability. Any application that is designed to be portable can be implemented in a portable fashion. Any application not so designed is unlikely to be portable, regardless of the "openness" of the underlying technologies. It is a key point, that will be repeated frequently, that open systems cannot be bought: they must be built. It is not sufficient for the operating system to adhere to standards. The applications you buy and the software you write must adhere to standards where possible, and design for portability where standards do not exist, if they are to be portable.

HP intends to continue to invest in standards-based technologies for the HP 3000. These technologies will be selected to support HP's strategy of making the HP 3000 interoperable with other systems, especially UNIX-based computers like the HP 9000 and NT-based computers such as HP's NetServers.

Specifications are not under the control of any single vendor. This requirement (which could just as easily have been written as "nothing written by Microsoft is an open system") is frequently used by the UNIX community to stress the importance of vendor independence in the standard setting process. It is left as an exercise for the reader to determine to what extent the committees that define standards are free from vendor influence (Hint: See the membership list for any standards body). Another reader exercise is to consider whether such a committee is more likely to respond in a timely manner to the needs of the marketplace than a vendor that has established a close working relationship directly with the user community. You should not be concerned with where the standards come from, but rather whether they accurately reflect your needs.

The fact of the matter is that standards are not standards until they are supported by multiple vendors. HP intends to continue to implement standard interfaces on the HP 3000 in response to demand from customers, regardless of whether those standards were originally defined at Microsoft, HP, IBM, or any other vendor. In each case, the decision to implement standards on MPE/iX has been (and will continue to be) driven by customer demand.

Common user interface. Even within a single implementation of UNIX, there is no consistency to the command-line interface. For X Windows based graphical interfaces for UNIX, there is a plethora of window managers and desktops. The industry is converging on a common desktop (called, appropriately enough, the Common Desktop Environment or CDE).

But is a common user interface really what you want, given the necessity to support different types of users and different types of hardware devices? A common user interface does facilitate portability; for example, an application that communicates with terminals using the curses user interface library will be more easily ported to a larger number of platforms than an application with a VPLUS user interface. But do not expect users to thank you for writing to the least common denominator. We have frequently heard developers state that it is best to write for Motif (an X-Windows variant), since X emulation is available on both PCs and Macintoshes. They would be wise to remember that the users who bought those PC's and Macintoshes could have bought workstations or X-terminals had they preferred to. By ignoring the fact that the users have a preference—sometimes a very strong preference—for a particular user interface, a software vendor risks losing the business of those users.

In later chapters, we will actually argue for the opposite requirement: rather than a common user interface, applications should be constructed to support multiple user interfaces. A single application should provide a graphical user interface to users on PC's or Workstations, a form-based interface to users on terminals, and allow for future extension to pen, voice, world wide web, multimedia, and other interface technologies. HP is committed to supporting the tools and technologies necessary to allow developers to use multiple user interface technologies on the desktop without compromising their ability to access data on the HP 3000.

Common Management Interface. Several of the above requirements deal with the system from a programmer's point of view, primarily in the portability of code and adherence to standards. A common user interface looks at the system from a user's point of view. The requirement for a common management interface looks at the system from a system administrator's point of view, and asks that a group of open systems not require operators and administrators to learn different procedures to backup, configure, manage output, and perform other system administration tasks on the various boxes.

As delivered "out of the box," no systems meet this criterion for openness. However, there are a number of system and network management tools that support multiple platforms. Here again, the responsibility is on the user to build the degree of openness required into the system configuration.

Compatibility over time. The final attribute of open systems to be discussed is compatibility over time. What use is an "open" technology if it will run on anybody's system today, but nobody's system tomorrow?

By this measure, MPE/iX is unparalleled in the industry. Code written for MPE systems over 20 years ago is still running on today's systems, without re-compilation. MPE users have never had to go through a conversion such as that entailed in moving from Solaris to SunOS, or even from HP-UX 9.0 to HP-UX 10.0. Products such as the NetIPC messaging facility and DSCOPY file interchange software have been dropped from HP-UX 10.0, forcing customers to re-write their software that used these facilities. They are still available, and will continue to be supported, on the MPE platforms. Compatibility over time, like system reliability, is a core requirement you should demand of your open systems supplier. In the chapters to follow, we will demonstrate numerous ways in which you can re-engineer your applications for improved functionality, increased performance, and portability. But development resources are always limited, and you will be limited in your ability to make these types of investments in your application software if you are constantly having to rewrite your software just to keep it running on top of operating systems or other software that does not provide a stable base over time.

Trading Hardware Vendor Lock-in for Software Vendor Lock-in

Through a combination of the open systems characteristics described above, there is a primary benefit that many people feel they are getting from investing in open systems. The benefit is that they are no longer locked in to a single hardware vendor.

This is good, if the primary problem you have is dissatisfaction with your hardware vendor. But what if your real frustration is with your software vendor or—heaven forbid!—what if what you really hate is UNIX, and you now find yourself facing fewer choices rather than more? Does Open Systems have anything to offer you?

It is possible to write completely vendor-independent code that removes any reliance on software vendors, and that does not use a least-common-denominator approach. Avoid any fourth-generation languages; write everything in an ANSI standard third-generation language such as C (or COBOL, if you prefer any sort of error checking). Develop your own data management software, software development tools, system administration utilities, report writers, and whatever else you need that isn't exhaustively covered by the existing standards. It would probably be best not to count on getting any business-related programming done in the next few years; you'll be too busy creating the infrastructure to allow you to write some code in the future.

Despite the impracticality of following this approach to the extreme described above, in later chapters we will explore a more usable design of just such a solution. By doing so, we will gain a clearer understanding of what the various middleware pieces actually do for us, and can therefore make better informed build-versus-buy decisions for the components that will be required to implement your Information Technology Architecture.

The promise of open systems was complete independence from vendors: the ability to spend tomorrow's IT budget without regard to yesterday's or today's investments. In reality, this is a promise that will probably never be kept. There is too much technology required in a typical business enterprise to allow an IT department to create it all from scratch. Yet every vendor—open systems notwithstanding—will attempt to make it more difficult to move to a competitor's product once you have selected theirs. Since you cannot go it alone, it becomes a matter of choosing your partners wisely.

If the software vendor you chose in the past seems today determined to drive you out of business with predatory upgrade pricing, then perhaps your architecture should allow you to gain independence from that vendor. But where your vendors are truly your business partners, providing products and services that add real value to your efforts, don't be afraid to rely on them. The authors hope that, regardless of whether your operating systems are MPE, HP-UX, or both, you will choose HP as a partner in meeting the challenges of providing Information Technology to your enterprise.

If Both MPE and HP-UX Are Open, Which Should I Use?

The answer is very possibly both, depending on what applications you need to run and what your data center requirements are. Briefly:·

- ***MPE is better*** at supporting large configurations, providing good (and predictable) performance under heterogeneous workloads, support of terminal-based OLTP, ease of management, compatibility over time, and unsurpassed reliability.
- ***UNIX is better*** at providing the largest choice in applications available, the best tools for software development, the earliest support for emerging technologies before they become standardized, and adherence to the broadest range of standards.
- ***MPE and UNIX are roughly equivalent*** in the ability to support client/server OLTP or Decision Support users, and as a database or application server in cases where the desired application or database software is available for both platforms.

Remember, there is no one best system for all situations. The best system is the one that most closely matches the business needs for whatever functions you plan to deploy on that system.

Today's IS organizations are faced with the most sweeping technological wave to date: the client/server wave. Never before have end users, as well as programmers, operators and IS managers been asked to adapt to such a total top-to-bottom revolution in their environments. The organizations in which they work, their responsibilities and their professional lives are all being profoundly shaken by the move to client-server. This wave is more than just a technical wave. It impacts the corporate culture, the fundamental ways information is managed and it determines by whom information will be owned. It challenges all the traditional assumptions of IS management. It changes all the rules. And the consequences for those who fail to adapt could be very ugly.

PART 2

Introduction to Software Architectures

CHAPTER 8

Introduction to Information Technology Architectures

We'll spend quite a bit of time in this book talking about a software architecture—what one is, why you need one, how to implement one—but we'll begin by proposing that there are actually three areas in the Information Technology department where the term "architecture" can be used. While all three will be touched on, only one will be the focus of the architecture discussions to follow.

One such area is in the software development environment. A **development architecture** is the collection of tools and processes by which analysts, programmers, and others involved in the development process design and develop programs. Most IT departments use fairly basic tools to accomplish these tasks, such that the term architecture may seem a bit grandiose. A small shop's development environment may consist of nothing more than a text editor and a compiler. At the other extreme, a large development organization may have dozens of tools to facilitate tasks such as structured analysis and design, database design, automated code generation, configuration management, versioning, preparation of documentation, testing, benchmarking, debugging, and many others. If such tools are used independently of each other, there isn't really a development architecture being used. But if the tools work cooperatively, such as in HP's SoftBench environment, then a development architecture can be said to exist. The creation of a development architecture is largely independent of the other architectures, and can thus be done without needing a full understanding of the architectural decisions made in other areas.

The primary focus of this book is on what can be called an execution, or **run-time architecture.** In later chapters, we'll examine all the pieces which make up an application—things such as the user interface, the database, networking, interfaces to operating system services, etc. The run-time architecture is primarily concerned with explicitly defining the responsibilities of each entity (for example, when data is input, which module is responsible for validating it—the user interface, the database, or the application logic?) and the interfaces between them. The technologies selected to fulfill requirements of the run-time architecture will also drive many of the requirements of the administration architecture (discussed below). Because of the interdependency of these architectures, it is a good idea to include the people responsible for designing and managing the administration architecture in the design of the run-time architecture as well. The technologies and tools selected for the run-time environment will have a definite impact on the supportability and ease of administration of the overall IT environment.

The third area is how the computer systems are managed on a day-to-day basis. This **administration architecture** covers many areas such as high availability strategies, security, software updates and distribution, and managing the network. Whereas the administration of the organization's IT resources is a separate task from application development, and is usually the responsibility of a different group of people, the administration of systems can be eased considerably if administration issues such as security and high availability are given consideration during the development of the run-time architecture.

CHAPTER 9

Defining an IT Architecture

Every day, Information Technology departments are being faced with questions such as these:

- Our manufacturing system no longer meets our needs. Should we migrate to a newer package, or try to enhance the existing one?
- We need to deploy a new application but have a mixture of system types. On what type of system should the new application be deployed?
- Our company acquired a new subsidiary whose systems are different from ours. Should we replace their systems with the ones that we use, or find a way to make the systems work together?

Whether you currently have an IT Architecture or not, you do have guidelines, or some sort of criteria, that you use in making the day-to-day decisions of running a data center. What application enhancements or bug fixes get top priority? What purchases will you make in the next 6-18 months? What development do you do internally, when do you purchase off-the-shelf applications, and when do you use contract programmers? If you make these decisions on anything other than a random basis, you have started to think about some of the areas that drive the need for an IT Architecture.

Throughout the remainder of this book, we'll show you how to define, implement and manage an Information Technology Architecture. Now, it's quite possible that you haven't had an IT Architecture before now, and if not, you may have gotten along just fine without one. So before jumping headfirst into the task of defining an architecture, the first question on your mind should be: Why bother?

Think for a moment of the person who most likely comes to mind when you think of an architect: someone who designs homes, office buildings, or other such structures. If you are building something with a unique design, you're going to need an architect to take your ideas and turn them into a design that can be constructed by people with the appropriate skills. Now, if you're building something you, or someone else, has built many times before—such as a tract home of a particular design—you may not need the design skills of an architect. You just need the blueprints that have already been created, and which your crew can then follow to create your building.

But we've already proven time and time again that, unlike home construction, software can be built without an architecture. Very good software, in many cases. What are we missing out on by just continuing to do things the way we always have? One critical limitation of most systems that are designed without an architecture is their inability to move smoothly into the future.

In the early days of America's space program, many top scientists, including Dr. Wernher von Braun, developed an "architecture" for the development of space. There was a recommendation to develop a manned orbital space station as a follow-on to Project Mercury, the program which first put Americans in space. This orbital space station could serve a number of functions, including meteorological observation and scientific experiments. It was also to be a critical component of the mission of landing a man on the moon. Through a technique known as Earth orbit rendezvous, a spacecraft would be launched from Earth to the station, where it could be refueled and checked out before continuing on to the moon. The station could also serve as a launch point or way station for many other types of missions.

In 1961, President Kennedy made the decision to land Americans on the moon before the end of the decade. With such an ambitious timetable, the NASA scientists reacted just as today's IT managers typically react to a shortened schedule. Everything not absolutely necessary to the single objective of landing a man on the moon was dropped. Instead of Earth orbit rendezvous, a mission profile known as lunar orbit rendezvous was chosen.

The Apollo program was one of the greatest technological triumphs in the history of mankind. Yet once it was done (terminated far short of its original goal of 10 moon landings), the U.S. space program never recovered its momentum. Because the infrastructure that would have supported a smooth transition to new missions was stripped out of the design, NASA floundered for years. Over thirty years after NASA had originally planned to have a permanent orbiting space station, the station has yet to be built.

You face the same decisions as NASA's top management. You can design an architecture and develop an infrastructure which will provide your organization a stable yet flexible foundation on which to build. It will take longer to develop than a single-minded effort that aims only to satisfy the organization's most pressing current application need. Or you can meet the short-term goals by leaving out anything that isn't a requirement for the immediate task at hand. We think you'll end up paying more over the long run by not developing an architecture, even though the architectural development is expensive in the short term.

Do all IT organizations need to develop an IT architecture? If you're going to operate a single system, dedicated to running a single off-the-shelf application package, then you don't need an IT architecture. The instructions from your hardware and software vendors should be your blueprints; after all, you aren't trying to do anything that hasn't been done many times before. If you're going to be running multiple applications, with each one independent of the others, the same is true: you have more work to do from a system administration point of view, but you still don't require the services of an "IT Architect."

Now we move on to a case that's more typical of the challenges of the IT department. You have a combination of application software packages, which may be in-house developments or third-party purchases, and they need to interface with each other. The financial packages need to know how much inventory is in the warehouse and what payroll expenses are. The production scheduling program needs to know what the marketing forecast is. Once you begin to design the interfaces that connect together these pieces, you are filling the role of an IT architect.

Now, we add in the complexities of today's IT challenges. The systems that you must interface are not homogeneous, but represent several different operating systems and vendors. They aren't all located in a single computer room, but are geographically dispersed. Some of them—the servers—are under control of the IT department, but the majority of them (clients) are on users' desks, where they may or may not be backed up and are almost certainly not secure. Software you do not control and have never heard of may be introduced onto these systems at any time. Business requirements are much more aggressive than they once were. Perhaps your system is used to batch up transactions for interfacing on a weekly or even monthly basis. Now you're probably interfacing the systems on a daily basis, but even this may not be good enough for some applications. You may have to provide up-to-the-minute access to any of your company's data, regardless of what system it resides on, to any other system on an as-needed basis.

While there has always been some need for "IT Architects," the changes caused in the industry by open systems have increased several fold the complexity of designing an IT architecture. In the early days of the HP 3000, for example, most of the choices were simple. For languages, FORTRAN and COBOL were the most popular choices. For a database, there was IMAGE; KSAM provided indexed files.

For the user interface, you most likely used VPLUS. Best of all, you were assured that all of these pieces would work together: the job of a 'system integrator' had never been heard of. Everything came from the same vendor, and had been designed and tested to ensure it all interoperated correctly.

Today, you can still make those same choices: all the products mentioned above are still available. But the resulting application will not be portable. It will not provide the ease of use of a graphical user interface, or the flexible inquiry capabilities of a relational data base. Your programmers' productivity will be less than with more recent tools that facilitate rapid prototyping and code reuse. So if you are starting out today, your choices are almost certainly going to be different. The products you choose will come from more than one vendor, and possibly encompass more than one hardware platform. It used to be that except for a few limited choices (COBOL or FORTRAN?), the tools you had to work with were preordained by the hardware platform you chose. Your job was then to develop and deploy the applications. Today, your job is to build the technology infrastructure: you should select the applications first, then the tools, letting those choices determine the hardware platforms required. It will be up to you to make the pieces fit, and work, together. Without an IT Architecture—a blueprint for this infrastructure—you aren't prepared to make the choices required.

You want to be able to pick the best tool for each job: the best program development environment, the best database management system, the best applications—based on the criteria that matter to you. With a robust architecture, you can do this, and make all the pieces play together.

Why Standards Aren't a Substitute for a Software Architecture

Everybody wants Open Systems. But many have not yet realized that Open Systems cannot be bought—they must be built. If you are committed to open systems, every decision you make—hardware, software, languages, applications, tools—will be restricted by the requirement. So before you jump on the bandwagon, find out what it is you really want when you say you want open systems. Is it application portability? Interoperability? The ability to change hardware vendors? Database vendors? Application vendors? Lower acquisition cost (which may be offset by higher operating costs)? Open has so many definitions that a blanket statement of "we want open systems" says nothing. Define the criteria by which openness will be measured, and to what extent openness is to be favored over other criteria. (Will you still prefer the "open" solution if it is 20 percent slower than the "proprietary" solution? If it fails twice as often?)

There is undoubtedly a move in the industry towards increasing adoption of open systems. These systems are most frequently implemented in addition to, rather than in place of, existing proprietary systems. You will have the most flexibility in your future IT directions if you set open systems requirements for all of your new purchases and new development. But, you should also develop architectural requirements in the areas of reliability, performance, productivity, system administration difficulty, and any others that you feel are important. There should be specific goals in each area, and a prioritization of the requirements so that when goals are found to be mutually exclusive it will be clear which goal should receive priority.

What are the factors that need to be considered in developing a software architecture? You should be considering at least the following:

- Functionality
- Data Integrity
- Performance
- Security
- Availability / Fault Tolerance / Resilience
- Support of Development Environment
- End-User Productivity
- Difficulty of Administration
- Interoperability
- Migration

An IT organization should think about their requirements in each of these areas. These criteria can be applied to the selection of hardware platforms, operating systems, databases, tools, and applications. An organization that says it will only choose UNIX-based solutions has decided to put the final two items, migration and interoperability, above all others. If no goals are set for other areas, such as performance and reliability, you can't be too surprised if the solution that is developed fails to meet your expectations in these area. It is far better to specify what is required for each of these areas than to assume that a particular solution strong in a few areas will meet your requirements in all of them. There are always trade-offs to be made; there is no one system or architecture that will be best in every area. Although there will be no one "ideal" solution, there are enough technologies available that you should be able to create an IT architecture that balances these attributes in the way that best serves the needs of your business.

Functionality

Functionality is perhaps the most obvious requirement in architectural design or product selection, and in most cases should be the highest priority. Functionality requirements are never static; it is the ever increasing demands for functionality that drive the industry forward and keep us all gainfully employed. Thus, determining whether an architecture or product meets your functionality requirements should also include whether that functionality is extensible to meet your future requirements. In the selection of packaged applications, functionality is frequently considered important almost to the exclusion of everything else; for example, an organization that has standardized on a hardware platform for all of its in-house development may consider the purchase of packaged software running on another platform, if there is nothing available for their preferred platform that meets the functional requirements.

While functionality is most typically the driving factor in the selection of applications or development tools, it is less frequently the pivotal factor in the selection of operating systems or databases. This is because, for the most part, operating systems and databases are functionally equivalent. Decisions on these components will be based on other factors.

Data Integrity

While everyone would agree that data integrity is a vital requirement, most organizations will not explicitly evaluate data integrity as a criterion in the selection of systems or databases. (In most cases, applications are not seen as having a significant impact; it is the responsibility of the underlying operating system, databases, and middleware to ensure data integrity.) Perhaps this is because all systems provide an adequate level of integrity—even the worst system in this regard is adequate for most uses. Or it may be because there are no benchmarks or other generally available measures to compare systems in this regard. While hard data is scarce, multi-platform shops that use HP 3000s consistently rank them highly for data integrity, on the same level as mainframe systems. UNIX-derived systems are regarded as somewhat less reliable, although the addition of add-on products can bring them up to comparable levels. Windows-based systems are seen as still less reliable. All of these systems are widely used in mission-critical roles; none of them should be considered "bad" in terms of data integrity. If your applications are truly mission-critical, however, and the cost of data loss to your company unbearable, then these small distinctions may become important.

Performance

With hardware becoming less expensive relative to the cost of program development, many IT departments are putting less concern into the area of designing for performance. It is certainly true that the advantage once sought by programmers hand-coding assembly routines is almost impossible to justify. Nearly every application, however, will have some performance constraints that need to be considered. On-line response time is still a critical measure for many applications. A design requiring substantial physical disk I/O to process a transaction may be unable to provide the required throughput, regardless of how much money you may be willing to throw at the problem.

With data storage requirements at many sites growing faster than the increase in speed of backup technologies, the time required to back up the system becomes a key operational constraint. At the same time, many IT departments are faced with the requirement of providing access to on-line systems for a greater portion of each day, in some cases requiring full application availability on a 24 × 7 × 365 basis. Needless to say, this requires a major restructuring of how batch processing will be handled. At the very high end, some shops are already running on the largest PA-RISC processors available, or if not, they may be experiencing growth rates that exceed the rate at which the product line adds new processing power on an annual basis. In either case, the developers must either find ways to process more efficiently, or restructure the application to allow it to be distributed across a number of physical systems.

Finally, with multiprocessor architectures taking an increasingly larger percentage of the total systems market in each year, batch or on-line applications that are single-threaded—that is, unable to make efficient utilization of the multiple CPUs provided in a multiprocessor system—will be unable to scale up effectively to larger configurations. The architecture discussions in the following chapters will assist you in taking all of these factors into account.

Security

Security can be implemented at many different levels. Operating systems are expected to provide some type of login security to provide unauthorized users from having any access to the system. Network interfaces are likewise expected to disallow access to the system from unauthorized users. Databases can provide another layer of security on the data that is stored therein. Finally, applications frequently implement their own security over and above that provided by the operating system and databases. It should be understood that security is only as strong as the weakest point among these. For example, an application that diligently checks that only a specified user can update particular records is defeated if the operating system security permits another individual to log in as that user. Security is not usually a major factor in product selection or architectural design, but becomes critical in the detailed design, implementation and administration of applications and systems.

Availability/ Fault Tolerance / Resiliency

We have already mentioned that many shops must now make applications available over larger time windows during each processing day. Another trend is that many HP 3000 shops are taking advantage of the increased processing capacity and lower cost of today's PA-RISC hardware by consolidating multiple older HP 3000s onto one or more larger PA-RISC boxes. In doing so, the cost associated with having the system unavailable increases proportionally. With 10 systems supporting 50 users each, 50 users are unproductive if one system is unavailable. With a single system supporting 500 users, 500 users are unproductive if that one system becomes unavailable. The HP 3000 has consistently proved to be among the most reliable systems in the industry, but for true round-the-clock availability, you will need more that just a single bullet-proof system. When developing an IT architecture, we will include defining the availability requirements for the system, and will evaluate hardware, software, and operational approaches to achieving the required level of system availability. Part 5 of this book will discuss the creation and administration of high availability systems in MPE and HP-UX environments.

Support of Development Environment

The increasing rate at which both business demands and technologies are changing requires that programmers become more productive. Programmer productivity as an architectural issue is addressed primarily in the area of tool selection. In order to achieve true openness and vendor independence, a third generation language such as C or COBOL should be used. Frequently, however, the productivity gain that comes from using a 4GL tool is so overwhelming that you may choose to forego some degree of openness by using such a tool. A good guideline is that if you could develop a particular piece of code in less than half the time using a fourth-generation tool, use the tool. Then, if you later need to move to a platform where the tool is not supported (or choose to eliminate the tool for any other reason, such as cost, vendor goes out of business, inability to support new features, etc.), throw the code away and completely redevelop in another 4GL that supports the new features/platforms/etc. that are now required. Assuming the new tool selected provides similar productivity to the one chosen today, you will still be ahead in overall effort, even having completely redeveloped the application.

The modular and layered approaches we will be advocating in the following chapters will also help you to segregate your code based on a number of criteria, with different approaches being suitable for different modules. Code that is long-lived and performance critical will provide more of a benefit from coding in a 3GL. Code that is short-lived, unlikely to be moved to another platform, and less performance critical should be developed using tools that provide the greatest productivity.

End User Productivity

Another area you will need to consider in developing your IT architecture is end-user productivity. For example, should you provide a graphical user interface or not? It is not true that GUIs always provide improved productivity. GUIs provide an easier learning curve, and are ideal for infrequent users or the user who must use a large number of applications, where consistency of user interface is crucial.

The benefit of a graphical user interface increases as the complexity of the tasks the user must do increases, and also if the number of different tasks within an application is large, making it difficult to remember all of the combinations of options possible. For heavy-duty "power" users of a single application, however, a GUI may just get in the way. An airline reservation system is a classic example of a cryptic but powerful user interface. Many UNIX tools and utilities follow the same model. The combination of a graphical user interface and keyboard-accessible shortcuts for power users is generally accepted as the best approach for balancing the needs of these different types of users.

Difficulty of Administration

An often neglected aspect of architectural design is consideration for the complexity of system administration. In client/server configurations especially, issues such as distribution of software to client platforms, backing up of systems that are not located in the data center, and being able to troubleshoot remote systems add greatly to the complexity of managing the enterprise's information technology. A properly designed architecture can minimize some of these difficulties, and where they are unavoidable, understanding the issues at the outset will help to ensure that you can develop the necessary policies and procedures to successfully implement the architecture.

Interoperability

It is an oft-repeated observation within IT circles that God was able to create the world in seven days because he didn't have an installed base. Programmers fresh from college with the idea that C is the 'one true language' and UNIX the 'one true operating system' speak of 'legacy systems' with contempt. Yet these systems are frequently the backbone of the business; they cannot be lightly tossed aside. Replacement of these applications is frequently impractical. Sometimes, the "legacy" application, whether it is a purchased application or an in-house development, still represents the best-in-class solution to the business problem it was designed to solve. Going through a costly conversion or replacement to move to software that provides no functional advantage is a dubious undertaking. Legacy systems that are no longer meeting the needs of the business should be updated or replaced; on the other hand, those which still meet the need for which they were intended should be considered part of the IT infrastructure on which new functionality will be built.

The existence of legacy systems does not need to be a hindrance in the creation or purchase of new applications. Many technologies are available to assist in integrating new applications with your legacy applications on either a batch or on-line basis. The HP 3000 is particularly strong in this regard, supporting a number of proprietary interface protocols (such as IBM's BSC and SNA family of products) as well as open systems protocols (such as ARPA TCP, UDP, and IP; CCITT X.25, X.3, X.28, X.29, and others) and Application Program Interfaces and architectures (such as BSD Sockets and DCE.) The databases available on the HP 3000—IMAGE/SQL, Allbase, and Oracle—all support gateway connection capabilities to allow interoperability with applications that may be built on a different database product.

The bottom line is that while the requirement to coexist with existing systems will need to be considered in the design or purchase of any application, it is not a requirement that new applications be on the same platforms, use the same databases, or otherwise be limited to the technology currently on hand. (Of course, cost may impose such a restraint).

Migration

For any software that is projected to have a life of more than a few years, the requirement to migrate the software in the future should be considered. Migration does not necessarily mean moving the application to another platform, although that is one possible scenario. It may be moving between architectures, such as between MPE V and MPE XL, or between MPE/iX and future architectures. It may be simply moving between one version of an application and another. While most applications are not affected by updates to an operating system, you should verify whether this is the case for applications that you purchase or create (on MPE, for example, heavy use of privileged mode could cause a problem in moving to a future version of the operating system). Updating to a new version of database software, or moving to a different database vendor are also types of migration that may be undertaken. All of these possible migration scenarios should be given some consideration; a sufficiently robust application architecture will allow most or all of these types of migrations to be supported if and when the need arises.

CHAPTER 10

Practical Matters

An IT manager's job doesn't just involve managing programmers and operators—there is also a budget to be managed. Architecture is cheap—we can design an elaborate system for not much more than the cost of designing a simple system. It's the implementation that's expensive. In this chapter we examine some of the things you'll have to fork out cold, hard cash for; things like computer systems and development tools.

Choosing Platforms

One of the biggest decisions faced by any IT organization is the selection of hardware platforms. Hardware still represents a significant portion of the total IT budget—frequently the largest single item, even though the trend has been downward for some time. Also, despite the promises of "open systems," changing hardware platforms is a difficult and expensive transition, so much so that many IT organizations will choose to avoid the hassles of a switch in hardware platforms even if their current platforms are no longer the best suited for their needs.

In increasingly large numbers, IT organizations are multi-platform. This makes the task of platform selection easier, even though it introduces complications in other areas such as system administration. In a multi-platform shop, frequently the selection can be simplified to finding the best platform for the immediate task at hand. This is obviously going to be easier than selecting a single platform that can meet all the organization's IT requirements for the foreseeable future.

The biggest obstacle preventing an organization from freely choosing hardware platforms on a case-by-case basis is the difficulty of system administration in a multi-platform environment. UNIX-based systems that may appear very similar to an end-user or a programmer may look totally different to the operations staff. (Indeed, the same thing was true of MPE's transition from the Classic architecture to PA-RISC; end users and programmers were isolated from changes between architectures to a much greater degree than the operations staff, who had to learn completely new procedures for installation, updates, booting, configuration changes, etc.).

The various Open Systems consortia have so far failed to successfully address system administration issues. The Open Software Foundation did propose a Distributed Management Environment (DME) as a companion specification to DCE. The specification is no longer under development. In the absence of any agreed upon specification, vendors have developed their own technologies for managing a multi-platform installation. Hewlett-Packard's OpenView family of products has become the de facto standard in this area. A multi-platform shop in which all platforms are controlled through OpenView software will avoid many of the headaches that have historically been associated with multi-platform operations.

Selecting OpenView as a framework for managing the data center can help narrow the list of candidates in the platform selection process, but still leaves many questions unanswered. It is beyond the scope of this book to develop a detailed platform selection model, but we will look briefly at factors that should be considered.

Some of the questions you will need to have answered before beginning the platform selection process are:

- What systems are we already committed to continuing to support due to legacy system requirements?
- What are the requirements for new applications in the future? Are the applications we need available on the platforms we currently have?
- What are the requirements for supporting more users? Can our existing systems handle any projected increases? If not, can they be upgraded to larger systems?
- How many different hardware platforms are we willing to support?

Based on the answers to the above, you can probably classify yourself into one of the following categories:

1. Our hardware platforms are already set; we have the right mix of systems to support our future needs.
2. Our hardware strategy needs to be simplified; we have too many different system types and need to eliminate some of them.

3. Our hardware strategy needs to be more flexible; our current systems cannot meet our future requirements, and the best strategy to meet future needs is a mixture of our current systems plus new systems with different capabilities.

4. We need a completely new hardware strategy; our current systems are not meeting our needs, and we want to replace them with different platforms.

Client Platforms

While terminals do not represent an additional hardware platform as such, you should note how many users are currently terminal-based. The cost of upgrading these users to PCs will be a major factor in determining whether it is practical to move all applications to client/server, GUI interfaces, or whether your architecture needs to incorporate continued support of terminal based users. A survey of user needs can determine whether it is possible to standardize on a single client platform throughout the organization. The most widely used client platform today is Windows 3.1; others in wide use are Windows 95, Macintosh, OS/2, and UNIX. Use of a single client platform throughout the organization is usually desirable, but the specialized needs of various departments (e.g., CAD/CAM, Desktop Publishing, software development) may cause several groups within the organization to have a preference for a specific system different from that selected for the rest of the organization. The cost/benefit tradeoffs from extending support to these additional platforms must be evaluated on a case-by-case basis.

Server Platforms

The hardware systems performing the role of server systems fall into several categories. There are the general purpose systems that may run a large number of applications; these systems are most typically mainframes or departmental servers. The recent trend has been more toward systems dedicated to a single function; of these the most common will be application servers and database servers. The HP 3000 is more commonly found in the general purpose role, and the HP 9000 in the dedicated server role, but both systems have been widely used in each capacity. Windows NT is expected to grab a large share of the server market, although it is too early to predict exactly how these systems will fit into existing IT environments.

In planning your hardware platform strategy for the future, you may have only a single type of server platform, or you may support several. UNIX systems such as the HP 9000 provide the greatest variety of available applications and databases today. Because of this, almost any organization planning to deploy new applications in the near future will find UNIX systems playing a role in their strategy. The same is very likely to be true of Windows NT systems by the end of the decade. Very few new applications are being deployed on mainframes; many IT organizations are phasing out the mainframes because their costs are far higher than comparable computing power in a distributed, open systems environment. Most proprietary systems are being phased out just as the mainframes are. A few exceptions, such as the HP 3000 and the IBM AS/400, look like they will survive the shake-out; however, they will be used almost exclusively by customers who already have a strong commitment to the platform or in specific vertical markets where these systems provide the best-in-class solutions.

In a nutshell, the platform decisions should depend on the same factor that has always been the most important differentiator in system selection: the availability of the software you need. In most cases, this will be application software. Based on the wide variety of application packages used at a typical IT installation, we expect to see many customers running a combination of MPE/iX, HP-UX, and Windows NT servers in the future.

Choosing Languages and Tools

In Chapter 8, we mentioned the Development Architecture as one of the areas of concern for an IT manager. While most development architectures are simple, they can also be quite complex. The build process for the MPE operating system, for example, is an elaborate process that requires the full-time efforts of several engineers. We won't attempt to develop or describe a development architecture within this book, but will try to cover briefly here how decisions made in the choice of development tools can impact aspects of the run-time architecture—especially portability.

The choice of a programming language will have an impact on portability, performance, supportability, development time—virtually every aspect of the application that really matters will be affected. Yet, most Information Technology organizations spend little if any effort trying to select the best language for a particular task. "If the only tool you have is a hammer, the whole world looks like a nail." The same is true of a programming department, or individual programmer, who has only mastered one language (or perhaps knows several, but believes that there is only one "true" language for serious programming). A programmer whose only tool is C loves to sneer at the COBOL programmer as an outdated dinosaur, but neither of them is a match for a programmer who is skilled in several languages and can select the right tool for the job at hand.

This is not to deny the costs involved with supporting multiple development languages and tools. Besides the obvious purchase, training, and support costs, the fact that not everyone will be proficient in all tools limits the flexibility in assigning engineers to projects.

The most important factor in selecting a language for development is its portability. Computer hardware technology continues to move forward at an increasing rate, while application lifespans have not appreciably shortened. (Yes, they become *obsolete* faster, but they don't seem to be *replaced* any faster.) Thus, the applications you write today are likely to still be around after the systems you write them on are gone. An ANSI-standard language, such as C, Pascal, or COBOL, is best; it will be available on the widest variety of platforms. The Kernigan & Ritchie variant of C is generally less desirable, but may be required depending on your choice of platforms. Fourth generation languages are generally not supported on as wide a variety of platforms as are the standard third generation languages, but may be selected when they support all of your required platforms.

Exception: There is no advantage (other than programmer familiarity with the language) in using a portable language for code that is inherently unportable. For example, code that implements a graphical user interface for a Windows-based PC will not be portable to other environments; you may as well use the proprietary Visual BASIC language rather than the more unwieldy C code needed to perform the same task. Likewise, converting your SPL programs that make heavy use of VPLUS, TurboIMAGE, KSAM, and MPE Intrinsics into C still won't permit them to be easily ported to another platform.

Performance is another area to consider in selecting languages, and in selecting development tools that have run-time components. Since third-generation languages out-perform fourth-generation languages in most instances, conventional wisdom has recommended avoiding 4GLs for performance-critical tasks. Improvements in 4GL technology, decreasing cost of hardware, and increasing costs of programming expertise have largely invalidated this rule. In many cases, eliminating a single disk I/O from a complex transaction will provide a bigger performance boost than recoding the entire transaction from a 4GL into a 3GL. Selective optimization of frequently accessed, performance critical parts of an application is generally more efficient than placing constraints on the development environment to maximize performance.

In developing for a multi-platform shop, having common development tools for the various platforms is an advantage. This can be achieved either through having the same tools available on each development platform, or by using one platform for development regardless of the platform on which the code will be executed.

Preserving Legacy System Investments

One of the strengths of the HP 3000 system throughout its history has been its unparalleled record of investment protection. The HP 3000 boasts a number of investment protection capabilities that, taken as a group, provide compatibility unparalleled in the industry. Some of the highlights are:

- MPE/iX's Compatibility Mode, along with HP's level of attention to backward compatibility, means that most software written for the first HP 3000s back in the early 70's can run on today's systems without recompilation.
- HP makes every effort to continue to support products on the HP 3000 for as long as possible. Thus, a customer's investments in using products such as DSCOPY and NetIPC are protected on the HP 3000, even though these products are no longer supported on the HP 9000.
- Even after a product has reached maturity, some level of investment continues to provide the most requested customer enhancements. Enhancements to IMAGE/SQL, VPLUS, and the RAPID family of products have all been introduced within the past year.

Because of these and other investment protection measures offered by the HP 3000, the decision to design, develop, and deploy software based on a new architecture (and perhaps new languages, new databases, new user interfaces, and other new technologies) does not mean that everything you currently have must be scrapped. Designing new software to coexist with legacy systems is admittedly more difficult than designing from scratch, but the extra design effort pays off with a greatly reduced implementation effort due to the savings of not having to replace software that is meeting your needs.

Much of HP's investment in the HP 3000 platform over the past few years has been in the area of coexistence with UNIX systems. This is in recognition of the fact that most new software development today is being done on UNIX based systems. The investments HP has made in the HP 3000 eases the porting of these UNIX applications to the HP 3000 when practical, or facilitates interoperability between the legacy applications on an HP 3000 and new applications on a UNIX system when porting is impractical or undesirable.

Some of the technologies that have resulted from these investments are designed to allow new technologies to be applied to older applications; as such, they should be considered as part of any strategy for moving to a new IT architecture while still supporting legacy applications. We'll examine a few of these technologies below.

IMAGE/SQL

IMAGE/SQL is the most widely used of these "bridge" technologies. It adds support of the widely used SQL (Structured Query Language), most commonly associated with relational databases, to the TurboIMAGE database. Also supported is Microsoft's ODBC (Open Data Base Connectivity) standard for client/server access to databases. With these two standard protocols, dozens of software packages such as spreadsheets and rapid development toolsets (for example, Visual Basic and Delphi) can be used to access IMAGE/SQL databases, even though these software packages have no specific knowledge of the IMAGE/SQL environment. Thus, open software—software not written for any specific database or platform implementation—can support the HP 3000 just as well as the UNIX or Windows based systems typically thought of when open systems are mentioned. You can also use this same capability in the applications you write. Rather than writing specifically to the TurboIMAGE intrinsic interfaces, which will make your software dependent on TurboIMAGE, you can use the SQL or ODBC interfaces in your applications. You then have flexibility to later move your TurboIMAGE data into an Allbase or Oracle database on the HP 3000, or into these or other relational databases on an HP 9000 or Windows based platform. An even better approach that combines the performance and power of the TurboIMAGE intrinsics with the portability of standard interfaces will be described in the chapters that follow.

NewFace

NewFace is a user interface tool that takes the same basic concept of IMAGE/SQL and applies it to the VPLUS user interface system of the HP 3000. Using the NewFace conversion tools, VPLUS forms files are converted to Dialog Manager dialog files. Unlike SQL or ODBC, Dialog Manager is a proprietary technology (supplied by ISA of Stuttgart, Germany), so the same degree of openness is not achieved, but the Dialog Manager run-time libraries allow the converted interface to be run on Windows based PCs and HP-UX Workstations or X-terminals. Once converted, the Dialog Manager graphical editor can be used to transform the user interface from the form-based appearance of VPLUS into a true GUI, with radio buttons, checkboxes, drop down lists, and other features typical of windowed user interfaces. The HP 3000 programs that drive the VPLUS user interface do not need to be changed; a NewFace provided XL intercepts the VPLUS intrinsic calls and translates them into messages that are sent to the NewFace run-time control program on the client system. Finally, the NewFace interception library is also available for HP-UX, so VPLUS applications that have been converted to use NewFace can also be moved to HP-UX systems if other dependencies (use of MPE or TurboIMAGE intrinsics, for example) are removed or handled in a similar fashion. Other products that provide the capability of updating the interface of VPLUS applications are covered in Chapter 24.

Starting From Scratch

Investment protection helps ensure that the applications and systems you purchase today will be available to you in the future for as long as they meet your needs. When your business requirements change such that today's systems and applications no longer fit, there are investment protection programs to help you move to the new systems that you require. For your applications, the transition is frequently more difficult.

The authors of this book have extensive experience in the area of application software porting. We can therefore state with some degree of authority that the porting of software between dissimilar platforms (a) frequently doesn't end up meeting your expectations, and (b) often wasn't a good idea in the first place. We'll start by examining the most common reasons why porting efforts fail, and then describe the practices that seem to work best.

Perhaps the most common reason for a failed port is that it was undertaken for political, rather than technical or functional reasons. The most common cause of such ports is a corporate edict to move to "open systems." While we support the objectives of open systems and believe that most companies should be moving in that direction, there are right and wrong ways to go about it. Porting applications that were designed for specific proprietary platforms, and which are meeting the needs of the business while running on those platforms, to another system without significant re-engineering of the application will almost always fail to deliver the benefits anticipated by management.

The reasons for this are many. For one, most forced marches to open systems are driven by visions of cost savings. This makes it highly unlikely that management will approve the expenses required to do the job right, as the payback time would slide beyond most managers' planning horizon. Also, as explained earlier, there is no real cost differential in the cost of owning and operating UNIX-based systems compared to the current generation of proprietary systems.

Besides the motivation for doing the port in the first place, most ports are unsuccessful because of the way they are done. Most porting efforts follow a path of least resistance; the idea being to minimize the amount of code that has to be changed. As an example, in porting an application to the HP 3000 from a UNIX platform, application developers have the opportunity to realize significant improvements in performance of terminal-based users by moving from a character mode implementation, which is typical of UNIX systems, to a block mode implementation such as VPLUS. Developers will usually choose to implement character mode terminal handling on the MPE system, with a result that the application can support fewer than half the number of users as a comparable application with block mode connections.

In almost every functional area—file and database handling, process management, interprocess communication, sharing of resources—there are opportunities to improve the performance, functionality, reliability, and supportability of applications by redesigning them to take advantage of features provided by the target operating system. In far too many porting efforts, all or most of these opportunities will be passed over in favor of keeping the code as close as possible to its original implementation.

What would be a better approach? There are several.

First of all, consider buying a package. Chances are, there are many more capabilities available in the packages available on the market today than when you made the "make or buy" decision for your current application. From a pure functionality standpoint, your custom designed application will always meet your needs better at the completion of design than an off-the-shelf package. But the purchased application, because of its need to support many companies that may do business in different ways, may be better suited to future needs if your company grows in unanticipated ways. Requirements other than business functionality—for example, support of graphical user interfaces, ad-hoc query capabilities, client/server architecture, etc.—are quite expensive to develop and support for a single copy of an application, but a developer who plans to sell many copies of the application can provide these capabilities at a reasonable cost.

If the application packages available on the market don't fit your requirements, we recommend you spend some time designing an application from scratch—even if you know that your budget won't allow it, and that you will be porting an existing application. Parts III and IV of this book will be given to just such an exercise. Designing from scratch helps give you a clear perspective, unencumbered by the baggage of your legacy implementation. When you have completed your new architecture, you can go through module by module, deciding in which cases the cost of development from scratch would be warranted, where the existing application is still a good fit and can be ported with few changes, and where an opportunity exists to put in a little more effort than a straightforward port to reap a big benefit.

We feel that regardless of whether you will build, buy, or port an application, the design from scratch exercise is an excellent way to develop an understanding for the feature set you want in your application. It also gives you a good starting point for the frequent case where there is not a single solution to the entire problem; you may end up buying some components, creating some new modules on a new platform, porting a few pieces, and leaving some components running on the current system. It's impossible to understand and evaluate such solutions without a firm understanding of each of the pieces such as will be gained by the design exercise.

Because application design is obviously strongly driven by the functional requirements of a particular application, and because these requirements will vary widely between readers, we will spend very little time in architecting the core of the application—the application logic itself. Instead, we will concentrate on the interfaces between the application and the various external components—primarily the operating system, databases, networking, and user interfaces. These interfaces constitute an "application framework," which should be generic enough that it can be reused for many different applications. By the time you have worked through the description of those components, you should feel comfortable moving on to the detailed definition of the application internals. Part 3, Designing a Software Architecture, covers high level design concepts, introducing fundamentals of object-oriented programming and client/server design principles. Part 4, Implementing a Software Architecture, will delve into more detailed design of the individual modules.

PART 3

Designing a Software Architecture

CHAPTER 11

Fundamentals of Software Architecture

The art of computer programming has changed considerably in the relatively short time it has existed as a profession. Unlike many professions in which you can learn a trade at the beginning of your career, and then apply that knowledge without change throughout your lifetime, the computer programmer must be prepared to learn his craft throughout his career. The tools and techniques that will ultimately be used may bear little resemblance to those used when first learning the job.

In this chapter, we will examine a number of characteristics of modern software architectures that are different from the characteristics of older software architectures. In an industry as young and dynamic as ours, many computer professionals working today have careers that have spanned all of the changes that will be described. We are currently in the midst of a changeover to a new programming paradigm called "object-oriented." While much of the terminology and technology surrounding object-oriented programming is new, much of it is just a restatement of things that good programmers have been doing for some time. In this book, we aren't going to teach you any radically new methods of doing systems analysis, design, or programming. We will, however, introduce the new terminology that is used in describing object-oriented systems, describe the architecture we're going to develop in those terms, and show how good practices you may already utilize can prepare you to move into this new arena.

Characteristics of Good Software Architectures

In descriptions of software architectures, you will often hear the terms ***modular***, ***layered***, ***object-oriented***, or ***tiered*** (as in two-tiered or three-tiered). These represent complementary, but different, aspects of how the software is divided into pieces. An architecture may have all of these characteristics or none of them. In general, the more of these characteristics an architecture possesses, the more flexible it will be. In addition to providing more flexibility, it should cost less to maintain over the long run. (As a trade off, it may also be larger, more complex, and take longer to initially develop.) Each of these characteristics will be explored in depth. In brief:

- Modular software is function-oriented. A modular design facilitates making changes in the business processes supported by the software.
- Layered software isolates application logic to the greatest extent possible from the implementation details of operating systems, databases, networks, etc. Layered software facilitates software portability.
- Object-oriented software is modular, incorporates data hiding, and includes software reusability as a design objective.
- "Tiered" is often used to describe a distributed hardware configuration, rather than a software implementation. In this book, we will use tiered to describe the software characteristics that allow the software to be distributed across multiple systems in a client/server environment.

Let's look at the changes involved in the adoption of each of these programming models.

Monolithic to Modular

One trend that has been prevalent in programming for some time is a move toward smaller compilation units. A typical COBOL program written for a mainframe environment in the 1970's might be tens of thousands of lines of code in a single monolithic program. The logic flow through the program might be very difficult to follow: most COBOL programmers learned their craft before it became unfashionable to use GO TO as the preferred method of controlling program flow. As the benefits of structured, or modular, programming began to be realized, the look of the typical program changed. The program was now broken down into smaller logical units. PERFORMing these discrete sub-units, and not using GO TOs indiscriminately to control the program flow, allowed the program to be seen as a collection of smaller well-defined units rather than as one huge program. In some cases, programmers took the next logical step of actually moving some of this code into separate programs altogether that would be CALLed from the main program, although COBOL did not facilitate this step as well as later languages.

Procedure based languages, such as Pascal and C, became much more prevalent during this time, because their structure is well suited to this new way of modularizing code. But nothing prevented the COBOL or FORTRAN programmer from incorporating the new thinking into his programs. Then, as now, it was not necessary to throw away your existing technology investments to take advantage of the latest technologies.

The breaking down of code into smaller functions was mirrored by changes in the way the program's run-time data was handled. Again, a large monolithic chunk of code tended to treat its data as monolithic, as well—everything went into a COBOL Working-Storage section (there was no alternative), usually with no indication of what parts of the program would access which data. With procedure-based languages, it was possible to create variables that were local to a particular function, as well as data that was global to an entire compilation unit or process. Making data local to a function helped provide greater control over it; the programmer could be confident that only the intended code could be modifying data values. This worked well when the data was only needed by a single function. For data used in several functions, some advocates of structured programming recommended that global variables always be passed explicitly into any module that might modify them. Although popular modular languages never enforced this restriction, those programmers who followed it would have an easier time understanding where global data was being used within a program. This set the stage for the introduction of object-oriented programming practices, which we'll come to shortly.

Imbedded Interfaces to Layered

When dinosaurs roamed the earth and the caveman programmers chiseled their programs onto stone tablets, portability wasn't a concern. The early mainframe era wasn't much different; computing resources were far too expensive to allow for elegant software architectures that could be ported to another system that probably hadn't been invented yet. But the minicomputer era brought very different economics to the industry, and for the first time it became practical to think in terms of creating software that might someday run on a different environment than the one for which it was initially created.

The most important design factor for creating portable software is having a layered software architecture. A modular software architecture, as described in the previous section, breaks software into small functional pieces. But each of these pieces may still interact with many different system-dependent or middleware components—the operating system, the database, the network, etc. In a layered software architecture, each of these interfaces to the system on which the application resides would be separated from the application itself. With a separate database interface layer, for example, if it becomes desirable in the future to change the database implementation, only this layer needs to be changed.

A properly layered software architecture provides all of the following benefits:

- Greater portability between platforms
- Easier adaptation to new technologies (different database, different networking protocols, new middleware layers, etc.)
- More flexibility in distributing tasks between client and server (or peers)
- Improved ease of maintenance

Procedure-Centric to Data-Centric

As discussed previously, the change in how code was organized was accompanied by a change in the organization of data. There was a further evolution in the relationship between code and data that went beyond merely reorganizing data into "global" and "local" units. Moving data that was unique to a task into the function responsible for that task removed much clutter from the set of data managed by a program, but did little to help manage the data that needed to be global in scope. Explicit passing of any global variables into any routine that modified them helped answer the question of "who's using the data," but did nothing to guarantee that the data was used in a consistent fashion (for example, one routine that modified a variable might perform a check to not allow a negative number to be stored, whereas another routine in the same program might omit this test). The large number of potential accessors, with no guarantee of consistent behavior, made maintenance and troubleshooting of such programs difficult. Another frequently encountered problem was that if it was necessary to change the format of the data for any reason, it became difficult to discover all the places in the code that might be affected by the change. Many IT organizations are now tackling the problem of expanding date fields to accommodate 4 digit years, and are encountering this problem head-on.

Thus, our next milestone in the evolution of flexible programming is the nearly-object-oriented concept of "data hiding." The reasoning is straightforward: the fewer ways in which a given piece of data can be modified, the smaller the chance of inconsistency in the way modifications are handled. Similarly, the fewer routines there are that know the physical representation of a piece of data, the smaller the impact of any change to that physical representation. The objective of data hiding is to minimize the number of routines that a) know the physical representation of a given data item, and b) may modify the contents of the data item.

There are numerous ways in which data hiding may be implemented. Many organizations will implement data hiding by agreement—there is no enforceable prohibition against directly accessing a data item, but routines are provided to read and write values to the data, and it is agreed that everyone will use these routines instead of bypassing them. In other environments, there may be security implemented on the actual data items such that only the approved routines will be able to access or modify them. This is particularly common with data that is sensitive or where the opportunity for mischief is great (e.g., payroll records).

There are several good examples of data hiding on any MPE system. In moving from the classic MPE V system to MPE XL, the internal representation of many data items changed from 16 bits to 32 bits to match the new architectural word size. Yet because most programmers never access these data items directly, but only through the MPE intrinsic interfaces, programs that represent these fields as 16 bit fields can in most cases continue to function without changes. (In those cases where the value stored in the field cannot be represented in 16 bits, the programmer will have to make modifications.) Another example is the TurboIMAGE database system, which implements data hiding at the record, rather than the data item level. If you use a particular field in a TurboIMAGE database, then any changes to the physical representation of that field will need to be reflected in your program. However, if you use a list parameter that returns only the fields you specify, then your program will be unaffected by any changes to other fields in the record. The record can be completely reordered, fields can be added or dropped, and your program will continue to work.

Introduction to Object-Oriented Concepts and Terminology

If the programs you create are modular, layered, and incorporate data hiding, then you are on the threshold of the next big step in programming evolution. In fact, the changes that have preceded this step have already incorporated most of the technical features of an object-oriented program. If you have mastered these techniques, then the next step is not so much one of learning to program differently, but rather to think about programs in a different way. **Object-oriented programming** is much more a shift in philosophy than the use of any specific tools or techniques. The small but crucial shift from a traditional mindset to an object-oriented mindset is a change in the way you think about code, data, and the relationship between them. In the traditional programming mindset, the program, procedure, or function is the primary focus of your efforts. (Even the job title of "programmer" implies that the code is main concern.) Data is merely what the program will operate on; data structures grow out of the program's processing requirements, and not out of any inherent properties of the data itself. To move to an object-oriented view, you don't have to become immersed in concepts such as "inheritance" and "polymorphism" from the start (yes, we'll get to them eventually—you'll have to keep reading). Just begin by thinking of the data as a standalone entity. Data is persistent; the data you put into the system today may still be needed by the business long after the programs you write today have been obsoleted. As business needs change, the way the data is accessed will change. So you should not structure the data based on today's access requirements; instead, the data must stand alone. Data base normalization rules are a good starting point; they provide an introduction to thinking about relationships between data items that will lead you to understand which ones really belong together because of inherent characteristics of the data, and not just processing convenience.

Once you decide to make this shift into an object-oriented way of thinking, the first question that arises is invariably, "What is an object?" It seems that every book on the subject tackles the question, usually with the result that the reader is more confused than ever. This is because the evangelists of object-oriented programming always seem to want to answer this question while avoiding reference to any widely understood data processing concepts, to emphasize how different this new paradigm is from everything that has come before. Most frequently, the question "what is an object" will be answered by items from the real world—a car, a telephone, a checking account. The answer you really need is that an object is a data structure. A "new and improved" data structure, with some things in it that your old-fashioned data structures don't allow, but just a data structure nonetheless.

Now given the huge amount that has been written about object-oriented, including new methods of analysis and design and entirely new development methodologies, languages, and tools, there must be more to it than just renaming data structures, right? We admit that the subject is more complex than our first approximation suggests. Yet we maintain that it is possible to evolve toward the object-oriented paradigm; it is not necessary to change every aspect of your IT organization to embrace the latest object-oriented methods. Our first approximation makes objects of data structures and the routines that directly manipulate them; this is the low-hanging fruit that is most easily 'objectified'. Doing so helps isolate the code in these structures from any changes that occur outside of the objects, and likewise protects external code from being affected by changes to these objects. To move further along the continuum toward full object-oriented-ness, look for other portions of the application that could benefit from similar protection. It may be an algorithm that you wish to be able to change; if so, the algorithm is a candidate for an object. It may be a file layout, a screen design, an interface between application modules, or a table: anything that you want to be able to vary independently of other portions of the application. In later chapters, we will propose making objects of the external service providers that an application interfaces with—databases, networks, operating systems, and the like. This allows the program to remain constant while the underlying service providers may change, thus achieving a far greater degree of software portability than is possible by the use of standards-derived interfaces.

To keep you COBOL programmers from being able to master object-oriented programming too quickly, the object-oriented gurus have created lots of new terms for things that aren't really new. We'll introduce the new terms now, and then use them throughout the remainder of the book. Whether you ever write a C++ program or not, there's no reason you shouldn't be able to understand all the basic philosophy and features that are behind the object-oriented programming movement.

Now that you know what an object is, you'll find that there are other terms for objects that are used more frequently. A **class** is the abstract representation of an object, and an **instance** is an actual use of the class. The run-time process of creating an instance of a class is called instantiation. For a parallel distinction from a non-object-oriented language, think of a C typedef statement as a class; then when a variable is declared to be of that type, you have created an instance. This terminology is from C++, and is fairly widely used. Some object-oriented languages use the term "template" for the abstract entity, so you will encounter this term in the literature as well. In this book, we'll use the term object whenever the distinction isn't important. Classes themselves can be either abstract or concrete. An abstract class is one that can never be instantiated; it serves only as a basis for defining other classes via *inheritance*, as will be described shortly.

A data structure in a traditional language is essentially a grouping together of data items. These data items are usually called *fields*; in an object-oriented language, they are called ***attributes***. The most dramatic difference between an object and a traditional data structure is that in addition to data items, the object can also contain code. In the procedure based languages such as C and Pascal, code can contain data—that is, a function can declare variables which are "owned" by that function. As we stated earlier, object-oriented thinking involves changing the way we think about programs from being based primarily upon the code, to being based primarily upon the data. Thus it should be no surprise that in an object-oriented program, code can be "owned" by the data. Program code that is contained within an object is called a **method**. The programmer who creates an object will try to provide a sufficiently complete set of methods that it will be unnecessary for any program code outside the object to directly access any of the object's attributes. This is called **encapsulation**. Thus, encapsulation is essentially a synonym for data hiding. Encapsulation can be implemented in any language, but object-oriented languages provide mechanisms to enforce it—data within an object can be declared private, and only the object's methods will be allowed to access it. In a traditional language, only disciplined programming practice will ensure that the encapsulation of data is not violated.

An object's set of methods provides an interface to the object's data that can remain consistent regardless of internal changes (changes to the actual physical representation of the data) or external changes (changes to the application programs that use the object). A payroll application would probably include employee "objects" and paycheck "objects," among others—just as a non object-oriented payroll application would have employee "records" and paycheck "records." As you learn more about good object-oriented practices, your objects will diverge somewhat from a traditional record design, but a basic similarity will exist in even the most "pure" object-oriented systems. One such divergence you will encounter early on will be finding that some of the attributes within an object should be objects themselves. This is typically the case if the attribute needs some specialized handling routines that are independent of any of the other attributes within the object. For example, if your object contains a date attribute, you may want to support returning the date in multiple formats—960228, 2/28/96, February 28, 1996. As you begin to write application code to access the object, you may find that the date attribute needs to be manipulated—comparing it to another date, adding or subtracting a number of days to this date, etc. In a traditional program, these manipulations would become part of the program logic. In an object-oriented environment, they become part of the object itself. Because these methods don't really have anything to do with the overall object—the paycheck record, or whatever it is that contains the date—it makes sense to make the date an object itself. This way, the paycheck object is not cluttered with methods that are not unique to a paycheck object, and the date object is now a self-contained piece of code that can be reused in this or other applications wherever dates are required.

If you adjust your terminology so that "data structures" are called objects, and if you implement strict data hiding by having all access to these objects be via a set of defined methods, is your program then object-oriented? Definitions vary, but most sources would probably say no. Aside from the use of objects, there are two additional features that are expected to be found in truly object-oriented programs. These features are **inheritance** and **polymorphism**. Whereas a program written in a traditional language such as COBOL can be made to provide some semblance of these features, it is the built-in support for these two concepts that really distinguishes an object-oriented from a non-object-oriented language.

Inheritance is a mechanism by which code (methods) and data (attributes) can be shared between different object classes. Inheritance derives its usefulness from the fact that in many programming problems, there are objects that are not identical—thus, they could not be represented simply as instances of the same class—yet have significant similarities, such that *some* of the attributes and methods from one class could be used in another. For example, consider a bank offering checking and savings accounts. If each type of account was represented by a class, there would be a lot of similarities between the classes. The attributes for account holder, branch, last activity date, and current balance could easily be defined identically. Methods that updated or reported the values of these items could likewise be identical. Other attributes, such as interest rate or per check charges, might be unique to one class or the other.

Inheritance is implemented by establishing a hierarchy of object classes. In the example above, a generic Account class would be defined, with two subclasses, CheckingAccount and SavingsAccount. The Account class is called a superclass of the CheckingAccount and SavingsAccount classes. Attributes and methods that are shared between the account types will be defined for the Account class, whereas those that are unique to a single account type will be defined as part of the definition of that subclass. Inheritance always follows a defined hierarchy; classes cannot arbitrarily inherit things from just any object that may have a useful attribute or method defined. For this reason, the development of the classes and how they will be arranged in the hierarchy is an area worthy of careful consideration. There are also implementation specifics to be considered; for example, some languages permit only single inheritance, in which a class can only be a subclass of one other class. Others permit multiple inheritance, where a class can be a subclass of several classes, inheriting from each of them. Languages that provide multiple inheritance must also provide some precedence mechanism for resolving cases where different definitions of identically named attributes or methods could be inherited into the same subclass.

If a particular attribute or method is defined within a class, any class which inherits from the class will by default pick up the defined attribute or method. If the inheriting class wants a different implementation of the method or attribute, it can **override** the inherited definition by redefining the method or attribute within the class. For example, we can create a new class NoOverdraftCheckingAccount, for a checking account with overdraft protection. The class would be a subclass of CheckingAccount, since it is in most respects just like the CheckingAccount class. If CheckingAcccount had a method HandleOverdraft(), we would override it in the new class. The implementation of HandleOverdraft() in CheckingAccount would make a pay or reject decision, add a charge to the account, and cause a NSF (Not Sufficient Funds) notice to be printed. In NoOverdraftCheckingAccount, the implementation of HandleOverdraft() would be different; it would call a method of the CreditCardAccount instance specified for this account to process a cash advance transaction, add the advance to our own account's balance, and then process the item that caused all the trouble. If the implementation of this one method were the only differences between a regular CheckingAccount and a NoOverdraftCheckingAccount, then you could argue persuasively that a simple if-then in the handling of overdrafts would have accomplished the same thing. However, in the real world there would probably be additional differences, and over time the code would likely diverge even further. Continuing to add additional cases and exceptions to a single code line creates just the maintenance headache that object-oriented code excels in avoiding. By making the objects separate, all the common code is reused. In any case where the logic must be different, having a distinct implementation in each subclass keeps the code simple and straightforward.

Because inheritance is only useful for sharing code between classes that are strongly related to each other, it is sometimes preferable to avoid inheritance, and instead use a technique known as object composition to build objects from a group of smaller objects. Object composition is also helpful in keeping the number of classes required to solve a problem manageable. If we expect either a large number of account types or a large number of variations on handling overdrafts, we may choose to create an OverdraftHandler object rather than creating new classes of accounts for every possible combination. An OverdraftHandler class can be subclassed for each different method of handling overdrafts. Each instance of a CheckingAccount includes an object of class OverdraftHandler, which allows any of the OverdraftHandler subclasses to be selected on an account-by-account basis. This allows the type of account and the type of overdraft handling to vary independently of each other, which may be (and probably is, in this case) a desirable capability. Useful behaviors and components should be made into their own objects. These can then be included wherever needed, regardless of the object inheritance hierarchy.

Some objects are created specifically to serve as containers for other objects, and are called (appropriately enough) container objects. Container objects may hold only a single type of object, or many. They may impose an ordering on the objects, or provide a structure such as a linked list or b-tree to facilitate retrieval of specific objects, or just be a random assortment (the junk drawer for object-oriented programmers).

Polymorphism is defined in the dictionary as "the quality or state of being able to assume different forms." It is not too much of a stretch to recognize this quality in the HandleOverdraft() method described above. To an application programmer, it appears that there is a single procedure called HandleOverdraft(), which is called regardless of the account type. And the programmer might assume that somewhere inside the implementation of HandleOverdraft() is conditional logic that performs different functions based on the account type. In reality, HandleOverdraft() is not one, but a set of procedures—our simple example had only a few account types, but there could have been dozens. At run time, which of the many implementations of HandleOverdraft() actually is invoked will depend upon the class of the object for which the method is invoked, and the types of the parameters. Another name for this capability is **overloading** a function—providing more than one implementation, based on the object type. Which implementation of HandleOverdraft() is executed may be resolved by the linker, called static binding, or at run time, called dynamic binding. Application logic is greatly simplified by providing overloaded function interfaces; in this case, the application programmer is freed from having to test the account type and perhaps call completely different interfaces, with different parameters, for what is conceptually the same task in each case.

Some languages such as C++ also allow this overloading to be specified not only for functions created by the programmer, but also for the language's built in operators. For example, we described a date object earlier. In a traditional language, we might create routines AddtoDate() and SubtractFromDate() to allow us to determine the date a given number of days before or after the date object. It is much more intuitive to simply override the "+" and "-" built-in operators for objects of class "date." Then, the simple statement `newdate = olddate + 30` will set newdate (an instance of class date) to the date that is 30 days after olddate (also an instance of class date).

Polymorphism and encapsulation together provide ease of maintenance and increased opportunities for code reuse by defining a firm boundary to objects: code inside the object should not be affected by changes to external routines, and likewise the external routines should not be affected by changes inside the object. Encapsulation allows an object's data to change while the interface to the object remains constant, and polymorphism allows an object's code to change while the interface to the object remains constant.

Polymorphism allows us to define several components that support identical interfaces, and defer selection of which object will actually be used until the moment it is actually used. For example, we can define an abstract base class for a File object, which supports an interface which consists of open, close, read, and write operations. We can create several subclasses of this object for different types of files—flat files, message files, KSAM files, TurboIMAGE datasets, etc. Each subclass would implement the file access methods as needed for that type of file. Applications can now be created that declare objects of the abstract type File when they are compiled, leaving open the possibility of any of the various subclasses of file being specified at run time. Then at run time, when an object is actually instantiated, the program can determine through whatever mechanism (command line parameter, configuration file entry, etc.) what type of file is actually desired. The application code is now completely independent of file types, and can be transparently extended to support new file types simply by adding new subclasses to the file object.

The terminology introduced in the preceding section will be used extensively throughout the remainder of the book because the architecture we will be defining has its roots in the application of object-oriented concepts to the objective of maximizing software portability.

Why Objects Are a Key Technology for Today's Software Architectures

Whether you adopt a true object-oriented language such as Smalltalk or C++, or develop in a traditional third-generation language such as COBOL or C, or use fourth-generation development tools, you should be incorporating object based thinking into the design of your applications. The rate of change in business today is faster than it has ever been, and all indications are that in the future, change will occur even more rapidly. If your development cycles are still measured in years, then the applications you are developing will be obsolete before they are ever deployed. Not obsolete in terms of the technology they use—you can always live with systems that aren't on the bleeding edge of technology—but obsolete in terms of being able to meet business requirements, a far more damaging limitation that you simply cannot accept.

Object technologies help you meet the business need of being able to re-engineer your applications to meet changing business conditions. A set of well-defined objects can be implemented once, and will persist with only minor changes through a number of re-engineering cycles. These business objects, which change little, are accessed through applications which can be rapidly deployed through the use of high-productivity development environments such as Visual Basic. The front-end applications can be revised or completely redeveloped as often as need dictates, while the business-critical data contained in the objects remains stable.

Implementing Objects in Traditional Languages

Many of the advantages of object-based systems can be achieved even when using traditional third- or fourth-generation development tools. Any language that supports the creation of user defined structures will allow you to group "attributes" into an "object."

Implementing encapsulation in a traditional language. You won't be able to include your access methods as part of the object, but the real benefit of providing a set of access methods doesn't depend on where the code actually resides. The methods can either be included at the source level (COBOL COPY-LIBs, C #includes) or the object code can be placed in a library for run-time access.

Implementing inheritance in a traditional language. In languages that don't provide inheritance, it is impossible to duplicate the functionality with the same robustness and flexibility as in languages designed for such a purpose. However, copylib or include files can be used (as they always have been) to allow certain methods or attributes to be included in different code modules, or in different places within the same code module. Thus the definition of those items that were common between the CheckingAccount and SavingsAccount objects can be placed in an included file incorporated into the definitions of both elements.

Implementing polymorphism in a traditional language. A "quasi-polymorphism" can be added to software through the implementation of a software switch layer. Using the HandleOverdraft() example, a HandleOverdraft() function would be called regardless of account type. Its implementation would be very simple; it would check the account type and call either HandleNormalOverdraft() or HandleProtectedOverdraft(), as required. Code that was common to both implementations—for example, if the account holder is charged a fee in either case—could be implemented in the switch layer, either before or after calling the class-specific function.

Why Client/server Is a Key Technology for Today's Software Architectures

There are several trends driving the current push toward client/server architectures. As with the trends driving the market toward object-oriented development, these trends show no sign of slowing. If your current development activities do not include any support for client/server architectures, you are almost certainly creating a competitive disadvantage for your business.

The most visible trend is the evolution of user interfaces to graphical, window based systems. The display devices required for these types of interfaces—bit-mapped displays—are not directly supported by the HP 3000, so if you want such an interface for your MPE applications, client/server is the only alternative. Furthermore, even if the hardware didn't require such an architecture, performance demands make it far more economical. Block-mode interfaces such as MPE's VPLUS or IBM's CICS place very little processing demand on the system, allowing a single system to support a large number of users with excellent response times. Character-based interfaces such as the UNIX curses system are far more CPU intensive. This is a primary reason why large UNIX installations almost always include some flavor of client/server architecture; the load created by of hundreds of character-mode users cannot be handled by even the largest available CPUs. Graphical interfaces, such as Microsoft Windows or OSF/Motif, represent another significant increase in processing requirements, such that a dedicated CPU per user is the norm for these systems. Thus, the demand for these graphical interfaces requires a move to a client/server design. We frequently hear requests from users to add more "GUI-like" features to VPLUS; for example, drop-down selection lists. Users want these capabilities made available on terminals so that they can provide a more modern user interface without incurring the expense of upgrading users to personal computers. Ironically, however, such capabilities will not avoid the need for such an upgrade, but rather accelerate it. These changes would make VPLUS far more CPU intensive, making it necessary to either upgrade the host system or move to a client/server configuration so that user interface processing could be off-loaded from the CPU.

A second driving factor is, once again, the increasing rate of change required to meet business needs. Because of business changes, a company may require a new application, only to find that the application doesn't run on the current hardware platform(s). Users may demand new office automation or decision support tools that require changes in desktop systems. These needs can only be met by bringing in new hardware. But it is not economical to convert all of the existing software to the new platforms. Instead, what is needed is a way for the various platforms to interoperate. Users can have the desktop system that best meets their needs; legacy applications can continue to run on the system best suited to support them; and new applications can be deployed on the platform which makes the most sense. Only through client/server technology can these systems be integrated into a cohesive "system" from the user's point of view, rather than a collection of incompatible systems.

There are a number of "models" that are commonly used to describe various types of client/server architectures. The following (shown in Figure 11.1) are the most common (source: Gartner Group):

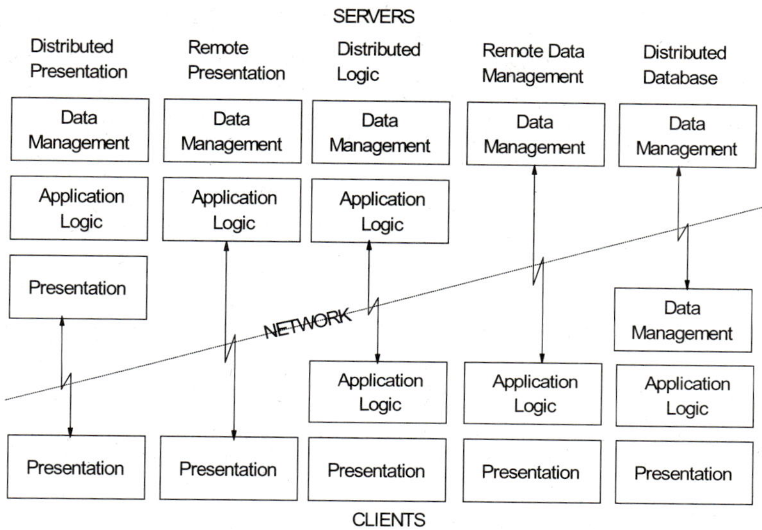

Figure 11.1 Client/Server Models

In the **Distributed Presentation** model everything except the user interface code resides on the server. The user interface code is split between the client and server systems. The X-windows system, upon which the OSF/Motif user interface provided on HP Workstations and X-terminals is based, provides the capability of having different user interface components run on different systems. Client/Server applications implemented with user interfaces based on X-windows are thus frequently based on a distributed presentation model. While we disagree with the characterization of VPLUS as a client/server tool (based on our belief that even sophisticated terminals do not have the processing capability to be considered a client), it nonetheless has a work breakdown typical of a distributed presentation application, and is useful as an example. A VPLUS application can pre-download forms layouts and simple data edits to a terminal, allowing initial processing of input data without interaction with the host. The form data is then uploaded to the host (server) for the execution of more complex logic such as that represented by the VPLUS field processing specifications. Tools that front-end legacy applications by providing a graphical user interface on a client system, such as the NewFace product for VPLUS-based applications, provide client/server capabilities based on the Distributed Presentation model.

The **Remote Presentation** model describes an architecture in which all the application logic is executed on a host (server) system, which is also where all of the application data is stored. The only functionality implemented on the client system is the user interface. Since the application and data reside on a single system, system management under this architecture is not very different from in a traditional host-terminal environment.

The **Distributed Logic** model has user interface code residing on the client, data management code residing on the server, and application logic split between the two systems. The client contains the logic required to assemble a transaction, while the server contains the logic necessary to execute and manage the transaction through completion. The most complex to implement, client/server purists view this as the "true" client/server architecture providing the greatest flexibility. You will frequently hear reference to "three-tier" client server; this is another way of referring to a distributed logic implementation.

The **Remote Data Management** or **Database Server** model describes a design in which the application runs on the client system, along with the user interface. The server system is used to store and coordinate access to the shared data. Specialized protocols to handle the communication between the client and server, most notably Microsoft's ODBC, have caused a surge in the use of this model, especially for decision support applications. The ODBC specification allows for tools such as spreadsheets to be written for the client end that can then extract information from any server database providing an ODBC interface. This is the model that is frequently referred to as "two-tier" client server.

The **Distributed Database** model puts user interface and application logic on the client, and splits the database between the client and the server. Application performance can be improved by having many requests for data satisfied by the client system. In simple implementations, only relatively static information is kept on the client system. More complex implementations will keep the most frequently accessed data on the client system, and methods for synchronizing the different copies of the data that may reside on the server and several different clients simultaneously.

Each of the above architectures can be further extended by replacing one server system—either a database or application server—with multiple systems providing the same functionality. The allocation of workloads across these multiple servers can either be statically determined as part of the system design, or dynamically allocated based on workload. An application server may be split up into multiple servers with each serving a certain number of users, or it may be split up functionally (accounts payable on system A, general ledger on system B). A database server may be split up based on access type (read only versus update), or certain datasets or tables may be placed on each system, or any of several other possibilities.

Components of a Hypothetical Architecture

In the remainder of Part 3, we will work through the design of a hypothetical architecture to provide co-existence across MPE, HP-UX, and Windows systems. The architecture is not offered as the one best way of providing this co-existence; rather it is used as an exercise in uncovering the issues involved and identifying the tradeoffs that must be made. The architecture will use object-oriented concepts as described previously, but not assume implementation in an object-oriented language. It will assume a client/server implementation, but provide to the largest extent possible flexibility to migrate between different client/server models as business needs change. It will incorporate layering and other features with the intent of allowing future technologies to be incorporated into the design with minimal changes to existing code. The specific features that will provide these capabilities are:

- Encapsulation and layering will be used to isolate core application logic from any dependencies on specific database, operating system, network, or user interface technologies.
- Business Rules will be implemented as part of application objects to ensure the consistency of critical business data regardless of how accessed.
- Application logic will be implemented as discrete transactions to provide flexibility in workload distribution across servers and to isolate the application from any changes in user interface technologies.
- An application messaging facility will be designed to provide capabilities to distribute the application while hiding the details of specific network protocols or differences in the underlying platforms.
- The application design will provide support for multiple user interfaces, recognizing that users today need access from different desktop platforms (PCs, Workstations, Macs) and that future technologies (voice, pen, multimedia) may be very different that todays.

CHAPTER 12

Evolution of HP 3000 Software Architectures

As we develop our ideas for an application software architecture, it helps to recap briefly what types of architectures have been used in the past. It is, after all, the limitations of these architectures that drive us to seek something better for new applications. Understanding where we have come from gives us a clearer understanding of where we would like to go.

This chapter will present a brief trip through the history of software architectures on the HP 3000. As you study the progression, don't be disturbed if you find that the model which best describes your current architecture is the first one described—the oldest model. The HP 3000 and its application development subsystems—TurboIMAGE and VPLUS—are so well suited to a particular architectural model that many, if not most, users have never seen a strong benefit to moving to a later model. Indeed, after studying everything we can present to you about what today's software architectures look like, you may still feel that the "classic HP 3000" model is the one best suited to your business needs. That must be the key consideration—not moving to the latest and greatest for the sake of change, but finding the model which best suits your business needs. If your business needs have changed little, then a radical shift in architecture probably isn't warranted.

The Classic HP 3000 Architecture

Figure 12.1 presents the classic HP 3000 application architecture. The program code is most likely implemented in COBOL. Data storage is most frequently TurboIMAGE, although KSAM and a number of flat-file formats are frequently used as well.

VPLUS is most commonly used to provide the user interface. Various system services, such as process management, are accessed via the MPE intrinsic mechanism.

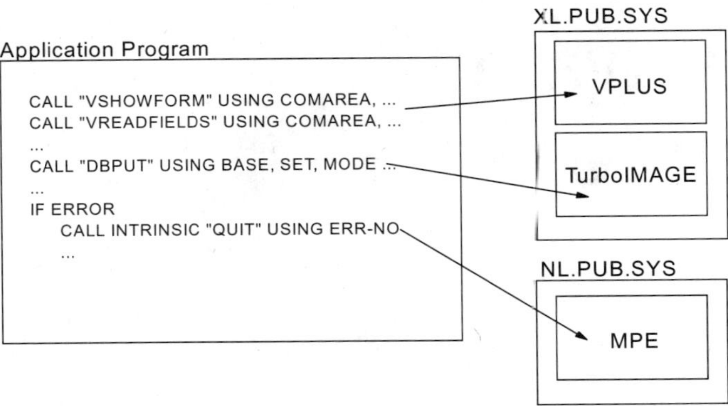

Figure 12.1 The Classic HP 3000 Architecture

This architecture is widely used for a number of reasons. One is its simplicity; there is nothing in the architecture which doesn't have to be there. Thus, development and maintenance are straightforward. The subsystem technologies are extremely well tuned to the HP 3000 environment, such that even with all the advances in past twenty years, the combination of components shown above will generally outperform systems built on a newer technology base.

The problem arises when there is a desire to change any of the components in this model. If you want to replace TurboIMAGE with a relational database, you are hindered by the fact that database access code is scattered throughout the entire application. If your application grows so large that it cannot run well on a single system, there is no straightforward way to distribute the application across multiple systems. If it ever became desirable to move the application entirely to another platform, you would be faced with a near rewrite to remove the dependencies on MPE intrinsics, TurboIMAGE, and VPLUS. The classic application architecture provides great functionality and performance, but very limited flexibility and no portability.

The Layered Architecture

A layered application architecture will address many (but not all) of the limitations of the classic architecture. The main difference between the classic and layered architecture is the creation of a software layer that separates the application code from the subsystems and operating system that provide the technological base for the application.

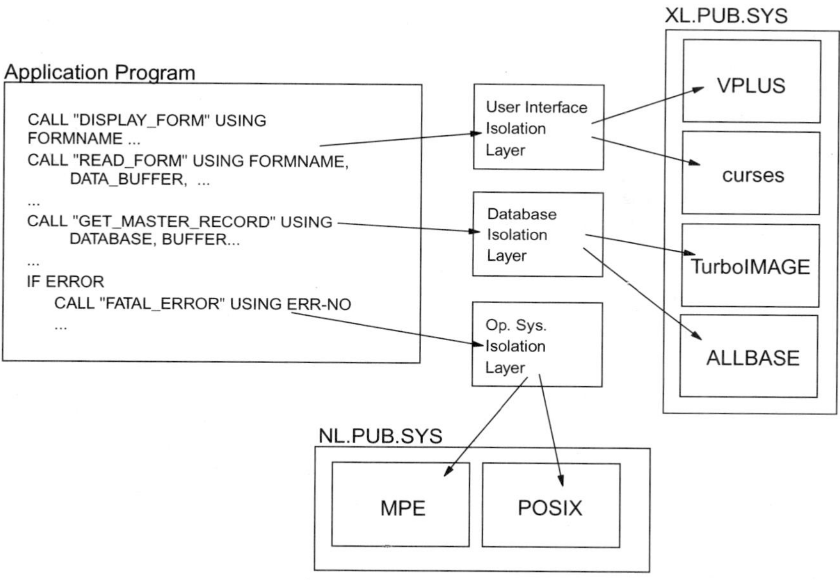

Figure 12.2 The Layered Architecture

Figure 12.2 depicts a layered application architecture which could be used for the same application. The insertion of a software isolation layer removes any direct dependencies between the application logic and the underlying subsystems. There are a number of advantages realized from this architectural change.

- Much of the code in the intermediate layer will be leveragable. For example, to display and collect data from a VPLUS form requires a relatively large number of calls (VGETNEXTFORM, VINITFORM, VSHOWFORM, VREADFIELDS, VFIELDEDITS, VFINISHFORM, VGETBUFFER). This entire sequence could be replaced by a single call, passing a form name and returning a data buffer. The intermediate user interface layer can be leveraged for all forms within the application, and even used in other applications.
- All data structures and logic specific to the subsystems can be moved out of the application logic, making the application more compact and maintainable.

- Application programmers need not be trained in the intricacies of VPLUS, TurboIMAGE, or MPE; they can simple write to a defined set of APIs (Application Program Interfaces) that are provided by the intermediate layer.
- If the interfaces to the intermediate layer are made sufficiently abstract, the underlying subsystems can be changed without affecting the application. For example, a VPLUS user interface could be replaced with a curses user interface, without changing the API used by the program. (This requires thoughtful design of the API. For example, do not pass the VPLUS COMAREA between the program and the intermediate layer; this is a VPLUS specific construct.)
- The application code itself is now portable. Components of the intermediate layer may be portable, depending on the subsystems accessed. Database access code for Allbase will be portable to HP-UX; code for TurboIMAGE will not be. For non-portable components, it will only be necessary to re-implement the specific module in question; compare this to the need to rewrite the entire application for the classic architecture.

As you can see, there are a number of advantages to using the layered architecture. The cost of such an architecture is the run-time penalty of processing additional procedure calls each time a subsystem is accessed. Most applications will be able to absorb this cost without a noticeable increase in response time or any measurable degradation in overall system performance. In reality, performance is more likely to improve as a result of this architecture. Rather than all programmers coding their own database access routines in varying fashions, you can have your best database programmer develop the intermediate layer. It will also be more practical to perform performance measurement and tuning on this single module than on the entire application.

The Client/Server Architectures

The Gartner Group describes five different models of Client/Server architecture: Distributed Presentation, Remote Presentation, Distributed Logic, Remote Data Management, and Distributed Database. We looked at these architectures earlier, but will now examine how they may be implemented in an HP 3000 environment. We will look at three of these in detail (the remaining two will be presented as variations of these three).

The Remote Presentation architecture, as shown in Figure 12.3, is the most widely used of the client/server architectures. This is perhaps because it solves the problem that forced the evolution of client/server architectures in the first place; the demands placed on the host system to support increasingly CPU intensive user interface technologies. If your users are satisfied with the look-and-feel of VPLUS forms based interfaces, then there may be no need for you to adopt a client/server architecture. But most users are demanding drop-down menu bars, scrollable pick lists, context sensitive help, and other features found on Graphical User Interface (GUI) based systems. If you try to implement these features on dumb terminals, you will find that they consume more CPU resources than VPLUS by a factor of 10 or more. Thus, you will be forced to either upgrade your CPU, support fewer users, or offload the processing of the user interface to a less expensive processor. It is this last option that is most economical, plus provides the greatest flexibility. CPU-intensive user interface processing is performed on the client system, while data access and application logic continue to be provided by the host (server) system.

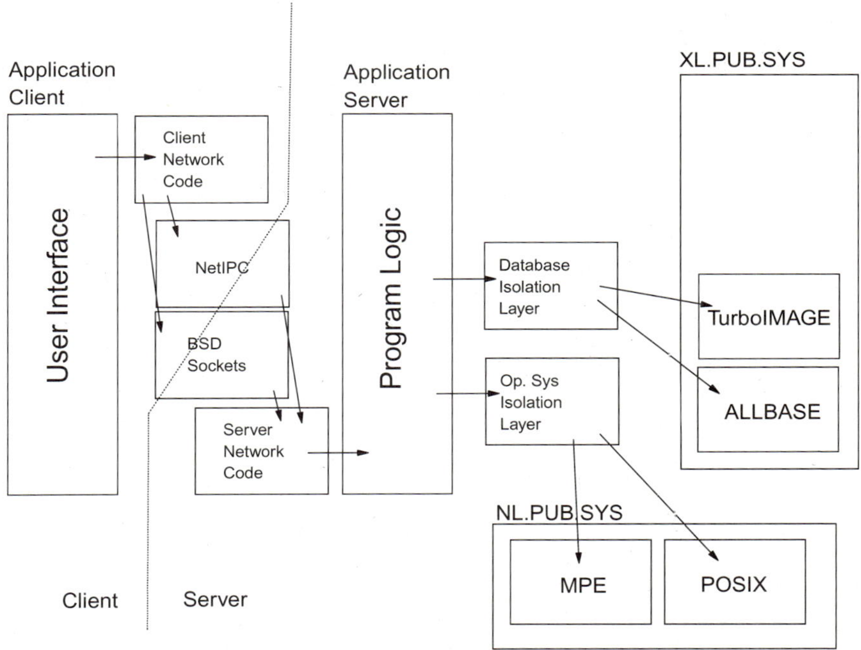

Figure 12.3 Remote Presentation Client/Server Architecture

In the Layered code model, we created a software layer that isolated the application logic from the specific user-interface technologies. This layer could provide transparent portability between, for example, VPLUS and curses. This is possible because both VPLUS and curses are screen-based interfaces; and while the mapping between functionality is not exact, a workable abstraction can be created to allow support of both environments.

Graphical interfaces such as Windows, Motif, or the Macintosh are quite different. This difference is more than just in appearance; there is a difference in the philosophy of how an application is controlled. Non-GUI applications typically have a standard program flow that is determined by the application designer. Users can influence this somewhat; for example, function keys can be used to navigate within the application. Compare this to the typical GUI application. Actions selectable from the application's menubar may give access to several dozen functions. Other than disabling selections that are not currently available, the application imposes no ordering of actions upon the user.

This different view of how an application is controlled leads to a different way of constructing applications. The older architecture is based on a prompt-and-response model; the application prompts for input (by displaying a form in the case of VPLUS), the user inputs data, and the cycle repeats. The new architecture is based on an event-action model. The application waits for the user to do something (an event), which may be selecting a menu item, entering data into a dialog box, or clicking on an icon, among others. The application responds to this by performing the indicated action, and then waits for the next user event. The application is controlled by the user interface; not the other way around. This change is indicated by the reorganization of the application modules in Figure 12.3; instead of the program code calling functions within the User Interface when user interaction is required, the User Interface now calls functions within the application logic module when an action is requested. This control of the application from the user interface is characteristic of all modern architectures, and will be seen in all the models we examine from this point forward.

The Distributed Presentation model (not shown) is a variant of this model in which a portion of the user interface logic continues to reside on the server.

The Distributed Logic model, as illustrated in Figure 12.4, moves portions of the application logic to the client in addition to the user interface. This permits tasks which are CPU intensive to be offloaded from the server system, or for certain tasks for which response times are particularly critical to be performed locally. For example, a production controller in a manufacturing environment may download a production schedule, and then perform analysis of various what-if scenarios on the client. If changes in the schedule are made, the results can then be transmitted back to the server. In a catalog order entry environment, the server would be accessed to determine the availability of merchandise, but processing such as calculating an extended price and adding sales tax can be performed locally in the client.

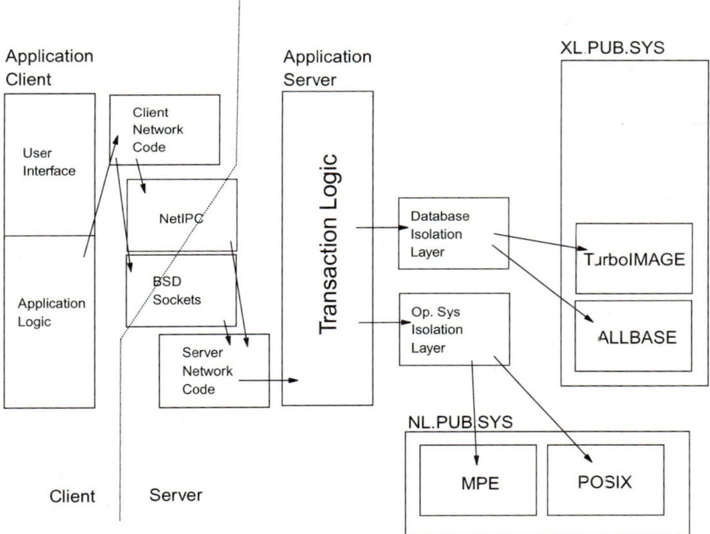

Figure 12.4 Distributed Logic Client/Server Architecture

Applications built upon the distributed logic model are frequently thought to be more complex than those built upon other client/server models. This is not necessarily the case. The perception arises primarily from the fact that in the other models, there is widely used middleware that handles the network interfaces. In a distributed logic implementation, the programmer is much more likely to be writing directly to a network API, rather than through a middleware layer. We feel that this is not as intimidating as it may at first seem, as our later discussions of creating a messaging module will illustrate.

In the Remote Data Management model (Figure 12.5), virtually all application logic is moved to the client. This is also referred to as the Database Server model, since all that remains on the server in this configuration is the database and code directly associated with data access. A database front-end provides the illusion of local database access; calls are made to this front-end as if it were the database engine. The front-end then sends the database requests over the network, using either a general-purpose mechanism such as BSD sockets or, more commonly, an API designed specifically for database communication, such as ODBC. A database process on the server receives messages from the client, performs the actual database operations, and returns requested information and status to the client. An advantage of this model is that the programmer can now take advantage of the latest generation of Rapid Prototyping / Rapid Development tools, such as Visual BASIC, Delphi, and PowerBuilder, while still enjoying the high reliability and performance of mainframe or minicomputer based database systems.

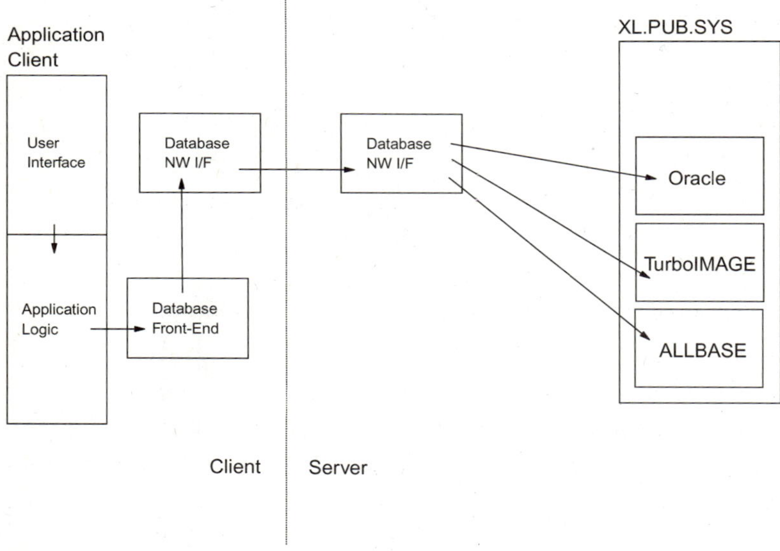

Figure 12.5 Remote Data Management Client/Server Architecture

The Distributed Database architecture (not shown) is a variant of the Remote Data Management architecture in which the database is itself distributed. It may be distributed between the client and server, or across multiple server systems. Maintaining the integrity of a distributed database in case of processing interruptions such as system failures is a far more complex task than maintaining integrity on a single system. Although it is possible to write code to manage this task yourself, organizations implementing a distributed database should consider implementing a Transaction Manager designed expressly for this purpose.

The various flavors of client/server architectures provide many advantages over the traditional host-terminal architectures. In each of the cases we have discussed so far, the distribution of work between the client and the server is fixed at the time the architecture is designed. An application architecture based upon the Remote Presentation model, for example, may not be easily adapted to allow additional processing to be added to the client at a later time. Since it is possible that the client/server model which best suits your processing needs may change over time, our final evolutionary step is to create an architecture which allows any of these client/server architectures, or a combination of them, to be used, with the capability of switching between models fairly easily when required.

The Maximum Flexibility Architecture

We'll refer to this final architecture as the Maximum Flexibility architecture, since that is its distinguishing characteristic. The design of this architecture, shown in Figure 12.6, includes the following features:

- To the programmers on the client side, all resources appear to be local.
- Local (client-side) isolation layer accesses local objects directly, and accesses remote objects via the messaging layer.
- Messaging middleware layer provides capability to send messages over various types of networks using different APIs. Ability to support asynchronous (non-blocking) messages.
- Single monitor process at server to handle incoming traffic from clients; can be replicated if needed to support workload.

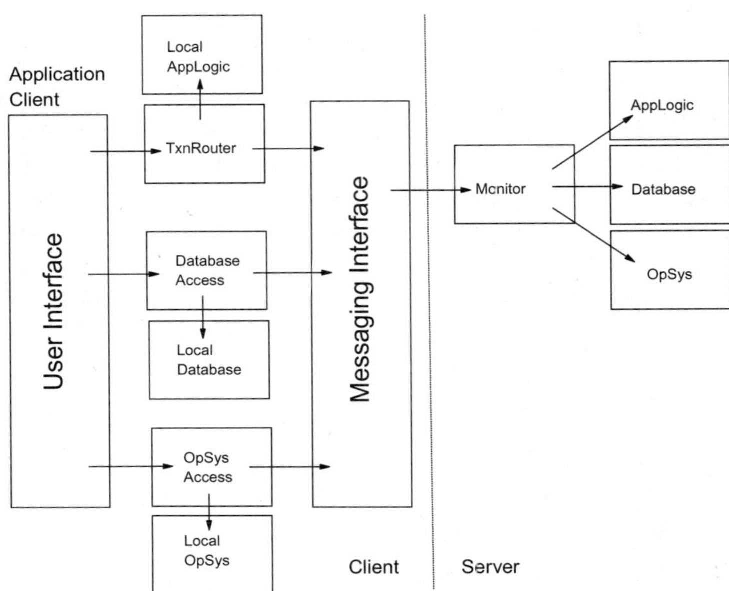

Figure 12.6 Maximum Flexibility Architecture

The design of this architecture was driven by two overriding objectives. First, it should work in the largest possible variety of configurations; flexibility is the number one requirement. This means that at every design point, the architecture strives to present the greatest number of alternatives. An architecture can be made simpler by limiting the choices at each of these design points; for example, if only MPE/iX and HP-UX need to be considered as operating systems, or if only one database technology needs to be supported. The architecture also provides the capability to be scaled anywhere from a single-user model on a PC, to a single multi-user system with terminal connections, to a client/server architecture based on any of the previously described models.

The second overriding objective is vendor independence. While many people today equate "open systems" with running on a UNIX-derived operating system, we have chosen to take the extreme position (at least within this architecture) that the required degree of openness is to be completely vendor independent. Thus, the architecture is designed to provide independence from hardware vendors, operating system vendors, database vendors, tool vendors, and stress relief medication vendors.

Exceptions will be noted where portions of the code are viewed as "throwaway"; that is, they can be redeveloped using another technology when required at a lower cost than designing them up front to support multiple underlying technologies.

In the client/server architectures described previously, the application always knew where to look for each component. In a Remote Data Management model, the database was on the server, while application logic was local. In the maximum flexibility architecture, the location of all components is flexible. For each component, there will be code on the client which receives requests from the user interface. This client code will then determine, by accessing configuration information which may be dynamically changing, where to go for the required service. It may be locally on the client, or on any of a number of servers which can be accessed over the network.

One component that is shown explicitly in this architecture for the first time is a monitor process running on the server. There is some such process in any client/server implementation, but depending on the architecture selected and middleware products used, it may be transparent to the programmer. The monitor is responsible for receiving the various messages that can be received from clients, and either processing them or passing them along to another process which will handle them.

Subsequent chapters will delve into each of the components of this hypothetical architecture in more detail.

CHAPTER 13

Designing the Database Module

The Maximum Flexibility architecture allows for the database to be placed on the client, on a single server, distributed between client and server(s), or distributed among multiple servers. The messaging mechanism has support for passing messages to or between databases, although this feature may not always be used. (Implementors also have the option of using a standard protocol such as ODBC, or using a proprietary multi-database tool such as EDA/SQL, or an API provided by a particular database vendor such as Allbase/NET.)

Detailed information on the implementation of database objects will be covered in Chapter 19, as will adding support for passing database information through the messaging facility. In this chapter, we will focus on higher-level characteristics of the database module. Readers familiar with relational database concepts will find most of this material to be a review; but readers experienced primarily with TurboIMAGE will learn some of the features of relational databases that have helped them gain a dominant share of the market.

Data Integrity

One of the primary concerns of an application designer is to ensure the consistency of the application's data. There are two levels of consistency that should be taken into account. **Physical Integrity** of the data is the most critical; it is essentially making sure that the ones and zeros you put into the database will come back out the same way. There is little that an application programmer can do about physical integrity of data; the database and operating system are responsible for this level of integrity. Some databases do provide either an application programmer or, more typically, a database administrator to make certain tradeoffs between performance and integrity (such as the AUTODEFER mode in TurboIMAGE), but these are essentially choices between a predetermined set of behaviors. Only the most determined (or paranoid) application developer will take on the responsibility for ensuring that data is physically written to disk; after all, the reason for buying a database in the first place was to not have to write such code yourself. This doesn't mean that your business doesn't have any responsibility to worry about physical integrity of the data; system administrators can employ technologies such as disk arrays, mirrored disks and shadowed systems to facilitate recovery when physical integrity is compromised.

The next level of integrity is **logical integrity**. If physical integrity is thought of as writing one record and making sure it was written correctly, logical integrity is ensuring that the relationship between multiple records is accurately recorded. For example, one type of logical integrity is ensuring that a key value is unique. Most databases will enforce this particular constraint, if specified in the database definition. Another example of logical integrity is **referential integrity**. This is guaranteeing that for any value entered into a particular field, that value exists in another defined location. For example, to enter a payroll record with a particular employee number value, that employee number must correspond to an entry in the table or dataset containing employee records.

Traditional network or hierarchical style databases, such as TurboIMAGE, provided referential integrity based on the physical structure of the database. Using the above example, by making the employees a master dataset with employee number as its key (or alternately, a detail dataset with an automatic master on the employee number), any detail data sets (such as payroll records) that define employee number as a search item will have a referential integrity constraint imposed. Specifically, you will not be able to add detail records for which there is no corresponding master entry, and you will not be able to delete a master entry that has any detail entries associated with it. The constraint is enforced by the database management software; a programmer who is unaware of the relationship between these records will not be able to corrupt the database by ignoring the constraint.

Relational databases, by their very nature, do not recognize any fixed relationships between tables or data items such as those represented by TurboIMAGE search items. A relational database which provides no specific facility for the specification and enforcement of referential integrity constraints would thus be far more likely to become inconsistent due to violation of the constraint than a TurboIMAGE database. Fortunately, this is not the case; all relational databases that we are aware of allow referential integrity constraints to be defined for any field. This is a superior approach, since there is no guarantee that all data items which could benefit from such a constraint will be search items in a TurboIMAGE implementation.

Another approach to referential integrity is available to those programmers using object oriented design. Since all access to the data object is via a set of defined methods, enforcement of the constraint can be coded into the method, making the data consistent regardless of the source of the change or the structure of the database.

A final type of logical integrity is any type of checking that a field meets specific criteria for valid values for that field. This could be making sure dates are validly formed, testing that payroll check amounts fall within an expected range, making sure that phone numbers have the correct number of digits, etc. Here, relational databases usually provide capabilities to define these types of constraints, but TurboIMAGE leaves any such testing completely to the application. Again, the object oriented approach of forcing all accessors through defined access routines—not allowing an application programmer to directly DBPUT or DBUPDATE the target dataset—allows the implementation of these constraints in a manner guaranteed to be applied to all transactions.

The Data Warehouse

If you've attended any trade shows or read any industry publications in the past year, you know that data warehouses are receiving a lot of attention right now. TurboIMAGE programmers have always been acutely aware of the impact of database design on performance. Because access paths are explicitly indicated in the database design, TurboIMAGE programmers are required to give consideration to how the data will be accessed when the database is designed. In relational databases, how the database will be accessed is frequently left to the database engine, allowing the programmer to be unaware of whether a particular query is efficient or inefficient with a chosen database design.

One of the ways in which the various database engines distinguish themselves from one another is in how well they can optimize various types of queries, and what facilities they provide a programmer to provide hints about data access intentions which can help in the optimization of these queries. The increasing sophistication of these optimization capabilities led the developers and users of relational databases to a breakthrough in thinking about database design: the realization that if you want to optimize a database design to support high-volume, online transaction processing, that you would design the database differently than if you wanted to optimize for ad-hoc inquiry capabilities. This realization might seem blindingly obvious to a TurboIMAGE programmer. This is because in TurboIMAGE, the database designer is responsible for defining the access paths to the data—what items will be search items, whether there will be sort items, etc. TurboIMAGE programmers understand intimately the trade-offs such as optimizing for retrieval speed at the cost of slower updates and similar topics. In relational databases, however, the database engine is responsible for finding the best access path to the data. Unless you explicitly look for the information, you won't even know how the database chooses to access the data. This makes relational databases easier to use, but tends to make the programmers and database administrators less aware of the performance impact of design choices in both the database and the application programs.

While programmers and database administrators may have been blissfully unaware of performance implications, database vendors most certainly were not. Increasing demands for performance of both OLTP and decision support application types have forced relational database vendors to recommend a split of data into different structures, depending on whether it should be optimized for OLTP access or for decision support access. The concept of a data warehouse was born. A data warehouse begins as a database optimized for ad-hoc queries, such as in decision support applications. Data warehouses are created by taking the data from the production databases and performing a number of filtering and transformation operations on the data. The data warehouse will then be updated on a regular basis, usually not more often than once a day or less often than monthly, to reflect changes in the production databases. (It is generally preferable to code any queries that must have up-to-the-minute accuracy to access production databases, rather than to try to keep a data warehouse in sync on a nearly real-time basis).

Moving data into the data warehouse is not just a matter of copying the data into a database that is differently organized. First, there is the decision of what data to move. A clear understanding of reporting requirements may allow much data to be filtered out. Next, summary data is created, so that reports that do not require detail-level information will not have to run through all of the detail records just to accumulate totals. The data warehouse will also include "meta data", or data about the data. This describes where the data comes from and how it has been processed into its current form. Meta data also describes any coded values in the data records; for example, if inventory records include a 1 for purchased parts and 2 for fabricated parts in a particular field, the meta data will describe this convention.

The newly rediscovered distinction between optimization for OLTP and optimization for inquiries seems to present an opportunity in the marketplace for a reemergence of non-relational databases. TurboIMAGE has always outperformed even the most highly tuned relational database in the performance of OLTP workloads (and likewise, been at a sizeable disadvantage in performance of ad-hoc workloads that don't follow the predefined access paths). It will be interesting to see if anyone in the marketplace takes advantage of this opportunity.

Because the data warehouse is not ever accessed directly by the application programs, it is not explicitly shown on any of our architectural diagrams, and is not taken into consideration in any of the module designs. Whether to implement a data warehouse or not is a decision that is independent of all of the architectural decisions we will be exploring. Data warehouses are frequently added after applications have been in production for some time, and not as part of the original design. Whether to implement a data warehouse at all, and whether to do it as part of the original design or as an add-on, should be decided based on the type of reporting requirements you have and the impact that the processing of these reports will have on production data processing.

Database Module Design

The database market is an extremely competitive one, which has led to an expansion of features in the various databases far faster than the standards can evolve to accommodate the new requirements. Since the functionality is being implemented ahead of any general consensus on what the standards will look like, the way that various features are implemented is frequently incompatible between the different databases.

In some areas of your architecture, it may be possible to take a least common denominator approach, and use only those features that have been incorporated into standards, or are at least implemented in a reasonably similar fashion between all the vendors. This isn't practical for the database layer; there are too many very valuable features you would be denying yourself if you used only ANSI standard SQL features.

The database module will be made up of a number of different types of objects, operating cooperatively. The objects that are accessed by the application logic should be View objects that represent a logical view of the data. There should be another group of Entry objects that represent the physical structure of the database; the actual record or entry formats. The View objects are responsible for updating the Entry objects. Information required to accomplish this may be stored within the objects themselves, or you may choose to use an external Data Dictionary. Making the Views and Entrys separate objects allows them to vary independently; a View may represent all or part of a single Entry, or fields from different Entrys (even Entrys in different databases), or you may even allow Views to represent data stored in non-database files such as KSAM. Each Entry and View object will support a standard set of methods, which can be called get, put, update, delete; or select, insert, update, delete; or any other terminology that you choose to adopt. A database object can be created for each different database engine to be supported. Implementation that is not easily portable between database engines, such as locking, should be implemented in these objects.

CHAPTER 14

Introduction to Messaging Mechanisms

In a client/server architecture, it is obvious that one of the features that the architecture will require is a method of communication between the client and the server. While all that is required of a messaging layer for many applications is just a way to deliver a message from a client to a server or vice-versa, this is also an area that is ripe for extension in a number of ways to provide additional capabilities.

Location transparency is a goal of most messaging middleware products. Location transparency means that when a client program needs a service that is provided by a server, it should be the responsibility of the middleware to locate an appropriate server, rather than have a hard-coded path stored on the client side. Location transparency may be as simple as having a central directory of servers. It is often extended to support dynamic reconfiguration, so that if a server goes down traffic for that server can be re-routed to another server providing the same capabilities. It may also incorporate some form of load balancing for when multiple servers provide the same services.

Security is another capability frequently provided at least in part by middleware products. Security measures may include encryption of data streams sent over the network, capabilities for authenticating users, and the ability to limit access to server systems to selected clients.

Messaging middleware is one of the areas of greatest activity in the client/server marketplace. If your needs are simple message delivery, you can develop your own. If you are looking for a more sophisticated capability set, and don't want to tackle the development of all of it yourself, you can choose from any number of middleware products that provide part or all of the messaging function for you.

The tools that you can use to build your messaging mechanism fall generally into three categories: message based, remote procedure call based, and SQL based. You may choose one of these as the backbone of your messaging facility, or you may use a combination of two or more. A high-level overview of the three basic types follows.

Message-based Communication Tools

The oldest and most widely used type of cross-system communication tools are the message-based tools. These include HP's proprietary NetIPC facility, and the Berkeley sockets (also BSD Sockets, or just sockets) facility and its derivative WinSock. The use of these facilities is fairly straightforward: a connection is opened between two processes running on different systems. Send and Receive functions are used to transfer messages between the processes. The content of the messages is completely up to the implementor; they may be fixed or variable length and may include any data types which are understandable by both sides (or that can be converted into an understandable format). A server program can be written to handle messages from a single client, or from a number of clients. (Likewise, a client program can communicate with one or more servers). The client and server code may in fact reside on the same computer; some systems, including the HP 3000, will detect this and use a "local socket" to reduce the overhead of sockets calls that need not be transmitted across a network.

Note that the connection is between two processes—implying that in order for a client to initiate a connection to the server, the server must already be running a program to receive the incoming connection[1]. This is what we referred to as the "monitor" process in the architectural overview. A typical HP 3000 implementation would be to run the monitor program from a batch job that is streamed at system startup time (you may already have such programs running on your system; for example, if you see a jobstream named JFTPMON running, it is the monitor for incoming FTP requests). On a UNIX system, such programs would run as daemon processes. There is a standard process called inetd (the Internet Services daemon) that runs on UNIX systems which handles a variety of incoming request types, including rcp, remsh, rlogin, ftp, and telnet. In addition to monitoring requests for these standard services, inetd can also accept incoming requests for user application servers. At the time of this writing, inetd is expected to be available for the HP 3000 as part of a 1996 release.

1. There is an exception to this in cases where the client has a way of invoking the needed server process on the remote server machine. Between two HP 3000's, the Remote Process Management (RPM) capability of the Network Services (NS) product provides this capability.

Our architecture does not assume availability of an inetd process, and thus includes the design of a monitor process. This monitor program is extensible to include capabilities beyond those provided by inetd. If all server systems to be accessed provide inetd capability, and you prefer the consistency of having a common access mechanism for all incoming requests, you may choose to move implementation of these additional features into the server portion of the application and use inetd as the monitor process. No other components of the architecture would require changes.

With a server running multiple applications, plus providing standard services such as telnet and ftp, how does a client get connected to the right server process? An IP address is not sufficient; it merely identifies the system. Sockets connections are made via a port number. The port number is like a telephone number: the client must know the port number that the server will be expecting a connection to come in on; the port number should be unique; and the server must be actively monitoring the port number for a connection to happen. Many assigned port numbers can be found in the file /etc/services. Port numbers below 1024 are reserved; even after selecting a value outside of this range you should check the /etc/services file for any possible collisions. It's a good idea to insert a comment with the number you have selected into the file to prevent collisions with future developers.

Remote Procedure Call Tools

Another group of inter-system communication tools are based on the concept of remote procedure calls. These include the Open Software Foundation's Distributed Computing Environment (OSF DCE) and Sun's ONC. Since programmers are already familiar with the concept of procedure calls to transfer control between different modules of code running on the same system, this method leverages familiar concepts by allowing the programmer to design the application modules as if they were to reside on the same system. Interface definitions are then created for any procedures which may be called across the network; these interface definitions are then processed by a special compiler which creates modules for both the client and the server systems. These modules contain stubs for each procedure that can be called. At run time, the client's call to a server procedure is received by the client stub (see Figure 14.1). The stub sends a message across the network to the server stub routine, passing it the parameters for the called procedure. The server stub then calls the target routine. Any parameters with changed values and any return value from the target routine are then formed into a message by the server stub and returned to the client stub, which then returns control to the calling program exactly as if the target procedure had been executed locally. Remote procedure calls protocols are inherently synchronous; that is, the calling process will be blocked until the called procedure completes, and then continue execution. Many applications will be blocked anyway whenever service by a server is required, but if your application can be doing other useful work while the server processes a request, you may wish to avoid the use of RPC-based tools.

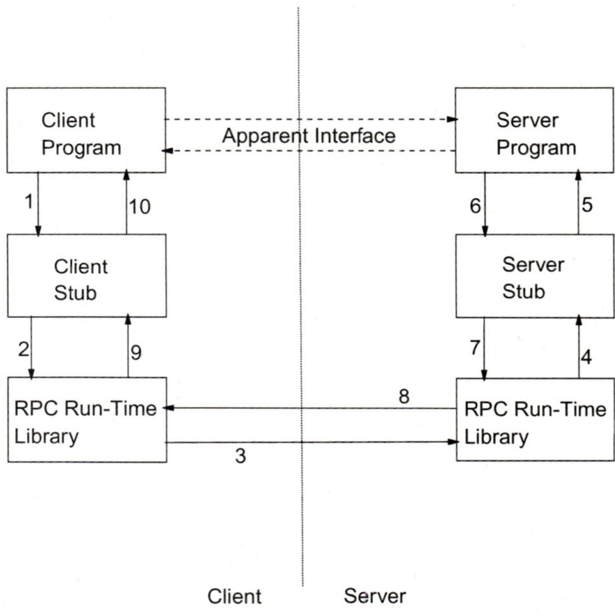

Figure 14.1 Running an RPC Application

SQL-based Tools

The final category of tools is those based on SQL-like syntax. Like the RPC tools, these tools attempt to simplify the task of writing a client/server application by hiding the network communications behind an access method that is already familiar to the programmer. In an application based on one of these tools, the client program is written as if it were accessing a local database. What actually happens is that the SQL calls are intercepted by a run-time library that resides on the client, and turned into messages that are sent across the network. A server program interprets the message, performs the requested access against the database, and formats the resulting data or status information into a message which is then sent back to the run-time library on the client. The client run-time library then presents the data back to the application program as if it had been obtained from a local database.

This approach is obviously well suited to an application which uses the database server model of client/server interaction, where all application logic resides on the client and the server houses only the database. An early problem with this approach was that it frequently required transferring huge blocks of data from the server to the client, which the client might then scan searching for only 1 or 2 records. If some of the data selection logic could be executed on the server, this overhead could be dramatically reduced. However, the SQL-based protocols only allowed access to the database, not to application code modules that might reside on the server. The solution, which you may be familiar with, is to store application code in the database, a capability referred to as **stored procedures**. The SQL syntax was then extended to provide for the invocation of these stored procedures via SQL statements. It should be noted that there is not a standard way of implementing stored procedures; each of the relational database vendors has a slightly different implementation, and use of this capability will impair the portability of your applications. The performance advantages of using stored procedures is significant enough that we recommend their use if you are using SQL-based communications tools; if you want both performance and portability, you should use a message-based or RPC-based tool instead that will allow your server based code to be kept outside of the database.

Maximum Flexibility Messaging Design

Note that in all three of these tool groups, the underlying communications facility is message-based; the RPC and SQL tools merely build additional layers on top of the messaging facility to isolate the user from the task of handling the messages. But this isolation also reduces the flexibility in terms of the types of information you can send across the network. We have chosen to use a messaging-based API as our primary interface to the messaging functionality required by application programs. However, the architecture is extensible to allow RPC or SQL-based interfaces to be layered on top of the primarily interface, allowing those models to be used when appropriate.

Future Directions in Messaging Middleware

Our architecture as designed is limited to the use of widely available technologies, and in particular technologies which are available to the HP 3000 developer. There are emerging trends in this area of the marketplace which any designer of object-oriented software will want to keep abreast of, even though there is not at yet any activity related to these technologies on the HP 3000 platform. Nothing in our architecture precludes extensions to incorporate these technologies at a later date.

Object-oriented middleware is beginning to move into the mainstream, and there are two primary architectures competing in the market today. One of these is the Object Management Group's (OMG) Object Management Architecture (OMA), of which the most widely known piece is the CORBA (Common Object Request Broker Architecture) for communication between objects across a network. More recently Microsoft has announced the Component Object Model (COM) architecture that fulfills the same purpose of providing the infrastructure for distributed object-oriented applications.

Both architectures address a similar set of requirements. These include the need to manage objects—to create them, keep track of them, delete them when no longer needed, and control access to them. Both architectures attempt to create guidelines for creating "plug and play" objects to allow the creation of customized user environments through the selection of various object components from different software providers. Both architectures also provide messaging facilities to communicate between objects, providing location transparency for both server providers and requestors.

One attractive feature introduced by the COM architecture is its built-in support for versioning of objects. The concept can be adapted for use in other architectural frameworks, including ours. Especially in a multi-vendor environment, software objects will evolve through various versions, and the task of ensuring that the desired version of each component is compatible with the desired versions of every other component could easily make the idea of the "plug and play" components unworkable.

The solution adopted by COM is to redefine the term "interface." As generally used in object-oriented terminology, an interface is simply the set of methods provided by an object to external callers. It could conceivably change during revisions of the software object. Thus, the interface changes as the object evolves over time. COM defines an Interface as a collection of methods that will not change, and that are viewed as a set—an object must implement all of the methods of any Interface it claims to support. If changes to the object result in the creation of new methods, deletion of old methods, or any changes to the external appearance and behavior of methods, a new Interface must be created to access these new features. The old Interface must either be supported exactly as before, or dropped altogether.

As an object evolves, it is expected that it will support multiple Interfaces. For example, version 1 of an application object may support 5 transactions. These would constitute its Interface, and the Interface would be named, as in IMyApp1. Version 2 of the object may add additional transactions. This would require that a new Interface be created, for example, IMyApp2. Requestors query objects for the Interfaces they want to use. Requestors designed to use the original Interface would ask for IMyApp1, and would be returned a pointer allowing access to the methods of that Interface. A new requestor may ask for IMyApp2, and would be given a different pointer allowing access to that set of methods. Requestors must be prepared to have a query for a particular Interface rejected, and handle it gracefully. For example, after another set of revisions that result in the creation of the IMyApp3 Interface, the object may drop support for some functions used in IMyApp1. If the object cannot support all of the methods of the Interface, it must tell requestors the Interface is not available by returning a null pointer. The requestor object would probably tell the user that the requested functionality is not available. This may not be the user's desired result, but it is far preferable to crashing the application by following a pointer to a nonexistent function.

Another developing trend is the emergence of a messaging model known as publish/subscribe. The previously described communication models are built upon the concept of communication between a single client and single server. Publish/subscribe is designed for those events which need to trigger the notification of multiple responders. The "publisher" is the system on which an event will occur; it may be either a client or a server. The "subscriber" is any system that wants to be notified when the event occurs; it may be a client, server, or peer of the publisher. The underlying implementation is still message based. The primary difference from the messaging described earlier is that rather than a single receiver, a notification list is built, and messages sent to each subscriber. One impact of this model is on how the subscribers must be structured. In a typical send/receive communication model, it is usually the case that the receiver is expecting a message, and in most cases is simply waiting for the message to be received. In the publish/subscribe model, the subscriber must be prepared to receive messages at any time. The subscribers must provide some mechanism to receive these messages, such as by polling or through a signal or interrupt.

As an example of how this could be used, consider a very dynamic environment in which a number of server systems are available to process client requests. Because of other process requirements, all servers are not available for these requests at all times—they may be being backed up, down for maintenance, or processing other critical tasks. To dynamically allow servers to be added or subtracted from the task, each server could "publish" two events—one to say that it is available to receive transactions, and another saying it will no longer accept transactions. At client startup, it polls the servers and builds a table of eligible servers, consisting of those which currently accept transactions. The client will then "subscribe" to the "change of status" events for each potential server. The Servers notify each subscribed client when their status changes, and the eligible server lists are dynamically updated.

CHAPTER 15

Application Logic

Up until this point, we have been working on an application framework—the environment that the application will run under. If done correctly, much of the development of this framework can be leveraged across multiple applications. This section is concerned with the code that forms the core of the application: the application transaction logic.

The key design criteria for the application logic is to make it **transaction** based. One advantage of doing this is to accomplish a clean separation between the application logic and the user interface. The easiest way to think of transaction based application logic is to imagine that the system you are designing is a batch system. As input, you expect a data record containing all the values necessary to complete the transaction. When complete, you will return status or any other necessary information to the caller. *There is no interaction with the user during the course of the transaction.* This doesn't mean that your application can't provide interactive feedback—validating a customer account number as soon as it is typed in, for example—but that this interactive feedback is separate from the transaction. The user interface can make as many separate queries as desired to create an interactive interface with the user, but once the user initiates the transaction (e.g. presses the enter key or an OK pushbutton), the user interface will package it up as a single discrete transaction to be passed to the application logic. The transaction logic will then validate the data, call the database layer to perform any adds, deletes, or updates, and return status information to the user.

Queries—read only transactions—can be thought of as a simplified subset of the transactions. The distinction is important in devising locking strategies, in which queries and transactions may have very different requirements, and in allowing for replicated data within an environment. In an environment supporting replicated data, queries need only access the most convenient copy of the data, whereas transactions are responsible for ensuring that all copies of the data have been updated. (In reality, middleware products will usually be given this responsibility, but if you are developing all components from scratch you must implement this capability yourself.)

Another reason for defining transactions is that they provide a logical unit of recovery in case processing is interrupted for any reason. A database system such as MPE's TurboIMAGE can be designed to ensure the physical integrity of the database, but without distinct transactions, logical integrity cannot be guaranteed. In an accounting system, for example, a transaction will usually consist of one or more debits and one or more credits. The database management software can guarantee that if a system interruption occurs, the debit or credit currently being processed will either be successfully written into the database, with any associated pointers correctly updated, or that it will be backed out entirely. However, unless the database management or higher-level transaction management software is aware of the beginning and end points of the overall transaction, some of the debits and credits comprising a transaction may be completed, while others are not, leaving the accounts out of balance.

In Chapter 23, we will describe the development of an Application Segment (AppSegment) class. An application segment is simply a group of transactions that the developer decides should be located on the same platform. Thus, the AppSegment class is a container for objects of the Transaction class. A Transaction Router (TxnRouter) object will be created to give the application transparent access to the various AppSegments and the Transactions they contain.

CHAPTER 16

Presentation

The presentation, or User Interface, layer presents a unique set of challenges to the architect. In developing layered software, the architect finds that regardless of the specific implementations of operating systems, networks, and databases, there are behaviors that can be modeled abstractly that can then be implemented satisfactorily in any number of different implementations. When trying to do this with the user interface, the creation of an abstraction layer that is robust and implementable on different technologies is nearly impossible. When the implementation constraints of certain user interface systems are added to the problem, it becomes next to impossible. A different approach is needed.

First, a bit more detail on why the solution that works so well for other architectural components is not satisfactory for the User Interface. There are two major difficulties; one conceptual, the other in implementation. The conceptual difficulty comes from the fact that differing user interfaces are far more dissimilar than different databases or operating systems. In designing an abstraction layer for a database, you know that the concepts of adding a record and deleting a record will be implementable, even if the record might be called a "tuple" in one database and an "entry" in another. The functionality of one can be mapped onto the other fairly well. For the user interface, however, the mapping is far less satisfactory. Form-based interfaces such as VPLUS cannot handle many of the behaviors expected of windows based interfaces. A program written for VPLUS will be designed to accept a very limited number of actions from the user at any particular time. Conversely, a windows application may, through menubar selections, allow a user to select from dozens of actions at any point. Some actions, such as dragging an object or iconifying a window, have no corresponding concept in a non-windowed environment. While it is possible to develop a user interface system that will simulate the appearance and behavior of windowed systems on dumb terminals, the CPU demands of processing such an interface, and the increased I/O traffic to the terminal device when compared to the block mode protocol, make this tradeoff unacceptable in all but the most lightly used applications.

The conceptual difficulty does not exist between all user interfaces. We can divide the various user interface technologies into classes, such as character based, form based, and window based. Within a class, much of the user interface design will be leveragable. So a design for Windows 3.1 could be leveraged for Motif or Macintosh, even if none of the code is leveraged. It is far less likely to be leverageable to VPLUS or even to a World Wide Web interface. In our object-oriented terminology, we can imagine creating abstract base classes for each of the classes of interfaces, and subclassing those for specific implementations. But an abstract interface that tries to represent different class of User Interfaces is likely to be unsatisfactory to the users of all of the user interfaces you are trying to support.

The difficulty in implementation stems from the fact that event-driven interfaces such as Microsoft Windows cannot be "called" through an API the way VPLUS is. Microsoft Windows is more than the user interface for the computer running it; it is in effect the operating system as well. A windows program consists largely of a series of callback functions that the windows system will invoke in response to user actions. In a nutshell, you don't call Windows; Windows calls you.

A final objective in designing the presentation layer for an application is to provide the maximum possible flexibility in implementing future technologies. This is a goal for all pieces of a well designed architecture, but we believe that there will be more radical changes in user interface technology in the future than in any other part of the technology infrastructure. In the past, you could assume that all application users would be sitting in front of a functionally identical terminal device, even though implementation might vary from a 3270 to a VT100 to a 2392. Today, you may need to still support those terminal users, while at the same time supporting users on PCs, Workstations, and/or Macintoshes. If you don't already need a World Wide Web interface to your application, chances are you will soon. In the future, you may need to support wireless mobile computing devices with pen or voice input, multimedia output, and other devices that haven't even been thought of. You cannot design a "object oriented user interface driver" that can support all of these possible futures. Instead, the architecture will sidestep the problem altogether by making no assumptions about how the user interface will interact with the user, and instead define the methods by which the user interface will interact with the application. This allows each implementation of an application user interface to be driven entirely by user requirements, exploiting the available user interface technologies without regard to maintaining a similar look-and-feel across implementations in other User Interface technologies.

The downside of this approach is duplication of work. If the application is to support terminal, Personal Computer, and World Wide Web interfaces, then three separate interfaces will have to be designed, coded, tested, and maintained. We believe that this is the right approach, however, for a number of reasons. First, there are now a large number of Rapid Prototyping / Rapid Development tools for creating user interfaces, such as Visual Basic. By moving business rules into the data objects, away from the user interface, the amount of code to be redeveloped for each implementation can be kept to a minimum. And finally, the user interface is the part of the code that becomes obsolete fastest anyway; it should be regarded as "disposable code."

PART 4

Implementing a Software Architecture

CHAPTER 17

Challenges of Multi-Platform Development

Among the many other flexibilities we are trying to design into our architecture is the capability to move source code from one platform to another, recompile, and have the software run as expected. If your only experience to date has been with proprietary systems, you may be under the impression that UNIX-derived systems have made this a "no-brainer." If your experience has been on a single brand of UNIX, you may be working under the same mistaken assumption, thinking that the code you have developed is equally suitable for any UNIX platform. The reality is that creating open software requires a lot of work. It won't happen by accident. Being aware of the ways in which systems differ—even open systems—will help you avoid creating incompatibilities where it is possible to avoid doing so. This awareness also allows you to provide capabilities for alternative implementations of the same functionality where a function cannot be implemented in a portable fashion. We'll divide the areas of concern into platform issues (issues related to the architecture of the system which code will run on), language issues, and linker issues.

Platform Issues

The first group of issues we will address are those related to the hardware platform. Since our objective is to achieve portability at the source code, rather than at the object code level, we are not concerned with differences in instruction sets or many of the other chip-level details of the hardware architecture. There are a few features of the hardware architecture, however, that are apparent even in software written in a high-level language. The most common of these are differences in word size, byte order, and alignment.

Word size is a fairly "visible" characteristic of architectures, meaning that most programmers know the word size of the system they are programming for. The most common word sizes are 16-bit (the "Classic" MPE machines, PC processors from the 8088 through the 80286), 32 bit (most systems today, including the HP 3000 MPE/iX and HP 9000 HP-UX systems based on PA-RISC 7000 series chips, and PC platforms based on 386, 486, and Pentium processors), and 64 bit (the DEC Alpha, upcoming PA-RISC systems based on the PA-8000 series chips). PCs running Windows 3.1 or Windows 95 are running on a 32 bit architecture, with much of the code being 16 bit. Windows NT is a completely 32 bit implementation of the Windows user interface, on top of a completely redesigned kernel that has more in common with systems such as MPE or VMS than with DOS or UNIX. All of the 64-bit systems which are in wide use today or in the near future also run 32-bit code to provide compatibility with older systems, just as the MPE/iX HP 3000 systems still run MPE V 16-bit code in compatibility mode.

In many cases, the word size of the underlying hardware doesn't matter to a programmer. The cases when a programmer has to be concerned are as follows:

- *In cases where a variable can be overflowed in some architectural representations of a variable.* For example, on MPE/iX, HP-UX, or Windows NT an `int` type variable in a C program will be allocated 32 bits, whereas on MPE V or Windows 3.1 platforms 16 bits will normally be allocated. The programmer must ensure that any values to be stored in that variable will not exceed the smallest physical representation that may be used to implement variables of that type. For example, if you are writing an application on MPE/iX but intend to also support it on 16-bit Windows systems, a variable declared as type int can only be used for values up to 32767 (if signed). You may prefer to declare your own data types, for example `U16, U32, S16, S32` for unsigned and signed 16 and 32 bit integers. (This could just as easily have been categorized as a compiler issue, rather than an issue of hardware word size. We include it here because the compilers originally chose their representation for int types to match the hardware word size. As Intel chips have moved from 16 bits to 32 bits, compilers still by default generate 16 bit integers. We're sure that on 64-bit PA-RISC implementations, compilers will still have the option to generate 32-bit integers, for backwards compatibility, as well as being able to generate the architecturally native 64-bit data types.)
- *In cases where data will be passed between architectures.* This can be because the data is placed into a static data structure, such as a file, which is to be moved between platforms, or because the data is being dynamically passed between platforms as in a client/server application. In either case, if two architectures with dissimilar word sizes try to reference a variable of type `int`, they won't be examining the same piece of data.

Storage allocation, which is essentially the number of bits that will be reserved for a variable of a particular type, is covered extensively in the HP Programmer's Reference Guides for the various languages. You should understand the difference in storage allocation for all of the various compilers and platforms your application will be expected to run on before you begin coding.

The next area of potential difficulty is byte ordering within a word. There are two different systems for how bytes will be ordered within numeric data types. The Intel architecture and DEC systems use an ordering known as "little endian," in which the least significant 8 bits are stored in the leftmost byte position within a word, and the most significant 8 bits in the rightmost byte position. Most other systems, including the initial implementations of PA-RISC, are big-endian, which is just the reverse. (Current and future PA-RISC hardware is actually bi-endian, capable of supporting either scheme. Since all MPE and HP-UX implementations use the big endian notation, this capability of the hardware is currently unused.)

As with the differences in byte size, most opportunities for difficulty arise when data is transmitted between systems. Messaging protocols such as BSD Sockets and OSF DCE provide the capability to translate fields between big-endian and little-endian notation. In BSD Sockets, it is up to the programmer to recognize when a field needs to be translated and explicitly call a routine provided for that purpose. DCE uses the Interface Definitions supplied by the programmer as a guide to when translation is required.

If a data field is not being moved between platforms, the byte order is irrelevant and should not cause any difficulty. An exception would be if the programmer expects to do any testing of specific bits, or is otherwise dependent on the internal representation of the data item. Data fields with any such dependency should not be implemented as numeric types.

The final architectural item to be aware of is data alignment. Like storage allocation, data alignment is actually a function of the compiler, but the compiler will be coded to produce a data alignment that is most efficient for the hardware architecture being targeted. Data alignment is only a factor for data structures or records, and affects the spacing between items within the record. As an example, consider a simple data structure made up of 2 16-bit fields. If the fields are 16-bit aligned, the structure will require 32 bits, and there will be no unused space. If the fields are 32-bit aligned, the structure will require 64 bits: the first data item in the first 16 bits, 16 empty bits, the second item in the third 16 bits, and another 16 unused bits. PA-RISC compilers align most data items on 32-bit word boundaries, although 64-bit alignment is used for some large numeric types. Data alignment is also discussed at length in the Programmer's Reference Guides for the appropriate languages. Compiler directives can be used to force 16-bit alignment in cases where compatibility with MPE V or other 16-bit architectures is required.

Language Issues

The next group of items to be considered are language differences. These include differences between different languages—for example, differences in representation of string data in different languages—as well as differences between implementations of the same language, for example, MicroFocus COBOL versus HP COBOL.

We will cover differences between different languages first. On some platforms, such as older IBM architectures, it is not even possible for one language to call a routine written in another language. If you are writing for such an environment, you have no choice but to keep everything that is expected to work together in the same language. On the HP 3000, where inter-language calling capability has always been a basic feature of HP's language products, and where the intrinsic mechanism hides most differences between languages, programmers are frequently unaware that there are any differences to be concerned about. To create portable code, you will need to be aware of potential difficulties and plan for them.

The biggest differences between languages are in the area of data types. Integer type data is the safest; it is usually represented the same by any compilers on a particular architecture. Real or floating point data is generally compatible between the languages that support it, but remember that these data types are not available within ANSI standard COBOLs (including HP COBOL). Also, classic MPE systems used a proprietary floating-point format, whereas PA-RISC systems use the IEEE floating point format. Intrinsics are available on both platforms for conversion between these representations, but it is up to the developer to explicitly invoke these whenever floating point data is transported between platforms. String or character data is represented in different fashions between different languages, but being aware of the different representations will allow programs in one language to read character strings written in another. For example, COBOL character data (`PIC X` fields) contain only the alphanumeric data expected. C character strings expect a terminating NUL character (ASCII 0). Pascal strings have the length of the string in the first 16 or 32 bits (architecture dependent) of the field, and possibly a housekeeping byte at the end, while Pascal packed arrays of characters are the same as COBOL `PIC X` fields.

In creating functions in one language that are to be called from another, you should be aware of how the case of function names is handled between different languages. This encompasses both language and platform issues, as some constraints on legal names may be imposed by the linker on a platform. On MPE systems, all languages but C downshift function names; C uses the actual case as specified. If a C routine is created with a mixed case name, other languages will have to use an aliasing capability (available through compiler directives) to be able to access the routine. Similarly, C programs should be aware that if a Pascal function called HandleError() was compiled and placed in a library, it will actually need to be called as handleerror() unless an alias was used to preserve the case when compiled in Pascal. (An exception to the standard case rules is MPE intrinsics, the names of which are all uppercase.) Hyphens in COBOL names will be changed to underscores; any language other than COBOL which attempts to access these routines will need to use the underscores to match the name correctly.

On MPE systems, the intrinsic mechanism is designed to hide many of these complexities from the programmer. The various compilers know that when a routine is declared to be an intrinsic, the name should be shifted into all upper case, for example. Each of the compilers will also put string data into the style of a Pascal packed array of characters (same representation as COBOL `PIC X` type) and take care of any other differences in data representation. The intrinsic mechanism also allows variable length parameter lists and default values for omitted parameters, functionality which is not otherwise available in some languages. Programmers can use the MPE intrinsic mechanism to create declarations for their own routines, and thereby gain these same benefits in their own code, but the intrinsic mechanism is a non-portable feature of MPE and thus is not generally recommended unless you will never need to move the code to another platform.

The difficulties above are all avoided if only a single programming language is used for the entire development effort. In a multi-platform environment, such as developing for a client/server configuration, there can be differences between different implementations of the same language. For example, MicroFocus COBOL, HP COBOL, and IBM COBOL will all have specific tools and extensions that are not covered by the ANSI standard, and these may be incompatible with other vendors' implementations. Even when the standard is adhered to, there are areas that the standard acknowledges will be machine-dependent, and other areas in which the standard does not specify correct behavior. As an example of the former, the `SELECT / ASSIGN TO` statement within the `FILE-CONTROL` section of a COBOL program will frequently involve machine-specific constructs. As an example of the latter, the program flow resulting from using a `GO TO` to exit from the middle of a `PERFORM`ed paragraph (which is considered bad form) is not specified by the standard. HP COBOL and IBM COBOL will behave differently given the same code in this case, and neither one of them can be said to be correct or incorrect, since the ANSI standard leaves the correct behavior undefined.

You can even encounter differences with different implementations of the same language on the same platform. A COBOL program on the HP 3000 may behave differently depending on whether it is compiled with the HP COBOL or the

MicroFocus COBOL compiler. In general, the HP COBOL is closely tied to the HP 3000 operating system and architecture, and should be used whenever it is important to interact with other languages on the platform, or when you need access to standard MPE file types. HP COBOL programs expect to be run from the MPE Command Interpreter, and programs are expected to access the MPE intrinsics for access to operating system services. MicroFocus COBOL programs are intended to be portable, and thus should not rely on MPE-isms. MicroFocus COBOL programs expect the underlying file system to be byte-oriented, as on UNIX and Windows platforms (MPE provides bytestream file types beginning with release 4.5). MicroFocus COBOL programs on MPE expect to be run from within the POSIX shell, and expect that access to operating system services will be via the POSIX C library functions, which are callable from within MicroFocus COBOL.

All languages are not created equal. You can standardize on a particular language for all your development, but the optimal solution is to choose the language best suited for each task. COBOL, for example, is an excellent choice for the development of the application's logic modules, but is very poorly suited to the construction of much of the middleware needed (because of its lack of support for call by value, pointers, and structured return types.) C is very well suited for exactly these types of tasks, but is inferior in error checking and syntactic clarity. C++ can be an improvement upon C in these areas, if properly used. Java is an object-oriented language that removes most of the shoot-yourself-in-the-foot opportunities that C and C++ are so famous for, while improving on portability. Java is definitely a language to watch; we believe that it will move from the specialized "applet imbedded in a web page" usage that is getting the most attention right now, into the role of a more mainstream programming language. Performance is an issue right now, but will improve: while Java performance may never reach the level of well-written and optimized C or COBOL, it will probably be sufficient for most applications.

One of the advantages in using C (C++ is included in any of the statements made about C unless specifically excluded) as a language for development of multiplatform applications is that, in addition to specifying the specifics of the language itself, the C standard also specifies a standard set of compiler directives. In writing COBOL, if we know that we need a particular `SELECT / ASSIGN` statement for one server platform, and a different statement when compiling for a different platform, there is no conditional construct we can use that is guaranteed to be understood by both compilers. Thus, we cannot have both versions of the code in-line, and are forced to adopt different copylibs for different platforms. But even the syntax for incorporating code from copylibs can vary between platforms. You may have no choice but to maintain separate code files for different platforms. Once this step is taken, it is far more difficult to keep the various versions of a code module in sync with each other than if the language permitted us to have different versions of the code in-line and control compilation with a set of generally understood compiler directives. The C preprocessor directives such as `#if`, `#define`, and `#ifdef` are part of the language specification, and provide programmers a way to control the compilation of machine-specific portions of their code in a way that is clearly understood by all C programmers.

Java takes a different approach to this problem by eliminating any implementation-specific variances. Things such as word size, byte ordering, and filename syntax do not vary across platforms with Java. This is because every platform on which Java runs must implement the Java Virtual Machine, for which all of these attributes have been defined. Thus, the Java compiler creates code for the Java Virtual Machine, which does not vary from one platform to another. At program run-time, a Java run-time interpreter or just-in-time compiler will execute the virtual machine instructions, making conversions as required to the underlying architecture. This also means that compiled Java code is portable between architectures. It is this feature that has made Java so popular on the World Wide Web, where a server can download a Java applet to a client system of unknown type, but it also means that Java applications can be developed on whatever system provides the best development environment, and then deployed throughout the enterprise across any system that has implemented the Java Virtual Machine runtime code.

Linker Issues

Once your code has been successfully compiled, you will use a link editor, or linker, to either convert it into an executable object file or place it in a library. Differences in the way linkers work can give rise to additional challenges for the developer of portable code. For HP-UX and MPE/iX programmers, these differences are less significant than they once were. Historically, HP-UX did not provide shared libraries (such as MPE's XLs or compatibility mode SLs), while MPE did not allow data to be shared between programs and libraries. HP-UX now supports shared libraries, and MPE/iX supports shared globals. The differences remaining between the systems are relatively minor. We will examine how shared global data and unresolved externals are handled between the two systems.

Shared Globals

Shared global data is data that is shared between compilation units without being explicitly passed between them. The most common example is the C errno variable. A C program can call routines that are in the C library, and if errors are encountered an errno variable will be set. This errno variable is declared in the calling program with extern storage class, and can be modified by code in any functions that the program calls, even though the variable is not explicitly passed into the function. (This really horrendous programming practice is the antithesis of data hiding, but it nonetheless caught on in the UNIX community. Go figure.)

MPE systems did not provide support for shared global data until the 5.0 release of MPE/iX. Shared Globals is enabled by specifying ;SHARE on the LINK or ADDXL link editor commands. If you are using the compiler scripts which perform compilation and linkage from a single CI command, the ;SHARE option will be specified for you. Code developed prior to MPE/iX 5.0 will need to be relinked on a 5.0 system to enable Shared Globals. Software that is expected to run on pre-5.0 MPE systems cannot use shared global variables. See the 5.0 Communicator (30216-90189) for more information on using shared globals.

Unresolved Externals

Anytime you create code that will be contained in more than a single compilation unit, the system's technique for resolving external references becomes important. The places where linkers will search for these references are in other object files, in relocatable (or static, or archive) libraries, and in executable (or shared, or dynamic) libraries.

If you link more than one object file in a single command, external references may be resolved between these different object files. Since the various object files are being compiled into a single program file or library module, the reference now becomes an internal reference. References which are resolved from relocatable libraries (MPE RLs, HP-UX archive (.a) libraries, Windows static (.LIB) libraries) are similar, in that the module which satisfies the reference will be copied into the target file being created, thus making these references internal also.

References which are resolved from an executable library (MPE XLs, HP-UX shared (.sl) libraries, Windows dynamic (.DLL) libraries) are different, in that the code is not copied into the target file, and the reference continues to be an external reference. This creates the possibility that a reference that is successfully resolved at link time may fail to resolve at run-time. This can be due to changes to the library, movement of either the program or library files, changes to path variables, or other factors. MPE, HP-UX, and Windows systems are different in how the link editor and loader anticipate and deal with these potential concerns.

The MPE link editor doesn't consider it a problem to have external references unresolved at link time. After all, the point in having separate compilation units is to allow code to be developed and maintained in pieces; you may have not created the libraries yet. MPE programmers frequently take advantage of "XL substitution" to test new functionality or alter the behavior of programs. This is done by having more than one XL that can be used to resolve the same references. The NewFace product, for example, uses its own XL to resolve calls to the VPLUS Intrinsics, allowing new functionality to be provided to VPLUS programs without changing or relinking them. The loader, on the other hand, wants to resolve everything. It will therefore want every external reference resolved before allowing the program to begin execution; any unresolved reference will cause the load to fail. This is true even if the unresolved reference happens to be some piece of code that might never be executed in a particular run of the program; for example, a call to an Oracle database in a program that checks at start-up whether to use TurboIMAGE or Oracle, and then makes the appropriate calls thereafter. Programs such as these can be loaded by specifying the ;UNSAT= parameter on the :RUN command. This causes all unresolved externals to be mapped to a routine that you specify, such as DEBUG, TERMINATE, or a stub routine that you create.

On HP-UX, the linker does expect to be able to resolve all external references, and returns an error if it is unable to do so. This is somewhat of a historical holdover, since on earlier versions of the system there were no shared libraries, and thus no possibility that references unresolved at link time would become resolved at run time. If there are no other errors in the link, a target file will be created, but will have its executable bit turned off. If you know that the unresolved externals are not a problem, and will be resolved correctly by the loader, you can simply `chmod` the file to turn on the execute bit(s) and continue. The HP-UX loader is actually two loaders: the exec() loader loads the program file, including any archive library modules, and cannot get unresolved externals. The dynamic loader, `dld.sl`, will be called as necessary to load shared library modules. By default, shared library modules will only be loaded when they are invoked, so you will not get errors from references that will never be executed. If desired, you can force the dynamic loader to load all referenced modules at program load time by specifying the `-bimmediate` option to the link editor. There is no way in HP-UX to provide additional or different libraries to be searched at run-time than those specified at link time; thus there is no equivalent to the XL substitution capability on MPE systems.

The Windows linker demands that all references be resolved at link time. Unlike HP-UX, you cannot simply "patch and go" if the linker fails with unresolved externals. The Windows linker also creates more work for the programmer by requiring that exports and imports be specified specifically, rather than by searching all modules in a list of libraries. When a dynamic link library (.DLL) is created, a module definition file (.DEF) must be created as input to the linker, which specifies each function that is to be exported by the DLL. For programs which wish to access the DLL, there are two alternatives. The DLL's module definition file can be processed by a utility called IMPLIB, creating an import library file (.LIB). This import library is then linked into the program file just as any other static library file. Or, you can create a module definition (.DEF) file for the program, which specifies each function to be imported by DLL name and function. The Windows loader fails if all referenced routines cannot be located at load time; neither deferred loading nor an UNSAT= type capability are provided.

CHAPTER 18

Engineering the Support Modules

For the remainder of Part IV, we will be doing a high-level design of the IT architecture we have discussed throughout the last several chapters. Again, the idea is not to present a one-size-fits-all, ready-to-wear application architecture, but rather to point out all of the design factors that must be considered, and show some alternative ways that various capabilities might be provided. In the next two chapters, we'll develop some of the infrastructure modules that are application independent (and thus highly reusable). Beginning with Chapter 21, we'll look at developing the application-specific modules.

In this chapter, we'll look at three infrastructure modules that need to be among the first pieces developed, as they will be used by everything that follows. These are the **directory** module, which is used by the various code objects to find each other; the **configuration** module, that allows our applications to indicate which of the different operating systems, databases, networks, or whatever they are running on; and the **error handling** module, which needs to be a part of any application.

Directory Module

Test implementations of various portions of the maximum flexibility architecture in C++ quickly pointed out the need for a directory object. When thinking about objects in an abstract way, we envision a group of objects that freely pass messages back and forth, requesting various favors from each other and receiving the requested data by means of arrows drawn between boxes on a diagram. When we actually try to implement this, passing these messages back and forth between objects requires that the sender obtain a pointer to the receiver. For the main program outer block, sending a message to an object that it has declared itself, this is trivial. Typical object designs, however, will not have all objects declared by the outer block. Some objects will declare other objects, and it isn't long before you have one object needing to send a message to another, and having no idea how to reach its target.

Object-oriented frameworks for application development provide code to handle the entire life cycle of objects, including creation, deletion, access control, etc. We have chosen to implement a stripped-down version of this capability as a directory object. We declare a directory object as the very first object created by the main program. A pointer to the directory object is kept in a variable with global scope, so that all objects created subsequently will have access to the directory object. It then becomes the responsibility of every object created to "register" itself by storing a pointer to itself in the directory. If an object is deleted, it should remove its entry from the directory, or set it to a null value.

C++ provides a convenient place to do these housekeeping tasks; all objects can have special functions which will be automatically invoked when they are created or destroyed. These routines are called constructors and destructors. We will put code in the constructor of each object to register with the directory object, and code in the destructor of each object to place a null value in the directory's pointer to the object.

It is possible, and perhaps even desirable, to create a generic object registry which has no foreknowledge of the name and number of objects that will be created, and that simply accepts incoming registrations and creates places to store them as they are received by dynamically allocating storage space. We did not find it necessary to be this sophisticated in our sample implementation. Since we knew the objects we intended to create, and how many of each, we simply created the necessary pointer variables as attributes of the directory object. When more than one of a particular object type could be created, an array of pointers was created. Two methods were then created for each directory entry—one to get the pointer (used by any object needing to send a message to the object), and one to set the pointer (used by the object's constructor and destructor functions). So for the configuration object, which is the next object to be discussed, we had one object pointer (there will only be one configuration object within an application), and methods GetConfigPtr() and SetConfigPtr() to access it.

Configuration Module

Most portable software is configured at compile time, through the use of compile switches. In C, the `-D` compiler flag, which functions the same as an in-line `#define` statement, is frequently used to specify the target configuration. So a single piece of code could be compiled with flags `-DMPEIX -DTURBOIMAGE -DNETIPC` to run in an MPE/iX, TurboIMAGE, and NetIPC environment, or it could be compiled with flags `-DHPUX -DSYBASE -DSOCKETS` to run in an HP-UX, Sybase, and Sockets environment. We are going a further step, and allowing application configuration to be specified at run-time. The configuration module is the code that contains the run-time equivalent of the compiler flags, specifying what environment the application is currently running under. Some configuration details will still need to be resolved at compile time; differences in architecture make it impossible to compile code that can run on both PA-RISC and Intel platforms (although future architectures may permit this).

The configuration module consists of a configuration object, which is the run-time data structure that will identify the configuration choices that are in effect, and a configuration file, which is read into the configuration object when the application is launched. The configuration file can be made simple or complex; it can be kept in some binary format that requires specialized programs to maintain, or it can be kept in an ASCII format so that any text editor can be used to make changes. While both approaches have their benefits, for the following discussions we will use a sample configuration file that is kept in an ASCII format such as that used by Microsoft Windows .INI files. (In fact, if you have the Microsoft Foundation Class Library as provided with the Microsoft C and C++ compilers, you can use the standard routines **GetProfileString** and **SetProfileString** as models for the development of your own routines to read and write the configuration file.)

Many of the choices described in the sample file below will not make sense until they are covered in later sections, but for purposes of understanding the configuration file layout a sample configuration file is presented here in its entirety:

```
[OPTIONS]
User Interface = Microsoft Windows 3.1
Local OpSys = Microsoft Windows 3.1

[SERVERS]
sonic, BSD Sockets, 3442, MPE/iX, MIKE.YAWN
capella, BSD Sockets, 6453, HP-UX, myawn

[CLIENTS]
csyserv6,NetWare 3.11, Microsoft Windows 3.1, 30100

[LOCAL RESOURCES]
database = pricedb, Oracle, C:\ORACLE\PRICING\DB01
application = schedule, C:\SCHED\SCHEDULE.EXE

[REMOTE RESOURCES]
database = empdb, sonic, IMAGE/SQL, ODBC
database = partsdb, capella, Oracle, OracleNet
application = inventory, sonic, INV0300.PUB.MFG
application = payroll, capella, /usr/local/apps/pr
```

This configuration file is typical of what might be found on a PC running Windows 3.1, and specifies the following configuration options:

- The operating system on the local system is Windows 3.1, which is also the User Interface.
- Two server systems that we may wish to connect to are identified. BSD sockets is the networking interface in both cases. Sonic is an MPE/iX server that we will connect to via TCP port 3442 and log on as MIKE.YAWN. (Note: Connection via BSD or NetIPC sockets does not require an MPE-style logon, but our application chooses to impose this requirement as a method of enforcing security. Also, we could have chosen to imbed passwords into the configuration file, but this would compromise security, so the user will be prompted for the passwords the first time a connection to the server is attempted). Capella is an HP-UX server that we will connect to via TCP port 6453 and log on as myawn.
- We identify one client system that may connect to us, csyserv6, via Netware 3.11. In many cases it is not necessary or desirable for the server system to know all of the clients that may try to connect; a simple client connection specification is shown here to suggest that you may want to consider such a requirement as an additional control at the server level of who can receive services.
- We have currently defined two types of resources—databases and applications—that may exist on either the local system or on one of the server systems defined above. For databases, the database name, type, and location are specified (and for remote databases, the protocol used for network communication). For applications, the name and location are specified. When an application exists as a single code module, the application entry points to that module. For distributed applications, the code pointed to by the application entry is actually a specific object called a Transaction Router, which will be described in an upcoming section. For performance reasons, the Transaction Router is best located locally on the client.

In a client/server configuration, a configuration file similar to the one above will exist on each system. Likewise, more than one configuration object will exist in a distributed application; each system will have a configuration object that describes both the local system and the other systems and resources that local application code may need to be aware of.

Like the directory module, the methods of the configuration module are essentially a pair of routines to get and set the value of each of the attributes that comprise the configuration. The "set" routines are currently used in only one place, which is the method used to load the configuration data from a flat file. More sophisticated implementations may allow some portions of the configuration to be dynamically configurable. The "get" routines are used primarily in the "middleware" layers of the application framework; when an application has requested a particular action be performed by calling a generic, portable interface, that portable interface must determine what the actual underlying service is that will be called upon to fulfill the request.

Error Handling Module

Another support module that should be among the earliest to be designed and implemented is some sort of error handling. Error handling can be simple or complex. A simple error handler may be nothing more than passing a status code back through several layers of code, and a catalog to convert the status code to a human-readable message at the user interface level. A lot of value can be added by creating an error stack; when an error is encountered, the code encountering the level pushes an error code onto the stack. Each level of code which is passed through on returning to the highest level caller may then push another error onto the stack which provides more detailed context information about what operation was in progress, what options were enabled, etc. Another possibility is that instead of pushing additional errors onto the stack, each level of code can add a tag to the error that provides this context information. It may be as simple as the procedure name, providing a quick trace of the code path resulting in the error, or each routine may create a more detailed tag that could include parameters passed or other information that may be useful in analyzing the failure. The error handling code may be extended further if you want the code to attempt to recover from certain types of error conditions itself. For example, a message transmission failure across the network may be retried some number of times before a failure is passed up to higher level code. In many cases, the information already being captured to present an error message to the user may be sufficient to allow some level of recovery. In other cases, you may find it necessary to capture additional information about the failure to allow a determination to be made about how to attempt recovery from the condition.

A sample implementation of an error handling object included the following methods:

• Push(message, severity)	Add an error to the stack
• Pop(message, severity)	Return the top error from the stack
• AddTag(message)	Add text to the topmost error in the stack
• Peek(index, msg, severity)	Look at any message in the error stack
• Clear()	Clear the error stack
• GetCount()	Returns the number of errors in the stack
• GetSeverity()	Returns the highest severity in the stack

Two additional methods, Send() and Receive(), are also necessary, but their specific parameters and implementation is heavily dependent on how the message facility (described in the next chapter) is implemented. In a distributed environment, an error may be encountered on the server side. An entry will be pushed onto the error stack, and as the application backs out of the failed routine additional errors or tags may be added. At some point, however, control will pass back to the client that initiated the failed transaction, and the contents of the error stack need to be transferred to an error stack on the client. There, additional errors or tags may again be added, or the client program may begin processing (POPing) the errors for purposes of recovery or reporting to the user.

CHAPTER 19

Creating the Database Interfaces

For the next six chapters, we'll be designing specific components to fit into the application framework previously described. The first component to be thus described will be the database interface module.

There are several ways to approach the design of a database interface, and the design chosen will differ based on your priorities. We have tried to create a design that allows views of data and physical layout of database entries to vary independently, and that also provides independence from any particular database implementation. This results in some sacrifice of performance, and more design and implementation effort, than if we just standardized on a particular database vendor.

Creating a Database Isolation Layer

If you have written any database programs, you already have a good idea of what a database interface could look like. If your experience is with TurboIMAGE, you're thinking DBGET, DBPUT, DBUPDATE; if your experience is with relational databases, you'll think in terms of SELECT, INSERT, UPDATE for the same functions. Whichever terminology you choose, the basic actions will be the same. We suggest that whatever your database interfaces end up looking like, you resist the temptation to call them directly from mainline application code. Database layouts may change over time; data may become distributed or consolidated in accordance with wherever your company happens to be in the perpetual cycle of centralizing and decentralizing; database engines may be changed; even platforms may change. The mainline code—which really means the user interface—should instead call a business transaction. That business transaction will in turn communicate with objects that represent logical views of the data. These objects will perform any necessary transformations to conform to the physical layout of the databases, and then call the underlying database engines to perform the desired operations. The relationship between these components is illustrated in Figure 19.1.

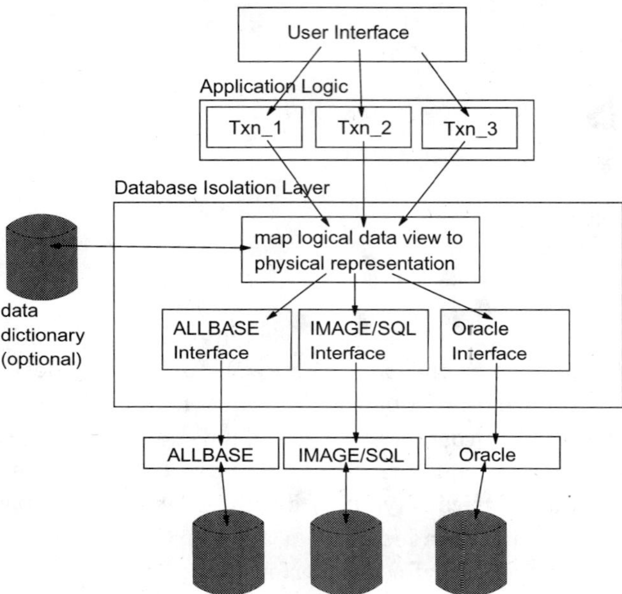

Figure 19.1 The Database Interfaces

The objective of the database isolation layer is to present a consistent interface to the application transactions, regardless of the underlying database engine, and yet to get as much as possible out of the underlying database engines in terms of performance and functionality. The isolation layer will therefore probably have more code unique to the different databases to be supported than code which is common to all of them.

Another function of the database isolation layer is to perform transformations between logical data layouts and the physical data layouts. For purposes of database normalization, or for organizational reasons, it may be that the data fields that make up a single business transaction are in fact spread across multiple database tables, or even across multiple databases. The business transaction really shouldn't be concerned with how the data is physically stored; therefore, the isolation layer should accept as input groups of fields that do not correspond to a single data entry in any database. This mapping of logical to physical record layouts may be implemented purely within the isolation layer, or it may be that an external data dictionary product is used to describe the various layouts and the mappings between them. The use of such a dictionary saves a lot of implementation detail, but it may be difficult to find one solution that is available on all the platforms you may need to support. A final function of the data dictionary or data objects is to enforce business rules. These consist of the integrity constraints such as those defined in Chapter 13 and any other data format or content restrictions that you wish to have consistently applied to the data.

Using IMAGE/SQL to Access TurboIMAGE

Given an objective of creating more portable code, it is natural to examine the IMAGE/SQL interfaces to TurboIMAGE as an alternative. We think that this deserves investigation anytime it is available as an option, but we also acknowledge that it will not always turn out to be the best solution.

TurboIMAGE data will always be more efficiently accessed by the TurboIMAGE intrinsics than by the SQL interfaces. So portability must be traded off for performance. Your priorities will determine in what cases to use IMAGE/SQL, and in what cases to use TurboIMAGE, but we do have a general rule of thumb: For two-tier client/server models, most typically in decision support or ad-hoc query applications, IMAGE/SQL's flexibility and support for a large number of front-end tools through the ODBC interfaces make it tough to beat. Unless you anticipate a huge number of inquires coming in from these types of interfaces, which raises a performance concern, the IMAGE/SQL front-end is probably your best bet. On the other hand, for high-volume transaction processing applications—applications which very likely were developed for TurboIMAGE at least in part because of its excellent performance characteristics for these types of workloads—we recommend that you continue to use the TurboIMAGE intrinsic interfaces. The database isolation layer described above still permits portability of the application; all the TurboIMAGE specific code will be confined within the database layer.

Other Approaches

There are other approaches besides the database isolation layer to achieve portability in your database code. One very widely adopted method is simply to standardize on a particular database engine. Code will then be easily portable to any platform on which the target database is available. Of databases available on the HP 3000, Oracle provides the greatest portability to other platforms. Allbase code can be ported to HP-UX only, and TurboIMAGE code will run only on the HP 3000. Our reason for developing the database isolation layer grows from our desire to expand the definition of portability to something more than just operating system platforms; as you will recall from Chapter 9, we aim to be equally free of dependencies on databases, networks, and any other technology which would be available from only a single vendor. As always, your priorities may be different, and the decision to standardize on a database vendor may be your preferred solution for database portability.

Another approach would be to try to write only "ANSI Standard" SQL. In an ideal world, this would be the best solution, allowing you to write code that was freely portable because it adhered to widely accepted standards. In reality, the functionality required by many applications simply isn't covered by the standards; things such as locking levels, handling of stored procedures, scrollable cursors, and how optimizations will be performed are likely to be incompatible between different databases that are all in conformance with the SQL standard.

A final approach may be to standardize on one vendor's interfaces, but use gateway products to allow other database engines to be used as well. All of the major database vendors—Sybase, Oracle, Informix, and Ingres—have database gateways that allow access for "foreign" databases through their version of SQL. In addition, the EDA/SQL product from Information Builders is essentially an SQL gateway product to over 60 different database implementations, including all of the databases available on the HP 3000. We have not tested any of these products for performance, functionality, and flexibility, but their availability indicates that the market agrees upon the need for access to multiple databases through a common interface.

CHAPTER 20

Creating the Messaging Interfaces

The messaging mechanisms are really the backbone of a client/server implementation. If you have not developed software previously that works in a networked environment, it may seem like an intimidating task. In reality, a client/server application that uses a VPLUS user interface and TurboIMAGE database will have far less of its code dedicated to the network interface than to the database or the user interface. If you have ever written programs that use message files or any other form of interprocess communication, you already know the sequence of tasks that must be performed; all that remains is to learn the specific networking APIs used to accomplish these tasks.

The client/server communications system could be designed around either a messaging model or a Remote Procedure Call (RPC) model. In an RPC model, every interaction between client and server must be exhaustively defined, with interface definitions written in a special language and passed through a separate compilation step. The RPC is thus actively involved in the execution of the transaction, reformatting data and providing other services to the application. On the other hand, a message based communication tool is simply a transport mechanism for moving messages between two endpoints. The format and content of the message can be anything which the sender and receiver agree on; it is not necessary for the messaging layer to understand the message formats (just as a postman doesn't need to understand the contents of mail being delivered). However, the messaging layer, like a postman, does need to be able to understand where you want a message to be delivered. Whereas the underlying network interfaces do the bulk of this work—making sure that a message gets to the right system, and to a specified TCP/IP port address on that system—we will specify how a monitor program that we design will understand enough of the message structure that once a message gets this far, it can be routed to the proper piece of code within our application for further processing. To continue the postal analogy, it's like having someone open all the mail addressed to "The Harris Family" and decide who in the family the message is actually intended for. (Our design isn't expected to have to deal with junk mail, but the monitor program could certainly screen it out should any show up.)

Basic Design

Figure 20.1 shows the basic functions that will be provided by any messaging API. The same API is used by both the client and server programs, although one call (network_select) is only used by the server. The API provides functions for:

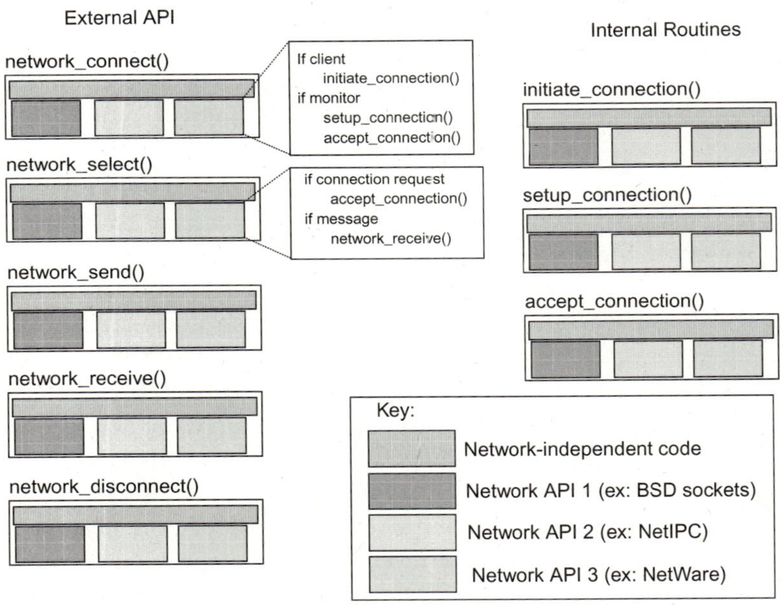

Figure 20.1 Message-based Client/Server API

Connection between Client and Server. At the highest level, our architecture provides a network_connect() call that can be used by either the client or the server. The parameters to the network_connect() call are a flag indicating whether we will be performing the role of a client or a server for this connection, and for clients, what resource we wish to access. When we are in the client role, the network_connect() routine will determine from the configuration object what system we will try to connect to. In either role, the network_connect() routine will also determine from the configuration object what underlying messaging mechanism will be used.

Because the steps required to establish a connection are different for the server than they are for the client, we have created different routines to handle the actual connection in each case. If we are in a server role, the network_connect() routine will call 2 intermediate level calls: setup_connection() and accept_connection(). Two different calls are needed, rather than a single call which completes the connection process, because the first performs one-time setup activity to identify the port where we expect the connection, whereas the second may be used repeatedly, because multiple client connections can be accepted through the same port address. This will be covered in more detail in the monitor section later in this chapter. The implementation of the setup_connection() and accept_connection() calls will vary based upon the underlying messaging mechanism to be used; in Berkeley sockets, for example, the setup_connection() call would make calls to the sockets APIs socket(), bind(), and listen(), while accept_connection() would call the sockets accept() interface. (Refer back to Figure 20.1).

If we are in the client role, our network_connect() interface would call an intermediate level initiate_connection() call. The Berkeley sockets implementation of initiate_connection() would call socket(), gethostbyname(), and connect(). Note that the intermediate level we pass through in these calls is solely for the purpose of portability across messaging architectures. If we knew that our messaging API would never change, we could make the lowest level calls directly. With this architecture, however, we need only change the intermediate level calls to support a new messaging architecture. To extend this architecture to support Netware SPX/IPX, for example, we add code to the setup_connection() call for the server that calls t_open, t_bind, and t_listen. The setup_connection() must find out from the configuration object what API will be used by incoming clients, and then make the appropriate lower-level calls.

Send and Receive. After establishing a connection, our messaging API needs to provide network_send() and network_receive() interfaces to allow messages to be sent in either direction. For the Berkeley sockets implementation, these would simply call the send() and recv() interfaces.

Select. The next interface is called network_select(). The network interface protocols upon which our messaging layer is built allow an N-to-1 relationship between clients and servers. Thus, an application server or network monitor program may have connections established with several clients. (This flexibility is provided by the architecture, but we have found that the model in which each client has its own server process to be the most trouble-free implementation.) The network_select() function allows us to monitor multiple connections, and returns to us the first one which has activity. This activity may be a new client requesting a connection (in which case the lower level accept_connection() routine would be called in response) or it may be an existing connection that has a message waiting (in which case the network_receive() routine will be called). Network_select() is implemented as a call to the sockets select() interface when BSD sockets is the messaging mechanism.

Disconnect. After communication is completed, each side should close the connection. The Berkeley sockets implementation of the network_disconnect() function calls the close() interface.

We have now created an interface that provides five calls—network_connect(), network_select(), network_send(), network_receive(), and network_disconnect()—that can be used by our client/server applications to provide all the necessary communications between systems. Our interfaces can be extended to support different types of messaging APIs such at Berkeley sockets, NetIPC, and Netware; they can also be extended with some effort to support an underlying RPC based mechanism such as DCE.

Implementation Details

We have already mentioned that the format of the messages being passed is irrelevant to the messaging routines themselves. They merely want a data buffer and a length parameter. However, we can build some additional intelligence into our monitor program to handle the routing of messages by using a consistent layout for identifying the target of each message.

We have therefore created a very basic high-level definition of each message to be passed, which divides the message content into four fields. The first field will be an integer value which contains a predefined constant identifying the target of the message. The second field, also an integer, identifies the message format; it tells the receiver what to expect in the data portion of the message. The third field is another integer value which contains the length of the fourth and final field, which is the message content. Only the final recipient of the message needs to know anything further about the layout of the fourth part of the message.

We have chosen 32 bits as the size for the integer fields. To make the code portable, they are all defined as type `U32`, a user-defined type. C `#define` statements are used to make the `U32` data type an `int` on 32-bit architectures, and a `long` on 16-bit architectures.

Our network_send() and network_receive() functions must also be prepared to deal with differences in byte ordering between platforms. APIs are available to perform the conversion between byte ordering schemes, but the developer must decide who calls these APIs, and when. There are several different approaches to this problem, of which the most common are the following:

- Some implementations designate a "network byte order." Any message placed on the network is ordered to conform to the network byte order. Thus, a system whose native byte ordering is the same as the network order will never need to perform reordering, whereas a system whose native byte ordering is different than the network order will always need to. When systems in a network are predominately of a particular ordering, designating this ordering as the network byte ordering minimizes the number of times that the reordering will have to be performed. It also allows systems to be ignorant of the native byte ordering of any other systems on the network; they need only be concerned with whether they match the network's ordering or not. The worst case scenario is one in which two systems which do not follow the network byte ordering scheme communicate with each other; each message is being reordered at each end, when in fact no reordering should have been necessary.
- Another possibility is to designate *when* messages will be reordered: before sending, or after receiving. This requires that each participant know the native byte ordering of the other participant. If they are the same, reordering is never necessary. If they are different, each participant will be responsible either to reorder all messages that they send, or to reorder all messages that they receive. The decision as to whether to reorder at the sending or receiving end is arbitrary; we can see no reason to prefer one over the other.
- A variation on the above is to have the receiver always responsible for reordering, if necessary, and to imbed the sender's byte ordering as part of the message. It would be specified in a single-byte character field (using an int field would mean we would have to know the contents of the field to read the field) that the receiver would check to know if numeric fields needed to be reordered. No unnecessary translations would be done in this design.
- The final option is to designate *who* is always responsible for performing the reordering. Either the client or the server is given this responsibility, and must then always ensure that messages sent or received are translated to the byte ordering of the other participant, if necessary. This is the scheme we prefer, with the responsibility being given to the client. It serves to offload the server, which is frequently an objective in client/server architectures. It also ensures that no unnecessary translations will be done.

In our sample implementations of this architecture, byte ordering was the only difference in systems that we needed to be concerned with. It is possible that you will encounter others. If you are communicating between IBM and non-IBM systems, you may need to perform ASCII to EBCDIC translations. If your data includes foreign language characters, you will find that not all systems represent these the same way, and translation between character sets may be required. The ROMAN8 character set used by the HP 3000 is different from the ISO 8859/1 character set used by personal computers, for example. In each case, the choices of where to perform the translation are the same as with byte ordering. All of these platform differences are handled completely within the messaging layer, and are invisible to the rest of the application code.

Designing the Monitor Program

We have already incorporated into our message format the ability to define both a target for messages, and a message identification field. These fields will be used by the server application program, but also by the monitor program which forms the final piece of the messaging mechanism.

There are several reasons for having a monitor program separate from the application server. One is that the monitor program can be very small, whereas the application would typically be much larger. Especially if the application is not used continuously during the workday, it is better to have it invoked only when needed. The smaller monitor program will always be active, but consumes less memory and other resources. Another possibility is that many different applications could all be served by the same monitor program, rather than having each application handle this task itself. This is another example of the code reuse we have tried to incorporate into every aspect of the architectural design. Finally, it is in keeping with the general philosophy of making our design both layered and modular; since the tasks performed by the monitor are logically distinct from the application's task, they should not be lumped together into a single piece of code.

The monitor needs to be running in order for any messages to be received, therefore it should be started as part of the system startup procedures. Once started, the monitor will use the network_connect() interface (and in particular, the setup_connection() routine) to wait for a client to connect.

Some client/server protocols are said to be "stateless"—that is, no information from one client/server interaction is retained for use in any subsequent interactions. Thus, tasks such as identifying the server and performing any logon and security checks must be performed each time a client/server interaction occurs. An example of a stateless interaction is the http protocol used by World Wide Web clients on the Internet (although there are workarounds that allow a client and server to maintain some state information, if desired). Because the logon and verification process can consume an appreciable amount of resources, we prefer to avoid using a stateless model for our client/server architecture. Thus, we have two distinct types of activities that the server side networking code must handle. There are incoming requests for connections, where the client identifies itself and any logon and authentication takes place, and then there is the processing of message traffic back and forth between the client and the server. These tasks can be physically separated, if desired, making one module responsible for handling connection requests, and another responsible for message traffic.

In making a decision about whether such functions should be combined or distributed, scaling factors should be taken into consideration. If there will be more message traffic than a single message monitor can handle, then the design needs to allow for replication of message monitors. Likewise, if there will be more connection requests than a single connection monitor can handle, then the connection monitor will also need to be designed to allow replication. We believe that in most cases a single connection monitor will suffice, but that multiple message monitors will frequently be required. A process indicates whether it wishes to look for only connection requests, only messages, or both by setting a flag field in the network_select() call. In this way, we don't need to create separate programs for connection requests and message traffic; a single program can handle either or both by setting the flag. As system traffic increases, we can create more monitor programs. Each monitor program can set the flag differently, so if connection activity is low enough to have a single process handle them all, we can have only one process set the flag to see connections.

When there is more than one process that will be performing some of the monitor duties, access to the underlying sockets becomes an issue. If you think of a socket as a file, then the server side program that establishes a connection with a client has in effect opened the file, and will be allowed to read and write to it. If another process is invoked to help handle the load, that process will need to have the same access to the socket. Unlike files, however, multiple processes cannot "open" the same socket. Instead, sockets depend on the behavior of the UNIX fork() and exec() process creation mechanism, by which a child process, when created, will inherit any open files and sockets that the parent has opened. In UNIX environments, a single process will monitor the connection socket, most commonly forking a child process for each incoming connection.

If your monitor program will only run on systems which provide the fork() mechanism, such as UNIX-derived operating systems and MPE/iX releases 4.5 and later, then this mechanism is very suitable. On MPE/iX 4.0, you must use CREATEPROCESS as the process creation interface, which will not inherit socket connections, but you can use the proprietary IPCGive and IPCGet intrinsics to give the socket connection from the parent to the child process. (These NetIPC intrinsics work with sockets created with both the NetIPC intrinsics and the BSD sockets API. However, the mix-and-match of NetIPC and BSD calls is not officially supported, and thus may not work the same way in the future.) MPE releases prior to 4.0 do not support the Berkeley sockets interfaces at all, but NetIPC intrinsics are available, and can be used to talk to clients that are written to use Berkeley sockets. If you need to support an architecture than does not have a fork()-like mechanism of passing sockets to a child process, and does not have an extension to do so such as the IPCGive intrinsic, then your only alternative is to use separate port connection addresses with separate monitor programs to provide scaling once a single monitor program becomes a bottleneck.

While many architectures will have application servers responsible for handling the message traffic once a connection has been established, we decided to have the monitor responsible for handling all messages. This follows from our desire to keep network-aware code separate from the application logic, and also provides some additional benefits. It is likely that the amount of traffic that can be handled by the monitor will not be exactly equivalent to the amount of transactions that can be processed by the application logic; it may be greater or less, depending on the complexity of the transactions. By separating these pieces, they can be scaled independently: If the network interface is the bottleneck, we can create more monitor processes, whereas if the application is the bottleneck, we can create more application servers. We also have the flexibility of creating a user interface that combines functionality from multiple applications; the front end can allow users to select various transaction types, and the messages thus created can be sent to the correct application servers. Finally, we have the capability of sending messages that aren't sent to an application server at all; we can create message types that are processed internally by the monitor, and message types that are passed to the server operating system or to a database engine.

This flexibility is achieved through the message target and message format fields described earlier. Consider an application implementation in which constants have been defined to represent the following message targets: APPLICATION_ONE, APPLICATION_TWO, MONITOR, SERVER_OPSYS, and DATABASE. The monitor program would itself be capable of processing any messages for which MONITOR was the target. Each such message would be assigned a unique message format identifier. (It is actually only necessary that the combination of message target and message identifier be unique, but we assigned a separate range of values to each target to avoid possibility of Stupid Programmer Errors.) For the monitor target, we defined three message formats: SHUTDOWN, LOGON, and LOGOFF. SHUTDOWN was a request for the monitor program to be stopped, and required no parameters. The LOGON message was used to identify the client to the server; it provides one place that security checks can be made. (Additional checks can be made at the application and database levels.) The LOGOFF message is used to release a connection to the server.

Most messages will be targeted at an application server. An application may be designed such that each client has a dedicated server, or it may be designed such that a server process can handle requests from a number of clients. In the first case, we would probably create a new message type to the server to request that an application be started on the client's behalf. In the latter case, the monitor would start a server process for an application if there was not one currently active, otherwise it would just pass the message along to the existing application server. More sophisticated schemes, in which the transaction volume is used to determine how many servers should be active, with the monitor controlling their activation and deactivation, can be created as extensions of the current design. The next leap forward from this would be a load balancing capability across multiple systems, and the ability to route transactions based on system loads and system availability. We believe that this routing is best performed at the client. The client could interrogate each server to determine loading, either for each transaction or at predetermined intervals, but we believe it more effective to use the publish/subscribe model as described previously to have the servers notify clients whenever server loads exceed defined minimum or maximum thresholds. If you are considering these types of designs, you have reached the complexity level where serious consideration should be given to middleware products such as transaction monitors that provide these types of capabilities.

Message Facility Extensions

The increasing acceptance of client/server architectures has driven a constant stream of innovation in the areas of messaging middleware. A few technologies that we haven't incorporated into our current design, but might want to include in the next revision, are message queues and a threaded monitor.

Any messaging middleware will have some sort of message queuing mechanism implemented internally, simply because to fail to do so may result in missed messages any time the server was unable to completely process a message before the next message arrived. Typically, however, these queues are hidden from the programmer; the API will allow access only to the first message in the queue. By making the queue explicitly visible to the programmer, additional features such as message priorities can be implemented, rather than a pure first-in, first-out ordering. To implement message queues on top of a network API that doesn't make its internal queues accessible, a program running a very small loop (and an ideal candidate for a thread—see the next paragraph) simply grabs messages from the network API and places them on its own queue, which can support multiple priority levels, monitor the overall queue length to determine server loading, and implement any other features the programmer finds useful. Message queues would also be useful on the client side; they would allow client programs to handle asynchronous events such as notification of servers going down, mail delivery, or even updates to client-local data within the client application program.

Threads are a relatively new model for process management that fits very well with the needs of a monitor program to handle many tasks simultaneously. A brief introduction to threads is given in Chapter 25. A threaded monitor program could have one thread building message queues from incoming message traffic, another thread handling messages designated for the monitor itself, and a variable number of threads (depending on load) routing messages from the message queue to application servers or other services. While the architecture as currently defined does not incorporate threads, the modular, layered nature of the architecture makes it extensible to a threaded implementation in the future.

CHAPTER 21

Creating the Operating System Interfaces

On an MPE system, when we talk about Operating System interfaces we typically think of the MPE Intrinsics (and perhaps the Architected Interface Facility). Since most readers are probably already familiar with the MPE Intrinsics, we'll use them as a starting point to talk about creating portable operating system interfaces.

The MPE Intrinsics manual divides the intrinsics into a number of groups based on functionality (with some intrinsics appearing in more than one group). Some of these groups represent tasks which will probably be handled similarly on other systems, even if the interface name and parameters are completely different. For these tasks, we can create an abstract interface which isolates the application program from any knowledge of the underlying operating system implementation. Other task groups may cover areas which are implemented in a very different fashion—if at all—on other systems, making the creation of an abstracted interface difficult. Fortunately, many of these tasks are seldom used, and you may be able to ignore them entirely in your implementation. For those which are required, workarounds will be evaluated.

The intrinsic groups described in the Intrinsics Reference manual are:

- Accessing Files
- Accessing Command Interpreter Features
- Getting System Information
- Managing Processes
- Managing Resources and System Information
- Programming for Localization

- Managing Message Catalogs
- Converting Data Types
- Sorting and Merging Data
- Handling Traps
- Managing Logging Facilities
- Debugging Applications
- Programming in Privileged Mode
- Managing USL Files
- Managing Data Segments
- Changing Stack Size
- Programming Switch

The intrinsics included in each of these groupings are as follows:
The **Accessing Files** group includes the following intrinsics:

FCHECK	FCLOSE	FCONTROL	FDELETE
FDEVICECONTROL	FERRMSG	FFILEINFO	FGETINFO
FLABELINFO	FLOCK	FOPEN	FOPEN
FPARSE	FPOINT	FREAD	FREADBACKWARD
FREADDIR	FREADSEEK	FRELATE	FRENAME
FSETMODE	FSETMODE	FSPACE	FUNLOCK
FUPDATE	FWRITE	FWRITEDIR	FWRITELABEL
HPERRDEPTH	HPERRMSG	HPERRREAD	HPFOPEN
HPFOPEN	PRINT	PRINTFILEINFO	PRINTOP
PRINTOPREPLY	READ	READX	

The **Accessing Command Interpreter Features** group includes the following intrinsics:

COMMAND	FINDJCW	GETJCW	HPCICOMMAND
HPCIDELETEVAR	HPCIGETVAR	HPCIPUTVAR	MYCOMMAND
PUTJCW	SEARCH	SETJCW	

The **Getting System Information** group includes the following intrinsics:

ALMANAC	CALENDAR	CLOCK	DATELINE
FFILEINFO	FGETINFO	FLABELINFO	FMTCALENDAR
FMTCLOCK	FMTDATE	HPERRDEPTH	HPERRREAD
HPERRMSG	JOBINFO	PRINTFILEINFO	PROCTIME
TIMER	WHO		

The **Managing Processes** group includes the following intrinsics:

ABORTSESS	ACTIVATE	CAUSEBREAK	CREATE
CREATEPROCESS	FATHER	GETINFO	GETORIGIN
GETPRIORITY	GETPROCID	GETPROCINFO	IODONTWAIT
IOWAIT	JOBINFO	KILL	MAIL
PAUSE	PROCINFO	PROCTIME	QUIT
QUITPROG	RECEIVEMAIL	SENDMAIL	STARTSESS
SUSPEND	TERMINATE		

The **Managing Resources** group includes the following intrinsics:

FREELOCRIN	GETLOCRIN	HPFIRSTLIBRARY	HPGETPROCLABEL
HPMYFILE	HPMYPROGRAM	LOCKGLORIN	LOCKLOCRIN
LOCRINOWNER	UNLOCKGLORIN	UNLOCKLOCRIN	

The **Programming for Localization** group includes the following intrinsics:

ALMANAC	CATCLOSE	CATOPEN	CATREAD
NLAPPEND	NLCOLLATE	NLCONVCLOCK	NLCONVCUSTDATE
NLCONVNUM	NLFINDSTR	NLFMTCALENDAR	NLFMTCLOCK
NLFMTCUSTDATE	NLFMTDATE	NLFMTLONGCAL	NLFMTNUM
NLGETLANG	NLINFO	NLJUDGE	NLKEYCOMPARE
NLNUMSPEC	NLREPCHAR	NLSCANMOVE	NLSUBSTR
NLSWITCHBUF	NLTRANSLATE		

The **Managing Message Catalogs** group includes the following intrinsics:

CATCLOSE	CATOPEN	CATREAD	GENMESSAGE

The **Converting Data Types** group includes the following intrinsics:

ASCII	BINARY	CTRANSLATE	DASCII
DBINARY	HPFPCONVERT		

The **Sorting and Merging Data** group includes the following intrinsics:

HPMERGEEND	HPMERGEERRORMESS	HPMERGEINIT	HPMERGEOUTPUT
HPMERGESTAT	HPMERGETITLE	HPSORTEND	HPSORTERRORMESS
HPSORTINIT	HPSORTINPUT	HPSORTOUTPUT	HPSORTSTAT
HPSORTTITLE	MERGEEND	MERGEERRORMESS	MERGEINIT
MERGEOUTPUT	MERGESTAT	MERGETITLE	SORTEND
SORTERRORMESS	SORTINIT	SORTINPUT	SORTOUTPUT
SORTSTAT	SORTTITLE		

The **Handling Traps** group includes the following intrinsics:

ARITRAP FINTEXIT FINSTATE HPENABLTRAP
RESETCONTROL XARITRAP XCONTRAP XLIBTRAP
XSYSTRAP

The **Managing Logging Features** group includes the following intrinsics:

BEGINLOG CLOSELOG ENDLOG FLUSHLOG
LOGINFO LOGSTATUS OPENLOG WRITELOG

The **Debugging Applications** group includes the following intrinsics:

DEBUG HPDEBUG HPRESETDUMP HPSETDUMP
RESETDUMP SETDUMP STACKDUMP

The **Programming in Privileged Mode** group includes the following intrinsics:

GETPRIVMODE GETUSERMODE

The **Managing USL Files** group includes the following intrinsics:

ADJUSTUSLF CLEANUSL EXPANDUSLF INITUSLF

The **Managing Data Segments** group includes the following intrinsics:

ALTDSEG DMOVIND MOVOUT FREEDSEG
GETDSEG SWITCHDB

The **Changing Stack Size** group includes the following intrinsics:

DLSIZE ZSIZE

The **Programming Switch** group includes the following intrinsics:

HPLOADCMPROCEDURE HPLOADNMPLABEL HPSETCCODE
HPSWITCHTOCM HPSWTONMNAME HPSWTONMPLABEL
HPUNLOADCMPROCEDURE LOADPROC UNLOADPROC

The strategies for handling each of these groups in a portable fashion are described below.

Accessing Files intrinsic group: This group of intrinsics is the most frequently used for most application-level programming. In addition to the obvious FOPEN, FREAD, and FWRITE type calls that will exist in some fashion on any target system, this group also includes interfaces such as FDEVICECONTROL, FSETMODE, and FFILEINFO that may be less easily mapped to similar functionality on other systems. Many application programs do not use the MPE file system intrinsics at all, relying instead on the file access mechanisms built into most languages. Since the language provided mechanisms are more portable, you should probably stick with this approach if it is what you are currently using. If you are currently using MPE intrinsics, you should look to see whether the mechanisms provided by the language you are using provide all the capabilities you need, or if your use of the MPE Intrinsics was done to gain additional functionality over and above that provided by your programming language. Designing a portable interface for your file system usage requires a thorough understanding of what features you are using and why. The HPFOPEN intrinsic call, for example, can be used to access a number of different file types, as well as physical devices; including options such as mapped access, nowait I/O, labeled tapes, and access to privileged files. Most applications that use HPFOPEN will not require the majority of the functionality provided, so attempting to create a portable implementation of the full HPFOPEN capability set is needlessly complex.

The creation of the exact interfaces that will be used will be based largely on the functionality needed, but also somewhat purely on designer preference for what makes a useful interface. There are several features provided via the MPE Intrinsic mechanism—such as extensible parameter lists—that are not provided by all compilers on all platforms. Likewise, we profess to a dislike of "magic numbers" in interfaces, where one must possess the secret decoder ring in order to know that an itemnumber of 11 with an itemvalue of 4 to HPFOPEN specifies read-write access. (Obviously, we're going to code these up as constants with meaningful names, but a distressingly large number of programmers will decline to do so, apparently under the philosophy that code that was difficult to write should be difficult to read, as well). The same is true for bitmaps that were used for aoptions and foptions in the older FOPEN interface. Given these biases, we tend to opt for a larger number of single-purpose (or limited purpose, anyway) interfaces instead of a single interface will a zillion options. So while access type—READ, WRITE, UPDATE—seems reasonable as a parameter to an open() call, the file type itself will be specified through use of different call interfaces, e.g., open_random, open_circular, open_short_mapped. This is done especially in the case where the parameters needed to open the file vary between the different file types. Remember that not all languages provide default or omitted parameter capabilities, and that in such languages a parameter that is only rarely used will still have to be passed by every caller in such implementations.

If coding in an object-oriented language that provides function overloading, the same philosophy applies, even though polymorphism can provide the appearance that a single interface is being created. An object class of File can have subclasses RandomFile, CircularFile, and SequentialFile, and each can (and should) have a method named open(). The three implementations may share a lot of the same code, or none, depending on how widely the file types vary. One advantage of object-oriented languages that is particularly helpful in this case is the ability to overload a function name even within the same subclass—so for example, the RandomFile() subclass may have more than one version of open() implemented, each with a different parameter list. This allows a very simple interface—such as open(filename)—when the default values are acceptable, while at the same time providing a more full-featured interface when a number of options need to be specified. In this way, the overloading capability provided in a language such as C++ allows you to re-implement the variable parameter list capabilities of MPE Intrinsics, but in a completely portable fashion.

Accessing Command Interpreter Features intrinsic group: This group of intrinsics provides the application program a way to access command interpreter features. While similar capabilities are available on HP-UX, providing access to a shell from within an application program, the difference in the shell versus the CI make a generic mapping of shell access to command interpreter access impractical.

For example, if an MPE program calls HPCICOMMAND and passes the command string `:LISTF @,2`, it would certainly not be sufficient on an HP-UX implementation to pass the same command string to a shell process. Command substitution is not necessarily 1 to 1; some of the information from a UNIX `ls -l` command corresponds to a `:LISTF ,2`; other parts correspond to a `:LISTF ,3`. The file type information displayed by MPE on a `:LISTF` has no direct correlation on UNIX, although the `file` command gives some information about the file's type. Additionally, even when the same information is presented, it may not be in the same format; for example, the UNIX `ls` command displays a file's size in bytes, while MPE's `:LISTF` command reports it in sectors.

To get around these various differences in the underlying command interface, it is best not to use a generic interface to the command facility. Instead, develop specific functions on a case-by-case basis for every instance where such access is required. For example, a call to HPCICOMMAND to obtain a list of files in a group would be replaced by a call to perform that specific function. The implementation of this call would still most likely call HPCICOMMAND on the MPE system, but could be designed to use a completely different mechanism on HP-UX, Windows NT, or another platform.

An alternative to this which may be applicable in some circumstances is to standardize on an underlying command mechanism that will be the same on all platforms where the application will be required to run. The POSIX shell provided on MPE/iX is in most respects the same as the Korn shell (ksh) available on HP-UX and other platforms. Migrating the command interpreter usage to the POSIX shell will in most cases permit the code to run unchanged on HP-UX. If there is no requirement to run on platforms that do not provide a compatible shell environment, this approach may work just as well as the function-specific interfaces.

Getting System Information intrinsic group: Several of the intrinsics listed here are also duplicated in other groups; for example, JOBINFO is also in the managing processes group, and FILEINFO is also in the accessing files group. The only intrinsics unique to this group are the time related functions. You will wish to create a set of routines that can return the current time and date to an application program. These values should be passed in the form of date and time "objects", which provide a variety of methods allowing the application program to request that the data be returned in the desired format.

Managing Processes intrinsic group: This group includes a number of routines for controlling processes, such as CREATE, ACTIVATE, SUSPEND, QUIT, TERMINATE, and PAUSE, as well as routines for interprocess communication (SENDMAIL, RECEIVEMAIL). We will discuss interprocess communication separately later in this chapter.

Process management is particularly tricky to provide in a transparent fashion between the traditional MPE systems and UNIX derived systems. This is due to the behavior of the UNIX `fork()` interface, which is the only method by which a new process can be created on most UNIX systems. `fork()` clones the existing process: after `fork()` is executed, two copies of the program will exist. They will have the same files open—even if the process initiating the `fork()` specified exclusive access upon opening them. They will both have all the same environment variable settings, and both programs will even continue execution with the statement immediately following the call to `fork()`. The only distinction will be in the value returned by the call to `fork()`—the parent process will see a return value of the child's process id, and the child process will see a zero. `fork()` is very well suited to certain types of process architectures; particularly a server process which listens for client requests and then forks() a process to handle the request. As a general purpose process creation mechanism—indeed, as the only process creation mechanism for many systems—its design is less than optimal. The majority of processes which call `fork()`—which incur a nontrivial amount of overhead in copying the exact process environment for the newly created process—will then immediately call `exec()`, which executes a new program, overlaying many of the things that have just been copied. Later versions of UNIX introduced a `vfork()` interface, to be used when a program will be calling `exec()` immediately after the `fork()`. `vfork()` avoids much of this pointless copying, and should be used instead of `fork()` whenever an `exec()` will be used to bring in a new program.

Because of the unique characteristics of the `fork()` interface—inheritance of the parent's environment, and execution of the child process beginning with the statement after the `fork()` statement—it is very difficult to emulate the behavior of the `fork()` call in a traditional process management environment, for example using MPE'S CREATEPROCESS intrinsic. On the other hand, duplication of the CREATEPROCESS functionality with `fork()` and `exec()` is relatively straightforward. Therefore, while in most cases we think it is a good idea for the abstract operating system interface layer to be as standard as possible—and therefore follow POSIX syntax to the greatest extent practical—this is one of the cases where we think the POSIX syntax is impractical if the code being developed will ever be required to run on a non-POSIX conforming operating system.

Managing Resources intrinsic group: Some of the intrinsics in this group are duplicates, which are better considered as part of the managing processes group. Those that remain are the intrinsics dealing with RINs—Resource Identification Numbers. RINs are a compatibility mode MPE mechanism for process synchronization, that is, coordinating access between multiple programs to system resources. The POSIX concept which provides the same functionality as RINs is semaphores. POSIX style semaphores can be used to implement this functionality on UNIX and MPE/iX, while RINs can be used to provide the same function on older MPE systems.

The **Programming for Localization**, **Managing Message Catalogs**, **Converting Data Types**, **Sorting and Merging Data,** and **Managing Logging Facilities** intrinsic groups represent areas in which MPE/iX provide capabilities to the application programmers which, on other operating systems, is left up to the programmer or a third-party supplier to provide. Even on the MPE/iX systems, many programmers either develop their own customized capabilities or rely on third-party packages to provide some of these services. Functionality from these groups should be implemented on an as-needed basis, and in whatever fashion best serves the immediate need; there are few if any standards that cover the functionality represented by these MPE Intrinsics.

The **Debugging Applications**, **Programming in Privileged Mode**, **Managing USL Files**, **Managing Data Segments**, **Changing Stack Size**, **Using the Compiler Library**, and **Programming Switch** intrinsic groups all involve very MPE-specific functionality. Several of these groups are used only for compatibility with the MPE V architecture, and provide functionality which is not required for either native mode MPE/iX applications or applications running under other modern operating systems. Other areas, such as the debugging intrinsics, may have counterparts on other systems but the specific behavior will be far different. Any functionality you are using in any of these categories needs to be evaluated on a case-by-case basis. In some cases, there may be a portable way to provide the functionality. In other cases, it will be necessary to either remove the code entirely, or have the specific functionality available only on the MPE/iX platform.

Now that we have covered all the functions that may be considered operating system interfaces, we can think about how our architecture should provide these functions. Many of the specialized functions will not be provided at all, unless needed. Others, like sort capabilities, will be capabilities built into whatever objects need them, but not seen as part of the operating system interfaces. Our architecture subdivides the remaining interfaces into File System, System Information, Process Management, User Information, Program Information, Interprocess Communication, and Process Synchronization objects. One reason for this further division is to allow multiple implementations of a given feature set on the same system. For example, on MPE/iX we support both traditional MPE Process Management (CREATEPROCESS, ACTIVATE, etc.) as well as POSIX-style process management (fork(), exec()). Similarly, there are several alternatives for Interprocess Communication on MPE/iX: Message Files, AIF:Ports, System V IPC, and others. On the Windows NT operating system, three different file system implementations are supported: The native file system (NTFS), the DOS File Allocation Table file system (FAT), and the OS/2 High-Performance File System (HPFS). Making these functional areas into separate objects allows the programmer to specify which subsystems should be used to provide the services required in each of these areas independently from the selection of the Operating System to run under. Table 21.1 shows some possible configuration values for the different OS objects available on MPE/iX, HP-UX, and Windows NT systems.

OS Area	MPE	HP-UX	Windows NT
File System	MPE_FS POSIX_FS NFS Netware_FS	HPUX_FS POSIX_FS NFS JFS	FAT HPFS NTFS
System Info	MPE_SINFO POSIX_SINFO	HPUX_SINFO POSIX_SINFO	WIN32_SINFO POSIX_SINFO
Process Management	MPE_PM POSIX_PM THREADS_PM	HP_UX_PM POSIX_PM THREADS_PM	WIN32_PM POSIX_PM THREADS_PM
User Info	MPE_UINFO POSIX_UINFO	HPUX_UINFO POSIX_UINFO	WIN32_UINFO POSIX_UINFO
Program Info	MPE_PINFO POSIX_PINFO	HPUX_PINFO POSIX_PINFO	WIN32_PINFO POSIX_PINFO
Interprocess Communication	MPE_MSGFILE MPE_PORTS SV_IPC POSIX_IPC	HPUX_IPC SV_IPC POSIX_IPC	WIN32_IPC POSIX_IPC
Process Synchronization	MPE_RINS SV_SEMA	HPUX_SYNC SV_SEMA	WIN32_SYNC

Table 21.1 Operating System objects on MPE/iX, HP-UX, and Windows NT

With the breakdown of various operating system services into the categories established above, it can be argued that there is no need for a separate operating system object at all. We have included one primarily for convenience; it is essentially a container to hold the file system, process management, and other objects which provide the operating system methods. It can also be responsible for "knowing" what configuration combinations are legal; for example, not allowing you to specify the FAT file system object for an MPE system. Figure 21.1 shows the same modules as in Table 21.1, but arranged to emphasize the physical location of the code. It is clearer from this representation that the POSIX file system object, for example, is implemented only once, and kept in a POSIX library. The source code that implements these functions is portable across MPE/iX, UNIX, and Windows NT systems. The MPE class, or abstract object, will allow specification of any of the valid options in each operating system subobject, as shown in Table 21.1; thus each of the legal components can be thought of as part of the class. At run time, when an instance of the MPE class is created, only one option is selected in each category;

and only the selected components are thought of as part of the instance. (This is an implementation choice only; it would be possible to expose all of the legal interfaces at the instance level, thus permitting an application to mix-and-match calls to the POSIX libraries and the MPE libraries, for example. We have chosen to avoid this because this mix-and-match approach does not always work as expected in all instances due to a number of differences in the POSIX and MPE environments.)

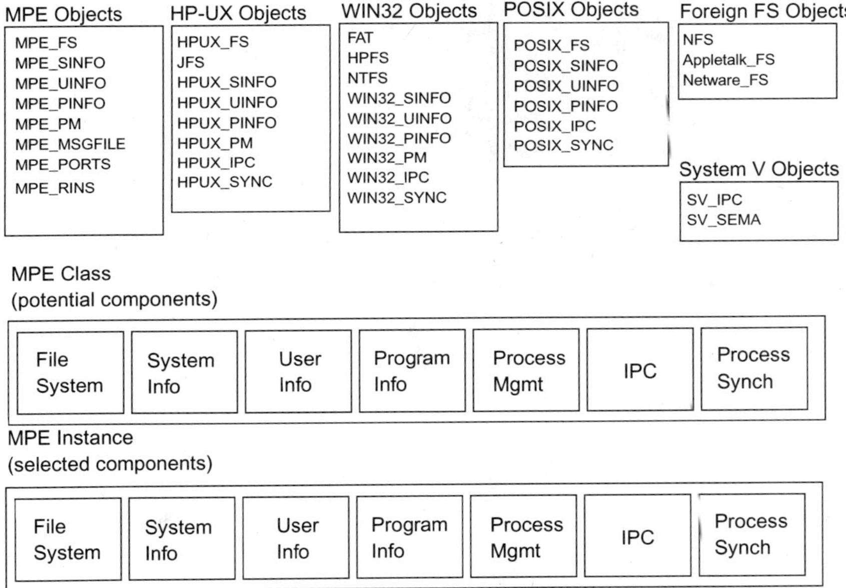

Figure 21.1 Operating System Object Inheritance Diagram

CHAPTER 22

Creating the Transaction Mechanism

Our sample Client/Server architecture, as you will recall, includes three software "entities" (each of which in turn comprises a number of software objects): the client, the server, and the monitor. It is the monitor which listens on a network port for incoming messages from clients. These messages include, among other attributes, a target field that designates the recipient of the message. The target may be the monitor itself (our architecture makes the monitor responsible for logon and logoff activity which forms the basis for security), the underlying operating system, a specified database, or a specified application. In this section, we will take a closer look at the types of messages that can be directed to the application.

Our architecture proposes three types of objects that will cooperate in the execution of business transactions. The first of these is the Transaction object. Transactions provide an Execute() method that is used to perform the business function the Transaction was designed to provide.

The second object, the Transaction Router (TxnRouter) object, is primarily concerned with finding a server on which to execute the desired Transaction. In a complex transaction, where either the transaction logic or the databases are not resident on a single system (being split either between the client and the server, or across multiple servers), the TxnRouter also takes on the responsibility of a Transaction Manager, ensuring that all pieces of the transaction have successfully completed before committing the transaction.

The third object type is the Application Segment (AppSegment). Simple applications will consist of a single AppSegment object which includes all the transactions which make up the application; in this case, the AppSegment is merely a container class for the Transaction objects which contain the executable code of the application. In a distributed environment, an application may be made up of multiple AppSegments, which may reside on multiple systems. The AppSegments are then interrogated by the TxnRouter object so that transactions can be directed to the appropriate server. In the simplest implementation, this interrogation may be replaced by a hard-coded listing of transactions within each AppSegment. (In all cases, the location of the AppSegment is kept in the Config object, which is typically initialized at run-time by loading values from a flat file). Figure 22.1 shows the steps involved in the execution of a typical transaction using these objects.

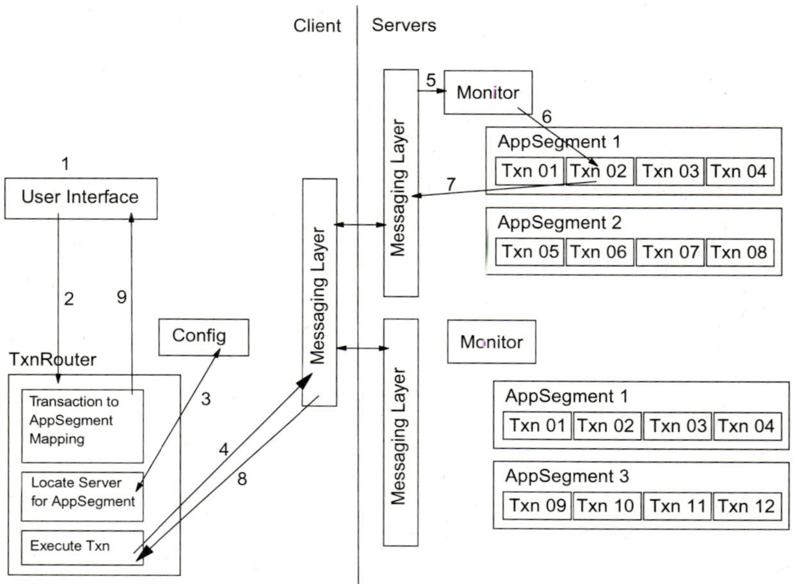

Figure 22.1 Relationship between TxnRouter, AppSegment, and Transaction objects

The flow of the transaction shown in Figure 22.1 is as follows:

1. The user selects the function to be performed, which corresponds to a particular transaction. The user interface gathers all the necessary information from the user to complete the transaction and invokes the Execute() method of the TxnRouter specifying the desired transaction.

2. The TxnRouter object must determine where the transaction will be executed. (It could turn out to be local, or on a remote server). This is done by first finding the name of the AppSegment which contains the desired location.

3. The TxnRouter then communicates with the Config file to find the server or servers on which the desired AppSegment is available. In cases where more than one server has the AppSegment available, it is a design decision as to what object is responsible for making a selection.

4. Based on the location information retrieved from the Config object, the TxnRouter sends a message to the AppSegment responsible for executing the Transaction. If the AppSegment is local (on the client), the message is sent directly to the object (not shown in diagram). If the AppSegment is remote, the message is sent to the messaging layer for routing.

5. The monitor on the selected server system receives the message. The Message Target field will identify the AppSegment that should receive the message, and the Message Format field will identify the Transaction to be executed.

6. The Application process appropriate for the selected transaction will be invoked by the monitor, and will execute the desired transaction.

7. The application server will send transaction completion information back to the client through the messaging facility.

8. The completion message is received by the TxnRouter. If this were a complex transaction, the TxnRouter may have to wait for multiple messages from distributed servers to complete the transaction.

9. The user interface running on the client receives a message indicating completion of the transaction.

Some of the methods that will be provided by each object to perform these tasks are described below.

The **TxnRouter** object. In a configuration in which multiple clients connect to a single server, and all application logic and databases reside on this server, the TxnRouter is unnecessary. If the systems for which you are providing the architecture are never expected to grow beyond this configuration, feel free to omit it. Alternately, a simple design can be implemented to provide the hooks for future expansion. The methods of a TxnRouter object should include:

- An Execute() method, which takes a transaction name and a data buffer as parameters. After locating the appropriate AppSegment (see following methods), the Execute() method either invokes the Execute() method of the desired transaction, if it is on the local system, or sends a message through the messaging facility to the AppSegment if it is on a remote system. If distributed transactions are supported, the Execute() method must locate and call ExecutePart() for each portion of the transaction. If all return a good status, it then calls Commit() for each part; if any fail, it calls Rollback() for all that reported completion. A commercial transaction monitor is recommended for implementing distributed transactions; the two-phase logic described here still has timing windows in which a failure can cause inconsistent data, although they are minimal.
- A FindServer() or FindServers() method, to which a transaction name is passed as a parameter, and from which is returned a server name (or list of servers) as found in the Config object. It is intended primarily for use by the Execute() method, and would probably not be made visible to external users of the object. If multiple servers exist, with the possibility of a particular transaction residing on more than one server, the architect must decide where in the code the decision will be made as to which server should receive each transaction. The logic can be placed in the FindServer() method, so that a single server name is always returned that represents the "best" target for the transaction. Or, a FindServers() method can return all servers that support the transaction, requiring that the Execute() method use its own algorithm to determine the best target system. If the selection logic is complex, you may wish to encapsulate it in its own object, and allow that object access to the FindServer() method so that they can cooperatively determine the best server to use.
- Select() is a method which allows the application to indicate to the TxnRouter what server should be used. It is optional; the expectation is that the TxnRouter itself will normally be responsible for server selection. This method provides flexibility in the case where there may be knowledge encapsulated in another object in the system which an application may use to make a decision regarding server selection.
- SetSelectMode() is another optional method to assist in the selection of a server. If the FindServer() method supports different algorithms for selecting a server, this allows the application to specify which algorithm should be used, for example, closest, least busy, round-robin, or largest capacity.

The **Transaction** object is fairly straightforward if all transaction execution is to be on one server and synchronous (that is, the client process is blocked until the transaction completes.) Adding distributed transactions and asynchronous execution capabilities can improve overall system throughput and flexibility, but at a cost of significant additional complexity. We recommend the simplest implementation be done first; the additional methods can always be added later.

- Execute(). This is the method which actually executes the transaction. In a straightforward implementation, this will be the only method defined by each transaction.
- ExecutePart(). An optional method of Transactions to allow distributed logic. The ExecutePart() method tells the targeted transaction piece to execute its logic and return a status, but to then wait for a Commit() or Rollback() method to be called to complete the transaction.
- Commit(). Completes a transaction that was executed via an ExecutePart() method.
- Rollback(). Cancels a transaction that was executed via an ExecutePart() method. Any data fields that were updated need to be rolled back to their values prior to the start of the transaction.
- ExecAsync(). Another optional feature of Transactions is to permit asynchronous execution, in which the caller will not wait for transaction completion. Status information will be held by the transaction until a WaitAsynch() call is done.
- ReportStatus(). For asynchronous transactions, reports the status (complete or pending) of the transaction.
- WaitAsync(). Called to complete an asynchronous transaction.

The AppSegment object is another container class. The Transactions within the AppSegment do all of the real work; it may not be necessary for the AppSegment object to have any methods at all. If some sort of workload balancing is desired, you may choose to have the AppSegment participate in this task by keeping track of the number of currently active Transactions via a ReportLoad() or similar method.

The TxnRouter and AppSegment objects together provide the infrastructure on which Transactions will be built. For the most part, the contents of the individual transactions are very application specific and beyond the scope of this book. However, there are some pointers to keep in mind in designing transactions, and this will be the topic of the next chapter.

CHAPTER 23

Creating Application Logic

The transition from batch-oriented systems of the mainframe era to the online systems of the minicomputer era allowed interfaces to become far more interactive. While there are online systems that did nothing more than replace punched cards with terminals, most applications provided more interaction for the user. When an account number is typed in, the account holder's name is presented for verification. When part numbers are entered in an order, the description of the item is displayed back to the user. When we try to create a transaction-based system, we tend to think of these user interactions as part of the transaction, dividing the transaction into a series of discrete steps: the user enters this, the computer responds; the user enters some more, the computer responds. The user presses OK, the computer writes the data into a database. In fact, everything up until the final interaction is not a part of the transaction, and it is vital that it be kept separate from the transaction logic. The actual transaction is still a batch operation: all the data required for the transaction is provided as input; the transaction executes in a single step that either succeeds or fails, and the user is informed of this success or failure. Anything else is not part of the transaction.

This is not to say that these other interactions should be eliminated; quite the opposite. It is the responsibility of the user interface code to provide as much feedback as possible to the user. Any field that can be verified, should be. Anywhere that a blank field can be replaced with a list of valid selections for the user to select from, do so. Just remember that these are user conveniences, and are a part of the user interface logic. Only when the user has finished this interaction, and is satisfied that everything is correct, does the actual transaction begin. By separating the user interaction from the transaction, we accomplish several things. For one, we minimize the time during which we will hold locks on any data during processing, increasing the amount of throughput achievable by the application. Also, we make it easier to support multiple user interfaces, since the user interface logic is completely separate from the transaction logic. The modular design allows us to make changes to either the transaction logic or to the presentation logic without impacting the other.

The application programmer must also understand the distinction between Transactions, which add, change, or delete data, and Queries, which merely read the data. Our architecture design did not specifically separate the two, intending for Queries to simply a subset of Transactions which do no updates, but you may choose to create separate Query objects for clarity. In a single-system architecture, they have about the same complexity. In some cases, queries do not need to be concerned with locking, although many databases will impose a locking requirement even on read-only transactions. Once you begin to distribute data, the Transaction-Query distinction becomes far more important. If data is replicated on several systems to improve data accessibility, queries need only to find one copy of the data to access. Transactions, on the other hand, must ensure that all copies of the data are updated. This may be the responsibility of the Transaction object program, or it may be handled by a distributed data base management system, or by a separate middleware product such as SharePlex/iX.

Distributing data and logic between systems introduces complexities that aren't encountered in a host-based application environment, or even in a simple client/server environment where only the user interface has been offloaded from the server. When application data is distributed, you encounter the risk that a failure during the execution of a transaction can cause data to become inconsistent, even though database management software on each system has ensured that the data on that one system is consistent. Database management software will ensure that a transaction is either completely committed, or rolled back, for a database on a single system. If the transaction is distributed, a failure may cause the transaction to be rolled back on one system, but committed on another. To prevent this, a two-phase commit is required. This is a protocol between databases that provides an additional check after each database has completed the transaction. If database A commits the transaction, it will verify that database B has also completed the transaction; if not, the transaction will be rolled back. This capability may be provided in the database management software, if you are using the same database on both systems, or it may be provided by a separate Transaction Monitor such as Encina or Tuxedo.

CHAPTER 24

Creating the User Interfaces

As described in the introductory sections, your approach to detailed design and implementation of the architecture will vary depending on how you plan to evolve your hardware platforms over time. In general, customers who plan to be "3000 centric" will not have to deal with many of the issues that arise from interoperability with HP-UX or Windows NT servers. However, even within the 3000 centric community, many customers are deploying Personal Computers as desktop devices. If all of your users will continue to use terminals, or all of the PC devices accessing the 3000 will do so through the use of software that emulates an HP terminal (e.g., Reflection, AdvanceLink, or Minisoft), then there is nothing new that your developers will have to learn in the area of user interfaces. Even if your underlying technology is not changing, however, you should consider implementing the layered software architecture as described throughout this section as a way of making your code more maintainable. VPLUS coding, for example, is not easily mastered by everyone. By separating the application logic, database logic, and user interface logic into separate software modules, it is not necessary that everyone on your programming staff be a "VPLUS guru."

If you are deploying Personal Computers, and want to take advantage of the Graphical User Interface (GUI) capabilities of these desktop platforms even when accessing traditional HP 3000 applications, then there are a number of ways to approach this. Again, if you have any application re-engineering projects to incorporate new functionality into the applications, it would be a good idea to take the opportunity to create more layered software. By creating application software that is transaction-based and includes no user interface code in the application core, you can then develop completely new user interfaces on the PC using tools such as

Visual Basic, PowerBuilder, or Delphi. Messaging interfaces such as those described earlier can be deployed on the PC's in dynamically linked libraries (DLLs) that will be accessible to programs written in these GUI environments. In cases where application logic is deployed fully on the client, with the server providing database management only, the ODBC protocol can be used for data access instead of the more complex messaging architecture described earlier.

Another approach that is especially appropriate for applications which do not need major reengineering is to use a VPLUS emulation tool to allow a new user interface to be created that mimics VPLUS when communicating with the application. Putting a graphical front end on an application that was not originally designed to support one is known as "facelifting" the application. (The converse, putting a character-based interface on an application designed to be graphical, is known as "defenestration.") There are a number of products available on the market to provide a VPLUS facelift:

- TVP/Wingspan, from Software Research Northwest, provides a VPLUS compatibility library for terminal-based applications. TVP/Wingspan allows the terminal interface to be enhanced with the addition of features such as drop-down selection lists and context-sensitive help. The TVP/Wingspan libraries are also available for the HP-UX platform, allowing these applications to be migrated to the HP 9000 in the future if the need arises (and if other HP 3000 dependencies such as TurboIMAGE, intrinsic calls, etc. are addressed as part of the migration effort).
- Faces, from API international; FrontMan, from MiniSoft; and *NUView*, from Chronological Ltd. and distributed by ACS (Advanced Computer Systems, Inc.), are "screen scraper" utilities that work in conjunction with a terminal emulator on PCs to allow VPLUS applications to be enhanced graphically. The application sends VPLUS screens to the terminal emulator as in a normal VPLUS application. You use the design tools provided to reformat the appearance of the data into a more graphical format (adding checkboxes, radio buttons, selection lists, etc.). The redesigned forms are seen by the user; the screen scraper is running along with the terminal emulator to transform the data between the VPLUS representation and the new graphical representation as the application runs. Of the user interface products described here, only these can be used for MPE V (systems before 1988) or Compatibility Mode applications. Because they depend on VPLUS to handle the server side of the user interface, they cannot be used to migrate applications to HP-UX.
- NewFace (available from M.B. Foster Associates in North America, or from HP in Europe) replaces VPLUS on the server side, and uses the Dialog Manager User

Interface Management System to provide support for both Personal Computers running Microsoft Windows and HP-UX workstations using the OSF/Motif user interface. No terminal emulation is required in this configuration; the NewFace client and server pieces communicate through one of several available networking protocols (WRQ PPL (serial), BSD Sockets, or WinSock). The Dialog Manager toolset provides extensive capabilities to customize and extend the user interface, including the incorporation of new code written in either C, MicroFocus COBOL, or the built-in Dialog Manager Rule Language. The NewFace server libraries are available for HP-UX to facilitate porting or co-existence needs.

Through the use of any of these products, applications can be given a graphical user interface with few, if any, changes to the application itself.

For customers deploying new applications, there are a number of factors to be considered, and a wide variety of choices on how to proceed. Questions you should be considering are:

- Where will the application logic reside? [3000 Server, 9000 Server, client, distributed] Do you want to allow the flexibility of moving some or all of the application logic in the future?
- What display devices need to be supported? [Terminals, PCs, Macintoshes, Workstations, X-terminals]
- How will these devices be connected [Serial, LAN, WAN, wireless]

Of all the modules that comprise your application, the user interface is the one in which it is most difficult to leverage code. If your application will support three different user interfaces, you may very well end up creating three completely different front-end programs. The difficulties have been covered previously, and include both technical issues (such as how Microsoft Windows callback functions must be written) and conceptual issues (finding a satisfactory mapping between event-driven functionality and prompt-and-response or forms-based user interfaces).

One characteristic that is natural to GUI environments, but quite foreign to environments such as VPLUS, is the idea of a central event loop. The event loop model is essentially this: the user interface builds the initial interface (creates whatever windows, fields, dialog boxes, etc.) and then waits for an event. The event may be characters typed, or a mouse button clicked. The user interface responds to this event—which may be as trivial as echoing a typed character, or as complex as executing a transaction after the “OK” pushbutton is clicked—and then waits for another event. A key feature of this event loop we’d like to appropriate for our non-

GUI interfaces as well is the extensibility of the event loop to deal with different types of events. In a typical VPLUS environment, we don't typically have a central location where we do the waiting. VREADFIELDS is used to wait for a function key or enter key to be pressed, and a typical VPLUS application may have dozens, or even hundreds, of calls to VREADFIELDS. So if we wanted to be able to handle a new event type—for example, receiving a message via our message queue that a server has gone down, and transactions for that system should be re-routed—there is no central place where we can check the message queue as part of our normal processing loop. We recommend trying to structure your user interface code so that a central event loop is always the main flow of control for the program, with all of the transactions, asynchronous event handling, and other capabilities of the program being accessed from this central point.

We feel that the best way to develop your front-end user interface modules is to use the best tool for the job on each platform, and not worry too much—for just this one module—about code leverage. Thus, you can feel free to use Visual BASIC or Delphi to create front-ends for your Windows users, knowing that the code will not be leveragable. But the productivity gain from using these products, as opposed to trying to create some portable C code to do the same thing, will free up more than enough time to allow you to create a separate user interface, using different tools, for your Macintosh users, or terminal users, or whatever other user group you must accommodate. You may also find that deciding to re-create, rather than re-use, frees you to customize each user interface to best suit the user community. If you have a variety of different display devices throughout your organization, hopefully it is not a random occurrence. If the accounting department uses PCs, and marketing uses Macs, and the engineers have UNIX workstations, then don't try to design a single user interface and implement it three times using different technology. Instead, understand what interfaces are needed by each of these different user groups, and develop a customized front-end that meets their specific requirements.

There are products that provide the capability of developing a portable user interface. These products, called User Interface Management Systems or UIMSs, provide a development environment that we feel is more productive than using a third-generation language, but not as good as the latest single-target tools such as Visual BASIC. Also, each tool will typically have a "native" environment which it matches most closely, and will generate code for other platforms that doesn't quite fit. If you've ever used a X-windows emulator on a PC, you know the feeling—function key mappings, or how items are arranged in menus, aren't what you expect. The result frequently leaves the user feeling that the design is inferior. If you must support a large number of user interfaces, you may find the tradeoff worthwhile, but our first choice is always to develop specifically for a given user interface.

CHAPTER 25

Future Directions for the Architecture

Accessing your Application Via the World Wide Web

One of the reasons we stressed the division between application logic and user interface logic is that while your application logic may be stable, user interface technology is changing rapidly. One example of this is the explosive emergence of the World Wide Web (WWW). Although at the current time, most WWW usage is for static information, such as displaying data sheets, there are several developments that promise to change this. One is the emergence of interactive capabilities on the Web. First there were CGI (Common Gateway Interface) extensions to the basic HTML (HyperText Markup Language) to provide form-processing capability; now we are seeing a rapid standardization on Sun's Java language to provide more interactive capabilities in the form of downloadable "applets." Several web browsers are adding plug-in modules to provide more interactive capabilities with less specialized programming effort than required by Java. Major credit card companies are working with the browser developers to develop sufficiently secure encryption and authentication services to allow commerce over the web. While many of the predictions about the importance of this "information superhighway" have been over-hyped, it is probably unwise to ignore the potential new markets represented.

There are three main areas that we see the World Wide Web technology having an impact. In order of how soon we expect them to be widely adopted, they are publishing static information, data warehouse interfaces, and application logic interfaces.

Publishing Static Information

This is where the World Wide Web is today. Thousands of companies that aren't even involved in any kind of high-tech business have seen the benefits of creating web sites in which they can advertise their products and services. Numerous different search engines have been developed that allow a user to find just about anything they want, anywhere on the web, through the means of a simple query. In addition to publishing material for external consumption, many companies have also created internal web sites (deemed "intranets") as an efficient way to distribute information to employees. Hewlett-Packard provides many such internal web sites; employees can "visit" HP Labs to see research papers, see what classes are being offered by training departments, look up benefits information, or gain on-line access to specifications and documentation for many different products. HP's external web servers provide access to data sheets, white papers, training schedules, press releases, and many other items. (Visit http://www.hp.com and http://jazz.external.hp.com to see for yourself.)

Data Warehouse Interfaces

We think one of the next big areas for the use of WWW technology will be on intranets for access to decision support information, in particular access to data warehouses. Our reason for putting this ahead of other uses, such as for business transactions, isn't because there is more demand for this than for more commerce-oriented applications, but rather because this use is internal, and thus less of a security concern, and it is less performance-critical. There is much to be learned about performance of WWW-based applications; right now suffice it to say that there is certainly cause for concern. The capabilities that have been built into today's web browsers and their accompanying search engines are very well suited to the kind of information retrieval and display that is needed in decision support applications.

Application Logic Interfaces

The next area for the Web to expand into is creating an alternate front-end for transaction processing applications. Some of these may appear only for internal users, but the more interesting concept is the idea of allowing customers direct access into your systems (in a controlled fashion, of course) to order merchandise or get other information. As an example, FedEx (http://www.fedex.com) has a web site at which you can enter a tracking number for a package you have sent, and immediately see the current location of the shipment. Services like these will help build customer preference for those companies with active participation on the web, in much the same way that a bank would find it hard to compete today if it could not offer ATM access to customer's accounts.

Adding Threads to the Architecture

Another technology that will find its way into more mainstream application is the technique of multi-threaded programming. Currently, this capability is used most often by database management systems and some messaging middleware products. Threads are sometimes referred to as "lightweight processes," lightweight meaning that the creation and execution of a thread is less resource intensive than creating a process via traditional interfaces to perform the same task. Threads are best explained by way of example, so we'll consider how our messaging module might be enhanced through the use of multi-threaded programming.

A thread is a process which is running the same program as its creator—in this way it resembles the POSIX fork() mechanism. However, when a thread is created, it begins execution with a function specified in the call that creates it. So if our monitor program is listening to a socket, and sees a connection request come in, it could create a thread to handle the connection, and have that thread begin execution with the accept_connection() routine. We now have the original thread—the main program—continuing to monitor for incoming messages, while this new thread handles the connection just received. The new thread may perform this one task and then die, but we would probably choose to have it continue to process all message traffic from the connection it established, terminating only after the client closes the connection.

Threads communicate with each other through a variety of specialized interprocess communication mechanisms, including mutexes (mutual exclusions, which are essentially semaphores) and condition variables, which are shared variables on which one or more threads can wait until another thread has placed a value in them. These constitute a fairly robust data sharing mechanism so that the various threads can cooperatively handle tasks of considerable complexity.

Threads are an excellent tool for allowing tasks to happen in parallel, improving throughput significantly over non-threaded implementations. Consider a complex transaction in which three different databases must be updated on a single system. In a non-threaded implementation, these updates would most likely happen sequentially. With threads, we can create one thread for each database and have the updates happen in parallel. Each thread would complete its update and signal the completion back to the originating thread. The threads would then wait for the next transaction affecting their database. The threads could also be created on a table (or dataset) level, providing parallel updates of tables within a single database. This capability has been implemented by a number of relational database vendors.

Understanding the overhead involved in thread creation relative to the task to be performed by the thread is a critical factor in optimizing performance of threaded applications. The best design is to not create threads to perform a single task and die, but rather to create a pool of specialized processors that will handle a number of different requests during the life of the thread.

Threads are available for the MPE/iX Operating System beginning with release 5.0, as part of the Distributed Computing Environment, although they can be used independently of other DCE components.

PART 5

Technologies for the System Administrator

CHAPTER 26

Yet Another History Lesson

In previous sections of the book, we've looked back in time at both the computing world and the "real world" over the past thirty or so years. For the remainder of the book, we'll be looking into networks and other technologies of concern to system administrators. These topics also have a rich history from which we can learn much.

It seems that anytime you get some Information Systems professionals together, as likely as not they will try to outdo each other in the competition for Old Computer Geezer. You know, conversations that go something like this:

> *"When I started, we had to type everything in on punched cards. And there was no typewritten text on these cards, either—if you wanted to know what was on the card, you better be able to read Hollerith code."*
>
> *"Gee, we didn't even get to get near the keypunch. We had to write everything longhand on coding sheets, and send them to the keypunch department."*
>
> *"You guys had it lucky. When I started, we toggled everything in directly from the front panel. None of these fancy mnemonics; it was just ones and zeroes"*
>
> *"You had ONES?"*

Yes, those were the days. While there isn't much that we miss about the mainframe era, we find that computer rooms today just aren't as impressive as they were in the midst of the mainframe era. Something about 20 or more tape drives in a row, jerking spasmodically in the background while the front panels of the mainframe created hypnotic patterns from hundreds of small status lights. The sounds of the card reader rifling through cards, and the chain printer alternately hammering away and throwing out reams of paper. Whether you knew what the various pieces and parts were all about or not, it was obvious that Something Important was going on here. Today, an equivalently powered system can sit unobtrusively in a single cabinet in the corner of your office. Getting here from there wasn't just a matter of miniaturization; the desktop or minicomputer system of today isn't just a tiny mainframe. Many changes have taken place, but none has as much impact as the emergence of the network, and the new computing models that it brought about.

Mainframe Environments

For most people who work in the IS industry, the term "mainframe" calls up images of a single large, multi-million dollar computer, probably based on a thirty year old architecture from a large vendor such as IBM. Today, most IS managers will boast that they are moving toward the use of less expensive computer platforms, including PCs, UNIX machines like the HP 9000 and RISC minicomputers such as the HP 3000. These changes are typically made in the name of cutting costs (which is probably true) and modernizing their IS environment. These IS managers are often surprised to learn that in spite of the fact that they've taken out their mainframe hardware, they are still running "mainframe environments."

The key characteristic which differentiates mainframe environments from other computer environments has nothing to do with what kind of hardware you're using. The distinguishing feature of a mainframe environment is centralization. If all processing takes place on a single computer, then the term "mainframe" applies to it. It doesn't matter whether the nameplate on the front reads IBM ES-9000, HP 3000, HP 9000, or HP NetServer. With apologies to Jeff Foxworthy, if the devices attached to your computer are "dumb" devices: (card readers, tape drives, disk drives, and terminals), then "it just might be a mainframe."

The centralization of mainframe computing hardware is frequently duplicated in the organization of the department running it. Just as no mainframe computer hardware is distributed outside the "glass house," neither is any computer access available outside its walls without the express say-so of the IS department. For batch applications, users submit work by physically bringing the work to be processed to a service desk adjoining the computer room; the work is logged in and scheduled for execution. After it is run, the output is placed in bins for collection by the users.

In mainframe environments, networks are nearly unheard of; first of all, because most companies had only a single mainframe, so what would you connect it to? Secondly, much mainframe processing was geared toward media that were easily transportable: magnetic tapes and card decks could be moved from one system to another far easier than a networked program could be created to transfer the data. Even disk-based data was typically stored on removable disk packs, so transferring data between systems was a simple matter of relocating the pack into a drive attached to the target system. This model is still in use for processing batch work at many mainframe installations.

Distributed Peripherals

The first use of networks to appear in the mainframe environment was not in system-to-system communications, but rather in allowing peripherals to be located outside the data center. By placing card readers or printers closer to the end-users, those users could submit their own jobs for processing and receive their output at a more convenient location. As the transition from batch to on-line systems progressed, terminals appeared throughout the organization, again providing input and output capabilities conveniently near the user, while maintaining all processing resources inside the confines of the computer room.

Introduction of the Minicomputer

When minicomputers first began to be installed in the early 1970s, they were hardly a threat to the mainframe environment. The capabilities of these new systems were quite modest in comparison to the mainframe systems, and were most likely to be deployed within a department of a large corporation. There, they were sometimes used to automate tasks that had never been computerized before, because a mainframe-based solution would have been too expensive. Or they were used for applications that had previously been handled on the mainframe but which represented a small portion of the total mainframe's workload. By putting them on their own smaller computer, they were able to avoid costly mainframe hardware upgrades.

The success shown by these companies in performing useful work on systems much smaller than the traditional mainframe led to widespread adoption of minicomputers by companies that had never before had a computer, being locked out of the mainframe era by the high cost of establishing a data center. These new adoptees had either been running their businesses on manual systems, or using a service bureau that provided either batch-only or timeshare access to a mainframe system that would be shared by a large number of smaller companies.

With minicomputer systems now deployed in companies along with mainframes—sometimes even sharing the hallowed ground of the data center—a leap forward is expected. Co-operative processing, data flowing freely between minis and mainframes; the ability to use each system for the tasks for which it is best suited: these things must be just around the corner. Of course, we know this wasn't the case. There were many barriers between these systems; some were organizational, but more than a few were technical. Chief among these was the lack of standard networking technologies that were supported by both types of systems.

Networks

As the cost of computing dropped, it became commonplace for a company to have more than one computer. Consequently, hardware vendors began to address the area of networking. At first, they focused on networking between the computers that they themselves manufactured; not between different brands of computers. A number of proprietary network protocols were marketed and widely used. IBM developed the SNA architecture for communications between IBM systems; HP developed the DS (later NS) architecture for communications between HP systems, and so forth.

At the same time, the US Government began to fund a project for hooking all sorts of computers together with something called TCP/IP, but because these weren't commercial computers, there wasn't much initial interest from the major players in the computer industry. Eventually, customer demand forced computer companies to begin to address multi-vendor networking issues and vendors realized that they would be shut out if they couldn't meet the customer's requirements for interoperability.

The first products to address these requirements were based on the proprietary networking protocols that were already in place. For example, when HP wanted to provide HP 3000 customers with the ability to network one of their MPE computers with an IBM machine, they designed networking products that would emulate a piece of IBM gear. HP, along with DEC, Data General and many other vendors, implemented an alphabet soup of products based on proprietary IBM networking protocols including RJE, NRJE, DHCF, IMF, and LU6.2. In the very early days of multivendor networking, these proprietary protocols acted as defacto standards. For example, some customers built networks between their HP computers and their DEC computers by having *both* machines masquerade as

IBM computers. This solution, although workable, was cumbersome and expensive. Better solutions were needed.

Standards organizations eventually got into the act, and the OSI (Open Systems Interconnect) standard for networking was born. OSI was the first major networking protocol that wasn't owned by an individual hardware vendor. The specification had been agreed to by all the major players, who agreed that OSI would be the future of networking, and would serve as the basis for all their multivendor network interoperability. Soon, OSI networking products began to appear in the marketplace for a wide variety of machines, including the HP 3000.

At the same time, research into TCP/IP was proceeding in parallel with and independent of the OSI committees. Before OSI networking had really gained a firm foothold in the commercial marketplace, TCP/IP had become the basis for a working multivendor heterogeneous network called the Internet.

Today, OSI networking is little more than a footnote in the history of heterogeneous networks. HP recently removed the HP 3000's OSI networking products from the corporate price list. The future of heterogeneous networking seems to be based entirely on TCP/IP.

The PC Revolution

Personal Computers, like the minicomputers, entered the corporate world as standalone "islands of automation" that weren't connected to the organizations' other Information Technology resources. Indeed, it was quite common for a middle manager to receive a printed report from the mainframe or minicomputer, and then key in data from that report to a spreadsheet on the PC for analysis. Then, they might start another program and re-key the same data into a graphics program to create a few presentation slides. Like the minicomputers that preceded them, PCs did not gain interoperability with the other IT systems until they had gained wide acceptance in a large number of organizations.

In part one of this book, we saw that the PC "revolution" was really a stealth operation; these systems snuck in the back door and quietly took their place alongside the dumb terminals used to access the mainframes and minicomputers. The first step at integrating these systems into the corporate IT infrastructure usually was the additional of terminal emulation software, allowing the user to reclaim valuable desk space by moving the functionality of the terminal into the PC and eliminating the terminal. The physical connection to the host system remained a serial connection, in most cases; there wasn't yet any reason to upgrade the connection speed.

It wasn't long before terminal emulators added an additional capability: the ability to download a file from the mainframe or minicomputer to the PC. This capability freed the user from the task of re-entering data from mainframe reports into PC based programs. It did create a large demand on the corporate IT department for various extractions and filtering of the corporate databases. Products such as Information Access were born, to give the end users a greater degree of self-sufficiency in getting the data they needed from the host systems.

Evolution of the Network.

As the types of devices connected to a network evolved, from peripherals attached to a single host to the heterogeneous mixture of clients, servers, and peripherals we have today, the network had to evolve as well. Early HP 3000 systems supported DS networks with serial connection speeds of up to 56K baud. (This was for a dedicated system-to-system link. Today, we want speeds faster than this for our dial-up access.) Network speeds grew to 10 megabits per second, and now to 100 megabits per second. Software demands grow just as fast, if not faster. For every new networking breakthrough that comes along, there is a software need for which the network just isn't fast enough.

The Wide Area Network

Wide Area Networks use technologies such as X.25, Frame Relay, ISDN and ATM to provide communications between widely distributed systems. With a local area network, or LAN, you typically own all of the pieces involved: the computers, cabling, routers, and other components that comprise the network. All of these pieces generally reside within the same building, or if not, within a small geographic area such as a corporate campus. With Wide Area Networks, the sites being connected are likely to be widely dispersed, perhaps even globally. You are more likely to depend on an outside provider, typically a phone company, to provide most of the pieces required, although private wide area networks do exist.

The X.25 network is based on the standards recommended by CCITT (Consultative Committee on International Telephony and Telegraphy). X.25 networks may be either a Private Packet Network (PPN) or a Public Data Network (PDN). Network diagrams usually represent X.25 networks as devices attached to a "cloud". The cloud represents the various switching and routing equipment, usually not owned by the company using the connection, which delivers packets between the various connected devices. In the PPN implementations of X.25, an X.25 switch is maintained at a local facility. The switch handles the configuration and control of the network. Configuration includes such items as line speed, line type, and whether the circuits will be switched or permanent. The configuration also provides information about the devices attached to the "cloud"; for example, identifying the use of an X.25 PAD (Packet Assembler/Dissembler) for remote printing and terminal sessions. By today's standards, X. 25 networks are slow, having a typical speed of 64 Kbps. However, they provide a very reliable connection due to the fact that error correction takes place at multiple levels within the OSI protocol stack.

X.25 networks provide multiple paths between the various attached devices, minimizing the effect of outages of specific hardware or network links. By contrast, inn a Point to Point configuration we have one system attached to another system via modem or other serial communications equipment. Unless you have an alternate route then when that one link goes down for whatever reason, the network is down. A positive feature of the Point to Point link is that this kind of link is generally easier to configure, since we don't have to specify many of the additional parameters one would find in an X.25 environment.

Today we are seeing other types of connections become more popular. ISDN or Integrated Services Digital Network is a circuit switching network. ISDN allows LAN technology to be extended across greater distances than supported by traditional LANs. ISDN can thus be used to "bridge" LANs at two different facilities, allowing workers at two sites to function as if they were all connected to the same LAN, for example. ISDN is also a popular technology with telecommuters, allowing a connection from home into the company LAN with performance comparable to what is available at your cubicle.

Internet technologies such as the World Wide Web can consume a lot of bandwidth, making typical dial up connections of 14.4K or 28.8K seem sluggish. ISDN links are therefore popular among web surfers, since they provide sufficient throughput for the large data transfers needed for graphics-rich interfaces.

In addition to ISDN, other types of Wide Area Network connections that are available in the USA include 56K and T1 connections. In Europe, the standards are different, and include 64K, 128K, 256K and so forth. 56K lines operate at a speed of 56K bits per second, and may be either leased line or switched. A leased line is a permanent connection between two points, while the switched line establishes a connection only when needed, reducing the cost. T1 lines provide 1.544 Megabits per second, which is broken down in 24 separate channels of 56K bits per second each multiplexed onto the single carrier line. Users not needed the full capability of a T1 line can lease a Fractional T1 line, using one or more of these 56K channels.

We are rapidly moving toward higher bandwidth Wide Area Networking protocols such as ATM and Frame Relay. With the need to provide video, audio and data over the same network, the speed of an X.25 network is no longer sufficient. We will cover ATM and Frame Relay technologies in Chapter 28.

The Client/Server Model and the Network

The latest trend affecting system administrators is the deployment of client/server solutions. In today's business environment the need to share more and more information requires that the user have fast access to a vast array of corporate data on demand. This new model of computing has placed new demands on the network, on the client systems, and on the servers. The impact of these changes, on the systems and on the people who administer them, will be examined in the next chapter.

CHAPTER 27

The Client/Server Environment

How client/server computing emerged has been the subject of many, often conflicting, stories. Whether it was a natural evolution of distributed computing between mainframes and minicomputers, or a technology in search of a problem to solve, is debatable. One thing it certainly was not was an answer to the "problem" of 'idle MIPS on the desktop.' If you were around for the early days of client/server, you no doubt heard this explanation, just as we did. Yet we never found anyone bothered by the concept of idle MIPS, on the desktop or anywhere else. It was a salesman's rationalization, to be used in the absence of any real ability to justify the technology they were proposing.

Now that the benefits of client/server computing are more generally understood, we have no need for this or other rationalizations. Yes, client/server can offload some processing from the server. But client/server solutions are far more processor-intensive than host-terminal applications. They will typically go far beyond consuming any excess capacity of desktop PCs: if you aren't on at least fast 486-based systems, deployment of client/server applications will probably force you to upgrade your desktop systems. Client/Server is not about offloading the server, but about doing things you simply couldn't have done on the server. Graphical User Interfaces, computationally intensive what-if and statistical analysis, pulling data from different sources to synthesize new insights into business problems: these are the types of things that client/server technology enables.

Some of the advantages to client/server computing are:

- The ability to provide a consistent, integrated front-end interface to the user, even though applications may be running across a heterogeneous mixture of hardware platforms, operating systems, and databases.
- Flexibility in choosing different servers for different applications or databases, and different clients for different user requirements, while still providing all necessary access from the different clients into the different servers.
- The modular design provides growth through plugging in additional components, rather than constantly upgrading a single monolithic system. This growth path can be less expensive (once the infrastructure exists) and also is more resistant to single points of failure.

Some of the disadvantages of client/server computing are

- Security, Backup and Recovery, Software Distribution and other system administration tasks are more complex.
- Problems are sometimes more difficult to diagnose (is it the application, the client system, the server system, or the network?)
- Client/Server configurations will have more parts, most likely from a number of vendors: networking hardware and software, middleware, databases, etc. The developer is forced into the role of "system integrator" to make sure all the pieces work together as needed.

The goal of most client/server environments is to provide the user with a single system image. Just as timesharing systems presented the user with the illusion that they had the resources of an entire system at their disposal, client/server gives the user the illusion of having all the resources of the configuration—servers, databases, applications—at their fingertips.

On a single system, tasks are often performed by several processes operating cooperatively. InterProcess Communication (IPC) mechanisms, such as message files or the AIF:Ports facility on the HP 3000, are used by these processes to share data and to coordinate flow of control and access to resources. For a client/server environment, we need an InterProcess communication facility that can operate over a network, and between dissimilar systems. The primary types of IPC mechanisms used in client/server environments include messaging, remote procedure call, and distributed SQL. Each of these was covered in Chapter 14. Different types of tools are appropriate in different situations, and you may find that your needs are best served by using a combination, rather than standardizing on a single InterProcess communication model for all your client/server needs.

Multi-tiered Computing

The different possible architectures in the client/server environment are sometimes distinguished by the number of distinct layers, or tiers, between application components. Tiers primarily denote distinctions between software layers. Physical distribution of the application across different systems can occur wherever there is a tier boundary. So, a three-tier architecture may reside on a single system, on two systems (a client and a server), or on three systems (a client, an application server, and a database server). A single-tier application is one which has no convenient place to separate it into a client/server configuration. This suggests that it cannot be distributed, but the reality is that a lot of middleware tools provide some capability to distribute applications that were not originally designed to be distributed.

The two tiered architecture usually describes a configuration in which the server provides database management functions only, with the user interface and application logic residing on the client. In such a configuration, communication between the client and the server is typically done via an IPC mechanism based on SQL syntax. All of the major database vendors have proprietary implementations of cross-system IPC tools that can be used for this purpose. The Microsoft ODBC protocol is perhaps the most popular mechanism for this type of communication.

In three-tiered architectures, the requests initiated by the client are not for database access, as with the two-tier model, but for business transactions. This means that part or all of the transaction logic is located on the servers. The application logic on the server will then issue the required database calls, which represent the boundary between the second and third tiers. Remember that this boundary may or may not represent an additional hardware layer; databases may be on the application server, or on a separate database server in the three-tier model.

Middleware

Middleware is a layer of software that supports multiple protocols, languages or platforms. In layered software architectures such as we have previously designed, middleware is the isolation layer that is used to make requesters of services independent from the providers or those services. In our architectural design, we built our own middleware in most places where an isolation layer was desired. Most IT departments will buy, rather than build, the middleware technology that they need.

Middleware includes application programming interfaces (APIs), global naming services, security services, system and network management tools, network transport interfaces and application development tools. Some examples of middleware include OSF DCE, ODBC, Microsoft's DDE (Dynamic Data Exchange) and OLE (Object Linking and Embedding) technologies. Middleware provides a consistent API across platforms, isolating the programmer from the specific components below the middleware layer. It thus helps to keep application code independent of platforms, network protocols and operating systems.

The World Wide Web In the Client/Server Environment

The Internet is fast becoming a major part of many client/server environments. Let's begin with a little of the history behind the Internet and then see how it fits into your computing model today.

The Internet was begun by the U.S. Department of Defense in the early 1970's as a network that connected military and research sites. A project of the Advanced Research Projects Agency (ARPA), the ARPAnet (as it was originally named) was designed to allow wide geographic distribution of computer systems to provide greater survivability in case of nuclear attack. The original development revolved around allowing computers of different types to be able to communicate together. In the late 1980s the National Science Foundation (NSF) expanded on ARPAs work with its own network known as the NSFnet. Their goal was to allow their supercomputers to work together, increasing their collective power.

The commercial use began very shortly after this time. While individual use of the Internet through service providers such as CompuServe, Prodigy, and America Online is rapidly growing, the fastest growing segment of Internet users is business. The current overall growth rate of the Internet is estimated at around ten percent a month. With over 30 million people using it to send email worldwide, this is one very large post office! Although the United States has by far the largest host distribution on the Internet, this network does span the globe. This has lead to the name World Wide Web being used to collectively refer to a number of services available over the Internet, but in particular the transmission of hyperlink-enabled documents that are read by Web browsers such as Netscape.

Today many companies are using the Internet for a number of purposes. The widest use of the Internet remains as a mail service. Another wide usage is for file transfers. These services are widely used to transmit data between companies, for example, allowing distributors and suppliers to communicate with each other. They are also widely used for intra-company communication, freeing companies from the need to maintain their own networks. By using the Internet rather than a private network, companies don't have to be responsible for the maintenance and repair of their backbone. They pay a fee only for their actual usage. While there are still many Private Packet Networks that utilize protocols such as X.25, the Internet is fast becoming the network of choice. The Internet has allowed global boundaries to virtually disappear when it comes to communication. In our own organization, we frequently find it more convenient to communicate with our coworkers around the globe by email rather than by phone. With time differences, varying quality of phone service in different countries, and the growing use of telecommuting and alternate work schedules, email becomes the easiest and most reliable form of communication.

Like all the other technologies we have to deal with, the Internet and the World Wide Web have introduced new terminology into our jobs. We've briefly define some of the terms you'll hear thrown about in discussions about the Internet.

The **World Wide Web** is sometimes used as a synonym for the Internet itself, but more commonly refers to the graphical information transmitted in **html** format over the Internet from **http** servers to **web browsers** running on client systems.

HTML is HyperText Markup Language, a format for specifying the appearance and behavior of documents transmitted over the web. HTML is platform independent. Thus, for example, you can specify that text should be bold, or italicized, but the selection of the specific font to be used is left up to the client. The most notable feature of HTML is the ability to embed hypertext links to other documents. These links are associated with a **URL** that points to another document (or to a different location within the same document). The link shows up to the user as highlighted text; if they are interested in the topic, clicking on the text takes them to the document identified by the URL.

HTTP is the HyperText Transfer Protocol. The World Wide Web supports several different transfer protocols for transmitting different types of information. For example, FTP is the protocol for file transfers. GOPHER is a protocol for some text transfers. HTTP is the protocol used for the transmission of HTML format documents.

Web Browsers are programs that are run on a client system, such as a PC or Workstation, to view information retrieved from various web servers. Web browsers are generally capable of supporting a number of different protocols such as ftp, gopher, news, and http, allowing access to information stored in many different formats at different locations. Because of its graphical nature, http is the dominant format in which you will find information. However, http is a static format; new formats and capabilities are now emerging which allow users to incorporate animation and other features. These will probably dominate the web in the future.

URL is a Uniform Resource Locator. URLs are addresses that identify the various resources on the web. They are in a format such as:

http: //www.hp.com

The portion before the colon, in this case http, identifies that protocol that should be used. The two slashes are used to preface a system name. In this case, the system we want to access is `www.hp.com`. Naming conventions are fairly consistent for system names, in general, by substituting the name of any company for "hp" in the above string, you would have the most likely address for that company's primary web site. Non-profit organizations will use `org` instead of `com`, e.g., `www.interex.org`. The system name may optionally be followed by path information that identifies a specific "web page" you want to access it. By omitting it, you come in at the highest level, or "home page," as determined by the web administrators of the system.

The Network

When networks were used primarily to move files between systems, the performance of the network didn't have much of a direct impact on the primary work being done on the system. In a client/server configuration, network performance is a critical component of overall application performance, that has to be evaluated along with CPU, disk, and memory as a potential bottleneck.

Network speeds have increased dramatically in response to increasing demands for improved throughput. The earliest serial networks provided speeds of up to 19.2 Kilobytes per second. LAN technologies in wide use today provide 10 Megabit to 100 Megabit per second transmission speeds, while technologies to be delivered in the near future will increase this to even higher speeds. On the horizon are technologies that promise speeds greater than 2.5 Gigabytes per second. New middleware and other technologies to permit distribution of workloads are lending credence to the statement "The Network Is the Computer"; such networks can serve as the virtual backplane of the computer of the future. Various components to provide processing power, data storage, and input and output services can be plugged into the network to create distributed computer systems that can grow to arbitrarily large capacities far in excess of the capabilities of any single supercomputer.

These high-speed networking capabilities have also enabled new breakthrough capabilities in high availability and disaster tolerance. In the past if a CPU failed, information processing came to a screeching halt. This halt would last as long as it took to repair the hardware, bring up the system, restore data to a consistent state, perhaps reapply logged transactions, and bring the application back online. Not only did this cost in lost productivity, but in user confidence as well. With products such as SharePlex/iX, processing can continue on a shadowed standby system after only a slight delay to the user after a system failure. The time for the application to switch can be less than a minute in some environments.

Because the network has become so important in support of client/server configurations and as an enabling technology for high availability solutions, we will look at network technology in considerably more detail in the following chapter.

CHAPTER 28

The Network

In this chapter we would like to provide the system administrator with the information necessary to plan and implement a networked system environment. We will cover technologies that are widely available today, as well as some of the technologies becoming available now that will be a major component of the network infrastructure you are likely to use in the near future.

The emergence of distributed computing and client/server is increasing the demands placed on corporate networks. Many networks grow ad-hoc with nodes being added haphazardly, and cables strung wherever needed, without any real planning. Without proper planning, maintenance can be a challenge, and the ability to grow the network may be severely constrained. Like all other aspects of an Information Technology strategy, the network design requires careful planning. The first step in planning your overall network design is the selection of a topology and transmission medium. Proper choices here will make your network easily extensible to meet future demands, while poor choices will leave you faced with the need to re-wire and re-implement large portions of your network should it grow beyond your original design.

Network Topology

The network topology refers to the way in which the various nodes (systems, terminals, printers, etc.) are connected to each other. One of the most common topologies is the star, as shown in Figure 28.1. In a star topology, there is a central point of control for the entire network, such as a single server system, or an X.25 switch. An advantage of this configuration is ease of administration, since it is all done through this central point of control. The disadvantage is that the central control point becomes a single point of failure that disables the entire network when it is down.

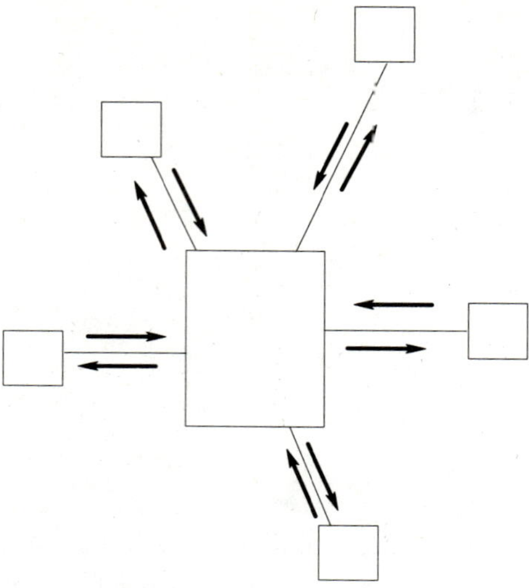

Figure 28.1 Star Topology

The Bus or Tree topology (see Figure 28.2) is another simple and widely used topology. The individual nodes attach at different points on the "backbone." This lends itself to ease of expansion but also requires more network administration since some configuration of each node is controlled from each individual node.

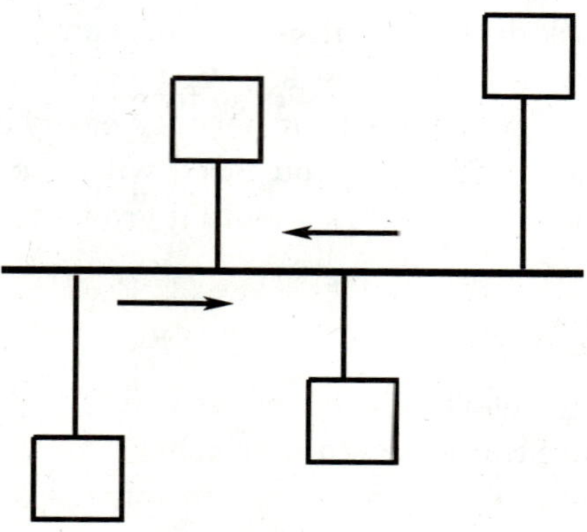

Figure 28.2 Bus or Tree Topology

A third topology is the ring (see Figure 28.3). This topology is a series of end to end links that combine to make up a closed loop. Each node forwards the packets that do not match their address. One disadvantage to this is if any node goes down, the network traffic flow will be interrupted since the down node will not be able to forward packets.

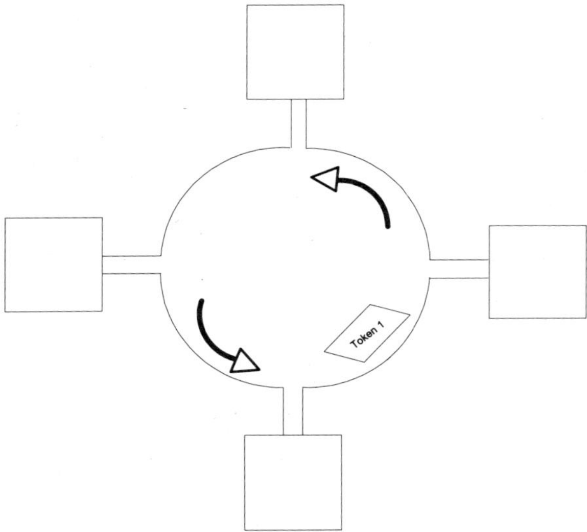

Figure 28.3 Ring Topology

Determining what protocol and transmission medium to use requires proper planning as well. The protocol establishes the format of the packet as well as the speed at which it will travel through the network. The transmission medium is the physical cabling through which packets flow. Usually the terms protocol and transmission are considered as synonymous, but they are different aspects of the network. The protocols and transmission media that we would like to cover in this section include 802.3/Ethernet (including ThinLAN, ThickLAN and EtherTwist), 802.5/TokenRing, FDDI (Fiber Distributed Data Interface) and 100VGAnylan. We will also touch on ATM, Frame Relay, ISDN and FibreChannel. Before covering the specific protocols and media, we've develop a foundation of basic network knowledge.

The OSI Network Model

Probably one of the most well known pictures in networking is the seven layer OSI (Open Systems Inconnection) model (see Figure 28.4). Each layer in the model has a well-defined set of responsibilities. Levels one through three (the physical, data link, and network layers) are sometimes referred to as the low-level protocols, whereas levels four through seven (the transport, session, presentation, and application layers) are referred to as high-level protocols.

The physical layer provides information regarding the physical interface between devices as well as the rules governing the passing of bits from one device to another. The four characteristics of the physical layer are Mechanical, Electrical, Functional and Procedural. The Mechanical characteristics describe the connector itself, for example, the popular 25-pin DB25 connector used for many RS232 connections. The Electrical characteristics define voltages, resistance, and other attributes of the connection. The Functional characteristics specify the use of each pin in the connector. For example, Pin 2 is Transmit, Pin 3 is Receive, and Pin 7 is Ground in the DB25 connector. The Procedural characteristics define the sequence of events that will be used; what signals are used in what order to control the communication flow over the connection.

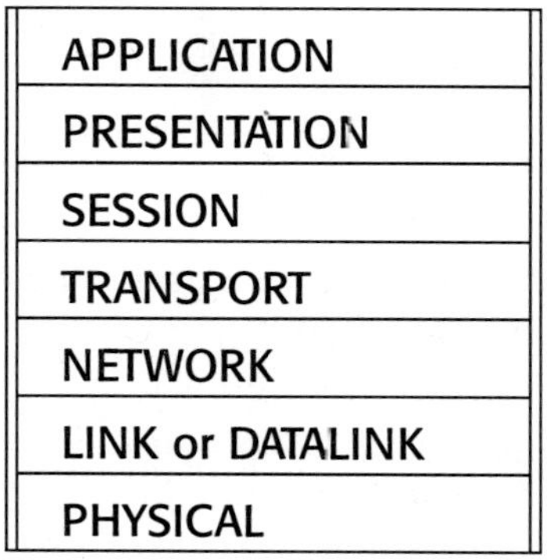

APPLICATION
PRESENTATION
SESSION
TRANSPORT
NETWORK
LINK or DATALINK
PHYSICAL

Figure 28.4 OSI 7-layer model

The Data Link layer is there to help the physical layer be more reliable by providing the means to activate, maintain and deactivate the link. The function of the data link layer is to build frames. Some frames, such as link control frames, are used to control the connection and do not contain data. The Data Link layer will build a data frame for each outgoing packet (and isolate and remove data frames from the incoming bit stream). In addition to the data itself, the data link layer generally adds sequencing, flow control, and quality of service parameters to the frame, although there are exceptions. For example, Ethernet, 802.2 LANs and FDDI Networks don't work this way, but X.25 networks do. The synchronization of the data transmission and handling of frame-level error checking and recovery are performed at this layer

The Network layer covers the communication between systems across the network, and also provides some of the information needed for the Transport layer. The network layer determines how the packets or frames are forwarded between stations. Congestion control information is also provided at this layer. The network addresses, connections and endpoint identifiers are some of the services provided at the Network layer. This is where the IP or Internet Protocol portion of TCP/IP protocol operates.

Layer four, the Transport layer, provides the mechanism to exchange data between processes on different systems. This layer is where error detection and recovery are performed. This layer verifies that packets are delivered in the order in which they were sent. In addition, establishment and release of the transport connection, and flow control on individual connections, are provided by the Transport layer. This layer may also use the congestion control information provided by the network layer.

The Session Layer, the fifth layer, controls the establishment and use of a connection between presentation entities, such as TELNET. The session layer may also provide services such as recovery, a checkpoint for failures, and specification of the dialogue type to be either one way or two way

The Presentation layer or layer six provides application programs and terminal handler programs with a set of data transformation services such as data translation, formatting and syntax selection. Compression and encryption are just a couple of examples of the formatting that can take place at this level.

The Application layer (layer seven) is where protocols such as LU6.2 or APPC (Advanced Peer-to Peer Communication) takes place. File Transfer Protocol, email and other session-enabled applications perform their functions here. For instance, File Transfer Protocol (ftp) allows hosts of different types to communicate at a high level, with all of the machine-dependent translations handled in lower layers of the stack.

Transmission Media and Protocols

802.3/Ethernet

Many people use the terms "Ethernet" and "IEEE 802.3" interchangably. In fact, 802.3 is a subset of Ethernet, but they are close enough that many people treat them as if they were the same. Since the HP 3000 and HP 9000 class equipment comes with the 802.3/Ethernet interface integrated, we would like to begin with it. This network link uses one of three cable types: ThinLan (50 ohm thin coaxial), ThickLan (75 ohm thick coaxial) or EtherTwist (unshielded twisted-pair). See Table 28.1 for specifications for each cable type.

Table 28.1 Cable Specifications for various 802.3/Ethernet Media

	ThinLan	ThickLan	EtherTwist
IEEE Cable Specification	10Base2	10Base5	10BaseT
Maximum Segment Length	185 meters	500 meters	100 meters (hub to node)
Minimum distance between nodes	0.5 meters	2.5 meters	N/A
Maximum nodes per segment	30	100	N/A
Maximum AUI cable length	50 meters	50 meters	50 meters

ThinLan is a very good fit for installations that are confined to a small area. ThickLan is generally used in a "backbone" configuration where greater distances between nodes in needed. EtherTwist has become the most popular medium in the business environment. PC networks that are dispersed in work areas on different floors of an office building are a good example of where EtherTwist is heavily used.

The IEEE 802 specification was defined by the Institute of Electrical and Electronics Engineers. It uses three layers to redefine the lower two layers of the OSI model. These layers are the Physical, Medium Access Control, and Logical Link Control layers. The physical layer provides the functions of encoding and decoding of signals, bit transmission and reception, and preamble generation and removal (the latter is used for traffic synchronization). The Medium Access Control (MAC) layer provides the management of communication over the link. The Logical Link Control (LLC) layer provides the service access points and assembles the data into a frame.

The IEEE 802 specification allows for three different Medium Access Control (MAC) techniques: Round-Robin, Reservation and Contention. These specify not only how access to the media is controlled, but also whether that control is centralized or distributed. In a centralized scheme a controller has to grant access to any station wishing to use the network. In the distributed method the stations dynamically determine the order. HP 3000 and HP 9000 implementations of IEEE 802 use the contention technique for Medium Access Control.

802.5/Token Ring

The 802.5, or Token Ring, protocol is widely used in IBM networks. Both the HP 3000 and the HP 9000 provide support for IEEE 802.5. This provides full interoperability with IBM Token-Ring networks. Token Ring supports four or sixteen mbps (mega-bit per second) transfer rates (see Table 28.2 for supported IBM cable types). In addition to Token Ring, there are other access methods in use in some ring configurations, such as register insertion and slotted ring. However, these methods are not nearly as widely used, and will not be covered in any detail here.

The Token is IEEE 802 standard for ring control and the oldest ring control technique. This technique, also known as the Newhall Ring, uses a small token frame that circulates around the ring. When the network is idle the token frame has a bit pattern indicating a "free" token. When a node needs to access the network it must wait until a token passes by. It then changes the free pattern to a pattern indicating a "busy" token. The node would then transmit its frame immediately behind the "busy" token. Since there is no "free" token on the network at the time no other node can transmit. The node that transmitted will wait until it receives the busy token back signifying the completion of its transmission. It will then change the busy back to a "free" token and put it back out on the network.

Table 28.2 Supported Cable Types for 802.5 (Token Ring) Connections

Data Grade	AWG	Type
Type 1	22	2-wire shielded twisted pair
Type 2	22	2-wire shielded or 4-wire unshielded twisted pair
Type 3	22, 24	twisted pair unshielded
Type 4	26	2 wire shielded twisted pair
Type 9	26	2 wire shielded twisted pair

AWG = American Wire Gauge

For 16mpbs transmission speeds, only shielded cable types are supported

Fiber Distributed Data Interface (FDDI)

FDDI offers an industry standard (ANSI compliant) solution for the system that needs a flexible, robust, high-performance network. FDDI is a great fit for a LAN backbone because of its high capacity and fault tolerance. FDDI offers 100 mbps transmission speeds with a maximum length of 2 kilometers between stations, up to 500 stations per ring, and a 100 kilometer maximum ring circumference. An FDDI network is made up of two independent rings. The dual rings provide redundancy and the ability to re-configure the network in case of failure. Hewlett Packard's HP 3000 and HP 9000 both provide a Single Attach (SAS) connection through a concentrator, and the HP 9000 also provides a Dual Attach (DAS) interface capability. It is recommended that you use a concentrator equipped with an FDDI DAS card to allow for an FDDI redundant topology. Without the redundancy, if the cable or a node on the cable fails, the network will be inoperable until the breakage is repaired. Hewlett-Packard's FDDI interface card is certified by both ANTC and University of New Hampshire IOP.

100VGAnylan

While most LAN technologies today are limited to 10 megabit speeds, two new technologies boost lan speeds to 100 megabits. These technologies are 100BaseT and 100VGAnylan. 100BaseT is only compatible with the Ethernet protocol, while 100VGAnylan supports Ethernet as well as Token Ring protocols (although you cannot mix both protocols on the same network.) 100VGAnylan is a great way increase the bandwidth of an existing 802.3 Ethernet or 802.5 Token Ring network, and is HP's preferred technology for 100 megabit networks 100VGAnylan is based on the emerging IEEE 802.12 standard. Both Twisted Pair and Fiber-Optic cabling are supported as transmission media. If you are currently using cabling that meets the requirements for 10BaseT or Token Ring then you will not need to upgrade your cable infrastructure. 100VGAnylan utilizes all four pairs in a twisted pair cable.

There are several considerations that need to be taken in account in the design of a 100VGAnylan network. The physical topology must be a star, with no branches or loops. At the heart of the 100VGAnylan network is a 100VGAnylan hub. To have a supported network you must have one or more 100VGAnylan hubs and two or more 100VGAnylan end nodes. 100VGAnylan networks can be multi-level, or layered. One hub is designated the root hub. Attached to the root hub can be nodes, or additional hubs, which are considered level 1 hubs. Attached to the level 1 hubs can be nodes or level 2 hubs, and so on to a maximum of seven levels between the root and the nodes. The maximum distance between the root hub and the nodes is 6 kilometers in a 2 level network. Adding additional levels to the network will reduce this distance, down to as little as 500 meters in a 7 level network.

You can also have network devices such as routers, bridges and switches in this network. In a four pair Unshielded Twisted Pair network, all four pairs are needed. You can not have any flat cable in the cabling structure. You can only have one active path between any two hubs on the network. While you may have more than one path for redundancy, only one can be active at a time. There are no limitations as to the maximum number of nodes. However there is a finite number of nodes that will allow peak performance. Once that number is surpassed the performance of the network will suffer. You can not mix packet formats on the network. They must either be all 802.3 Ethernet or 802.5 Token Ring. You can not have any more that seven bridges between any two nodes on the network.

Asynchronous Transfer Mode (ATM)

Asynchronous Transfer Mode is a very high speed solution for both local and wide area networks. Deployed mostly as a backbone transmission medium, ATM provides 155 mbps speed over multi-mode fiber or UTP category 5 unshielded twisted pair wiring. ATM utilizes cell-switching technology to carry data and real-time voice and video packets. ATM may very well become the networking technology that will form the future infrastructure of the Internet as well as most corporate networks. Being able to use the same connection protocol between LAN and WAN systems is becoming more and more important. ATM is the first technology that can be used in both environments. While 802.3, 802.5 and FDDI require network equipment to attach to a wide area network, ATM can be used in both. ATM has been chosen as a key component of Broadband-ISDN wide area networks. By using cell-switching, ATM allows full bandwidth speed to every user. This allows users requiring a guaranteed amount of bandwidth, for example when transmitting video, to be given a fixed portion of the total available bandwidth. The small size of the cell greatly enhances its use in the transmission of video, voice and data traffic. ATM can support speeds ranging from 51 mbps up to 2.4 Gbps and greater.

FibreChannel

FibreChannel is a serial point to point channel between desktop workstations, mass storage subsystems, peripherals and host systems. The serial nature of the connection allows FibreChannel to extend 100 mbps transmission capabilities to distances that exceed those supported by any other network technologies available today. Unlike the previous transmission media we have discussed, FibreChannel is not only a network medium, it can also be used to attach peripherals, systems and other devices together and allow data to be transmitted at greater than standard network speeds.

FibreChannel is one way to open up the communications bottleneck caused by limited transmission speed of existing network protocols. There are many applications where FibreChannel can be used today. One use is as a communications link between systems that need to share large amounts of data quickly. Another use is to create a shared resource environment in which FibreChannel allows various mainframes, minicomputers, workstations and desktop PC's to communicate together in a large geographical environment. Another place for FibreChannel is in the area of data storage. Today applications such as document imaging create a need for large amounts of data to be stored in a central location, and a requirement to dramatically increase the speed of retrieval and storage of this data. FibreChannel allows users of clustered workstations to deploy new classes of data and communication intensive applications with a speed that before now could only be achieved by a super computer. Many applications today are running on fast processors at greater than 100MHz, yet spending much of their time waiting for data to be retrieved from other nodes on the network.

FibreChannel defines three different classes of service. Class One is a physical or circuit-switched connection. Class Two is a connectionless, frame switched link that provides guaranteed delivery with an acknowledgment of receipt. Class Three is a connectionless service that allows data to be sent rapidly to multiple attached devices without requiring an acknowledgment. An optional mode that is available is called intermix. This mode reserves the full FibreChannel bandwidth for a dedicated connection but also allows connectionless traffic to share the link if there is additional bandwidth available.

Topologies supported by FibreChannel are switch based, Point to Point, and Arbitrated Loop. Although the Arbitrated Loop is the least expensive to implement, it is constrained by severe distance limitations and having to share bandwidth. In the switched and point-to-point topologies, a node can have full bandwidth due to access being controlled by the switch. One thing to be cautioned of when deciding whether to use FibreChannel in place of a traditional network type connection is FiberChannel only performs a simple hardware-level error correction.

In TCP/IP networks, new nodes can be added somewhat arbitrarily, as long as their address does not conflict with nodes already on the network. FibreChannel requires that each node or device be defined to the system.

Frame Relay

Frame Relay is often called "fast X.25." Frame Relay transfers data at the Data Link layer, allowing the network to deal only with the Physical and Data Link layers. By bypassing the upper protocol layers, frame relay networks achieve greater speeds than more robust network protocols. Because these layers are bypassed, Frame Relay does not provide error checking or packet sequencing as in X.25 networks. Frame Relay is a simple connection oriented frame transport service. Information frames are relayed over LAN or WAN as well as the internetworking devices that are used to connect these systems. Frames are groups of data at the Data Link Layer. Datagrams are groups of data at the Network layer. The protocols that Frame Relay uses can manage permanent virtual circuits or establish switched virtual circuits. By including LAN traffic in a Frame Relay frame, multiprotocol support is supplied.

ISDN (Integrated Services Digital Network)

ISDN came into being as a way to group transmission lines together. As phone companies provided a greater range of services to customers, including voice, LAN, modem, and video transmission capabilities, the ability to provide all of these services over a single line became very desirable. ISDN is a packet switching network protocol that allows all of these different types of traffic to be transmitted over the same line.

An advantage of ISDN connections is that they are routed over completely digital networks. In other common connection types, it is rare to be able to send a message in its digital form all the way through the network. Various switches along the path are likely to be analog, requiring that the data be converted from digital to analog, and then back again for other segments. In the Integrated Digital Network (IDN) fully digital paths are available. ISDN is the common structure and signaling method used on the IDN. ISDN is a result of a working group from CCITT (known today as ITU-T, International Telecommunications Union Telecommunications). In its basic form ISDN was designed for a 64 kbs speed. Increased speeds are available by using the N-ISDN or Narrow Band ISDN standard.

The benefits of ISDN are its international appeal and open systems approach as well as the multiple services it can provide from File Transfer to e-mail, directory services and facsimile transmission. Data, voice, and video can all be transmitted over a single line.

Network Address Planning

In addition to planning your topology and protocol, your network address scheme is also very important. If not properly planned and maintained, future growth can be severely impaired. We will cover the different address schemes in a TCP/IP environment, as well briefly look at some of the more popular non-TCP/IP addressing schemes.

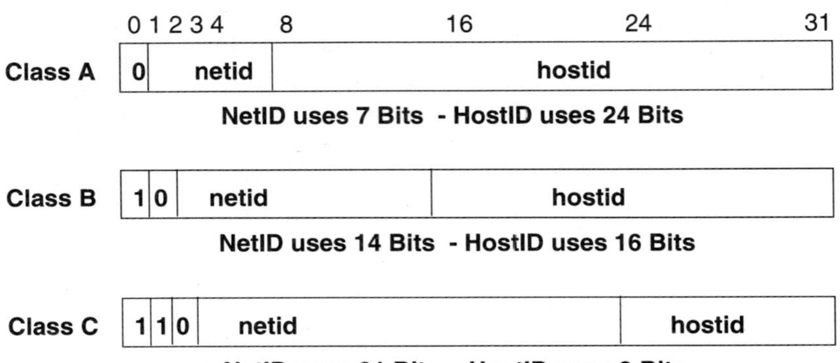

Figure 28.5 Classes of IP Addresses

Internet Protocol (IP) Addresses

An Internet Protocol address is a thirty-two bit address which uniquely identifies a node on a network. These thirty-two bits are subdivided into a network and host number, with the point of the division varying depending on the address class (see Figure 28.5). For readability, IP addresses are typically written in dotted decimal notation. This representation divides the address into four octets, of eight bits each. This allows each octet to represent a value between 0 and 255.

There are four classes of Internet Protocol addresses. An "A" class address is used only for the largest networks; nearly 17 million nodes can be addressed in a class A network. In a A class address, the first octet is used to represent the network number, while the remaining three octets (24 bits) identify a host. The first octet is further restricted in that the first bit must be a zero, since this is the convention to designate a class A address. This means that the first octet of a class A address will always be in the range of 1 to 126 (the value 127 is reserved). This limitation of 126 class A networks has resulted in the internet running out of class A addresses, and an extended address format is under consideration for introduction in the future.

A class B address uses the first two octets to represent the network number, and the final two octets to represent the host. This allows addressing for about 65 thousand nodes in a B class network. The first two bits of the first octet will always be "10" in a class B address. This means that B class addresses will be in the range 128.1.0.0 through 191.254.255.255. With only slightly more than 16 thousand class B networks available, these addresses have also been nearly depleted.

A C class address is used for smaller networks. The first three octets (24 bits) designate the network, while the final octet (8 bits) designates the node. This permits addressing for up to 254 hosts on a class C network. The "C" class address range is from 192.0.1.0 through 223.255.254.254. The first octet of a C class address will always contain "110" in the first three bits.

There are other special address conventions used in IP addresses (see Table 28.6). An address that is all zeros would implies "this" host. All zeros in the network portion along with the host address would imply this host on "this" network. An address that is all ones is a limited broadcast for the network. The network address followed by all ones in the node portion signifies a directed broadcast for the network. Any address that with the value 127 in the first octet designates a loopback connection.

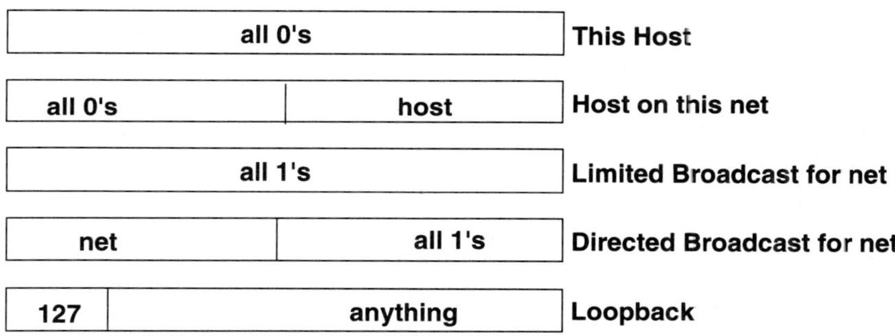

Figure 28.6 Special IP Address Conventions

Subnetting IP Addresses

The hostid portion of an IP address can be further subdivided into a subnet and a host id. Subnets allow a single network to be divided into a more manageable group of smaller networks. This assists in network traffic management over routers and bridges. It is up to the network administrator to decide how to divide the network, depending on the number of separate networks (subnets) desired and the number of nodes needed in each subnet. In a class B network, the hostid portion of the address is 16 bits. What are some of the ways this field could be subnetted?

- We could use 15 bits for the subnet, and 1 bit for the host. This creates somewhat more than 32 thousand subnets, each with one node. Not particularly useful.
- We could use 12 bits for the subnet, and 4 bits for the host. This creates just over four thousand subnets, each with 16 nodes. That's still a lot of networks, and the number of nodes could easily be exceeded by many workgroups.
- We could use 8 bits for the subnet, and 8 bits for the host. This creates 255 subnets, each with 255 nodes. This may be a workable configuration.
- We could use 6 bits for the subnet, and 10 bits for the host. This creates 64 sub nets, each with 1024 nodes. This is another reasonable configuration.

As you see, you can arbitrarily subdivide the hostid field anywhere you like; it doesn't have to be at an octet, or any other boundary. You can do the same thing with a Class A address; since the hostid field in these networks is 24 bits, you can create larger subnets, and more of them, than with class B addresses. Similarly, you can subnet a Class C address, with the number of subnets and nodes per subnet being far more limited.

Once you've decided how you want to subdivide your network, you create a network parameter called a subnet mask to identify how long the network and subnet fields are. The subnet mask is stated in dotted decimal notation just as IP addresses are, but are easier to understand in binary representation. The purpose of a subnet mask is simply to document where you have chosen to break the subnet and hostid fields within your network. To build a subnet mask, you simply use a 1 to denote each bit that should be considered part of the subnet, and a 0 to denote each bit that should be part of the host id. The bits that comprise the network id—the high-order 8 bits in a class A address, and 16 bits in a class B address—must be set to 1 in the subnet mask.

Thus, for our four examples above, we would create subnet masks as follows:.

Table 28.3 Subnetting IP Addresses

Network Bits	Subnet Bits	Host Bits	First Octet	Second Octet	Third Octet	Fourth Octet	Dotted Decimal Notation
16	15	1	11111111	11111111	11111111	11111111	255.255.255.254
16	12	4	11111111	11111111	11111111	11110000	255.255.255.240
16	8	8	11111111	11111111	11111111	00000000	255.255.255.0
16	6	10	11111111	11111111	11111100	00000000	255.255.252.0

Dividing the network into subnets can really simplify the administration of a large network. It can also help in reducing the amount of traffic over the "backbone". When you use a bridge or router to physically separate the different subnets within your network, the traffic from each subnet won't arbitrarily "roam" through the entire network. With the use of gateways and routers the entire network can still be reached, but only traffic that needs to cross subnet boundaries will do so.

If your network is isolated and will never be connected to other Internet Protocol networks then you can "build" your own IP address. But we highly recommend that you obtain an assigned IP address. This way if you ever attach your system to the Internet (World Wide Web), you can rest assured you will not have a duplicate address. IP addresses are assigned by Government Systems, Inc., who can be reached at the following address:

Government Systems, Incorporated
ATTN: Network Information Center
14200 Park Meadown Center
Suite 200
Chantilly, VA 22021
email: hostmaster@nic.ddn.mil
formerly - DDN Network Information Center (NIC)

Other address schemes

While we have covered the TCP/IP address scheme rather deeply we would also like to discuss some of the other LAN protocols and their address schemes. Let's review what a protocol is. The protocol provides the rules regarding packet structure, addressing or naming and the procedures for locating other devices on the network.

The NetWare network operating system uses an addressing scheme known as **IPX**. A full IPX address is made up of both a network and a host address. The host address is a 48 bit number. For most applications, the host address is the Medium Access Control (MAC) address. This is also referred to as the station or the physical address. An IPX network address is a 32 bit number. Each must be unique with hexidecimal values from 00000001 to FFFFFFFE.

Digital Equipment's **DECnet** address is a 16 bit address which consists of a 6 bit area number from 1 to 63 and a 10 bit node number from 1 to 1023.

An AppleTalk node address is made up of a 16 bit network number, from 1-65279, and an 8 bit node identifier from 1-253. The AppleTalk nodes will dynamically determine their own network number.

Routers and Bridges and Hubs, Oh My

With the growth and segmentation of networks today the network equipment that is used can have as much of an affect on the performance of the network as do the protocol, transmission medium and hosts. In this discussion we will try to assist you in understanding more about the use of bridges, routers and other network equipment.

The hub or repeater is a network device that can be used to connect many devices to a network as well as to extend the network. It amplifies and retransmits all signals, including collisions. A network that contains no network equipment other than hubs is what we define as a flat network. All traffic on the network will be seen by all nodes on the network. While hubs have their place in the design of a network, one of their major limitations is that they do nothing to reduce collisions.

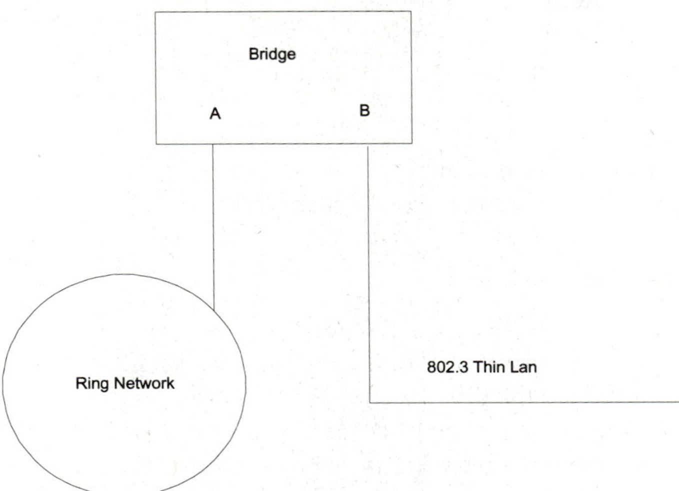

Figure 28.7 Bridge

Bridges are used to connect separate networks together. The concept of a bridge is to examine each packet and either keep it on the local network or send it across to the other network (see Figure 28.7). Bridges generally are "smart" enough to hold tables that allow the bridge to decide whether to transmit the packet to the other network or not. Today, there are "learning" bridges available that need very little if any configuration. Bridges operate at the MAC level so they do not serve as a "gateway" unless the bridge itself has routing capabilities. In a flat network configuration, any fault that occurs it will impact the entire network. For example, if you had a node that was generating a high volume of invalid traffic, it could bring the entire network down. In a bridged network, this failure would be contained to the side that contained that node only. While this may still impact a significant number of nodes, at least the effect contained to some degree

In addition to improving network reliability, another reason to use bridges is to improve performance. Network performance does decline with each added node or extended distance. By dividing a very large network up into smaller work areas divided by bridges, performance over the entire network can be enhanced. Bridges are used very heavily in Wide Area Networks. In a WAN environment a bridge is used to "extend" the network to the distant location. In the bridged WAN, you must take the same precautions you do with a LAN. Security can be enhanced in some bridges today by configuring only the MAC addresses that are allowed to communicate across the bridge. A bridge also allows a network that has reached its configuration limit to be extended (see sidebar for example).

Bridge example:

The ABC Manufacturing Company is housed in a three story building. The first floor contained accounting, information services and manufacturing management. The second floor is where engineering was housed and the third floor was occupied by marketing and personnel. Utilizing an HP 3000 as their business server each area used directly connected terminals. The engineering department also had HP-UX 700 workstations that were connected by a ThinLan LAN. Each department wanted to start using PC's rather than terminals to communicate with the 3000 as well as utilize spreadsheets, graphics programs and word processing functions. The system administrator decided to install a location wide 802.3 EtherTwist network. Cabling all the PC's on a floor together and using a hub in the wiring closet of each floor, they connected all of the departments to the HP 3000. This ran fine for a little while. Engineering decided that they would like to connect their network as well so they could upload information to manufacturing real-time. When the two networks were connected not only did they see a dramatic decrease in response time from the HP 3000 but they also started to other problems with their PC applications. The network administrator had a performance analysis performed on the network and found that the network was overloaded. The LAN was averaging over 40% utilization. In the current environment each packet that was transmitted was received by all nodes on the network. Thereby slowing down not only the network but each system would have to process each packet at least to the point of realizing that the address wasn't theirs. The decision was made to take engineering back off of the network. Rather than do that though the network administrator decided to segment the network into two parts. Engineering would be on one segment, the rest of the company on the other. Using a bridge between the two allowed engineering to still upload the data on a real-time basis and yet keep their inter-department traffic from flowing all through the network. The bridge would only forward packets addressed to a node that was not on the engineering side. Also any node on the company side of the bridge could still send data to engineering.

The company experienced dramatic growth over the next year and doubled the amount of PC's in marketing. Again all the other users experienced a slow down on their systems. The Network administrator decided to replace the two remaining hubs with bridges again segmenting her network into 2 more sections. Not only did the users see a dramatic increase in response time from the HP 3000, but also found their file sharing activities between each other and their network printers was much faster!!

Today the routed network is becoming more and more popular. Routing sends packets from one location to another over one of many possible paths. While a bridge has to store routes to all hosts it connects, a router only needs to store routes to another network and to the hosts directly connected to its own network. You can think of a routed environment as a network of networks. A router operates at the network layer. In this way a router can connect different types of networks. Unlike a bridge that typically has only one path to send the traffic over, a router can pick the best route if more than one is available in which to forward the packet. In the LAN environment a router can significantly reduce network traffic thereby improving overall network performance. (see sidebar). Another plus to the routed network is the improvement in LAN security. Unless the address of an intruding device is recognized by the router it will not forward the packet unless bridging has been enabled.

The saga continues!!.. Routing example:

During that same year the company decided to put a manufacturing plant on the west coast as well as the southeast. Each plant was connected to the corporate office using a data line and a remote bridge. Knowing that they had used a class C address scheme, the network administrator saw that they were about to run out of IP addresses. She requested an IP address from the Network Information Center so if they ever decided to attach to the Internet they would know they had a unique IP address. They were assigned a B class address of "131.10."

On one particular occasion the line between the plant on the west coast and corporate went down. This line was down for over two days. With no communication between the two plants a lot of production was held up. This could not happen again! Since a bridge really only knows one way to get to it's destination, the decision was made to implement a routed network. This was also a good time to convert to the new B class address.

Since the network was basically divided into five segments and knowing that she shouldn't use an address of all zero's or one's, she decided to apply a mask of 255.255.240.00. By going to a routed network the company would have at least two ways to reach each facility in the future. Also by using a subnet mask, the network administrator could manage the assignment of IP addresses much easier in the future.

Network standards and why we need them

Standards have developed and adopted in nearly every facet of the computer industry, but nowhere are they more important than in the area of networking. Networking, after all, is the part of the computer environment which by definition has to be compatible with different computing elements. Even if you are willing to buy all of your computer hardware from one vendor, it is unlikely that every peripheral, network component, length of wire, and netware-aware software module that you need to run your business will be available from the same source.

Standards are important not just for making the components work together today, but also for providing a foundation for future technologies. For example, suppose you have recently built a network using category 5 unshielded twisted pair wire, supporting protocols that provide 10mbps throughput. If an when you need to move to newer protocols supporting 100 mbps speeds, these protocols can run on the same wiring. While there is no guarantee that such upgrades will always be possible, the fact that the Category 5 UTP was a widely utilized standard made it more economical to build upon the standard technology if at all possible.

Standards are important for the LAN protocols as well as for the transmission media. If each of the vendors work to meet the standards set forth by organizations such as IEEE, CCITT, and others, then the user doesn't have to wonder whether they can change out one piece of network equipment for another and not affect their running network. Standards are approved by different committees that have been formed to ensure that each party involved strives to meet common measurements specifying the operation of their equipment. Organizations such as IEEE work to ensure that IEEE 802.3 is the same whether it is running over a DECnet or an IPX network. It is because of these standards that we now have the opportunity to ease our dependance on a single vendor for hardware, software and networking.

CHAPTER 29

Management of the Environment

Network Management

In today's computing environment, management of the network has become a very demanding task. Can you imagine not knowing what databases are running on your system? How about not knowing what accounts, groups or users are established on your system? The network has these same types of attributes that can and should be monitored.

We know of customers who spend thousands of dollars monitoring their systems' performance but have never had a network audit performed. With the clustered environment and the use of RPC's and other network based application technologies the network can make a big difference in the overall performance of the environment. It is better to view your systems as an "environment" rather than just a group of systems, and understand the ways in which the various parts can affect each other. The administrator's responsibilities in this environment include managing, monitoring and maintaining the network.

One of the first areas of concern regarding network management is having a valid network map. We have seen maps drawn on napkins, scrap pieces of paper, and white boards. The media isn't important, but maps drawn on these media aren't going to last very long. Of course, just how long is a network map valid? At the individual node level, probably not as long as it takes for the "napkin map" to fade away. But there is higher-level information about LAN segments, routing equipment, subnetting decisions and the like that will tend to be more permanent than the location of a particular node, and this information should be documented in a similarly long-lived media.

Network maps should properly be drawn before the network is built. A proper network map should include all network addresses, node names, pertinent data regarding each node, network equipment and LAN segments. What is more typical is to find a network map drawn only when it becomes necessary in troubleshooting the network; and then as likely as not, the problem will turn out to be one that could have been avoided had the configuration been documented in the first place.

Another difficulty that is encountered is maintaining the network map. Not only do nodes, addresses and other attributes change on a regular basis, but the personnel involved will also change. A network map should document not only the hardware components that comprise the network, but the persons who are responsible for each portion of the network. People such as the System Administrator, Network Administrator, Security Administrator should be included in the documentation. Phone extensions, home phone or pager numbers should also be included; essentially, anything an operator or user will need to know when the network is down should be documented in a single location.

Now that we have our network properly documented, let's look into what it will take to maintain the network at its peak performance. It is not a difficult matter to attach a LAN Probe or Network Advisor to your LAN segment. With these or other LAN measurement instruments such as LAN and Protocol Analyzers you can not only tell what your network traffic looks like but where the offending node may be if you are having network problems. There can be many reasons for having network problems. The most frequent problems are caused by mis-configurations, broken or damaged transmission media, or traffic that exceeds the designed capacity (the bandwidth) of your network.

Some network maintenance agreements include a yearly performance analysis. The time to perform an analysis is not while you are having problems. Our suggestion is to have an analysis performed when the network is first put into production. With this information, you have a base line that you can always use for comparison either when problems arise, or to determine trends by comparing this base line to subsequent analyses. Most customers will wait until the network is in trouble before they have an analysis performed. This analysis or audit is not primarily intended as a troubleshooting tool, but as a planning tool. Most system administrators know approximately how many users, systems and additional processes they will be adding to the environment over the coming year. That information coupled with a good network analysis can really help when it comes to system upgrade sizing. A network audit or analysis should include the average bandwidth utilized by the network, the addresses generating and receiving the most traffic, average collision rate and average connection rate. If you can divide up the audit on different segments of the LAN, you might want to find the busiest segments and look at subdividing these further to reduce the overall network utilization. Another item to look for is dropped packets. Most devices today will keep a record of network errors that can be used to track down potential problem areas.

The staff involved in the management of the network should be a formal organization. In the past the different divisions within the IS staff didn't communicate on a regular basis. While they might have gotten together during staff meetings, the information shared was generally limited to troubleshooting an on-going problem or discussion of something new coming down the line. Today these different departments have to communicate more often. The communications or networking people will have to be involved in decisions that in the past they would not have been. This includes areas such as determining operating systems for the clients, designing and implementing security for systems on the network, and even application development, especially if RPC technologies are used. In a successful implementation of a client/server environment, everyone from the user all the way to top management will have to be involved. Be sure to include your networking and communications staff in planning meetings where client/server systems are being discussed. They'll be responsible for making it all work in the long run, and their inputs should be solicited at every step of the process.

Another area that requires proper management for a network is the naming and address conventions. We have seen numerous problems on customer sites where someone added a node to the network and didn't check with the networking staff to determine what address to assign. In one case, an engineer diligently checked the workstations on the local LAN segment and selected an address not in use by any of them. Unfortunately, it turned out to be the address used by the server. Every time a call was made to the server both the server and the new node tried to respond, bringing the entire network to a halt. A map of addresses associated with node names should be maintained at all times. This map should be controlled by one department or individual. In today's Network Information Services (NIS) and Domain Name Server (DNS) environments it is imperative that the host tables on the master servers be maintained properly. Even if you aren't using these tools you should always know what addresses and names are in use on your network.

In summary the key to network management is documentation. Network maps that include as much information as possible, lists of names and addresses of all network nodes, and procedures for the proper maintenance of these documents are the tools that any network administrator must have to do the job right.

Distributed Management

In today's distributed client server environment, the management of the systems can be a very difficult task. Some of the challenges facing administrators today are maintaining reliability, backup and recovery, system availability, and software distribution.

System reliability is affected by many components, including the applications themselves, the network, databases, and human error. Chapter 30 will look at high availability strategies and products in greater detail. Application designers also have a responsibility to consider high availability topics, such as logging errors and proving recovery mechanisms for which retries or other software-level recovery mechanisms are appropriate.

Software distribution in a client/server environment is another administration challenge. Multiply the number of users by the number of different applications or other software packages, and then multiply again by the number of updates to these you may experience in a year. The total number of 'incidents' of software distribution in a year can be staggering. Without an automated distribution capability, the chances that some of these will be of the wrong version or have other problems is quite great. Today with products such as Hewlett-Packard's OpenView Software Distributor, applications as well as operating systems can be "pushed" out over the network from a central site.

Another element you need to consider is going to be ultimately responsible for the environment. Are users responsible for "pulling" the latest application updates to their local clients, or will they be "pushed" out when the central site decides it is appropriate? Will backups of client local data be initiated by the users, or by the central site? While one of the attractive features of client/server technology is to free users from the "tyranny" imposed by a centralized decision making process, users typically aren't willing to take on the discipline required to ensure smooth operation of the environment. Add to this that expertise is usually centralized, and that support contracts frequently recognize only the central site as being able to receive support, and you have built a strong case that control of backups, software distribution, and similar issues is best maintained centralized, with input solicited from all involved.

Backing up the system is not the only concern. Management concerns of all types have to be considered. Should your company adopt a one vendor approach to hardware? Is there a corporate standard for applications on an individual's PC? If a user decides to load a copy of software that is not licensed should you require them to remove it or will it be up to the user to be responsible for the problems that might arise from this action? There are many areas that we could go into with regard to this topic but we would like to leave you with this one main thought. Whether to distribute your management does not have to be tied to whether you have distributed your environment or not. You can have a distributed environment but maintain a centralized management approach. Whether you decide to distribute management or not is an important question, and the correct answer for a particular site hinges on many factors. Technology, although important, is frequently not the decisive factor; corporate culture, user sophistication, and capabilities of the centralized IT function are likely to play a larger part in the decision that the technology itself.

CHAPTER 30

High Availability

The HP 3000 is one of the most reliable computer systems you can buy. In survey after survey, HP 3000 owners cite one reason for their loyalty to HP. They like the reliability of the HP 3000. There are two reasons for the HP 3000's near legendary reliability. First there is the simplicity of the PA-RISC hardware design. Secondly, there is the quality of the system software. HP uses an exhaustive test suite to ensure the "stay-up-ability" of each new release of the MPE/iX operating system and its related subsystems, particularly the IMAGE/SQL database management system. For this reason, many HP customers think of the HP 3000 first when building applications that have special needs for availability. In a survey that was done July of 1994, customers that use HP 3000 systems together with UNIX systems were asked which machine they preferred for heads down transaction processing and mission critical applications. Seventy-five percent expressed a strong preference for the HP 3000.

Mission critical applications require highly reliable computer systems, but perhaps even more importantly, they require that system managers put extraordinary efforts into managing those systems. This is true regardless of whether the systems are HP 3000s, UNIX systems, NT servers, or non-HP platforms. There is no substitute for performing regular backups and maintenance according to the guidelines established by your hardware vendor—whether it's Hewlett-Packard or another company. System management practices for high availability are not complex—they're actually very simple. But they must be done regularly and without fail. The HP 3000's fundamental reliability has long emanated from, and in large measure depended upon the ready availability of information and training for system operators and administrators.

It's difficult to measure the expertise of the "typical" system administrator. There are no readily agreed-upon metrics that can be used, and no historical records to which those metrics could be applied. But there is anecdotal evidence to suggest that today's system administrators are not as well equipped to provide high availability environments as there counterparts were ten or even five years ago. Engineers who work in HP's customer support organization, the Response Center, report that a significant number of the problems that they deal with on a day to day basis are caused, not by failures of hardware or software components, but rather by operator errors, ignorance and outright incompetence. This has always been true, but as one engineer put it, "in recent years the situation seems to have gotten worse. It's as if everybody were running their computer room with summer help. And you know what they say about summer help. Some are help. Some are not."

The reason for this trend is not hard to understand. Over the last thirty years, one trend in the IS industry has continued unabated—hardware has gotten cheaper and more reliable. At the same time, the human resource costs associated with managing IS have gotten higher, and in many companies the willingness to invest in human resources has eroded. One operator expressed it to me this way.

> *"Back in the 1970s, we used to spend millions on hardware. In the context of a million dollar hardware budget, spending a few thousand on training didn't seem like a big deal. It was less than 1% of the overall budget. Today, the price of hardware has dropped to a fraction of what it used to be. And this has driven IS budgets down dramatically. I've seen some smaller companies whose total annual IS budgets are well under $100,000. The trouble is that they're still expecting to spend 1% of that (or less) on training. They don't seem to realize that although hardware has gotten cheaper, people haven't. If anything, the kinds of environments that they're running today require that the operators and system administrators have more expertise than ever—because we aren't just running one computer. We're trying to run heterogeneous networks made up of lots of different kinds of computers, from different vendors. That requires more investment in training—not less. You wouldn't believe the number of people I've met in this business who haven't had any formal training since they got out of college. They're trying to pick up the knowledge that they need in their spare time. And it just isn't possible. Things are changing too quickly."*

Companies that have skimped on training often discover that the fundamental reliability of the HP 3000 can sometimes actually work against them. Sometimes, when HP 3000 installations go for years without a system problem, they can be lulled into a false sense of security. System administration procedures that were designed to protect against problems are gradually forgotten and operators begin to fail to rigorously observe the backup schedules. Inevitably, a hardware failure will eventually happen, and without proper backups recovery can become very complicated if it's possible at all.

The availability of up-to-date information is critical to maintaining a high availability environment. As of this writing Hewlett-Packard is providing HP 3000 customers a package of high availability fact sheets at no charge. You can obtain this package by Faxing your name, phone number and shipping address to Hewlett-Packard at 612-430-3388. You'll be sent product data sheets, technical white papers and other information by return mail. These fact sheets, in addition to the various high availability white papers that are presented each year at the Interex conference, provide system administrators with the information that they need to manage their systems for the best possible reliability.

High Availability is one of those buzzwords that everybody in the computer industry seems to be using, but nobody can really define clearly. Obviously, it has something to do with reliability. (I've talked to dozens of HP 3000 customers who've told me that they have no need to plan for "high availability" because, "we're using an HP 3000—and that *is* the most highly reliable platform that there is—isn't it?" The fact is that even in the reliable HP 3000 world, there are levels and degrees of reliability and availability. When management embarks on a campaign to improve system availability, there are at least five key areas that need to be investigated and understood.

1. Is the requirement for a Reliable or for a Continuously Available (fault-tolerant) environment?
2. How much planned downtime can be tolerated? How can it be minimized?
3. How much un-planned downtime can be tolerated? How can it be minimized?
4. Exactly how much does downtime really cost? Can the cost of High Availability solutions be justified by the amount of downtime (both planned and unplanned) that can be eliminated?
5. How do I plan a high availability environment? What steps are involved?

We've talked a good deal in this book about using UNIX and MPE/iX systems together. It's impossible to talk about the reliability of HP systems in this context without comparing these two strategic HP product lines. We've noted that HP customers have tended to prefer the HP 3000 for mission critical applications because of it's reliability. This is not to suggest that the HP 9000 is not reliable. After all, the hardware components that underlie both systems are virtually identical. Today, HP-UX has advanced to the point where it can be just as reliable as MPE/iX, as long as proper system management procedures are observed.

In a mainframe environment (see chapter 26), planning a high availability environment meant figuring out ways to make the computer more reliable. The computer could have been an HP 3000, an HP 9000, or even a traditional IBM ES-9000 mainframe—the point was to manage it so that it could be used as a high availability *system*. In today's environments, planning high availability means figuring out ways to manage the network and the different kinds of computers (plural!) that are attached to the network to provide a high availability environment that covers all of these components. This is a much trickier proposition.

While the products and configurations may be different between HP-UX and MPE/iX, the strategic analysis and planning of this environment are very similar. With that in mind this chapter will address both platforms from a high-level point of view.

High Availability Strategies

The first thing that must be determined is exactly what is meant by the term "High Availability." We realize this may seem like a moot point but it really isn't. There are many levels of customer uptime needs and therefore there are many different environments to support these needs. Each company has different requirements. For the purposes of this discussion we'll consider four levels and degrees of high availability.

1. The base configuration to start with is the "***reliable***" system.
2. This environment is enhanced by the "***protected***" system products being added.
3. The next step up the availability chain is achieved by adding the "***highly***" available products.
4. The ultimate goal to be achieved is the "***continuously***" available system also known as the fault tolerant system.

A ***reliable*** system consists of an environment that is robust without spending extra money specifically on High Availability solutions. A reliable system environment will typically include basic reliability technologies.

A "***protected***" system is one that has been enhanced by utilizing component redundancy. For example technologies such as disk mirroring (available for both HP 3000 and HP 9000 platforms), and disk arrays, will greatly reduce the recovery time if a failure should occur. In the protected environment the goal is automatic detection and recovery from faults through redundant hardware and the software needed to support it. It's important to understand that these environments build on one another. You can't use these technologies to make a "silk purse out of a sow's ear." More specifically, if a system is fundamentally unreliable because it's not being properly managed, adding disk mirroring isn't going to help. You must cover the basics first.

To the reliable and the protected system we add the products necessary to achieve the ***"highly available***" system. In this environment the goal is to recover from failure with a very short ***application*** interruption. This is achieved through the use of products such as SharePlex/iX-Netbase (for the HP 3000) and MCServiceGuard (for the HP 9000). In order to reach this goal this system must have redundant system components and software support which allows an application to be transferred from one system that is failing to another system. The time frames for this to take place varies from one to thirty minutes. Also by using the Journaled File System even the one minute time frame can be reduced!

The top rung on the ladder is the "***continuously available***" or fault tolerant system. A continuously available environment has transparent failure recovery, twenty four hour availability, no planned downtime. While this sounds very close to highly available the difference is in this environment the goal is to never have to recover. It is not necessary for instance to justify the need to power down the systems for a repair or update of any kind. While this goal is achievable, it is not without significant cost. Not only in the systems and software requirements but the physical plant requirements as well.

Reliable Systems

Perhaps the best examples of basic reliability technology are Powerfail Recovery and the Uninterruptable Power Supply (UPS). Since the 1970s, HP 3000s have included a technology called Powerfail Recovery to minimize the impact of interruptions in the power. This technology uses an internal battery with software integrated into the MPE/iX kernel to ensure that interruptions in the power do not cause data corruption. A UPS is an external power supply which automatically takes over in the event of a power failure. Today, UPS technology is bundled with HP 3000 and 9000 systems.

Another key reliability technology is a journaled file system, (JFS). Without a JFS, any system failure can result in corruption in user files and databases, which must be repaired manually by the system administrator. Many popular operating systems lack this key technology.

- For example, "classic" MPE/V systems such as the HP 3000 S/70 did not have a journaled file system. After a system failure corruption typically manifested itself in the form of "broken chains" in TurboIMAGE databases. These had to be repaired manually by the system administrator.
- Similarly, UNIX systems typically require that a "file system check" (fsck) utility be run after each operating system shutdown to seek out any corruption that may have resulted. This can take many minutes—even hours—depending on the number and size of the file systems being checked. Repairs may have to be made manually by the system administrator.
- Microsoft's MS-DOS file system (which is also used by Windows 3.1), suffers from a similar weakness. Corruption on a PC's hard drive can be pinpointed using the "chkdsk" or "scandisk" command, but repairs must be made by the system administrator.

JFS technology monitors each change that's made to the file system in a way that ensures that in the event of a failure, recovery is quick and automatic. The HP 3000's file system has made use of journaling technology since the inception of the Series/900 (RISC) machines in the 1980s. HP literature calls this technology "integrated transaction management" and its inclusion in the HP 3000 operating system made broken chains a dim memory. Today they are almost unheard of on modern MPE/iX systems. A JFS file system type was bundled with HP-UX Release 10.0. Users that are upgrading from an earlier HP-UX release must convert traditional HFS file systems to the new JFS type. Then, in the event of a system failure (UNIX calls them system "panics"), the fsck program can find and fix any corruption in a JFS in seconds. Recovery is fast and automatic.

JFS technology is used to recover from corruption that results from software failures. It cannot compensate for disk failures. On reliable systems, peripherals, particularly disks, must be carefully selected for their reliability. In an open systems environment, standards such as SCSI have made it possible to comparison shop for disks and buy the least expensive ones you can find. This is one reason why the open systems strategy is so attractive, particularly for companies that are downsizing, or simply trying to contain costs. But it's at least as important to remember that in a high availability environment, you get what you pay for.

If you're trying to build a highly reliable system, you should carefully qualify and limit the number of vendors with whom you choose to do business. You may pay a little more, but when something goes wrong, (and eventually something will), there will be fewer people to call, and you'll lose less valuable time sorting out the problem. More importantly, when you choose to buy the most critical components of your system from a single vendor, then you can be relatively certain that all of these components will have been tested by the vendor to ensure that they work—not only individually—but together. By contrast, suppose that you choose to buy each of your system's hardware components, peripherals, system management software products and support services from the lowest bidder. You may find that your company is the only one trying use that particular combination of technologies. In essence, *you're* testing it.

This is an argument that has been used to justify the use of single-vendor hardware platforms like the HP 3000. But it also makes good sense when putting together highly reliable UNIX systems. Just because it's possible to use third-party disk drives with an HP 9000 doesn't mean that it always makes good business sense to do so. If an application is mission critical, then the peripherals should be able to support them in a mission critical environment. Today hardware has reached a very high mark in reliability, and it's easier than it used to be to compare the reliability of hardware components from different vendors. Mean Time Between Failure is a measure of reliability that is widely used. There are formulas to calculate Mean Time Between Failure as well as other measures such as MTTR (Mean Time To Repair), and AFR (Annualized Failure Rate). It is not difficult today to have a reliable environment. There are some things that can be done to enhance this environment without adding to your system's cost.

In an HP 3000 environment, utilizing User Volume Sets can improve your recovery time in the event of a failure. The easy thing to do is to put all your applications and data on a single System_Volume_Set. This works fine until you encounter a failure on any of the disks. Recovering from such a failure requires that you recover the entire system. All the data on all the disks must be restored from a backup. A far better alternative is to divide your disk sub-system up using User_Volume_Sets. In the event of a failure, you may find that you only have to recover the volume that was affected by the failure.

Lets say for instance that you have a failure on the system disk. If you're using User_Volume_Sets, recovery can be relatively quick. After the failed disk has been repaired you would effectively "install" the system back on your system volume set and re-configure your user volume sets. You would *not* have to "restore" the rest of your system. Not only can this save recovery time but also save time in not having to rebuild your databases or repair other application type problems that occur as a result of a failure. It does take time to plan how you want to lay out your User Volume Sets but it's pretty clear that it is well worth the time to plan and implement this strategy.

Backup time can be reduced as well if you utilize User Volume Sets. The System_Volume_Set would not require backing up as often as the user volumes do. This not only saves time but tapes as well. Using user volume sets can also assist you in planning your backup strategies. If you have a particular user group that the only time they are not on the system is during lunch, then use that time to back that volume set up. This way they have their system when they need it. A main point that we would like to bring out regarding User Volume Sets is the cost. There is no additional software to buy; the necessary technology is bundled with MPE/iX. By keeping your hardware and software up to date and maintaining support agreements in case you do have a failure as well as utilizing a UPS, achieving a "reliable" system is not very difficult.

The *Protected* system

In the protected environment the goal is automatic detection and recovery from faults through redundant hardware and the software needed to support it. You will have to purchase the hardware and software necessary to put this environment in place.

In an HP9000 environment by utilizing Mirror/UX software and duplicating your disk sub-system you can drastically reduce the effects of a disk failure. Some people have confused disk mirroring with the kind of mirroring that is offered with RAID disk arrays. With any disk storage device there are at least four key points of failure: the disk mechanism itself, the disk controller, the channel and the cable that connects them. With disk mirroring, all four of these components are duplicated. If any component of the primary disk fails, the mirrored disk takes over. RAID drives may only offer duplication of some of these components. We'll examine RAID in more detail a little later on.

Here's an example of how disk mirroring might be used. Consider an HP 9000 system that has the need for four disk drives. The first is the root and primary swap volume. The next three house the database, application and user space. In the Mirror/UX environment you can mirror all the disks (resulting in a configuration with eight volumes). But you may not need to duplicate all the hardware. If for instance you have the space available and you only want to mirror the root and swap volume, you can do this on any of the other volumes.

There's a common mistake that system administrators make in setting up a root mirror. You must mirror all the necessary file systems to ensure that the system will remain operative in the event that you lose the root volume. For example, on a 9.0 system you need to ensure that you have mirrored the **usr** file system as well as the entire root directory, i.e. **/dev**, **/etc** and **/bin** as well as the primary swap. This will ensure that your system will remain operative in the event that the primary disk fails.

Another area that must not be overlooked is the need to have the "mirror" disk on a different I/O channel from the primary disk (the one being "mirrored"). To fully take advantage of what you are trying to accomplish with mirroring you need to have your "secondary" or "mirror" volume on a completely different I/O path. While this is not a requirement, without doing this you really are only protected in case of a disk failure.

The main point in mirroring in our opinion is to keep the system from going down in case you have a failure in the disk sub-system. This is to prevent a single point of failure. This includes cabling and termination of the I/O bus. Taking our example a little further. Let's say we can put our root and primary swap on one disk. We then need to mirror that entire disk to another disk on a separate I/O channel. The other three disk should also be mirrored on this second I/O channel. Not only will the secondary disk be available to keep the system running in case of a disk failure you now are covered if you lose the I/O channel that the disks are attached to. While you might not feel you need to mirror the user space if you lose that disk you are still in a recovery mode that will impede your users.

In an HP 3000 environment, you can use the Mirror/iX product to achieve similar levels of protection. In this environment the mirror or "secondary" disk has to be of the same type as the primary or on-line disk. As of this writing the System_Volume_Set can not be mirrored. In order to ensure that the system disk is protected, we would suggest that you utilitize the User Volume Set approach and install your System_Volume_Set on RAID array. The User Volumes can be on stand-alone disks that are mirrored and with the system on an array you are covered in case of failure.

In both environments there is an acronym that has been used by some engineers to describe a stand alone configuration: JBOD or Just a Bunch Of Disk. One of the advantages to the JBOD configuration is the flexibility that you have in placement of data, power source and racking. Mirror/UX as well as Mirror/iX handle the access to the multiple copies of the data whether you are handling a disk failure or in a normal mode of operation.

RAID is an acronym for Redundant Arrays of Inexpensive Disks. There are several different RAID levels, offering various levels of protection from failure. A Level 0 Array has no check disk, and no data protection. User data is sector interleaved or block striped across a group of disks, and if any disk fails the data must be recovered from a backup. Since there is no data protection with RAID level 0 the only benefit is the potential for increased performance due to the data being spread across multiple disks.

On RAID Level 0/1 devices, the data is sector interleaved across groups of mirrored disks. Disk mirroring with products such as Mirror/UX or Mirror/iX can be thought of as an implementation of RAID level 1. RAID Level 2 uses multiple check disks which maintain the integrity of data using something called Hamming Code. RAID Level 3 uses a single check disk. It maintains data integrity using Parity and is the data is byte interleaved or byte striped. RAID Level 4 also uses a single check disk using Parity, but the data is sector interleaved. RAID Level 5 has no single check disk. Data and parity are spread across all disks, sector interleaved or block striped.

Disk Arrays can be used in a mirrored configuration for protection. A disk array can prevent data loss by utilizing a "parity" disk. If one of the disk mechanisms should fail, the parity mechanism (or "mech") will keep the disk operational until the failed mech can be replaced. This replacement can take place on-line without having to power the disk drive down. After the failed disk has been replaced a re-build function is then performed on-line and the data can be re-built by using the parity mech.

By using disk mirroring and RAID technologies you can effectively eliminate the impact on your business of many different types of failures. But one area that still can be a problem is data corruption. Data corruption can be caused by defects in application software or system software. If data corruption should occur on one of the primary disks, then that same corruption will be copied to the mirror disk. Disk mirroring and RAID do not reduce or eliminate the need for proper system management procedures such as regular backups. If you are going to implement mirroring as well as disk arrays, you need to ensure that you have the underlying items such as power, air conditioning and other environmental needs well planned.

While we have spent quite a bit of time discussing disk sub-systems there are other areas that require attention as well. If your environment is very much dependent upon its LAN or WAN, then you need to take this into consideration. For example, many companies use HP's SNA products to let their HP 3000 communicate with a corporate mainframe. In a protected environment, strict uptime requirements dictate the use of RAID and disk mirroring, as we've seen. Similarly, you might consider the use of multiple links between their two systems. A leased-line would give access to the mainframe, but you might also use an X.25 link or a satellite link as backup in case the leased-line went down. Today, many people are looking at the public Internet as a substitute for leased lines. Today, the public Internet represents a low cost alternative to other forms of wide area networking, but performance and reliability may not be up to the requirements of mission critical applications. Not only should all these links be in place at all times they should also be tested on a regular basis to ensure that they would work if they were needed.

In the Local Area Network environment hardware such as bridges, hubs and routers should be duplicated or at the bare minimum alternate routes set up in case of failure. In many cases today the failure of the LAN is at least equivalent to the system failing. Don't forget the goal of a protected system is automatic detection and recovery from faults through redundant hardware and the software needed to support it.

The Highly Available system

The goal in the protected system environment is the reduction of recovery time for the system in the event of a failure. In the highly available environment the goal is subtly different: to reduce the amount of time that the application is down while recovering. For instance, in the protected environment a system should not shut down due to a disk failure. But what happens if the processor fails? While the data may be protected due to disk redundancy the application will be down until the processor is repaired. In a highly available environment the application will be automatically "switched" to another CPU to continue running. There will be a slight interruption in application service while it is being switched over, but in most cases end users will not be inconvenienced. In the HP9000 environment the product that can be used for this is MCServiceGuard. HP 3000 use SharePlex/iX-NetBase.

MCServiceGuard—Conceptual Overview

MCServiceGuard is a dramatically different product from its predecessor, SwitchOver/UX. It's important to understand the difference. The switchover environment was designed to offer a standby solution in case of a CPU failure. In a SwitchOver environment the two CPU's had to be the same hardware type. Disc subsystems were cabled together but could not be shared. The primary CPU transmitted a constant signal called a heartbeat. The standby system listened to it. If the primary system ceased to send the heartbeat then the *standby* CPU would shut itself down. Assuming the root disk of the primary system, the secondary system would reboot and continue to run the applications that the primary had been running.

This represented a serious limitation. If the standby CPU had been running a secondary application it would stop. The secondary application would go offline until the primary CPU was back in operation. The main objective was ensuring that the primary application continued running. The cost was temporarily losing the secondary application. Given some of the downtime examples we looked at in a previous chapter this approach would still be acceptable to sustaining the loss due to a down CPU.

A positive aspect of the SwitchOver/UX environment was the protection against a single point of failure. This should be the top priority in any highly available environment. For example, you might have one standby CPU for up to 3 primaries in a SCSI or 7 primaries in a HP-FL disk environment. The switchover functionality is transparent to the application—no special interfaces to the operating system or the SwitchOver product itself are necessary.

On the other hand, SwitchOver/UX does not have the ability to detect a failure in an application or a service failure. As long as the heartbeat is being transmitted, the secondary system will continue to behave as if all is well. SwitchOver does not offer the option of having a standby LAN card that could switch automatically in case the primary LAN card failed. Time to reboot after a failure of course was dependent on how long it took to FSCK the root volume as well as the normal time that a reboot would take.

While there are many positives to the SwitchOver/UX product, MCServiceGuard offers much more flexibility. In the current release of MCServiceGuard you can have from one to four CPU's in a cluster. These CPU's do not have to be the same hardware type. A small system such as an E55 *can* serve to standby for an application running on a mainframe class system such as a T500, (although such a wide disparity might not be practical).

ServiceGuard is focused on application availability. This is contrasted with SwitchOver, which was focused on one class of problems—CPU failure. MCServiceGuard monitors not only the CPU but applications, services and other items that each member of the cluster depends upon to run. MCServiceGuard allows all of the nodes in the cluster to interrogate each other checking to see if the application or service being monitored is in fact operating. Through the use of multiple LAN interfaces you can guard against various kinds of LAN failures. If a failure occurs, the LAN interface can be switched automatically with only a slight interruption of LAN traffic.

Through clustering, the nodes cooperate to increase the availability of a service. In case of an application failure ServiceGuard can resume operations in a very short period of time. Only one cluster node will run a package at any given time. The package manager ensures this. Node failures such as panics, powerfailures, hangs and network card failures or disconnects (whether un-terminated or due to other transmission medium problems) along with abnormal termination of a monitored process are just a few of the failure types that MCServiceGuard will monitor for. Unlike the switchover environment, MCServiceGuard does not "take over" the failed CPU's root disk. This means we don't use valuable time performing an FSCK on a root volume before we can re-start the application.

Let's look at an example in which we have two nodes on the network, called "cba" and "abc." A typical failure and recovery would follow this sequence. Node "cba" detects a cluster application on Node "abc" has failed. The application or "package" is then switched to Node "cba." Before the package is started, Node "cba" does the following. A "start" script is run that, among other things, activates the volume group that the application needs in order to run. It also "assumes" the failing node's Network Address so the application can still be reached. It runs a crash recovery routine on the package and then starts the application.

The time between failure detection and execution of the "run" script on the new node is typically less than a minute (assuming JFS is being used). One thing to keep in mind when planning this environment is the possible need to obtain some consulting during both the planning and implementation phases. The main goal of MCServiceGuard is to reduce the amount of interruption time to an application due to a failure.

SharePlex/iX-NetBase—The highly available solution for the HP 3000

SharePlex/iX-NetBase, is a very flexible product for HP 3000 systems much like MCServiceGuard. With SharePlex/iX-NetBase you can loosely couple or cluster your systems. This provides much greater flexibility by providing a single-system view to the user. SharePlex/iX-NetBase also provides cluster operations and management features as well as shared cluster-wide facilities for managing print queues, batch queues, file systems and peripherals.

SharePlex/iX-NetBase can span LANs as well as WANs. The main objective of SharePlex/iX-NetBase is to provide application and system availability. Since SharePlex is supported over a WAN you also have the added benefit of having your own "disaster" recovery system in case of a geographical disaster. If an entire datacenter is destroyed, processing can be automatically shifted to a secondary site. Applications in a SharePlex cluster can be moved from one system to another for performance reasons. SharePlex supports clusters made up of different types and sizes of CPU's, including MPE/V as well as MPE/iX systems.

Another feature of SharePlex/iX-NetBase is the option to use peripherals such as printers throughout the cluster. SharePlex ensures that a spoolfile that has been "moved" to a different system printer is actually printed before the original copy is destroyed. Just as in the MCServiceGuard environment you must work to eliminate all single points of failure. Redundant disk's, multiple paths to the disk's, additional LAN cards for protection, mirroring software along with disk arrays for full disk protection.

By utilizing the HPOpenView System Manager the operator can have one "view" of the systems they are supporting. HPOpenView System Manager is a very straight-forward product that can be utilized right away. Many of the operator functions can be automated, tested and verified complete using HPOpenView System Manager. The minimum requirements are at least two HP 3000's networked together with SharePlex/iX running on both systems.

SharePlex/iX-NetBase is a product that can come "bundled" with many different options:

- ***Master Print/Spooling Management***—allows a user to print to any spooled printer on the network as long as it is configured in SharePlex/iX,
- ***Network File Access***—allows users and applications access to data and programs on the other HP 3000's in the cluster,
- ***Shadowing***—provides a complete system and data/application replication system.

Shadowing is an entry level product. SharePlex/iX can be ordered as a "bundle" to include all, or at an entry level which would include the shadowing product only. Other things to consider with SharePlex/iX are the opportunity to move users and applications to a different system in the cluster while performing maintenance activities on their "home" system.

Just like MCServiceGuard we would suggest that SharePlex/iX requires a fair amount of planning. Not only to install and configure but the "what ifs" as well. The flexibility of SharePlex/iX-NetBase coupled with the additional products of Print Management and NFA make it a most viable product to ensure your HP 3000 is in a highly available environment.

The most important thing to remember is to not have any single points of failure. If your disk sub-systems aren't protected by either mirroring, disk arrays or both, what good will MCServiceGuard or SharePlex/iX-NetBase do for a disk failure? Using the same logic, while your disk systems may be protected through these measures what happens if you have a failure on the CPU or LAN? For MCServiceGuard or SharePlex/iX-NetBase to work to it's maximum level there should not be any single points of failure, you need to provide duplicate paths to disks, duplicate LAN interfaces, mirrored and high available disk arrays.

The Continuously Available system

In the Continuously Available system environment NO downtime is the goal. While this can be accomplished it is not without cost. In many ways this cost is not in the hardware and software alone, but also includes the physical plant. In this environment nothing can be allowed to bring the system down including geographical, natural and other types of disasters. ALL hardware must be redundant. System components as well as peripherals. Not only do they have to be redundant but they must be "hot swap-able." But more importantly, they have to be able to "switch" to the alternate hardware automatically. If you lose a power supply you should never see a problem. After supplying a warning message and possibly a test-fail led, the system should simply run on the "alternate" supply. The defective supply can then be "hot swapped". Like the previous environments there should be no single points of failure.

For instance, in the computer room environment, there must be a source of back-up power such as a Motor Generator and additional air conditioning that can be automatically switched in case of primary unit failure. At the software level, it must be possible to patch and test the operating system and applications without having to shut the system down. Generally these environments also have very stringent security as well as "hardened" equipment rooms. Don't forget that some failures can occur as a result of internal sabotage. Providing the Continuously Available environment requires extensive planning.

The Costs of Planned and Unplanned Downtime.

We've looked briefly at a number of high availability products, which can be used to achieve various levels and degrees of application and system availability. All these products can cost a lot of money and before investing in any of them, you need to be able to justify their costs. In reviewing your environment you need to consider what downtime—both planned and unplanned—is costing you. Unplanned downtime is the result of a failure of some sort. Planned downtime is due to routine maintenance. Planning for a high availability environment involves an analysis of both unplanned and planned downtime. Do you have to take your application away from your users to perform a backup? Can you update your application software as well as your Operating System without affecting your users? Activities such as these are called planned downtime operations.

It's important to understand the cost of planned and unplanned downtime. This represents, in simple terms, the amount of money that the company loses if a particular application is offline for a specified period of time—typically one hour. Downtime costs can run into millions of dollars per hour. For example, in a manufacturing environment, a system shutdown that lasts for over thirty minutes can force a plant to shut the production line down. To calculate the cost of downtime, you'd need to analyze the cost of actually being down, as well as the cost of stopping and starting the line. Material waste is often the biggest cost because anything that is in the production line when it is shutdown may need to be thrown away.

Here's another example. Imagine you get off of an airplane and walk up to a rental car agency counter. Before you even get the chance to say hello the clerk tells you their computer system is down and they cannot write up a rental agreement and they aren't sure how long it will be before they can. Your first inclination would be to walk approximately thirty feet to the next counter and rent your car from another company. This represents a permanent loss of business to the rental car company. While the amount of your rental might not appear to be significant, imagine the cost of similar occurrences taking place all over the country at the same time!! This can add up to a very significant loss of revenue.

Lets look at one more example of the cost of downtime. Consider the case of a company which determined that they could perform their maintenance activities after the stock exchanges closed. They had automated the backup process and could change their tapes during the day. So their planned downtime was really not going to cost them any productivity loss. The question then became do they really need any of the high availability strategies available today? During the planning process we determined that planned or unplanned downtime during the day could very well cost them two hundred thousand dollars a half-hour. How would you answer the previous question? Do they need to look into High Availability?

Another area that often goes unnoticed when deciding whether to implement a High Availability solution is the user confidence area. We have a customer that had a very heavily used printer. As a matter of fact we would submit that this printer was one of the most important peripherals on their system. Since the printer was so heavily used it required additional maintenance. These activities required the printer to be down while they were being performed. The information services personnel understood this. But the users did not. As a matter of fact, as far as the users were concerned the printer was "broken" again!! The printer wasn't "broken," it was down so we could perform preventative maintenance to keep it from breaking at an inopportune time. But after looking at this from the users point of view the printer WAS broken. If they couldn't get their printouts when they needed them, the printer was useless to them. Needless to say it did not take too long for the user community to completely lose faith in this printer. Too much downtime whether planned or unplanned can cause irreparable damage if the user community loses faith in the system.

If you do not have a need for your system during the off hours then planned downtime can be handled very easily. But that is only if you never have an unplanned downtime event. On the other hand if you are in an environment that can not stand any downtime then products that allow you to perform on-line backup, on-line database management and control are necessities. Again, like one of the previous examples you need to also look at the cost of unplanned downtime. While today's hardware is more and more reliable it still can and does fail.

In Summary

In today's environment downtime, whether planned or unplanned, is becoming more and more unacceptable. By determining your downtime cost and proper planning, you can reduce the effects that an untimely downtime event can have on your productivity. You need to first determine what type of environment you are striving to maintain. Do your needs require a ***reliable***, ***protected***, ***highly available*** or ***continuously availabl***e system? In all of the environments other than the reliable system the primary goal should be to eliminate all single points of failure. By utilizing mirroring, array disks, MCServiceGuard, SharePlex/iX-NetBase and on-line backup products such as TurboStore 24x7 True On-Line backup and Omni-Back II, you greatly improve the availability of your system while reducing the recovery time if an unplanned downtime even should occur.

CHAPTER 31

Security

For almost as long computer systems have been used in business, there have been attempts to use them to defraud and steal. Even the earliest batch systems were systematically abused and manipulated. These early computer crimes were typically perpetrated by company insiders who modified "home grown" application software to line their own pockets. When the perpetrators were caught, the corporate victims often declined to press charges, fearing that the publicity would destroy public confidence in the firm. As a result, many of the early examples of computer fraud come down to us primarily in rumors and anecdotes. Police reports and court records are few and far between.

In the banking industry, it was rumored that one major financial institution lost hundreds of thousands of dollars over a period of years, when a programmer was asked to write a routine that would calculate interest on passbook accounts. The programmer realized that when you multiplied an account balance by an interest rate, you got a result of dollars, cents and fractions of a cent. Instead of rounding the result to the nearest penny, the programmer simply added the "roundings" to his personal account. At the end of each week, he emptied the account of whatever cash had accumulated. He was only caught, the story goes, because a female bank teller became curious about the bookish young man from the computer department who seemed to have a limitless supply of cash. Her questions attracted the attention of the young man's manager, who called him into his office one afternoon in hopes of getting some advice with his investments. Imagine his surprise when the programmer, upon being asked about his fiscal resources, broke down and confessed what he had done.

In another example, a retailer decided to replace an aging credit application. The batch system had been one of the first business applications that the company had put in place, written in a now-obsolete low level language. As part of the design process for the new on-line system, a thorough audit of the old software had to be completed, so that the new system's logic would reflect the old one wherever it was appropriate. Imagine their surprise when the audit uncovered a table of credit card numbers, buried deep in the bowels of the batch application and labeled "SPECIAL-ACCOUNTS". Any charges to these "special" accounts simply vanished from the books—the card owners were never billed. In order to balance the books, the application diverted the missing charges, sometimes one penny at a time, to accounts belonging to other customers. So a person who charged $27.74 in the housewares department might instead be billed in the amount of $27.75. As near as the investigators could tell, the special accounts had been there for almost ten years when they were uncovered, and if anybody had noticed the discrepancy in all that time, they had apparently decided that it was easier to pay the extra penny than it was to complain about it. It was assumed that any customer who filed a "one cent complaint" with the local store would almost surely be paid off without any record of the complaint being filed with the corporate office. An investigation revealed that the "special" accounts belonged to an individual who had once been employed by the company as a programmer, but who had left the company two years earlier. The last charges to a "special" account were received shortly after his departure. He had bought nearly seven hundred and fifty dollars worth of Hawaiian shirts, swimsuits, beach towels, and an electric guitar.

Application programmers must have a trusted relationship with their employers, because ultimately they are the ones that tell the company's computers what to do. Both of these crimes were committed by people whose trusted relationships with their employers gave them special access to the datacenter, and to the software that resides there.

In both of these cases, a company was robbed—not using a gun or a knife—but using a piece of software—an application program. In mainframe environments, applications are stored inside the walls of the "glass house" where they could be protected from tampering. One of the cardinal rules of the mainframe environment is that applications that programmers create or modify should not go into production without an audit to detect fraud. And in order to prevent programmers from circumventing this audit, they should *never* be given free access to the data center.

Today, physical access to "the glass house" is much more tightly controlled than it once was. IS managers now have a wide variety of high tech tools available to them for keeping unauthorized people out of the datacenter (key cards, retinal scanners and voice printing, just to name a few). But at the same time, networks are making the walls of the "glass house" irrelevant. Many of the applications that used to reside in the datacenter have migrated to desktops all over the enterprise. How will we protect the applications from dishonest or malicious users? Worse, we are now entering an age when at least limited access to corporate data will be extended to applications that reside outside of the enterprise. Will the next wave of computer crime be committed by users on the public Internet?

It's interesting to note that the 1987 Computer Security Act assigns responsibility for all damages due to electronic fraud or abuse to the company whose computers were used to perpetrate the fraud—*not* to the perpetrator. This is particularly worth thinking about if you are the one responsible for your company's system security. Who do you suppose the company will turn to if the security of that system is compromised?

Computer security encompasses three areas: privacy, availability and system integrity. Privacy ensures that access to valuable data and programs can be controlled. As was saw in the previous chapter, availability is the provision of service and access to data regardless of circumstances and conditions. Integrity is the ability of the system to provide and maintain accurate information for the users. In order for the systems integrity be maintained error-checks must be performed on a regular basis. Verification methods must be continually updated as the need requires.

One of the tools that many persons go by today to measure how secure their systems are is the Department of Defense "Orange Book." This is a publication the purpose of which is to provide guidance to manufacturers so that they will know what security tools and technologies are necessary to meet a high level of security requirements. The Orange Book also provides vendors with a clear statement of the security requirements that they must meet if they are going to bid on a government contract. Users are provided with a measure to put against products with regard to security.

The Orange Book stipulates four evaluation divisions. They are; A-Verified Protection, B-Mandatory Protection, C-Discretionary Protection and D-Minimal Protection. The protection features in each division are cumulative to the previous division.

Division D is for minimal protection and has only one "class." This class is for the "evaluated" system. To qualify for this division a system has to only have minimal protection.

Division C has two classes.

- Class C1 stipulates that access can be controlled by the user, that identification and authentication of users can be performed and that a TCB or Trusted Computing Base domain is protected. A TCB is the combination of protection mechanisms within a computer system. Items such as software, hardware and firmware are responsible for enforcing a security policy. To qualify as a TCB one or more of these items must be present.
- Class C2 states that a system has access control for individual users and has the capability to log access and secure reuse of storage objects. The key item here is that access control be at the individual user level not just at the group or account level.

Division B has three classes.

- Class B1 maintains mandatory access control and associates sensitivity labels with each subject and storage object under its control to include items such as processes, files, segments, devices and I/O channels and an informal statement regarding the security policy model must exist.
- Class B2 mandates a structured protection mechanism such as a clearly defined and documented formal security policy model that requires mandatory and discretionary access control enforcement to be extended to all subjects and objects of the system as defined in class B1. There must be clear configuration management and detailed design documentation.
- Class B3 is measured by minimized complexity of the security requirements, the definition of a security administrator, to signal not just record security relevant events and provide reliable recovery procedures and also be highly resistant to penetration.

Division A has only one class. Class A1 stipulates no additional architecture beyond that of class B3 but that security specification and verification techniques be developed as well as provide extensive documentation relevant to the assurance all of the measures have been correctly implemented.

The security environments provided by computer operating systems can be measured against the specifications of the Orange Book's divisions and classes. For example, both MPE/iX and HP-UX can be made secure enough to comply with Class C2. MPE/iX requires the addition of the Security Monitor product, and HP-UX requires that the system be configured as a "trusted system." The important thing to understand is that with either operating system, the only shortcut to making a system totally secure is to simply power it down. If it can't be accessed, it can't be broken into. Short of that, good system security is a matter of proper system management. Computer "Hacking" is little more than a methodical search for mistakes that have been made by sloppy or naive system administrators.

In order to begin providing good security measures let's go over some of the elements that make up security. We will drill down further on some of these items as we go along. Every system manager needs a documented security policy and a security plan that addresses all three of the security areas, availability, integrity and privacy. Every System Administrator needs to be aware and knowledgeable about security requirements. And the user community should be security-conscious.

By contrast, "conventional wisdom" sometimes suggests security practices that are ineffective or downright destructive. For example, some system administrators have tried to make ignorance a key piece of their security plan. They reason that keeping the design of the security plan hidden from users will hamper their efforts to defeat it. This just a plain bad idea, rooted in an atmosphere of distrust. How can your users become security conscious if they are kept in the dark as to what is expected of them?

The security policy should define responsibilities and duties of the system administrator, security administrator and the users. This policy should be derived from contributions from all levels that it applies too. The policy should be visible to anyone to whom it applies. As previously mentioned, don't hide it.

A security plan consists of tools and actions that should be utilized to protect the system. This plan should be detailed, (but not so detailed as to prevent it from being implemented). Items such as backup schedules, checking log files, password management and security audits are just a part of this plan. When putting this plan together keep these protection issues in mind.

- What actions need to be performed to provide sufficient protection?
- Who will be responsible for performing these actions and are there any physical protection requirements?
- There are three areas that need to be considered when developing a security plan.
    1. The People involved, and their specific responsibilities under the plan
    2. The physical resources that will be required, and
    3. The procedures and actions that need to be performed, how often and by whom.

Responsibility is a key part of any security plan. Users, system administrator and the security administrator must share responsibility for the security of the system. Users should be well trained in what is expected of them. Procedures for logging in, the security policy itself and such basic practices as ensuring that terminals or PC's are not left logged on to the system while unattended should all be part of basic user training. Users must also be held responsible for locking up data that might have been printed or stored on diskettes, tapes and other media. They should also be aware of password policy and cautioned against sharing passwords with other users.

The system administrator's responsibilities include maintaining the availability and integrity of the system. The security administrator should be more concerned with protecting system software, verifying new releases of vendor supplied software with particular attention to security patches and the performance of security audits.

The physical part of a security plan involves making sure the system, console and other sensitive equipment is kept in a secure area, with proper access controls (locks, key cards, etc.) in place. Of course, controlling the doorway to the computer room is only part of the solution. Providing end users access to the system console can open up a variety of security problems. The HP 3000 operating system provides the operator with a command (:CONSOLE) which can be used to make it possible to enter console commands from a terminal other than logical device 20 (the terminal typically located on top of the CPU). Users who have been authorized to use the :CONSOLE command can "pull" the console to their own terminals in order to check on the status of a batch job or printout. In the past, the console could only be moved to terminals wired to a DTC (i.e., connected to the HP 3000 using RS-232). But as of release 5.5, the console can be "pulled" across a network. This means that, more than ever, console access must be carefully controlled and monitored, because any user who can pull the console to his desktop can also bring the system down by simply typing the appropriate operator commands.

Perhaps the most important but least well understood security issues are those associated with networking. Consider an Ethernet LAN. The wires of a LAN are, in this respect, like the surface of a pond. Throw a stone into the pond, and ripples from the stone are transmitted across the surface. You can't send a ripple from point A to point B without also sending it to every other point on the surface of the pond.

A similar situation arises when you send a message (i.e., a packet) across a LAN. If a user at a PC sends a packet to a server, the packet is transmitted from the PC to *every* device that's attached to that segment of the LAN. At the same moment it arrives at the server for which it was intended, it is also arriving at every other server, PC, printer, workstation or device on the same LAN. Ordinarily, the networking software on these other devices will look at the IP address of the packet and, determining that it's not addressed to them, will simply ignore it. But, software exists (if you know where to get it, and it's not hard to find on the World Wide Web) which can put a PC into (I'm not making this term up), "promiscuous mode." This means that the PC will accept every packet that comes across the LAN, regardless of to whom it's addressed. These software packages (sometimes distributed through "hacker" bulletin boards) will look for "interesting packets" (containing character strings such as "Password:"). These packets are stored in a log file for later analysis by the hacker. If your office's LAN cables are easily accessible, then you might want to give some thought to what would happen if an office "visitor" were to attach a device to your network that would enable them to obtain passwords, port numbers and other kinds of sensitive data.

We've already talked about the importance of controlling access to the datacenter. It's particularly important that you exercise strict controls over who can access your system's backup tapes. With these a person could very well restore them to another system (or PC) and obtain very sensitive data. Encrypted files, copied from a backup tape, can be subjected to the thorough and painstaking attempts to break the encryption when transferred from your system to a hacker's PC or workstation. The security plan must specify who is responsible for performing, updating and maintaining the procedures or actions necessary to insure the plan is properly enforced.

If security is your responsibility, these are some of the questions you should be continually asking yourself. Where am I exposed? Is the network secure? Am I covered in case I have a malicious user? Do I have modems on my system and are they secure? In this chapter we will drill down further to clarify these questions as well as provide information that could lead to even more questions that you need to answer. Remember that just answering these questions won't make your computer room any more secure than it today. That can only be achieved by having the discipline to follow through on the answers, and changing any procedures that are in place that leave you exposed.

The answer to the question, "Where am I exposed," can be very long and detailed. Virtually every company has some exposure. The computer or equipment room itself, and the network are two obvious places to begin your investigation. If you have users, programs, and modems, you almost certainly have some security exposure. As application software migrates from the datacenter to people's desktops, it's more critical than ever that end users be aware of some of the techniques that hackers have used to break security, including Trojan Horses, Trap Doors, Time Bombs and viruses.

Like the famed Horse of ancient Greece, a Trojan Horse program looks harmless on the outside, but contains something that's very unpleasant. For example, every—based PC contains a file called AUTOEXEC.BAT. It is executed automatically every time the PC is powered up or re-booted. If a PC is left unattended, an unscrupulous office visitor might make a change to AUTOEXEC.BAT, so that unbeknownst to the PC's owner, every time the machine is powered up in the morning, it automatically makes a copy of some file containing sensitive data. It may even email the copied file to the visitor. Trojan Horse programs are typically "disguised" as frequently used system files (such as AUTOEXEC.BAT) or as innocuous games.

Although Trojan Horse programs can be created for HP 3000s, they are difficult to "plant" on MPE/iX systems. This is because in order for a program to do anything malicious, it must typically be linked with a special program capability such as Privileged Mode (PM). And programs that are linked with special capabilities can only execute if they are placed in groups that also have these special capabilities. The key to keeping dangerous Trojan horse software off of your HP 3000 is to know exactly what groups have PM capability, (this can be displayed using the LISTGROUP command), and to check the system regularly to ensure that there have been no changes. This can be done as part of your regularly scheduled backups.

For example, a programmer might create a "Trojan Horse" program that disguises itself as CI.PUB.SYS, (the program that displays the MPE "colon prompt," and interprets and executes MPE commands). But in order to do its dirty work, the Trojan Horse program would have to be placed in the PUB.SYS group, or in another group that has all the special capabilities of the program. By default, MPE/iX prevents non-SM users from copying any kind of software into PUB.SYS. A hacker who wants to break into an MPE system will look for files in PUB.SYS (or in other PM groups such as PRV.TELESUP) that have had their access rights disabled using the :RELEASE command. If a file in PRV.TELESUP or PUB.SYS has been :RELEASED, then any user on the system has permission to read or write that file. In other words, using the :RELEASE command on a program that resides in a PM group makes it possible for a hacker to replace the program with one of their own. System managers who control access to groups with special capabilities have gone a long way toward protecting their systems from Trojan Horses and other security breaches. If you need to change the security attributes of a file in a PM group, use the :ALTSEC and :ALTFILE commands with an Access Control Definition (ACD). In this way, you can grant the specific permission needed to the specific user who needs it. This eliminates the security breaches that can be created by using the inadvisable use of the :RELEASE command.

Another term that you frequently hear in discussion of security issues is the "trap door." "Trap door" routines are sequences of code that are concealed inside a legitimate program. They're sometimes originally written for debugging purposes—

and may circumvent security policies of your application or your system. Trap doors may be used (or abused) to allow users to "sneak" into the system.

Trap door programs for UNIX systems may assign root user privileges to the person running the program. Similarly, "trap door" programs for MPE systems may grant some or all special capabilities to the calling session. Operating system software is not immune to trap doors. In the early days of UNIX, there were a number of known trap doors that were often exploited by hackers. Over time, these have been eliminated. Today, with UNIX systems being commonly used for mission critical, commercial applications, all known trap doors in HP-UX have long since been removed. And if a new one comes to light, HP quickly makes patches available to close it. The key to keeping trap doors off of your system is to ensure that all patches relating to security are promptly installed on your system, and to maintain control of any and all software that is stored on your system. On HP 3000s, strict limitations on access to groups that have special capabilities (SM, OP, PM, etc.) is the key to eliminating trap doors.

Another programmatic technique that has been used to interfere with security is the "time bomb." The time bomb is actually a variation on the Trojan Horse. It is typically disguised as a program that either belongs on your computer (like AUTOEXEC.BAT) or that is harmless (like a game). The program emulates the behavior of the "real" program until a certain time or date is reached. Then it does something different (and typically destructive). Time bombs are sometimes used by software vendors for legitimate purposes. For example, many software companies distribute free copies of their products to prospective customers, but these free copies contain "time bombs." which ensure that the software will cease to operate (if you haven't decided to pay for it) when a certain date arrives.

A computer "virus" is a combination of a Trojan Horse and a time bomb. A virus typically attacks a system by being imbedded in another program like a Trojan Horse. But unlike an ordinary Trojan Horse, a virus program secretly copies the "time bomb" logic to another part of your system. On a PC, it might be copied to your hard disk's "boot sector," which is executed whenever your system is rebooted. Or it might be copied across your LAN to affect other PCs in your office. In this way, computer viruses can be "transmitted" not unlike biological viruses. Viruses can be secreted inside of any executable software object. Most viruses are concealed in compiled programs, but certain kinds of viruses have been transmitted using other executable media—including interpreted programs, command files and scripts. There's even a virus that has been transmitted via word processing documents by disguising itself as a macro used by a popular word processing program.

These are just some of the examples of security problems in the programming area. By verifying all software that is loaded on the system you can protect yourself against all of these potential security breaches. One of the quickest ways to endanger your computer system today is by downloading free software from the internet. Many companies have installed firewalls as a protection against outsiders who try to use the Internet to break into their systems. But this is no protection against a PC user who downloads software from a bulletin board. There have been cases in which seemingly innocuous programs (games are the most common transmission medium) have infected not only the PC of the person who downloaded the software, but also all of the systems that are on that network, perhaps even the firewall!

Most system managers look to the outside for security problems, but we must also look inside the company as well. According to one FBI study, 85 percent of "computer break-ins" are perpetrated, not by outsiders, but by trusted employees who misuse their access to sensitive data. Disgruntled employees and employees who have been terminated have been known to leave damaging software behind.

Predictably, most of the attention paid to security is directed at high-tech hacking techniques like the ones we've just discussed. But the most over-looked security breaches are often the simplest—proper management of passwords. Password policy isn't the hardest thing to establish, but it can be one of the most difficult things to maintain.

A new term that has surfaced recently in the computer security world is "shoulder surfing." This may be a new entry to the jargon, but refers to one of the oldest hacker's practices: looking over a user's shoulder as he or she types in passwords or other sensitive information. The most stringent password policies can not prevent this security problem. Shoulder surfing can be covert, bold or sublime. The bold shoulder surfer simply walks up to a user and asks him or her to sign on to a particular account or area to look for something. The shoulder surfer carefully observes the user typing the password and remembers the sequence. The sublime shoulder surfer is more sneaky. He'll come up to you and ask a question that they know will require you to sign on to a particular area. If you don't fall for it, then, well, not everyone who surfs "hangs ten" every time. Shoulder surfing is one of the key reasons why end users need to be trained to be security conscious. The best defense is an end user community that won't hesitate to report suspicious behavior. . . .

The password protection scheme supported by your computer's operating system may be sufficient to meet your security needs. In most instances your security and password policies should enforce practices such as password aging, format requirements as well as other restrictions. System passwords should be changed regularly and frequently. While this might not seem significant think how many people might have left that company over a period of years. If they had access to your system passwords while they still worked for your company, there's little to stop them logging on, leaving behind software goodies such as Trojan Horses or viruses and doing a lot of damage.

Password aging determines how long a given password is allowed to stay valid. With some operating systems such as HP-UX 10.01, users are required to change passwords within a certain specified period of time, or the login is disabled. The system administrator is required to enable the login again. Similar functionality is available on MPE/iX with the addition of the Security Monitor product. Password aging guarantees that the passwords are being changed on a regular basis. How long should a password be valid? This question can only be answered by you but we suggest that passwords should be changed at least in six-month increments.

Another area that often time goes overlooked is the format of a password. Here again some operating systems are taking this into account. They won't let you set up a password that doesn't have at least one numerical character. This prevents users from adopting obvious passwords such as their own names. The most secure passwords are long character strings (at least 8 characters, preferably more) consisting of random combinations of letters and numbers.

The most common technique used by hackers to break security is to simply guess the password. Lists have been published on hacker bulletin boards commonly used accounts and passwords. For example, one hacker board has a complete list of the passwords that HP routinely assigns to MANAGER.SYS and MGR.TELESUP when initially installing a new HP 3000 system. This list also contained logons and passwords typically used by popular vendors of software for the HP 3000. Similar lists exist for other systems—including UNIX systems and (increasingly) NT systems. If a vendor installs software on your system, insist that they remove all unnecessary logons when they're done. If they need an account on your system, be certain that you change the password as soon as they leave. If you haven't changed these passwords, I can't overemphasize the importance of doing so. Put this book down and go do it. Now.

Hackers can easily guess the passwords associated with user accounts with passwords that have some kind of meaning to the user such as a date. The most commonly used passwords are based on some portion of the user's name, address, birthday, anniversary or just a particular key stroke sequence. Children's names, ages and birthdates are also very popular. Given that you know the person whose password you are trying to decipher which one do you think would be easier to guess, "PSEB253Y" or "may1273"? Password policy should disallow the use of simple keyboard sequences like "asdf." Don't use visible things from your office or desk. Make sure you use different passwords for different systems. Don't store your password in a function key for ease of use. Do not toggle back and forth between two set passwords to get by the password aging parameters. Don't use words from the dictionary spelled correctly or backwards. And ensure that your users are security conscious, so that they'll understand the reasons behind these rules.

In the UNIX environment passwords are encrypted in a file called /etc/password. This file is accessible to anybody on the system, so the encryption represents UNIX's sole line of defense against hackers. Luckily, UNIX's encryption algorithm is very good. For one thing, it's "one way" encryption. This is best explained using an example. Suppose my password is gulliblegoose. UNIX encrypts this password and stores the encrypted string in /etc/password, along with other information relating to my userid. The encrypted password string will appear as a random string of characters. The important thing to understand about UNIX encryption is that there's no way to decrypt that string. In other words, even if you know what the encrypted string is, it's mathematically virtually impossible to work your way backwards from the encrypted string to the original string.

This should lead you to wonder how UNIX verifies your password when you logon. Common sense would tell you that it must somehow decrypt the encrypted string in /etc/password. But we've already said that this is virtually impossible to do (even for UNIX). Instead, when you attempt to logon to a UNIX system, the operating systems encrypts the string that you enter when you try to logon. Then it compares the encrypted string that you entered at logon time with the encrypted password that's stored in /etc/password. If they match, then you're permitted to logon.

A hacker who's bound and determined to break through a computer system's security might resort to using a computer program to help him. For example, we've seen that on UNIX systems, passwords are stored in a file called /etc/password. The passwords are encrypted, but other information is stored in "clear text" (i.e., without any encryption at all). Software can be used to mechanize the process of trying to guess passwords.

Perhaps the most widely used program of this type is Cracker (also known simply as "crack" in some versions). Cracker is available on a number of hacker bulletin boards, most of which are accessible on the Internet. If a user installs cracker on your computer, he (or she) can use it to look at each entry in /etc/password. System administrators have the option of storing all sorts of information in this file. User names, phone numbers, mailstops and so forth are frequently found in /etc/password. Cracker picks up whatever information it finds in /etc/password. The program then encrypts it using the same algorithm that UNIX uses, and compares the results against the encrypted passwords stored in the password file. To the extent that the end users decide to use easily guessable passwords, (their own names, phone numbers, mailstops, etc.), cracker can be used to guess them and easily circumvent your system security. On a typical UNIX system, the /etc/password file is relatively small. Cracker can be used to compare the unencrypted user information against the encrypted passwords, and the whole password file can be processed in a matter of seconds. You can protect against this kind of attack by ensuring that your users don't use obvious passwords such as their own names, logon Ids, and so forth.

Some companies have a security policy that insists that every password contain a mixture of alphabetic and numerical characters. This eliminates the use of names and phone numbers (which may be available in the password file). But it's not enough. Cracker can be configured to circumvent this policy, by spelling whatever information it finds forwards and backwards, and comparing the resulting encrypted string to the passwords. It can be configured to substitute strings of numbers at the beginning and end of each prospective password that it tries. If that fails, it can even be programmed to try similar processing with every word in the English dictionary.

Using Cracker in this way means that the hacker who is running it won't be able to process your password file in a matter of seconds. Encrypting every word in the dictionary could take hours. A hacker who is running Cracker on your system will probably be noticed long before he has time to compare every word in the dictionary with the passwords used on your system. For this reason, hackers have learned that it's more effective to use ftp to copy your password file to their own system, where they can allow Cracker to run for days, if necessary.

It has been said that HP 3000s are intrinsically more secure than UNIX systems. If there's any truth to that at all, I suspect it's because there are more UNIX computers than MPE/iX computers in use today, which means that hackers have less interest in studying techniques for attacking MPE/iX security. The fact is that system security on virtually any operating system can be circumvented by a determined hacker who has a working knowledge of the operating system's internals, particularly if the system administrator has been sloppy in managing system security.

Unlike UNIX, MPE/iX does not store its passwords in a file, but rather in an internal system table. To access the MPE/iX password table, a Cracker-like program would have to be linked with privileged mode (PM) capability. MPE/iX only allows PM programs to execute if they reside in a group that has this capability associated with it. Therefore, HP 3000 system administrators can best defend themselves against software-based security attacks by controlling PM capability carefully. The system should frequently be audited to ensure that only authorized users and approved groups have PM capability. And the contents of PM groups should be carefully managed.

For example, a programmer with a working knowledge of HP's Architected Interface Facility (AIF) product could easily write a program to display the MANAGER.SYS passwords. Programs with names like "god" have even been distributed which temporarily grant the user running them with every MPE capability, including PM. But a user who obtains copies of these programs cannot run them on your system unless they are able to place them in a PM group, such as PUB.SYS or PRV.TELESUP. This means system managers need to be particularly careful about managing access to these groups, (see the notes in the section on Trojan Horses earlier in this chapter).

On both MPE/iX and UNIX, operating system defects occasionally create situations which allow end users to give themselves PM capability. For example, there was once a notorious defect in the QUERY program on HP 3000s. A knowledgeable user could run QUERY with the DEBUG option, and set a breakpoint at a certain location. When execution was interrupted at that point, the end user would have PM capability, which allowed him to use DEBUG commands to give himself other capabilities, including SM. Similar defects have surfaced from time to time on UNIX systems. It's important, therefore, that system administrators keep themselves up to date on the latest patches to their operating systems. When a vendor discovers a security "hole" in their software, and classifies it as a "known problem," it typically means two things: first, there's a patch to fix it, and second, the problem is known, not only to the vendor, but to hackers as well. Security patches should be installed as soon as possible.

I'm covering these tricks in this book, not to make you a better hacker, but rather to make the point that your security policies (particularly your password policy) are critically important. A password like MARY may be easy to remember—but it will also be easily guessed by programs like Cracker. A password like A234BC#HH looks more difficult. But it's virtually "Cracker-proof." Security policies that include a regular audit of the password file can be used to ensure that users choose secure passwords. This is perhaps the most important reason why you need to understand how hackers go about trying to break your system's security. One way that you can enforce these policies is to periodically use programs like Cracker to try to guess the passwords yourself. If you can get through your security, then a hacker can.

The best way to ensure that the password can not be deciphered is to allow no access what so ever to the /etc/passwd file. This can be accomplished in many ways. One is to enable "trusted system" level security. A trusted system doesn't use the normal /etc/passwd file when checking security. Instead, things like encrypted passwords are stored somewhere else, where programs like Cracker cannot access them. The only drawback today in making your system "trusted" is that NIS will not operate. NIS requires the /etc/passwd file be intact. In today's HP-UX 10.01 a system can be configured as "trusted" through the SAM utility. Not only can it be enabled but unlike previous versions of HP-UX it can also be disabled.

Let's look at a couple more areas that should be considered when putting together your security plan.

The network can be a valuable place for the "hacker" to gain information regarding your system. Oddly enough, one area of concern is the "trusted" host. UNIX systems provide users with a number of convenient utilities such as rlogin, remsh and rcp. Some of these have been ported to MPE/iX, and are even available as "shareware" on MPE systems. These were not intended to be used in a trusted host environment. Users may be able to gain access to your system with these utilities without having to enter a password. The trusted host concept should be used carefully if these utilities are part of your system's operation.

Another area to watch out for is the use of packet sniffers and network analyzers. A packet sniffer is a device or piece of software that is used to diagnose network connection problems. It is typically nothing more than a PC running specialized software for troubleshooting. This device captures all packets that cross the network, and store them in some kind of cache or logfile. Notice the operative word is "all." These packets can contain passwords. Passwords are not encrypted until they arrive at the computer onto which the user is trying to logon. By default, when a user enters a password in response to a prompt, the password is transmitted to the host as clear text (i.e., unencrypted). Packet sniffers can (and will) see them.

Network analyzers are used to gather network performance data over a period of time. Like a sniffer, it captures packets and the information contained in those packets. This could include passwords, sensitive business data and other things you might not want to disclose. Most systems also have trace diagnostics that can be started from the host, and which will behave like a sniffer. If a user has the root password, there's little to stop them from running these diagnostics. If the permissions on the diagnostic program are not correct, root users can start the diagnostic and log the information they want. In the HP-UX environment the /etc/services and /etc/inetd.conf files should be used to control network services.

Modems are important tools, but they can be one of the most vulnerable areas with regard to security. Modems provide an invaluable service to the system administrators, remote programmers and remote service personnel. Modems provide wide access to your machine, and typically don't provide encryption. Hackers have used modems to provide dial tone playback to record phone numbers and other information. A modem disconnect doesn't always terminate the session that was in progress on that modem. An end user who calls in to a modem might find a root session already in progress. Modem phone lines can even be tapped.

One of the easiest ways to prevent unauthorized access to the system via a modem is to have a password on the modem port. Callback modems are another popular option. These can be set up to respond to a call by dialing a preconfigured phone number. They are typically used to allow employees to dial in from home. The employee, working out of his home, calls the callback modem and hangs up. A few seconds later, the callback modem calls the employee's home number, and the employee's modem answers, making the connection. If an unauthorized caller dials a callback modem from another location, the callback modem will not call him back—it will only call its preconfigured phone number.

Callback modems can be fooled. For instance some modems are configured to dial out on the same line that was used to dial up the modem. This represents an exposure. A hacker can call this line, then keep the connection open after the system cuts its end of the circuit. The modem will then attempt to dial out on this same line. The hacker (who still has the line open) uses a tape recorder to play back a dial tone, fooling the callback modem into thinking it has received a dialtone from the phone company. It opens a connection to the hacker's phone line and dials its preconfigured number. The hacker ignores this and answers the "call" with his own modem. The callback modem, thinking it has reached its preconfigured number, makes the connection, providing the hacker with a log in prompt. Callback modems should not dial out on the same line that was used to dial them. They should be configured to use a different line.

There are programs available to help a security administrator watch out for problems. A couple of these are COPS and Cracker. COPS is a collection of UNIX programs that attempts to tackle different areas of security. COPS stands for Computer Oracle and Password System. The security administrator can obtain this via an anonymous FTP from cert.sei.cmu.edu. In addition to some of the items we covered in this chapter, COPS also checks directory and file ownership issues and other such related items.

The Cracker program that was mentioned earlier also has a legitimate purpose. System administrators have used to find common eight character DES-encrypted passwords. This tool comes in real handy to assist in enforcing password policy by looking for passwords that can be hacked by comparing them to a standard dictionary search. It also checks for accounts with no passwords. Cracker, like COPS, is designed to run on a UNIX system.

In Table 31.1 please find references to security related organizations that provide items such as newsletters, training and conferences. Some also provide assistance in emergency situations.

Table 31.1 Security Organizations

Association for Computing Machinery (ACM)
USENIX

ACM Headquarters
USENIX Association
11 West 42 Street
2560 Ninth Street, Suite 215
New York, NY 10036
Berkely, CA 94703

IEEE Computer Society
Computer Security Institute (CSI)

IEEE Computer Society
Computer Security Institute
1730 Massachusetts Avenue N.W.
600 Harrison Street
Washington, DC 20036-1903
San Francisco, CA 94107

National Institute of Standards and Technology
(NIST)
Computer Emergency Response Team (CERT)

NIST Computer Security
email - cert@sei.cmu.edu
Division A-216
(412) 268-7090
Gaithersburg, MD 20899

In today's environment, security is one of the leading concerns where the commercial use of the Internet is involved. While most of us think of a firewall as the only security we need when we connect our business to the Internet that is only one small part. The three categories that fall out regarding the Internet are authentication, confidentiality and integrity.

In it's most simple form authentication is proving the user is who they say they are. Today authentication while being still somewhat sketchy is improving. Much of the new work that's being done in the security area is being driven by the intense level of interest in the World Wide Web. Some Web servers allow user level authentication ranging from simple password protection to network domain exclusion. When data is passed between a Web server and a browser, the data can be encrypted before it is transmitted across the network. This is particularly important for electronic commerce applications, which require the transmission of sensitive pieces of information such as credit card numbers. But in order for this to work, the browser and the server must use the same encryption algorithm. Today, there are multiple "standards" for data encryption, and it's not clear which one will eventually be accepted.

Basically, there are two kinds of encryption commonly used with Web applications. The first involves the use of a secret key, and the second involves the use of public and private keys.

Text which is not encrypted in any fashion is sometimes referred to as "clear text." There are many algorithms that can be used to encrypt clear text. As kids many of us played with "decoder rings" which simply substituted different characters for one another. This substitution algorithms are very easy to break. In fact, any encryption algorithm that has the clear text to be encrypted as its only input can be broken using the same techniques used with decoder rings. For this reason, the encryption algorithms typically used with the web have two inputs: the clear text to be encrypted, and a second character string called a "secret key."

The use of secret keys can be demonstrated using the crypt command, which is available on most UNIX systems (including the HP 9000). Suppose you have a file called "invite.txt," which contains some ASCII text. This file can be encrypted using the crypt command. The file, invite.txt, is used as input to the command. The output is directed to another file, called invite.crypt, as shown:

```
crypt <invite.txt >invite.crypt
```

The crypt command will prompt the user for a key. This can be any character string. The crypt command is also used to decrypt the file by simply reversing the process. The input of the crypt command is redirected to reference the encrypted file (invite.crypt).

```
crypt <invite.crypt >decrypted.txt
```

Once again, the user is prompted for a key. The same character string that was used to encrypt the file must be specified to decrypt the file. Otherwise, crypt will simply produce a file of random garbage.

The use of secret keys results in an encryption algorithm that is very difficult to break. But it may not be practical for Web applications. Secret keys depend on an agreement between the client and the server to use the same key. If the client and server "meet" on the internet for a single transaction (to order a pizza, for example), there may be no opportunity to establish an agreed upon key. Fortunately, there's another way. It involves the use of public and private keys.

In this scheme, information is encrypted and decrypted using keys, but the key that's used to encrypt the data is different from the key that's used to decrypt it. An example will serve to show how this can be useful. Suppose a bank starts to allow its customers to use the Web to access their accounts. They might provide their customers with a browser, and a public encryption key. This key (which could even be hard coded inside the browser) would be used to encrypt information passed from the browsers to the server (located at the bank). The public key can be used to encrypt information, but it cannot be used to decrypt it.

Therefore it doesn't matter if an unauthorized person finds out what the public key is, because all the banks customers use the same key, and it cannot be used to decrypt anything. When the encrypted messages arrive at the bank's server, they are decrypted using a second key called a private key. This key is known only to the bank, and must be protected from unauthorized persons.

When the bank is ready to send information back to its customers, it can be encrypted using the private key, and decrypted using the public key (exactly the reverse of the process that the customers used to send encrypted messages to the bank). Messages encrypted using the private key are not very secure, because they can be decrypted using the public key. And the public key is hardly a secret; it's in the hands of all the bank's customers. Therefore this kind of encryption allows customers to send secure messages to the bank—("My account number is 12345, and my password is ABCDE"). But the bank must assume that its replies could be intercepted and read by unauthorized persons. Therefore the replies should not contain any sensitive information. (That is, the bank should reply "Your password is correct," not "ABCDE is the correct password.")

These encryption techniques are used in a variety of ways to ensure that the data transmitted across the Web is safe from prying eyes. Perhaps the most common security protocols are the Secure Sockets Layer (SSL) and Secure HTTP (S-HTTP). SSL is a transport level or session encryption protocol which enables a secure channel in which messages are encrypted. This provides private and reliable communication between client and server, and server authentication. S-HTTP is a document level protocol to provide security of documents on the WWW. S-HTTP provides the capability to authenticate clients and servers, support digital signatures, negotiate security levels based on application needs and provide secure communication through existing firewalls. Digital signatures provide message authenticity (e.g., entire e-mail messages) using a sophisticated hash algorithm based on the sender's private key. There are other security protocols including the "Pretty Good

Privacy" program (PGP), Smart Cards and Kerberos. These protocols are not interchangeable, (so, for example, a server using S-HTTP will not work properly with a browser using SSL). At this time, no single security protocol has achieved the level of acceptance required to make it a defacto standard.

It's important to investigate security protocols thoroughly before investing in a Web server package for use with commercial applications, or before standardizing on a browser for use in a large enterprise.

Confidentiality is making sure your documents are "secure" from being seen by other parties while traveling through the maze of locations along the Internet. Integrity is ensuring the information is protected from modification. The use of encryption is the process used today to ensure confidentiality. There are many programs available today. Browsers such as Netscape and NCSA Mosaic provide encryption. Another well known encryption protocol available today is Pretty Good Privacy or PGP.

Today many contracts, purchase orders, invoices and many other such documents travel through this electronic post office. And we might add that unless some sort of encryption method is used, this information becomes public knowledge as soon as it is transmitted the first time. We would think most companies would consider this information to be most private. Also take into consideration how often mail is delivered to the wrong party. This occurs with email as well. Not only can it be delivered to the wrong address but, it can also be "detained" long enough to be modified and then sent on it's way. While this might seem a little far-fetched, consider how often corporate espionage occurs today. When you are putting your security policy into place you might consider adding a portion regarding encryption. While this may seem a little scary at first, consider the consequences that come along without encryption.

To ensure your system is secure, available and the integrity of the data has not been compromised, please take the time to develop a security policy as well as a security plan. Not only should you develop these items you need to enforce them. Through vigilance and encouragement, your users will be much more productive and security conscious.

CHAPTER 32

When It All Fails and How To Be Prepared For Most Disasters

The year was 1989. Two dramatic disasters took place. Hurricane Hugo slammed the coast of South Carolina and continued its deadly path inland as far as Charlotte, North Carolina. Less than a month later, a magnitude 7.1 earthquake centered under a mountain called Loma Prieta rocked the San Francisco bay area.

You might be thinking that it is during times such as these that most companies think of their Disaster Recovery Plans. This is not true. At times like these, it's too late to be thinking about Disaster Recovery. It's time to be practicing it. A Disaster Recovery Plan or DRP can be one of the most important documents your company has. It might not have a face value like your company's stock certificates, but if your company doesn't have one (that works) you can rest assured that the face value of your company's stock will drop.

The word "disaster" conjures up images of fires, earthquakes, hurricanes and riots. But a DRP should not be limited to planning for catastrophe. Good DRPs document the procedures to follow in the face of more mundane disasters. These include everything from the failure of a critical hardware component such as a disk drive to the total destruction of the datacenter. While most companies have some idea of what they would do in case of a disaster, many do not have these procedures documented anywhere. The system administrator keeps this information in his or her head. But what good does that do your company if the system administrator is not there when disaster strikes? Most disaster recovery plans address the data that resides on the computers in the "glass house," typically mainframes and minicomputers. But what good does that do your company if data that's critical to the business is stored outside of the glass house? What about the data that resides on people's desktops?

Every disaster recovery plan is unique, because every business is unique. But there are three common components to all good DRPs.

1. An honest and intelligent assessment of the risk to your business.
2. A well thought out contingency plan.
3. A detailed look at your backup strategy.

Risk Assessment

The first step you will need to take will be to define your risk. What impact would a disaster have on your business? What would be the long term cost to your company? To accomplish this task, begin by performing an audit of your systems. The following information should be obtained.

- The amount of data you currently have on your systems. This includes all the systems, from the mainframes, minicomputers and servers that reside the "glass house" to the client systems on people's desktops.
- The type of data on each system. (For example, is it a database server or an email gateway?)
- The value of the data. (How long can your business survive without it? How difficult will it be to recreate it?)

During this audit do not forget your LAN and other equipment that is not located in the computer center. The use of special forms can assist in obtaining remote information.

By contracting with specialized consulting firms this audit can be performed from an objective point of view. These firms specialize in gathering this information. Upon completion of the audit, divide your data into the following categories. This classification will assist you in deciding which backup and recovery parameters are most appropriate.

1. Is the data business critical? This term has been much overused in recent years. People are very much inclined to classify their own responsibilities this way, so it's important to be honest with yourself. If the data were to simply "go away," would the business survive? And if so, how long?

2. Is the data less than business critical? If the business would survive the loss of the data, but the cost to the business would be significant, then it may fit in this category.
3. Is there no need to worry about the data? Disaster planning audits often have the unexpected by-product of turning up files and applications that are no longer necessary. Eliminating an application is a difficult decision for an IS manager to make, and it shouldn't be made lightly. There's an element of risk involved in taking an application off-line. A week after it's shut down, it may turn out to be essential in some corner of the enterprise that you hadn't thought of. A thorough audit of your applications can reduce this risk to an acceptable level.
4. Is the data dynamic or unchanging? Protecting dynamic data is more difficult than data which only changes occasionally and then under carefully controlled conditions. (For example, software which changes only when new versions are installed).

Risk is a precise measurement of the financial impact of data loss. Some risks may be affordable. For the business to be at risk the loss data has to be beyond the "affordable" level. It must have a high probability of occurrence. There will be gray areas in all risk assessment data. To find just how at risk you are you must match the probability and loss characteristics of various exposures. One suggested way to accomplish this is to use a scenario.

A scenario can be a synopsis of events or conditions leading to an accidental loss. There are many ways to express this scenario. There are many parties involved in identifying these areas of possibility. Engineers and actuaries use their expert judgment and the parameters that you provide them with to accomplish this task. The more scenarios you can come up with the more accurate your assessment of the risk factor can be. Each scenario should be constructed from the departmental level all the way to the corporate level.

Are the scenarios that you concoct accurate? When disaster really strikes, will it strike just as you predicted in your scenario? While you can never be certain, you can ensure that a wide range of probabilities are evaluated. Make certain that all uncertainties are documented and communicated to all interested parties. If not, the final outcome can be skewed and decisions made from this data could be costly. The credibility of the analysis will be questioned. The more specific the scenario is the better. The more gray areas the larger this problem becomes. Do not forget these scenarios can range from a disk failure to complete destruction of your facility.

In calculating your costs associated with a Disaster Recovery Plan we suggest you determine how much a **Business Impact Analysis** or BIA will cost. This figure will vary with how detailed you want the plan to be. Highlighted areas of a Business Impact Analysis might be.

- How long will current inventories hold?
- How deep are your retained earnings and how long before they are depleted?
- What business areas depend **SOLELY** on your information systems?

While you might be able to do this yourself there are firms who specialize in this area. They can also provide a much needed assessment to assist you in performing risk analysis and other areas of concern. Most of these areas can be calculated and utilized in a well thought-out and factual presentation to management.

Contingency Planning

A key component of your Disaster Recovery Plan will generally be the contingency plan. The contingency plan is the portion of your DRP that deals with how your company will operate during and after a disaster. A contingency plan will have a cost associated with it alone. Let's look at some of the concepts that will be used in designing a contingency plan for your company.

ABC Company, A small company with daily revenues of $80,000.00.

	Under Normal Conditions	Disaster w/o Plan	Disaster w/ Plan
Revenue:	$80,000.00	$ 0.00	$80,000.00
Expenses:	-50,000.00	-50,000.00	-50,000.00
Outage Exp.:	- 8,000.00	- 8,000.00	- 8,000.00
DRP Active:			- 4,000.00
Profits:	$22,000.00	-58,000.00	$18,000.00

The simple table above shows the bottom line of a sample contingency plan. The numbers aren't meant to be realistic. It's just a sample. The **Revenue** and **Expense** portions of this calculation are based on normal, every day figures. In this example the cost of contingency coverage is included. The **Outage Expense** line takes into account the actual cost associated with the disaster such as repairs, temporary quarters and other areas of concern. **DRP active** is the cost to activate your contingency plan. We will cover the different methods of contingency coverage in more detail later in this chapter.

As we can see in this example the company comes out better with a disaster recovery plan that includes a contingency plan that costs rather than none. This area may very well be one of the most difficult to promote to upper management. In calculating these figures be sure you use realistic figures. One way of guaranteeing failure is to use figures that are blown WAY out of proportion. This example is not a complete analysis by any stretch of the imagination.

Another area you should keep in mind is what your personnel will do if they have to travel during a disaster? Will they use a corporate credit card or will they incur the expenses to be reimbursed upon return? Also what if they have problems of their own due to a geographical disaster? You really need these persons but you also cannot expect them to walk away from home and family problems. One alternative you may look into would be contracting with a personnel agency as a contingency. These agencies could provide you with temporary people at the location of your Hot Site facilities. As well, some of the Hot Site vendors may have persons you can utilize. These things must be taken into consideration and should be documented as well as tested on a regular basis.

In promoting contingency planning the first obstacle you may encounter could be the cost of such coverage. We've all heard statements like these:

"Well, we have been successful so far, why do we need this?"

or

"We didn't put this plant here because of the hurricanes."

Disaster recovery is generally not a popular topic at Directors' meetings. Therefore, you will need to be prepared to be able to deliver your message in a quick and powerful way. Emphasizing the potential loss of profit is the best way to get upper management's attention. One thing is for sure, a company WILL lose money in case of a disaster. With or without a plan that works and the cost associated with that plan. No matter how small or large. The only difference being the amount of the loss.

Some of the areas of loss you must look at are tangible as well as intangible. You can demonstrate loss of revenue, additional expenses, reconstruction costs, etc., but what about the areas such as customer confidence and customer satisfaction? Granted if the disaster is such that the news services carry the story there might be a little sympathy, but as you know, there is little room for sympathy in the business world. People will have to order those goods from someone. Why not let it be you?

A DRP and its associated contingency plan can be designed to enable you to simply take orders, or it can be designed to enable you to act on them. Your normal expenses will continue to build and will have to be taken care of. Be sure to estimate your costs relative to the day to day operation of the business. This figure may (or may not) change in the face of a disaster. There may be costs associated specifically with the disaster. Try to foresee the unexpected things that will definitely occur at the time of a disaster.

Contingency coverage comes in many different flavors. Each has a cost directly related to the availability and access that it provides. The different options that are available today in contingency plans are

- Hot Site,
- Cold Site,
- Electronic Vaulting,
- Mobile/Portable Site,
- OEM Insurance and
- Quick Ship.

Let's look at each of these alternatives in a little more detail.

A **Hot Site** will provide you with an operationally ready data center offering you specific hardware platforms and configurations for immediate availability upon notification of a disaster. Some companies are large enough to have multiple sites, and will use them to implement a hot site arrangement. The clustering technologies that are available for the HP 3000 and HP 9000 make the implementation of hot sites more practicable than ever. (See the chapter on high availability for a more detailed discussion of the value of clustering systems using SharePlex or MCServiceGuard.) One thing you need to keep in mind is the impact this can have on the remote system and its user community. If your company is not willing to invest in setting up a second physical datacenter, hot sites can still be an option. Some consulting firms offer a subscription generally lasting a year or more, during which time they commit to making a hot site available to you at very short notice. There is generally a limit to how long you can use this facility. While this may be an expensive alternative you may find this is exactly what your company needs.

A **Cold Site** is a computer room that is ready environmentally but without the hardware you will need. These sites, like the Hot Sites are available on a subscription basis. Generally the length of a subscription is from one to three years. The cost associated with this alternative may be more attractive to the Hot Site plan but do not forget you still have to get the hardware there. This alternative is generally used AFTER the depletion of your available time at a Hot Site. Most Hot Site vendors will include this in their service as well.

Electronic Vaulting is a relatively new type of service that allows your data to be "vaulted" to a Hot Site in order to speed up the recovery process. While the cost of this service is currently a little high, you may find the cost outweighs the delay in the time it will take you to make your Hot Site ready for action.

The **Mobile or Portable-Site** alternative works well for small hardware configurations or emergency office situations. Mobile sites are stand-alone systems trucked into the area ready for operation. A Portable site is assembled after arriving on the site. This is a very popular alternative since the equipment needed will come to you.

OEM Insurance is being offered today by major hardware vendors such as Digital Equipment and Wang. Under the terms of this agreement, the vendor will replace the damaged equipment on a priority basis. This service is added as a percentage of your overall support cost. Equipment with equal or greater processing power is guaranteed.

Quick Ship is an option to ship your replacement equipment quickly. You are charged a fee to search for the equipment you require. While your normal leasing cost will continue you probably will also have to pay an additional cost once a Quick Ship is requested.

We have evaluated your risk factors, assisted with contingency planning as well as alternatives to your recovery needs. Do not forget that there are professional organizations that are available to help you in these as well as other areas. It could very well pay you to utilized them.

Backup Strategies for the 21st Century

Most system administrators have a knee-jerk reaction to the suggestion that they review their backup strategy.

> *"Backup strategy? Of course we have a fully tested, comprehensive backup strategy! We perform nightly partial backups of our systems, together with weekly full backups. We follow the procedures that HP (or IBM or DEC or whatever hardware vendor sold them the system) gave us."*

Conscientious system administrators understand that regular backups are one of the most basic components of their system management tactical plan. Any suggestion that they review it tends to draw a "been-there, done-that" sort of response. They just **know** that they're covered. Which is exactly why they get in trouble.

System administrators that have been around for a while tend to think in mainframe terms when it comes to backup strategies. This is reflected in their language, which is peppered with terms like "backing up the system" (as if there were only one "system" to back up). The trouble is that in today's enterprises, data is no longer concentrated on one system, or even in one room. As we have discussed repeatedly in this book, data now resides everywhere—from the mainframes and/or minicomputers in the glass house to the systems on people's desktops. The backup strategy must ensure that regular consistent backups are made of all the critical data that resides on all of these systems.

Most IS managers are pretty good about making sure that "regular" backups are done. The consistency of the backups is another issue, however. Consider the case of a company that was using a home-grown client/server application to run their business. The applications consisted of two pieces: the client module, which was PC-based, and the server module, which ran side by side with a number of other applications on the company's HP 3000. Most of the data that was owned by this application was physically stored on the HP 3000, although parts of it (particularly graphical data) were stored in the form of GIF files on the PCs. Their backup strategy consisted of using a network-based backup product to copy the PC data to the HP 3000. TurboStore was used to backup the data on the HP 3000 (including the backed-up PC files).

They thought they were prepared for any eventuality, until one autumn evening, disaster struck. A fire reduced their offices to rubble. Their disaster plan had called for copies of their nightly backup tapes to be stored at another location, safe from the flames. The company had a "cold site" with procedures in place to get the necessary HP 3000 and desktop hardware installed in a matter of 24 hours. All that was left to do was to restore the data from the backups. A few hours later, the HP 3000's files had been restored from the TurboStore backups, and the network backup tool had been used to recover the data that resided on the desktop computers. The HP 3000 was working, the PCs were working, and the network was working.

Imagine the reaction, then, when the client/server application refused to work. Application programmers and analysts pored over the problem until they isolated the flaw. The problem turned out to be in the backup strategy. The IS manager who had written the DRP had forgotten that it wasn't good enough to ensure that both the HP 3000 and the PCs were being backed up regularly. It was just as important that the PC backups and the HP 3000 backups *both represented the same point in time*. Whether you're doing full backups nightly, or weekly full backups together with nightly partial backups, the point of backing up your data is to ensure that, in the event of a disaster, the system can be restored to the state it was in at the time of the last backup. That means that *all* the data in the backup, regardless of what computer or what kind of computer it came from, must represent a single point in time (namely, the time of the last backup).

If you're using the :STORE and :RESTORE commands that come bundled with the HP 3000, your backup operations involve chasing all the users off the system, which effectively "freezes" the data on your HP 3000, before starting your backup. You can think of your backup as a snapshot of how the data on your system looked at the time you started the backup job. If you're using TurboStore to do on-line backups, you can let your end users back on the system while the backup job is running and the on-line backup will represent a snapshot of how the system looked at the time the backup job started running. Any changes that are made while the backup is running are not reflected in the backup.

In a client/server environment, you must ensure that the backup of your application data is consistent—that the backup represents a single point in time—even if that backup consists of the output of multiple backup tools, running on multiple platforms. This is an aspect of distributed systems that has been known to slip by some IS managers (particularly inexperienced ones). In the rush to distributed, client/server systems, a backup strategy that's based on the older host-based paradigm is no backup strategy at all. As companies move toward heterogeneous distributed environments, the backup strategy must be continuously re-evaluated and re-tested to ensure that it will work if (when!) things go wrong.

Once you are certain that your backup strategy is capable of producing regular, consistent backups, the next thing to address is the workability of the recovery portion of your contingency plan. Below are some of the questions you will need to answer with regard to backup and recovery.

- Where do you store your tapes?
- How current is the backup set you have access to?
- Do you trust the data that the tapes contain?
- What format is the data stored in?

With the many different types of off-line storage devices available today and the opportunity to back-up different platforms at the same time to one or more devices concurrently, backing up the system just is not what it used to be.

High availability products are no substitute for a good backup strategy. Remember that your backup strategy represents your insurance against all kinds of problems above and beyond hardware failures. Consider the case of a company that had purchased disk mirroring as a high availability product. They decided that since they had mirroring in place, there was no further need to backup the system. After all, wasn't mirroring supposed to help you keep your system available all the time? This may sound like a good idea in theory, but they found out the hard way one day about data corruption. A bug in their application software caused the data on the primary disk to become corrupt. Disk mirroring, being unable to tell the difference between an application that was working correctly and one that was behaving "strangely," dutifully copied the corruption to the secondary pair. There was no hardware failure. But their database needed to be restored from the backup that they didn't have.

There are many strategies available today for performing back-ups on an HP 3000. The traditional strategies that are covered in HP's basic system management classes recommend doing a full backup each night or a daily partial backup with a full backup being done on a weekend. This was fine in the early days of the HP 3000, when the average system had only a few hundred megabytes of disk storage on-line. In today's world, a surprising number of HP 3000 users are managing over a terrabyte of disk storage. Some companies literally cannot perform a full backup. Their systems cannot be unavailable to their users for that long. In these situations alternative methods come into play. Strategies such as near-line storage and other archival methods may be appropriate.

Near-line storage is the utilization of a hierarchical data storage manager. On-line disk drive storage is very expensive compared to off-line tape storage. Near-line takes the middle and allows data to be stored on an optical device for immediate retrieval if the data is needed by an application or user. The data is moved off of on-line disk storage to the near-line optical storage when it is not needed. For instance you may store data to near-line if the file has not been opened during a two-week time frame. If the file still is not accessed for another two-week time frame, you might then store it to tape for off-line storage. If during the two-week time frame the file is actually on the optical device and an application or user needs it, the file will then be loaded back to memory with only a slight delay to the user. After the file has been modified it will then be stored back to the on-line disk to begin the wait for movement back to the near-line optical device.

When devising the recovery portion of your plan be sure to note the time it takes you to back the system up. Recovering your system will take at least this long (if not longer). You will also need to devise your storage plan with regard to recovery. As we asked earlier, how long will it take you to get your latest tape set ready to restore? You must also decide how much data you are prepared to lose considering your last back-up will not actually be current to the minute.

In working on your DRP keep your backup and recovery methods in mind. Be sure to test them. Especially the recovery method. The time to test is not when you are actually going through a disaster.

Your plan should be updated on a regular basis. A major re-organization, an application addition or deletion are good triggers for updating your DRP. A good time frame is every six months. Most companies go through some sort of change during that time. While some companies only update their plans on an annual basis, an updated plan will be valid for only three months following the revision. Your recovery team should be meeting more frequently than every 12 months. If you only review your plan every year, how familiar do you think you really are with it? For a DRP to be effective the players involved should know this plan in and out. That is hard to do if you only test or look at your plan on a yearly basis. Things you will find that change with the most frequency are:

- Contact Names
- Telephone numbers, home as well as work extensions and pagers
- Home addresses
- Alternate contact names and information

These items should be updated quarterly. Consider your vendors as well. They will also have changes. What about your contingency vendors? They should be notified of any changes that have occurred on a regular basis or they might not be as ready to help when the time comes. The basic information that we have been discussing can be handled during a regular revision meeting. Some changes could actually require major modifications to the plan. Major organizational changes such as departmental shuffling, adding and moving facilities and reorganization of the management structure or changes to your operational plan could trigger a modification to your DRP. New products, services and application changes are just a few examples of this. It is a good idea to actually re-visit the basic aspects of your DRP as well. Risk and business impact analysis can become obsolete with changes at the organizational level. One suggestion is to perform risk and business analysis on a yearly basis. This way you maintain the foundation of the plan.

Do not forget your people. As personnel changes occur your plan can be at risk. Do they know where they fit into the plan? Do they know their part in it? If these persons are actually involved as a trigger point or in the recovery process, they must know what to do in order for the plan to work. The best way to handle this is to have the recovery teams meet on a regular basis to go over the plan and their role in it. As new members are brought in, the team should meet to ensure each player understands their own role. A Disaster Recovery Plan is never really finished, it should be updated and maintained on a continual basis.

How often you test your DRP is of great importance. We suggest you test at least every six months. Most testing can be of the planned type but some tests should be unplanned. We realize you cannot interrupt plant and business operations during this test but your Disaster Recovery Team can be tested without notification. Just be sure they know it is a test before it gets too far along.

Consider one company that used HP's Customer Network Center to maintain and support their Wide Area Network. They decided they were going to test their plan. They notified the CNC regarding this test and told them to not respond to any failure information or calls for help. They wanted to make this test as real as possible. During the test they actually had a real disaster. The X.25 switch they had on site failed when they tried to bring it back up. All calls to the CNC were ignored. Well, they HAD said to ignore them. A Customer Engineer happened to arrive at the site for an unrelated problem. They did get it repaired in a timely fashion and completed their test successfully. Just keep in mind while testing to be sure to let people know you are testing and have plans in place should the test actually become real!

A Disaster Recovery Plan is a strict requirement in today's business environment. Ensure you have a plan in place that is current, tested and ready to go when you need it.

CHAPTER 33

The Server Operating Systems—Using MPE/iX and UNIX Together

Here's an interesting quotation:

> *"Today, more and more System Managers are feeling rather embattled. For some reason or another the systems that they have managed, maintained and supported are becoming obsolescent. Or so they are being told. Time and time again in User Group meetings all over the world the question arises, what are we to do with our systems?"*

What systems are being talked about above? Is it HP 3000 users bemoaning the industry's interest in UNIX? Or is it OS/2 users worried about the move to MS/Word? Or could it be UNIX users worried about the move to NT? The fact is that all operating systems are becoming obsolescent. Sooner or later, every operating system is going to be replaced by something different—maybe it will even be something better. No operating system, data base, chipset or platform represents the be-all-and-end-all of the computing industry.

What does this mean to you? In the not so distant past, system buyers focused on choosing the "right" operating system—that is, the one that wasn't going to "go away." Companies talked about "strategic" operating systems. The cruel fact is that regardless of what operating system you're using, one day it will "go away." It's no good wasting time trying to figure out which is the "right" operating system. There are far more important questions to be considered. Should we centralize or distribute our systems? Is the client/server movement practicable for us? Will we actually improve our information systems by going to a client/server environment? Where does my MPE/iX system fit into this equation? Why would I want to introduce UNIX or any other platform into my MPE/iX environment? In this chapter we would like to help you explore some of the reasons you may decide to bring your systems into the world of coexistence by introducing a UNIX platform into your environment.

If your MPE/iX system is meeting all of your needs then there's little need for you to worry about using anything else. But the operative word here is "ALL." To it's credit, MPE/iX is one of the most robust operating systems on the market today. The reliability, ease of management and OLTP performance of MPE/iX are unrivaled.

On the other hand, little new application development is taking place on MPE/iX. Most of the few new applications that have appeared on the HP 3000 over the last few years were developed on UNIX platforms and ported to MPE/iX using Oracle or the POSIX shell. For every new HP 3000 application, there are dozens of new applications for UNIX, and increasingly, many new applications for NT as well.

Today, many HP 3000 users are putting UNIX systems in place, not to replace their HP 3000, but to supplement it, and to gain access to new applications, without having to worry about the impact on their current applications. A company that's running a manufacturing application on an HP 3000 might choose to use a UNIX-based financial package, or to move their program development efforts to a UNIX platform.

By using a UNIX system for in-house development you can effectively build a "firewall" between your production and development environments. Generally speaking production and development do not make good system "partners." By utilizing this approach you can protect your users from "bugs" that are inherent in a development stage. Another attractive aspect of UNIX is the availability of client/server Database Management Systems. A few, (Oracle and an older version of Ingres) are available on MPE/iX. But many others, including Informix, ADABASE and Sybase are not.

Today, Oracle provides a product called the "Oracle Transparent Gateway" that make it easy to integrate Oracle databases with IMAGE or ALLBASE databases on the HP 3000. This technology is useful for integrating Oracle-based applications running on an HP 9000 with IMAGE/SQL based applications running on an HP 3000. At this writing, Sybase's "Open Client / Open Server" technology is in the process of being ported to the HP 3000 and will provide similar functionality.

In the not-so-distant-past, conventional wisdom dictated that the most cost effective way for a company to use multiple computer applications was to put them all on a single mainframe-class computer and run them side-by-side. The logic was that the most expensive thing in your data center was the hardware, so it made sense to run as many applications as possible on each box. Today, hardware is much less expensive than it used to be. Using multiple computers, even multiple kinds of computers, makes a lot of business sense.

A much-discussed alternative to using UNIX systems together with HP 3000s is getting rid of the HP 3000 and moving everything to UNIX. The low cost of UNIX hardware seems to make this an attractive alternative. Porting traditional proprietary MPE/iX applications to UNIX can be difficult, time consuming and costly. Few application providers have done so successfully. What's worse, some customers who have "bit the bullet" and moved their HP 3000 processing to UNIX completely have discovered that they did not get all of the benefits they expected once the conversion was complete. UNIX hardware is cheap, but the low cost of hardware is often offset by the costs associated with managing UNIX systems.

As we have discussed in part one of this book, "open" means among other things, application portability, interoperability, providing a common user interface as well as a common management interface. The key element though has to be compatibility over time. Taking these items into consideration MPE/iX is as open if not more so than some UNIX systems available today. As of release 5.5, MPE/iX now comes bundled with inbound and outbound TELNET as well as File Transfer Protocol. Today's MPE/iX system can communicate with any other system that can provide these services.

To communicate between a PC and a UNIX system you will need some sort of terminal emulation if you are going to be utilizing a session type connection. There are many available on the market today. Most UNIX system providers include or bundle TELNET into the operating system.

To communicate between a PC and a MPE/iX system you will again need some sort of terminal emulation package on the PC. As well the MPE/iX system now includes TELNET. To communicate between the MPE/iX system and a UNIX system you will need to use TELNET on the HP 3000 as well as the UNIX system.

To transfer files across either of the three platforms you may use the File Transfer Protocol or FTP. As well NFS or Network File System is available on all three systems. The implementation that you will find on the HP 3000 is currently supplied by a third party vendor, Quest systems.

UNIX has forced standards on the industry as a whole thereby allowing many different platform types to coexist. With POSIX applications are much more portable. TCP/IP is fast becoming the LAN protocol of choice with it's ease of use as well as being one of the foundations of the Internet. SQL and ODBC allow virtually any DBMS to communicate with IMAGE and ALLBASE on the MPE/iX system.

The positives far outweigh the negatives when deciding whether to introduce UNIX into your MPE/iX environment. Take the time to really evaluate the issues surrounding going completely to either UNIX, Windows NT or staying completely on MPE/iX. The purpose of open systems is to provide your users with as many options as possible while maintaining the integrity of your systems. By taking full advantage of what is available today with an eye toward the future you will insure your information systems success over the long haul.

Many of our customers today utilize open systems to their fullest. Some are on what you might call the "bleeding" edge. These forward thinking customers are leading the way into the future with great ideas that are inspired by the opportunities that open systems can provide.

MPE/iX In The Client/Server Environment

The Hewlett Packard series 3000 MPE/iX system is a great fit in today's client/server environment. As we have previously discussed it is an open operating system that also provides ease of management, reliability and great OLTP performance. By utilizing currently available Relational Database Management Systems such as Oracle and Ingres you can use your 3000 as the top of the tier so to speak. If you are currently using an HP 3000 as your central server you already have most of the data there. Utilize this data storage point. As well you can use the 3000 as a database server. The two options you have are to migrate your data to either Oracle or Ingress or you might choose to use Image/SQL or ALLBASE to keep your current database intact.

You can utilize POSIX, C, MicroFocus COBOL and other languages as tools to port your current MPE/iX only applications as well as develop newer network-centric applications.

By bringing your HP 3000 into a DCE or Distributed Computing Environment you can develop and deploy portable distributed applications. DCE provides among other things RPC's, CDS or Cell Directory Service, Kerberos security as well as DTS or Distributed Time Service. As was discussed earlier, you will find that DCE is more of a foundation for computing than a mechanism. Applications should be developed with DCE in mind.

One of the key items today is the availability of Internet access. The HP 3000 can make a great web server. Taking the 3000's outstanding security and it's quick and robust recovery from power failure it can provide the sturdy server that is required today.

Each platform whether it be UNIX, MPE/iX or Windows NT has their own set of positive as well as negative attributes. The challenge facing each of us the information industry is to utilize each to their fullest and provide coverage for the shortfalls. An open system is not purchased today it is built. And it takes time if you are to build it correctly. Ensuring compatibility over time should be a major concern to you and by planning with that in mind, you can rest assured you will be ready to take advantage of each new development the future has to offer.

CHAPTER 34

Windows NT—The New Network OS

Windows NT is fast becoming a major force in today's client/server computing environment. The "NT" portion of the name stands for "New Technology." That might be a little misleading. Most of the features found in Windows NT have been around in other Operating Systems for a long time. Windows NT seems to have taken a lot of its traits from UNIX. NT is a multi-threaded, preemptive multi-tasking operating system with full 32-bit memory addressing. It supports Windows, DOS, the WIN32 GUI, character based applications as well as POSIX compliant and character based OS/2 1.x applications. It can run on multi processor systems as well as single CPU systems without modification and it supports Intel processors as well as some RISC chips. It comes complete with E-mail and group scheduling capabilities bundled.

The driving force behind Windows NT acceptance is not necessarily any of the "new" functions but the rapid availability of applications. If we look back at the introduction of other operating systems we would find that most of the application vendors starting ramping up once the Operating System took hold in the market place. For instance UNIX was accepted at the research and academic levels long before it was accepted in the commercial environment. When UNIX first hit the streets so to speak it was the technical users that realized the benefits first. It didn't take long for it to become commercially viable but it didn't happen over night. Windows NT has started out with so many applications being able to run on it instantly, including applications that are in great demand today.

Any Intel 486 based or higher system will run Windows NT. Albeit you will probably need to add memory and other items. But NT will still operate in that environment. NT runs most existing DOS and Windows applications. Windows NT offers robust security and Kernel solidity. In today's mission critical environments this is a major requirement. Windows NT is not a GUI running on top of Windows. Contrary to popular opinion, it was written from the ground up.

The need to re-train your user base is not required since most PC users today are running some sort of Windows based application and GUI. It is also very scaleable. Unlike DOS and DOS/Windows, NT prevents a single application from pulling down the entire system. As previously mentioned there is a myriad of applications that will run on Windows NT. It also supports Windows Object Linking and Embedding (OLE) version 2.0 to enable data sharing between applications even over the network.

Windows NT has Peer to Peer Networking built in by using the basics of LAN Manager and Windows For Workgroups. It also has built in drivers to support NetBUI, IPX/SPX, TCP/IP and other transports. NT is compatible with Novell NETWARE, Banyan VINES and Micro Soft LAN Manger. Not to be left out, the NT server product (which does carry an extra cost) provides mainframe as well as Apple Macintosh connectivity.

In today's computing environment security is also a major concern. Windows NT server is rated as C-2 compliant. Windows NT supports multiple user accounts on the same NT system. Each account includes a username, password and privileges assigned by the administrator. Users can customize their work areas with regard to files and directories as well as their File and Program Manager along with their own Control Panel settings. These modifications will remain applicable with each logon. This is commonly known as a profile. Just like UNIX you can have a user as well as a global profile.

You will find a lot of similar features in Windows NT that you find in UNIX today. Windows NT has its origins in a variation of the UNIX kernel called Mach. Windows NT like UNIX provides RPC support, a major requirement in today's client/server application environment. Like UNIX, NT talks to devices via device file drivers. One of the major differences though is in the choice of the Windows GUI. The UNIX community is still trying to settle on a common GUI.

Along with the above features, NT also supports disk striping as well as mirroring. This is especially important in today's mission critical environments. It also supports RAID technology for high availability environments.

Let's look a little deeper into the hardware required for Windows NT. Windows NT was designed to run on multiple hardware architectures namely of the PC type. Today it is capable of supporting the following three PC processors, Intel x86, MIPS RISC and Digital Equipment's Alpha AXP RISC. As well it is supported on some workstation processors as well: the Motorola 68000 and Power PC processor along with a wide variety of architectures used in UNIX workstations. The low end Intel 386 is becoming more and more rare in today's commercial environment so let's spend a little time with the upper end 80486xx's along with the Pentium.

The 80486 processor has the following three feature sets. It uses the same architecture as the 80386, as well as a built-in math coprocessor and a high speed memory controller to improve performance. The largest improvement in performance came from the introduction of the cache controller. This improved the speed with which the processor could access memory. Cache is reading more than what is asked for and storing the additional data in memory. The improvement comes from being able to cache reads to keep from having to go back to disk each time more data is needed in memory. The 486 also has a 32-bit data bus along with a 32-bit memory addressing scheme. Today you can find 100 MHz processor speeds in the 80486 range.

The Pentium followed along the original path the 80386 system introduced regarding the external architecture with one exception. It incorporated a 64-bit data bus. This doubled the speed at which data could be moved. The Pentium also doubled the amount of cache to further enhance memory performance. The Pentium also incorporated two data paths to enable the processor to execute two instructions at one time. This is known as multi-threading. This advantage is not automatically utilized. Software must be written to take advantage of it. Windows NT as well as some other OS's such as UNIX will do just that. Since Windows NT does support multi-threading it is a good idea to use Pentium processors at the minimum in order to ensure the performance gains that are available. Another reason to choose a Pentium class server is the availability of the Intel PCI bus. The PCI bus is a high performance bus that uses a mezzanine approach to solve problems associated with the local bus. The mezzanine approach, as its name infers, layers an interface between the microprocessor and the main bus. Through the use of special circuitry, the microprocessor is buffered from the PCI bus. Another attractive feature of the PCI bus is its capability to detect installed hardware and to set parameters such as interrupt levels, DMA channels and addresses automatically.

Windows NT supports three different File Systems. The FAT or File Allocation Table that is used in DOS systems today, the HPFS or High Performance File System that is used in OS/2 environments and the NTFS or NT File Systems. The features that are available with the NTFS are, complete support for Windows NT security, long file names (up to 256 characters) and the availability of disk logging to allow the rolling back of incomplete updates due to a system failure. This last feature is especially needed in the commercial environments of today. There are some requirements regarding the file system choice. The boot partition has to be at least 90 MB for an Intel x86 system. The partition must be configured with the FAT File Systems if you are using a RISC based server and must be at least 110 MB in size. The system volume cannot be stripped or part of a volume set.

While we have spent a little time on some of the features and functions available in Windows NT we must now compare some of these features with other operating systems available today.

In the high availability arena it is a requirement to have disk mirroring as well as raid support. While both of these functions come bundled in Windows NT each one has a few problems. In mirroring if the system has to be brought down after a mirror set has been "broken" then we lose one of the most attractive features. In HP-UX today the availability of breaking a mirror set in order to perform on-line backup is a feature that is used extensively. As well, in some cases we have seen drives that have failed removed, repaired and re-synched without having to shut the system down. This capability is a necessity in most high availability environments. As well in the Windows NT environment if the boot disk is mirrored and a failure occurs on the primary volume a lot of extra things have to be done. These items include using an emergency floppy disk to boot the system with. After that even more steps are required to re-apply the mirror. In HP-UX if the primary root volume fails the system shouldn't go down as long as the mirroring was done properly. This assumes that all of the file systems that the root volume requires are mirrored as well. When a root volume is mirrored the secondary volume must have all of the items that any boot disk has in order to make it bootable. These items include a LIF, a boot area as well as LVM requirements such as among other things a Boot Data Reserved Area. If you do have to re-boot you should only have to change the boot path and boot with no quorum and the system should come back up. When the primary disk is repaired you can re-sync, or you can shut down and re-boot from the primary volume, in which case the re-synching will be performed automatically.

While the availability of RAID and software array technology being bundled with Windows NT is a plus, don't forget this is a software implementation of something that is taken care of by hardware in the HP-UX world. Anytime software has to handle the array or parity disk concept, it will inherently take away resources from other processes to perform this function. Until this is performed at the hardware level then this feature might very well be a detriment due to the performance cost.

Some of the other areas to look into while comparing Windows NT to UNIX are Network File Systems, parallel processing and the availability of built in utilities and extensions to the Operating System.

While UNIX may be much larger than Windows NT this is mainly due to the available utilities, applications and extensions to the OS that UNIX has built in. When UNIX first hit the market it also was relatively small. But as acceptance in the commercial market increased, so too did the size of UNIX. This increase is directly related to the addition of utilities that make the system and network administrator's life much easier. We would suggest that the trade in space was well worth the gain in customer satisfaction.

The availability of transaction logging is another feature that Windows NT shares with UNIX. This type of logging is a relatively new feature among UNIX users. A transaction log holds transactions until they have been completed. This way if there is a failure before the completion of the pending I/O the system will recover much faster. Rather than have to perform a full FSCK or File System Check the Operating Systems searches through the transaction log. If there are any incomplete transactions they will be "rolled back." The difference that we see between Windows NT implementation and that of HP-UX is that in the NT environment any data associated with this roll back will be lost. Thereby putting the integrity of the data at risk. We would suggest that this is a little dangerous in a mission critical environment.

While Windows NT can allocate memory in a similar fashion to UNIX one element that is missing is the ability to de-allocate bad memory addresses. This feature that became available with HP-UX 10.01 is a great addition to the mission critical environment. In the past if a memory address failed with what is called a double-bit parity error, the system went down and stayed down until that memory board could be replaced or was removed entirely from the system. As of HP-UX 10.01 this section of memory could be de-allocated and the system return to service. The de-allocation is of a 4k size keeping performance from suffering. We didn't see that in our research of the Windows NT memory section. In today's mission critical environments, anything that will prevent a system from being down is an advantage.

While Windows NT does have connectivity to IBM's SNA environment, it is limited to 3270-type terminal emulation and LU6.2 type peer-to-peer communication. Today we see many customers using the 3770 or Remote Job-Entry Subsystem emulation. The RJE subsystem is utilized in many places to send up accounting type jobs such as payroll and general ledger applications to be run on the mainframe but printed locally using the HP-UX system as a print server.

Let's compare Windows NT with another popular Network Operating System. Novell's NetWare.

Like Windows NT, Novell's NetWare is a multi-tasking, multi-threaded operating system that supports up to a 4 Giga-byte memory space. There are many features of NetWare.

NetWare 3.x and 4.x have full 32-bit memory addressing available. By utilizing NetWare Loadable Modules or NLM's, the server can be linked in to provide services such as Communication, database and messaging services. As well archive and backup, network management services as well as the support to store non-DOS files to disk. The NetWare environment is also very open allowing DOS, Windows, OS/2 and UNIX workstations to be attached to the network served by a NetWare server. By utilizing a protocol-independent structure known as Open Data-link Interface or ODI, NetWare can provide simultaneous support for different protocols on the network. As well by installing the Open Data-link Interface Network Support or ODINSUP network driver you can have the ODI and the Network Driver Interface Specification or NDIS coexist on the same network. NetWare can dynamically configure itself to match current usage conditions. This allows the dynamic configuration of memory usage, directory caching, number of volume directory entries, size of the open file table, routing buffers, turbo FAT indexing, service processes and active transaction tracking system transactions.

The NetWare file system boasts of some of the following features.

Elevator seeking allows the disk system to prioritize incoming read requests relative the current location of the read head of the disk drive. This allows the read to head to "pick" data up as it passes addresses thereby reducing random head seeks.

File caching like UNIX allows the number of reads be reduced by holding in memory the files that are accessed most often. This allows the system to read from memory which is much faster than having to return to the disk each time more data is needed.

The use of background writes can really speed up I/O. This allows the operating system to write data to the disk during the times that requests to the disk are at a minimum.

File compression and block suballocation are features that assist in the storage of data on the disk. File compression as implemented by NetWare can increase disk space by up to 63 percent. Users and administrators can determine which files should and should not be compressed. Block suballocation allows a partially used disk block to be divided into 512-byte sub-blocks for storage of small files or fragments of files.

Four Gigabyte file sizes are allowed and volumes can span multiple drives or spindles. The file system can support more than 2 million files and directories and allows 100,000 open files.

One of the neat features is the recovery of deleted files. This feature can be adjusted by the administrator to allow a minimum amount of time that a deleted file can be kept recoverable. As well you can mark files for immediate purge. The deleted files can be kept until the disk runs out of free space and at that time the oldest files will start being actually purged. This feature is at the file level allowing deleted files to exist even if the directory has been purged.

There are many more features of Novell's NetWare product but we would like to compare just some of the areas that are most notable between NetWare and Windows NT.

In this discussion we will compare Novell's NetWare version 4.1 to Windows NT Server version 3.51.

In the area of Directory Services NetWare 4.1 allows a single login to the network as well as to services. Windows NT allows limited single login to the network only. Windows NT doesn't have location-independent login and as of yet isn't interoperable with X.500. To move a user you can drag and drop in the NetWare environment but you have to delete and recreate in Windows NT. While this might be considered a favorable feature Windows NT doesn't have a single point of administration but NetWare does.

In the file services area an advantage with NetWare 4.1 is the ability to suballocate blocks for more efficient storage of data. Windows NT doesn't allow this. NetWare also has mirrored server capability whereas that capability is just now being introduced in the Windows NT environment.

It appears that NetWare 4.1 still has many more print services features than Windows NT today. Printing has been a mainstay in the Novell arena for a long time. They have plenty of experience in the network printing area.

In the realm of interoperability NetWare seems to again have more available than Windows NT. In the UNIX environment, NetWare has full SNMP support and built-in IP routing. Windows NT does not support IP routing and has limited SNMP support at this time. Another feature that is used very heavily today is the Networked File System or NFS. NetWare allows bi-directional file system mounting along with printer sharing. Windows NT as of this writing does not allow either of these.

While there are many more areas that can be used to compare Novell's NetWare and Windows NT, we think these comparisons can get you started.

Deciding what Network Operating System to utilize is a very important decision that can affect your systems growth opportunity down the road. It is our opinion that at this time Novell's NOS is more tried and true than the current release of Windows NT. But each environment has different needs and those needs should be the basis of your NOS decision. Given time we think that Windows NT will become a very effective operating system in most areas of the computing environment. The comparisons above between Windows NT and UNIX and Novell's NetWare are based on the products that are available today. Windows NT is still in its infancy stage and we expect even better things to come. Don't let the shortcomings that are there today hold you back from looking into its applicability in your future computer needs.

Fitting In Today

In today's environment Windows NT as well as Novell's NetWare products has become an integral part of the computing enterprise. The opportunity to offload items such as printer services, file sharing and word processing from the mainframe or mini to servers dispersed throughout a work area has proven to most beneficial with regard to performance. Following the logic that we have been utilizing in the previous sections, the Net servers today is doing more and more work by fitting in the middle tier of a three tier environment. By utilizing SQL type databases, a Net Server can do most any operation that a Mini or Mainframe can do today. In some customer environments you will find Net Servers racked in cabinets that are 1.6 meters in height. From a distance these systems look like their older siblings the mini. You may find two or more "systems" divided among these different servers. For instance you may find accounting and general ledger on one server, manufacturing on another and inventory control on yet another server. All three of these servers and their appropriate "clients" will be inter-connected on the same backbone LAN. In this environment the LAN now becomes the bus that will carry all the data to and from the respective servers. Again, in this environment the LAN can also become the bottle neck.

In today's mission critical environments the need for highly available solutions require a system be as battle hardened as possible. The PCs or net servers of today meet and exceed this quality need. One of the features of being able to "split" our applications up across multiple servers is that if one goes down you may very well remain operational in the other areas until that system is back on-line. If all of these systems were housed under one CPU if you will and that system goes down, then the entire information system is down until the fault is repaired. As was previously mentioned, there are high availability products that allow you to keep this from occurring in the server market today. But as we have just seen it is also available in the net server market as well.

The Windows NT and NetWare servers fit very nicely as gateways to the mainframe. Most medium to large corporations still have valuable data on the mainframe that most clients still require. Not only can the workstation servers provide the gateway to this data but can also provide the gateway for the client to store large amounts of data at the mainframe level. The limited amount of disk space in some net server environments can be overcome by utilizing the vast amounts of space on the mainframe as a data repository. In today's multi-window environment the client can very easily have a window open to the net server, the mainframe and it's own local applications allowing the user to basically operate at three levels at one time.

We see Windows NT and NetWare servers as being the gateway to the three tier model that can include your current legacy systems. Either as the client only or as both the client and the middle tier or server. This all depends on how your distributed applications are written.

It is difficult to find a better solution for your network printing needs than by utilizing Novell's NetWare printing services. Why not let this same technology help enhance your current environment by utilizing the full network application potential that Windows NT and Novell's NetWare offer you today.

The future that is being painted today is very bright. In the previous discussion we used the term "Network Operating System" a lot. Well, Windows NT is not just a NOS. It is an Operating System that has connectivity to networking built it. It is by all rights a stand alone Operating System. Today the PC is still pretty much relegated to the desktop except in some cases as servers where they still handle desktop functions such as word processing, spreadsheets and communications. Some customers are venturing out to utilize net servers as systems that serve as both a UNIX workstation supplying the horsepower to run engineering applications and word processing and spreadsheet applications to provide reports all in the same system. In the not too distant past an engineer may have had two systems on their desk. One for running graphic intensive CAD/CAM applications and a PC to run the word processing applications needed to create the reports needed to run the business. Already in today's environment PCs have become powerful enough to handle this charge but the UNIX workstations typically still have more power. So in an effort to combine the two Windows NT will finally allow this to happen. Both types of applications will be found under the same operating system on the same system. Makes one wonder where the name Windows NT Workstation came from doesn't it?

With the cooperative work being done to supply a RISC based chip that can run on both platforms, PC and Workstation that is, Windows NT is positioned to take full advantage of this situation. Given the next release of Windows NT and the possible enhancements that are being talked about we can't see why Windows NT cannot be the operating system on large server class systems as well. With the use of SQL database calls and the major RDBMS suppliers such as Sybase systems, Oracle and Ingress already providing connectivity for Windows NT this may very well be a reality much quicker than expected. In the overall scheme of OLTP, Windows NT can fit very well in this environment. Another area of concern today is the mission critical environments. Hopefully the next release of Windows NT will provide the much needed server mirroring or clustered environment. One must ask the question though. Just what is mission critical? We would think that everyone has a different answer to that question since each application in most environments are mission critical at some time or other.

Another approach that may very well occur will be the mainframe desktop PC. Given the high speeds that the PC is approaching today and combining that with

RISC processors and an Operating System that can handle most of the applications in BOTH environments, this is becoming more of a possibility. It is our understanding that the next release of Windows NT may very well provide an implementation of MIT's Kerberos security. This would allow a security server to handle all security verification be placed on the network. This type of security arrangement is a necessity in distributed computing environments. Given Windows NT's interoperability with Novell's NetWare and other operating systems along with the availability of RPCs, we see the distributed computing environment as being a positive step for the PC based servers in the future.

One thing to keep in mind as you go forward into the future is co-existence. If in planning your future growth you keep in mind that all operating systems, hardware platforms and applications be required to be inter-operable then your growth will not be limited. Planning this environment properly while not being the easiest thing in the world, can mean the difference between your being locked out when new technology becomes available or standing at the ready to incorporate it easily.

CHAPTER 35

Where's the HP 3000 Going?

This past year has been a busy one for Hewlett-Packard's MPE/iX lab. At this writing, Hewlett-Packard is putting the finishing touches on the 5.5 release of MPE/iX. It is slated to ship to customers sometime late in 1996 and contains an abundance of new functionality for HP 3000 customers, representing the latest in a burst of improvements for the HP 3000. This eruption of HP 3000 related activity actually began in 1995. Hewlett-Packard released the 5.0 platform release in February of that year, followed by an upgrade to 5.0 (that is, a patch containing new functionality) called Express 2. On November 22, 1995, Hewlett-Packard kept the pressure on when they began shipping another MPE/iX 5.0 upgrade, this one called Express 3. And with the 5.5 release hot on *its* heels, you can't fault the Hewlett-Packard engineering team for not being productive.

In stark contrast to the almost unbelievable strides that have been made in the development of hardware over the years, the software developers who create operating systems such as MPE/iX are still grappling with many of the same fundamental problems that they've faced since the 1970s. In recent years, the art of programming has been transformed by the availability of a wealth of client/server software engineering tools. And while it's true that these have made coding a much more efficient process than it was back in the days when we used to write COBOL programs on pads of paper, somehow they don't seem to be solving the problem.

Today, there are innumerable development methodologies from which to choose. In my own career, I've personally been involved in projects that were developed using the "code-it-first-and-design-it-later" method, (virtually guaranteed to produce software that does not work), the "code-it-first-and-ask-the-users-what-they-want-later" method (guaranteed to produce software that nobody will use), and the time honored “don’t-bother-testing-my-code-because-everything-I-do-is-perfect” method, (works for me—um, well, most of the time, anyway). . . .

The trouble is that software development isn’t a pure science, like mathematics or physics. Unlike those sciences, programmers must sooner or later deal with the people who actually want to use the fruits of their labors. People tend to want software to do what *they* want it to do, not what the programmer’s spec sheet says it should do. People tend to want their software now, not when the programmer’s schedule says it’s going to be finished. And people tend to want their software to work reliably, all the time, not just during the programmer’s test suite.

Although technology is an important element in software development projects, at Hewlett-Packard, engineers in the MPE/iX lab have discovered that there’s another, much more important element to be considered. Effective communications between end users and the programmers is the real key to success. In many application software projects, the end users work in offices right next door to the programmers. In theory, communications shouldn’t be a problem. But it often is anyway.

In spite of this, the MPE/iX lab has pumped out two major releases and two updated Express Releases in the past 18 months. And not only has the quality not been compromised, it has by all accounts improved. MPE/iX continues to be widely recognized and revered as one of the most reliable operating systems available today. For most customers, the update to 5.0 was flawlessly smooth. In survey after survey, the HP 3000 has scored higher customer satisfaction scores than any comparable machine, and users typically point to the MPE/iX operating system as the primary reason for its reliability and ease of use.

The success of MPE/iX can be traced to Hewlett-Packard’s adoption of a tactic called “Customer Focused R&D”. As the computer industry moves into the last years of the century, “customer focus” is becoming one of those buzzwords that everybody talks about, but that relatively few actually act on. Managers throughout the industry solemnly declare that they are “focused on their customers,” or even “customer driven”—but when push comes to shove, they fall back on business practices that are tried and true, (well, tried, anyway).

In the early 1990s, the MPE/iX lab was plagued with the same problems faced by virtually every software development project in the world. Projects were taking far too long to design, develop and deliver—and during the development process, the needs of the customers refused to remain stationary. In some cases, projects were begun in response to loud and clamorous customer demands, only to have the finished projects languish on the shelf, because by that time customers were clamoring for something else.

By 1993, the words "customer focused R&D" had become much more than a buzzword in the MPE/iX lab. Rather, the whole software development process had begun to change, until it was totally driven from beginning to end by HP 3000 customers, not by Hewlett-Packard marketers, engineers or managers. By the time 5.0 development got under way in 1993, projects in the MPE/iX lab were being launched, not with requests from marketing, but with service requests originating with customers. Today, no MPE/iX lab engineer can begin to design or build a software product without the direct participation of customers. No design decision can be made, no code can be written without specific, direct customer input. Customers are involved throughout the development lifecycle of each project—so that if customer requirements change, the project changes with them.

Prior to this revolution, all managerial decisions relating to MPE/iX were made on Hewlett-Packard's campus in Cupertino, California. But by the beginning of 1994, much of the "say-so" about what would (and would not) be developed had moved into the hands of customers, geographically spread out all over the world. When development changed, Hewlett-Packard's traditional tools for managing the development process had to change too. An entirely new planning methodology called "Solutions Planning" was created. Solutions Planning is HP's bridge between its customers and the R&D community.

Solution Teams for 5.5

Solution Team	Team focus: satisfying customer requirements for...
High Availability	Minimizing system downtime, both planned and unplanned.
Platform Evolution	Hardware technology, including PA-RISC processors and peripherals.
Coexistence	Tools and technologies for integrating HP 3000 applications with those running on other platforms, especially (but not exclusively) HP-UX.
Desktop Integration	Tools and technologies for using HP 3000s together with desktop devices such as personal computers and desktop printers.
Application Evolution	Providing tools for the development and porting of HP 3000 applications.
Patch Process	Providing tools to reduce the amount of downtime associated with routine software maintenance.
Customer Delight	Ease of use and other requirements aside from those addressed by other solution teams.

At the core of the solutions planning process are "Solution Teams." In engineering organizations, people have traditionally been organized around *technologies*, rather than around solutions. For example, in the 'old days,' the engineers in the MPE/iX lab were organized into a file system team, a dispatcher team, database teams, networking teams and so forth. This organization sometimes became a barrier to getting things done, because the things that customers wanted invariably involved many different technologies. That meant that lots of different teams had get involved, and their efforts had to be coordinated. Delays were inevitable.

Hewlett-Packard management decided to try something different. The MPE/iX lab was reorganized. Based purely on feedback from customers, seven solution teams were formed (see Table, "Solution Teams for 5.5") to develop the various technologies that were to go into the Express 3 update to MPE/iX 5.0 and into Release 5.5.

These were the business needs vocalized by customers at the time 5.5 was getting under way. It's important to understand that this list of business needs isn't carved in stone. The teams may change (and in fact they are already changing) in response to the changing business environment. The only requirement imposed by Hewlett-Packard is that the solutions reflect the company's key HP 3000 strategies. Each solution team is expected to offer specific, measurable value to customers across multiple technologies.

For example, the solution team that's focused on Coexistence with UNIX was charged with creating enhancements to MPE/iX and its subsystems that would allow better networking interoperability and application portability with UNIX systems. This brings many different technologies into play, including database gateways, standard networking protocols and features, UNIX-like programming commands, common system management tools, etc. In a solutions team environment, the technology does not become a barrier to getting things done. As a result, each and every solution team made significant contributions to the 5.5 release.

New High Availability Features

TurboSTORE/iX 7x24 True-On-line	This product provides the HP 3000 with the capability of doing "true" on-line backups. Eliminates the need to have users logoff the system in order to begin the backup. Users don't have to leave their applications, and can continue to do productive work.
On-line DTC/TIO Configuration	Allows the system administrator to add and delete serial devices such as terminals and printers to the DTC configuration without having to restart the system
On-line Disk/Tape Configuration	Allows the system administrator to add, delete and change the configuration of tape and disk devices without having to restart the system. On-line configuration of disks, tapes, DTCs, and terminal input/output devices eliminates system downtime while restoring TIO connections or updating configurations.
Subsystem Dump	In the event of a system abort, this feature allows the system operator to dump specific subsystems. By avoiding a dump of the full system, and dumping only the file system part of MPE/iX, error recovery can be greatly speeded up. On first release, the file system is the only subsystem supported. Working with the Hewlett-Packard response center, this can facilitate the solution of complex system problems.
Additional File System Resiliency	Changes have been applied to the file system to reduce the number of system aborts due to file system problems. If the operating system encounters a problem such as a bad pointer, those errors can now go to an error stack, where they can potentially be handled by application code, avoiding system aborts.
Shareplex/iX-NetBase enhancement requests	Shareplex/iX-NetBase is now integrated with the MPE/iX Transaction Manager. In the event that the secondary system goes down, it will automatically resync with the primary system when it comes back up, eliminating the need to do a full backup and restore. Joint effort by Hewlett-Packard and Quest labs.

The high availability solution team is focused on delivering new MPE/iX functionality and new products designed to increase system and data availability by reducing planned and unplanned downtime. Planned downtime refers to periods of time during which the system is not usable because of system backups or other routine maintenance. Unplanned downtime means periods when the system is not usable because of an unexpected interruption in service, such as a hardware failure or system "crash." Hewlett-Packard is constantly striving to improve reduce both kinds of downtime by improving the basic reliability of the MPE/iX software, and by making products available which are targeted at those customers which may have special high availability needs.

On 5.5, there are several new high availability features and products available (See Table of New High Availability Features). Ironically, the fundamental reliability of the HP 3000 can sometimes work against it. There is no better way to ensure your system stays up than to manage it carefully, performing regular backups and maintenance according to the guidelines established by Hewlett-Packard. System management practices for high availability are not complex—they're actually very simple. But they must be done regularly and without fail.

Sometimes, when HP 3000 installations go for years without a system problem, they are lulled into a false sense of security. System administration procedures that were designed to protect against problems are gradually forgotten and operators begin to fail to rigorously observe the backup schedules. Inevitably, a hardware failure will eventually happen, and without proper backups recovery can become very complicated if it's possible at all. High Availability products alone cannot make your system bullet proof, but a combination of the right products and good system management practices can get it very close.

What the Platform Evolution Team Delivered

The platform evolution team is focused on ensuring that a growth path is always available to HP 3000 customers. As their businesses grow, the platform evolution team is charged with ensuring that new hardware platforms and peripherals are there to meet the challenge.

In November 1995 Hewlett-Packard introduced a number of new hardware platforms, including versions of the 996 Corporate Business Server supporting up to 8-way multiprocessing. These high end systems, based on the 120 MHz PA7150 chip, give up to a 15 percent performance increase over previous Corporate Business Servers. The 969KS/100-400 was also introduced, based on a 120 MHz PA7200 chipset, giving up to a 20 percent performance increase over the previous 959KS servers. Eight to thirty two user license levels were added to all 9x8 and 9x9KS servers, ensuring that customer costs were kept to a minimum. In addition, a CD-ROM Drive is now bundled with all new systems for software distribution and reading MPE/iX software documentation on-line. Release 5.0 Express 3 also added support for greater than 10,000 spool files and support for IMAGE/SQL data sets larger than 4 Gigabytes.

In Release 5.5, MPE/iX will increase the maximum memory size supported from 2GB to 3.75 GB on the 995/996 Corporate Business Servers. In the future, MPE/iX will be supported in the 9x9KS and 99x Servers using Hewlett-Packard's new PA-RISC revision 2.0 architecture, (the PA-8000 chipset).

In the peripherals arena, with 5.0 Express 3 Hewlett-Packard also brought a new High Availability Storage System (HASS) to the HP 3000 platform. A key feature of the HASS system is "hot pluggable" or "hot swappable" devices. This means that HASS fast/wide SCSI disks can be physically added or removed from the cabinet without having to first power the unit down, greatly reducing the amount of downtime required for routine maintenance or recovery from a disk failure.

The HASS system features automatic hot pluggable fast/wide differential (FWD) SCSI disks, redundant hot pluggable power supplies and cooling fans, industry-leading reliable disk modules and dual SCSI buses. This new system is supported on Express 3 (i.e., an update to 5.0). Available in deskside and rack-mount versions, HASS supports single-ended SCSI and FWD SCSI as well as primary and secondary storage all in the same enclosure. In its initial release, HASS will include the new 2GB and 4GB low profile disk drives and the DDS-2 DAT tape drive. A new optical library called the C1100B is also supported as of Express 3 which can be used by Filenet Imaging Software.

In release 5.5, MPE/iX will support the long awaited Fast Wide Differential Disk Arrays. Also in 5.5, additional high availability functionality called "hot-add" will be enabled on the HASS cabinet. Essentially, this will allow you to add disk capacity without shutting down the whole system. This is different from the "hot-swap" capability, which is more typically used for repairs.

Coexistence Features

Network printing	Allows the HP 3000 spooler to send printed output to LAN-connected printers, such as HP/LaserJets connected to the LAN via a JetDirect card. This can be done using Novell's IPX/SPX transport mechanism if Netware for the HP 3000 is being used. In most cases, customers will choose to use the industry standard TCP/IP transport mechanism. TCP/IP-based network printing is bundled with MPE/iX.
Inbound TELNET	A user who is logged onto a computer that supports outbound TEL-NET access (such as an HP 9000) can establish a session on a net-worked HP 3000 using this technology. The HP 3000 has supported outbound TELNET since 5.0, allowing MPE/iX users to log onto net-worked UNIX computers.
Show network connections	TCP/IP can, under some circumstances, be used to run programs on HP 3000 without first logging on or establishing a session. This tech-nology allows system administrators to monitor this activity. Show network connections allows the operator to see who, what device, and what programs are connected to the system on the network. (Note: just for TCP/IP connections, NOT serial or NetWare).
inetd, bootp, tftp	The Internet Daemon (inetd) is a system process which is widely used by networked applications on UNIX platforms. Bootp is used to initialize devices (such as printers) on a LAN. And the trivial file trans-fer protocol (tftp) is a simplified version of ftp, used for copying files across a network. The availability of these technologies on 5.5 will make it easier to port networked applications to MPE/iX.
POSIX enhancements	The POSIX environment has been enhanced in 5.5 to make the port-ing of UNIX applications even easier. A few examples: script files now can specify which shell program they are to use in the 1st line. The fork/exec command (formerly one of the slowest POSIX APIs) has been highly optimized. Support has been added to the POSIX.2 (MKS) shell program for the lp command family (lp, lpstat, cancel), and the tar command has been enhanced so that it can be used to back up MPE/iX filetypes (e.g. KSAM and IMAGE/SQL) to tape. Time stamps on POSIX files will now be updated ONLY if writes are actually performed, not just if they files have been opened. This is more con-sistent with the way UNIX handles timestamps.

According to the best market research available to Hewlett-Packard, roughly a third of HP 3000 customers now have HP-UX based HP 9000 computers installed side-by-side with their MPE/iX machines, and roughly 70 percent are currently planning projects to use their HP 3000s in conjunction with other HP computers. In spite of this widespread interest in UNIX, this does not appear to represent a desire on the part of most MPE/iX customers to migrate to HP-UX. HP's estimate is that 35 percent of the HP 3000 installed base has some interest in moving to UNIX, but only about 5 percent of HP 3000 users are actively pursuing the replacement of their HP 3000s with HP 9000s.

Instead, the vast majority of these installations report that they plan to continue using both kinds of computers for the foreseeable future. IS managers have come to see the value of heterogeneity, using different kinds of systems together. In response to this, Hewlett-Packard has begun delivering tools and technologies to allow better integration of applications and operations across architectural boundaries.

The coexistence team has two fundamental value propositions. First, they make it possible for HP 3000 customers to achieve new levels of interoperability, which is the ability to tie unlike systems together on a single network without sacrificing network functionality. Second, they make software portability a reality in the MPE/iX world. This is the ability to leverage development resources across multiple dissimilar platforms. The Table above, "Coexistence Features," shows the MPE/iX enhancements delivered into 5.5 by the coexistence team.

Desktop Integration Features

ALLBASE/SQL and Image/SQL version G.1 (also available on Express 3)	Enhancements in the new release of ALLBASE/SQL and IMAGE/SQL provide dramatic performance improvements. • The SQL interface for IMAGE databases is now aware of 3rd party indexes and TurboImage search items. This greatly reduces the need for serial database reads and speeding up response to data queries. • Row level locking improves IMAGE/SQL concurrency, making it much more practical to use SQL-based client/server applications and traditional IMAGE-based OLTP applications at the same time. • The ODBC driver used by IMAGE/SQL and ALLBASE/SQL has been tuned to give better performance. • Support for ODBC on Windows 95 is planned for mid-1996.
Enhancements to Netware for the HP 3000	HP 3000 users that are using Netware/iX can now route HP 3000 printed output to networked printers (such as HP/LaserJets connected to the LAN via a JetDirect card). Improved NetWare/iX-MPE/iX File Integration is planned to be available shortly after Release 5.5.

The purpose of the desktop integration solution team is to enable users to better access data and applications on their HP 3000. The tools and technologies that we develop are used to enable client/server computing. Customers are using client/server technology to improve end user productivity and to facilitate communication between desktop devices and the HP 3000. The technologies and products delivered by the desktop integration team in 5.5 are detailed in the Table above, Desktop Integration Features.

A few years ago, when Hewlett-Packard first introduced IMAGE/SQL, a lot of customers who were interested in client/server did some "tire kicking" with the new product. And while the first version of IMAGE/SQL met many customers' needs, others found that the performance was not up to their requirements. If performance is an issue, you should take a second look at IMAGE/SQL now that the G.1 version is available. HP has done a lot of work to improve client/server performance with IMAGE/SQL. Customers will notice a significant increase in retrieval speeds with this update. For example, one product manager at HP has been using Microsoft Excel with ODBC to retrieve customer requests out of an IMAGE/SQL database. Prior to these enhancements, the retrieval took 30 minutes. Now that IMAGE/SQL is aware of IMAGE search items, this retrieval runs in 10 seconds."

Application Evolution Features

POSIX Developer's kit	The MPE/iX (POSIX) Developer's Kit will be bundled with MPE/iX 5.5. This was formerly a separately priced product, required to write programs that take advantage of MPE's POSIX application program interfaces (APIs).
C++ for Object Oriented Programming	The g++ compiler from GNU, which is used to compile C++ applications on MPE/iX systems, is available for HP 3000 users. G++ is a superset of C which includes a number of extensions for writing object-oriented software. Customers can obtain a copy of this compiler from Hewlett-Packard's WorldWideWeb site, http://jazz.external.hp.com.
DCE	DCE is available from Hewlett-Packard as a separate orderable product with MPE/iX 5.0 Express 2.

The Applications Evolution team's charter is helping customers to evolve their HP 3000 applications to meet their changing business needs. The team focuses on enhancing the development environment and on working with application developers to add new applications to the HP 3000 platform. Several new programming languages and tools are now available for the HP 3000, as shown in the table above, Application Evolution Features.

Customer Delight Features

Console switching over LAN (available on Express 3)	For many years, the :CONSOLE command has allowed the operator to move the console from LDEV 20 to another terminal. Up until now, however, the console could only be moved to a serially connected terminal. Now it can be switched to a terminal (or PC running terminal emulation software) that is connected to the HP 3000 via the LAN.
UDC Access Rights (available on Express 3)	Up until now, in order for a user to be able to execute a User Defined Command (UDC), they had to have read access to the UDC file. In some instances, this created a potential security "hole". Now users can execute UDCs even if they have only Execute access to the UDC file. In this way they can use the UDC without being able to see how it works.
CI Vars (available on Express 3)	A number of new Command Interpreter variables are now included in MPE/iX: HPSTREAMEDBY, HPLASTJOB, HPOSVERSION, and HPRELVERSION.
Stream Jobs without passwords	Batch jobs no longer need to have the passwords hard-coded into the !JOB statement, eliminating potential security problems. This is accomplished through PASSEXEMPT, a new parameter to the JOBSECURITY command. This allows the system administrator to turn off the requirement that passwords be hard-coded.
POSIX directory in HPPATH (available on Express 3)	The HPPATH system variable has traditionally been used to specify which MPE/iX groups are searched for executables when a user types a command. This variable can now optionally also specify POSIX directories, in addition to MPE/iX groups.
POSIX files as command files (available on Express 3)	A command file can now be assigned a POSIX filename, (for example, a name longer than 8 characters or containing lowercase characters).
VPLUS enhancements	The VPLUS facility, which is used by most HP 3000 applications to manage the use of forms on terminal screens, has been enhanced. FORMSPEC allows field-to-field copies and VREADFIELDS can now sense the position of the cursor.
IMAGE Jumbo Datasets (available on Express 3)	IMAGE/SQL has been enhanced to allow datasets to grow beyond the 4GB limit specified in earlier versions.

Invariably, there are many technology requests that come to Hewlett-Packard which don't fit neatly into categories like "high availability" or "coexistence." The Customer Delight Solution team is charged with finding the enhancements that customers are most interested in, and implementing them. The table above, "Customer Delight Features" shows the new MPE/iX features brought to 5.5 (and to MPE/iX 5.0 Express 3) by the Customer Delight team

The enhancements to the patch process are really part of our high availability strategy for HP 3000 customers. The ability to apply multiple patches without having to repeatedly take the system down means that our customers will be able to reduce the amount of downtime that they need to plan for in order to do routine MPE/iX maintenance. And this is without having to buy any additional products. The table below, "Patch Process Enhancements" details the MPE/iX enhancements delivered by the Patch Process team.

Patch Process Enhancements

Patch/iX	This new process represents an alternative to using AUTOINST and AUTOPAT . All patches, including PowerPatch and reactive patches, can be installed in one process, instead of having to reboot the system after EACH patch installation. This process qualifies all the patches in a set, to ensure that prerequisite patches (some patches require that another patch be previously installed). are included. This new process also includes an easy-to-use screen driven interface.
Stage/iX	Stage/iX allows you to stage multiple patch environments. So you can back out a patch by rebooting without having to go through the installation process again. For instance, if you need to try out a new patch or configuration change, but don't want to throw away the old one, you can keep both on the system at the same time, selecting the desired environment at boot time.
Electronic Patch Delivery	Patches are on the WWW on the Hewlett-Packard Supportline web site: http://us.external.hp.com.

Hewlett-Packard is very serious about involving its customers in the evolution of the HP 3000 platform. In December of 1995, the company aired one of its video broadcasts to reaffirm Hewlett-Packard strategies for the HP 3000. According to CSY's new General Manager Harry Sterling, the MPE/iX lab and marketing organizations would now focus on three objectives.

- Enabling the growth of customers' existing HP 3000 core applications.
- Facilitating the integration of new solutions around customer's existing HP 3000 core applications.
- Providing a smooth transition for customers evolving to new application environments.

This is a natural part of the Solutions Planning process; as customer business requirements evolve, the division's objectives evolve with them. The thing that doesn't change is Hewlett-Packard's dedication support its customers.

Among the HP 3000 enhancements you can expect to see after 5.5 are the expansion of the coexistence program to include not only UNIX, but also NT and PC LANs. In this way we will continue to protect the customer's investment in Hewlett-Packard technology. This gives Hewlett-Packard users the flexibility to add functionality using the platform that you choose. We also plan to continue growing our system platform and peripheral product offerings in the years to come.

For almost as long as the HP 3000 has been around, people have wondered and worried about it's future. Hewlett-Packard, in the meantime, continues to focus on it's most important asset—its customers. And as long as Hewlett-Packard continues in that vein, HP 3000 customers can look forward to a future that's bright. The marketing and technology investments being made in the HP 3000 platform today are part of an overall strategy called "Customer Choices." A key component of the Choices program is realizing that the HP 3000 doesn't fit the same way into every customer's IT organization, and thus not all customers will use the system the same way. We hope that we have provided some information of value to all customers, regardless of how you are currently using your HP 3000 systems, and how you plan to use them in the future.

The first customer segment identified in the choices program are those customers for whom their use of the HP 3000 is not expected to change much in the future. The applications that are in place meet the business needs. The IT organization at these customers is probably focused on application enhancements, or add-on products such as graphical front-ends. In most of these organizations, the HP 3000 is their primary computing platform, both today and in the future. For these customers, our message is that the HP 3000 continues to provide investment protection through the continued support and enhancement of "traditional" MPE-based technologies such as TurboIMAGE. At the same time, new technologies are available, such as DCE, World Wide Web server capability, and multi-threaded programming support. You can choose how quickly you want to be evolving to these new technologies, if at all. Technologies that catch on, and solve a business problem, continue to be added to the HP 3000 platform.

The second customer segment is those customers needing to add new applications to meet the demands for new or changed business functionality. These new applications may be deployed on the HP 3000, an HP 9000, a Windows NT server, or other platforms. For these customers, the primary concern with the HP 3000 platform is the ability to integrate these new applications into the legacy environment. The software architecture described in Parts II through IV of this book can help provide such integration. POSIX on the HP 3000 helps in porting software to the HP 3000, while networking software such as DCE and the ARPA services (ftp, TELNET, and others) help the 3000 to interoperate with applications residing on different platforms, such as the HP 9000 or Windows NT.

The final customer segment is those customers replacing their existing applications with new ones. In some cases, the new application will be on the HP 3000. In other cases, it will be on a new platform. For these customers, the software architecture discussions are the key thing they should focus on to ensure that their new technology investments will be viable over the long term. Transitions from legacy applications to new applications don't happen overnight. Interoperability of the new applications with the current applications is frequently thought of as a transitional phase, but may turn out to be a long-term need.

We'd like to hear your thoughts and ideas. We can be reached at:

Mike Yawn myawn@cup.hp.com

George Stachnik stachnik@cup.hp.com

Perry Sellars sellars@c3133aps.ssr.hp.com

THE END

Bibliography

Costa, Janis Furtek, *Planning and Designing High Speed Networks Using 100VGAnylan*, Printice Hall PTR, 1995

Cowart, Robert, *WindowsNT Unleased*, Sams Publishing, 1995

Ellsworth, Dr. Jill H. and Matthew V., *The Internet Business Book*, John Wiley & Sons, Inc, 1994

Gamma, Erich, Richard Helm, Ralph Johnson and John Vlissides, *Design Patterns: Elements of Reusable Object-Oriented Software*, Reading, Massachusetts: Addison-Wesley Publishing Company, Inc., 1995

Garfinkel, Simson, *PGP:Pretty Good Privacy*, O'Reilly and Associates, Inc., 1995

Haywood, Drew, *Inside Windows NT Server*, New Riders, 1995

Keast, Cathy and Amede Hungerford, *Designing for Client/Server, Interex Proceedings,* 1995

Overman, James, Sue Meloy, Walter Murray, Jim Scaccia and Don Jenkins, *Avoiding Pitfalls in Multi-Language Programming*, Interex Proceedings, 1995

Ruley, John D., David Methuin, Martin Heller, Arthur German Iii, Eric Hall, *Networking Windows NT 3.51*, 1995

Sanville, Elizabeth, *HP COBOL II vs Micro Focus COBOL*, HP internal analysis document 1995

Sheldon, Tom, *Lan Times*, Osborne Mcgraw-Hill, 1994

Stallings, William, Phd, *Local Area Networking*, Macmillan Publishing Company, 1987

Index

A

B

C

D

E

F

P

Q

R

S

T

U

V

W